Growing Up in America
An Atlas of Youth in the USA

Growing Up in America
An Atlas of Youth in the USA

Rickie Sanders & Mark T. Mattson

Macmillan Library Reference USA
Simon & Schuster Macmillan
New York
Prentice Hall International
LONDON • MEXICO CITY • NEW DELHI • SINGAPORE • SYDNEY • TORONTO

Macmillan Library Reference USA
Simon & Schuster Macmillan
1633 Broadway
New York, NY 10019

Manufactured in the United States of America.

Printing Number
1   2   3   4   5   6   7   8   9   10

Library of Congress Cataloging-in-Publication Data

Sanders, Rickie.
     Growing up in America : an atlas of youth in the USA / Rickie Sanders,
Mark T. Mattson.
p. cm.
     ISBN 0–02–897262–7
1. Children—United States—Statistics.   I. Mattson, Mark T.
II. Title.
HB 1323.C52U649   1997
305.23'0973—dc21   97–39575
                                                                         CIP

This paper meets the requirements of ANSI/NISO   Z39.48-1992
(Permanence of Paper).

CONTENTS

INTRODUCTION
Noteworthy Trends   2
Overview of the Chapters   5
Defining children   6

CHAPTER 1
Demographic Profile of America's Children   7
  1.1 Introduction   8
  1.2 Rural-Urban Contrasts   10
  1.3 Dependency Ratio   13
  1.4 Infant and Child Mortality   14
  1.5 The Changing Face of America's Children   16
  1.6 Adoptions/Foster Care   19

CHAPTER 2
America's Children: How They Live   59
  2.1 Introduction   60
  2.2 Defining and Measuring Poverty   61
  2.3 Poverty Among Children   62
  2.4 The Youngest Victims   64
  2.5 Homelessness   66
  2.6 Child Care   68
  2.7 Welfare   77

CHAPTER 3
The Health of America's Children   103
  3.1 Introduction   104
  3.2 Immunizations   105
  3.3 Runaways and Homeless Youth   107
  3.4 Sudden Infant Death Syndrome   109
  3.5 Children with HIV/AIDS   111
  3.6 Lead Poisoning   112

3.7 The Legacy of Teen Suicide   113
3.8 Child and Adolescent Mental Health   114
3.9 Teenage Sexuality   115
3.10 Substance Abuse   117
3.11 Dental Care and Dental Care Utilization   117
3.12 Birth Defects   118

CHAPTER 4
Children and the Criminal Justice System   129
  4.1 Introduction   130
  4.2 The Juvenile Court System   130
  4.3 Conditions of Confinement/Facilities
        for Juvenile Offenders   136
  4.4 Youth as Agents of Crime and as Victims   140

CHAPTER 5
Children in the Educational System   157
  5.1 Introduction   158
  5.2 School-Age Population   158
  5.3 The American School System   162
  5.4 Student Performance   172
  5.5 Issues in Contemporary Education   177

CONCLUSIONS
Children: Our Future   237

APPENDIX   239

SOURCES & REFERENCES   263

INDEX   273

FIGURES AND TABLES

INTRODUCTION FIGURES

1   Children and the elderly as a proportion of the U.S. population. (page 2)

2   Poverty rates for children and the elderly, 1959-1995. (page 3)

CHAPTER 1 FIGURES

1.1.1   Distribution of children throughout the United States, 1996. (page 9)

1.1.2   Percent of state population that is under the age of 18, 1996. (page 24)

1.1.3   Children under the age of 5 as percent of county population, 1995. (pages 26-9)

1.1.3a   Children between the ages of 5 and 17 as a percent of county population, 1995. (pages 30-3)

1.1.4   Percent of population in major metropolitan statistical areas that are below the age of 18. (page 24)

1.2.1   Poverty rates by location of primary residence, 1967-1988. (page 10)

1.2.2   Income by residence, 1950-1980. (page 11)

1.2.3   Persistently low-income nonmetropolitan counties in the United States, 1985. (page 12)

1.2.4   Migrant worker streams in the United States. (page 34)

1.2.5   Total MEP (Migrant Education Program) participants in each state, 1995. (page 35)

1.2.6   Migrant allocation in thousands of current dollars, 1995-96. (page 36)

1.3.1   Ratio of children to the elderly, 1940 to 1988, and projections to 2030. (page 38)

1.3.2   The percent of state population that is under age 5, 1993. (page 39)

1.3.3   The percent of state population ages 5 to 17, 1993. (page 40)

1.3.4   The percent of state population that is under the age of 18, 1993. (page 41)

1.3.5   Percent of population over age 65 compared with that under age 18. (page 42)

1.3.6   Number of children under age 18 for every person 65 years of age and older, 1993. (page 38)

1.3.7   Percent of children and elderly in poverty, 1970-1994. (page 38)

1.4.1   Infant mortality rate (IMR) per 1,000 live births, 1990. (page 43)

1.4.2   Percent change in infant mortality rate, 1970-1990. (page 44)

1.5.1   United States population ages 0 to 19, by race, 1950. (page 17)

1.5.2   United States population ages 0 to 19, by race, 1995. (page 17)

1.5.3   Legal immigration by area of origin, 1951-1990. (page 17)

1.5.4   Hispanic children under age 18 as a percent of the total Hispanic population in each state, 1990. (page 47)

1.5.5   Asian American children under age 18 as a percent of the total Asian American population in each state, 1990. (page 48)

1.5.6   African American children under age 18 as a percent of the total African American population in each state, 1990. (page 49)

1.5.7   Native American children under age 18 as a percent of the total Native American population in each state, 1990. (page 50)

1.5.8   White children under age 18 as a percent of the total white population in each state, 1990. (page 51)

1.6.1   Number of adopted children, 1990. (page 53)

1.6.2   State implementing reimbursement programs for nonrecurring adoption costs including maximum payments, 1992. (page 21)

1.6.3   Average monthly adoption assistance claims, 1992. (page 53)

1.6.4   States that allow access to confidential adoption records upon mutual consent: a) consent process through confidential intermediary; b) mutual consent registries; c) mutual consent without a formal registry and; d) states with access to birth certificates upon request from adult adoptee. (page 54)

1.6.5   Substitute care population, fiscal year 1988. (page 54)

CHAPTER 2 FIGURES

2.1.1   Children, by relative income levels, 1939-1988. (page 60)

2.1.2   Poverty rates by age, 1959-1995. (page 61)

2.1.3   Poverty rates for children under age 6, compared to the national rate, by state, five-year average, 1990-94. (page 82)

2.1.4   Rate of children under age 6 in poverty, by state, five-year average, 1990-94. (page 83)

2.3.1   Gap between poor and affluent children found in the Luxembourg Income Study of 18 countries, 1995. (page 63)

2.3.2   Distribution of the poor, by race and age, using three measures of poverty. (page 64)

2.3.3   Distribution of the poor, by family type, using three measures of poverty. (page 85)

2.3.4   Percent of children living in poverty that are African American in each state, 1995. (page 86)

2.3.5   Percent of children living in poverty that are Asian American in each state, 1995. (page 87)

2.3.6   Percent of children living in poverty that are Hispanic in each state, 1995. (page 88)

2.3.7   Percent of children living in poverty that are Native American in each state, 1995. (page 89)

2.3.8   Percent of children living in poverty that are white in each state, 1995. (page 90)

2.3.9   Percent of people with selected characteristics who exited poverty in 1993. (page 85)

2.4.1   Poverty rates for children under age 6 in 13 industrialized nations. (page 91)

2.4.2   Trends in ranking and child poverty. (page 91)

2.4.3   Number of poor children under 6, 1972-1992. (page 91)

2.4.4   Poverty rate by race, 1995. (page 65)

2.4.5   States that fund programs targeted toward young children, 1995. (page 92)

2.5.1   Shifting demographics of homeless families, 1987-1995. (page 67)

2.5.2   Disruptive childhood experiences of homeless mothers. (page 67)

2.5.3 Number of residences in year prior to home-lessness, 1995. (page 67)

2.6.1 Primary care for youngest preschool child, employed mothers, 1965-1993. (page 70)

2.6.2 Labor-force participation rates of women with youngest child age 2, 1975-1995. (page 76)

2.6.3 Trends in percent of children in single- and two-parent homes, 1960-1991. (page 95)

2.6.4 Trends in living arrangements of children. (page 95)

2.6.5 Primary child care arrangements used by families with employed mothers for preschoolers, 1993. (page 95)

2.6.6 The maximum number of infants that one adult can supervise and care for according to each state. (page 96)

2.6.7 The number of child care centers in each state accredited by the National Association for the Education of Young Children (NAEYC). (page 97)

2.6.8 The number of family child care providers in each state that meet standards set by the National Association for Family Child Care. (page 97)

2.6.9 Requirements of each state about meeting the immunization standards of the Centers for Disease Control and the American Academy of Pediatrics for attending out-of-home child care programs. (page 98)

2.6.10 The condition of playground surfaces in each state. (page 98)

2.6.11 The amount each state spends on child care out of every $100 collected in state tax revenues. (page 99)

2.6.12 The maximum number of toddlers that one adult can supervise and care for according to each state. (page 99)

2.7.1 Historical trends in AFDC enrollments in thousands of children, 1970-2000. (page 80)

2.7.2 AFDC recipients as a percent of total U.S. population and AFDC child recipients as a percent of children in poverty, 1970-1994. (page 80)

2.7.3 Maximum AFDC benefits for a 3-person family by state, 1996. (page 100)

2.7.4 Change in AFDC need standard for a 3-person family by state, 1970-1996. (page 100)

2.7.5 Change in maximum AFDC benefits for a 3-person family by state, 1970-1996. (page 101)

2.7.6 Total AFDC administrative expenditures, 1970-2000. (page 82)

2.7.7 Level of reported state effort to promote responsible fatherhood. (page 101)

CHAPTER 3 FIGURES

3.1.1 Children under age 19 by type of health insurance coverage. (page 104)

3.1.2 Percent distribution of Medicaid recipients and program payments, by eligibility group, 1992. (page 104)

3.1.3 Medicaid users (in millions), by eligibility group, 1975-1992. (page 105)

3.1.4 Medicaid payments, by eligibility group, 1975-1992. (page 105)

3.1.5 Federal aid to states and local government by type. (page 106)

3.2.1 Percent of children appropriately immunized by age two, by state, 1994. (page 119)

3.2.2 Exemption rationale from immunization requirements in each state. (page 120)

3.3.1 Reasons runaways left home according to national runaway switchboard callers. (page 107)

3.3.2 Definition of runaways. (page 108)

3.3.3 Total incidence of runaways, 1988. (page 108)

3.4.1 SIDS deaths, 1983-89 and 1990-94. (page 122)

3.4.2 Number of SIDS deaths for the United States, 1983-1991. (page 122)

3.4.3 Rate for SIDS by race and year in the United States, 1983-1994. (page 122)

3.4.4 Rates of SIDS deaths for various races in the United States, 1990. (page 110)

3.5.1 AIDS deaths by race and sex under age 15. (page 123)

3.5.2 Pediatric AIDS cases by exposure category and race (cumulative total), 1995. (page 111)

3.5.3 Pediatric AIDS cases as a percent of cumulative cases, July 1993 to June 1994. (page 124)

3.5.4 Top ten metropolitan areas for AIDS cases in children less than 13 years old. (page 123)

3.6.1 Ratio of children screened to number confirmed with elevated blood lead levels, 1993-94. (page 125)

3.6.2 United States blood lead level confirmation protocols (in microns per deciliter), 1993-94. (page 125)

3.6.3 Geometric mean blood lead levels (BLLs) for persons aged less than 75 years, by age group, 1976-1980 and 1988-1991. (page 125)

3.6.4 Percentage of children aged 1-5 years with blood lead levels greater than or equal to 10mg/dL, by urban status, household income, and race/ethnicity, 1988-1991. (page 113)

3.7.1 Leading causes of death in adolescents 15 to 19, 1992. (page 126)

3.7.2 United States suicide rates per age group, 1994. (page 126)

3.7.3 Suicide rates by young age groups, 1980-1993. (page 126)

3.7.4 Suicide rates by age/sex, Native Americans and Alaskan Natives per 100,000 population, 1989-1991. (page 126)

3.8.1 The percentage of resident patients under 18 years in state and county mental hospitals, 1990. (page 127)

3.8.2 States with separate child and adolescent units in departments of mental health, 1992. (page 127)

3.9.1 Percentage of women ages 15 to 19 who have ever had intercourse, 1982, 1988, and 1990. (page 116)

3.10.1 Percent of adolescents aged 12-17 using selected substances in the last month, 1972-1993. (page 127)

3.11.1 Annual number of dental visits for U.S. children 5-17 years of age, by race and dental insurance status, 1989. (page 117)

3.12.1 Birth defects surveillance programs, 1994. (page 128)

3.12.2 Leading causes of infant death in the United States, 1990. (page 128)

3.12.3 Infant deaths due to birth defects by type in the United States, 1990. (page 128)

CHAPTER 4 FIGURES

4.2.1 Age at which criminal courts gain jurisdiction of young offenders, 1997. (page 131)

4.2.2 State statutes requiring sealing or expungement of juvenile records. (page 154)

4.2.3 Statutory provisions for dissemination and access to juvenile law enforcement records. (pages 134-35)

4.2.4 One-day counts of juveniles in jails, 1985-1990. (page 136)

4.2.5 Custody rates of juveniles held in public juvenile facilities, 1989. (page 146)

4.3.1 Percent of juveniles residing in facilities, by type, 1979-1991. (page 137)

4.3.2 Number of admissions to juvenile facilities by facility type, 1978-1990. (page 137)

4.3.3 Average annual cost per resident offender: includes juveniles and adults, 1988. (page 148)

4.3.4 Average daily resident population figures for public facilities administered by state and local governments (includes juveniles and adults), 1988. (page 149)

4.3.5 Juvenile custody rates per 100,000 persons from 10 years of age up to statutorily defined maximum age of original juvenile court jurisdiction in each state, 1989. (page 150)

4.3.6 Percent of juvenile facilities that conform to federal standards pertaining to living space, health screening, assessment criteria on classification, supervision staff ratios, teacher-to-student ratios, educational needs assessment criteria, educational availability, and teacher certification, 1991. (page 151)

4.3.7 Percent of confined juveniles in facilities whose average daily population exceeds reported design capacity by facility type, 1987-1991. (page 138)

4.3.8 Percent of confined juveniles in facilities that conform to minimum supervision staffing ratio, by facility type, 1987-1991. (page 138)

4.4.1 Percent of total arrests that are juveniles in each state, 1995. (page 152)

4.4.2 Juvenile arrest rates for violent crime, 1972-1992. (page 141)

4.4.3 Juvenile arrest rate for murder, 1972-1992. (page 153)

4.4.4 Juvenile arrest rate for rape, 1972-1992. (page 153)

4.4.5 Juvenile arrest rate for robbery, 1972-1992. (page 153)

4.4.6 Juvenile arrest rate for aggravated assault, 1972-1992. (page 153)

4.4.7 Juveniles and young adults at risk for victimization. (page 154)

4.4.8 Violent crime victimization rates for juveniles in 1991. (page 154)

4.4.9 Homicide victimization rate among African American and white youth, 1976-1991. (page 142)

4.4.10 Homicide victimization rate among youth by sex and age. (page 142)

4.4.11 Trend in child reporting rates, 1976-1992. (page 144)

4.4.12 Victims by type of maltreatment. (page 155)

4.4.13 Relationship of perpetrator to abuse victim. (page 155)

4.4.14 Age of victims of child abuse, 1992. (page 155)

4.4.15 Race/ethnicity of victims of child abuse, 1992. (page 155)

CHAPTER 5 FIGURES

5.2.1 Racial composition of public elementary and secondary schools, fall 1986 and fall 1993. (page 159)

5.2.2 Percent of state enrollment that is African American, 1994. (page 188)

5.2.3 States with disproportionately large ethnic school enrollments, fall 1995. (page 189)

5.2.4 Percent of state enrollment that is Hispanic, 1994. (page 190)

5.2.5 Percent of state enrollment that is Asian and Pacific Islander, 1994. (page 191)

5.2.6 Percent of state enrollment that is Native American, 1994. (page 192)

5.2.7 Percent change in the number of children ages 0 to 21 served under Individuals with Disabilities Education Act, by state, 1990-91 to 1993-94. (page 193)

5.2.8 Children served under the Individuals with Disabilities Act by type of disability, 1992-93. (page 161)

5.2.9 Percent of disabled students that are diagnosed with learning disabilities, 1992. (page 194)

5.2.10 Comparison of disabilities by ethnic background, 1990. (page 161)

5.3.1 The structure of education in the United States. (page 162)

5.3.2 Enrollment in public elementary and secondary schools grades K-8 and 9-12, 1949-2005 (projected). (page 163)

5.3.2a Trends in preschool enrollments, 1965-1993 (percent of population 3 and 4 years of age enrolled in school). (page 164)

5.3.3 Projected percent change in enrollment in public schools for grades 9 to 12, by state, fall 1993 to fall 2005. (page 197)

5.3.4 Projected percent change in enrollment in public schools for grades K to 8, by state, fall 1993 to fall 2005. (page 198)

5.3.5 Public expenditures for education as a percent of gross domestic product (GDP), selected countries, 1991. (page 199)

5.3.6 State commitment of GSP to education as compared to national commitment of GDP, 1993. (page 199)

5.3.7 Revenues sources for public education, grades K through 12, 1995. (page 165)

5.3.8 Total expenditures for public education, by function, 1992-93. (page 165)

5.3.9 Expenditures for instruction as a percent of current expenditures for public schools, by state, 1992-93. (page 200)

5.3.10 Teacher salaries in public elementary and secondary schools, by state, fall 1993-94 (1994-95 constant dollars). (page 201)

5.3.11 Current expenditures per pupil in average daily attendance in public elementary and secondary schools, by state, 1992-93. (page 202)

5.3.12 Percent change in teacher salaries in public elementary and secondary schools, by state, 1979-1995 (1994-95 constant dollars). (page 203)

5.3.13 Expenditures for education compared to revenues, 1992-93. (page 204)

5.3.14 Expenditures per student in public elementary and secondary schools, by state, 1993-94. (page 205)

5.3.15 Educational effort: public revenues per student in public elementary and secondary schools as a ratio of personal income per capita, by state, 1993. (page 206)

5.3.16 Public revenues per student in public elementary and secondary schools, by state, 1993-94. (page 207)

5.3.17 Teacher salaries as a percent of personal income per capita by state, 1994. (page 204)

5.3.18 Immunization inventory: percent of population 2 years old fully immunized against preventable disease, by state, 1994. (page 208)

5.3.19 Percent of high school dropouts among persons 14 to 34 years old, by sex and race/ethnicity, October 1970 to October 1994. (page 169)

5.3.20 Average income according to education level, by race, March 1993. (page 169)

5.3.21 States requiring testing for certification of teachers: a) basic skills tests; b) content knowledge; and c) in-class observations, 1996. (page 209)

5.3.22 Percentage of 12th grade students whose parents reported that school personnel contacted them at least once during the current school year for various reasons, 1992. (page 170)

5.3.23 The percentage of secondary school courses taught by teachers without formal training in the subject matter, 1990-91. (page 210)

5.3.24 The percent of secondary school teachers with a degree in main teaching assignment, 1991. (page 211)

5.3.25 The percent of teachers reporting that they participated in various in-service or professional development programs, 1994. (page 212)

5.3.26 Public and private elementary and secondary pupil-teacher ratios by level, fall 1955 to fall 2005. (page 171)

5.3.27 Student-teacher ratio for public schools K-12, by state, fall 1994. (page 213)

5.3.28 Total public elementary and secondary teachers, by state, fall 1994. (page 214)

5.4.1 Fourth grade reading proficiency scores, 1994. (page 174)

5.4.2 Eighth grade math proficiency scores, 1992. (page 175)

5.4.3 Distribution of scale scores on reading literacy assessment, by age and country, school year 1991-92. (page 222)

5.4.4 Distribution of proficiency scores on mathematics assessment, by age and country, 1991. (page 223)

5.4.5 Distribution of proficiency scores on science assessment, by age and country, 1991. (page 224)

5.4.6 Event dropout rates, by ethnicity, October 1972-1994. (page 177)

5.4.7 Event dropout rates, by income, October 1972-1994. (page 177)

5.5.1 Percent of school districts that are largely comprised of minority enrollments, 1993. (page 178)

5.5.2 Distribution of poor students in schools, 1992. (page 178)

5.5.3 Revenues for public elementary and secondary schools by source of funds, 1919-1920 to 1993-94. (page 227)

5.5.4 Disparity in funding in educational investment, 1995. (page 228)

5.5.5 Percent of students ages 12 to 17 reporting drug use of any illicit drug between the years of 1979 and 1994. (page 229)

5.5.6 Percent of students ages 12 to 17 reporting use of marijuana between the years of 1979 and 1994. (page 229)

5.5.7 Percent of students ages 12 to 17 reporting use of hallucinogens between the years of 1979 and 1994. (page 229)

5.5.8 Percent of students ages 12 to 17 reporting use of cocaine between the years of 1979 and 1994. (page 229)

5.5.9 Percent of students ages 12 to 17 reporting use of heroin between the years of 1979 and 1994. (page 230)

5.5.10 Percent of students ages 12 to 17 reporting use of alcohol between the years of 1979 and 1994. (page 230)

5.5.11 Percent of students ages 12 to 17 reporting use of cigarettes between the years of 1979 and 1994. (page 230)

5.5.12 Percent of infants born with one or more health risks, 1992. (page 231)

5.5.13 Labor-force participation rate for women with children under 6 years old, 1970-1993. (page 184)

5.5.14 Labor-force participation rate for women with children ages 6 to 17, 1970-1993. (page 185)

APPENDIX FIGURES

1 Asian Americans or Pacific Islanders as a percent of county population in U.S., 1995. (pages 240-43)

2 African Americans as a percent of county population in U.S., 1995. (pages 244-47)

3 Hispanic population as a percent of county population in U.S., 1995. (pages 248-51)

4 Native Americans and Alaskan Natives as a percent of county population in U.S., 1995. (pages 252-55)

5 Birth rates in counties of the U.S., 1995. (pages 256-59)

6 World infant mortality rates, 1996. (page 260)

7 World birth rates, 1996. (page 261)

8 World life expectancy, 1996. (page 262)

INTRODUCTION TABLES

1 The status of children, selected years, 1960-1994. (page 4)

CHAPTER 1 TABLES

1.1.1 Resident population, number of children, and children as percent of state population, 1995. (page 25)

1.1.2 Counties with the largest percent of residents under age 18, 1992. (page 25)

1.1.3 Counties with the smallest percent of residents under age 18, 1992. (page 25)

1.1.4 Fertility rates for racial and ethnic groups, 1992. (page 25)

1.2.1 The working poor by residence, 1973 and 1987. (page 34)

1.2.2 Aid to Families with Dependent Children (AFDC) and Supplemental Security Income (SSI) recipients and payments, by state, 1990-94. (page 37)

1.2.3 Racial/ethnic profile of MEP-eligible population, 1989-1990. (page 13)

1.2.4 Enrollments/participants in migrant education during the regular school year, 1984-1990. (page 13)

1.3.1 Federal, state, and local government purchases of goods. (page 38)

1.4.1 Infant mortality rates for selected countries and U.S. nonwhite population, 1991. (page 14)

1.4.2 Infant mortality rates for the 20 largest U.S. metropolitan areas, 1988. (page 15)

1.4.3 Number of infant deaths, mortality rate, and percentage of deaths attributed to each cause, by race, United States, 1990. (page 45)

1.4.4 Number and percent of low birth weight and very low birth weight by age and race of mother, 1990. (page 16)

1.4.5 Infant, neonatal, and postneonatal deaths and mortality rates, by specified race in the United States, 1988. (page 46)

1.4.6 Deaths, by selected causes and selected characteristics, 1990. (page 46)

1.5.1 Children by race and state, 1990. (page 52)

1.6.1 Percentage of finalized adoptions and children awaiting adoptive placement, 1989. (page 55)

1.6.2 Proportion of special needs children in foster care, awaiting adoption, and adopted, 1984-89. (page 55)

1.6.3 State substitute care populations, fiscal years 1990-92 (based on VCIS data). (page 55)

1.6.4 Children entering, in, and leaving substitute care, by age, 1989. (page 56)

1.6.5 Outcomes for children who left care, fiscal year 1989. (page 56)

1.6.6 Race/ethnicity of children entering, in, and leaving care, 1989. (page 56)

1.6.7 Reasons children entered substitute care, fiscal year 1989. (page 56)

1.6.8 Federal foster care expenditures under Title IV-E, fiscal year 1993 (in millions of dollars). (page 56)

1.6.9 Foster care basic monthly maintenance rates for children, ages 2, 9, and 16, 1987-1992. (page 57)

CHAPTER 2 TABLES

2.2.1 Poverty thresholds by size of family and number of related children, 1995 (in dollars). (page 84)

2.2.2 The cumulative effect of taxes and transfers on poverty estimates, 1994-95 (numbers in thousands). (page 84)

2.3.1 Expected years of childhood poverty out of first 15 years of life. (page 63)

2.3.2 Incidence of short-term and persistent poverty of children by race. (page 63)

2.4.1 Percentage of poor children under 6 covered by entitlements, by family type, 1968-1992. (page 93)

2.4.2 Percentage of poor children under age 6 living in mother-only and two-parent families, 1968-1992. (page 93)

2.4.3 Selected characteristics of parents of poor and non-poor children under age 6, 1968-1992. (page 93)

2.5.1 Composition of the homeless population by percent and category, 1995. (pages 68-9)

2.5.2 Profiles of homeless children, by family characteristic, by age, 1987 and 1992. (page 94)

2.5.3 Estimated number of U.S. homeless children and youth under age 16 at any given time. (page 94)

2.5.4 City data on the homeless, 1995. (page 94)

2.6.1 Labor-force participation rates of women with children under 18, by marital status and age of youngest child, 1995. (page 70)

2.6.2 Federal payments to states for AFDC child care and transitional child care, in thousands of dollars, fiscal years 1991 and 1997 (estimated). (page 71)

2.6.3 Overview of federal programs that support child care. (pages 74-5)

2.6.4 Eligibility for specified benefits for full-time employees, 1995. (page 76)

2.6.5 How frequently states inspect child care centers. (page 96)

2.7.1 Medicaid characteristics by race/ethnicity, age and poverty level. (page 81)

2.7.2 AFDC and combined benefits as a percent of 1996 poverty guidelines. (page 81)

2.7.3 Characteristics of families who received Aid to Families with Dependent Children (AFDC), 1969-1994. (page 102)

2.7.4 Summary of changes enacted by the Personal Responsibility and Work Opportunity Reconciliation Act (PRWORA), August 1996. (page 102)

2.7.5 Cumulative percentage of women leaving welfare by duration of time on welfare and type of exit, 1995. (page 81)

2.7.6 Cumulative percentage of women returning to AFDC by duration of time off AFDC and type of exit, 1995. (page 81)

2.7.7 Events associated with endings of AFDC spells, by percent, 1986 and 1993. (page 82)

CHAPTER 3 TABLES

3.2.1 Recommended child vaccination schedule of the Public Health Service's Immunization Practices Advisory Committee. (page 107)

3.2.2 Summary of state immunization requirements applicable to any or all grades K to 12, school year 1993-94. (page 120)

3.2.3 Measles outbreaks with greater than 100 reported cases, 1991. (page 121)

3.4.1 Infant deaths and infant mortality rates (IMR) per 1,000 live births, by cause of death. (page 110)

3.5.1 AIDS cases by age at diagnosis and exposure category, through December 1993. (page 123)

3.6.1 Top cities confirmed lead poisoning with levels greater than 10 microns per deciliter in children. (page 125)

3.7.1 Suicide mortality rates for Native Americans and Alaskan Natives and all races within the U.S., by age and sex, 1990 (rate per 100,000 population). (page 114)

3.12.1 Leading categories of birth defects. (page 118)

CHAPTER 4 TABLES

4.2.1 Police disposition of juvenile offenders taken into custody, 1993 (1993 estimated population). (page 147)

4.3.1 Agencies administering juvenile facilities run by state authorities, 1991. (page 147)

4.3.2 Total number of juvenile facilities, 1979-1991. (page 139)

4.3.3 Percent of juveniles in facilities that conform to assessment criteria on providing basic education, by facility type, 1991. (page 139)

4.3.4 Deaths in juvenile detention and correctional facilities by region, 1988. (page 140)

4.4.1 Total arrests by state and proportion of arrests that are juvenile, 1995. (page 156)

4.4.2 Changes in arrests of persons under age 18, 1983-1992. (page 156)

4.4.3 Child abuse and neglect-related fatalities, 1985 and 1993. (page 156)

CHAPTER 5 TABLES

5.2.1 Ten-year flows of immigration to the United States and their impact on the total United States population, 1830-1990. (page 195)

5.2.2 Enrollment of fifty largest school districts, fall 1993. (page 195)

5.2.3 Number of children served under Individuals with Disabilities Education Act and Chapter 1 of the Education Consolidation and Improvement Act, State Operated Programs, by age group and state, 1990-91, 1991-92 and 1993-94. (page 196)

5.3.1 Public school districts and enrollment, by size of district, 1988-89 to 1994-95. (page 215)

5.3.2 Enrollment in educational institutions, by level and control of institution, fall 1980 to fall 2000. (page 215)

5.3.3 Enrollment in grades K-12 in public elementary and secondary schools, by region and State, fall 1995 to fall 2005. (page 216)

5.3.4 Total expenditures of educational institutions related to the gross domestic product (GDP), by level of institution, 1959-1960 to 1995-96. (page 216)

5.3.5 Revenues for public elementary and secondary schools, by source of funds, 1919-1920 to 1992-93. (page 217)

5.3.6 Source of revenues for public elementary and secondary schools, by state, 1992-93. (page 217)

5.3.7 Estimated total expenditures of educational institutions, by level, control of institution, and source of funds, 1959-1960 to 1995-96 (in billions of current dollars). (page 218)

5.3.8 Personal income per capita (PIC), revenues per students, and educational effort by state, 1993 (1993 current dollars). (page 218)

5.3.9 States requiring testing for initial certification of teachers, by authorization and test used, 1996. (page 219)

5.3.10 Percentage of 12th grade students whose parents reported that school personnel contacted them at least once during the current school year for various reasons, by race/ethnicity, 1992. (page 220)

5.3.11 Teachers teaching "out of field," by state, 1995. (page 221)

5.3.12 Public and private elementary and secondary teachers and pupil-teacher ratios, by level, fall 1955 to fall 2005 (projected). (page 220)

5.3.13 Student/teacher ratio, public elementary and secondary schools, by state, fall 1994. (page 221)

5.4.1 Average reading proficiency (scale score), by age, ethnicity, and sex, selected years, 1975-1992. (page 222)

5.4.1a Average reading proficiency (scale score), selected years, 1971-1992. (page 225)

5.4.2 Average writing proficiency (scale score), by grade, ethnicity, and sex, selected years, 1984-1992. (page 225)

5.4.3 Average mathematics proficiency (scale score), by age, ethnicity, and sex, selected years, 1973-1992. (page 223)

5.4.4 Average science proficiency (scale score), by age, ethnicity, and sex, selected years, 1973-1992. (page 224)

5.4.5 Percent of population with high school diploma or equivalency, by race and gender, 1971-1995. (page 226)

5.4.6 Percentage of 10th to 12th grade dropouts who reported various reasons for dropping out of school, by sex and race/ethnicity, 1992. (page 225)

5.5.1 Percent of high school students who reported experience with violence on school property, 1993. (page 227)

5.5.2 Percent of students responding to questions about crime on or near school campuses, 1993. (page 179)

5.5.3 Steps school principals have taken to prevent violence in the classroom. (page 227)

5.5.4 Percentage of students in grades 6-12 who report agreement or strong agreement with statements about the school discipline, by school and by family characteristics. (page 232)

5.5.5 Percent of teachers indicating item is a serious problem in their school, by type and control of school, 1993-94. (page 232)

5.5.6 Percent of high school seniors reporting drug use, by type of drug and frequency of use, 1980-1995. (page 233)

5.5.7 Home-schooled children and requirements in the U.S., 1991. (page 233)

5.5.8 Gifted and talented students and programs, 1994. (page 186)

5.5.9 Special placements of white students, 1992. (page 234)

5.5.10 Special placements of African American students, 1992. (page 234)

5.5.11 Special placements of Hispanic students, 1992. (page 235)

5.5.12 Special placements of Asian American students, 1992. (page 235)

5.5.13 Special placements of Native American students, 1992. (page 236)

ACKNOWLEDGEMENTS

Many people contributed time, advice, and support to this project. Thanks go to the hundreds of public and private organizations; international, federal and state agencies; research institutes; and members of the academy who provided information and data. We are also grateful to Andy Ambraziejus and his production staff at Macmillan who worked diligently to get us to this point. We also applaud Catherine Carter, our editor.

Gracias to Tom Bole, Charles "Bud" Boenecke, William "Beau" Bradley, Braley Crandall, Harley Etienne, Charlene Howard, Bill Kampf, Scott Snyder, and Agnes Zidros—Geography and Urban Studies students at Temple University who contributed their Internet and cartographic skills.

A special acknowledgment goes to Susan Clampet Lundquist and Gerald Kreig whose timely analysis of the impact of welfare legislation and school violence is provided in Chapter 2, Section 6 and Chapter 5, Section 5.

Finally we are indebted to our children and all the children of America—for whom this volume was intended. What we have done can only be partial given the limitations of time and ability.

Introduction

"Many things we need can wait, the child cannot. Now is the time his bones are being formed, his blood is being made, his mind is being developed. To him we cannot say tomorrow, his name is today."

—*Gabriela Mistral*

NOTEWORTHY TRENDS

Persons under the age of 18 make up only about 26.0 percent of the U.S. population. Yet, for casual observers and scholars alike, this segment of the population—children—is the most accurate barometer of the health and vitality of the nation. As expressed by Marian Wright Edelman, founder of the Children's Defense Fund, "no country can be more than its children and the world it creates for them."

From the end of the American Revolution, prosperity and growth have been the order of the day. Since the mid 1970s, however, American society has been dramatically restructured. American economic growth has been slowed by global and national forces or trends such as rising interest rates, the internationalization of capital, deindustrialization and the associated shift to a service economy, and massive labor migrations. Although the causes and implications of these changes are not fully understood, it is clear they are having significant effects on the lives of American children and their families. *The Summary Report of the National Commission on Children* has highlighted several trends as particularly noteworthy.

The first of these trends is demographic, as illustrated by the rapid growth of the elderly as a percentage of the U.S. population. The elderly currently make up 14.0 percent of the U.S. population. Children currently make up 26.0 percent (Figure 1). Between 1997 and 2032, as the baby boom generation enters the ranks of senior citizens, the percentage of the population that is elderly will eventually surpass the percentage under age 18. Further, as life expectancies increase, births are expected to decline, resulting in a smaller ratio of children to elderly. Whether the pressures exerted by the elderly will erode the well-being of children remains to be seen. Critical entitlement programs that provide much needed support for children will have to compete more vigorously with income-maintenance programs for the elderly. Since these benefits are indexed to the Consumer Price Index, they have risen with inflation. Benefits to children have not. Prior to 1975, poverty rates for the elderly surpassed those for children. Subsequent to 1975, as the numbers of elderly increased, the economic situation of children worsened relative to the elderly (see Figure 2, page 3).

A second recent trend in American politics, "fiscal conservatism" has also had far-reaching effects on children and families. During the 1960s and 1970s, the U.S. government established programs to ensure that children were adequately maintained.

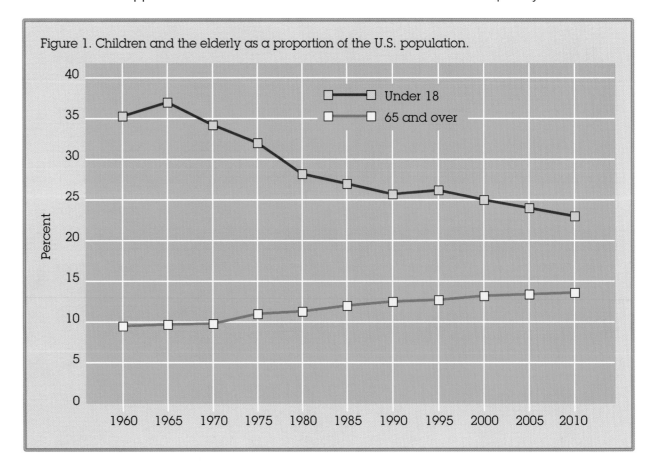

Figure 1. Children and the elderly as a proportion of the U.S. population.

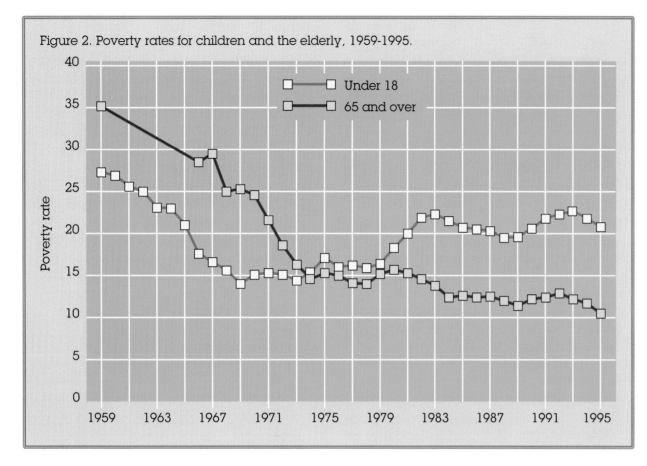

Figure 2. Poverty rates for children and the elderly, 1959-1995.

children in single-parent homes, usually headed by the mother. In 1970, about 12.0 percent of the nation's children lived with only one parent. By 1989, this figure had increased to roughly 16.0 percent. Children living in mother-only families are especially likely to be poor. About 43.0 percent of mother-only families are poor, compared to only about 7.0 percent of those in two-parent households.

Finally, although America is one of the richest and most politically stable countries on Earth, today a policy debate exists concerning the formula that determines the dollar amounts paid by the public and private sectors for the maintenance of children. Some European countries routinely offer financial support and generous social insurance benefits to strengthen families with children. The government of the United States stands alone among those of the industrialized countries, characterized by its traditionally limited response to child care, social support, and the reform of workplace policies.

In the United States, the meeting of these needs has historically been the responsibility of the family. Among the 122 signatories to the United Nations Convention on the Rights of the Child, a landmark international treaty that sets out a comprehensive vision of the basic efforts nations must make to assure the viability of their children, the United States is noticeably absent.

These 3 trends provide a valuable context for understanding the condition of America's children. As scholars continue to analyze precisely how the social, demographic, and politico-economic trends discussed above have affected and will con-

These programs helped families meet basic needs such as adequate housing, nutrition, health care, and protection against abuse and neglect; they also helped to provide broader supports for child care, special education, parents' job training, and recreation. In 1981, President Reagan signed into law the *Omnibus Budget Reconciliation Act*, which transferred the responsibility for public child care maintenance from the federal government and handed it over to state and local governments and the private sector. This shift signaled a withdrawal of the federal government's commitment to providing opportunities for children and their families.

More recently, the Welfare Reform Act signed into law in 1996 threatens the safeguards of poor children by prohibiting the payment of welfare benefits to mothers who are minors and by denying increased benefits for children born to mothers currently on welfare. While the long-range goal of this legislation, a decrease in the demand for welfare services by instilling a sense of responsibility and family planning among welfare recipients is commendable, the children affected by this change must bear the immediate effects of living with less.

A third trend, social change—particularly the high divorce rate and the increase in out-of-wedlock births—has placed more

tinue to affect the lives of American children, universally accepted conclusions are not immediately forthcoming. Some interpretations highlight the unsurpassed technological and material wealth and abundance that blanket a large number of America's children from birth. They point to the fact that the United States has long had in place a highly developed social insurance scheme, to provide material assistance for children. Moreover, the infant and child mortality rates have fallen by more than 50.0 percent between 1970 (20 deaths per 1,000 live births) and 1993 (8.4 deaths), and life expectancies have increased by a similar percentage.

Due to the wealth of the United States and its large GDP, the majority of children have adequate access to health care and, compared to millions of children in many other countries around the world, especially developing countries, live relatively free from disease and disability.

At the same time, a growing number of statistics point to the worsening of the status of today's children (Table 1). Since 1960, educational performance as measured by SAT scores has declined. Suicide rates among adolescents aged 15-19 kept increasing noticeably until the early 1990s. Now the rate remains constant at around 11.0 per 100,000. Moreover, the homicide rate among adolescents increased from 4.0 per 100,000 in 1960 to 20.3 per 100,000 in 1994. Births to unwed mothers have increased, as has the number of children living with only one parent. While high school graduation rates remained at a constant 19.0 percent from 1950 to 1993, the rate of high school students who drop out actually decreased from 15.7 percent in

1973 to 13.3 percent in 1994 (see Chapter 5, section 5.4). Even among those who complete high school, a substantial number lack command of basic skills. Many are culturally illiterate—they do not possess the basic skills they need to thrive in the modern world. Even conducting an employment interview or opening a bank account is beyond their reach.

Globally, America ranks third in per capita gross domestic product. However, national economic power has not provided a better life for many. Eight to ten million children lack some form of health insurance. A typical problem that can be indirectly traced to a shortfall of financial resources is the incidence of babies born at low birth weight caused by an absence of pre-natal medical care. Reported rates of child abuse and neglect, often associated

with families weakened by the stress of economic deprivation, tripled between 1976 and 1986, and increasing numbers of children were separated from their families for longer and longer periods of time.

Today, one in five American children is poor, while teen violence has reached epidemic proportions, and death by firearms ranks high as a cause of death for America's teens. In 1996, the United States General Accounting Office estimated the nationwide population of homeless children at between 41,176 and 106,543 individuals, with another 2 million who are "precariously housed"—at imminent risk of becoming homeless. Underlying these issues is an important racial dimension. Differences in economic conditions between minority and white children are striking. African American, Native

Table 1. The status of children, selected years, 1960-1994 (children are under age 18 unless otherwise specified).

	Year					
	1960	1970	1980	1988	1992	1994
SAT scores						
Verbal	477.0	466.0	424.0	428.0	423.0	423.0
Math	498.0	488.0	466.0	476.0	476.0	479.0
Suicide rate, ages 15 to 19	3.6	5.9	8.5	11.3	11.1	10.9
Homicide rate, ages 15 to 19	4.0	8.1	10.6	11.7	19.3	20.3
Children in poverty (%)	26.9	15.1	18.3	19.5	22.3	21.8
Births to unwed mothers (%)	5.3	10.7	18.4	25.7	26.6	31.0
Children living with one parent (%)	9.1	11.9	19.7	24.3	26.6	26.7
Married women in the labor force with children under age 6 (%)	18.6	30.3	45.1	57.1	59.9	61.7

Note: Rates are per 100,000. Suicide data and data for births to unwed mothers listed for 1992 are from 1990. Suicide data and data for births to unwed mothers listed for 1994 are from 1993.

American, or Hispanic children are much more likely to live in impoverished households than their white counterparts.

These disturbing realities provide the context for this atlas. Our primary purpose is to describe the condition of America's children, portray their world, and gauge the prospects for their future. In the face of mounting pressures, policymakers and those in education and human services have begun to collect background information to develop policies that are responsive to the needs of children. Despite these efforts, data on the American child remain sketchy and widely dispersed in myriad texts, special-purpose publications, edited volumes, and reports. Beyond compiling basic information in a single source, *Growing Up in America* paints a picture of how children live, who they are, how well educated they are, and the state of their health. By using the format of an atlas, our route to that goal is different from conventional studies on this topic. We use maps and illustrations to aid the reader in the visualization of information and to offer an alternative framework from which to pose questions and explore answers. *Growing Up in America* is an analytical reference work that brings together statistics and information on the policy issues. This study is a companion to previous investigations; we hope its contribution is greater insight into the spatial relationships bound within the data. We hope to leave in the mind of the reader a sense of how and where life in America comes together for children—the current social and economic landscape of America, a patchwork of states stitched together by the common threads of national policy.

OVERVIEW OF THE CHAPTERS

Chapter 1 furnishes the reader with a demographic profile of America's children. Descriptive information pertaining to the geographic distribution of topics such as major causes of death, infant mortality rates, age structure, and racial identity is presented through tables, graphs, and maps. We use these demographics to frame policy and planning questions that emerge in later chapters. Typical questions asked include, Who is the average American child? How has this child changed over the past fifty years? What is life like for this child? What does this child think about drugs, school, the future? What forces shape the child's life? ideas? Where do windows of opportunity exist that could lead to an improvement in the child's life?

America's Children: How They Live, chapter 2, provides a picture of how America's children live. Its primary focus is on child poverty. It highlights the federal role in alleviating poverty (AFDC, food stamps, child support contributions), and issues relating to children's homelessness. Throughout the chapter, comparisons are made with children's living conditions in other countries.

The physical, mental, and emotional health of American children is examined in chapter 3. It provides information on health care accessibility, physician contact, health insurance, Medicare/Medicaid, and federal and state guidelines regulating children's care. Teen suicides, HIV/AIDS, and lead poisoning are examined.

Chapter 4 deals with general issues pertaining to children and the criminal justice system—crimes committed by juveniles and offenses committed on juveniles. Important in this chapter is information on incarceration (state and federal spending), detention, and state/federal expenditures on rehabilitation and incarceration. A number of philosophical issues deserve treatment under this topic. The question of when a juvenile should be treated as an adult and whether or not juvenile records should be permanently sealed are two issues that are also explored.

No atlas of children would be complete without a chapter on education. Schools constitute a venue where many of the problems confronting children converge; they are also the sites of human capital formation. Increasingly they are becoming the setting in which values are taught and discipline is enacted. In that regard, education is perhaps the single most important element in children's lives. In chapter 5, we look at the variables that are critical in improving the quality of schools across the United States. In addition, we analyze the government's commitment to educating its youth—funding amounts and sources. State-by-state comparisons give us a sense of regional variation.

In our conclusions we consider the practical utility of attempts to paint a picture of "the American child." Based on what we found, there is considerable variation in the lives of American children. We further pose questions arising out of recent policy actions that give increasingly more power to states. We leave this task convinced that by looking at spatial patterns, we have informed the on-going policy discussions surrounding children's lives.

Defining Children

Like many other aspects of an individual's life, childhood is more socially than biologically determined. For some, childhood is defined in functional terms. When an individual is financially independent or assumes responsibility for a family, that person is no longer considered a child.

For others, childhood is defined more in formal terms, dependent upon some external event—the age at first intercourse or graduation from high school.

Chronological age may also define childhood. In the United States, for instance, one magically crosses the threshold into adulthood at 18. Most states (though not all) set the minimum age for voting, driving, purchasing alcohol, and defending the country at 18.

The status accorded to childhood and the types of lives, roles, expectations, and responsibilities envisioned for children also differ among groups. Some groups place children at the center of childhood. Others see children as "pre adults," judged by adult standards and expected to conform to adult rules. The child is a small man or woman and expected to behave accordingly. Infancy, then, is "prehuman," early childhood is brief, adolescence unrecognized, and the generation gap non -existent. Childhood is merely a preface to the more important life stage, "adulthood."

Notwithstanding these differences, the condition of childhood is universal; reflecting the time of emotional, financial, and physical dependence on parents/caretakers.

The various phases of childhood are marked by important age-related physiological and sociopersonal thresholds that relate to locomotive capability, emotional development, and intellectual activity. For the first four weeks of life, the newborn is helpless and totally dependent on others for survival. Touch, smell, and taste are the first senses to develop. From about 4 weeks to 24 months, most infants begin to sit, crawl, and move about. By the end of about 24 months, the toddler can fix an object in his or her line of vision. Increased locomotion makes the two year old an active explorer.

Early childhood begins around age 3 and lasts until about age 6. Before early childhood, physiological development presents such enormous demands that virtually no other development takes place. During the early childhood and preschool years, intellectual development is greater, and psychosocial, intellectual, and emotional development is more rapid than in any other comparable life stage. The preschooler can master swimming, learn several languages at once, and seek out and create novel experiences.

At about 5 years of age, children show abrupt changes in behavior and begin to reduce their physical and emotional attachment to their mothers. This marks the beginning of the early school years.

During the early school years, physiological growth stabilizes. The child moves out of the microcosm of family and embraces the meso system—the school, sports, friends. At this age, the young child's intellectual, emotional, and locomotive acumen is developed enough to allow him or her to move beyond the aural and visual field of the mother and take responsibility in increasingly varied geographical settings. In this stage, growth is more stable and seemingly quiescent, as if the child were preparing for what will be demanded by puberty.

The period between 10 and 14 years brings on the onset of puberty. Puberty is characterized by accelerated physical growth and intense psycho-social adjustment. Dependence on adults for basic needs is practically nil, but at the same time the adolescent is not yet an adult. In previous stages, most individuals experienced the same events at roughly the same time. With puberty, however, timing among individuals varies considerably. As a rule, boys develop later than girls. This is a very stressful phase involving identity issues and image problems.

The final phase of childhood is adolescence. In many ways, the young person beyond age 14 is already beyond childhood but not yet recognized as an adult. Physical development does not cease during this stage but slows down relative to the pace of development in previous stages. Intellectual and psycho-social development also slow down.

Chapter 1

Demographic Profile of America's Children

1.1

INTRODUCTION

In a country as large and as diverse in population as the United States, one could expect that attitudes toward childrearing, parenting, and what children's lives should be like vary considerably in terms of both geographic location and population demography. Until very recently there were few if any questions asked about children or the condition of their lives. Traditionally, to handle challenges like meeting the basic physical needs or soothing the emotional distress of children, parents and teachers proceeded on the assumption that they should do things exactly the way their parents and teachers had done. Profound change in this area began in the 1940s when industrial production for the American effort in World War II opened the door to full time employment for many women and mothers. As women entered the workforce, the need to place them on the same educational footing as men became apparent. In the 1960s, the civil rights movement and the end of legal segregation accelerated the shift away from the "traditional" pre-war ways of doing things. Energized by these two events, contemporary American society is still struggling to improve the lives of children, and to guarantee that children's lives will be "better." Hardly a day passes without some new idea about the way in which children should be brought up and educated or without some public official recommending passage of a law aimed at changing the basic structure of children's lives. Part of

this results from the vast number of new opportunities, resources, and support available to parents in the United States to change the way children are reared. Another part, however, stems from our current ideas about the value of children. They represent the next generation of workers and embody the nation's hope for a continued, perhaps improved, existence. For parents, they offer fulfillment, a chance to care for and help mold another human being. Taking both these nationalistic and personal motives together, it becomes clearer why improving the condition of America's children has become a fundamental element in the lives of many Americans.

For children living in middle- or upper-income homes, changes in the way they are raised and educated are primarily in the hands of their parents and the local school board. However, children who come from poor families, in either urban or rural settings, with a low local tax base, must rely to a greater degree on governmental agencies for social, health, and educational programs. This fact of American life forces poor families, those with the least political clout, to do battle with more powerful groups, many of whom wish to maintain the status quo or even roll back the gains previously won for poor children. It is this duality of circumstances between the poor and non-poor and the political competition for resources at the local, state, and federal level, that makes the task of improving the lives of all children in America a difficult one.

A second component of the problem has to do with the fact that there is no easy and direct way of knowing how to

improve children's lives. In other words, no one individual or interest group possesses what a philosopher might describe as "perfect knowledge" on this subject. What this means is that even among groups that could be labeled as "pro-child," differences in opinion exist as to what course of action should be taken.

Finally, the assessment of results achieved by shifts in official policy are often recorded separately and viewed piecemeal. To determine (after all is said and done) if children's lives have actually been improved, gains and losses always need to be examined concurrently to get the "big picture." To accomplish this assessment, one needs a clear perspective on the demographics of children—where they are, how they got there, their racial identity, and their age structure. What do the statistics tell us about children in America? How do children in America compare with other underrepresented groups such as the elderly or the disabled? From what causes do they die? What factors have made them who they are? In this chapter, we begin to paint a picture of America's children. Though we pay particular attention to the condition of the poor, minorities, and those with special needs, we are concerned with all children.

DEMOGRAPHICS OF CHILDREN

Children make up 26.6 percent of the U.S. population. They number 69,840,000 (see Table 1.1.1, page 25). This has not always been the case. During the 1940s, children were approximately 31.0 percent (numbering 40,386,000), and in 1970 69,702,000 children accounted for only 34.0 percent of the total U.S. population. It is expected that the percentage of the total American population below the age of 18 will decrease even further in the future due to shrinking numbers of women of the childbearing age, changing lifestyles, and declining fertility rates.

SPATIAL DISTRIBUTION

The distribution of children across the American landscape is remarkably uneven (Figure 1.1.1). Although California is the state with the largest number of children, Utah is the state with the highest percentage of its population below age 18 (see Figure 1.1.2, page 24). In Utah, one of every three residents is a child. In the District of Columbia, the figure is one of every five. Four factors that contribute to the greater concentration of children in different regions are religious beliefs (Mormons and Catholics disapprove of birth control and promote the concept of large families among their congregations), economies based on family farming where children are employed to help with the chores, the more complex interconnections woven by the slave economy of the old South and race, and the settlement of areas largely by immigrant populations. States west of the Mississippi River, which are receiving areas for many migrants, have much higher percentages of children than do states to the east. These western states stand to capture most of the nation's future growth.

Counties with the largest proportion of children are also concentrated in the west (see Figures 1.1.3 and 1.1.3a, pages 26-33). In fact, no county outside the west placed in the top twenty-five counties with the largest number of residents under age

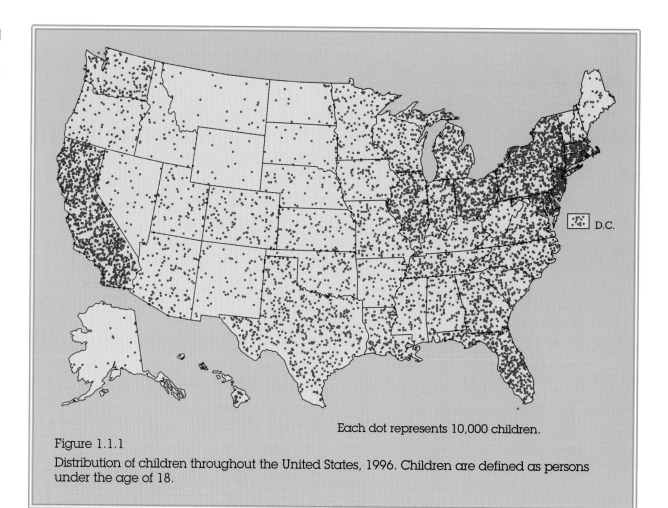

Each dot represents 10,000 children.

Figure 1.1.1
Distribution of children throughout the United States, 1996. Children are defined as persons under the age of 18.

18. Forty-four percent of the top 25 are in Utah. In four Utah counties, 1 of every 2 persons is below the age of 18 (see Table 1.1.2, page 25). Table 1.1.3 shows the U.S. counties with the smallest number of residents under 18 (see page 25).

Outside the west, areas with a high concentration of children are in the South Atlantic and the West South Central States. The higher than average distribution of children in these states can be explained by the larger number of minorities in those states. Minority women tend to have more chil-

dren than do non-Hispanic white women (see Table 1.1.4, page 25). Thirty-one percent of the nation's children are minorities. There is also a smaller concentration of counties with large percentages of children in Alaska and the Upper Midwest.

Figure 1.1.4 shows the percentage of the population in major metropolitan statistical areas (MSAs) that is below the age of 18 (see page 24). In MSAs east of the Mississippi River, percentages of children are lower and do not exceed the average.

1.2

RURAL-URBAN CONTRASTS

One of every five children in America lives in a rural area. For most of them, particularly those who live near census-designated "metropolitan areas," life is not dramatically unlike that of their urban and suburban counterparts. However, for those who live in rural areas plagued by isolation and low population density where government services are few and public-service needs go unmet, concentrated, long-term impoverishment is the norm. For this population group, life is more like that in the nation's inner cities. Children lack access to parks, recreation facilities, public transportation, quality education, and affordable competent child care. Education illustrates the dilemma many rural areas (with limited tax revenues, small size, isolation, and lack of administrative staff) find themselves in. The incentive to increase investments in education is lacking, because the youth, once educated, only move away because of the lack of good local jobs. Still another illustration of the issues affecting children in impoverished rural areas is day care. The absence of professional day care for children, unavailable to isolated families due to a lack of transportation and financial resources, prevents them from maximizing their incomes because it ties up a parent or older child with baby-sitting duty.

It has been argued that the rural "underclass" is perhaps the most neglected segment in American society. The overall poverty rate, though not as high as inner city poverty, in 1988, was higher than in typical urban areas (Figure 1.2.1). Moreover, during the period 1950 and 1980, income for rural nonfarm households declined relative to both urban and rural farm households (see Figure 1.2.2, page 11). Children growing up in these areas are indeed truly disadvantaged.

Pockets of concentrated, rural poverty are spread throughout the nation; however, the highest concentration of persistently low-income nonmetropolitan counties is in the South—Louisiana, Mississippi, Alabama, Arkansas, Tennessee, Kentucky, Georgia, and the Carolinas. These states contain 43.5 percent of the nation's rural population under the age of 18 (see Figure 1.2.3, page 12), and as remnants of the old South, still are home to large numbers of African Americans descended from slaves.

One of the distinguishing characteristics of the rural poor is their work effort. Approximately, twenty percent of poor rural households worked full-time, year round (see Table 1.2.1, page 34), yet the low wages diminished opportunities for these families to successfully move out of poverty.

About 80.0 percent of America's children live in metropolitan areas. Almost 50.0 percent of the United States population lives in the 37 metropolitan areas that have at least 1 million population. Minority chil-

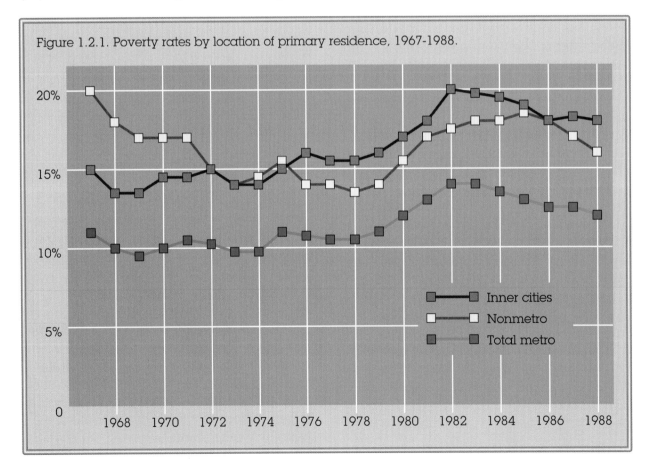

Figure 1.2.1. Poverty rates by location of primary residence, 1967-1988.

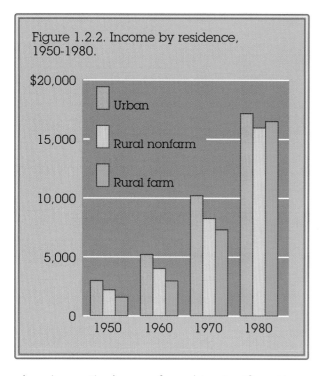

Figure 1.2.2. Income by residence, 1950-1980.

- Urban
- Rural nonfarm
- Rural farm

$20,000

15,000

10,000

5,000

0

1950   1960   1970   1980

dren in particular are found in significantly higher numbers in metropolitan areas. New York-New Jersey-Connecticut (19.8 million), Los Angeles-Riverside-Orange County (15.3), Chicago-Gary-Kenosha (8.5), Washington-Baltimore-Hagerstown (7), and San Francisco-Oakland-San Jose (6.5) are the top 5 consolidated metropolitan areas in terms of total population. California (92.6%), New Jersey (89.4), Arizona (87.5), Utah (87.0) and Rhode Island (86.5) are the states with the largest percentage of total population living in urban areas. In 1990, 30.0 percent of urban children lived in poverty as compared to 22.2 percent of rural children. Unlike their rural counter-parts, for a child born into urban poverty, the household is likely to be headed by a female on welfare; unemployment is wide-spread and chronic, and crime and juvenile delinquency are prevalent.

HIGHLIGHT:
CHILDREN OF SEASONAL AND MIGRANT FARM WORKERS

Children of seasonal and migrant farm workers constitute only a small proportion of rural children in poverty. These children almost always come from families with low incomes, live in inadequate housing, and are susceptible to serious health problems from a lack of adequate preventive health care. What aggravates their situation and puts them among the most underprivileged groups in American society is their constant mobility. Traveling as they do from place to place with their families in search of employment, they stay at any one place for only a short time. This means that the chil-dren change schools perhaps two to three times a year, while some must go back and forth between schools located both within and outside the United States. Few of these children have access to social programs such as Aid to Families with Dependent Children (AFDC) or food stamps (see Table 1.2.2, page 37 for AFDC summary).

There are three primary streams of migrant workers in the United States—the western, the central, and the eastern. Northern Mexico and southern Texas are the sending areas for both the western and central streams (see Figure 1.2.4, page 34). These areas are dominated by Mexicans. The eastern stream is more eth-nically diverse. Blacks living in rural Florida migrate up the coast working in Georgia, South Carolina, North Carolina, New Jersey, Pennsylvania, and New York. Puerto Ricans, Haitians, Mexicans, and Southeast Asians make up the bulk of this stream. Some migrants in each stream are citizens of the United States, others are refugees,

others are under contract with foreign governments for specific harvests, and some are illegal workers.

Using 1991 data supplied by the National Agricultural Workers Survey, the National Commission on Migrant Education (an agency within the federal Department of Health and Human Services) found that most migrant youth are the sons and daughters of Hispanic immigrants who have limited English proficiency. Nearly 85.0 percent are between the ages of 6 and 16, and most (approximately 50.0 per-cent) are concentrated in 3 states: California, Texas, and Florida. This scenario is quite different from that in the early 1980s, when the typical migrant farm worker was a U.S. citizen (African American or non-Hispanic white) or a Mexican immigrant.

At any time during the year, there are approximately 587,000 migratory children in the United States. The vast majority (over 65.0 percent) of these children are U.S. citi-zens by birth. Of the total, 65.0 percent travel with or join their parents and do not do farm work; 6.0 percent travel with par-ents and work on farms; and the remaining 29.0 percent travel on their own and do farm work.

The education of the children of migrant farm workers is administered at the federal level by the Department of Health and Human Services through the Migrant Education Program (MEP) and the Migrant School Record Transfer System (MSRTS). The racial/ethnic composition of the migrant education program eligible population is overwhelmingly Hispanic (see Table 1.2.3, page 13) Of all Migrant Student Record Transfer System enroll-

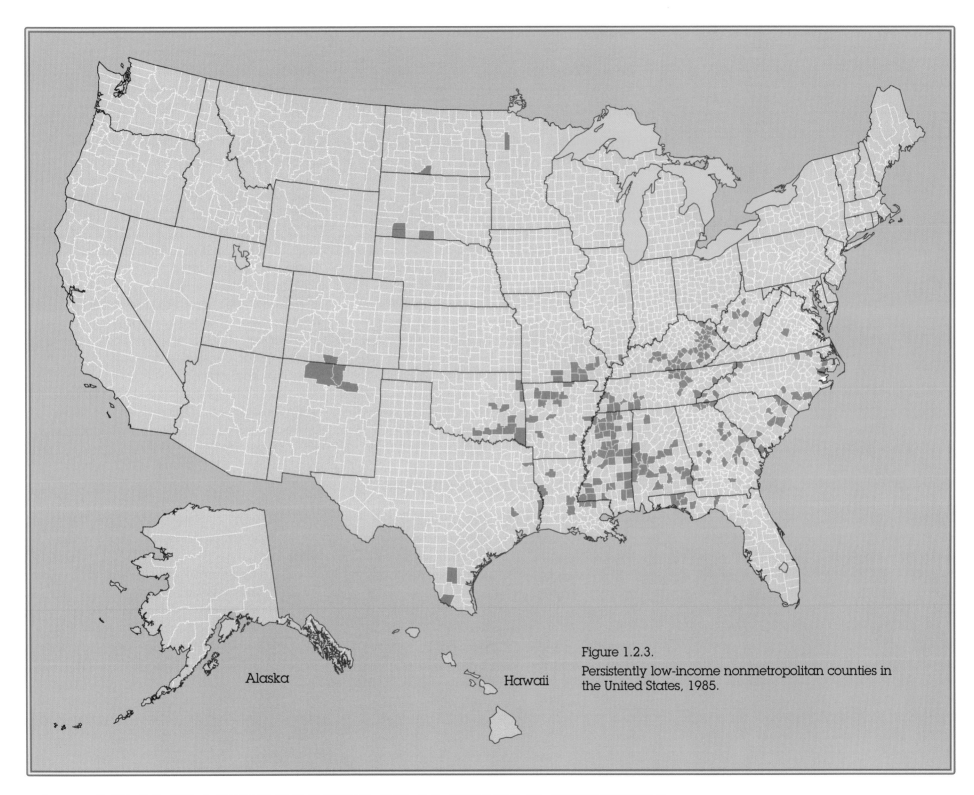

Alaska

Hawaii

Figure 1.2.3.

Persistently low-income nonmetropolitan counties in
the United States, 1985.

DEMOGRAPHIC PROFILE OF AMERICA'S CHILDREN

Table 1.2.3. Racial/ethnic profile of MEP-eligible population, 1989-1990.				
	MSRTS		RTI	
Race/ethnicity	Regular term	Summer term	Regular term	Summer term
Asian/Pacific Islander	3.0	3.0	3.0	<1.0
Black	5.0	2.0	3.0	1.0
Hispanic	79.0	85.0	74.0	86.0
Native American	2.0	1.0	1.0	2.0
Non-Hispanic white	11.0	8.0	20.0	11.0

Table 1.2.4. Enrollments/participants in migrant education during the regular school year, 1984-1990.			
School year	MSRTS enrollments	MEP participants	Percent served
1984-85	438,958	311,615	71.0
1985-86	440,733	323,601	73.0
1986-87	448,914	300,674	67.0
1987-88	471,619	308,249	65.0
1988-89	513,137	333,042	65.0
1989-90	550,865	360,839	66.0

ments, only a portion actually participate (see Table 1.2.4, page 13 and Figure 1.2.5, page 35), and dropout rates are high. Because of the labor needs of the family, approximately 40.0 percent drop out before the 6th grade. Statistics contained in the MSRTS note the lack of fluency in English as critical. Over one-third of migrant children are one or more grades behind grade level, and over 40.0 percent are estimated to be achieving below the 35th percentile in reading. With the exception of Hawaii, every state in the United States receives some funding to support its migrant education (see Figure 1.2.6, page 36). The bulk of the funds go to the three states with the largest number of migrant children—California, Texas, and Florida. California alone receives one third of the total nationwide allocation to migrant education. Michigan, Oregon, Alaska, Pennsylvania, and Washington also rank high in receipt of funds for migrant education.

Medical research undertaken by the Migrant Clinicians Network reveals that the demographic patterns, socioeconomic status, lifestyle characteristics, and disease categories of migrant workers' children are more typical of conditions in the Third World than of conditions in the U.S., one of the most powerful and affluent nations in the world. Fewer than half of migrant children under 16 receive the recommended number of annual checkups. Older children are more likely to be immunized because immunizations are administered at school. Only one-third have received an annual dental check-up, as compared with 50.0 percent of children in the total population.

Two out of every 1,000 migrant children die in infancy, and 45 out of 1,000 die by age 2. By age 5, the cumulative mortality rate is 46 per 1,000! By comparison, the infant mortality rate for black infants is approximately 22 per 1,000. For the nation as a whole, infant mortality is 9 per 1,000, with cumulative mortality by age 5 at 17 per 1,000. The corresponding level of mortality among migrant children is 1.6 times greater than that of the United States population. Clearly, the children of migrant agricultural workers are at greater risk and suffer more problems than the general population of the United States. The issues surrounding the need for a health policy and research agenda focused on migrant farmworker children is much needed.

1.3

DEPENDENCY RATIO

Perhaps more important in understanding the condition of America's children than their numbers and where they are located is their ratio to the elderly (the dependency ratio). As shown in Figure 1.3.1, the dependency ratio in the United States has steadily declined since 1940 (see page 38). Currently the ratio is 2:1; in 1940, however, it was 4.5 to 1. If these trends continue, by the next century the ratio will be 1:1. Figure 1.3.5 contrasts the percent of population under 18 with the percent of population over age 65 by state (see page 42). Florida, West Virginia, Pennsylvania, Arizona, and Iowa stand out as states with greater than average proportions of the elderly.

States west of the Mississippi River have larger percentages of their populations below 18 (see Figures 1.3.2 to 1.3.4, pages 39-41). Figure 1.3.6 provides regional comparisons (see page 38). Some demographers are concerned that as America's population grows older and children become a smaller proportion of the population, the needs of the elderly and the childless will enter into competition with the needs of children. As the pool of public funds shrinks, voters might be more inclined to represent their interests and undermine the political viability of child-related expenditures. As seen in Table 1.3.1, aggregate government purchases for children increased by almost 3.0 percent per year over the period 1960-1988 (see page 38). For adults, the increase was 6.8 percent per year. Similarly, purchases per person for children increased approximately 3.0 percent per year but for adults the increase was 5.2 percent per year. This disparity in resource allocation between the young and old may in part be responsible for the emergence of children as the most numerous group living at the bottom of the economic ladder. Since the 1970s, poverty among the elderly has been cut by more than half, but children's poverty has experienced an increase of about 8.0 percent over the same period. In 1994, Roughly 12.0 percent of all persons aged 65 and over and 21.0 percent of all children (18 years old or younger) were at or below the poverty line. (see Figure 1.3.7, page 38).

1.4

INFANT AND CHILD MORTALITY

The infant mortality rate (IMR) describes the number of deaths of children under the age of 1 year old per 1,000 live births in a given year. It is the most widely used indicator of a nation's health and well-being. In 1950, the United States ranked third

among all nations in its ability to prevent infant mortality. The 1979 Surgeon General's Report on Health Promotion and Disease Prevention set the goal of reducing the IMR to fewer than 9 deaths per 1,000 live births by 1990. With an overall infant mortality rate of 9.2, the United States has essentially succeeded in achieving its goal. This rate is down significantly from 26 per 1,000 in 1960 and 20 per 1,000 in 1970.

Despite this decline, the United States has a much higher infant mortality rate than the Republic of Korea, Japan, Hong Kong, and all of the Western European countries. Among countries with a similar GDP per capita ($20,000 or more), the United States has the highest infant mortality rate. Even more important, among non-whites, the infant mortality rate approximates that found in many lesser developed countries (Table 1.4.1). The infant mortality rate for black infants (17.0) is roughly twice that for white infants (7.7). The infant mortality rate for Hispanic infants is 7.8, approximately the same as for whites. For Indians and Alaska natives, the infant mortality rate is currently 9.7 per 1,000 live births, down significantly from 36.8 in 1966. This current figure is still 25.0 percent higher than the rate for white infants.

Infant mortality rates are highest in the southeastern United States (see Figure 1.4.1, page 43). The District of Columbia leads the nation with an infant mortality rate of 20.7, placing the area in the same category with countries like Trinidad/Tobago. Among metropolitan areas, Detroit led the nation with an infant mortality rate of 12.3 (see Table 1.4.2, page 15). Since 1970, every state in the United States has

experienced a decrease in its infant mortality rate. Maine, Nevada, Vermont, Texas, and New Hampshire led the nation with reductions of 60.0 percent or more. North Dakota, Georgia, Rhode Island, and the District of Columbia showed the least

Table 1.4.1. Infant mortality rates for selected countries and U.S. white and nonwhite population, 1991.

Country	Infant Mortality Rate
Sweden	4.0
Japan	5.0
Finland	6.0
Canada	7.0
France	7.0
Hong Kong	7.0
Netherlands	7.0
Norway	7.0
Switzerland	7.0
United Kingdom	7.0
Australia	8.0
Austria	8.0
Belgium	8.0
Denmark	8.0
Germany	8.0
Ireland	8.0
Italy	8.0
New Zealand	8.0
Singapore	8.0
Spain	8.0
USA, white	8.6
Korea, Republic of	9.0
USA	9.0
Greece	10.0
Israel	10.0
Portugal	10.0
Cuba	11.0
Czechoslovakia	12.0
Costa Rica	14.0
Kuwait	14.0
Jamaica	15.0
Malaysia	15.0
Poland	15.0
Hungary	16.0
Sri Lanka	16.0
Bulgaria	17.0
Chile	17.0
USA, nonwhite	17.0
Colombia	18.0
Yugoslavia (former)	19.0
Trinidad/Tobago	20.0

Table 1.4.2. Infant mortality rates for the 20 largest U.S. metropolitan areas, 1988.

Metropolitan area	IMR per 1,000 infant population (1)
Detroit-Ann Arbor-Flint, MI CMSA	12.3
Chicago-Gary-Kenosha, IL-IN-WI CMSA	11.9
Philadelphia-Wilmington-Atlantic City, PA-NJ-DE-MD CMSA	11.7
Washington-Baltimore, DC-MD-VA-WV CMSA	11.5
Atlanta, GA MSA	11.3
Miami-Fort Lauderdale, FL CMSA	11.1
Cleveland-Akron, OH CMSA	11.0
New York-Northern New Jersey-Long Island, NY-NJ-CT-PA CMSA/NECMA (2)	10.9
Tampa-St. Petersburg-Clearwater, FL MSA	10.7
Phoenix-Mesa, AZ MSA	9.9
St. Louis, MO-IL MSA	9.7
Houston-Galveston-Brazoria, TX CMSA	9.6
Los Angeles-Riverside-Orange County, CA CMSA	8.9
Seattle-Tacoma-Bremerton, WA CMSA	8.9
Dallas-Fort Worth, TX CMSA	8.8
Pittsburgh, PA MSA	8.6
San Francisco-Oakland-San Jose, CA CMSA	7.8
Minneapolis-St. Paul, MN-WI MSA	7.8
Boston-Brockton-Nashua, MA-NH NECMA	7.7
San Diego, CA MSA	7.1

Notes:

(1) Excludes births to and deaths of nonresidents of the United States. Data are by place of residence. Metropolitan statistical areas (MSA's), consolidated metropolitan statistical areas (CMSA's), and New England County Metropolitan Areas (NECMA's) are defined by the U.S. Office of Management and Budget as of December 31, 1992. Data includes infants under 1 year, excluding fetal deaths rates per 1,000 registered live births.

(2) Includes parts of New Haven County, CT, not in the CMSA; excludes parts of Litchfield and Middlesex Counties, CT, in the CMSA.

change (see Figure 1.4.2, page 44).

Although not all of the factors responsible for the decline in the nation's infant mortality rate are clear, the introduction of new "surfactant" medications (which cause the tissues of underdeveloped lungs in premature babies to separate and inflate) ranks high as a contributing factor. Since these medications were introduced, the rate of infant deaths due to respiratory distress syndrome (RDS) and short gestation/low birth weight has decreased considerably among white infants. Deaths from both causes have remained virtually unchanged among African American infants.

In 1990, the single largest cause of death in the first year of life among all children born in the United States was from various congenital abnormalities. This was followed by sudden infant death syndrome (SIDS), complications relating to short gestation/low birth weight (less than 2,500 grams at birth), and RDS (see Table 1.4.3, page 45). The rank order of these four leading causes of death differed between white and black babies. Among African American infants, the leading cause of death was from disorders relating to short gestation and low birth weight. For white infants, congenital abnormalities were the number one cause of death, and the risk increased if these infants were born with low birth weight, short gestation, RDS, and pneumonia.

Research has shown that health of infants was strongly associated with the age of the mother; higher rates of low birth weights were linked with anatomical immaturity of the mother (see Table 1.4.4, page 16). This theory has been challenged, and more recent studies have linked birth weights to family structure, family income, the mother's socioeconomic status, her diet during pregnancy, and her ability and willingness to obtain early and continuing prenatal health care. Most women who do not receive prenatal care are uninsured or underinsured, or are Medicaid recipients.

Infant mortality rates are higher for African American children than for white children. African American children were twice as likely to die before one year than were white children. Historically, this 2:1 ratio has been fairly constant.

Approximately two-thirds of all infant deaths are neonatal (deaths occurring before the first 28 days of life) and are generally related to maternal health. The remaining one-third—postneonatal mortality (deaths from the 28th day through the end of the first year)—occur in the environments that infants experience after leaving the hospital (see Table 1.4.5, page 46). Accordingly, these deaths are strongly related to socioeconomic conditions. Sudden infant death syndrome, the second largest cause of death among infants, has been associated with low maternal education, first pregnancy before age 20, and socioeconomic status. Neonatal mortality among Alaskan Indians and Native Americans has typically been lower than the rate for all races in the United States for that same year.

In 1990, the major causes of child mortality (children age 1 to 14 years) were accidents / adverse effects, followed by cancers and homicides / legal intervention. Here again, differences between whites and African Americans were notable. Among whites, only 4.1 percent of all deaths resulted from homicides / legal intervention. For African Americans, the figure was greater than 10.0 percent. White children were more likely to commit suicide than African American children. Suicides constituted 2.0 percent of all deaths of white children and less than 0.1 percent for African American children. For whites, the top three causes of child mortality were accidents, cancers, and heart disease. For African Americans, homicides ranked second as a cause of death. Males aged 5-14 were more than two times more likely to commit suicide than females, and females were much less likely to die as a result of homicide / legal intervention than males (see Table 1.4.6, page 46). As with infant mortality, death rates among American children aged 5-14 were generally higher than those in other countries.

1.5

THE CHANGING FACE OF AMERICA'S CHILDREN

Aside from recent policy-making trends that have diverted funding away from children's programs, another reason for the increased concern about children is the changing racial composition of the country and the vast economic disparities among racial / ethnic groups.

Though today's minority groups have many differences, all continue to suffer economic, political, and social disadvantages because of their racial or ethnic identity. To compound the problem, differences in race / ethnicity, class, income, and living conditions also lead to growing inequalities. As noted in the previous section, infant mortality rates are more than 50.0 percent higher among minorities than among whites; poverty rates among minority youth are also higher than among white youth, as are deaths from homicides and high school dropout rates. The country continues to be challenged in its effort to develop effective, equitable policies that address the needs of disadvantaged groups.

The changing racial / ethnic composition of America's children is revealed in Figures 1.5.1 and 1.5.2 (see page 17). In 1950, approximately 90.0 percent of all of America's children were white. Blacks and other minorities made up less than 12.0 percent of the population under 18. By 1990, the higher birth rate among minorities and the large influxes of immigrants from Latin America and Asia contributed to change this situation dramatically. Figure

Table 1.4.4. Number and percent of low birth weight and very low birth weight by age and race of mother, 1990.

Race	Age of mother	Total births	Low birth weight		Very low birth weight	
			Number	Percent	Number	Percent
All races	All ages	4,158,212	289,418	7.0	52,915	1.3
	Under 15	11,657	1,545	13.3	371	3.2
	15 to 19	521,826	48,324	9.3	9,286	1.8
	20 to 24	1,093,730	77,300	7.1	13,915	1.3
	25 to 29	1,277,108	78,486	6.2	13,838	1.1
	30 to 34	886,063	56,444	6.4	10,309	1.2
	35 to 39	317,583	23,283	7.3	4,431	1.4
	40 to 44	48,607	3,869	8.0	737	1.5
	45 to 49	1,638	167	10.2	28	1.7
White	All ages	3,290,273	187,179	5.7	31,314	1.0
	Under 15	4,974	512	10.3	124	2.5
	15 to 19	354,482	26,714	7.5	4,796	1.4
	20 to 24	837,572	48,203	5.8	7,828	0.9
	25 to 29	1,051,760	53,108	5.1	8,536	0.8
	30 to 34	739,209	39,358	5.3	6,626	0.9
	35 to 39	261,787	16,412	6.3	2,892	1.1
	40 to 44	39,309	2,754	7.0	494	1.3
	45 to 49	1,180	118	10.0	18	1.5
African American	All ages	684,336	90,523	13.3	19,953	2.9
	Under 15	6,338	995	15.7	241	3.8
	15 to 19	151,613	20,358	13.5	4,303	2.8
	20 to 24	217,274	26,620	12.3	5,758	2.7
	25 to 29	168,217	21,983	13.1	4,853	2.9
	30 to 34	99,514	14,253	14.3	3,299	3.3
	35 to 39	35,592	5,440	15.3	1,300	3.7
	40 to 44	5,581	842	15.1	191	3.4
	45 to 49	207	32	15.5	8	3.9

1.5.3 provides a detailed picture. Thirty-eight percent of Asians and 50.0 percent of the Hispanic foreign-born arrived in America during the period 1980-1990 alone. White children declined to 68.7 percent of the population, while minority children increased to more than 30.0 percent.

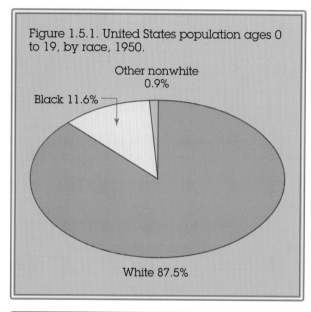

Figure 1.5.1. United States population ages 0 to 19, by race, 1950.

Other nonwhite 0.9%

Black 11.6%

White 87.5%

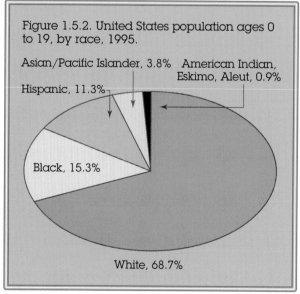

Figure 1.5.2. United States population ages 0 to 19, by race, 1995.

Asian/Pacific Islander, 3.8%   American Indian, Eskimo, Aleut, 0.9%

Hispanic, 11.3%

Black, 15.3%

White, 68.7%

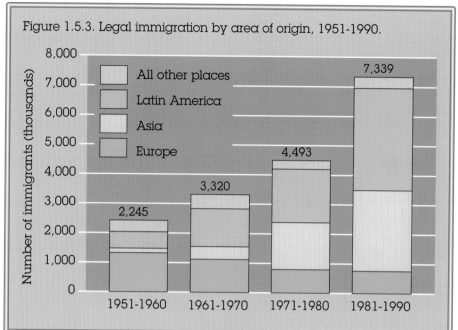

Figure 1.5.3. Legal immigration by area of origin, 1951-1990.

Number of immigrants (thousands)

All other places
Latin America
Asia
Europe

2,245   3,320   4,493   7,339

1951-1960   1961-1970   1971-1980   1981-1990

In Hawaii and the District of Columbia, minority children surpassed white children in number as inferred by Table 1.5.1, page 52. As reflected in the 1980 census, the United States began its gradual move away from being a predominantly white, European culture to a diverse, multicultural nation. What follows is a description of the child population in each of the major racial/ethnic groups in the United States today.

HISPANIC CHILDREN

Hispanic children are 12.0 percent of the total child population, estimated at 7,632,531. Children of Mexican, Cuban, Puerto Rican, Central and South American, Brazilian, Dominican, or Haitian origin make up the bulk of this population. Two-thirds of these children are of Mexican origin. In 1990, 70.0 percent of all Hispanic children lived in 5 states—California, Texas, New York, Florida, Illinois (see Table 1.5.1, page 52 and Figure 1.5.4, page 47). Most Hispanic children lived in states located on the U.S.-Mexico border, in states close to the Caribbean, and in states like California, Texas, New Jersey, New York, Florida, and Illinois that received large numbers of immigrants during earlier migration streams. Vermont, South Dakota, and Massachusetts had the lowest number of Hispanic children. Los Angeles and Chicago are the cities with the largest number of Hispanic children.

Hispanic children have an infant mortality rate of 7.6 deaths per 1,000 live births. A larger percentage are under 5 years of age than non-Hispanics, and a larger percentage are more likely to be living in a two-parent married couple family than African Americans. Hispanic children are less likely to be enrolled in prekindergarten. Approximately 1 in 5 Hispanic 3- and 4-year-olds are enrolled in prekindergarten. Hispanic youth (ages 16-24) are much more likely to drop out of school. Nearly 30.0 percent between 16-24 had dropped out of high school as of October 1992.

ASIAN AND PACIFIC ISLANDER CHILDREN

Three percent (1,908,132) of American children belong to this group, which includes Chinese, Japanese, Filipino,

Korean, Vietnamese, Laotian, Cambodian, Indians, Pacific Islanders, Samoans, Tongans, Fijians, Tahitians, Thai, and Hmong. California, Hawaii, New York, and Texas are the home states for 60.4 percent of all children in this group. Outside Hawaii, where Asian and Pacific Islander children account for 59.8 percent of all Hawaiian children, California far surpasses all other states with 38.9 percent of the total Asian and Pacific Islander child population in the United States (see Table 1.5.1, page 52 and Figure 1.5.5, page 48).

The Hmong and Cambodians are the most recent arrivals among this group, with a median age of 13-years and 19-years respectively. The proportion of Asian and Pacific Islander families maintained by a husband and wife was 82.0 percent and 73.0 percent—in line with the national average of 79.0 percent. Asian American children are less likely to grow up in a female-headed household. Two groups, however, had proportions above the national average—Cambodians and Hmong. Asian and Pacific Islander children are more likely to complete high school than other groups, and in general Asian American males have higher rates of high school graduation than do Asian American women. The high school graduation rate for all Asians and Pacific Islander was 78.0 percent; the national rate was 75.0 percent. About 11.0 percent of Asian American families were in poverty in 1989, slightly higher than the 10.0 percent for all American families. Hmong and Cambodian families had the highest family poverty rates—62.0 percent and 42.0 percent respectively. The lowest poverty rates were for Filipino (5.0 percent) and Japanese (3.0 percent) families.

AFRICAN AMERICAN CHILDREN

In 1990, there were 9,318,151 African American children in the United States. California, Florida, Georgia, New York, Texas, and Illinois had the largest number of African American children (see Table 1.5.1, page 52 and Figure 1.5.6, page 49). Over 90.0 percent lived in states east of a line extending north from Texas through the panhandle of Oklahoma, Missouri, Illinois, and Lake Michigan, and west of a line through Vermont, New Hampshire, and eastern Massachusetts. This pattern corresponds to that of initial settlements in the South followed by waves of the great migration to the Northeast and the Midwest. Blacks make up 11.0 percent of the population; black children make up 15.0 percent of the population of U.S. children. New York, California, Texas, Florida, and Georgia are home states for 35.9 percent of all African American children in the United States. Montana, Vermont, Wyoming, Idaho and South Dakota each had fewer than 2,500 African American children. Idaho stands out as the state with the lowest percent of African American children. About 40.0 percent of the black population resides in 10 consolidated metropolitan statistical areas (CMSAs), 7 of which are the most populous in the nation.

Infant mortality statistics suggest that African American infants are twice as likely to die or be of low birth weight as are white infants. Black children have higher death rates than whites, though significant improvements have been made.

The high school dropout rate for African American children declined from 16.0 percent in 1980 to 14.0 percent in 1990. Slightly more than 50.0 percent of all black children live in single-parent families. This represents an increase from 47.0 percent in 1980 and is 3 times more than the comparable rate for whites. The share of black children living with two parents declined from 58.0 percent in 1970 to 38.0 percent in 1990. Approximately 40.0 percent of African American children below age 6 live with mothers who never married. Black children are more likely to live with a grandparent than are white or Hispanic children.

AMERICAN INDIAN AND NATIVE ALASKAN CHILDREN

As of 1990, there are nearly two million American Indians, Eskimos, Inuits, and Aleuts living in the United States. Nearly two-thirds are concentrated in 10 states—Oklahoma, California, Arizona, New Mexico, Alaska, Washington, North Carolina, Texas, New York, and Michigan (see Table 1.5.1, page 52 and Figure 1.5.7, page 50). Oklahoma has the largest American Indian population. Twenty-two percent of all American Indians lived on reservations and trust lands. More than 31.0 percent of American Indians 3-years old and older living on reservations and trust lands are enrolled in school.

In 1990, 39.0 percent of the American Indian population was under age 20. Twenty-seven percent of all American Indian families were headed by a single female; this compares with 17.0 percent for the country as a whole.

In 1990, 66.0 percent of the 1,080,000 American Indians 25 years old and over were high school graduates—compared with 56.0 percent in 1980. Only about

10.0 percent of American Indians completed a bachelor's degree or higher (the national rate is 20.0 percent). Twenty-seven percent of American Indian families were in poverty in 1989, compared with 10.0 percent of all U.S. families.

NON-HISPANIC WHITE CHILDREN

Two-thirds of the 64 million U.S. children are non-Hispanic whites. White children are more dispersed across the continental United States than are children of all other groups (see Table 1.5.1, page 52 and Figure 1.5.8, page 51). States in the upper Northeast and the Midwest generally have larger numbers of white children. For the most part, white children tend to be concentrated in less urbanized states. Maine, West Virginia, and New Hampshire have the largest percentage of white children. Though white children are much more likely to live in families with high incomes and much less likely to experience poverty, their lives have changed considerably since the 1950s. The percentage of white children who lived in traditional families, where the father is a full-time worker and the mother a full-time homemaker, declined from approximately 47.0 percent in 1950 to 20.0 percent in 1990. As with all other groups, the number living in two-parent households also declined from 83.0 percent in 1980 to 80.0 percent in 1990. Another trend that has altered the family life of America's white children is the increase in the number born to unmarried mothers. In 1960, only 2.3 percent of all white children were born out of wedlock. By 1987, that number had increased to 16.7 percent. The rate of high school graduation has remained stable for white children since the mid-1970s. About 90.0 percent of whites aged 18-24 have completed high school.

Some researchers have noted a deterioration in the emotional and psychological well-being of American children. Among white children in particular, studies cite rising adolescent suicide rates and a growing number of children with chronic emotional problems. Most children, however, are not depressed or unhappy with their lives.

1.6

ADOPTIONS/FOSTER CARE

No consideration of the condition of America's children would be complete without an examination of children placed in the public welfare system for care. This includes those in foster care who are waiting to be placed as well as those placed in adoptive homes through the public welfare system. According to the Child Welfare League of America, adoption is "for children who cannot be cared for by their birth parents and who need and can benefit from the establishment of new and permanent family ties established through legal adoption." Currently there is no single agency responsible for collecting data on adoptions handled by the public welfare system. Private, independent adoptions are not required to report data in any way.

Unlike adoption, foster care is temporary placement for children who will eventually be returned to their family of origin.

ADOPTIONS

In 1990, there were 118,779 children in adoptive placement. It is estimated that there are 1 million adopted children living with adoptive parents; two to four percent of U.S. families include an adopted child, and there are 5 million adopted individuals of all ages. In recent years, a number of issues have become important regarding the practice of placing children in adoptive homes. The most pressing is certainly the need for accurate and complete information from all adoption agencies. Between 1944 and 1975, the Children's Bureau and the National Center for Social Statistics collected data on adoptions based on court records. Since 1975 however, no single agency has responsibility for collecting data on adoptions. Most recent data are provided by the Adoption Information Improvement Project (AIIP), the National Council for Adoption, and the Voluntary Cooperative Information System (VCIS). Data on international adoptions are collected by the Statistics Division of the U.S. Immigration and Naturalization Service.

In the United States, states are under no obligation to report data, and thus their reporting is often incomplete and sporadic. Moreover, the agencies include data on "formal" adoptions only. Informal adoptions—which occur when a birth mother allows another person to take parental responsibility for her child without obtaining legal approval or recognition—are excluded altogether. Informal adoption arrangements are common in minority communities. Additionally, the VCIS includes data only on those children who have passed through the public welfare system. Private adoptions are only occasionally reported, and independent adoptions are seldom if ever reported.

With these shortcomings in mind, it is possible to provide an overview of adoption trends and characteristics of adoptees in the United States.

The AIIP and the Adoption Technical Assistance Project (ATAP) reported that there were 118,779 adoptions in the United States in 1990 (see Figure 1.6.1, page 53). This is a 1.0 percent increase over the 1987 figure of 117,585. The American Public Welfare Association's (APWA) Voluntary Cooperative Information System, which reports on adoptions of children who are part of the public child welfare system, noted that in fiscal year 1989, 16,000 public agency adoptions were finalized. Eighteen thousand children and youth were placed in a nonfinalized adoptive home. The overwhelming majority of these children (approximately 85.0 percent) were under age 12 (48.0 percent were 5 and under). Non-Hispanic white children (54.9 percent of all adoptions) were most likely to be adopted. This figure, however, represents a significant decline from the 1982 figure of 68.5 percent. Roughly 29.0 percent of adopted children were black. Approximately, sixty-four percent of adopted children had one or more special needs (see Table 1.6.1, page 55). Special needs children may include those who have suffered physical and/or emotional abuse, neglect or abandonment by the biological parents, children who are part of a sibling group, religious group, and/or racial minority or are physically handicapped. It may also include children who are poorly served by the foster care system and have drifted from home to home.

Characteristics of children *awaiting* adoptive placement differ in some respects. They were generally older, minority, and had been in foster/substitute care for a longer time. Nearly 45.0 percent of children awaiting adoptive placement had waited two years or more and, like adopted children, an overwhelming percentage had special needs (see Table 1.6.1, page 55).

Over the years, there has been an increase in the percent of foster care children with special needs who were adopted (see Table 1.6.2, page 55). This improvement in adoption rates for this group is due in part to the flexibility that states now have in using the special needs category. The Title IV-E adoption assistance program gives to states the ability to provide financial assistance to adoptive parents who adopt children with special needs and who are SSI or AFDC eligible. It also authorizes federal matching funds for states to pay the nonrecurring one-time adoption expenses of parents of special needs children, regardless of AFDC or SSI eligibility (see Figure 1.6.2, page 21). This has served as an incentive to adoption.

As of January 1987, federal reimbursement under Title IV-E was capped at $2,000 and covers such costs as attorney fees and probate court fees. Payments vary by state and may be adjusted if circumstances change. Payments may also be discontinued when the child reaches 18 (or 21 depending on the state guidelines) or if the parents are no longer legally responsible for support of the child. Figure 1.6.3 shows average adoption assistance claims for 1992 (see page 53). The average payment was $664. One reason that the level of reimbursement was so low is that many

items are already covered under the states' existing adoption program.

Another adoption issue revolves around the guidelines of confidentiality and anonymity in the adoption process. Of particular concern is balancing the rights of the adoptive parents, the adoptee, and the birth parents. When faced with disputes over just how confidential and how anonymous the adoption process should be, courts seek to maintain the sanctity of the adoptive pact on the one hand while acting in the "best interest of the child" on the other. The "access" issue has adoption advocates strongly divided, and the Uniform Adoption Act (proposed by the National Conference of Commissioners on Uniform State Laws) has not been able to devise a procedure that is acceptable to a majority of states. Figure 1.6.4 identifies states that allow access to confidential adoption records upon mutual consent (see page 54).

The controversy over transracial adoption is another important issue in adoption discussion. The term "transracial" refers to the matching of children and parents who are racially different.

Initially, transracial adoptions were largely the result of international adoptions. Slightly over 7,000 Korean and Japanese children were adopted by American families (mostly white) between 1948 and 1962. By the 1960s, growing concern in Korea about "irregularities" in the adoption process as well as nationalistic resentment reduced the number of Korean children available for adoption. In the early 1960s and 1970s, black/white transracial adoption reached its peak. In 1971 alone, 2,500 black children were

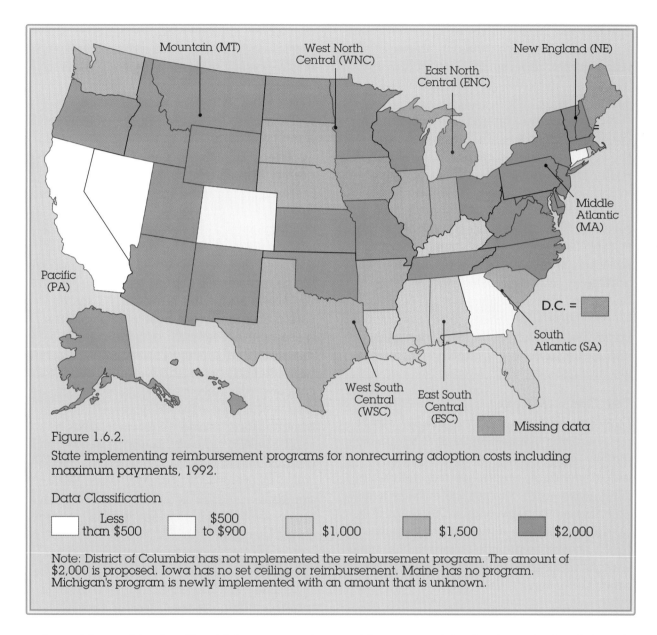

Figure 1.6.2.

State implementing reimbursement programs for nonrecurring adoption costs including maximum payments, 1992.

Data Classification

Less than $500 $500 to $900 $1,000 $1,500 $2,000

Note: District of Columbia has not implemented the reimbursement program. The amount of $2,000 is proposed. Iowa has no set ceiling or reimbursement. Maine has no program. Michigan's program is newly implemented with an amount that is unknown.

adopted into white families. This prompted the National Association of Black Social Workers to question whether sufficient efforts were being made to find black families for black children and later led to a resolution strongly opposing the placement of black children with white families. Black/

white transracial adoptions declined sharply afterwards. Similarly, Native American opposition to transracial adoption led to the passage of the Indian Child Welfare Act of 1978, which curtailed years of transracial adoption of Indian children.

The Vietnam conflict added to the num-

ber of transracial adoptions during the 1970s. When U.S. involvement ceased, however, the number of Vietnamese children adopted by white Americans decreased to a very small number. Currently, the largest number of transracial adoptions involve Hispanic children from Colombia, El Salvador, and Mexico. Transracial adoptions of children from Central and South America now number nearly 1,000 annually. As with Asians, African Americans, and Indians, opposition to the adoption of Hispanic children by white families is increasing.

In many instances, information is too sketchy to paint a comprehensive picture of adoption in the United States. If policy makers and advocates are to make informed decisions and develop workable programs and policies, more accurate and more inclusive information is needed. A highlighted box on page 23 provides a listing of adoption information needed on a national level.

FOSTER CARE

Foster care/substitute care is intended to provide protection and placement for children in cases where it is in the best interest of the child to no longer live with the family of birth. No one knows exactly how many children are currently in foster care. As with adoption, the primary source of national data on foster care is Voluntary Cooperative Information System (VCIS). Based on research conducted between 1982 and 1989, they estimated the number of children in foster care in 1991 to be 429,000. VCIS includes in this figure all children in foster family care (relative and non-relative) group homes, child care facilities, emergency shelter care, supervised independent living, nonfinalized adoptive placements, and any other arrangement. This number represents an increase over previous years. Table 1.6.3, on page 55 provides estimates of substitute care populations by state for 1990-1992. Figure 1.6.5, on page 54, maps their spatial distribution. Only 11 states experienced a decline in their foster care populations over the period 1986-1988. VCIS provides statistics on characteristics of children entering, in, and leaving substitute care. Here are some of their major findings:

1. AGE

Children, 13-18, are the largest percentage of those entering and leaving care in 1989. Children 6-12, however, were the largest percentage in care (see Table 1.6.4, page 56). It is difficult to determine precisely the outcome for that particular group. Data indicate that 63.0 percent of the children who left care during 1989 were reunified with their family of origin (see Table 1.6.5, page 56).

2. RACE / ETHNICITY

Table 1.6.6 provides a description of the race/ethnicity of the 1989 foster care population (see page 56). Of note is the percentage entering and the percentage leaving for each group. For all groups, the percent is roughly the same. The only group for which the percentage leaving care is not comparable to the percentage entering care is African Americans, who are over represented in the foster care system.

3. DISABILITY / HEALTH STATUS

With less than a third of the states reporting, the American Public Welfare Association (APWA) found that 16.6 percent of children in foster care in1989 had one or more disabling conditions.

Protective service (neglect, abuse, etc.) was the most frequently given reason for placement in substitute care (see Table 1.6.7, page 56).

In the United States, there is a strong belief that children should remain with their natural parents in their natural home. Foster care is regarded as a temporary living arrangement. Ideally, children should remain in foster care for as short a time as possible. In most instances, the goal is family reunification. With 23 states reporting, APWA data reveal that the median length of time in continuous care during 1989 was 17 months.

Two federal programs, both part of the Social Security Act, have had significant impact on foster care/substitute care. They are discussed below.

THE CHILD WELFARE SERVICES PROGRAM (TITLE IV-B)

The Child Welfare Services Program was initially designed to provide aid to homeless, dependent, and neglected children in rural areas. Later, monies were made available to train social workers. States were asked to provide a match to the federal funds as well as provide evidence that child welfare programs were coordinated with other social service delivery programs. Child Welfare Services Program (CWSP) monies were to be used for child day care, foster care maintenance payments, and adoption assistance payments. Despite a recognition of the importance of child welfare services, the CWSP was never funded adequately, and, until fiscal year 1980, no more than $56.6 million was ever actually appropriated in any year for the program. There were no income eligibility requirements for the receipt of Title IV-B child welfare services, and reporting requirements were minimal.

TITLE IV-E AID TO FAMILIES WITH DEPENDENT CHILDREN FOSTER CARE PROGRAM

The AFDC-FC program had considerably greater impact on the lives of children. States were required to provide foster care maintenance payments to AFDC eligible children who had been removed from the home of a relative. The program stated if the child received or would have been eligible to receive AFDC prior to removal from the home and if the removal and foster care placement were based on a voluntary placement agreement, or a judicial determination that the child's welfare would be best served if he or she were removed; the care and placement of the child are the responsibility of a public agency. Maintenance payments for such costs as food, shelter, clothing, school supplies, incidentals, liability insurance, and reasonable travel to the child's home for visits. States are responsible for providing Medicaid coverage. Table 1.6.8 provides federal foster care expenditures under Title IV-E for 1993 (see page 56). Note that expenditures for California and New York are half the entire federal allocation. Table 1.6.9 shows basic monthly maintenance rates for each state. States were allowed to set rates at any level based on age; thus they differ significantly by age and state (see page 57).

Several points were significant about the AFDC-FC legislation. First, unlike the CWSP, the AFDC-FC program was part of the larger AFDC program and therefore is an open-ended entitlement program—that is, the federal government must pay for all the children who meet the eligibility requirements. Second, the legislation did not permit the funds to be used for anything other than out-of-home placement. Adoption assistance or family reunification could not benefit from AFDC-FC funds. Thus, the major federal child care program created an incentive for states to place children in foster homes and keep them there. Third, the AFDC-FC program required minimal review of the quality of care and gives only lip service to the importance of encouraging family ties. A recent Government Accounting Office (GAO) investigation of the program found that children reimbursed by AFDC-FC

stayed in care longer than nonfederally supported children and that few family reunification efforts were documented.

Practitioners, policy makers, and researchers have recently identified several issues of importance for foster care. A major issue, as noted above, is certainly the commitment to family reunification / kinship care, preventive services, or adoption-related services. Though the dominant view is that children should be with their families, the creation of policy to support this effort lags behind. Still another issue is the training given to foster parents. How this training is best structured, who pays, and what forms training should take are some of the more pressing questions. Unnecessary

removal from the home is also an issue confronting foster care practitioners. Addressing this is more problematic since the basis for decision making is more philosophical (interventionist vs. non-interventionist) than with other issues. Another issue is monitoring the foster care system— the quality of care, appropriateness of placement, and so forth.

The policy questions spawned by these issues should continue to generate lively debate. Improvement of the system will be a long, arduous process. Effective solutions depend in part on a thorough understanding of the issues and people involved.

Adoption Information Needed on a National Level

Information regarding the number of adoptions

- State maintenance of minimum adoption information data base
- Uniform definitions and methods for counting
- Systematic reporting of all adoptions to a responsible federal agency with penalties for noncompliance
- Case specific data, e.g. relative v.s. nonrelative adoption (confidentiality maintained)
- Breakdown of placement arrangements (public, private, independent)

Information regarding child characteristics

- Numbers of children relinquished
- Demographic information on each child
- Special needs status
- Reasons for entry
- Length of time in substitute care
- Placement history
- Current care arrangements
- Available subsidies

- Goals
- Reasons for discharge from substitute care

Information regarding birthparents

- Demographic information
- Reason for termination of parental rights for birthmother and biological father
- Information on other children
- Medical history (drug abuse, genetic information, prenatal care)

Information regarding adoption seekers

- Number of persons seeking to adopt
- Numbers who successfully adopt
- Movement into and out of the adoption seeking process and reasons
- Demographic information
- Characteristics of desired child(ren)
- Previous relationships of adopted children with adoptive parents
- Waiting times for adoption

- Subsidies received
- Previous adoptions/placements

Information regarding adoption outcome

- Numbers of adopted children
- Demographic information
- Characteristics of adoptive family
- Disrupted Adoptions
- Dissolved Adoptions
- Post adoption services

From: *The Future Of Children-Adoption*, 1993.

For other discussions of needs and suggestions for future national data collection efforts, see Maza, P. (1990). "What We Do—and Don't—Know About Adoption Statistics." Permanency Report, Child Welfare League of America. *Permanent Families for Children*, 21, (3), Spring. Department of Health and Human Services. See also Title IV-B and Title IV-E of the Social Security Act; "Data Collection for Foster Care and Adoption." *Federal Register*, 27 September 1990, 55,188:39540-39571.

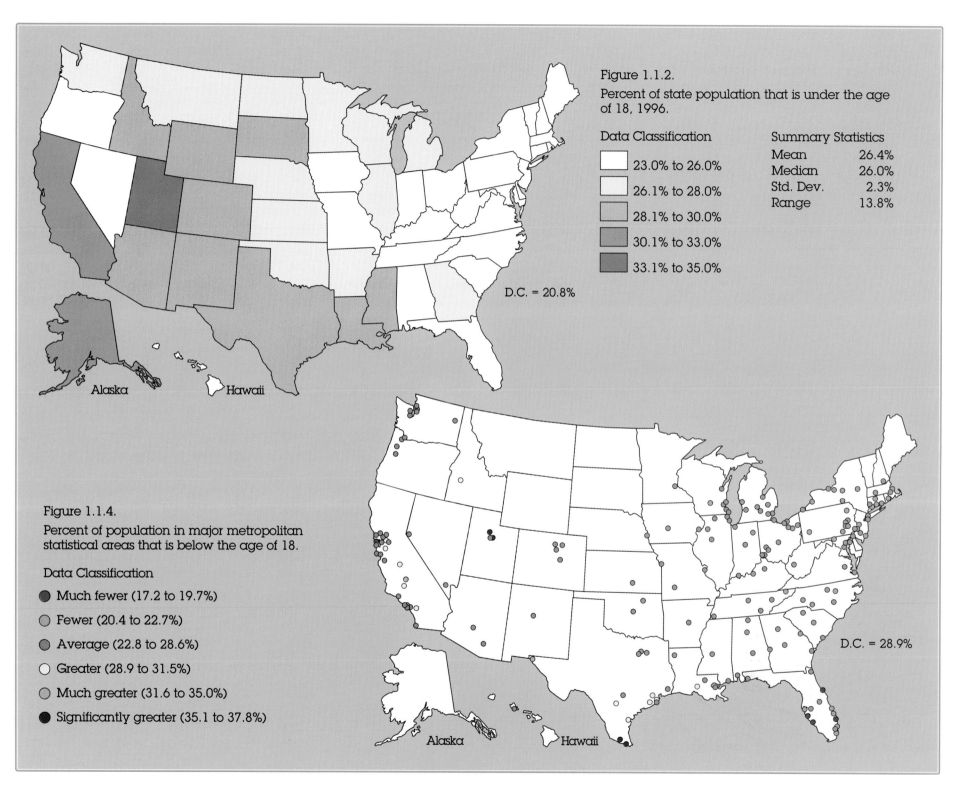

Figure 1.1.2.
Percent of state population that is under the age of 18, 1996.

Data Classification

- 23.0% to 26.0%
- 26.1% to 28.0%
- 28.1% to 30.0%
- 30.1% to 33.0%
- 33.1% to 35.0%

Summary Statistics

Mean	26.4%
Median	26.0%
Std. Dev.	2.3%
Range	13.8%

D.C. = 20.8%

Figure 1.1.4.

Percent of population in major metropolitan statistical areas that is below the age of 18.

Data Classification

- Much fewer (17.2 to 19.7%)
- Fewer (20.4 to 22.7%)
- Average (22.8 to 28.6%)
- Greater (28.9 to 31.5%)
- Much greater (31.6 to 35.0%)
- Significantly greater (35.1 to 37.8%)

D.C. = 28.9%

Table 1.1.1. Resident population, number of children, and children as percent of state population, 1995.

	Total	Under 18	Percent under 18
Alabama	4,253	1,080	25.4
Alaska	604	189	31.3
Arizona	4,218	1,193	28.3
Arkansas	2,484	650	26.2
California	31,589	9,794	31.0
Colorado	3,747	1,081	28.8
Connecticut	3,275	798	24.4
Delaware	717	179	25.0
Dist. of Columbia	554	115	20.8
Florida	14,166	3,371	23.8
Georgia	7,201	1,923	26.7
Hawaii	1,187	309	26.0
Idaho	1,163	347	29.8
Illinois	11,830	3,126	26.4
Indiana	5,803	1,487	25.6
Iowa	2,842	725	25.5
Kansas	2,565	693	27.0
Kentucky	3,860	973	25.2
Louisiana	4,342	1,239	28.5
Maine	1,241	305	24.6
Maryland	5,042	1,272	25.2
Massachusetts	6,074	1,432	23.6
Michigan	9,549	2,520	26.4
Minnesota	4,610	1,246	27.0
Mississippi	2,697	762	28.3
Missouri	5,324	1,381	25.9
Montana	870	236	27.1
Nebraska	1,637	443	27.1
Nevada	1,530	398	26.0
New Hampshire	1,148	295	25.7
New Jersey	7,945	1,963	24.7
New Mexico	1,685	500	29.7
New York	18,136	4,537	25.0
North Carolina	7,195	1,799	25.0
North Dakota	641	171	26.7
Ohio	11,151	2,860	25.6
Oklahoma	3,278	878	26.8
Oregon	3,141	797	25.4
Pennsylvania	12,072	2,909	24.1
Rhode Island	990	238	24.0
South Carolina	3,673	945	25.7
South Dakota	729	206	28.3
Tennessee	5,256	1,310	24.9
Texas	18,724	5,401	28.8
Utah	1,951	675	34.6
Vermont	585	147	25.1
Virginia	6,618	1,613	24.4
Washington	5,431	1,419	26.1
West Virginia	1,828	421	23.0
Wisconsin	5,123	1,353	26.4
Wyoming	480	136	28.3
United States	262,754	69,840	26.6

Table 1.1.2. Counties with the largest percent of residents under age 18, 1992.

County	State	Percent
San Juan	Utah	43.3
Emery	Utah	43.0
Duchesne	Utah	43.0
Millard	Utah	42.9
Apache	Arizona	41.7
Uintah	Utah	41.4
Box Elder	Utah	40.6
Jefferson	Idaho	40.4
Davis	Utah	40.2
Uinta	Wyoming	39.8
Wasatch	Utah	39.5
Starr	Texas	39.4
Sevier	Utah	39.3
Bethel Census Area	Alaska	39.0
McKinley	New Mexico	38.8
Bingham	Idaho	38.6
Navajo	Arizona	38.4
Rolette	North Dakota	38.2
Lincoln	Wyoming	38.1
Sanpete	Utah	38.0
Maverick	Texas	38.0
Fremont	Idaho	37.9
Utah	Utah	37.7
Glacier	Montana	37.1
Webb	Texas	36.7

Table 1.1.3. Counties with the smallest percent of residents under age 18, 1992.

County	State	Percent
Williamsburg (city)	Virginia	9.2
Radford (city)	Virginia	12.7
Arlington	Virginia	15.1
Alexandria	Virginia	15.4
Charlotte	Florida	15.6
Harrisonburg	Virginia	15.6
Sarasota	Florida	15.7
San Francisco	California	16.1
Llano	Texas	16.4
New York	New York	16.6
Pitking	Colorado	16.8
Watauga	North Carolina	17.1
Monroe	Florida	17.4
Martin	Florida	17.6
Citrus	Florida	17.6
Whitman	Washington	17.8
Pinellas	Florida	17.8
Pasco	Florida	17.9
Montgomery	Virginia	17.9
Charlottesville (city)	Virginia	18.0
Centre	Pennsylvania	18.3
McDonough	Illinois	18.4
Monroe	Indiana	18.4
Hernando	Florida	18.4
Fredericksburg (city)	Virginia	18.6

Table 1.1.4. Fertility rates for racial and ethnic groups, 1992.

Race/ethnicity	Fertility rate
Non-Hispanic	
White	1.9
African American	2.5
Asian/Pacific Islander	2.3
American Indian/Eskimo/Aleut	2.9
Hispanic	2.7

Note: Fertility rate is defined as the average number of children born per woman.

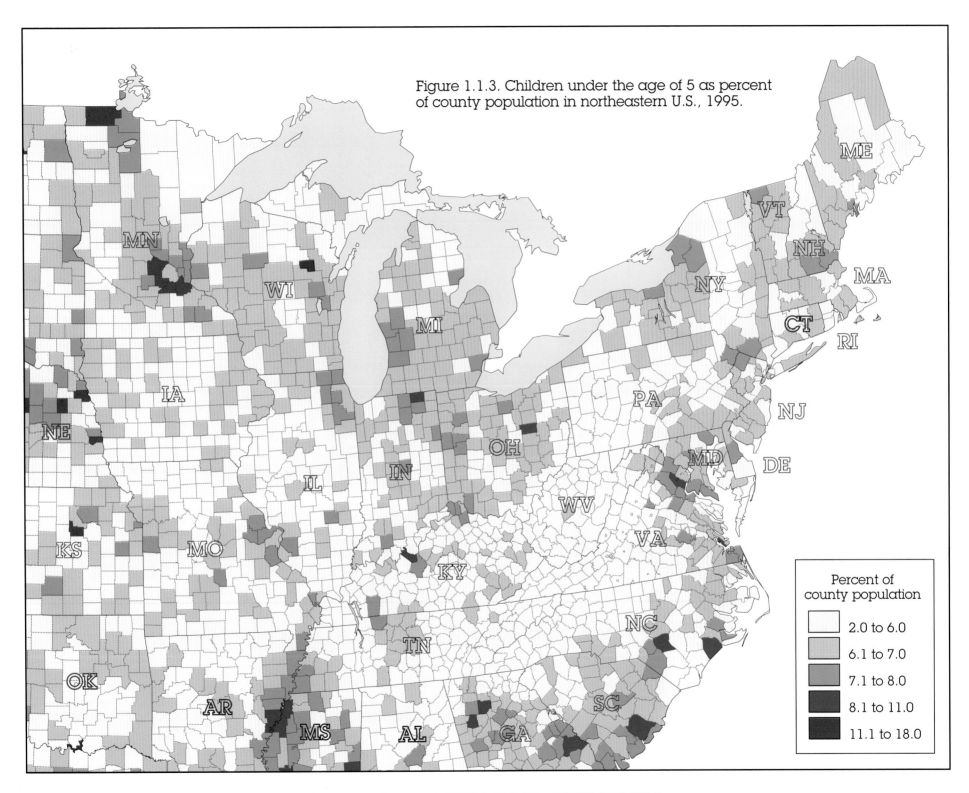

Figure 1.1.3. Children under the age of 5 as percent of county population in northeastern U.S., 1995.

Percent of county population

	2.0 to 6.0
	6.1 to 7.0
	7.1 to 8.0
	8.1 to 11.0
	11.1 to 18.0

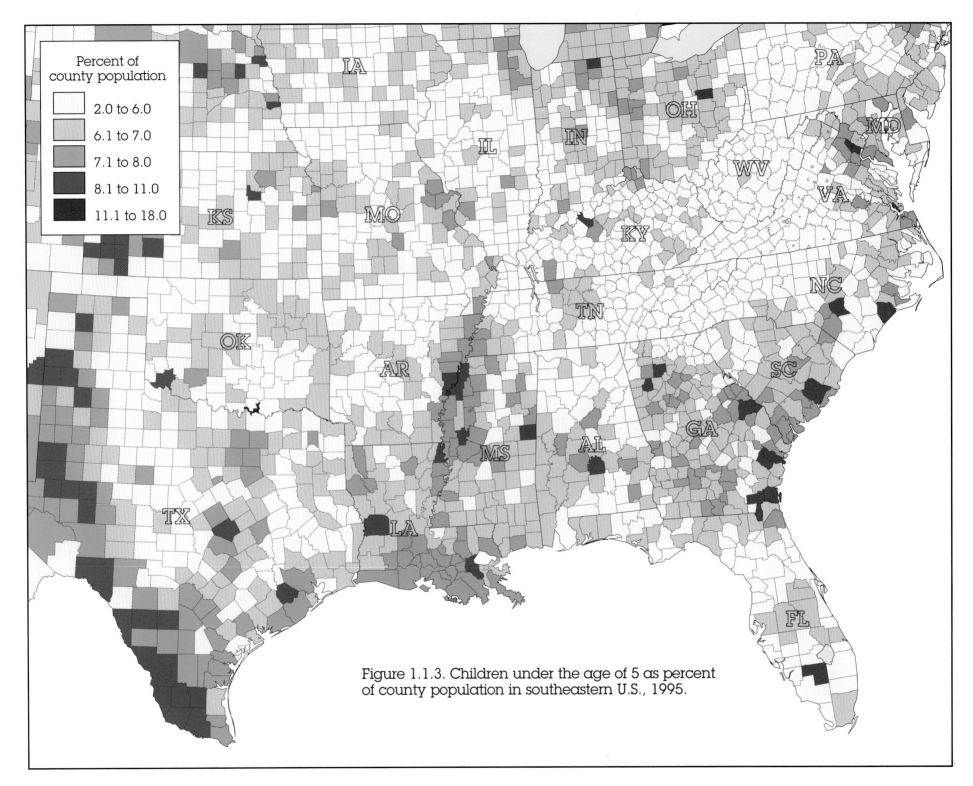

Figure 1.1.3. Children under the age of 5 as percent of county population in southeastern U.S., 1995.

Percent of county population
- 2.0 to 6.0
- 6.1 to 7.0
- 7.1 to 8.0
- 8.1 to 11.0
- 11.1 to 18.0

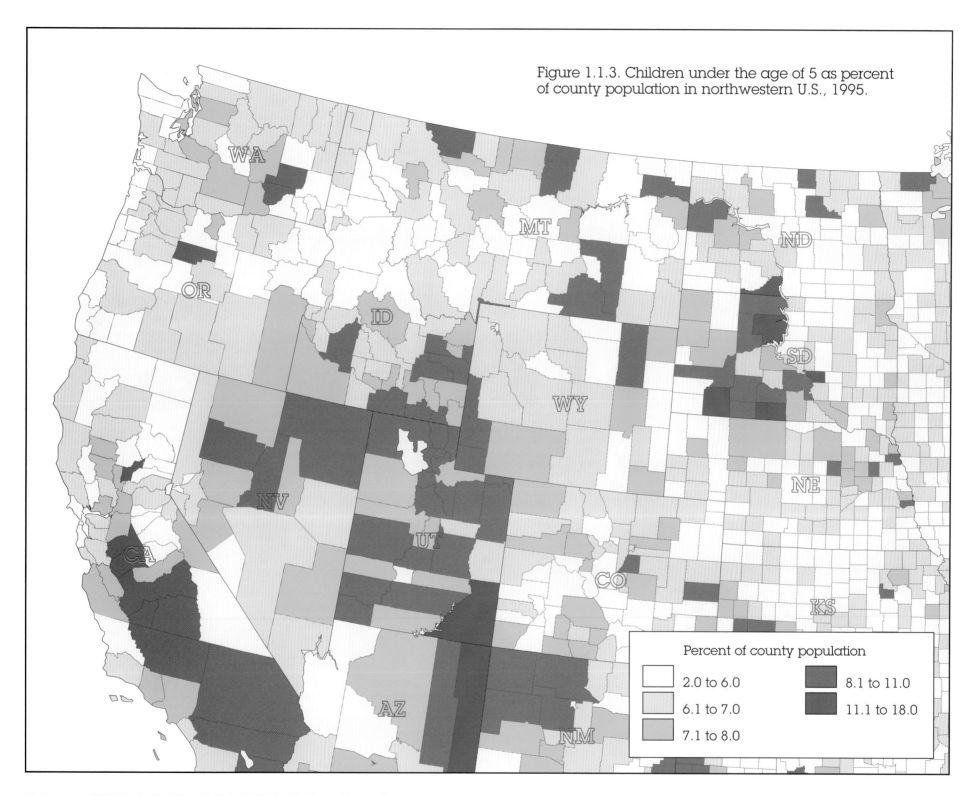

Figure 1.1.3. Children under the age of 5 as percent of county population in northwestern U.S., 1995.

Percent of county population

2.0 to 6.0	8.1 to 11.0
6.1 to 7.0	11.1 to 18.0
7.1 to 8.0	

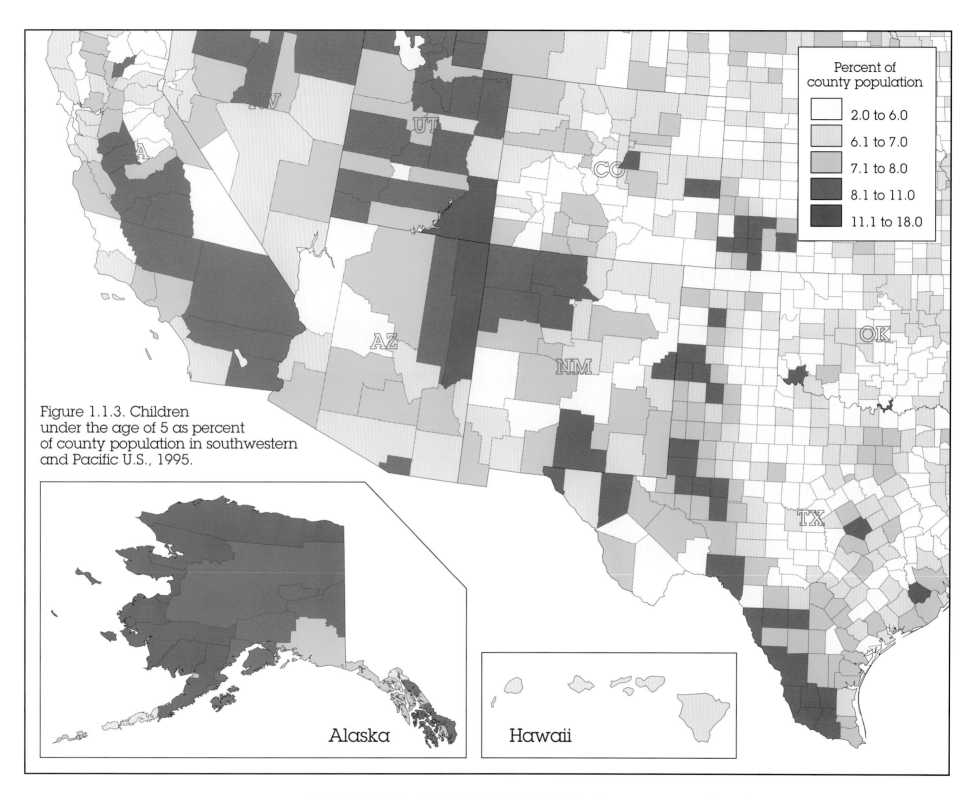

Figure 1.1.3. Children under the age of 5 as percent of county population in southwestern and Pacific U.S., 1995.

Percent of county population

- 2.0 to 6.0
- 6.1 to 7.0
- 7.1 to 8.0
- 8.1 to 11.0
- 11.1 to 18.0

Alaska

Hawaii

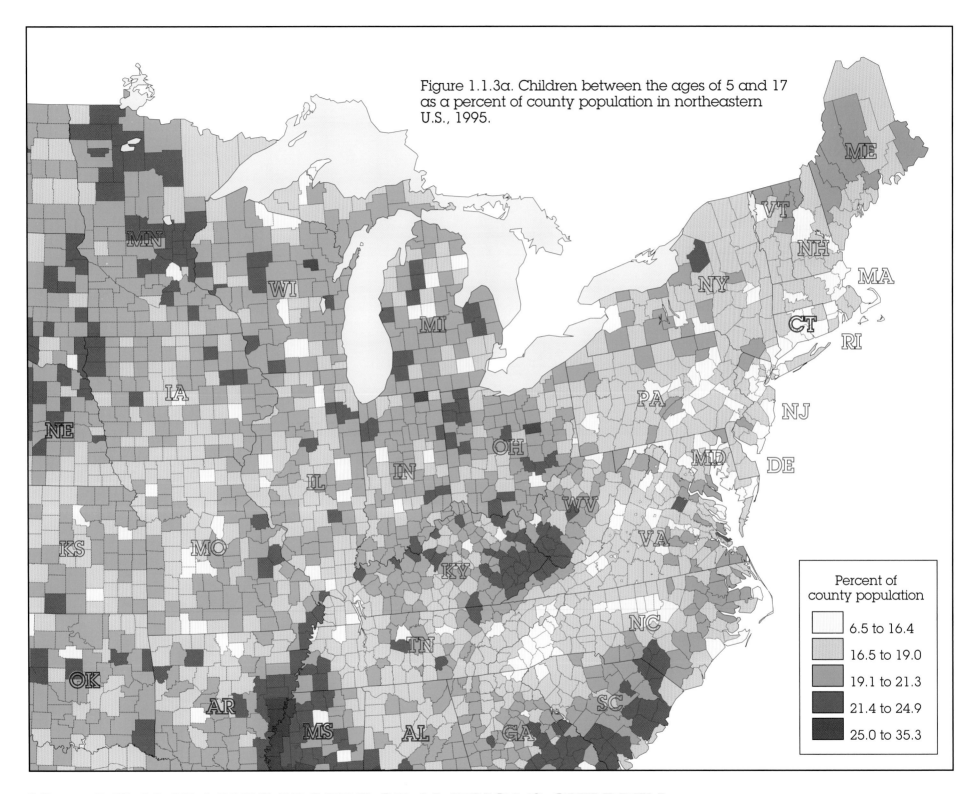

Figure 1.1.3a. Children between the ages of 5 and 17 as a percent of county population in northeastern U.S., 1995.

Percent of county population

	6.5 to 16.4
	16.5 to 19.0
	19.1 to 21.3
	21.4 to 24.9
	25.0 to 35.3

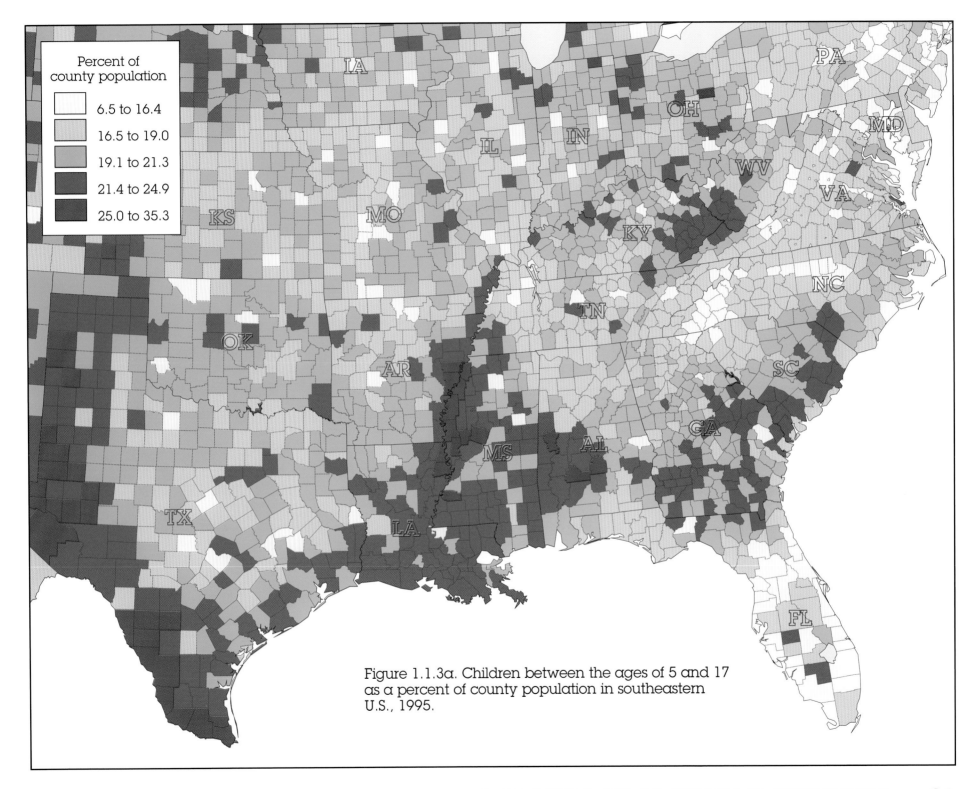

Figure 1.1.3a. Children between the ages of 5 and 17 as a percent of county population in southeastern U.S., 1995.

Percent of county population

- 6.5 to 16.4
- 16.5 to 19.0
- 19.1 to 21.3
- 21.4 to 24.9
- 25.0 to 35.3

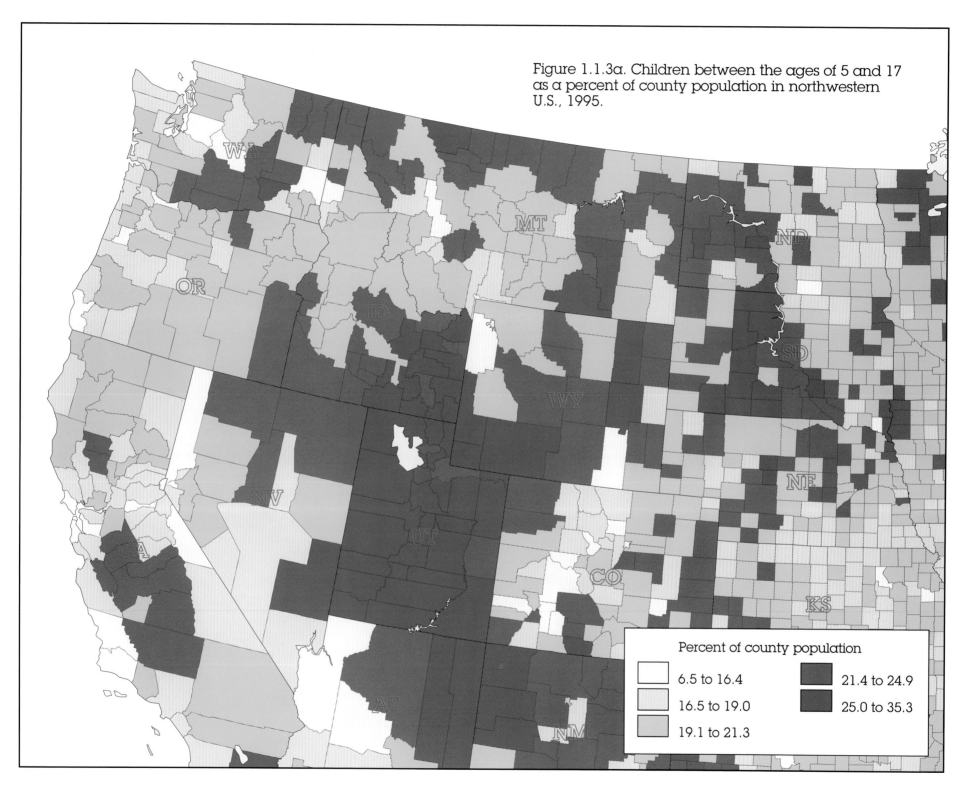

Figure 1.1.3a. Children between the ages of 5 and 17 as a percent of county population in northwestern U.S., 1995.

Percent of county population

6.5 to 16.4	21.4 to 24.9
16.5 to 19.0	25.0 to 35.3
19.1 to 21.3	

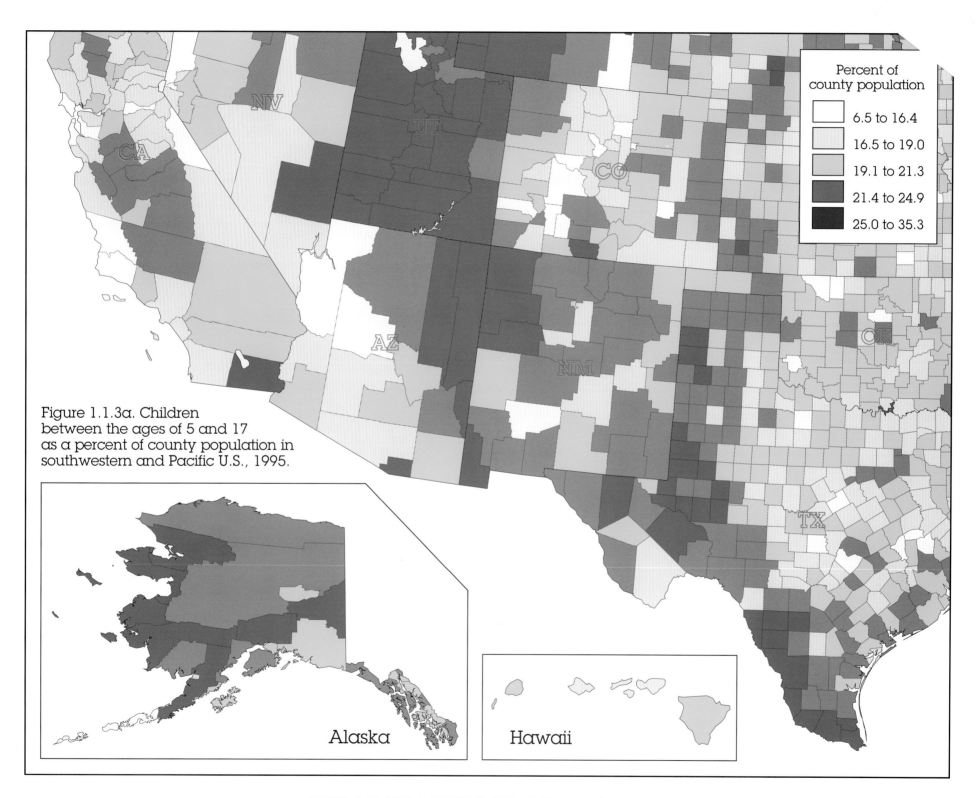

Figure 1.1.3a. Children
between the ages of 5 and 17
as a percent of county population in
southwestern and Pacific U.S., 1995.

Percent of
county population

	6.5 to 16.4
	16.5 to 19.0
	19.1 to 21.3
	21.4 to 24.9
	25.0 to 35.3

Alaska

Hawaii

Table 1.2.1. The working poor by residence, 1973 and 1987.

Item	United States 1973 (1)	United States 1987 (2)	Metro 1973	Metro 1987	Nonmetro 1973	Nonmetro 1987
Poor householders who worked	51.6	47.2	47.6	44.0	57.3	54.9
Poor householders who worked full-time (3)	18.3	14.6	15.5	12.8	22.2	18.8
Poor householders who did not work	48.4	52.9	52.4	56.0	42.7	45.3
Main reason for not working						
Ill or disabled	32.2	23.4	25.0	20.6	44.8	31.9
Keeping house	43.0	41.0	51.6	44.7	27.8	30.1
Going to school	3.4	5.7	4.2	6.3	2.0	4.1
Unable to find work	3.6	11.2	4.6	9.9	2.0	15.1
Retired (4)	n/a	16.6	n/a	16.3	n/a	17.5
Other	17.8	2.0	14.6	2.2	23.3	1.3
Poor families with						
No workers	38.1	42.8	42.4	45.9	32.1	35.4
One worker	41.9	39.1	42.0	38.2	41.8	41.3
Two or more workers	20.0	18.1	15.7	15.9	26.1	23.4

Notes:

(1) 1973 data based on metro/nonmetro designations from the 1970 census. Data include families whose householders are in the armed forces.

(2) 1987 data based on metro/nonmetro designations as of June 1984. Family data are based on the "householder" concept while the 1973 family data are based on older "head" concept. Changing from the head to the householder concept had minor effects on poverty statistics. Data do not include families whose householders are in the armed forces.

(3) Full-time work is defined here as working at least thirty-five hours per week for at least fifty weeks per year.

(4) Retired included in "other" in 1973.

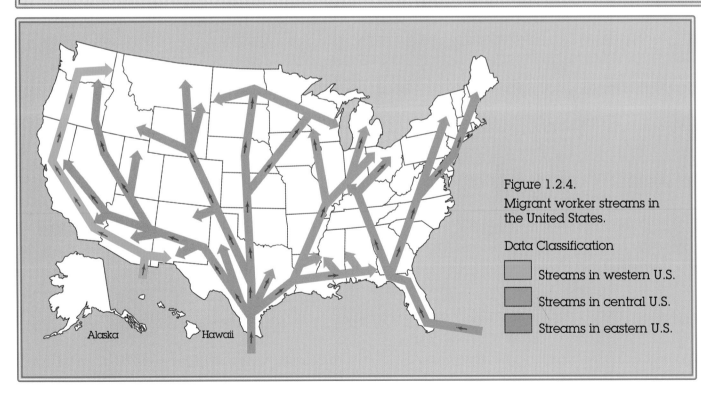

Figure 1.2.4.

Migrant worker streams in the United States.

Data Classification

Streams in western U.S.

Streams in central U.S.

Streams in eastern U.S.

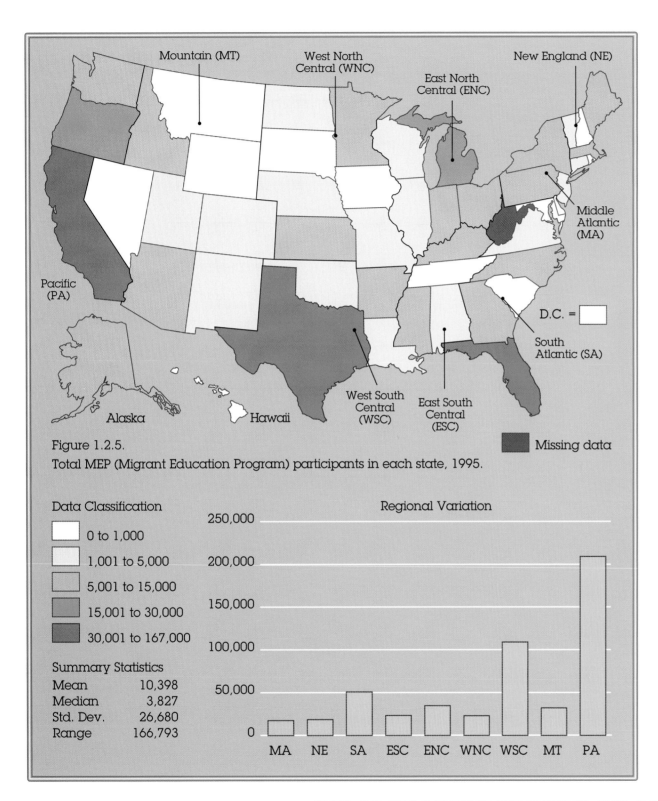

Figure 1.2.5.
Total MEP (Migrant Education Program) participants in each state, 1995.

Data Classification

- 0 to 1,000
- 1,001 to 5,000
- 5,001 to 15,000
- 15,001 to 30,000
- 30,001 to 167,000

Summary Statistics

Mean	10,398
Median	3,827
Std. Dev.	26,680
Range	166,793

Regional Variation

Total MEP allocations and number of MEP participants by state, 1995.	MEP allocations	MEP participants
Alabama	2,555,058	4,944
Alaska	9,923,035	11,227
Arizona	6,837,496	14,244
Arkansas	3,487,308	8,385
California	91,969,523	166,793
Colorado	3,425,526	4,142
Connecticut	2,160,250	3,663
Delaware	401,964	424
Dist. of Columbia	192,504	337
Florida	23,568,013	33,068
Georgia	4,606,706	9,942
Hawaii	0	0
Idaho	4,811,568	6,996
Illinois	1,771,460	2,696
Indiana	2,775,795	6,181
Iowa	306,293	528
Kansas	6,417,579	11,736
Kentucky	6,896,880	12,447
Louisiana	1,905,641	3,991
Maine	3,465,036	5,064
Maryland	265,330	486
Massachusetts	2,725,170	8,274
Michigan	11,973,962	19,167
Minnesota	2,336,932	5,332
Mississippi	1,341,990	5,595
Missouri	814,257	1,911
Montana	706,733	724
Nebraska	2,293,375	2,219
Nevada	502,728	526
New Hampshire	97,518	95
New Jersey	947,831	1,662
New Mexico	1,242,065	3,417
New York	5,700,409	8,970
North Carolina	4,231,568	5,041
North Dakota	515,740	1,152
Ohio	1,881,507	5,923
Oklahoma	1,286,237	1,166
Oregon	11,740,813	18,494
Pennsylvania	5,525,208	6,899
Rhode Island	152,990	345
South Carolina	567,294	686
South Dakota	603,875	198
Tennessee	98,994	396
Texas	43,427,913	95,703
Utah	1,130,828	2,045
Vermont	944,829	1,177
Virginia	787,429	1,125
Washington	13,286,402	12,938
West Virginia	99,881	N/A
Wisconsin	644,427	1,085
Wyoming	174,973	339

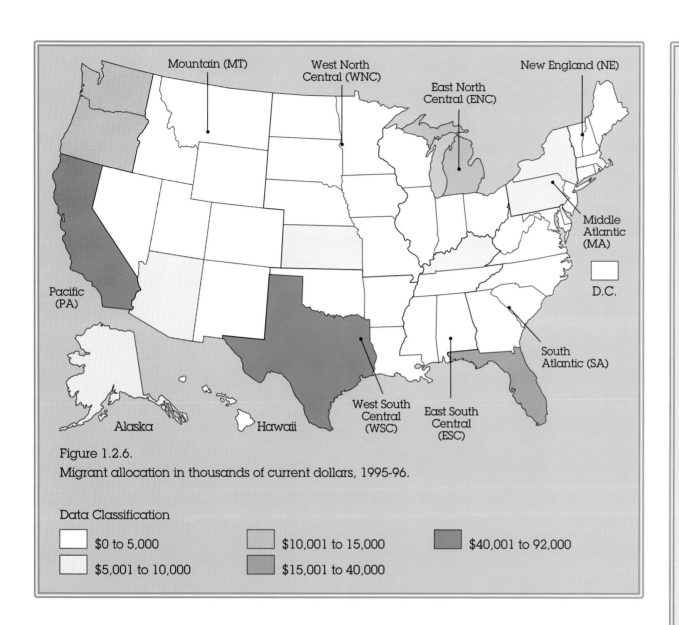

Figure 1.2.6.

Migrant allocation in thousands of current dollars, 1995-96.

Data Classification

- ⬜ $0 to 5,000
- ⬜ $5,001 to 10,000
- ⬜ $10,001 to 15,000
- ⬛ $15,001 to 40,000
- ⬛ $40,001 to 92,000

Migrant allocations in current dollars, 1995-1996.	Migrant allocation 1995-1996
Alabama	2,555,058
Alaska	9,923,035
Arizona	6,837,496
Arkansas	3,487,308
California	91,969,523
Colorado	3,425,526
Connecticut	2,160,250
Delaware	401,964
Dist. of Columbia	192,504
Florida	23,568,013
Georgia	4,606,706
Hawaii	0
Idaho	4,811,568
Illinois	1,771,460
Indiana	2,775,795
Iowa	306,293
Kansas	6,417,579
Kentucky	6,896,880
Louisiana	1,905,641
Maine	3,465,036
Maryland	265,330
Massachusetts	2,725,170
Michigan	11,973,962
Minnesota	2,336,932
Mississippi	1,341,990
Missouri	814,257
Montana	706,733
Nebraska	2,293,375
Nevada	502,728
New Hampshire	97,518
New Jersey	947,831
New Mexico	1,242,065
New York	5,700,409
North Carolina	4,231,568
North Dakota	515,740
Ohio	1,881,507
Oklahoma	1,286,237
Oregon	11,740,813
Pennsylvania	5,525,208
Rhode Island	152,990
South Carolina	567,294
South Dakota	603,875
Tennessee	98,994
Texas	43,427,913
Utah	1,130,828
Vermont	944,829
Virginia	787,429
Washington	13,286,402
West Virginia	99,881
Wisconsin	644,427
Wyoming	174,973

| | Aid to Families with Dependent Children (AFDC) | | | | | | Supplemental Security Income (SSI) | | | |
| | Recipients (in thousands) | | Payments for year (in millions) | | Average monthly payment per family | | Recipients (in thousands) | | Payment for year (in millions) | |
	1990	1994	1990	1994	1990	1994	1990	1994	1990	1994
Alabama	132	124	63	92	115	155	133	162	351	558
Alaska	24	37	62	113	651	740	5	6	14	24
Arizona	144	198	146	268	268	311	45	69	139	259
Arkansas	73	66	57	58	190	188	76	94	187	310
California	2,023	2,682	5,107	6,113	637	556	873	1,014	4,278	5,174
Colorado	109	115	138	158	320	321	38	55	110	203
Connecticut	135	171	309	397	571	553	32	43	96	162
Delaware	22	26	30	40	292	293	8	10	22	36
District of Columbia	54	75	87	127	380	389	16	20	54	79
Florida	420	645	443	826	263	282	222	317	653	1,160
Georgia	320	390	333	430	265	254	159	194	415	646
Hawaii	44	65	100	163	581	652	14	18	51	76
Idaho	17	24	20	30	266	285	10	16	29	57
Illinois	656	713	868	932	342	322	177	260	593	1,107
Indiana	164	203	174	229	263	263	60	86	174	324
Iowa	96	105	154	169	371	356	33	41	86	139
Kansas	77	82	103	124	332	347	25	36	65	127
Kentucky	204	195	185	199	224	210	115	156	337	578
Louisiana	279	260	188	169	167	165	133	179	378	679
Maine	62	61	104	107	422	393	24	30	56	87
Maryland	198	227	304	313	370	324	60	79	185	308
Massachusetts	282	288	647	730	556	553	119	157	397	643
Michigan	684	619	1,232	1,136	464	430	143	207	483	870
Minnesota	177	169	355	379	512	513	40	60	110	215
Mississippi	176	147	86	82	120	123	114	140	300	480
Missouri	218	260	237	287	274	260	85	110	237	400
Montana	29	34	40	49	344	344	10	13	29	48
Nebraska	44	42	60	62	336	330	16	21	42	70
Nevada	25	41	28	48	278	275	11	19	33	69
New Hampshire	21	29	35	62	431	451	7	10	19	33
New Jersey	323	324	459	524	352	358	105	140	340	562
New Mexico	67	105	66	144	273	352	32	43	90	152
New York	1,031	1,273	2,337	2,993	556	543	415	564	1,557	2,542
North Carolina	255	322	257	356	237	227	149	182	403	592
North Dakota	16	15	24	26	359	381	7	9	18	27
Ohio	657	634	896	940	328	318	156	236	483	972
Oklahoma	129	127	135	166	279	296	60	72	158	246
Oregon	99	107	150	197	374	395	32	45	95	168
Pennsylvania	549	611	827	927	382	367	191	252	635	1,060
Rhode Island	52	63	104	136	499	499	17	23	53	89
South Carolina	118	133	97	115	203	186	90	108	234	360
South Dakota	19	18	22	25	272	307	10	13	26	44
Tennessee	230	281	176	216	186	164	140	175	384	602
Texas	673	794	431	544	165	159	295	390	755	1,286
Utah	47	48	65	77	347	364	13	20	38	75
Vermont	25	27	51	65	527	549	10	13	31	46
Virginia	158	190	181	253	265	282	95	125	257	431
Washington	237	289	447	612	452	494	62	88	208	368
West Virginia	109	109	112	126	249	260	47	64	146	255
Wisconsin	236	214	441	423	464	462	86	110	288	467
Wyoming	16	15	20	21	313	310	3	6	9	19

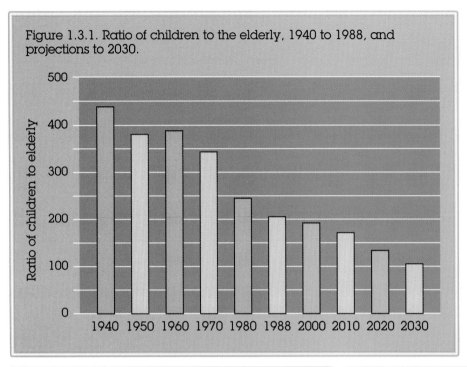

Figure 1.3.1. Ratio of children to the elderly, 1940 to 1988, and projections to 2030.

Table 1.3.1. Federal, state, and local government purchases of goods.

	1960	1970	1980	1988	1960-1988 (% change per year)
Aggregate purchases					
Children	83.1	141.6	154.3	188.1	2.9
Adults	34.0	102.8	160.2	228.7	6.8
Not allocated by age	381.0	461.7	450.3	545.7	1.3
Number of persons					
Children	64.5	69.7	63.8	63.8	0.0
Adults	116.1	133.5	162.8	182.0	1.6
All ages	180.7	203.2	226.5	245.8	1.1
Purchases per person					
Children	1,289.0	2,032.0	2,420.0	2,946.0	3.0
Adults	292.0	770.0	984.0	1,257.0	5.2
Not allocated by age	2,109.0	2,272.0	1,988.0	2,220.0	0.2

Note: Aggregate purchases are measured in billions of 1988 constant dollars. Number of persons are measured in millions. Purchases per person are measured in 1988 constant dollars.

Figure 1.3.6. Number of children under age 18 for every person 65 years of age and older, 1993.

Figure 1.3.7. Percent of children and elderly in poverty, 1970-1994.

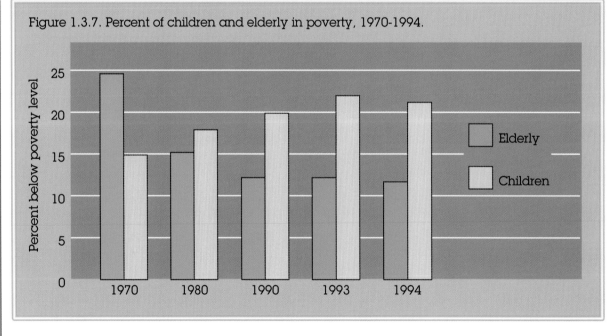

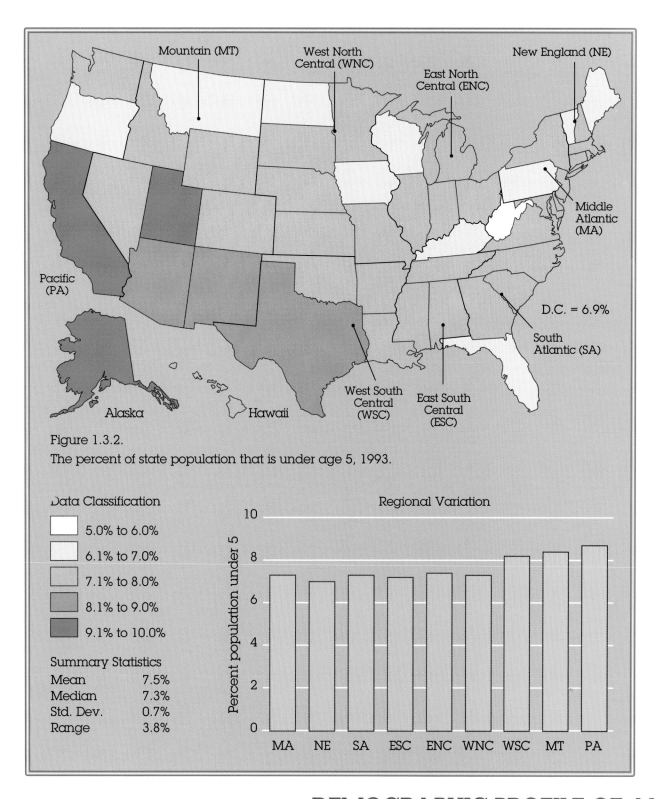

Figure 1.3.2.

The percent of state population that is under age 5, 1993.

Data Classification

- 5.0% to 6.0%
- 6.1% to 7.0%
- 7.1% to 8.0%
- 8.1% to 9.0%
- 9.1% to 10.0%

Summary Statistics

Mean	7.5%
Median	7.3%
Std. Dev.	0.7%
Range	3.8%

Percent of the state population that is under age 5, 1993.

	Population under 5	Percent under 5
Alabama	300,627	7.2
Alaska	57,485	9.6
Arizona	325,001	8.3
Arkansas	171,886	7.1
California	2,829,525	9.1
Colorado	267,858	7.5
Connecticut	233,734	7.1
Delaware	52,838	7.5
Dist. of Columbia	40,044	6.9
Florida	951,972	7.0
Georgia	540,885	7.8
Hawaii	93,971	8.0
Idaho	85,923	7.8
Illinois	913,246	7.8
Indiana	405,868	7.1
Iowa	190,426	6.8
Kansas	185,592	7.3
Kentucky	261,187	6.9
Louisiana	341,914	8.0
Maine	80,598	6.5
Maryland	377,955	7.6
Massachusetts	427,520	7.1
Michigan	704,986	7.4
Minnesota	332,762	7.4
Mississippi	207,779	7.9
Missouri	375,153	7.2
Montana	58,746	7.0
Nebraska	116,387	7.2
Nevada	109,745	7.9
New Hampshire	80,469	7.2
New Jersey	580,420	7.4
New Mexico	136,579	8.4
New York	1,374,737	7.6
North Carolina	503,005	7.2
North Dakota	44,041	6.9
Ohio	806,361	7.3
Oklahoma	235,095	7.3
Oregon	211,573	7.0
Pennsylvania	811,543	6.7
Rhode Island	71,285	7.1
South Carolina	274,851	7.5
South Dakota	55,468	7.8
Tennessee	360,584	7.1
Texas	1,534,008	8.5
Utah	180,023	9.7
Vermont	38,857	6.7
Virginia	471,542	7.3
Washington	395,873	7.5
West Virginia	107,953	5.9
Wisconsin	354,741	7.0
Wyoming	34,059	7.2

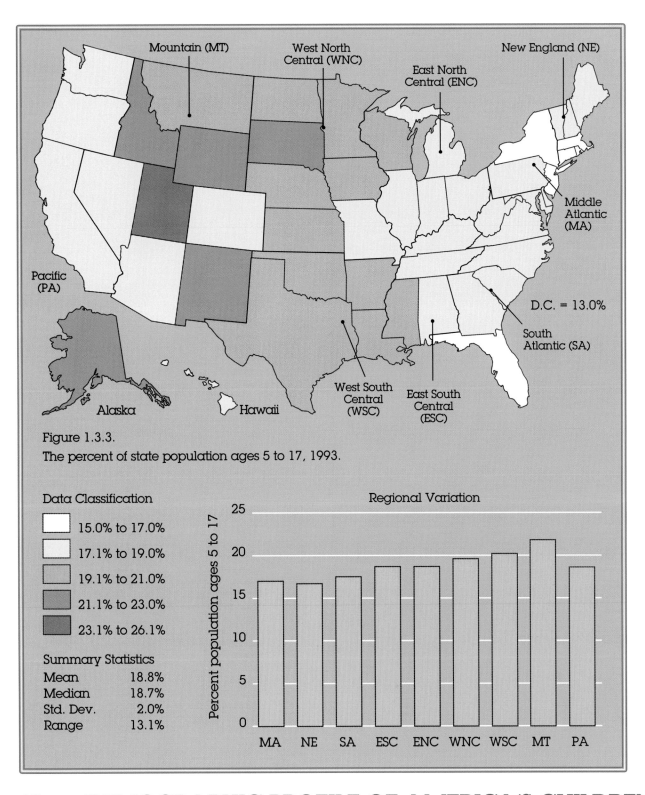

Figure 1.3.3.
The percent of state population ages 5 to 17, 1993.

Data Classification

	15.0% to 17.0%
	17.1% to 19.0%
	19.1% to 21.0%
	21.1% to 23.0%
	23.1% to 26.1%

Summary Statistics

Mean	18.8%
Median	18.7%
Std. Dev.	2.0%
Range	13.1%

Regional Variation

(bar chart: Percent population ages 5 to 17 — categories MA, NE, SA, ESC, ENC, WNC, WSC, MT, PA)

Percent of the state population ages 5 to 17, 1993.

	Population age 5 to 17	Percent age 5 to 17
Alabama	775,646	18.5
Alaska	131,709	22.0
Arizona	744,692	18.9
Arkansas	462,791	19.1
California	5,763,619	18.5
Colorado	670,285	18.8
Connecticut	540,859	16.5
Delaware	122,274	17.5
Dist. of Columbia	74,957	13.0
Florida	2,217,270	16.2
Georgia	1,299,784	18.8
Hawaii	205,064	17.5
Idaho	246,525	22.4
Illinois	2,154,523	18.4
Indiana	1,063,283	18.6
Iowa	543,702	19.3
Kansas	498,195	19.7
Kentucky	710,174	18.7
Louisiana	901,100	21.0
Maine	226,332	18.3
Maryland	862,589	17.4
Massachusetts	965,385	16.1
Michigan	1,801,273	19.0
Minnesota	895,036	19.8
Mississippi	550,037	20.8
Missouri	988,114	18.9
Montana	173,193	20.6
Nebraska	322,746	20.1
Nevada	242,373	17.5
New Hampshire	203,396	18.1
New Jersey	1,315,972	16.7
New Mexico	343,511	21.3
New York	3,092,643	17.0
North Carolina	1,200,960	17.3
North Dakota	128,067	20.2
Ohio	2,053,119	18.5
Oklahoma	634,351	19.6
Oregon	569,605	18.8
Pennsylvania	2,060,069	17.1
Rhode Island	163,872	16.4
South Carolina	677,364	18.6
South Dakota	153,206	21.4
Tennessee	907,620	17.8
Texas	3,649,373	20.2
Utah	484,941	26.1
Vermont	105,108	18.3
Virginia	1,116,249	17.2
Washington	997,002	19.0
West Virginia	326,360	17.9
Wisconsin	986,806	19.6
Wyoming	104,421	22.2

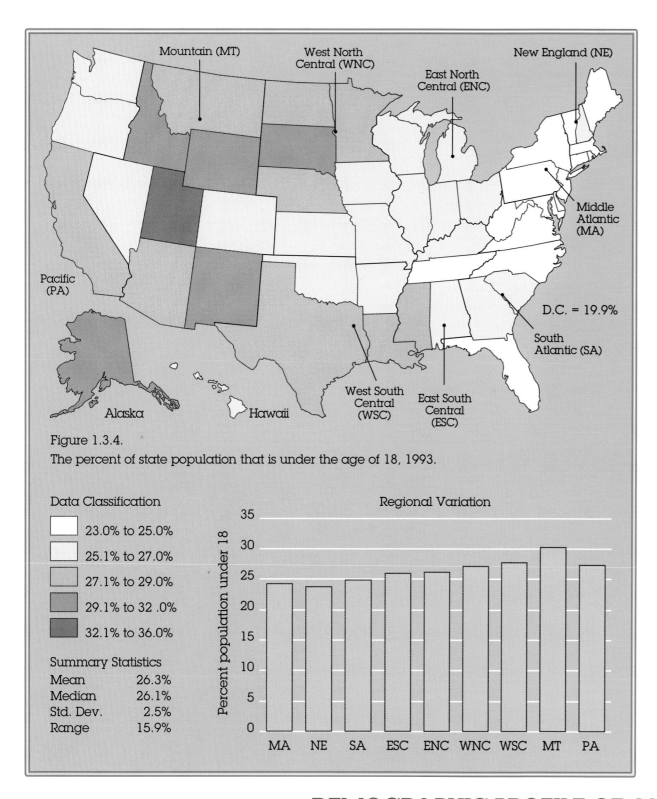

Figure 1.3.4.

The percent of state population that is under the age of 18, 1993.

Data Classification

☐	23.0% to 25.0%
☐	25.1% to 27.0%
☐	27.1% to 29.0%
☐	29.1% to 32 .0%
☐	32.1% to 36.0%

Summary Statistics

Mean	26.3%
Median	26.1%
Std. Dev.	2.5%
Range	15.9%

Percent of the state population under age 18, 1993.

	Population under 18	Percent under 18
Alabama	1,076,273	25.7
Alaska	189,194	31.6
Arizona	1,069,693	27.2
Arkansas	634,677	26.2
California	8,593,144	27.5
Colorado	938,143	26.3
Connecticut	774,593	23.6
Delaware	175,112	25.0
Dist. of Columbia	115,001	19.9
Florida	3,169,242	23.2
Georgia	1,840,669	26.6
Hawaii	299,035	25.5
Idaho	332,448	30.2
Illinois	3,067,769	26.2
Indiana	1,469,151	25.7
Iowa	734,128	26.1
Kansas	683,787	27.0
Kentucky	971,361	25.6
Louisiana	1,243,014	28.9
Maine	306,930	24.8
Maryland	1,240,544	25.0
Massachusetts	1,392,905	23.2
Michigan	2,506,259	26.4
Minnesota	1,227,798	27.2
Mississippi	757,816	28.7
Missouri	1,363,267	26.0
Montana	231,939	27.6
Nebraska	439,133	27.3
Nevada	352,118	25.4
New Hampshire	283,865	25.2
New Jersey	1,896,392	24.1
New Mexico	480,090	29.7
New York	4,467,380	24.5
North Carolina	1,703,965	24.5
North Dakota	172,108	27.1
Ohio	2,859,480	25.8
Oklahoma	869,446	26.9
Oregon	781,178	25.8
Pennsylvania	2,871,612	23.8
Rhode Island	235,157	23.5
South Carolina	952,215	26.1
South Dakota	208,674	29.2
Tennessee	1,268,204	24.9
Texas	5,183,381	28.7
Utah	664,964	35.8
Vermont	143,965	25.0
Virginia	1,587,791	24.5
Washington	1,392,875	26.5
West Virginia	434,313	23.9
Wisconsin	1,341,547	26.6
Wyoming	138,480	29.4

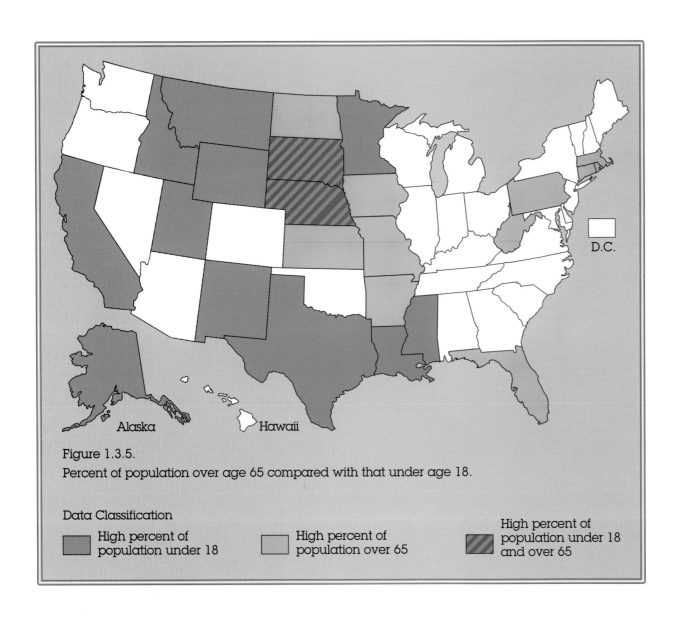

Figure 1.3.5.
Percent of population over age 65 compared with that under age 18.

Data Classification

High percent of population under 18

High percent of population over 65

High percent of population under 18 and over 65

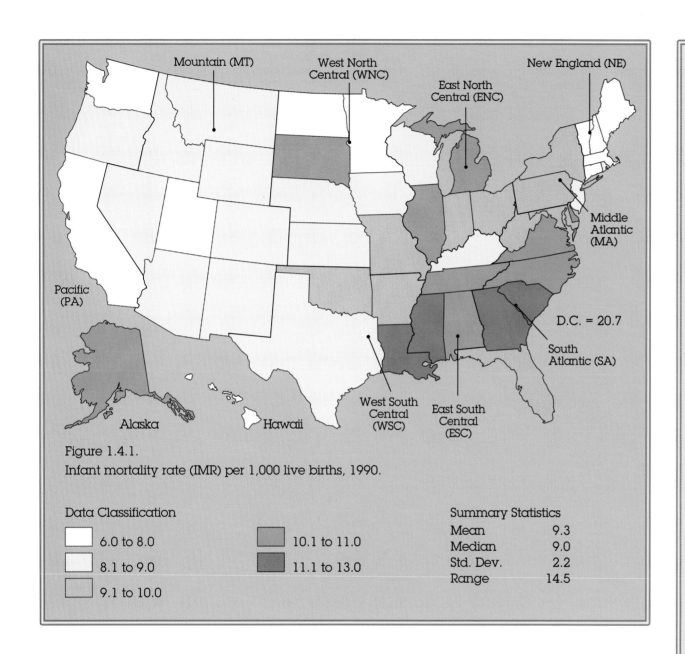

Mountain (MT)

West North Central (WNC)

East North Central (ENC)

New England (NE)

Middle Atlantic (MA)

Pacific (PA)

D.C. = 20.7

South Atlantic (SA)

Alaska   Hawaii

West South Central (WSC)

East South Central (ESC)

Figure 1.4.1.
Infant mortality rate (IMR) per 1,000 live births, 1990.

Data Classification

6.0 to 8.0	10.1 to 11.0
8.1 to 9.0	11.1 to 13.0
9.1 to 10.0	

Summary Statistics

Mean	9.3
Median	9.0
Std. Dev.	2.2
Range	14.5

Infant mortality rate (IMR) per 1,000 live births, 1970 and 1990.

	1970 (IMR)	1990 (IMR)
Alabama	24.3	10.8
Alaska	22.6	10.5
Arizona	17.7	8.8
Arkansas	21.6	9.2
California	17.2	7.9
Colorado	19.9	8.8
Connecticut	17.1	7.9
Delaware	19.6	10.1
District of Columbia	29.1	20.7
Florida	21.5	9.6
Georgia	22.1	12.4
Hawaii	18.6	6.7
Idaho	17.1	8.7
Illinois	21.5	10.7
Indiana	19.4	9.6
Iowa	18.7	8.1
Kansas	17.6	8.4
Kentucky	19.6	8.5
Louisiana	24.9	11.1
Maine	21.0	6.2
Maryland	19.4	9.5
Massachusetts	16.8	7.0
Michigan	20.5	10.7
Minnesota	17.4	7.3
Mississippi	28.5	12.1
Missouri	19.5	9.4
Montana	21.5	9.0
Nebraska	19.4	8.3
Nevada	24.0	8.4
New Hampshire	18.0	7.1
New Jersey	19.9	9.0
New Mexico	21.0	9.0
New York	19.4	9.6
North Carolina	24.2	10.6
North Dakota	14.3	8.0
Ohio	18.7	9.8
Oklahoma	21.3	9.2
Oregon	15.9	8.3
Pennsylvania	20.2	9.6
Rhode Island	10.8	8.1
South Carolina	22.9	11.7
South Dakota	19.1	10.1
Tennessee	21.3	10.3
Texas	21.2	8.1
Utah	14.9	7.5
Vermont	17.6	6.4
Virginia	20.6	10.2
Washington	18.7	7.8
West Virginia	23.0	9.9
Wisconsin	16.8	8.2
Wyoming	20.0	8.6

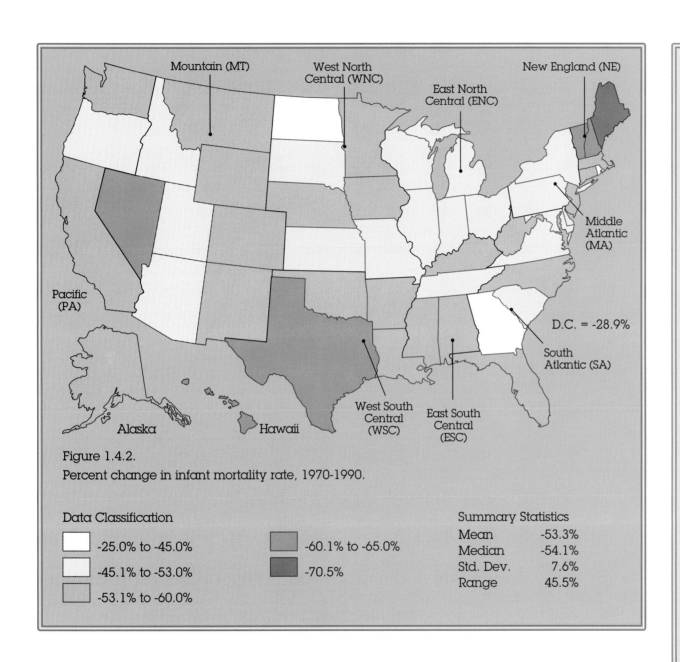

Figure 1.4.2.
Percent change in infant mortality rate, 1970-1990.

Data Classification

☐	-25.0% to -45.0%
☐	-45.1% to -53.0%
☐	-53.1% to -60.0%
☐	-60.1% to -65.0%
☐	-70.5%

Summary Statistics

Mean	-53.3%
Median	-54.1%
Std. Dev.	7.6%
Range	45.5%

Percent change in mortality rate between the years of 1970 and 1990.

	1990 infant mortality rate	Percent change
Alabama	10.8	-55.6
Alaska	10.5	-53.5
Arizona	8.8	-50.3
Arkansas	9.2	-57.4
California	7.9	-54.1
Colorado	8.8	-55.8
Connecticut	7.9	-53.8
Delaware	10.1	-48.5
District of Columbia	20.7	-28.9
Florida	9.6	-55.3
Georgia	12.4	-43.9
Hawaii	6.7	-64.0
Idaho	8.7	-49.1
Illinois	10.7	-50.2
Indiana	9.6	-50.5
Iowa	8.1	-56.7
Kansas	8.4	-52.3
Kentucky	8.5	-56.6
Louisiana	11.1	-55.4
Maine	6.2	-70.5
Maryland	9.5	-51.0
Massachusetts	7	-58.3
Michigan	10.7	-47.8
Minnesota	7.3	-58.0
Mississippi	12.1	-57.5
Missouri	9.4	-51.8
Montana	9	-58.1
Nebraska	8.3	-57.2
Nevada	8.4	-65.0
New Hampshire	7.1	-60.6
New Jersey	9	-54.8
New Mexico	9	-57.1
New York	9.6	-50.5
North Carolina	10.6	-56.2
North Dakota	8	-44.1
Ohio	9.8	-47.6
Oklahoma	9.2	-56.8
Oregon	8.3	-47.8
Pennsylvania	9.6	-52.5
Rhode Island	8.1	-25.0
South Carolina	11.7	-48.9
South Dakota	10.1	-47.1
Tennessee	10.3	-51.6
Texas	8.1	-61.8
Utah	7.5	-49.7
Vermont	6.4	-63.6
Virginia	10.2	-50.5
Washington	7.8	-58.3
West Virginia	9.9	-57.0
Wisconsin	8.2	-51.2
Wyoming	8.6	-57.0

Table 1.4.3. Number of infant deaths, mortality rate, and percentage of deaths attributed to each cause, by race, United States, 1990.

Race	Rank	Cause of death	Number	Rate (1)	% distribution
Black (2)	1	Disorders relating to short gestation and unspecified low birth weight	1,912	279.4	15.6
	2	Sudden infant death syndrome	1,578	230.6	12.8
	3	Congenital anomalies	1,530	223.6	12.4
	4	Respiratory distress syndrome	984	143.8	8.0
	5	Newborn affected by maternal complications of pregnancy	571	83.4	4.6
	6	Infections specific to the perinatal period	291	42.5	2.4
	7	Newborn affected by complications of placenta, cord, and membranes	291	42.5	2.4
	8	Accidents and adverse effects (3)	289	42.2	2.4
	9	Pneumonia and influenza	235	34.3	1.9
	10	Intrauterine hypoxia and birth asphyxia	231	33.8	1.9
		All other causes (residual)	4,378	639.7	35.6
		Total causes for black	12,290	1,795.9	100.0
White	1	Congenital anomalies	6,418	195.1	25.8
	2	Sudden infant death syndrome	3,643	110.7	14.6
	3	Disorders relating to short gestation and unspecified low birth weight	2,004	60.9	8.1
	4	Respiratory distress syndrome	1,798	54.6	7.2
	5	Newborn affected by maternal complications of pregnancy	1,044	31.7	4.2
	6	Newborn affected by complications of placenta, cord, and membranes	657	20.0	2.6
	7	Accidents and adverse effects	609	18.5	2.4
	8	Infections specific to the perinatal period	569	17.3	2.3
	9	Intrauterine hypoxia and birth asphyxia	505	15.3	2.0
	10	Pneumonia and influenza	375	11.4	1.5
		All other causes (residual)	7,261	220.7	29.2
		Total causes for white	24,883	756.3	100.0
Total	1	Congenital anomalies	8,239	198.1	21.5
	2	Sudden infant death syndrome	5,417	130.3	14.1
	3	Disorders relating to short gestation and unspecified low birth weight	4,013	96.5	10.5
	4	Respiratory distress syndrome	2,850	68.5	7.4
	5	Newborn affected by maternal complications of pregnancy	1,655	39.8	4.3
	6	Newborn affected by complications of placenta, cord, and membranes	975	23.4	2.5
	7	Accidents and adverse effects	930	22.4	2.4
	8	Infections specific to the perinatal period	875	21.0	2.3
	9	Intrauterine hypoxia and birth asphyxia	762	18.3	2.0
	10	Pneumonia and influenza	634	15.2	1.7
		All other causes (residual)	12,001	288.6	31.3
		Total for all races	38,351	922.3	100.0

Notes:

(1) Deaths at <1 year of age per 100,000 live births in specified group.

(2) Due to limitations in data set used to describe racial differences, only black and white races are used. A Death Data Set—used to more accurately estimate infant mortality rates for other racial groups—was not yet available for 1990.

(3) When a death occurs under "accidental" circumstances, the preferred term within the public health community is "unintentional injury."

Table 1.4.5. Infant, neonatal, and postneonatal deaths and mortality rates, by specified race in the United States, 1988.

Race	Infant (1) Number	Infant (1) Rate (2)	Neonatal Number	Neonatal Rate	Postneonatal Number	Postneonatal Rate
All races	42,155	8.9	26,707	5.4	15,448	3.5
White	25,925	8.5	16,346	5.4	9,579	3.1
African American	11,840	17.6	7,695	11.5	4,145	6.2
Native American (3)	414	9.0	187	4.1	227	4.9
Asian American	714	4.9	451	3.2	263	1.7
Hispanic	3,245	8.1	2,017	5.0	1,228	3.0
Other	17	5.2	11	3.4	6	1.9

Notes:

(1) Infant is less than one year old; neonatal is less than 28 days old; postneonatal is 28 days to 11 months.

(2) Rate equals deaths per 1,000 live births.

(3) Native Americans include deaths among Aleuts and Eskimos.

Table 1.4.6. Deaths, by selected causes and selected characteristics, 1990.

Age, sex, and race	Total	Heart disease	Cancer	Accidents and adverse effects	Cerebro-vascular diseases	Chronic obstructive pulmonary diseases	Pneumonia and flu	Suicide	Chronic liver disease, cirrhosis	Diabetes mellitus	Homicide and legal intervention
All races											
Both sexes, total	2,148,463	720,058	N/A	91,983	144,088	86,679	79,513	30,906	25,815	47,664	24,932
Under 1 year old	38,351	794	90	930	148	55	634	0	16	4	332
1 to 4 years old	6,931	282	513	2,566	45	55	171	0	7	7	378
5 to 14 years old	8,436	308	1,094	3,650	73	115	134	264	7	24	512
Male, total	1,113,417	360,788	N/A	61,938	56,697	49,416	36,898	24,724	16,627	20,266	19,604
Under 1 year old	21,856	442	48	509	88	32	365	0	8	3	178
1 to 4 years old	3,969	141	280	1,574	22	40	88	0	2	1	208
5 to 14 years old	5,127	169	621	2,418	36	71	71	195	2	14	299
Female, total	1,035,046	359,270	N/A	30,045	87,391	37,263	42,615	6,182	9,188	27,398	5,328
Under 1 year old	16,495	352	42	421	60	23	269	0	8	1	154
1 to 4 years old	2,962	141	233	992	23	15	83	0	5	6	170
5 to 14 years old	3,309	139	473	1,232	37	44	63	69	5	10	213
White											
Both sexes, total	1,853,254	637,364	N/A	76,934	124,526	80,179	70,806	28,086	21,478	38,696	12,153
Under 1 year old	24,883	501	69	609	89	38	375	0	13	3	181
1 to 4 years old	4,866	181	413	1,861	33	31	118	0	4	7	190
5 to 14 years old	6,272	226	897	2,747	55	59	100	223	5	15	267
African American											
Both sexes, total	265,498	75,111	N/A	12,419	17,407	5,655	7,563	2,111	3,753	8,114	12,144
Under 1 year old	12,290	254	17	289	52	15	235	0	3	1	141
1 to 4 years old	1,768	90	81	591	10	22	40	0	3	0	170
5 to 14 years old	1,839	70	154	745	15	53	28	31	2	8	232

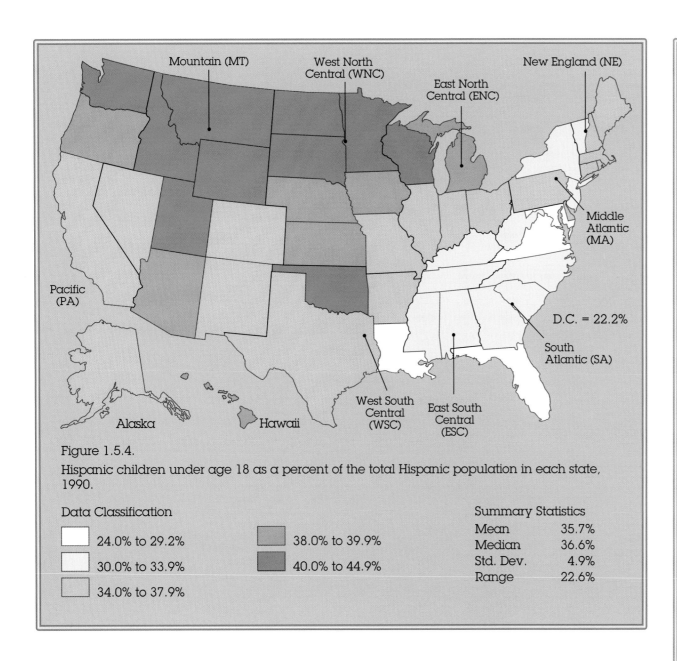

Figure 1.5.4.

Hispanic children under age 18 as a percent of the total Hispanic population in each state, 1990.

Data Classification

24.0% to 29.2%

30.0% to 33.9%

34.0% to 37.9%

38.0% to 39.9%

40.0% to 44.9%

Summary Statistics

Mean	35.7%
Median	36.6%
Std. Dev.	4.9%
Range	22.6%

Hispanic children under 18 years as a percent of total Hispanic population in each state, 1990.

	Hispanics	
	Under 18	% Under 18
Alabama	7,931	32.2
Alaska	6,747	37.9
Arizona	265,698	38.6
Arkansas	7,454	37.5
California	2,736,906	35.6
Colorado	152,749	36.0
Connecticut	77,361	36.3
Delaware	5,584	35.3
Dist. of Columbia	7,262	22.2
Florida	391,962	24.9
Georgia	32,677	30.0
Hawaii	31,172	38.3
Idaho	22,494	42.5
Illinois	331,027	36.6
Indiana	36,650	37.1
Iowa	12,863	39.4
Kansas	36,719	39.2
Kentucky	7,101	32.3
Louisiana	26,797	28.8
Maine	2,520	36.9
Maryland	36,280	29.0
Massachusetts	107,256	37.3
Michigan	77,211	38.3
Minnesota	22,524	41.8
Mississippi	5,273	33.1
Missouri	21,287	34.5
Montana	5,113	42.0
Nebraska	14,714	39.8
Nevada	42,302	34.0
New Hampshire	3,944	34.8
New Jersey	222,698	30.1
New Mexico	203,308	35.1
New York	675,278	30.5
North Carolina	23,939	31.2
North Dakota	2,090	44.8
Ohio	52,526	37.6
Oklahoma	34,636	40.2
Oregon	43,730	38.8
Pennsylvania	86,169	37.1
Rhode Island	16,105	35.2
South Carolina	9,746	31.9
South Dakota	2,316	44.1
Tennessee	10,281	31.4
Texas	1,618,785	37.3
Utah	35,108	41.5
Vermont	1,102	30.1
Virginia	46,964	29.3
Washington	86,257	40.2
West Virginia	2,589	30.5
Wisconsin	39,328	42.2
Wyoming	10,378	40.3

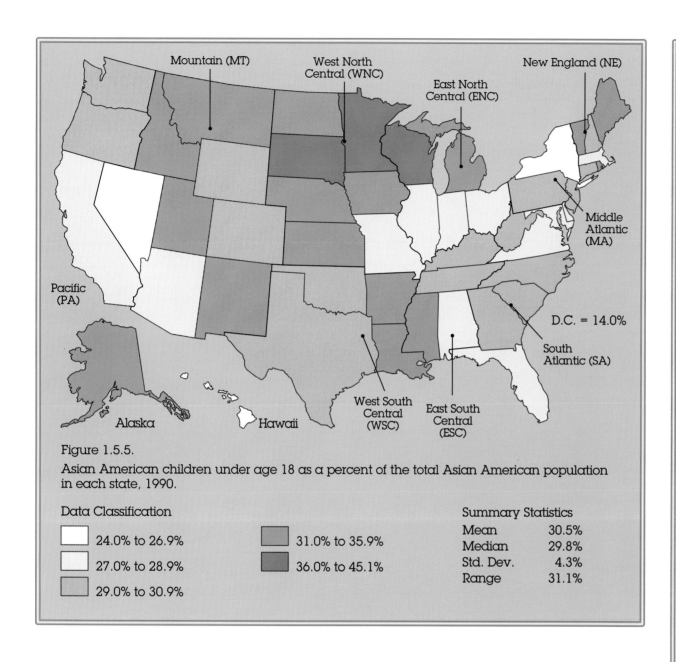

Figure 1.5.5.

Asian American children under age 18 as a percent of the total Asian American population in each state, 1990.

Data Classification

☐ 24.0% to 26.9%	☐ 31.0% to 35.9%
☐ 27.0% to 28.9%	☐ 36.0% to 45.1%
☐ 29.0% to 30.9%	

Summary Statistics

Mean	30.5%
Median	29.8%
Std. Dev.	4.3%
Range	31.1%

Asian American children under 18 years as a percent of total Asian American population in each state, 1990.

	Asian Americans	
	Under 18	% Under 18
Alabama	6,278	28.8
Alaska	6,234	31.6
Arizona	15,458	28.0
Arkansas	4,010	32.0
California	811,013	28.5
Colorado	18,138	30.3
Connecticut	14,804	29.2
Delaware	2,617	28.9
Dist. of Columbia	1,570	14.0
Florida	43,359	28.1
Georgia	22,583	29.8
Hawaii	178,161	26.0
Idaho	3,006	32.1
Illinois	81,314	28.5
Indiana	10,194	27.1
Iowa	8,713	34.2
Kansas	10,160	32.0
Kentucky	5,361	30.1
Louisiana	14,220	34.6
Maine	2,245	33.6
Maryland	38,423	27.5
Massachusetts	41,297	28.8
Michigan	34,644	33.0
Minnesota	35,127	45.1
Mississippi	4,282	32.9
Missouri	11,888	28.8
Montana	1,461	34.3
Nebraska	4,025	32.4
Nevada	9,875	25.9
New Hampshire	2,747	29.4
New Jersey	80,394	29.5
New Mexico	4,421	31.3
New York	172,746	24.9
North Carolina	15,337	29.4
North Dakota	1,073	31.0
Ohio	26,351	28.9
Oklahoma	9,733	29.0
Oregon	20,642	29.8
Pennsylvania	42,056	30.6
Rhode Island	6,304	34.4
South Carolina	6,603	29.5
South Dakota	1,124	36.0
Tennessee	9,584	30.1
Texas	96,157	30.1
Utah	11,747	35.2
Vermont	1,038	32.3
Virginia	45,171	28.4
Washington	64,553	30.6
West Virginia	2,185	29.3
Wisconsin	22,987	42.9
Wyoming	822	29.3

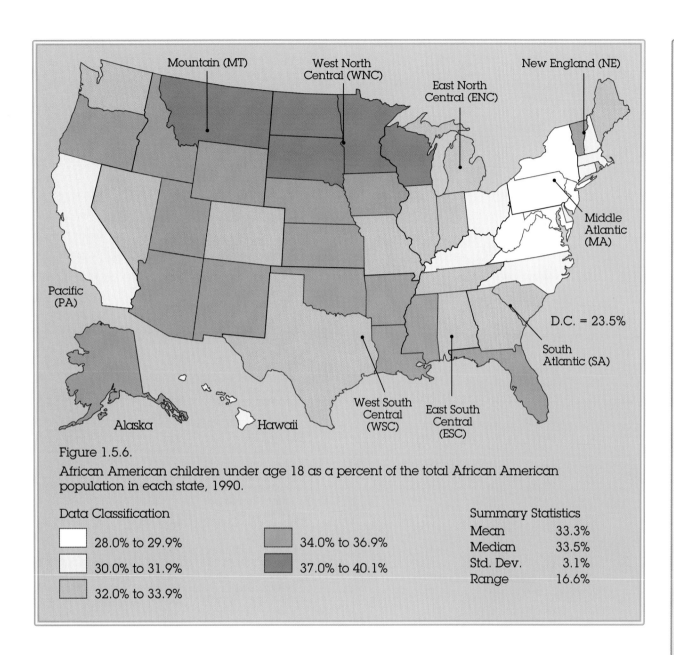

Mountain (MT)
West North Central (WNC)
East North Central (ENC)
New England (NE)
Middle Atlantic (MA)
D.C. = 23.5%
South Atlantic (SA)
Pacific (PA)
Alaska
Hawaii
West South Central (WSC)
East South Central (ESC)

Figure 1.5.6.

African American children under age 18 as a percent of the total African American population in each state, 1990.

Data Classification

☐	28.0% to 29.9%
☐	30.0% to 31.9%
☐	32.0% to 33.9%
☐	34.0% to 36.9%
☐	37.0% to 40.1%

Summary Statistics

Mean	33.3%
Median	33.5%
Std. Dev.	3.1%
Range	16.6%

African American children under 18 years as a percent of total African American population in each state, 1990.

	African Americans Under 18	% Under 18
Alabama	342,957	33.6
Alaska	7,903	35.2
Arizona	37,910	34.3
Arkansas	136,478	36.5
California	664,849	30.1
Colorado	42,607	32.0
Connecticut	85,572	31.2
Delaware	35,537	31.6
Dist. of Columbia	93,907	23.5
Florida	608,799	34.6
Georgia	578,113	33.1
Hawaii	8,349	30.7
Idaho	1,237	36.7
Illinois	552,333	32.6
Indiana	143,887	33.3
Iowa	17,649	36.7
Kansas	48,646	34.0
Kentucky	83,079	31.6
Louisiana	465,143	35.8
Maine	1,706	33.2
Maryland	341,501	28.7
Massachusetts	93,340	31.1
Michigan	419,804	32.5
Minnesota	37,123	39.1
Mississippi	337,656	36.9
Missouri	178,716	32.6
Montana	881	37.0
Nebraska	20,952	36.5
Nevada	26,546	33.7
New Hampshire	2,282	31.7
New Jersey	40,090	29.3
New Mexico	10,392	34.4
New York	834,844	29.2
North Carolina	448,547	30.8
North Dakota	1,314	37.3
Ohio	368,389	31.9
Oklahoma	80,194	34.3
Oregon	16,255	35.2
Pennsylvania	320,400	29.4
Rhode Island	13,135	33.8
South Carolina	348,361	33.5
South Dakota	1,238	38.0
Tennessee	252,083	32.4
Texas	657,030	32.5
Utah	4,144	35.8
Vermont	691	35.4
Virginia	339,594	29.2
Washington	50,333	33.6
West Virginia	16,326	29.0
Wisconsin	98,060	40.1
Wyoming	1,269	35.2

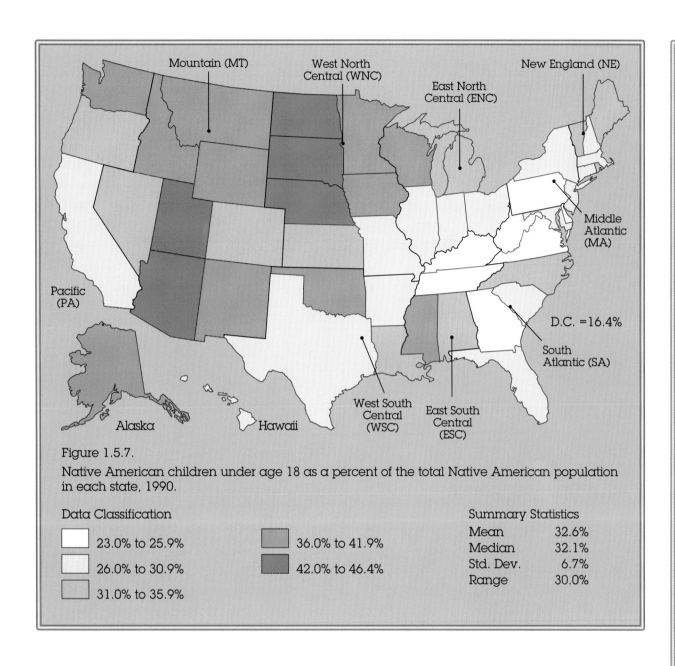

Figure 1.5.7.

Native American children under age 18 as a percent of the total Native American population in each state, 1990.

Data Classification

☐	23.0% to 25.9%
☐	26.0% to 30.9%
☐	31.0% to 35.9%
☐	36.0% to 41.9%
☐	42.0% to 46.4%

Summary Statistics

Mean	32.6%
Median	32.1%
Std. Dev.	6.7%
Range	30.0%

Native American children under 18 years as a percent of total Native American population in each state, 1990.

	Native Americans Under 18	% Under 18
Alabama	5,695	34.5
Alaska	34,793	40.6
Arizona	85,481	42.0
Arkansas	3,691	28.9
California	74,102	30.6
Colorado	9,222	33.2
Connecticut	1,737	26.1
Delaware	499	24.7
Dist. of Columbia	240	16.4
Florida	9,556	26.3
Georgia	3,444	25.8
Hawaii	1,576	30.9
Idaho	5,126	37.2
Illinois	6,180	28.3
Indiana	3,663	28.8
Iowa	2,778	37.8
Kansas	7,270	33.1
Kentucky	1,431	24.8
Louisiana	6,545	35.3
Maine	2,123	35.4
Maryland	3,412	26.3
Massachusetts	3,574	29.2
Michigan	19,028	34.2
Minnesota	20,513	41.1
Mississippi	3,316	38.9
Missouri	5,653	28.5
Montana	19,882	41.7
Nebraska	5,237	42.2
Nevada	6,303	32.1
New Hampshire	555	26.0
New Jersey	3,892	26.0
New Mexico	54,414	40.5
New York	18,983	30.3
North Carolina	26,531	33.1
North Dakota	11,637	44.9
Ohio	5,395	26.5
Oklahoma	94,153	37.3
Oregon	13,358	34.7
Pennsylvania	3,816	25.9
Rhode Island	1,360	33.4
South Carolina	2,334	28.3
South Dakota	23,467	46.4
Tennessee	2,490	24.8
Texas	18,643	28.3
Utah	10,855	44.7
Vermont	543	32.0
Virginia	3,607	23.6
Washington	29,415	36.1
West Virginia	590	24.0
Wisconsin	15,125	38.4
Wyoming	3,905	41.2

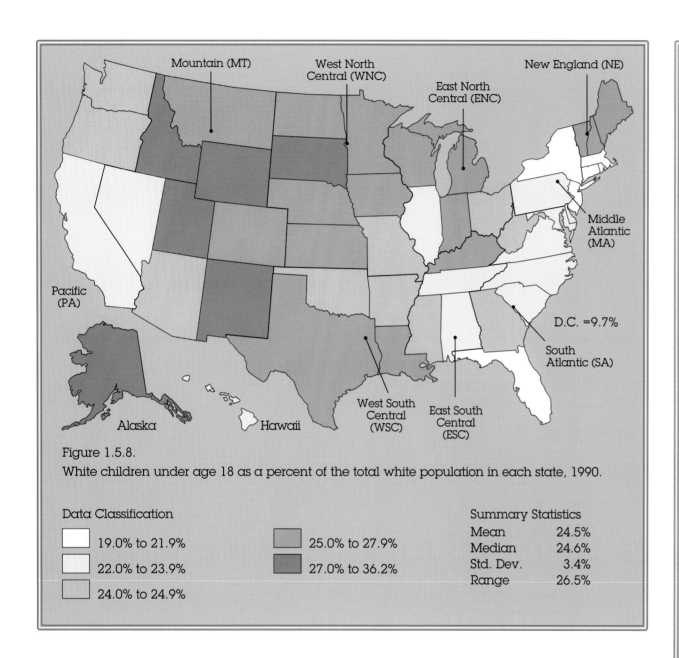

Figure 1.5.8.
White children under age 18 as a percent of the total white population in each state, 1990.

Data Classification

- [ ] 19.0% to 21.9%
- [ ] 22.0% to 23.9%
- [ ] 24.0% to 24.9%
- [ ] 25.0% to 27.9%
- [ ] 27.0% to 36.2%

Summary Statistics

Mean	24.5%
Median	24.6%
Std. Dev.	3.4%
Range	26.5%

White children under 18 years as a percent of total white population in each state, 1990.

	Whites	
	Under 18	% Under 18
Alabama	702,288	23.6
Alaska	121,324	29.2
Arizona	711,165	24.0
Arkansas	474,518	24.4
California	4,761,644	23.2
Colorado	729,274	25.1
Connecticut	609,042	21.3
Delaware	122,001	22.8
Dist. of Columbia	17,428	9.7
Florida	2,128,358	19.8
Georgia	1,108,636	24.1
Hawaii	85,012	23.0
Idaho	287,036	30.2
Illinois	2,121,856	23.7
Indiana	1,280,279	25.5
Iowa	684,188	25.5
Kansas	575,852	25.8
Kentucky	861,525	25.4
Louisiana	735,337	25.9
Maine	302,090	25.0
Maryland	767,036	22.6
Massachusetts	1,151,345	21.3
Michigan	1,954,534	25.2
Minnesota	1,065,642	25.8
Mississippi	400,198	24.5
Missouri	1,108,098	24.7
Montana	198,618	26.8
Nebraska	392,348	26.5
Nevada	235,958	23.3
New Hampshire	271,858	25.0
New Jersey	1,318,050	21.5
New Mexico	309,428	27.0
New York	2,904,600	21.7
North Carolina	1,106,877	22.1
North Dakota	160,702	26.6
Ohio	2,285,221	24.0
Oklahoma	635,544	24.6
Oregon	653,923	24.8
Pennsylvania	2,377,565	22.6
Rhode Island	196,318	21.4
South Carolina	558,418	23.2
South Dakota	172,129	27.0
Tennessee	947,248	23.4
Texas	3,372,537	26.4
Utah	584,936	36.2
Vermont	140,437	25.3
Virginia	1,097,308	22.9
Washington	1,068,616	24.8
West Virginia	424,479	24.6
Wisconsin	1,132,643	25.1
Wyoming	125,556	29.4

Table 1.5.1. Children by race and state, 1990.

	Hispanics		Asians		African Americans		Native Americans		Whites	
	Under 18	% under 18	Under 18	% under 18	Under 18	% under 18	Under 18	% under 18	Under 18	% under 18
Alabama	7,931	32.2	6,278	28.8	342,957	33.6	5,695	34.5	702,288	23.6
Alaska	6,747	37.9	6,234	31.6	7,903	35.2	34,793	40.6	121,324	29.2
Arizona	265,698	38.6	15,458	28.0	37,910	34.3	85,481	42.0	711,165	24.0
Arkansas	7,454	37.5	4,010	32.0	136,478	36.5	3,691	28.9	474,518	24.4
California	2,736,906	35.6	811,013	28.5	664,849	30.1	74,102	30.6	4,761,644	23.2
Colorado	152,749	36.0	18,138	30.3	42,607	32.0	9,222	33.2	729,274	25.1
Connecticut	77,361	36.3	14,804	29.2	85,572	31.2	1,737	26.1	609,042	21.3
Delaware	5,584	35.3	2,617	28.9	35,537	31.6	499	24.7	122,001	22.8
District of Columbia	7,262	22.2	1,570	14.0	93,907	23.5	240	16.4	17,428	9.7
Florida	391,962	24.9	43,359	28.1	608,799	34.6	9,556	26.3	2,128,358	19.8
Georgia	32,677	30.0	22,583	29.8	578,113	33.1	3,444	25.8	1,108,636	24.1
Hawaii	31,172	38.3	178,161	26.0	8,349	30.7	1,576	30.9	85,012	23.0
Idaho	22,494	42.5	3,006	32.1	1,237	36.7	5,126	37.2	287,036	30.2
Illinois	331,027	36.6	81,314	28.5	552,333	32.6	6,180	28.3	2,121,856	23.7
Indiana	36,650	37.1	10,194	27.1	143,887	33.3	3,663	28.8	1,280,279	25.5
Iowa	12,863	39.4	8,713	34.2	17,649	36.7	2,778	37.8	684,188	25.5
Kansas	36,719	39.2	10,160	32.0	48,646	34.0	7,270	33.1	575,852	25.8
Kentucky	7,101	32.3	5,361	30.1	83,079	31.6	1,431	24.8	861,525	25.4
Louisiana	26,797	28.8	14,220	34.6	465,143	35.8	6,545	35.3	735,337	25.9
Maine	2,520	36.9	2,245	33.6	1,706	33.2	2,123	35.4	302,090	25.0
Maryland	36,280	29.0	38,423	27.5	341,501	28.7	3,412	26.3	767,036	22.6
Massachusetts	107,256	37.3	41,297	28.8	93,340	31.1	3,574	29.2	1,151,345	21.3
Michigan	77,211	38.3	34,644	33.0	419,804	32.5	19,028	34.2	1,954,534	25.2
Minnesota	22,524	41.8	35,127	45.1	37,123	39.1	20,513	41.1	1,065,642	25.8
Mississippi	5,273	33.1	4,282	32.9	337,656	36.9	3,316	38.9	400,198	24.5
Missouri	21,287	34.5	11,888	28.8	178,716	32.6	5,653	28.5	1,108,098	24.7
Montana	5,113	42.0	1,461	34.3	881	37.0	19,882	41.7	198,618	26.8
Nebraska	14,714	39.8	4,025	32.4	20,952	36.5	5,237	42.2	392,348	26.5
Nevada	42,302	34.0	9,875	25.9	26,546	33.7	6,303	32.1	235,958	23.3
New Hampshire	3,944	34.8	2,747	29.4	2,282	31.7	555	26.0	271,858	25.0
New Jersey	222,698	30.1	80,394	29.5	40,090	29.3	3,892	26.0	1,318,050	21.5
New Mexico	203,308	35.1	4,421	31.3	10,392	34.4	54,414	40.5	309,428	27.0
New York	675,278	30.5	172,746	24.9	834,844	29.2	18,983	30.3	2,904,600	21.7
North Carolina	23,939	31.2	15,337	29.4	448,547	30.8	26,531	33.1	1,106,877	22.1
North Dakota	2,090	44.8	1,073	31.0	1,314	37.3	11,637	44.9	160,702	26.6
Ohio	52,526	37.6	26,351	28.9	368,389	31.9	5,395	26.5	2,285,221	24.0
Oklahoma	34,636	40.2	9,733	29.0	80,194	34.3	94,153	37.3	635,544	24.6
Oregon	43,730	38.8	20,642	29.8	16,255	35.2	13,358	34.7	653,923	24.8
Pennsylvania	86,169	37.1	42,056	30.6	320,400	29.4	3,816	25.9	2,377,565	22.6
Rhode Island	16,105	35.2	6,304	34.4	13,135	33.8	1,360	33.4	196,318	21.4
South Carolina	9,746	31.9	6,603	29.5	348,361	33.5	2,334	28.3	558,418	23.2
South Dakota	2,316	44.1	1,124	36.0	1,238	38.0	23,467	46.4	172,129	27.0
Tennessee	10,281	31.4	9,584	30.1	252,083	32.4	2,490	24.8	947,248	23.4
Texas	1,618,785	37.3	96,157	30.1	657,030	32.5	18,643	28.3	3,372,537	26.4
Utah	35,108	41.5	11,747	35.2	4,144	35.8	10,855	44.7	584,936	36.2
Vermont	1,102	30.1	1,038	32.3	691	35.4	543	32.0	140,437	25.3
Virginia	46,964	29.3	45,171	28.4	339,594	29.2	3,607	23.6	1,097,308	22.9
Washington	86,257	40.2	64,553	30.6	50,333	33.6	29,415	36.1	1,068,616	24.8
West Virginia	2,589	30.5	2,185	29.3	16,326	29.0	590	24.0	424,479	24.6
Wisconsin	39,328	42.2	22,987	42.9	98,060	40.1	15,125	38.4	1,132,643	25.1
Wyoming	10,378	40.3	822	29.3	1,269	35.2	3,905	41.2	125,556	29.4

Figure 1.6.1.
Number of adopted children, 1990.

Each dot equals 50 children.

Figure 1.6.3.
Average monthly adoption assistance claims, 1992.

Each dot equals 25 children.

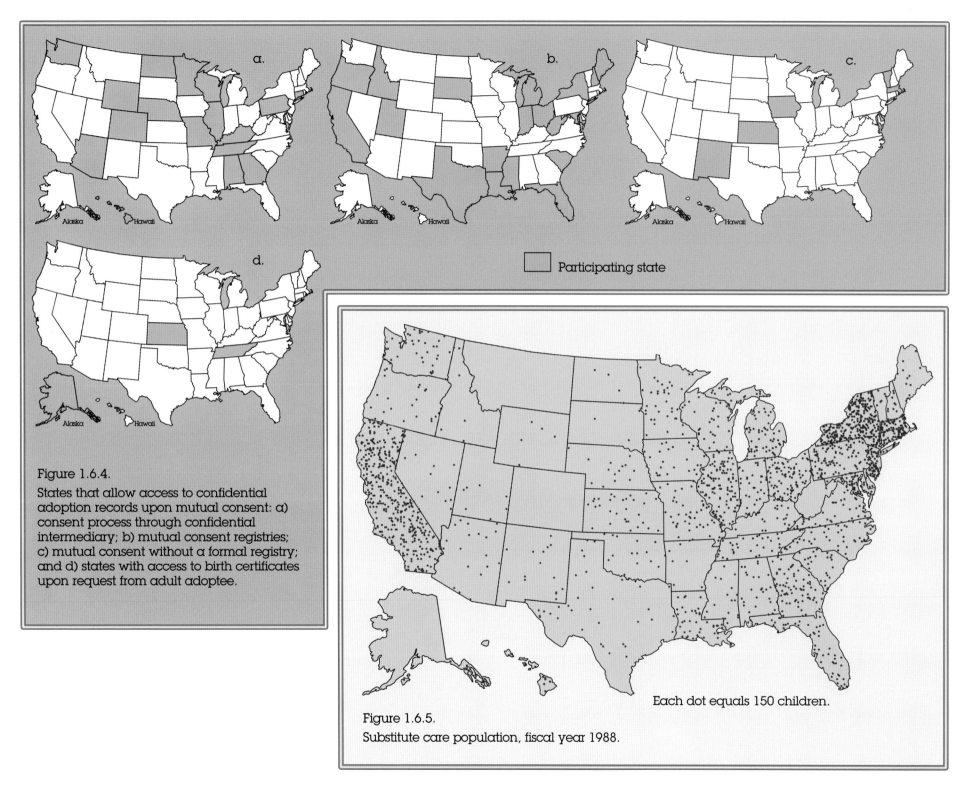

Participating state

Figure 1.6.4.

States that allow access to confidential adoption records upon mutual consent: a) consent process through confidential intermediary; b) mutual consent registries; c) mutual consent without a formal registry; and d) states with access to birth certificates upon request from adult adoptee.

Figure 1.6.5.
Substitute care population, fiscal year 1988.

Each dot equals 150 children.

Table 1.6.1. Percentage of finalized adoptions and children awaiting adoptive placement, 1989.

	Finalized adoptions	Children awaiting adoptive placement
Age		
0 to 1 year	6.0	3.1
1 to 5 years	48.0	32.7
6 to 12 years	36.6	42.5
13 to 18 years	9.1	20.5
19 years and older	0.2	1.1
Unknown	0.1	0.1
Race/ethnicity		
White	54.9	47.0
Black	28.9	42.2
Hispanic	10.2	6.6
Other	3.8	2.5
Unknown	2.2	1.7
Special needs status		
1 or more special needs	63.7	63.6
No special needs	35.7	26.1
Unknown	0.6	10.3
Time awaiting adoptive placement		
0 to 6 months		22.7
6 to 12 months		14.2
1 to 2 years		16.3
2 years or more		45.3
Unknown		1.5

Table 1.6.2. Proportion of special needs children in foster care, awaiting adoption, and adopted, 1984-89.

Status	1984	1985	1988	1989
Number of children in foster care	276,000	276,000	340,000	383,000
(Percent with special needs)	22.0	18.0	22.0	17.0
Number of foster children awaiting adoption	17,000	16,000	18,000	20,000
(Percent with special needs)	43.0	51.0	64.0	64.0
Number of foster children adopted	20,000	16,000	19,000	16,000
(Percent with special needs)	57.0	62.0	59.0	64.0

Table 1.6.3. State substitute care populations, fiscal years 1990-92 (based on VCIS data).

	Fiscal year		
	1990	1991	1992
Alabama	4,420	4,383	4,133
Alaska	3,852	1,942	1,496
Arizona	3,379	3,618	3,909
Arkansas	1,351	1,326	1,981
California	79,482	80,880	83,849
Colorado	3,892	5,519	4,390
Connecticut	4,121	4,202	4,252
Delaware	N/A	655	638
District of Columbia	2,313	N/A	2,152
Florida	10,664	10,235	9,928
Georgia	15,179	15,500	16,999
Hawaii	1,659	1,600	1,214
Idaho	548	877	1,235
Illinois	20,753	23,776	29,542
Indiana	7,492	8,126	8,455
Iowa	3,425	4,609	3,606
Kansas	3,976	7,112	7,838
Kentucky	3,810	6,422	6,966
Louisiana	5,379	5,799	5,722
Maine	1,745	1,814	1,944
Maryland	6,473	4,859	5,816
Massachusetts	11,856	13,232	13,147
Michigan	9,000	11,282	11,121
Minnesota	7,310	7,898	7,895
Mississippi	2,832	2,830	3,169
Missouri	8,241	7,143	8,171
Montana	1,224	1,494	1,691
Nebraska	1,543	2,660	2,985
Nevada	2,566	1,563	1,664
New Hampshire	1,505	2,095	2,630
New Jersey	8,879	8,451	8,024
New Mexico	2,042	2,304	2,118
New York	63,371	65,171	62,705
North Carolina	7,170	9,619	10,275
North Dakota	393	695	759
Ohio	18,062	17,298	17,099
Oklahoma	3,435	3,803	2,892
Oregon	4,261	3,996	4,031
Pennsylvania	16,665	17,508	18,491
Rhode Island	2,680	3,311	2,755
South Carolina	3,286	3,698	5.066
South Dakota	567	613	674
Tennessee	4,971	5,217	5,312
Texas	6,698	7,200	9,965
Utah	1,174	1,405	895
Vermont	1,063	1,088	1,162
Virginia	6,217	6,590	6,305
Washington	13,302	13,956	11,327
West Virginia	1,997	1,997	2,315
Wisconsin	6,037	6,403	6,812
Wyoming	484	605	907

Table 1.6.4. Children entering, in, and leaving substitute care, by age, 1989.

Age range	Percent		
	Entering	In care	Leaving
Under 1 year	15.8	3.2	3.9
1 to 5 years	26.8	31.6	26.7
6 to 12 years	26.6	32.2	24.7
13 to 18 years	30.2	30.6	40.8
19 years and older	0.4	1.8	3.6
Age unknown	0.2	0.6	0.3
Median age	7.5	N/A	10.6

Table 1.6.5. Outcomes for children who left care, fiscal year 1989.

Reunified	63.0%
Adopted	7.8%
Emancipated/reached majority age	7.1%
Other	18.1%
Unknown	4.0%

Table 1.6.6. Race/ethnicity of children entering, in, and leaving care, 1989.

Race/ethnicity	Percent		
	Entering	In care	Leaving
White	53.7	48.1	53.4
Black	30.6	34.3	28.2
Hispanic	10.5	9.7	10.4
Other	4.3	7.2	4.5
Unknown	0.9	0.7	3.5

Table 1.6.7. Reasons children entered substitute care, fiscal year 1989.

Reason	Percent
Protective service	46.8
Parent condition or absence	23.5
Status offense/delinquent	11.2
Relinquishment of parental rights	0.9
Handicap of child	1.6
Other	12.6
Unknown	3.4

Table 1.6.8. Federal foster care expenditures under Title IV-E, fiscal year 1993 (in millions of dollars).

	Maintenance payments	Child placement services and administration	Training	Total	Child placement services and administration as a percent of total
Alabama	1.5	3.1	0.1	4.7	65.4
Alaska	2.0	2.4	0.0	4.4	54.9
Arizona	7.8	9.4	0.7	18.0	52.4
Arkansas	2.3	4.9	2.6	9.8	50.3
California	232.2	227.6	18.3	478.1	47.6
Colorado	4.9	14.4	1.0	20.3	71.1
Connecticut	4.9	10.4	0.7	15.9	65.1
Delaware	0.4	0.9	0.1	1.3	68.7
District of Columbia	4.4	6.8	0.0	11.2	60.7
Florida	14.6	28.9	2.4	45.9	63.0
Georgia	8.5	14.3	1.7	24.5	58.3
Hawaii	0.8	2.1	0.0	2.9	73.2
Idaho	0.7	1.4	0.0	2.2	64.7
Illinois	73.9	40.4	3.3	117.6	34.3
Indiana	22.9	14.7	0.0	37.7	39.1
Iowa	7.4	5.8	0.4	13.7	42.7
Kansas	7.4	10.6	1.3	19.4	54.8
Kentucky	12.7	17.0	4.4	34.1	49.9
Louisiana	16.6	10.9	1.1	28.6	38.2
Maine	7.2	1.3	0.9	9.4	14.0
Maryland	23.8	17.4	3.4	44.6	39.0
Massachusetts	26.5	30.6	0.4	57.4	53.2
Michigan	47.4	54.4	1.5	103.3	52.6
Minnesota	18.7	12.4	1.9	33.0	37.6
Mississippi	1.6	2.2	0.3	4.1	54.3
Missouri	12.7	14.7	1.7	29.1	50.5
Montana	3.3	1.3	0.0	4.6	28.6
Nebraska	5.4	3.2	1.6	10.2	31.4
Nevada	1.6	1.2	0.1	2.9	41.7
New Hampshire	3.7	3.6	0.1	7.4	49.0
New Jersey	11.9	13.3	0.2	25.3	52.5
New Mexico	3.6	1.2	0.7	5.5	22.2
New York	416.0	345.5	17.7	779.2	44.3
North Carolina	14.3	3.2	0.1	17.6	18.4
North Dakota	2.5	2.4	0.5	5.4	45.1
Ohio	44.8	43.2	3.9	92.0	47.0
Oklahoma	5.1	2.6	0.5	8.2	32.1
Oregon	7.3	6.8	0.0	14.1	48.2
Pennsylvania	125.9	48.3	6.3	180.5	26.7
Rhode Island	3.2	4.8	0.1	8.1	59.0
South Carolina	4.7	3.5	0.7	8.8	39.1
South Dakota	1.3	1.3	0.0	2.6	49.0
Tennessee	9.1	5.3	1.3	15.8	33.9
Texas	38.5	32.1	1.6	72.2	44.5
Utah	3.0	2.8	0.1	6.0	47.0
Vermont	4.2	2.4	0.1	6.7	35.6
Virginia	4.5	6.6	2.4	13.4	49.1
Washington	8.1	11.6	0.2	19.9	58.3
West Virginia	2.2	1.6	0.4	4.3	37.2
Wisconsin	18.9	23.7	0.0	42.6	55.6
Wyoming	0.8	0.3	0.0	1.1	28.6

Table 1.6.9. Foster care basic monthly maintenance rates for children, ages 2, 9, and 16, 1987-1992.

	Age 2				Age 9				Age 16			
	1987	1990	1991	1992	1987	1990	1991	1992	1987	1990	1991	1992
Alabama	168	181	181	199	188	202	202	222	198	213	213	234
Alaska	428	na	na	588	478	na	na	523	565	na	na	621
Arizona	223	250	247	295	223	250	247	284	282	309	305	362
Arkansas	175	195	195	300	190	210	210	325	220	240	240	375
California	294	345	345	345	340	400	400	400	412	484	484	484
Colorado	235	284	296	302	266	284	296	302	318	338	352	359
Connecticut	268	319	386	497	302	355	424	506	350	407	478	572
Delaware	264	296	301	301	266	289	304	304	342	383	391	391
District of Columbia	304	304	304	304	304	304	304	304	317	317	317	361
Florida	233	296	296	296	233	296	296	296	293	372	372	372
Georgia	300	300	300	300	300	300	300	300	300	300	300	300
Hawaii	194	529	529	529	233	529	529	529	301	529	529	529
Idaho	138	198	198	198	165	205	205	205	204	278	278	278
Illinois	233	268	268	295	259	299	299	329	282	325	325	358
Indiana	226	281	281	405	245	330	330	462	280	398	398	518
Iowa	159	198	198	258	201	243	243	289	285	300	300	356
Kansas	187	225	304	305	245	304	304	305	280	386	386	386
Kentucky	248	250	265	263	263	265	288	285	300	303	333	330
Louisiana	199	283	283	283	232	316	316	316	265	349	349	349
Maine	244	296	296	296	250	304	304	304	291	353	353	353
Maryland	285	535	535	535	285	535	535	535	303	550	550	560
Massachusetts	362	410	410	410	362	410	410	410	433	486	486	na
Michigan	315	326	332	354	315	326	332	354	395	408	416	442
Minnesota	285	325	341	358	285	325	341	358	375	421	442	464
Mississippi	130	145	145	175	150	165	165	205	160	175	175	250
Missouri	174	209	209	212	212	255	255	259	232	281	281	286
Montana	283	294	307	318	283	294	307	318	354	368	384	402
Nebraska	210	222	222	326	210	222	291	393	210	222	351	463
Nevada	275	281	281	281	275	281	281	281	330	337	337	337
New Hampshire	200	200	200	200	251	251	251	251	354	354	354	354
New Jersey	203	213	244	256	215	226	259	272	253	266	305	320
New Mexico	236	258	258	258	247	270	270	270	259	281	281	281
New York	312	353	353	353	375	424	424	424	434	490	490	490
North Carolina	215	265	265	265	215	265	265	265	215	265	265	265
North Dakota	240	250	260	260	287	300	312	312	345	400	416	416
Ohio	240	269	289	297	270	305	328	342	300	341	366	381
Oklahoma	300	300	300	300	360	360	360	360	420	420	420	420
Oregon	200	220	285	295	234	258	295	306	316	348	363	378
Pennsylvania	558	285	303	330	558	361	319	392	558	432	377	450
Rhode Island	223	274	274	270	223	274	274	270	275	335	335	330
South Carolina	138	182	182	182	158	209	209	209	208	275	275	275
South Dakota	188	227	237	237	230	278	291	291	276	334	349	349
Tennessee	139	255	255	225	190	226	226	226	224	267	267	267
Texas	243	390	420	554	243	390	420	554	274	390	420	554
Utah	198	300	300	300	198	300	300	300	225	300	300	300
Vermont	210	371	371	321	249	371	371	321	268	447	447	397
Virginia	193	239	246	246	244	280	288	288	309	354	365	365
Washington	184	265	270	278	227	327	332	342	268	387	392	405
West Virginia	161	161	161	161	202	202	202	202	242	242	242	242
Wisconsin	163	194	231	231	224	240	257	257	284	304	324	324
Wyoming	300	300	400	400	300	300	400	400	330	300	400	400

Chapter 2

America's Children: How They Live

"How old would you be if you didn't know how old you were?"
— *Satchel Paige*

2.1
INTRODUCTION

The Great Depression was a time of economic deprivation for virtually all Americans. In the years following, the economic situation improved notably. Using income level as the exclusive indicator of poverty, the percentage of children in relative poverty actually declined after the Great Depression (Figure 2.1.1). One of the most striking features of children's lives during the past decade is the increase in the number of children in poverty. The overall poverty figure for children (under 18) increased during the decade 1979-1988 and for the first time surpassed the rate for all other groups, reversing the traditional pattern in the United States where poverty was a phenomenon which primarily affected the elderly (see Figure 2.1.2, page 61). By the late 1980s about 20.0 percent of America's children lived in poverty as compared with 13.0 percent for the rest of the population, including the elderly.

There are many explanations for the increase in child poverty. Some argue that child poverty increased because of the general widening of United States income inequality due largely to global economic restructuring (social and economic dislocations). They point to the economic recession of the early 1980's which fueled job losses and layoffs, reduced work hours, and contributed to a decline in the number of jobs that pay adequate wages as a

prime factor. Others cite the increase in single parent households and the change in living arrangements of children. The recent rise of mother-only families is important and, according to some, accounts for substantial increases in overall welfare dependence among poor children. Linked to this, fiscal conservatives point to federal welfare programs which, because of their "increasingly generous" economic rewards encourage unemployment, nonemployment, out-of-wedlock childbearing, and welfare dependency.

Data from 1986 to 1991 suggests that

the child poverty rate in the United States, though still troublesome, has actually declined from 22.9 to 20.8 percent. The earned income tax credit (EITC) and the federal food stamp program have been singled out as important factors in the decline. According to the Children's Defense Fund, however, child poverty has become more pervasive around the nation and less concentrated in the large cities. New York, West Virginia, Kentucky, Mississippi, Louisiana, Texas, and New Mexico have poverty rates, for children under 6, that are significantly higher than the national rate

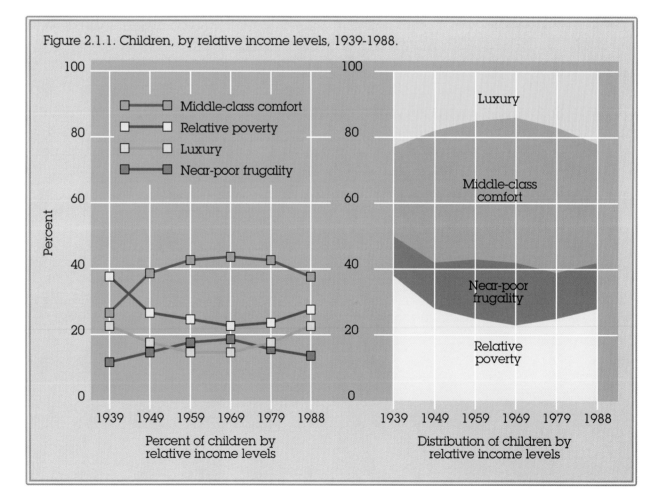

Figure 2.1.1. Children, by relative income levels, 1939-1988.

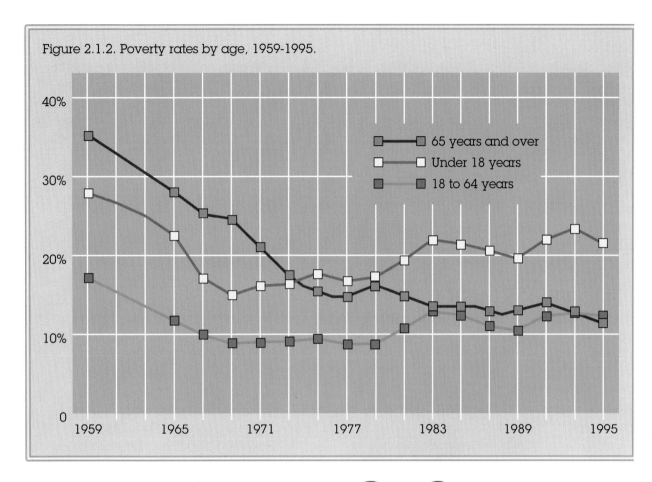

Figure 2.1.2. Poverty rates by age, 1959-1995.

Legend:
- 65 years and over
- Under 18 years
- 18 to 64 years

(Y-axis: 0, 10%, 20%, 30%, 40%; X-axis: 1959, 1965, 1971, 1977, 1983, 1989, 1995)

(see Figure 2.1.3, page 82). West Virginia, Mississippi, and Louisiana stand out as having the highest absolute child poverty rates in the nation during 1990 and 1994 (Figure 2.1.4, page 83).

After defining and measuring poverty, we describe how America's children live. We pay particular attention to trends in child poverty; impacts of family structure, especially the connection between single family homes and child poverty; the federal role in alleviating poverty; the implications of persistent poverty; and the link between housing, homelessness, and child poverty.

2.2
DEFINING AND MEASURING POVERTY

Poverty is defined by the Committee on National Statistics of the National Research Council as the condition or quality of being poor or in need. It is a situation characterized by a low level of material goods and services or a low level of resources to obtain those goods and services. It is an arbitrary construct based on a number of implicit and explicit social judgments, regarding what constitutes a "need" and what constitutes "well-being" and what

constitutes a "resource."

Formal measurement of poverty in the United States is fairly recent. The current definition is based on research undertaken by Mollie Orshansky in the early 1960s. Orshansky, a staff economist working for the Social Security Administration, began with a set of minimally adequate food budgets based on the Economy Food Plan—the least expensive of four food plans designed by the U. S. Department of Agriculture. She determined that food represented about 1/3 of after-tax income for the typical family. To obtain the poverty thresholds, the minimally adequate food budget was multiplied by a factor of 3. A family's resources (cash income before taxes) was compared with the appropriate threshold to determine if that family was impoverished. Orshansky's measure of poverty was accepted by policymakers at the Council of Economic Advisors and other researchers. With only minor modifications (adjusting for price inflation), the Orshansky thresholds still form the basis for the official poverty statistics (see Table 2.2.1, page 84).

As noted in the Poverty Measurement Working Paper by Daniel Weinberg "Measuring Poverty: Issues and Approaches" published by the U.S. Bureau of the Census, re-examinations of the poverty thresholds have occurred several times in the last 30 years. Though minor changes in measurement have resulted, there has been no full-scale redefinition of what constitutes poverty. What remains consistent is agreement that when one defines the level of resources needed to be non-poor, one must also determine which resources are to be counted.

Numerous groups maintain that the

current measure of poverty needs to be revised—it no longer provides an accurate picture of the extent of economic poverty among population groups or geographic areas of the country. Nor does it provide an accurate picture of trends over time. They note that the current measure has remained virtually unchanged over the past 30 years. Yet, during that time there have been marked changes in the national economy and society, and in public policies that have affected well-being. The National Academy of Sciences Committee on National Statistics has recently recommended that the government redefine the way it measures poverty. They recommend specific changes in the income measure, changes in the poverty thresholds and changing the survey instrument used. Specifically, they recommend adding non-cash benefits to the current money-income measure, subtracting taxes, subtracting work expenses, subtracting child-care expenses, subtracting child support and subtracting medical out- of-pocket expenses. Poverty thresholds are to be based on basic needs: food, clothing, and shelter. The panel also recommends that the government use the Survey of Income and Program Participation (SIPP) rather than the Current Population Survey (CPS). Though both surveys are produced by the United States Census Bureau. The CPS was first published in 1947 and uses a large sample size and simple questionnaire. The SIPP is newer (1984), and derives its greater descriptive quality by surveying a smaller sample in much greater detail, thereby reducing the number of non-responses. On the downside, the SIPP takes longer to interpret and publish (6

months to a year) and so by the time the data gets into the hands of policy-makers, it may no longer reflect the actual situations. Table 2.2.2, on page 84, shows the effect on poverty estimates when cumulative effects of taxes and transfers were considered. As is clear, using alternative approaches to measuring and adjusting poverty has a noticeable impact on the number and percent of people considered to be poor.

But, just what does being poor mean to a child? We know that being poor means feeling at risk. Poor children live and play in neighborhoods that generate multiple threats. Beyond that, being poor means that the odds are stacked against you. Poverty to a child is based on an evaluation of the child's surroundings in relative terms—comparing one person's situation with that of others. Children may feel poor when they compare themselves with others, even if they have the resources needed to meet basic needs. The girl who lives in a three-bedroom row house in a lovely neighborhood might consider herself poor when her peers live in five-bedroom single-family houses. The boy who does not have $150 sneakers may consider himself poor relative to his peers who seem to have so much more.

Understanding what it means to be poor is not simple. It is significantly more than statistics and measurements. According to James Garbarino, Director of the Cornell University Family Life Development Center, "the phenomenology of poverty is dominated by the experience of deprivation and exacerbated by widespread promulgation of highly monetized affluence as the standard." All of this could

potentially place children (whether incidentally or deliberately) in the position of being victims of rage and despair, neglect and abuse. The challenge of eradicating child poverty is both an academic endeavor as well as an ideological endeavor. Achieving a more comprehensive scope to the definition of poverty.

2.3
POVERTY AMONG CHILDREN

In many ways, America's children live better than most children worldwide. They have more leisure time, more consumer goods, spend more money on clothes and enjoy an overall higher standard of living. As the country struggles to maintain its global position however and undergoes new technological demands and changes in employment structure, America's children have been among the first to experience the tension in this transition. They have either reaped windfall benefits or become the targets. Using the Luxembourg Income Study database, the National Center for Children in Poverty undertook an international comparative study of poverty rates, real income levels and relative income positions. They found that in the United States, low-income children were worse off than their counterparts in most other countries, while high-income children in America were better off than their counterparts (see Figure 2.3.1, page 63). In exploring this theme of how children in the United States live, we focus on the overall context of income

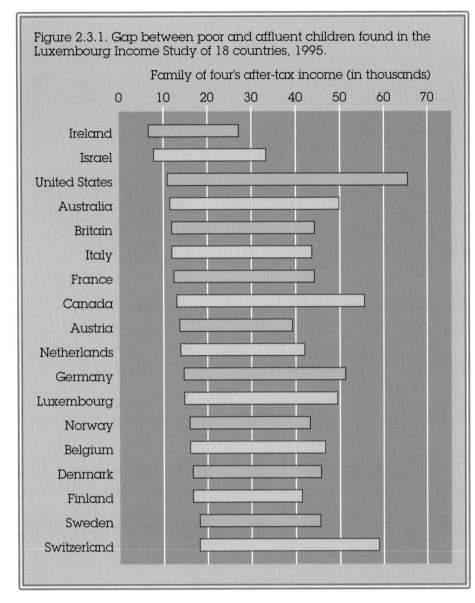

Figure 2.3.1. Gap between poor and affluent children found in the Luxembourg Income Study of 18 countries, 1995.

Family of four's after-tax income (in thousands)

nomic situations related to the demographic and social characteristics; and (2) the work undertaken by Greg J. Duncan, Director, Survey Research Center, University of Michigan, and co-author Willard Rogers *A Demographic Analysis of Childhood Poverty* (1984).

Children under 18 years and individuals 65 years and over tended toward longer spells of poverty. Among children, however, 47.6 percent—the largest percentage of all groups—were chronically poor. Using similar data from Duncan and Rogers, whereas 2.6 percent of all individuals experienced mid- to long-run (persistent) poverty, 4.8 percent of all children lived in persistently poor families. Duncan and Rogers provide some insights into our understanding of the persistence of poverty. They note in their demographic analysis of childhood poverty that differences in chronic poverty occur based on regional location, household status, and metropolitan/non-metropolitan status. While "locational factors," such as region

and metropolitan/nonmetropolitan status, figure prominently in understanding poverty among African Americans, characteristics of households have a greater influence on the poverty of white children. Duncan and Rogers observed that "being born to a white, never married female increases the expected number of years of child poverty by almost 700 percent (from 0.8 years to 6.2 years)." By comparison, the increase in expected number of years of child poverty for African American children increases

Table 2.3.1. Expected years of childhood poverty out of first 15 years of life.

	Non-Black	Black
All households	0.8	5.4
Characteristics of household at birth of child		
Never-married mother	6.2	6.0
Teenage mother	1.2	5.4
Education of head:		
8 years	1.2	5.6
12 years	0.7	5.3
Characteristics of household throughout childhood (15 years)		
Head disabled	3.3	10.9
Lived in South	0.8	6.4
Lived out of South	0.7	4.3
Large city	0.7	3.9
Rural area	1.1	8.1
1-parent	3.2	7.3
2-parent	0.5	3.0

Table 2.3.2. Incidence of short-term and persistent poverty of children by race.

	Rate	
Poor	White	Black
1 to 4 years out of 15	19.8	32.3
5 to 9 years out of 15	4.6	17.7
10 to 14 years out of 15	0.6	24.0
All 15 years of childhood	0.0	4.9

inequality which places children in poverty.

Not only are U.S. children more likely to be in poverty, they are more at risk of staying in poverty for longer periods of time. This is supported by both: (1) the Survey of Income and Program Participation (SIPP)—which also measures movement into and out of poverty and provides analysis of eco-

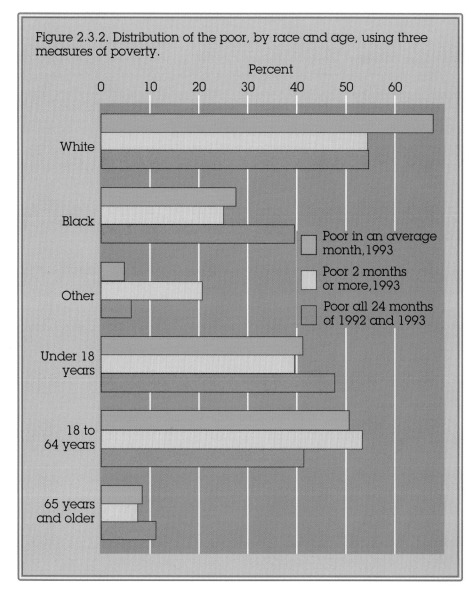

Figure 2.3.2. Distribution of the poor, by race and age, using three measures of poverty.

Percent

Legend:
☐ Poor in an average month, 1993
☐ Poor 2 months or more, 1993
☐ Poor all 24 months of 1992 and 1993

only 10 percent (from 5.4 years to 6.0 years). When race is isolated, the situation becomes disturbing. Almost 30 percent of all black children were persistently poor. This compares to 0.6 percent for all white children (see Tables 2.3.1 and 2.3.2, page 63). Black children spend over one-third of their first 15 years in households that are

poor while white children spend only 5 percent or less than one year.

Figure 2.3.2 shows the percent of the population, by race and age, that was poor during various times between 1992 and 1993. More whites experienced poverty than members of other races. Likewise, children were more likely to remain in poverty for longer periods of time. Among various family types, female-headed households were more likely to be poor for 24-month periods (see Figure 2.3.3, page 85). The maps found in Figures 2.3.4 to 2.3.8 illustrate the geographic distribution of American children living in poverty by ethnic/racial background (see pages 86 to 90). For all groups child poverty is localized in certain regions.

As some of America's children persist in poverty for longer and longer periods of time, exiting poverty becomes more difficult. Figure 2.3.9, on page 85, shows that almost 30 percent of married-couple families and 25 percent of whites exited poverty (poor in 1992 and then not-poor in

1993). The elderly and children made up a larger fraction of the chronically poor than the percent defined by the average monthly measure. Among children, only 18 percent were successful in exiting poverty.

2.4
THE YOUNGEST VICTIMS

Children under six are particularly vulnerable to the effects of poverty. In the United States, between 1987 and 1992, the number of poor children under six grew from 5 to 6 million and the poverty rate for children under six reached 26 percent. The young child poverty rate is significantly higher in the U. S. than in other Western industrialized countries and is higher than the rate for any other age group (see Figure 2.4.1, page 91).

According to the National Center for Children in Poverty, the increasing number of poor young children in America reflects a 20-year progressively worsening trend. The significance of this increase in numbers cannot be overstated (see Figures 2.4.2 and 2.4.3, page 91). "Poverty gives rise to many types of deprivation and many of our youngest children suffer severe consequences in terms of physical, emotional, intellectual, and psychological development. As children in poverty grow into adolescence and adulthood they are more likely to drop out of school, commit crimes as juveniles, have children out of wedlock and be unemployed. In addition, there is a huge economic cost to the nation as a whole which threatens the productivity and competitiveness of America's future."

These increases in young child poverty occur in concert with growing income inequality (Figure 2.4.4). Such concentrated poverty endangers the social cohesion of the nation and undermines the prospect of civil authority.

Reasons for the increase in poverty among the youngest citizens are unclear and solutions are not simple. The tendency is to blame the federal government for its lack of responsiveness and failure to intervene in a timely and concerned manner. Before government can move, however, it needs more information on the true circumstances that contribute to higher poverty rates among younger children as well as clear targets. A significant finding in the work undertaken by the University of Wisconsin Madison Institute for Research on Poverty, suggests that the "current patchwork of entitlements inadequately

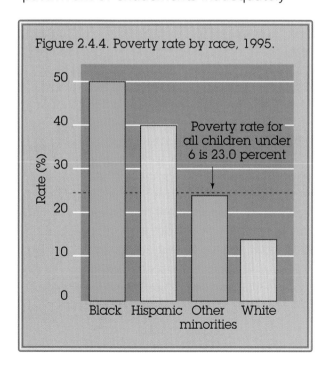

Figure 2.4.4. Poverty rate by race, 1995.

Poverty rate for all children under 6 is 23.0 percent

protects poor children in two parent families," because both parents work. They maintain that one way of raising a substantial portion of the nation's poor young children out of poverty is through policies that reward the efforts of two parent families (see Tables 2.4.1 and 2.4.2, page 93). Children in two-parent families consistently fewer benefits. Recent findings reveal other patterns that are not consistent with public "myths" about poor children and their families. For instance:

(1) The majority of the poor do not resemble the stereotypical inner-city "underclass." Large numbers are non-Hispanic white; most do not receive welfare; nearly two-thirds live outside of central cities; and they do not have significantly more preschool aged children than the non-poor. (see Table 2.4.3, page 93). The poverty rate among children under 6 living in urban areas was 35 percent, compared to 19 percent in suburban areas and 28.0 percent in rural areas. Most recent figures suggest that the poverty rate is increasing faster in the suburbs than elsewhere.

(2) More than half, 55 percent of poor children under 6 were African American or Hispanic.

(3) A majority of poor children under 6 had parents who worked full-time or part-time.

(4) Unemployment accounted for the poorest families.

(5) Of the six million children under 6 living in poverty, just under half lived in extreme poverty, in households

with a combined family income below 50 percent of the federal poverty line.

(6) Full-time employment does not guarantee that families will not be poor.

Given the recent trend toward shifting responsibility from federal to state governments, the state role in the current policy landscape becomes more important. In 1966, the National Center for Children in Poverty (NCCP), based at Columbia University School of Public Health, released the first edition of *Map and Track: State Initiatives for Young Children and Families. Map and Track* identified the states whose governments supported programs that provided: supplemental health insurance for children, supplemental funds for federal Head Start and prekindergarten programs, and supports at least one state-funded, comprehensive program strategy targeted to young children and their families (see Figure 2.4.5, page 92). The findings of the NCCP are encouraging. Thirty-nine states are supporting one or more state-funded comprehensive program strategies explicitly targeted to young children; 29 states maintain state-funded prekindergarten programs; 14 states provide supplemental funds for Head Start and 19 (almost 25.0 percent) provide supplemental health care for children. Even with these encouraging findings and the growing awareness of the seriousness of the issue, America's youngest citizens still fall behind other Western countries. Jane Knitzer and J. Lawrence Aber, of NCCP, point to some difficult issues as well (1992). They note that many of the young children's initiatives build on or use federal dollars. Alternatively they use state dollars to supplement basic services supported by federal dollars. If federal dollars shrink, the pressure on states will surely increase. If a concerted effort among federal and state government is absent, ensuring the well-being of children will be much more difficult.

2.5
HOMELESSNESS

The problem of homelessness gained national attention during the mid-1980s. Although no methods exist to measure the number of homeless people with absolute precision, it is agreed by most experts that homelessness is rising. From an economic perspective, the trend in homelessness over the past decade is puzzling; it runs counter to what might have been expected given that during the decade the country recovered from its steepest recession since World War II, and one of its vital signs, employment, actually improved.

Homelessness is a condition in which individuals and families have no residence—owned, leased, or shared—in which they can live safely, healthfully, and legally both night and day, and in which they can meet their social and basic needs in privacy and with dignity. After shifting from its original manifestation of being a one-time "emergency" situation due to fire, personal calamity, or temporary unemployment; the homeless problem in the 1980s came to be seen as a "housing" problem—linked to poverty, but temporary.

Most recently, homelessness (in the 1990s) threatens to take another radical turn and present itself still differently—sustained, long-term, and severe—a total and complete loss of dignity.

"What happened? I worked hard all my life and here I am. And I was working. I had my clothes, my plants, and my son. How could this happen to me? I had a good head on my shoulders; I made good decisions. Here I thought things were going to work out and all of a sudden, wow! This happens to other people. This doesn't happen to me."

—Executive Summary and Recommendations—Homelessness in Pennsylvania: How Can This Be?, authored by Phyllis Ryan, Ira Goldstein, and David Bartelt.

Table 2.5.1, on page 68, from the U.S. Conference of Mayors Status Report on Hunger and Homelessness in America's Cities, breaks down the Composition of the Homeless Population of 29 U.S. cities for the year 1996. Today in the United States it is estimated that over 400,000 families are homeless. Another 2.5 million families double or triple-up with friends and relatives—just one step away from official homelessness.

Family homelessness is a more complex phenomenon than homelessness in general. A typical homeless family in the early 1980s consisted of a middle-aged woman with adolescent children. Now it is a twenty-year-old mother with children under age 6. The average age of homeless children today is 3 years old, while in 1987 the average age was 7 (see Figure 2.5.1, page

67 and Table 2.5.2, page 94). A consequence of younger homeless parents is a lower level of educational attainment and hence a less productive work history. Poverty, a common theme in all homelessness, is more pervasive in family homelessness. The causes of family homelessness are exacerbated by other intractable and complicated problems such as domestic violence, child abuse, substance abuse, foster care, an ineffective educational system and inadequate health care. Children are often the "hidden silent homeless." Comprehensive and reliable data describing the total number of homeless children living in the United States does not exist. Professionals in the field estimate that children account for approximately 27.0 percent of the domestic homeless population. The General Accounting Office estimates that there are approximately 26,000 homeless children and youth under the age of 16 living in shelters and hotels in urban centers (see Table 2.5.3, page 94). Children and families constitute the largest and fastest growing segment of the homeless population. Children comprise two-thirds of all individuals living in shelters.

Policy-makers are struggling to understand the "new" homelessness. With the implementation of federal and state budget cuts in the human health and welfare field which began in the early 1980s, and the continued shift from an industrial to a high-tech service-based economy, and high levels of immigration, an increasing number of families may lose in the competition for jobs and find themselves homeless. While family histories and family dynamics (see Figure 2.5.2, page 67) and the number of residences in the year prior to becoming

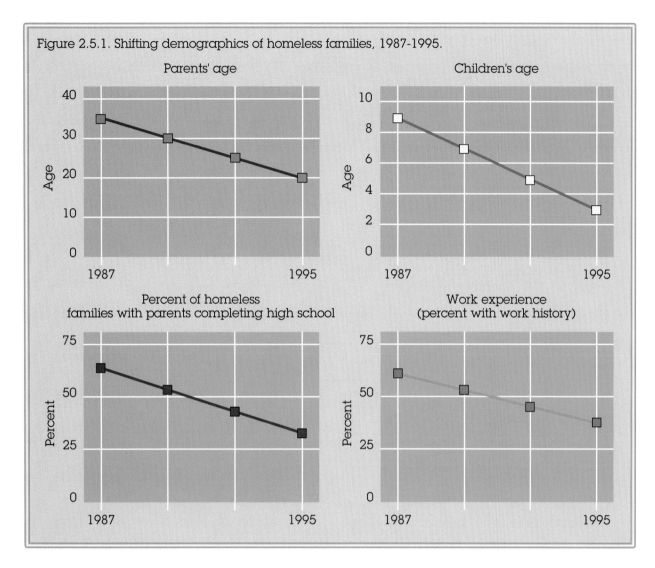

Figure 2.5.1. Shifting demographics of homeless families, 1987-1995.

Parents' age

Children's age

Percent of homeless families with parents completing high school

Work experience (percent with work history)

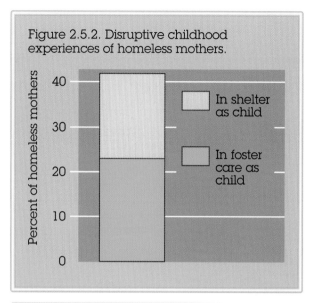

Figure 2.5.2. Disruptive childhood experiences of homeless mothers.

In shelter as child

In foster care as child

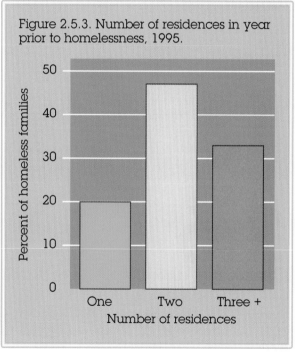

Figure 2.5.3. Number of residences in year prior to homelessness, 1995.

homeless (see Figure 2.5.3) are cited as primary problems, the bleak reality is that for many of today's homeless, no other way is known. Most homeless mothers are raising their children just as they themselves were raised. According to Homes for the Homeless, Inc., even if a family makes it to permanent housing, "a staggering 50 percent (one in two families) return to shelters in less than a year." There is a lack of affordable housing and inadequate public assistance benefit levels in most cities. The most significant increase for emergency shelter during the past year has come from families with children and yet, in the cities sampled, families are turned away (see Table 2.5.4, page 94).

Other facts about homeless children and youth are located in a highlighted box on the following page.

Table 2.5.1. Composition of the homeless population by percent and category, 1995.

	Families	Single men	Single women	Youth	Mentally ill	Substance abuser	Employed	Veteran
Alexandria	41	47	11	0	26	79	27	16
Boston	32.2	56	10.8	0.9	—	—	28	30
Charleston	32	54	9	5	40	65	36	30
Charlotte	33.8	41.9	15.5	8.8	15.7	35.3	27.2	19.2
Chicago	37	43.5	19.3	—	7.9	21.5	8.8	5
Cleveland	22	52	23	2	25	50	15	10
Denver	32	48	20	2	18	32	11	28
Detroit	26	58	12	4	3	50	19	19
Kansas City	74	11.9	13.9	0.1	—	—	—	—
Los Angeles	—	—	—	—	—	—	—	—
Louisville	31	47	10	12	—	—	8.4	12.5
Miami	30	45	20	5	45	60	15-20	15-20
Minneapolis	78	18	4	—	10	35	15	25
Nashville	8	68	23	1	2	33	7	4
New Orleans	16	57	14	13	22	42	15	26
Norfolk	28	52	19	>.1	—	—	—	—
Philadelphia	63.3	24.5	11.9	0.3	>4	34.6	9.2	7.2
Phoenix	30	60	5	5	20-50	21-34	23	28
Portland	49	37	13	1	—	—	—	7
Providence	—	—	—	—	18	—	13.5	4
Saint Louis	68	20	12	0	22	40	12	7.6
Saint Paul	42	51	8	—	5	6	13	36
Salt Lake City	28	60	10	2	57	32	37	35
San Antonio	58.6	28.9	11.4	1.1	40	31	24	22
San Diego	18	68	10	4	22	24	18	29
San Francisco	25	55	15	5	43	52	8	40
Santa Monica	18	42	30	10	30	65	—	30
Seattle	—	—	—	—	—	—	—	—
Trenton	77	11	11	1	25	85	>10	1

2.6
CHILD CARE

Children as a group are nearly totally dependent on the individual and collective actions of a number of social and economic institutions. The ability of these institutions to meet the needs of children has important consequences for the structure and quality of life for American society. Child care is perhaps the most critical of these institutions.

Somebody other than parents "minding the kids" is not new—either a friend, relative, sitter, family child care, or a center took care of the kids. In 1965, most children were cared for by a relative. By 1993, the percent cared for by a relative was down to 29.0 percent and the percent cared for in a center had increased to 30.0 percent (Figure 2.6.1, page 70). Issues surrounding early childhood programs emerged in the late 1980s. Several things prompted heightened attention to child care. First, there is considerable interest in the impact of child care on children.

Preschoolers are in the midst of forming personalities, developing cognitively and learning social skills; child care providers can and do have a major impact on these processes and their outcomes. Second, there has been a dramatic increase in labor-force participation of mothers with children under 2 (see Figure 2.6.2, page 76). Child care serves the broader purpose of enabling mothers with young children to join the paid labor-force. Third, there have been fairly dramatic changes in family structure over the past decade. Most children grow up in single-parent mother-only

Table 2.5.1 (cont.). Composition of the homeless population by percent and category, 1995.

	African American	White	Hispanic	Asian	Native American	Single-parent families	Family members who are children
Alexandria	76	19	3	0	1	87	57
Boston	45	45	10	—	—	95	62.7
Charleston	73	26	1	0	0	80	65
Charlotte	73	23.6	1.7	0.5	1.2	60	60
Chicago	82.6	9.5	7.2	0.4	0.3	97.6	67.5
Cleveland	78	19	2	0.5	0.5	95	70
Denver	23	50	16	0	5	60	65
Detroit	93	6	7	0.2	1	99	70
Kansas City	61.4	27.8	9.7	10	0.1	43	49
Los Angeles	—	—	—	—	—	—	—
Louisville	—	—	—	—	—	88	64
Miami	55	15	28	>1	>1	70	65
Minneapolis	70	15	3	2	10	75	62
Nashville	51	45	2	0	1	67	60
New Orleans	66	31	1	1	1	80	71
Norfolk	88	11	1	0	0	92	60
Philadelphia	89.2	7.2	3.5	0.1	—	89.4	71.3
Phoenix	15	64	15	1	5	80	60
Portland	23	55	15	1	4	80	59
Providence	—	—	—	—	—	89	50
Saint Louis	85	14	0.3	0.7	0	65	50
Saint Paul	51	31	14		4	95	69
Salt Lake City	8	70	13	1	8	67	70
San Antonio	23.8	25.8	50.1	0.2	0.1	73	76
San Diego	39	38	23		—	90	60
San Francisco	47	31	13	5	4	73	87
Santa Monica	43	35	17	2	3	78	15
Seattle	—	—	—	—	—	—	—
Trenton	58	26	1	0	1	88	67

homes (see Figures 2.6.3 and 2.6.4, page 95). Again, child care facilitates labor force participation of mothers. Finally, child care has been a significant issue in recent debates over how to move welfare recipients from dependency to employment and self-sufficiency.

Child care is a relatively young and growing field. Over the past 3 decades, child care arrangements have shifted from parents or relatives to centers or child care homes. In 1993, organized child care facilities served almost half of America's preschoolers (see Figure 2.6.5, page 95).

This shift has prompted concern over issues of quality, availability, and affordability. See Figures 2.6.6 through 2.6.12, pages 96-99 for state performance on various dimensions of child care quality.

CHANGING PATTERN OF EMPLOYMENT AMONG PARENTS

A growing proportion of children live in mother-only families. At the turn of the century, most children lived in breadwinner-homemaker families—two-parent households where the father worked outside the home to support the family and the mother stayed at home to care for the children. In 1950, only 12.0 percent of women with children under six were in the paid labor-force. By 1986 that proportion had grown to over 50.0 percent. The Bureau of Labor Statistics reports that in the recent past, the labor-force participation rate for women with very young children has increased from one-third to one-half. Labor-force participation rates for all mothers have increased markedly and, unlike in the past when mothers were more likely to join the paid work force when children were older, the trend now is for women to enter the labor force when children are younger.

The most notable increase in working among mothers has been for women in married-couple families. In contrast to earlier generations, most women now remain in the labor-force after they marry and have children. Regardless of marital status, rates of labor-force participation among women increases with age of youngest child (see Table 2.6.1, page 70). Clearly, what was once the exception regarding working wives and mothers is now the rule and one result of this shift is an emerging demand by working parents for an accommodation of their child care needs.

Coupled with these changes in living arrangements is the increasing diversity among the American population—economic, labor-force participation, racial/ethnic. This growing diversity has impacts on the nature and content of the care that children will need.

As the country ponders ways to move welfare recipients toward employment and self-sufficiency, child care is viewed as critical to that process.

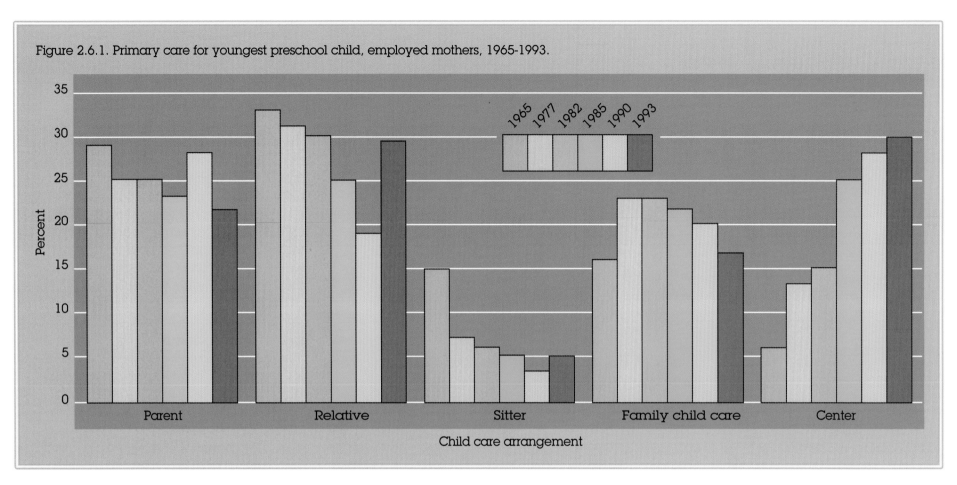

Figure 2.6.1. Primary care for youngest preschool child, employed mothers, 1965-1993.

Legend: 1965, 1977, 1982, 1985, 1990, 1993

Child care arrangement: Parent, Relative, Sitter, Family child care, Center

Table 2.6.1. Labor-force participation rates of women with children under 18, by marital status and age of youngest child, 1995.

Marital status	Age of youngest child						
	Under 3	Under 6	Under 18	3 to 5	6 to 13	6 to 17	14 to 17
All women with children under 18	58.7	62.3	69.7	67.1	75.1	76.4	79.5
Married, spouse present	60.9	63.5	70.2	67.2	74.9	76.2	79.6
Divorced	65.8	73.3	82.0	77.8	83.7	85.2	88.6
Separated	57.2	59.3	66.1	61.3	70.9	71.5	73.1
Widowed	45.3	58.9	61.2	65.1	62.5	61.7	61.0
Never-married	48.7	53.0	57.5	61.7	67.3	67.0	65.4

CHILD CARE AND DEVELOPMENT BLOCK GRANTS

Soon the federal government will send checks to states to reform the system of welfare. For 1997 estimates see Table 2.6.2, page 71. With this money (and some of their own), states will be expected to implement welfare-reform guidelines set at the federal level. As well, states will be expected to continue to provide maintenance during the transition. According to Judith Havemann (*Washington Post* staff writer, October 22, 1996), the problem with transforming the old system into the new world of welfare reform is "uneven payment." In other words, according to Havemann, "if you're a state on the low end of the federal payment scale you have relatively little money with which to provide child care, transportation, training or public service jobs for those welfare recipients you're trying to move into work." She describes this as the key obstacle. If states fail to meet federal standards because they lack federal resources and/or unwilling to make up the difference on their own, they will be docked up to 21.0 percent of their total grant, setting them even further back in the race to reform.

Further, Havemann notes that some states, like Wisconsin, already have legislation providing for universal jobs and child care for every welfare recipient. Others, like Alabama (whose welfare payments have been among the lowest in the nation), however, confront an enormous challenge. Wisconsin will get $1,450 for each poor child in the state. Alabama will get $379. Louisiana will get $357 and Vermont will receive $2,778.

The formula—simply matching the funding that states provided under the old system and turning it into a block grant—is fair argue "pro-reform" advocates. Others, however, maintain that "if a parent who has been getting $164/month goes to work and requires child care that costs $300, the state loses." By contrast, if Wisconsin, which has been paying $517/month, puts a person in a job that requires a $400/month child care subsidy, the state makes $117 on every case. States that operated generous welfare programs were rewarded and those that did not were penalized. "The rich will get richer and the poor get poorer."

INTERNATIONAL COMPARISONS

Use of early childhood programs is increasing worldwide. The factors promoting the rise in child care worldwide are the same as those promoting increased child care use in the U.S.—economic pressures that promote employment by mothers and the lack of an extended family-support system.

Another factor contributing to the

Description of Conference Action on HR 3734—the Personal Responsibility and Work Opportunity Reconciliation Act of 1996/Title VI: Child Care

The conference report approved by the House of Representatives provides maximum state flexibility and funding to reform welfare through the creation of a broad cash welfare block grant. This block grant would provide states with at least their 1995 level of funding over the coming years. A total of $16.4 billion per year would be provided under the basic block grant.

The conference report would consolidate the major child care programs into a single block grant, the Child Care and Development Block Grant (CCDBG), to assist low- and moderate-income parents in paying for child care. This approach will eliminate the gaps, disruptions, and paperwork caused by separate programs. Funds made available through the block grant would total $15 billion over 7 years (1996-2002). In addition, the proposal would authorize $1 billion each year in discretionary funds. The block grant would contain provisions which give parents choice and authority in deciding where to send their child to day care. As well, it would give parents the option of receiving assistance through vouchers or cash.

Table 2.6.2. Federal payments to states for AFDC child care and transitional child care, in thousands of dollars, fiscal years 1991 and 1997 (estimated).

	FY 1991	FY 1997	Percent change
Alabama	2,820	14,915	528.9
Alaska	415	2,980	718.1
Arizona	2,354	21,262	903.2
Arkansas	4,348	2,875	66.1
California	11,331	64,681	570.8
Colorado	3,649	7,168	196.4
Connecticut	5,301	18,767	354.0
Delaware	1,300	5,964	458.8

	FY 1991	FY 1997	Percent change
D.C.	2,799	4,276	152.8
Florida	20,678	42,016	203.2
Georgia	13,231	49,109	371.2
Hawaii	249	2,237	898.4
Idaho	756	1,754	232.0
Illinois	8,468	57,523	679.3
Indiana	12,828	30,453	237.4
Iowa	2,204	8,590	389.7
Kansas	3,233	7,302	225.9
Kentucky	5,027	16,032	318.9
Louisiana	12,741	16,220	127.3
Maine	1,354	2,596	191.7
Maryland	9,509	25,745	270.7
Massachusetts	24,889	64,944	260.9
Michigan	14,467	16,791	116.1
Minnesota	11,342	21,909	193.2
Mississippi	574	7,758	1351.6
Missouri	1,196	23,519	1966.5
Montana	1,144	2,560	223.8
Nebraska	5,152	11,790	228.8
Nevada	1,057	1,647	155.8
New Hampshire	1,621	4,924	303.8
New Jersey	2,195	15,996	728.7
New Mexico	2,026	4,907	242.2
New York	29,289	61,954	211.5
North Carolina	7,306	82,051	1123.1
North Dakota	1,554	2,030	130.6
Ohio	9,394	73,349	780.8
Oklahoma	7,983	22,580	282.9
Oregon	6,260	21,384	341.6
Pennsylvania	N/A	54,965	N/A
Rhode Island	1,821	7,993	438.9
South Carolina	541	6,588	1217.7
South Dakota	983	1,346	136.9
Tennessee	4,492	42,896	954.9
Texas	20,803	58,943	283.3
Utah	6,275	13,454	214.4
Vermont	1,626	4,786	294.3
Virginia	4,320	21,986	508.9
Washington	8,355	58,575	701.1
West Virginia	2,169	9,260	426.9
Wisconsin	8,242	20,407	247.6
Wyoming	957	3,242	338.8

Accreditation Standards

Several voluntary systems exist nationally to establish higher-quality standards than are required by law for both child care centers and family child care homes.

Child Care Centers

One of the most widespread accreditation systems for centers is that created by the National Association for the Education of Young Children (NAEYC). In this system, center-based programs conduct self-evaluations involving staff and parents. Professional validators from NAEYC conduct visits to determine whether or not standards have been met, and if they have, programs are accredited for three years. Standards are designed for programs that serve children from infancy through age eight in centers caring for 10 or more children; school-age programs are eligible if a majority of children are eight years old or younger. As of January 31, 1996, there were 4,523 accredited centers in the United States and 16 foreign countries, and another 8,815 centers were in the process of becoming accredited.

Family Child Care Homes

In 1988, the National Association for Family Day Care (now the National Association for Family Child Care, or NAFCC) began a program of voluntary accreditation for family child care homes. The process includes self-evaluation as well as external validation of aspects of program operation, including health and safety, nutrition, indoor and outdoor play environments, interactions, and professional responsibility. Accreditation of family child care homes is less common than accreditation of child care centers. As of early 1996, only 1,083 providers were accredited, and another 272 were in the process of becoming accredited. All but six states had accredited providers. These six states were Louisiana, Mississippi, Nevada, New Mexico, South Carolina, and South Dakota.

Note: The National Association for Family Child Care is working with the Family Child Care Project at Wheelock College, and a national network of providers, parents, and others to develop a new accreditation process and instrument, scheduled to replace the current system in 1998. Also refer to Figures 2.6.6 through 2.6.12, pages 96 to 99 for state accreditations status and Table 2.6.5, on page 96, for inspection frequencies for individual states.

From: The Davis and Lucile Packard Foundation, *The Future of Children*, vol. 6, no. 2 (1996).

Understanding Head Start

Head Start is administered by the Administration for Children, Youth and Families of the Administration for Children and Families in the Department of Health and Human Services. In 1994, there were 40,295 Head Start classrooms nationwide that served three fourths of a million children.

Head Start began in the 1960s as a program to help prepare children from low-income families for school and life. Currently, it is the single largest federally funded early childhood program ($3.5 billion in 1995). The program targets 3- and 4- year-old children and provides them with a wide range of services in four areas: education; health services; social services; and parent involvement. Typically programs are part-day and operate on a school year calendar. This often makes it difficult for working parents to participate.

Grants for Head Start programs are awarded to local public agencies, private nonprofit organizations, and school systems to operate programs at the community level. The fiscal year 1995 appropriation was $3.5 billion. Between 1990 and 1994, acting on favorable reports of the impact of the program, Congress doubled funding for the program. Federal funds cover 80.0 percent of costs. The remaining local-match of 20.0 percent may be waived or matched in-kind. In 1994, the federal cost per child was $4,345.

increased use of child care worldwide is the recognized development importance of early childhood education. Support for this comes from recent research from Australia, Canada, Colombia, France, Germany, India, Ireland, Japan, etc., which suggests that the achievement gap between low-income children and their more advantaged peers is narrowed through participation in preschool programs. Children's cognitive development, learning skills, and personality and social development are all increased. This has been difficult to confirm in the U.S. due to racial/ethnic divisions, vast rural urban disparities, and large variation in abilities to afford quality preschool services—all of which complicate findings. Likewise, there is little evidence that interventions do much to reduce the unequal opportunities that often confront children from different social, cultural, and economic backgrounds.

Preschool facilities and services are unevenly distributed both within and among countries. Availability and quality of preschool programs tend to be much higher in rich industrialized nations than in poor developing ones. Likewise, access to preschool facilities is much greater in urban centers than in rural areas, and enrollment rates for children from upper- and middle-income homes exceed those for poor children.

Government involvement in the provision of preschool services takes different forms in different countries, from full funding and direct sponsorship of programs to a more modest role of regulating programs provided by the private sector and paid for by parents. In the U.S., government steps in only in special circumstances. Parents are expected to care for their own children, seeking assistance in the private market.

When families fail or the market cannot provide, the state intervenes to offer benefits or provide a safety net. The most visible public child care interventions are Head Start (see highlighted box on the preceding page) and state prekindergarten programs used by the majority of states to provide support for children who are at risk of school failure.

Historically, AFDC is the primary income support for child care for poor U.S. families, giving mothers and eligible families cash benefits based on the number of children in their care. By contrast, in the social democratic policies of the Scandinavian countries, such as Sweden, the supports provided by the government are not treated as marginal or as required only by a few unfortunate individuals, but are considered essential to enable citizens to achieve a basic standard of living. Governments provide generous benefits (subsidized child care) to all citizens who are seldom obliged to meet income criteria to qualify for assistance (as noted in the work of Siv Gustafsson and Frank Stafford (1995)—professors of economics at the University of Amsterdam and Institute for Social Research at the University of Michigan—*Links Between Early Childhood Programs and Maternal Employment in Three Countries*). An intermediate approach exists in the Netherlands and its neighbors like Austria, France, Germany, and Italy. In these countries, government has a more limited role but reliance on the private market as a source of essential services is also limited. Policy is shaped by the interplay of powerful political interest groups, e.g., the Christian church.

In the Asian and Pacific Rim, research has been directed more on the goals and outcomes of early childhood programs than on the policy context. In Japan, Singapore, South Korea, Hong Kong, and Taiwan, where very traditional Confucian values intermingle in a context of rapid industrial growth, most (90.0 percent) children attend preschool by age three. The focus of preschool programs is on preparing children for the academic demands of school. With such a large proportion of 3- to 6-year-olds in preschool, the attention of policy-makers turns to questions of program design and approach. Findings confirm European research results that attending preschool yields significant benefits, though short-lived.

In the developing world (Latin America, Africa and parts of Asia), preprimary education is viewed as a strategy for promoting national development. Preschool programs are often funded by outside sources (IBRD, UNESCO, UNICEF, etc.), and are increasingly employing an approach that engages local communities in the design, operation, and evaluation of programs. The full impact of early childhood programs has not been felt. Barriers to success include inadequate nutrition and health problems. Preschool programs often link nutritional supplements and health education with programs offering cognitive and psychosocial stimulation.

International research confirms basic conclusions drawn from studies conducted in the U.S. (Boocock 1995). Attendance at preschool programs is associated with cognitive gains and improved performance in school (as long as the program is not of very poor quality as are some forms of child care in the U.S.). Research has also shown that the benefits of early childhood programs are greater for children from disadvantaged backgrounds.

According to Gustafsson and Stafford (1995), it is important to consider the full range of incentives and barriers to child care that are embedded in any nation's social system. What these examples show, however, is how national policies have incorporated ideas of motherhood, education, economic development, and the intersecting needs of women and children in different ways.

FINANCING CHILD CARE

The amount of money spent on child care reflects more than parental choices. Reported expenses reflect what families can afford to pay for child care, but not always the amount necessary to acquire adequate child care. Two-parent families with both parents in the labor-force might work different shifts to avoid the necessity for outside child care. Leaving a child unsupervised because of lack of money might be another response among both poor and non-poor households.

Because of the linkages with the broader social purpose of enabling family members to work, the question of who should pay for child care—employers, parents, government—is a complicated issue. Currently, it is estimated that about 50.0 percent of the total funding for child care for children from birth through school age comes from parents, 45.0 percent from federal, state, and local government and perhaps 5.0 percent from business, philanthropy, and other donations.

All levels of government provide funding for child care, the federal government providing the most. The bulk of federal funding goes to: (1) Head Start; (2) the

Table 2.6.3. Overview of federal programs that support child care.

Program	Statutory authority	Federal funding support	Fiscal year 1995 outlays (in millions)	Target population
Child care for AFDC recipients	Social Security Act	Open-ended, federal match at Medicaid rate	633	AFDC recipients who need dependent care to accept or maintain employment, or to participate in state-approved education/training
Transitional Child Care assistance (TCC)	Social Security Act	Open-ended, federal match at Medicaid rate	192	Families that lose AFDC eligibility due to employment (increase in income or hours worked)
At-risk child care	Social Security Act	Funding ceiling, federal match at Medicaid rate	279	Low-income families not receiving AFDC who need child care to work, and are at risk of welfare eligibility if care not provided
Child Care and Development Block Grant	Omnibus Budget Reconciliation Act of 1990	Funding ceiling, 100 percent federal funding	933	Families with incomes at or below 75 percent of state median income, with parents engaged in work or education/training.
Child and Adult Care Food Program	National School Lunch Act of 1946	Open-ended, 100 percent federal funding	1,461	N/A
Title XX Social Services Block Grant	Social Security Act	Funding ceiling, 100 percent federal funding	448	State discretion
Head Start	Discretionary authorization	Omnibus Budget Reconciliation Act of 1981	3,393	Low-income children and families

Child and Adult Care Food Program; (3) Title IV-A "At Risk"; (4) the Child Care and Development Block Grant; (5) Title XX Social Services Block Grant; (6) Transitional Child Care; and (7) Child care for AFDC recipients. See Table 2.6.3 above and its continuation on the following page for a description. Hoffert, Helburn and Howes; and Stoney and Greenberg in work done for the Packard Foundation—*The Future of Children,* (1996)—note five major areas of concern about providing child care:

(a) Complicated funding—this has been addressed somewhat with the passage of the new welfare reform legislation which eliminates many federal programs that funded child care for families.

(b) Limited availability of services/space concern here revolves around the number of children left without adult supervision and/or the number of children who potentially need child care and go unserved .

(c) Lack of affordable child care—over the recent past, the amount paid by parents per hour of child care has increased dramatically. In part this is due to demand outstripping supply, but also results from the preference for center-based, child care programs among middle/upper-income families.

(d) Quality—Helburn and Howes in their work for *The Future of Children* reported findings from a 1995 study that found that about 15.0 percent of children in child care centers are in centers of such poor quality that their health or development is threatened (1996).

(e) High turnover rates among child care

Table 2.6.3 (cont.). Overview of federal programs that support child care.

Program	Eligible children	Provider requirements	Reimbursement rates to providers
Child care for AFDC recipients	Children under age 13 (unless incapable of self-care or under court supervison)	Must meet applicable state and local standards	Cost up to $200 per month (less than 2), and $175 per month (2 or older) Not more than the 75th percentile of local market rate
Transitional Child Care assistance (TCC)	Children under age 13	Must meet applicable state and local standards	Same as AFDC
At-risk child care	Children under age 13	Must meet applicable state and local standards or, if not regulated and with the exception of relatives, be registered	Same as AFDC
Child Care and Development Block Grant	Children under age 13 (unless incapable of self-care or under court supervison)	Must meet applicable state and local standards or be registered (including relatives). With exception of relatives, must also meet certain health and safety standards	No limit
Child and Adult Care Food Program	Children under age 13, migrant children under age 16	Must meet applicable state and local standards	Meal rates are indexed to inflation, rates vary by family income
Title XX Social Services Block Grant	State discretion	Must meet applicable state and local standards	No limit
Head Start	Children from poor families who have not reached the age of compulsory school attendance	Must meet federally established standards with respect to health, education, parental involvement, nutrition, and social services	No limit

workers—low wages are the primary reason for the high turnover rates found in child care centers. Wages for child care providers are among the lowest of any profession, according to Goodman (1995). He also notes that earnings for child care workers have fallen in recent years. What this means for children is that they have less opportunity to form stable, nurturing relationships with their caretakers.

Many agree that relying exclusively on parents, government, or businesses to fund child care will not address the many issues confronting child care in America. A sizeable number, however, believe that because of the benefits to be gained for the country as a whole in terms of human resource development, the role of government should be expanded.

In her work, "What Does it Cost to Mind our Preschoolers?," Lynne Casper (1993) seeks to define and measure the cost of child care. She notes that based on data from the SIIP, there were 8.1 million families with preschoolers who required day care during the time their mothers were at work.

Of these 56.0 percent paid an average of $74/week for care or about 8.0 percent of their monthly income. Families with 2 or more preschool aged children paid about $110 per week for child care while families with one child paid only $66/week. Married-couple families spent a smaller proportion of their family income on child care (7.0 percent) than did single-parent families (12.0 percent). Families with older mothers paid more for child care than did families with younger mothers—on average $14/week more. The proportion of income spent on child care by younger mothers, however, was greater than the proportion spent by older mothers. Casper also noted that families whose mothers have more education pay on average $10/week more for child care than families whose mothers have less education.

Child care expenditures also vary by region and metropolitan residence. Residents in the Northeast pay on average $85/week, compared to residents in the South who pay $69/week. Likewise, residents in non-metropolitan regions spend less (actual amounts and percentage) than their metropolitan counterparts. Just as child care expenses vary regionally, they also vary over time. From 1986 to 1993, child care expenses have increased from an average of $40/week to $70/week. Similarly, the percent of monthly income spent on child care has increased from 6.3 percent to 7.3 percent.

Recently, employers are being asked to contribute to child care expenses. Data from the employee benefits survey reveal that employers provide the following family benefits to employees (Table 2.6.4).

Employer support for child care is less than other employee benefit programs. In 1995, 35.0 percent of employees were eligible for severance pay while only 8.0 percent of all employees were eligible for employer-assisted child care. Also, a gap exists between higher and lower paid workers in terms of child care support. Fifteen percent of professional workers were eligible for child care support from their employer as opposed to only 3.0 percent of those in blue-collar jobs and 7.0 percent of those in clerical positions.

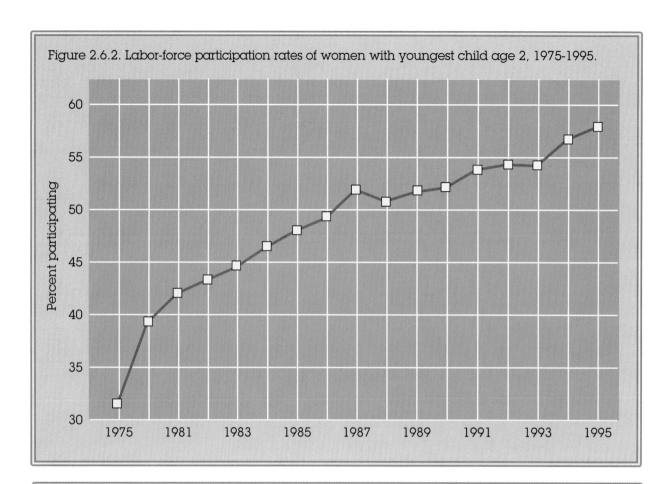

Figure 2.6.2. Labor-force participation rates of women with youngest child age 2, 1975-1995.

Table 2.6.4. Eligibility for specified benefits for full-time employees, 1995.

Marital status	All employees	Professional, technical, and related employees	Clerical and sales employees	Blue-collar and service employees
Employer assistance for child care	8	15	7	3
Employer-provided funds	4	7	4	2
On-site child care	3	8	2	4
Off-site child care	1	2	1	6
Adoption assistance	11	18	1	4
Severence pay	35	47	43	24

2.7
WELFARE

Children are a popular rallying point for social issues, particularly poverty. Their plight generates sympathy among both policy makers and the general public. In America, the poverty that affects children is largely perceived as resulting from personal deficits in their adult caretakers. As a result, anti-poverty policies are not as comprehensive in the U.S. as in other industrialized nations. The United States, for example, is the only western industrialized nation which does not have some form of universal cash benefit for families with children. In limiting benefits to poor adults, America limits benefits to children.

The main anti-poverty programs—referred to as "welfare"—which affect children can be categorized under two main types—*in-kind benefits* and *cash assistance*. According to the summer/fall 1997 edition of the Packard Foundation's *The Future of Children*, federal expenditures for in-kind programs have increased by 135.0 percent (excluding Medicaid for the elderly and disabled) since 1975. Expenditures on cash assistance have decreased by 8.0 percent. This is especially troublesome since there has been a 19.0 percent increase in the number of children receiving cash aid.

This section briefly describes the main *in-kind* and *cash* benefit anti-poverty programs which affect children. In this section, we also summarize the effect of the recent changes in the federal safety net.

IN-KIND PROGRAMS

The *Food Stamp* program was authorized in 1964 and was designed to increase the purchasing power of low income households in order to maintain a nutritionally adequate low cost diet. It is classified as an entitlement program which enables households which meet the income eligible criteria to receive food stamps—often, a major share of total household resources for many low income families. Interestingly more than 60.0 percent of households receiving food stamps include children; only 40.0 percent however er receive any form of cash assistance. Legally, states are permitted to count as income the value of a family's food stamps and accordingly, states could reduce the amount paid to a household. To date, no state has done so. The Food Stamp program does, however, consider AFDC payments to be countable income and food stamp benefits are reduced by about 30 cents for each AFDC dollar.

Assistance through the *Special Supplemental Food Program for Women, Infants and Children* (WIC) was initiated in 1972 to supplement the nutritional needs of low income pregnant women, infants and children. WIC is not an entitlement program and is limited by federal funding levels which have never been adequate to reach all who are eligible. (*Future of Children*, 1997)

The primary federal program designed to enhance early development in children is *Head Start*. Head Start (see Section 3.6) is funded subject to a 20.0 percent local match (which may be in-kind or waived). It is targeted at low income families with 3 and 4 year old children. Federal funding for

---

President Signs Welfare Bill: Significant Child Care Impacts Anticipated

On August 22, President Bill Clinton signed the personal Responsibility and Work Opportunity Reconciliation Act of 1996, H.R. 3734, H. Rept. 104-725. The Act will affect a broad range of low-income programs. The principal changes for child care include:

(1) Repeal of the AFDC Child Care, Transitional Child Care, and At-Risk Child Care programs. With the repeal comes the elimination of any open-ended federal funding for child care, and elimination of state duties to guarantee child care for families receiving AFDC or leaving AFDC due to employment;

(2) Creation of a single Child Care and Development Block Grant. Under this block grant, states will generally be eligible to receive a level federal child care funding equivalent to the level received in 1994 or 1995 without being required to contribute state funds. Also, a capped amount of

additional funding will be available to states that maintain their previous level of state spending and contribute additional state matching funds; and

(3) Repeal of the AFDC Program, and replacement with a Temporary Assistance for Needy Families Block Grant. States may use the block grant to assist needy families, subject to a 60-month limit on using federal TANF funds to provide that assistance, but states will have no obligation to assist any family for any period of time. States will face steadily increasing work-participation rates for families receiving assistance, which may require commitment of substantial amounts of child care resources.

From: The Davis and Lucile Packard Foundation, Center for the Future of Children, *The Future of Children*, vol. 6, no. 2 (1996).

Head Start in FY 1995 was $3.5 billion, the largest amount for any single tax- or expenditure-based child care/early education program. Although Head Start is the largest of these federally funded program, only 38.0 percent of eligible 3 and 4 year olds are served.

The federal government also provides *in-kind* benefits to low income families to assist with housing costs. This assistance is largely in the form of public housing and *Section 8* rent subsidies. Even though safe and decent housing is an important element in the lives of children, housing assistance is not an entitlement and less than half of all households who receive cash assistance also receive housing assistance.

Enacted in 1965, *Medicaid* plays a critical role in the health of low income children by providing health insurance to all who are income eligible. States must provide Medicaid to families receiving cash assistance under AFDC. In 1986, Congress extended Medicaid coverage to certain groups of women and children not enrolled in AFDC. In addition, states have the option to provide coverage to pregnant women and infants under age 1 with incomes less than 185.0 percent of the Federal poverty level. According to the U.S. Census Bureau, almost 1 out of every 4 children was covered by Medicaid in 1995. Among African American children, the figure was 1 out of every 2. Also, younger children are more likely to be covered by Medicaid than older children. (see Table 2.7.1, page 81). Even with the new provisions in Medicaid coverage, 9.8 million children under age 18 had no health insurance at any time in 1995. According to the Child Welfare League, two thirds of these uninsured children live in families with incomes above the poverty line and nine out of ten have working parents (Child Welfare League of America, 1997).

DIRECT ASSISTANCE PROGRAMS

Low income children who are disabled may be eligible for cash assistance through *Supplemental Security Income* (SSI) monthly benefits. The Urban Institute estimates that 890,000 children received more than $4 billion in SSI benefits in 1994. SSI benefits play an important role in alleviating poverty. Without this benefit, according to Plotnick (1997), 63.0 percent of recipient children would be poor.

The *Earned Income Tax Credit* (EITC), enacted in 1975 and expanded in 1993, lowers tax rates for income eligible families with children. Almost 19 million families were provided an estimated $25 billion of assistance through the EITC in 1996.

The cash assistance program most identified with "welfare" in the mind of the general public is *Aid to Families with Dependent Children* (AFDC). AFDC was begun in 1935 and initially targeted children in families with only one parent present. This was changed in 1990 when AFDC was extended to needy two parent families. In 1995, over 9 million children received AFDC monthly (see Figure 2.7.1, page 80). AFDC serves 6l.0 percent of children in poverty, a decline since 1975 when it served 72.0 percent (see Figure 2.7.2, page 80).

As an entitlement program, AFDC nor combine benefits met poverty levels for 1996. (see Table 2.7.2, page 81). Figure 2.7.3, page 100, shows maximum AFDC benefits by state. Over time, both need standards and maximum benefits established by states have changed significantly (see Figure 2.7.4, page 100 and 2.7.5, page 101). Similarly, other costs associated with implementing the program-notably administrative-have changed over time (see Figure 2.7.6, page 82).

Over the years, as AFDC benefits have declined, food stamp benefits have been used to offset the decline. Even with this, combined benefits for a 3 person family has dropped from $962 (in 1972) to $699 (1996). This 27.0 percent shrinkage was due largely to shrinkage in AFDC benefit levels (Green Book, 1996).

Contrary to the popular stereotype of the "welfare queen" (welfare mothers receiving large amounts of money from the government), the median monthly benefit level in 1996 was approximately $390. Plotnick, in *The Future of Children* (Summer/Fall, 1997) notes that "In the median state, combined AFDC and food stamp benefits... equaled 65.0 percent of the federal poverty threshold." Table 2.7.3, on page 102, describes the changing demographics of families who received AFDC from 1969 through 1994. Over this period, the average AFDC family size has decreased from 4.0 to 2.8. The proportion of AFDC families headed by teen mothers has also decreased and the majority of AFDC families in 1994 were headed by a mother over 24 years old. Reflecting on the trend in the population overall, the percentage of AFDC families with a single parent has increased from 27.9 percent to 55.7 percent over the period.

Since a significant element in the new welfare legislation concerns increasing the flexibility of states in distributing funds, it is important to briefly describe past state responsibilities and performances in anti-poverty program administration. The Urban Institute estimated that before the enactment of TANF (Temporary Assistance to Needy Families), states paid between 20-50 percent of AFDC, depending on the state. States would apply to the federal government for waivers in order to implement special initiatives. These initiatives included: strengthening child support enforcement. See Figure 2.7.7, page 101, for states implementing enforcement strategies, expanding employment and education opportunities, limiting benefits for families who have additional children while on assistance, and requiring Medicaid recipients to enroll in a managed care organization.

With the passage of the Personal Responsibility and Work Opportunity Reconciliation Act (PRWORA) in August, 1996, significant changes have been made to the anti-poverty federal safety net. The Center on Budget and Policy Priorities estimates that the act will cut low income programs by almost $55 billion over the next six years, with most of the cuts affecting programs other than AFDC. The Urban Institute has predicted that 1.1 million children will be pushed into poverty with these cuts, and that the overall depth and severity of child poverty will increase by 20.0 percent. The major alterations to welfare through the PRWORA include:

(1) Converting entitlement programs to state block grants;

(2) Instituting stricter work requirements;

(3) Setting lifetime limits of receipt;

(4) Cutting food stamp allotments; and

(5) Barring legal immigrants from accessing certain programs.

As portions of this legislation are currently being challenged, some items in the above list may be subject to change. See Table 2.7.4, on page 102, for a summary of changes.

By converting AFDC cash assistance from an entitlement program to state block grant (TANF), the federal government has essentially capped funding. Poor families who meet the income eligibility criteria are no longer entitled to receive cash assistance. This means that if a poor family applies to the state for cash assistance after the state has spent all its monies, they could be denied benefits. Although there is a contingency fund in case of a recession or population increase, advocates are concerned that funding levels will be vastly inadequate if/when a state economy takes a turn for the worse. States are not required to contribute as much funding to TANF as they did previously to AFDC. They are allowed to withdraw up to $40 billion from the funding stream between 1997 and 2002. Proponents of the new reform measures argue however that the state block grant is expected to provide states with more flexibility in distributing funds and planning programs designed for specific needs of the state. Following certain general guidelines, each state was required to form a plan for spending the funds and setting requirements for its caseload. States can differ in terms of their work requirements, lifetime limits and restrictions on illegal immigrants.

A key element in welfare reform legislation recently has been transitioning welfare recipients into work. PRWORA requires that at least 25.0 percent of a state's caseload must participate in work activities in fiscal year 1997. Before a household reaches two years of cash assistance, the adult(s) in the household must work at least 30 hours a week by fiscal year 2000 or 20 hours if there is a child under 6 years old in the household. Research indicates that most recipients leave the welfare rolls between 4 to 5 years of initial enrollment, but then cycle back on welfare (see Tables 2.7.5 and 2.7.6, page 81). Significantly, the most frequent event associated with ending AFDC spells in 1993 was increase in earnings of females. This was a change from 1986 when marriage, remarriage or reconciliation ranked highest (see Table 2.7.7, page 82). Cycling is due to the type of jobs commonly available to low income women. These jobs are characterized by low wages, no benefits and little job security. Advocates for children and their parents argue that the issue is not finding a job as quickly as possible for welfare recipients, but rather providing a stable job with a livable wage and a full array of supports such as affordable quality child care and health insurance.

Child care (see Section 2.6) and health insurance coverage (Chapter 3, section 1) are elements of support needed for a welfare recipient to make the transition to the work force. PRWORA placed all federal child care programs in a single child care block grant. There is no longer an entitlement for child care assistance. Parents with children under six are not penalized for failing to meet work requirements if they cannot find affordable child care, but their time spent receiving cash assistance is still counted toward their lifetime limit. If a welfare recipient finds a job which does not offer health insurance, the recipient may still be able to receive Medicaid coverage for herself/himself and the family for one year if the income is below a certain level. Medicaid coverage was only directly changed for legal immigrants under the new law, but for non-immigrants, Medicaid eligibility is no longer linked to receipt of cash assistance. As a result of this "delinking" there is a separate eligibility process for Medicaid and TANF. Concern is that eligible children may lose their benefits or not apply for them due to the more complex application process.

Half of the spending cuts in PRWORA come from the Food Stamp Program. According to the Center for Budget and Policy Priorities, food stamp cuts total $27.7 billion over 6 years. The food stamp allotment will be reduced from $.80 per person per meal to $.66 per person per meal by 2002. Two thirds of the benefit reductions will affect families with children, including working poor families. Families with children are expected to lose an average of $435 annually in food stamp benefits by 1998. PRWORA also has restricted the eligibility criteria for children to qualify for SSI benefits. The Center for Budget and Policy Priorities has estimated that by 2002, approximately 315,000 low income children formerly eligible for SSI will lose their benefits. This restriction of SSI not only limits cash benefits but also makes some children ineligible for Medicaid, thus depriving them of their health insurance as well.

Children of legal immigrants are particularly affected by PRWORA cuts. Forty percent of the net savings of the reform legislation are gained by cutting benefits to legal immigrants, according to the Center

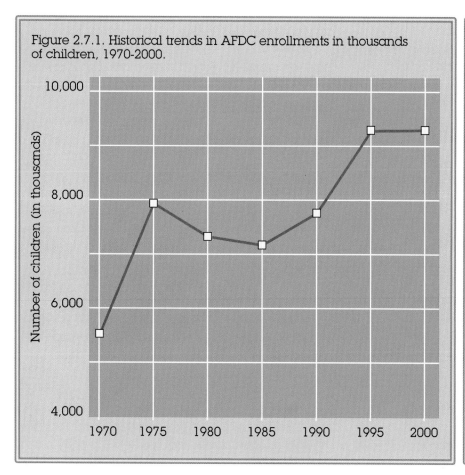

Figure 2.7.1. Historical trends in AFDC enrollments in thousands of children, 1970-2000.

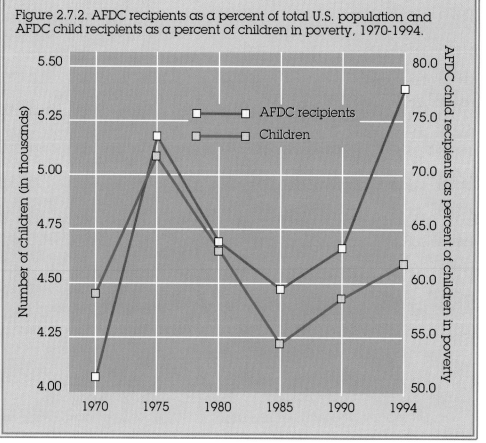

Figure 2.7.2. AFDC recipients as a percent of total U.S. population and AFDC child recipients as a percent of children in poverty, 1970-1994.

for Budget and Policy Priorities. Most legal immigrants are barred from receiving food stamps or SSI benefits. Excluding refugees and asylees, legal immigrants who enter the U.S. after August 1996 are not able to receive TANF or Medicaid for five years or until they become citizens.

In sum, the recent cutbacks in the federal safety net of anti-poverty programs may adversely affect millions of children. By cutting funding for food stamps, restricting eligibility for cash assistance through TANF and SSI, and by barring legal immigrants from receiving key benefits, federal policies are in effect, endangering the health, safety and future opportunities for children in the United States.

Table 2.7.1. Medicaid characteristics by race/ethnicity, age and poverty level.

	Percent
Percent of children covered by Medicaid in 1995	23.2
White	18.3
African American	45.4
Hispanic	37.4
Percent of people in poverty covered by Medicaid in 1994	
0-5 years	71.5
6-10 years	65.3
11-18 years	52.4
19-44 years	36.9
45-64 years	29.4
65 or older	28.7

Table 2.7.2. AFDC and combined benefits as a percent of 1996 poverty guidelines.

	Combined benefits	AFDC benefits
Alabama	44	15
Alaska	92	68
Arizona	61	32
Arkansas	48	19
California	79	56
Colorado	67	39
Connecticut	81	59
Delaware	60	31
District of Columbia	67	39
Florida	57	28
Georgia	55	26
Hawaii	95	57
Idaho	58	29
Illinois	64	35
Indiana	56	27
Iowa	67	39
Kansas	69	40
Kentucky	53	24
Louisiana	47	18
Maine	66	39
Maryland	63	34
Massachusetts	76	52
Michigan (Washtenaw Co.)	71	45
Minnesota	74	49
Mississippi	40	11
Missouri	56	27
Montana	67	39
Nebraska	63	34
Nevada	61	32
New Hampshire	75	51
New Jersey	68	39
New Mexico	65	36
New York (New York City)	78	53
North Carolina	54	25
North Dakota	67	40
Ohio	60	32
Oklahoma	57	28
Oregon	71	43
Pennsylvania	67	39
Rhode Island	79	51
South Carolina	47	18
South Dakota	67	40
Tennessee	46	17
Texas	46	17
Utah	67	39
Vermont	82	60
Virginia	62	33
Washington	77	50
West Virginia	52	23
Wisconsin	73	48
Wyoming	62	33

Table 2.7.5. Cumulative percentage of women leaving welfare by duration of time on welfare and type of exit, 1995.

Duration in months	Work exits	Other exits	All exits
1 to 12	25.4	30.4	55.8
13 to 24	31.7	38.3	70.0
25 to 36	35.0	42.3	78.2
37 to 48	39.0	43.6	82.6
49 to 60	40.9	45.4	86.3

Table 2.7.6. Cumulative percentage of women returning to AFDC by duration of time off AFDC and type of exit, 1995.

Duration in months	Work exits	Other exits	All exits
1 to 12	39.4	49.5	44.9
13 to 24	52.5	61.8	57.6
25 to 36	57.8	69.3	64.2
37 to 48	62.5	74.3	69.1
49 to 60	65.0	76.6	71.5

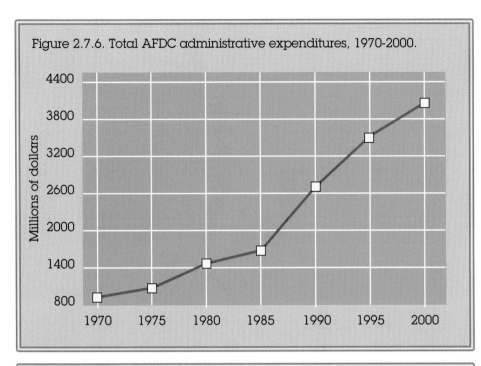

Figure 2.7.6. Total AFDC administrative expenditures, 1970-2000.

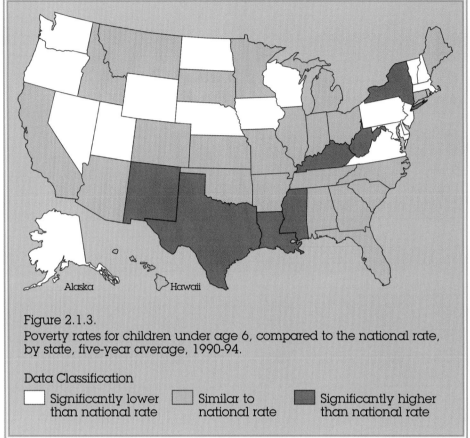

Figure 2.1.3.
Poverty rates for children under age 6, compared to the national rate, by state, five-year average, 1990-94.

Data Classification

Significantly lower than national rate	Similar to national rate	Significantly higher than national rate

Table 2.7.7. Events associated with endings of AFDC spells, by percent, 1986 and 1993.

Event	1986 study (annual data)	1993 study (annual data)
Marriage, remarriage, or reconciliation	34.6	11.4
No eligible child left in household	11.2	3.1
Increase in earnings of female head	21.3	45.9
Increase in earnings in others in family	4.9	N/A
Increase in transfer income	14.2	7.3
Disability	N/A	1.5
Move	1.8	6.9
Other, including unidentified	11.8	24.1

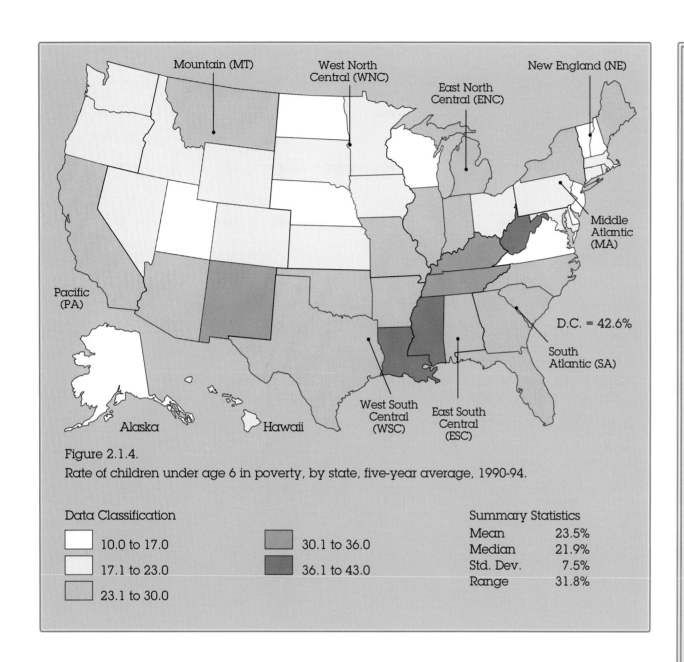

Figure 2.1.4.

Rate of children under age 6 in poverty, by state, five-year average, 1990-94.

Data Classification

☐ 10.0 to 17.0	■ 30.1 to 36.0		
☐ 17.1 to 23.0	■ 36.1 to 43.0		
☐ 23.1 to 30.0			

Summary Statistics

Mean	23.5%
Median	21.9%
Std. Dev.	7.5%
Range	31.8%

Number and rate of children under age 6 in poverty, by state, five-year average, 1990-1994.

	Poor young children (in thousands)	Poverty rate
Alabama	112	28.1
Alaska	9	15.9
Arizona	91	23.8
Arkansas	56	27.2
California	867	27.1
Colorado	75	21.7
Connecticut	59	20.3
Delaware	7	13.0
Dist. of Columbia	25	42.6
Florida	323	27.0
Georgia	152	24.5
Hawaii	20	19.4
Idaho	23	21.9
Illinois	301	26.1
Indiana	148	26.6
Iowa	44	17.5
Kansas	48	19.8
Kentucky	105	35.5
Louisiana	163	41.4
Maine	23	23.5
Maryland	85	17.1
Massachusetts	93	19.0
Michigan	238	27.7
Minnesota	84	21.3
Mississippi	100	39.3
Missouri	130	28.2
Montana	19	24.7
Nebraska	26	16.3
Nevada	22	18.0
New Hampshire	11	10.8
New Jersey	116	16.2
New Mexico	47	32.5
New York	470	28.8
North Carolina	140	24.7
North Dakota	8	16.5
Ohio	207	21.6
Oklahoma	82	28.0
Oregon	48	18.2
Pennsylvania	204	20.3
Rhode Island	16	21.0
South Carolina	88	27.3
South Dakota	15	22.5
Tennessee	135	31.3
Texas	523	29.1
Utah	26	11.7
Vermont	8	13.5
Virginia	97	17.0
Washington	78	17.7
West Virginia	53	40.0
Wisconsin	69	16.5
Wyoming	7	17.1

Table 2.2.1. Poverty thresholds by size of family and number of related children, 1995 (in dollars).

	One	Two	Three	Four	Five	Six	Seven	Eight	Nine or more
				Number of persons in family					
Total	$7,763	$9,933	$12,158	$15,569	$18,408	$20,804	$23,552	$26,237	$31,280
Number of related children under 18									
None	$7,763	$9,985	$11,921	$15,719	$18,956	$21,803	$25,088	$28,058	$33,752
One	—	10,504	12,267	15,976	19,232	21,890	25,244	28,306	33,916
Two	—	—	12,278	15,455	18,643	21,439	24,704	27,797	33,465
Three	—	—	—	15,509	18,187	21,006	24,328	27,350	33,086
Four	—	—	—	—	17,909	20,364	23,627	26,717	32,462
Five	—	—	—	—	—	19,983	22,809	25,913	31,609
Six	—	—	—	—	—	—	21,911	25,076	30,835
Seven	—	—	—	—	—	—	—	24,863	30,644
Eight or more	—	—	—	—	—	—	—	—	29,463

Table 2.2.2. The cumulative effect of taxes and transfers on poverty estimates, 1994-95 (numbers in thousands).

	1995		1994		1994-1995 difference	
	Persons in poverty	Poverty rate	Persons in poverty	Poverty rate	Persons in poverty	Poverty rate
Selected income definitions						
Definition 1 (current measure)						
	36,425	13.8	38,059	14.5	-1,634	-0.7
Definition 2 (definition 1 less government cash transfers)						
	57,643	21.9	59,730	22.8	-2,087	-0.9
Definition 4 (definition 2 plus capital gains and health benefits)						
	55,558	21.1	57,526	22.0	-1,968	-0.9
Definition 6 (definition 4 less Social Security, payroll, and federal income taxes)						
	58,388	22.1	60,673	23.2	-2,285	-1.1
Definition 7 (definition 6 plus the Earned Income Tax Credit [EITC])						
	55,061	20.9	57,624	22.0	-2,563	-1.1
Definition 8 (definition 7 less state income taxes)						
	55,505	21.0	57,977	22.2	-2,472	-1.2
Definition 9 (definition 8 plus nonmeans-tested government cash transfers)						
	37,176	14.1	39,570	15.1	-2,394	-1.0
Definition 11 (definition 9 plus the value of Medicare and regular-price school lunches)						
	36,177	13.7	38,572	14.7	-2,395	-1.0
Definition 14 (definition 12 plus the value of Medicaid and other means-tested government non-cash transfers)						
	27,190	10.3	29,038	11.1	-1,848	-0.8

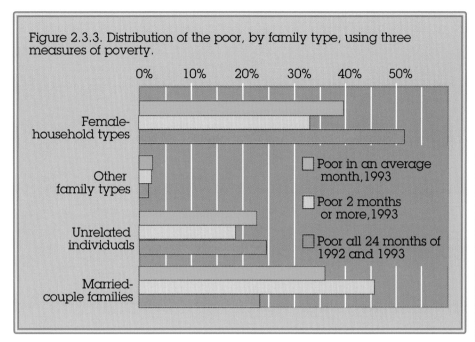

Figure 2.3.3. Distribution of the poor, by family type, using three measures of poverty.

Female-household types

Other family types

Unrelated individuals

Married-couple families

☐ Poor in an average month, 1993

☐ Poor 2 months or more, 1993

☐ Poor all 24 months of 1992 and 1993

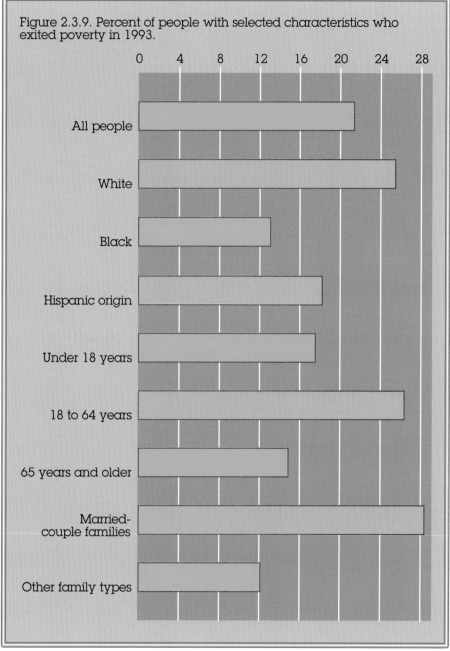

Figure 2.3.9. Percent of people with selected characteristics who exited poverty in 1993.

All people

White

Black

Hispanic origin

Under 18 years

18 to 64 years

65 years and older

Married-couple families

Other family types

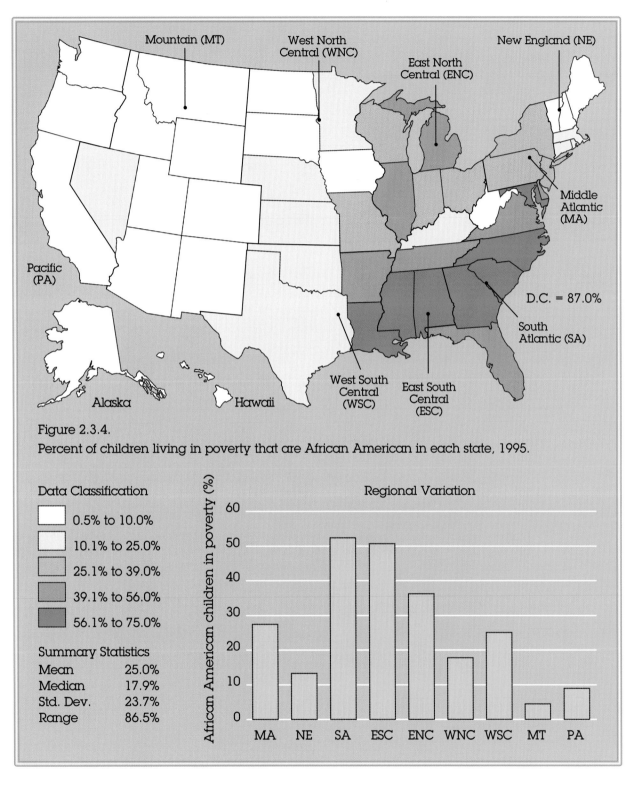

Figure 2.3.4.

Percent of children living in poverty that are African American in each state, 1995.

Data Classification

	0.5% to 10.0%
	10.1% to 25.0%
	25.1% to 39.0%
	39.1% to 56.0%
	56.1% to 75.0%

Summary Statistics

Mean	25.0%
Median	17.9%
Std. Dev.	23.7%
Range	86.5%

D.C. = 87.0%

Number of children living in poverty in each state and the percent that are African American, 1995.

	Total children in poverty	% African American
Alabama	255,465	62.8
Alaska	20,093	5.4
Arizona	301,884	4.2
Arkansas	157,689	44.4
California	2,094,255	9.3
Colorado	178,062	7.7
Connecticut	109,022	21.6
Delaware	20,553	51.6
District of Columbia	30,287	87.0
Florida	618,734	39.3
Georgia	350,231	64.9
Hawaii	37,240	2.6
Idaho	56,864	0.5
Illinois	575,552	40.6
Indiana	211,418	26.5
Iowa	104,914	7.9
Kansas	101,299	18.4
Kentucky	235,815	16.2
Louisiana	386,850	67.0
Maine	42,332	1.0
Maryland	132,688	58.0
Massachusetts	225,866	13.1
Michigan	472,529	39.9
Minnesota	152,872	11.4
Mississippi	250,176	74.4
Missouri	234,304	30.7
Montana	46,580	0.5
Nebraska	62,335	14.1
Nevada	46,723	17.9
New Hampshire	21,145	1.7
New Jersey	260,257	31.4
New Mexico	192,418	1.8
New York	1,069,234	25.7
North Carolina	277,970	56.8
North Dakota	30,355	0.7
Ohio	509,116	32.0
Oklahoma	191,233	18.0
Oregon	125,914	4.4
Pennsylvania	470,601	26.5
Rhode Island	37,198	11.9
South Carolina	192,508	70.9
South Dakota	40,559	0.8
Tennessee	253,929	41.8
Texas	1,798,615	14.1
Utah	87,254	1.5
Vermont	17,163	1.2
Virginia	202,529	50.8
Washington	206,653	7.0
West Virginia	115,887	6.8
Wisconsin	201,298	26.5
Wyoming	21,914	1.6

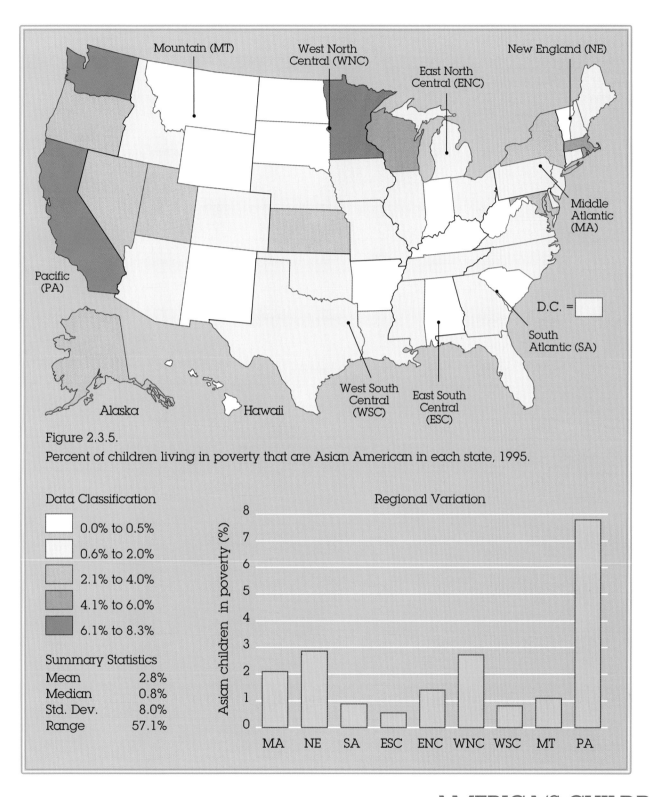

Figure 2.3.5.

Percent of children living in poverty that are Asian American in each state, 1995.

Data Classification

	0.0% to 0.5%
	0.6% to 2.0%
	2.1% to 4.0%
	4.1% to 6.0%
	6.1% to 8.3%

Summary Statistics

Mean	2.8%
Median	0.8%
Std. Dev.	8.0%
Range	57.1%

Number of children living in poverty in each state and the percent that are Asian American, 1995.

	Total children in poverty	% Asian American
Alabama	255,465	0.5
Alaska	20,093	2.5
Arizona	301,884	0.7
Arkansas	157,689	0.4
California	2,094,255	7.4
Colorado	178,062	1.8
Connecticut	109,022	0.8
Delaware	20,553	0.7
District of Columbia	30,287	0.8
Florida	618,734	0.8
Georgia	350,231	0.7
Hawaii	37,240	57.3
Idaho	56,864	1.0
Illinois	575,552	1.3
Indiana	211,418	0.5
Iowa	104,914	1.8
Kansas	101,299	2.2
Kentucky	235,815	0.4
Louisiana	386,850	1.1
Maine	42,332	0.8
Maryland	132,688	2.1
Massachusetts	225,866	4.1
Michigan	472,529	1.0
Minnesota	152,872	8.3
Mississippi	250,176	0.7
Missouri	234,304	0.8
Montana	46,580	0.5
Nebraska	62,335	1.2
Nevada	46,723	2.2
New Hampshire	21,145	1.7
New Jersey	260,257	1.8
New Mexico	192,418	0.4
New York	1,069,234	2.3
North Carolina	277,970	0.8
North Dakota	30,355	0.5
Ohio	509,116	0.7
Oklahoma	191,233	0.7
Oregon	125,914	3.0
Pennsylvania	470,601	1.8
Rhode Island	37,198	5.5
South Carolina	192,508	0.4
South Dakota	40,559	0.5
Tennessee	253,929	0.6
Texas	1,798,615	0.8
Utah	87,254	2.6
Vermont	17,163	0.4
Virginia	202,529	1.7
Washington	206,653	6.1
West Virginia	115,887	0.2
Wisconsin	201,298	5.4
Wyoming	21,914	0.4

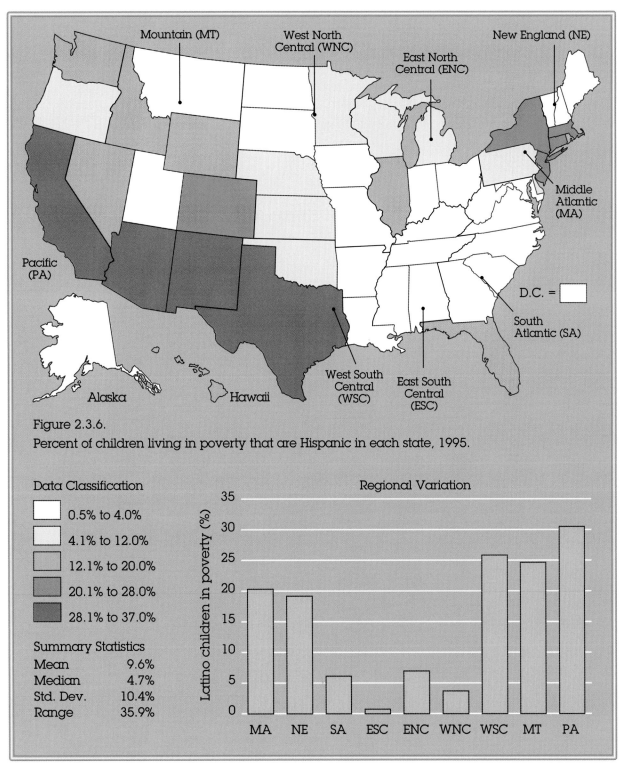

Figure 2.3.6.

Percent of children living in poverty that are Hispanic in each state, 1995.

Data Classification

- 0.5% to 4.0%
- 4.1% to 12.0%
- 12.1% to 20.0%
- 20.1% to 28.0%
- 28.1% to 37.0%

Summary Statistics

Mean	9.6%
Median	4.7%
Std. Dev.	10.4%
Range	35.9%

Regional Variation

Number of children living in poverty in each state and the percent that are Hispanic, 1995.

	Total children in poverty	Percent Hispanic
Alabama	255,465	0.7
Alaska	20,093	4.0
Arizona	301,884	29.8
Arkansas	157,689	1.5
California	2,094,255	34.1
Colorado	178,062	27.2
Connecticut	109,022	27.5
Delaware	20,553	6.3
District of Columbia	30,287	5.5
Florida	618,734	15.1
Georgia	350,231	2.0
Hawaii	37,240	14.2
Idaho	56,864	13.5
Illinois	575,552	13.9
Indiana	211,418	3.6
Iowa	104,914	3.1
Kansas	101,299	8.1
Kentucky	235,815	0.8
Louisiana	386,850	1.5
Maine	42,332	1.0
Maryland	132,688	3.1
Massachusetts	225,866	22.0
Michigan	472,529	4.7
Minnesota	152,872	4.2
Mississippi	250,176	0.6
Missouri	234,304	1.8
Montana	46,580	4.0
Nebraska	62,335	6.2
Nevada	46,723	18.2
New Hampshire	21,145	3.3
New Jersey	260,257	22.9
New Mexico	192,418	36.5
New York	1,069,234	25.2
North Carolina	277,970	1.8
North Dakota	30,355	2.1
Ohio	509,116	3.1
Oklahoma	191,233	6.2
Oregon	125,914	11.3
Pennsylvania	470,601	8.2
Rhode Island	37,198	17.1
South Carolina	192,508	0.8
South Dakota	40,559	1.6
Tennessee	253,929	0.9
Texas	1,798,615	35.5
Utah	87,254	1.6
Vermont	17,163	0.8
Virginia	202,529	2.5
Washington	206,653	13.2
West Virginia	115,887	0.7
Wisconsin	201,298	6.2
Wyoming	21,914	12.4

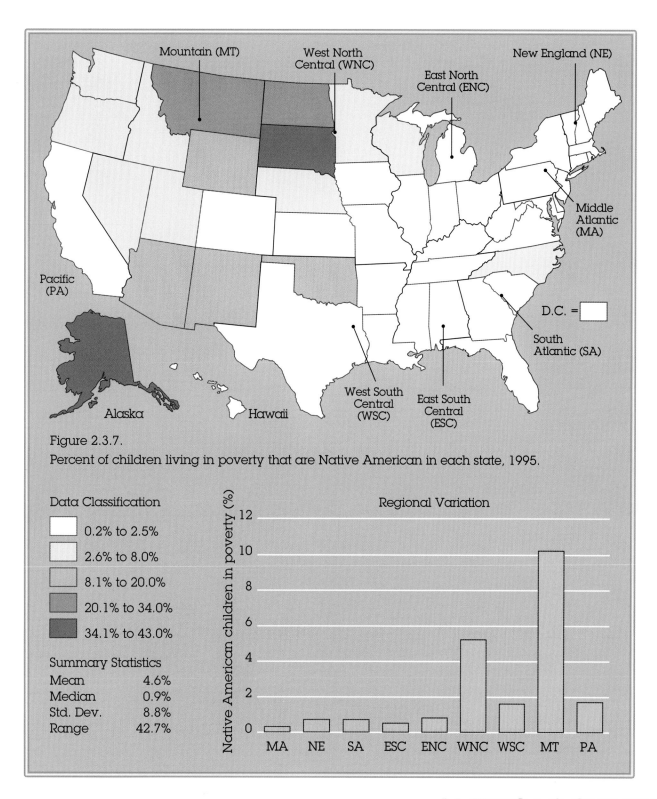

Mountain (MT) West North Central (WNC) East North Central (ENC) New England (NE) Middle Atlantic (MA) Pacific (PA) D.C. = South Atlantic (SA) Alaska Hawaii West South Central (WSC) East South Central (ESC)

Figure 2.3.7.

Percent of children living in poverty that are Native American in each state, 1995.

Data Classification

- 0.2% to 2.5%
- 2.6% to 8.0%
- 8.1% to 20.0%
- 20.1% to 34.0%
- 34.1% to 43.0%

Summary Statistics

Mean	4.6%
Median	0.9%
Std. Dev.	8.8%
Range	42.7%

Regional Variation

Native American children in poverty (%)

MA NE SA ESC ENC WNC WSC MT PA

Number of children living in poverty in each state and the percent that are Native American, 1995.

	Total children in poverty	% Native American
Alabama	255,465	0.6
Alaska	20,093	42.9
Arizona	301,884	14.8
Arkansas	157,689	0.7
California	2,094,255	0.9
Colorado	178,062	1.7
Connecticut	109,022	0.3
Delaware	20,553	0.4
District of Columbia	30,287	0.2
Florida	618,734	0.4
Georgia	350,231	0.3
Hawaii	37,240	1.1
Idaho	56,864	3.6
Illinois	575,552	0.2
Indiana	211,418	0.5
Iowa	104,914	1.1
Kansas	101,299	1.9
Kentucky	235,815	0.3
Louisiana	386,850	0.8
Maine	42,332	1.4
Maryland	132,688	0.5
Massachusetts	225,866	0.6
Michigan	472,529	1.3
Minnesota	152,872	6.8
Mississippi	250,176	0.6
Missouri	234,304	0.6
Montana	46,580	22.0
Nebraska	62,335	4.5
Nevada	46,723	3.7
New Hampshire	21,145	0.6
New Jersey	260,257	0.3
New Mexico	192,418	13.8
New York	1,069,234	0.4
North Carolina	277,970	2.8
North Dakota	30,355	20.4
Ohio	509,116	0.3
Oklahoma	191,233	16.7
Oregon	125,914	3.4
Pennsylvania	470,601	0.2
Rhode Island	37,198	1.2
South Carolina	192,508	0.3
South Dakota	40,559	34.9
Tennessee	253,929	0.4
Texas	1,798,615	0.3
Utah	87,254	5.6
Vermont	17,163	1.5
Virginia	202,529	0.3
Washington	206,653	4.9
West Virginia	115,887	0.3
Wisconsin	201,298	3.2
Wyoming	21,914	9.0

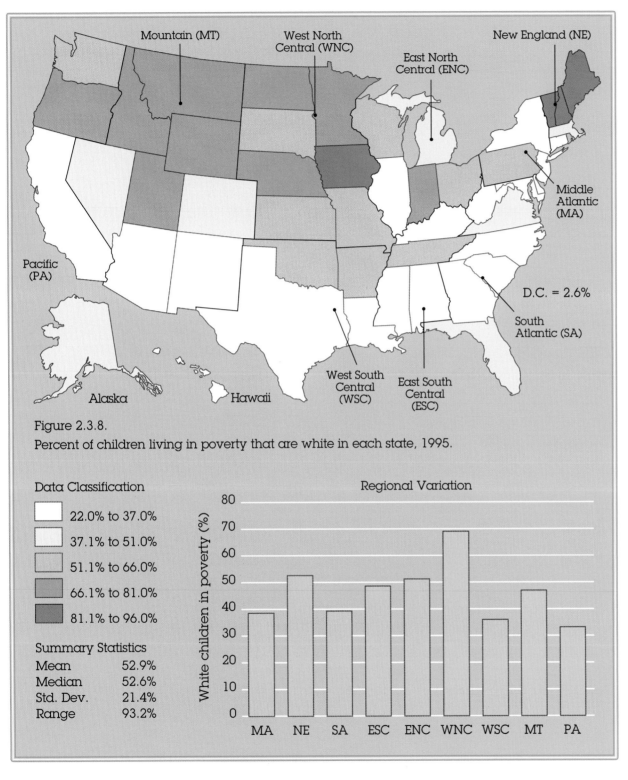

Figure 2.3.8.
Percent of children living in poverty that are white in each state, 1995.

Data Classification

☐	22.0% to 37.0%
☐	37.1% to 51.0%
☐	51.1% to 66.0%
☐	66.1% to 81.0%
☐	81.1% to 96.0%

Summary Statistics

Mean	52.9%
Median	52.6%
Std. Dev.	21.4%
Range	93.2%

Regional Variation

White children in poverty (%): MA, NE, SA, ESC, ENC, WNC, WSC, MT, PA

Number of children living in poverty in each state and the percent that are white, 1995.

	Total children in poverty	Percent white
Alabama	255,465	35.2
Alaska	20,093	44.1
Arizona	301,884	34.5
Arkansas	157,689	52.6
California	2,094,255	28.2
Colorado	178,062	49.5
Connecticut	109,022	33.9
Delaware	20,553	36.7
District of Columbia	30,287	2.6
Florida	618,734	40.9
Georgia	350,231	31.1
Hawaii	37,240	22.3
Idaho	56,864	73.0
Illinois	575,552	35.5
Indiana	211,418	66.8
Iowa	104,914	84.9
Kansas	101,299	64.7
Kentucky	235,815	82.1
Louisiana	386,850	29.1
Maine	42,332	95.5
Maryland	132,688	34.8
Massachusetts	225,866	46.5
Michigan	472,529	50.6
Minnesota	152,872	67.1
Mississippi	250,176	23.6
Missouri	234,304	65.2
Montana	46,580	71.8
Nebraska	62,335	71.3
Nevada	46,723	49.0
New Hampshire	21,145	91.3
New Jersey	260,257	32.3
New Mexico	192,418	35.1
New York	1,069,234	32.0
North Carolina	277,970	36.7
North Dakota	30,355	75.9
Ohio	509,116	62.0
Oklahoma	191,233	55.0
Oregon	125,914	72.5
Pennsylvania	470,601	57.6
Rhode Island	37,198	54.5
South Carolina	192,508	27.2
South Dakota	40,559	61.7
Tennessee	253,929	56.1
Texas	1,798,615	34.1
Utah	87,254	74.2
Vermont	17,163	95.8
Virginia	202,529	43.6
Washington	206,653	60.3
West Virginia	115,887	91.9
Wisconsin	201,298	55.1
Wyoming	21,914	70.9

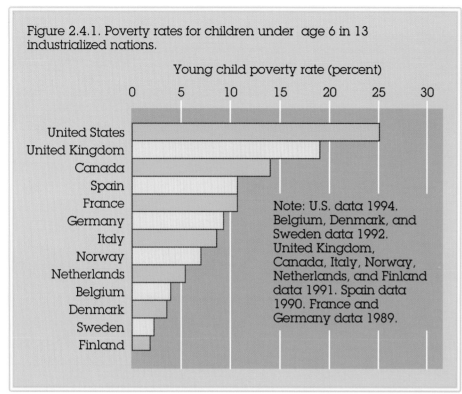

Figure 2.4.1. Poverty rates for children under age 6 in 13 industrialized nations.

Young child poverty rate (percent)

Note: U.S. data 1994. Belgium, Denmark, and Sweden data 1992. United Kingdom, Canada, Italy, Norway, Netherlands, and Finland data 1991. Spain data 1990. France and Germany data 1989.

Figure 2.4.3. Number of poor children under 6, 1972-1992.

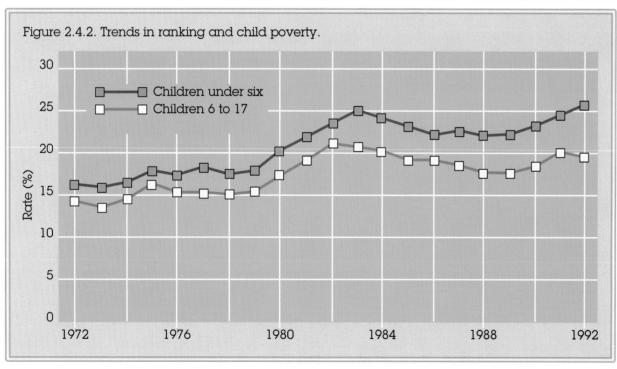

Figure 2.4.2. Trends in ranking and child poverty.

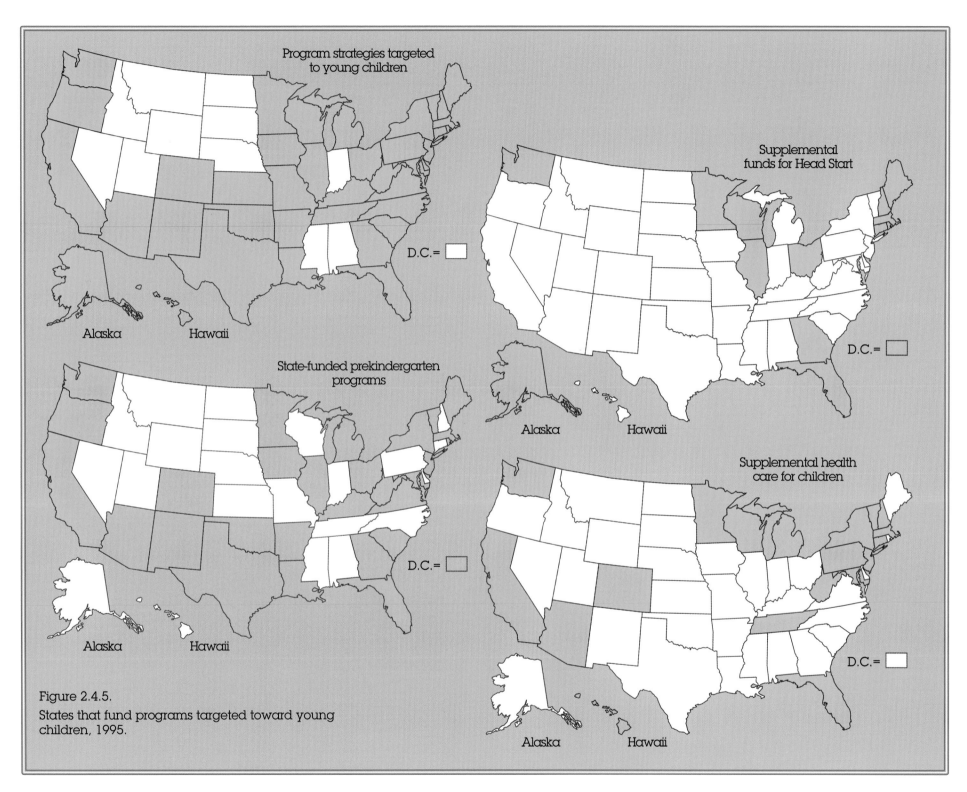

Program strategies targeted
to young children

D.C.=

Supplemental
funds for Head Start

D.C.=

State-funded prekindergarten
programs

D.C.=

Supplemental health
care for children

D.C.=

Alaska   Hawaii

Alaska   Hawaii

Alaska   Hawaii

Alaska   Hawaii

Figure 2.4.5.

States that fund programs targeted toward young
children, 1995.

Table 2.4.1. Percentage of poor children under 6 covered by entitlements, by family type, 1968-1992.

	Non-cash medical coverage		Subsidized housing		Food stamps		Cash welfare	
	Mother-only	Two-parent	Mother-only	Two-parent	Mother-only	Two-parent	Mother-only	Two-parent
1968	—	—	—	—	—	—	57.7	7.8
1969	—	—	—	—	—	—	55.2	9.7
1970	—	—	—	—	—	—	58.8	12.5
1971	—	—	—	—	—	—	71.1	11.7
1972	—	—	—	—	—	—	73.0	9.9
1973	—	—	—	—	—	—	63.8	15.1
1974	—	—	—	—	—	—	76.4	18.7
1975	—	—	—	—	—	—	72.1	10.2
1976	—	—	21.9	7.7	—	—	66.1	11.2
1977	—	—	24.6	14.7	—	—	71.2	21.4
1978	—	—	23.9	13.3	—	—	69.7	17.4
1979	—	—	27.5	11.2	—	—	68.8	10.1
1980	—	—	29.9	9.9	69.3	48.7	69.6	15.5
1981	81.0	54.8	29.0	13.0	70.7	51.2	66.2	11.4
1982	77.9	58.4	31.1	9.4	72.3	44.9	67.4	8.8
1983	78.3	62.8	30.8	22.2	68.8	47.3	61.6	16.0
1984	78.3	62.1	42.7	11.2	69.0	44.2	66.2	10.4
1985	74.5	68.1	34.0	13.1	60.2	52.3	55.2	11.4
1986	78.7	65.0	36.3	17.6	67.2	42.5	64.0	17.7
1987	79.7	62.4	36.0	15.3	65.6	36.2	61.4	12.5
1988	81.7	56.9	34.5	17.7	65.0	44.5	64.8	13.3
1989	85.5	53.3	44.3	19.8	71.6	36.5	61.8	11.1
1990	83.3	61.5	39.0	15.5	69.8	49.7	61.1	10.7
1991	87.5	59.0	58.0	17.0	70.8	53.3	62.4	12.3
1992	85.4	60.5	38.4	23.3	68.7	58.7	63.2	18.3

Table 2.4.2. Percentage of poor children under age 6 living in mother-only and two-parent families, 1968-1992.

	Percent	
	Mother-only	Two-parent
1968	33.1	66.9
1969	34.0	66.0
1970	38.8	61.2
1971	43.8	56.2
1972	45.5	54.5
1973	49.7	50.3
1974	52.6	47.4
1975	46.8	53.2
1976	53.6	46.4
1977	58.8	41.2
1978	54.9	45.1
1979	57.9	42.1
1980	57.6	42.4
1981	54.4	45.6
1982	60.0	40.0
1983	58.3	41.7
1984	56.1	43.9
1985	57.2	42.8
1986	60.5	39.5
1987	64.6	35.4
1988	63.2	36.8
1989	66.9	33.1
1990	62.4	37.6
1991	65.3	34.7
1992	62.0	38.0

Table 2.4.3. Selected characteristics of parents of poor and non-poor children under age 6, 1968-1992.

Variable	Poor	Non-poor
Age in years	28.7	31.9
Number of families per household	1.3	1.1
Received food stamps (%)	37.0	3.0
Received welfare (%)	40.0	2.0
Race (%)		
Non-Hispanic white	69.0	89.0
Black	27.0	7.0
Other	4.0	4.0
Married (%)	43.0	93.0
Female family head (%)	60.0	9.0
Completed schooling (years)	10.7	12.9
Number of children under age 6	1.5	1.4
Primary family of household (%)	81.0	98.0
Live in central city (%)	35.0	23.0

Table 2.5.2. Profiles of homeless children, by family characteristic, by age, 1987 and 1992.

Characteristics	1987	1992
Average per family	1.0	2.0
Average age (years)	7.0	3.0
Age range: under 6 years	15.0	78.0
Age range: 6 years and over	85.0	22.0

Table 2.5.3. Estimated number of U.S. homeless children and youth under age 16 at any given time.

Category	Best estimate	Range Low	Range High	Source	Confidence
Literally homeless					
Urban					
Shelters and hotels	25,522	18,265	32,779	Surveys	High
Churches	4,094	2,340	6,570	Opinion	Low
Public places	9,016	4,512	24,072	Opinion	Low
Other	7,651	5,168	10,446	Opinion	Low
Suburban	14,427	7,213	21,641	Pop. rates	Moderate
Rural	7,357	3,678	11,035	Pop. rates	Moderate
Total	68,067	41,176	106,543	Varies	Moderate
Precariously housed doubled-up	185,512	39,362	296,452	Opinion	Low

Table 2.5.4. City data on the homeless, 1995.

	% increase in request for emergency shelter	% increase in requests by families for emergency shelter	Shelter beds	Traditional housing units	Family break-up for shelter	Family leave during the day	% need unmet	Families turned away	Others turned away
Alexandria	-13.0	-2.0	same	same	no	yes	N/A	yes	yes
Boston	10.0	0.0	increase	increase	yes	no	0.0	yes	no
Charleston	10.0	0.0	increase	same	no	no	0.0	yes	no
Charlotte	20.0	9.6	same	same	yes	no	30.0	no	yes
Chicago	N/A	N/A	increase	same	no	no	0.0	yes	no
Cleveland	10.0	15.0	same	increase	yes	yes	N/A	no	yes
Denver	20.0	20.0	same	increase	no	yes	25.0	yes	yes
Detroit	20.0	10.0	decrease	increase	no	yes	50.0	yes	yes
Kansas City	0.0	0.0	same	increase	yes	yes	28.0	yes	yes
Los Angeles	N/A	N/A	N/A	N/A	N/A	N/A	N/A	yes	no
Louisville	0.0	0.0	increase	increase	yes	no	N/A	N/A	no
Miami	20.0	0.0	increase	increase	no	no	20.0	yes	yes
Minneapolis	-50.0	-29.0	decrease	same	no	yes	50.0	yes	yes
Nashville	10 to 50	N/A	same	same	yes	yes	50.0	yes	yes
New Orleans	N/A	N/A	same	increase	yes	yes	30.0	yes	yes
Norfolk	-31.0	46.0	same	same	no	N/A	N/A	yes	yes
Philadelphia	-33.0	-36.0	decrease	decrease	yes	no	18.0	yes	yes
Phoenix	10.0	10.0	same	same	no	yes	41.0	yes	yes
Portland	26.0	23.0	increase	increase	yes	no	18.0	yes	yes
Providence	N/A	N/A	same	same	yes	yes	35.0	yes	yes
St. Louis	2.0	6.0	same	increase	yes	yes	<0.1	no	yes
St. Paul	3.5	23.5	same	same	yes	no	8.0	no	no
Salt Lake City	N/A	N/A	same	increase	no	no	0.0	no	no
San Antonio	36.0	38.0	same	increase	yes	no	25.0	yes	yes
San Diego	10.0	10.0	decrease	same	no	no	25.0	no	yes
San Francisco	0.0	0.0	decrease	increase	no	no	10.0	yes	yes
Santa Monica	0.0	5 to 10	same	same	yes	yes	30.0	no	yes
Seattle	N/A	N/A	N/A	N/A	N/A	N/A	N/A	no	N/A
Trenton	N/A	-15.0	same	increase	yes	N/A	N/A	yes	yes

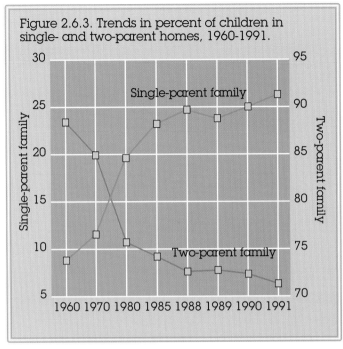

Figure 2.6.3. Trends in percent of children in single- and two-parent homes, 1960-1991.

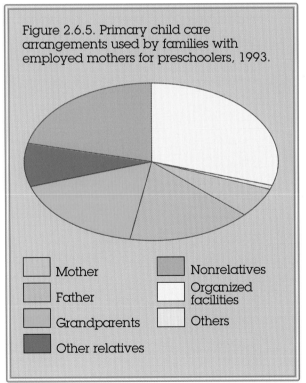

Figure 2.6.5. Primary child care arrangements used by families with employed mothers for preschoolers, 1993.

Mother
Father
Grandparents
Other relatives
Nonrelatives
Organized facilities
Others

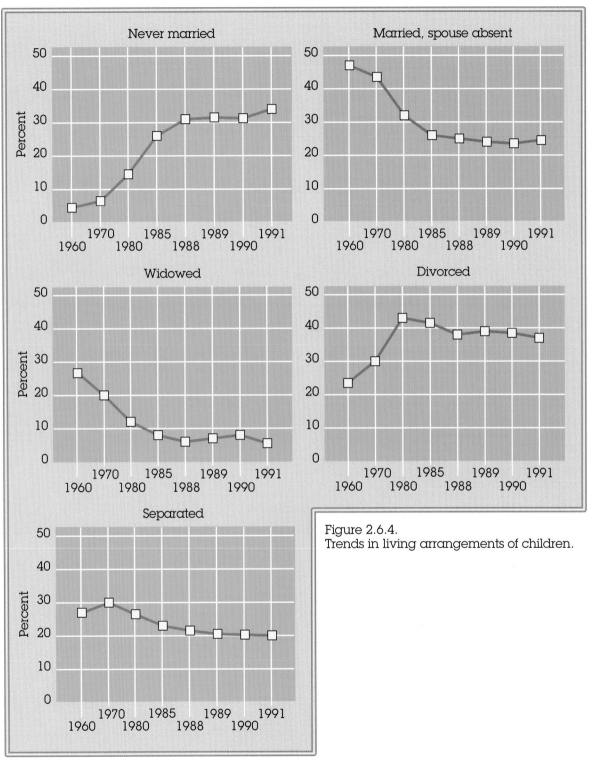

Never married

Married, spouse absent

Widowed

Divorced

Separated

Figure 2.6.4.
Trends in living arrangements of children.

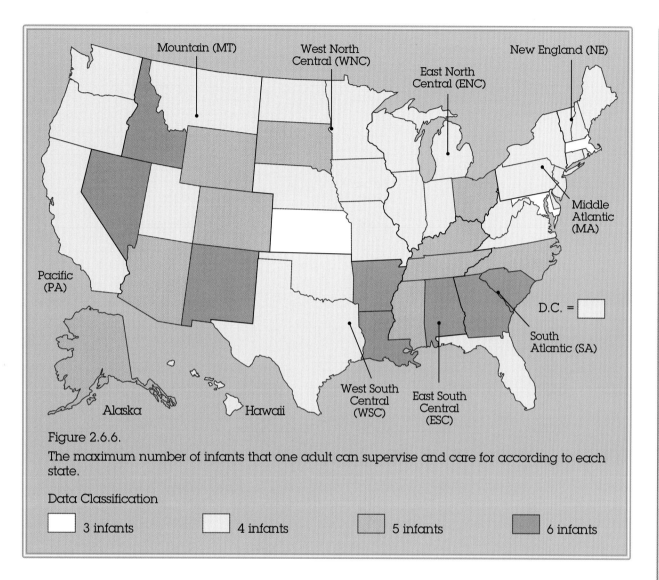

Figure 2.6.6.

The maximum number of infants that one adult can supervise and care for according to each state.

Data Classification

☐ 3 infants	☐ 4 infants	☐ 5 infants	☐ 6 infants

Table 2.6.5. How frequently states inspect child care centers.

	Frequency
Alabama	every 2 years
Alaska	every 2 years
Arizona	once a year
Arkansas	four x's a year
California	once a year
Colorado	once a month
Connecticut	every 2 years
Delaware	once a year
Dist. of Columbia	1 to 3 x's a year
Florida	3 x's a year
Georgia	once a year
Hawaii	once a year
Idaho	every 2 years
Illinois	once a year
Indiana	3 x's a year
Iowa	once a year
Kansas	once a year
Kentucky	once a year
Louisiana	once a year
Maine	once a year
Maryland	once a year
Massachusetts	every 2 years
Michigan	alternating yrs
Minnesota	every other yr
Mississippi	once a year
Missouri	2 x's a year
Montana	2 x's a year
Nebraska	every 2 years
Nevada	2 x's a year
New Hampshire	once a year
New Jersey	every 3 years
New Mexico	2 x's a year
New York	every 2 years
North Carolina	once a year
North Dakota	2 x's a year
Ohio	2 x's a year
Oklahoma	3 x's a year
Oregon	2 x's a year
Pennsylvania	once a year
Rhode Island	2 x's a year
South Carolina	2 x's a year
South Dakota	once a year
Tennessee	2 x's a year
Texas	1 to 3 x's a yr
Utah	3 x's a year
Vermont	2 x's a year
Virginia	2 x's a year
Washington	every 3 years
West Virginia	once a year
Wisconsin	once a year
Wyoming	once a year

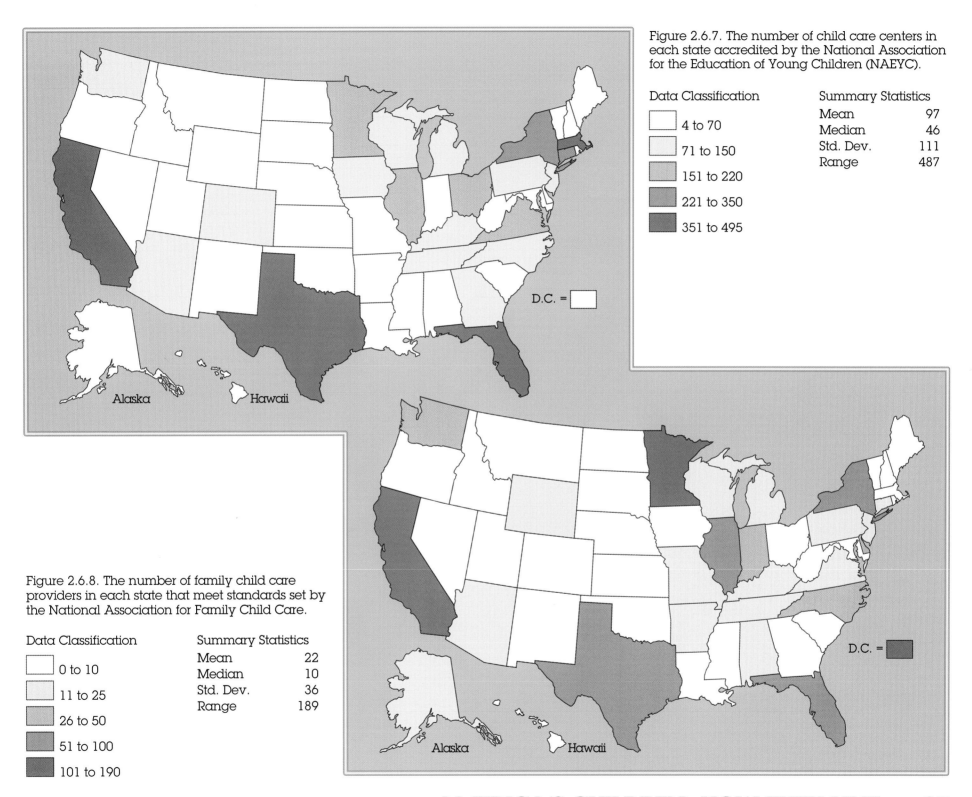

Figure 2.6.7. The number of child care centers in each state accredited by the National Association for the Education of Young Children (NAEYC).

Data Classification

4 to 70
71 to 150
151 to 220
221 to 350
351 to 495

D.C. =

Summary Statistics
Mean   97
Median   46
Std. Dev. 111
Range   487

Alaska   Hawaii

Figure 2.6.8. The number of family child care providers in each state that meet standards set by the National Association for Family Child Care.

Data Classification

0 to 10
11 to 25
26 to 50
51 to 100
101 to 190

Summary Statistics
Mean   22
Median   10
Std. Dev. 36
Range   189

D.C. =

Alaska   Hawaii

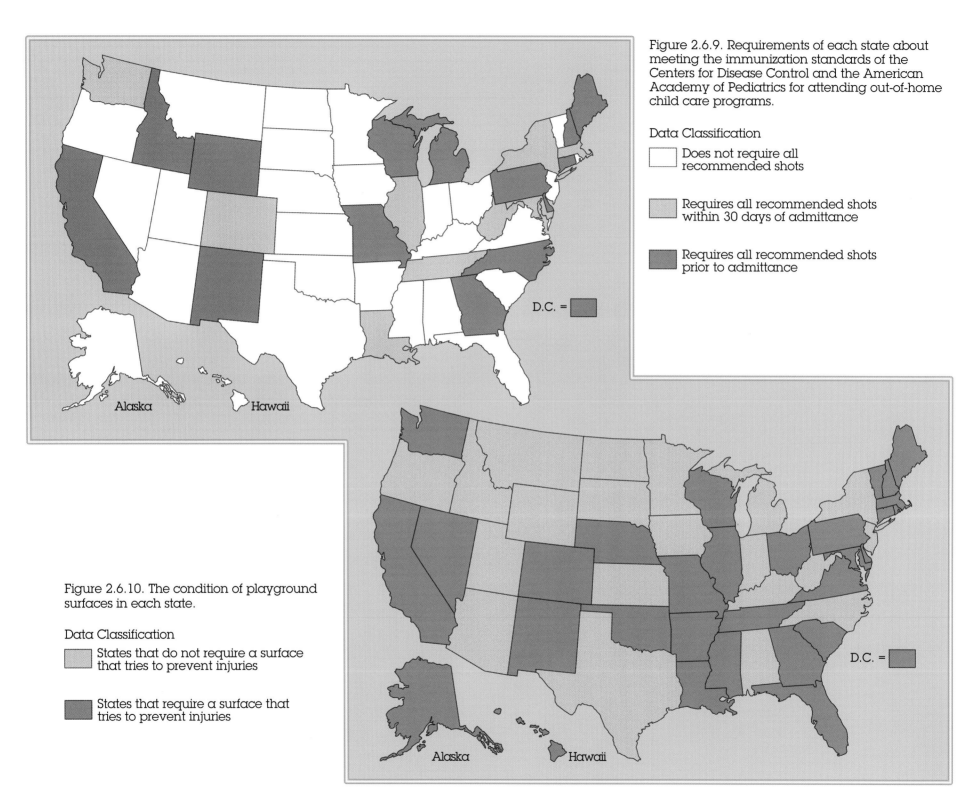

Figure 2.6.9. Requirements of each state about meeting the immunization standards of the Centers for Disease Control and the American Academy of Pediatrics for attending out-of-home child care programs.

Data Classification

Does not require all recommended shots

Requires all recommended shots within 30 days of admittance

Requires all recommended shots prior to admittance

D.C. =

Figure 2.6.10. The condition of playground surfaces in each state.

Data Classification

States that do not require a surface that tries to prevent injuries

States that require a surface that tries to prevent injuries

D.C. =

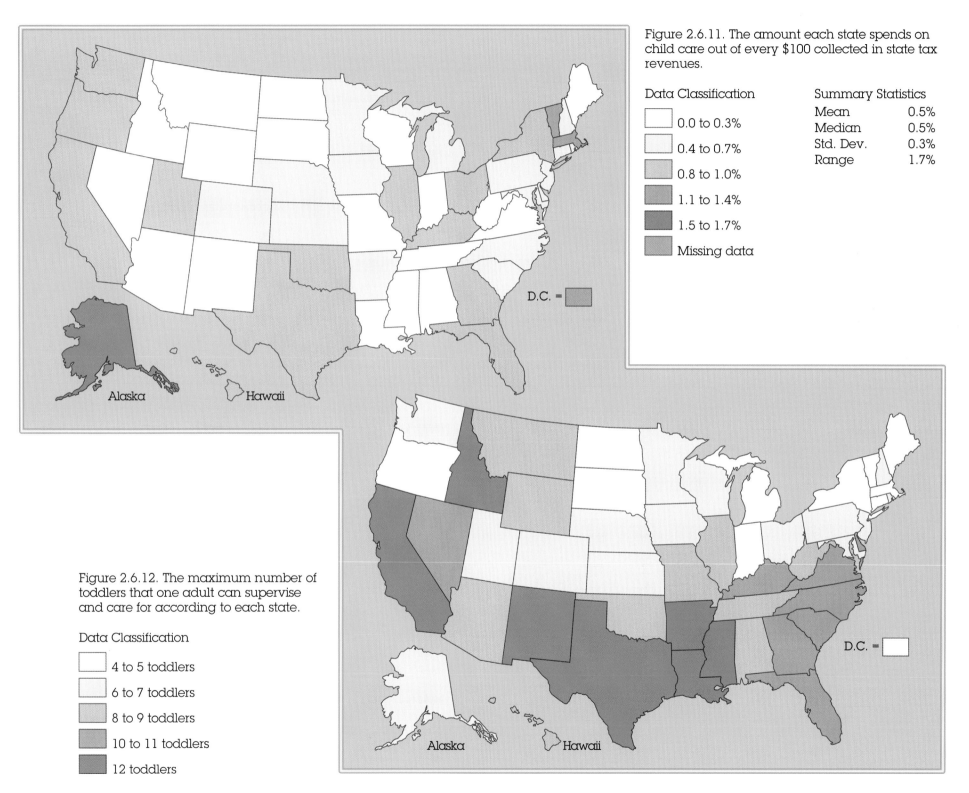

Figure 2.6.11. The amount each state spends on child care out of every $100 collected in state tax revenues.

Data Classification

- 0.0 to 0.3%
- 0.4 to 0.7%
- 0.8 to 1.0%
- 1.1 to 1.4%
- 1.5 to 1.7%
- Missing data

Summary Statistics

Mean	0.5%
Median	0.5%
Std. Dev.	0.3%
Range	1.7%

D.C. =

Alaska   Hawaii

Figure 2.6.12. The maximum number of toddlers that one adult can supervise and care for according to each state.

Data Classification

- 4 to 5 toddlers
- 6 to 7 toddlers
- 8 to 9 toddlers
- 10 to 11 toddlers
- 12 toddlers

D.C. =

Alaska   Hawaii

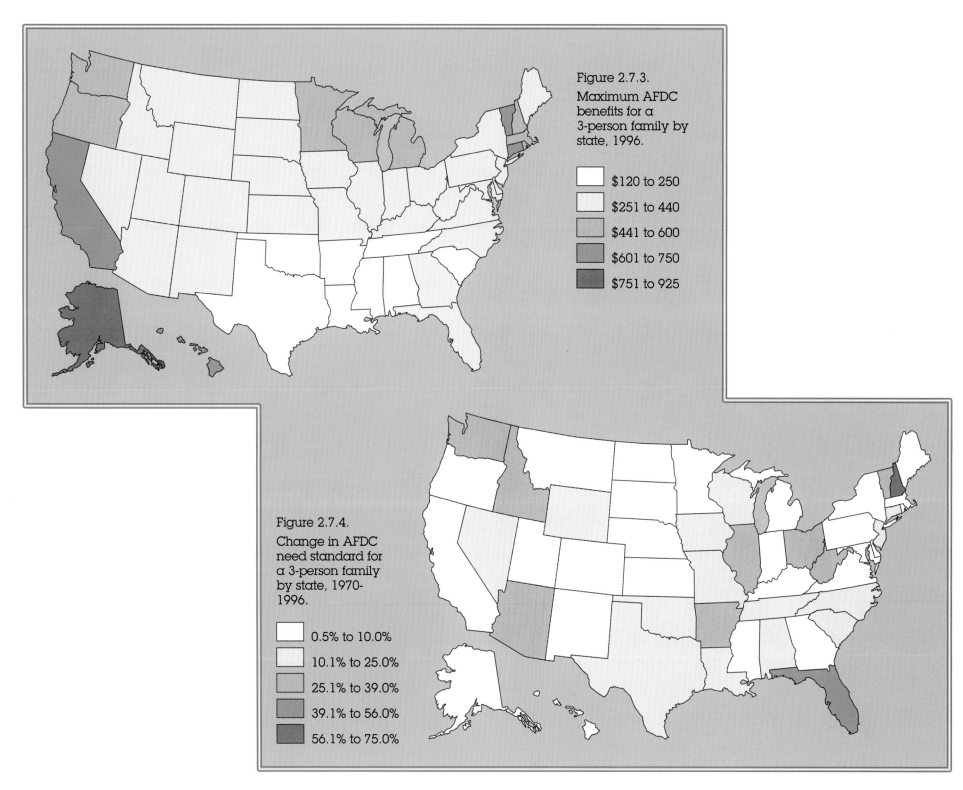

Figure 2.7.3.

Maximum AFDC benefits for a 3-person family by state, 1996.

- $120 to 250
- $251 to 440
- $441 to 600
- $601 to 750
- $751 to 925

Figure 2.7.4.

Change in AFDC need standard for a 3-person family by state, 1970-1996.

- 0.5% to 10.0%
- 10.1% to 25.0%
- 25.1% to 39.0%
- 39.1% to 56.0%
- 56.1% to 75.0%

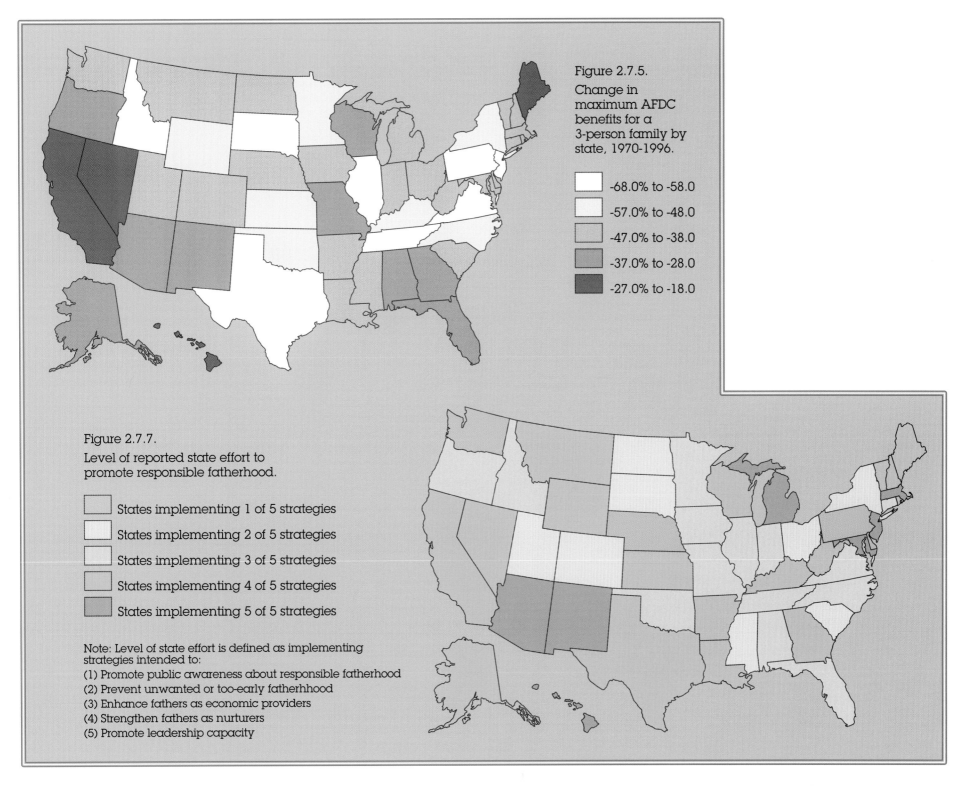

Figure 2.7.5.
Change in maximum AFDC benefits for a 3-person family by state, 1970-1996.

- -68.0% to -58.0
- -57.0% to -48.0
- -47.0% to -38.0
- -37.0% to -28.0
- -27.0% to -18.0

Figure 2.7.7.
Level of reported state effort to promote responsible fatherhood.

- States implementing 1 of 5 strategies
- States implementing 2 of 5 strategies
- States implementing 3 of 5 strategies
- States implementing 4 of 5 strategies
- States implementing 5 of 5 strategies

Note: Level of state effort is defined as implementing strategies intended to:
(1) Promote public awareness about responsible fatherhood
(2) Prevent unwanted or too-early fatherhood
(3) Enhance fathers as economic providers
(4) Strengthen fathers as nurturers
(5) Promote leadership capacity

Table 2.7.3. Characteristics of families who received Aid to Families with Dependent Children (AFDC), 1969-1994.

Characteristic	1969	1973	1975	1979	1983	1986	1988	1990	1992	1994
Average family size	4.0	3.6	3.2	3.0	3.0	3.0	3.0	2.9	2.9	2.8
Percent children in single-parent family	27.9	31.5	31.0	37.8	44.3	48.9	51.9	54.0	53.1	55.7
Percent mothers under 20	6.6	N/A	8.3	4.1	3.6	3.3	3.4	7.9	7.6	6.3

Note: Data for percent of mothers under 20 for years 1979, 1983, 1986, and 1988 is for mothers under 19.

Table 2.7.4. Summary of changes enacted by the Personal Responsibility and Work Opportunity Reconciliation Act (PRWORA), August 1996.

Pre-PRWORA	PRWORA
AFDC cash assistance was an entitlement.	TANF cash assistance is funded through a block grant to the states.
Recipient could receive benefits as long as income-eligible.	After 60 months of cumulative receipt, person no longer eligible.
Fifteen percent of non-exempt caseload was required to participate in work-related activities.	In FY 1997, 25% of caseload must be working at least 20 hours a week. Recipients are required to work at least 20 hours/week within the first 2 years, with few exemptions.
More children were eligible for SSI benefits due to expanded definition of disability.	Restricted eligibility criteria for SSI may disqualify over 300,000 children by 2000.
Legal immigrants who are income-eligible could qualify for SSI, food stamps, Medicaid, and AFDC.	Legal immigrants who were in the U.S. before August 1996 can qualify for Medicaid and TANF benefits (depending on the state). Most legal immigrants will lose SSI and food stamp benefits.
Food stamp allotments amounted to $0.80 per person per meal.	By 2002, food stamp allotments will be cut to $0.66 per person per meal.

Chapter 3

The Health of America's Children

"And no grown-up will ever understand that this is a matter of so much importance"
—Antoine de Saint-Exupery

3.1

INTRODUCTION

Healthy children are essential for the future of any country. Guaranteeing that children's health be protected and that children have access to adequate health care has long been a basic feature of United States law and policy. Because of the enormous wealth in the United States and the large share of the GNP spent on health care, America's children fare far better than millions of children in other countries around the world. Despite its enormous wealth, however, the United States has not yet established universal health care for all children. It is disturbing to find that millions of children lack health insurance, public or private.

Faced with the onslaught of illness and inability to pay, many Americans wait until the illness becomes life threatening before seeking care in a hospital emergency room. Routine primary and preventive care is often times unavailable. Health care reform and its successful implementation should remedy this.

About 64.0 percent of children under age 18 in the United States are covered through private insurance providers, particularly the employer provided group plans of their parents. Outside of employer group plans, Medicaid is the largest insurer for persons under age 18. Seventeen percent of America's children are covered by

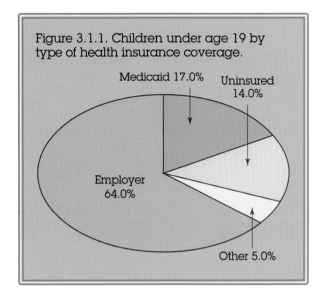

Figure 3.1.1. Children under age 19 by type of health insurance coverage.

Medicaid 17.0%
Uninsured 14.0%
Employer 64.0%
Other 5.0%

Medicaid. Fourteen percent lack any coverage whatsoever (Figure 3.1.1).

Medicaid is a government insurance program for the poor. It is administered by each state, but the federal government provides matching funds. The Federal government provides broad national guidelines to the states under which they (1) establish their own eligibility standards (2) determine the type, amount, duration and scope of services (3) set the rates of payment for services (4) administer their own programs. Medicaid programs vary considerably from state to state as well as within each state over time. The following groups

are entitled to Medicaid assistance: (a) families with children receiving AFDC; (b) low income (not exceeding 133 percent of the federal poverty level) pregnant women and children under 6; (c) low-income aged, blind, and disabled persons who qualify for SSI; (d) special protected groups; and (e) persons with emergency medical conditions who are not citizens or nationals of the United States or aliens lawfully admitted for permanent residence or permanently residing in the United States. Though most Medicaid recipients are low-income parents and children (approximately 70.0 percent), they account for only about 29.0 percent of Medicaid expenditures. The bulk of Medicaid expenditures are for institutional care for the aged and disabled (Figure 3.1.2).

In recent years, the number of persons eligible for Medicaid benefits as well as the

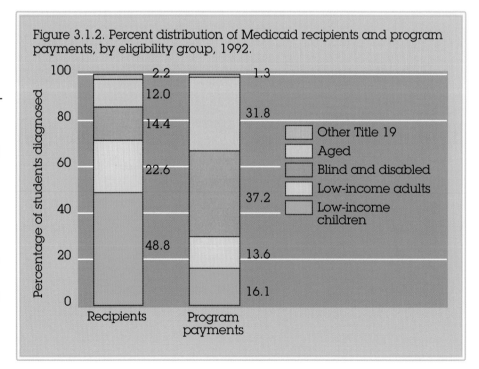

Figure 3.1.2. Percent distribution of Medicaid recipients and program payments, by eligibility group, 1992.

	Recipients	Program payments
Other Title 19	2.2	1.3
Aged	12.0	31.8
Blind and disabled	14.4	37.2
Low-income adults	22.6	13.6
Low-income children	48.8	16.1

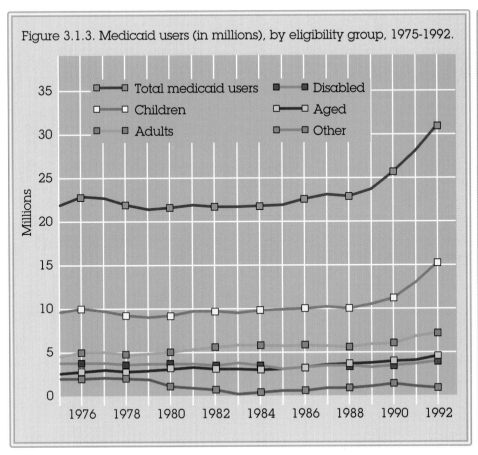

Figure 3.1.3. Medicaid users (in millions), by eligibility group, 1975-1992.

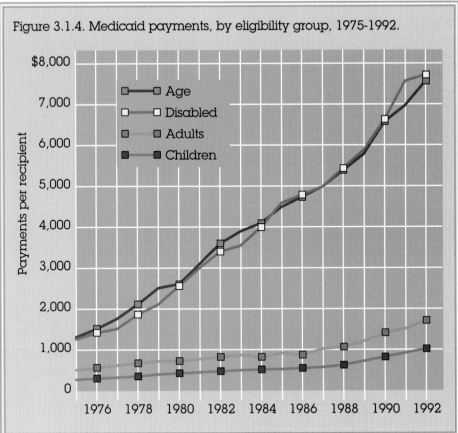

Figure 3.1.4. Medicaid payments, by eligibility group, 1975-1992.

amount of Medicaid expenditures has increased. Four reasons account for the increase. First, many states increased their need standards for AFDC, enabling more families to qualify for cash assistance. Second, the number of female headed households increased. Third, many organizations mounted public information programs to increase participation in AFDC. Finally, the number eligible were increased because states had insufficient programs initiating Medicaid assistance during the period. Overall, the Medicaid program experienced a 41.6 percent increase in total numbers during the time period 1975-1992 (Figure 3.1.3). Medicaid payments to indi-

viduals experienced a similar pattern. Per child payments increased over fourfold, from about $228 in 1975 to about $971 in 1992 (Figure 3.1.4). In spite of the fact that the program is one of the fastest growing federal programs (federal assistance to Medicaid increased from 13.7 percent in 1975 to 36.4 percent in 1991, see Figure 3.1.5, page 106), it is generally seen as being inefficient, overly complicated, and ineffective.

Medicaid does not provide protection to all low income children in need of insurance. Only 50.0 percent of children older than six are served by Medicaid.

3.2

IMMUNIZATIONS

Widespread immunization of children is the most effective of the preventive health services available. In the United States, widespread immunization has been effective in reducing the prevalence of the most common childhood diseases, for example, polio, measles, mumps, rubella, and pertussis (whooping cough). The United States Public Health Service recommends that children receive the vaccination series of four doses of diphtheria and tetanus toxoids

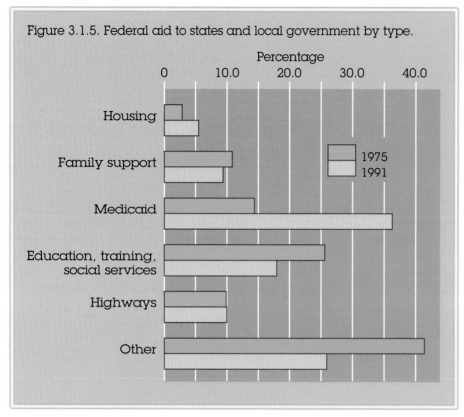

Figure 3.1.5. Federal aid to states and local government by type.

Percentage

Categories (top to bottom): Housing, Family support, Medicaid, Education, training, social services, Highways, Other

Legend: 1975, 1991

---

and pertussis (DTP) vaccine, three doses of oral polio vaccine (OPV), one dose of measles-mumps-rubella (MMR) vaccine, and three or four doses of Haemophilus influenzae type b (Hib) by the time they are 2 years old. In addition, the hepatitis B vaccine has been recommended since 1991 for the universal immunization of infants (see Table 3.2.1, page 107). The United States has achieved over 97.0 percent immunization of children by school age and has reduced the incidence of preventable diseases by more than 90.0 percent. America's immunization program has largely been a public health success story.

Recent research, however, has highlighted an important gap in the United States program. Approximately 20.0 to 30.0 percent of America's children do not receive a complete series of immunizations by their second birthday, a year 2000 objective (see Figure 3.2.1, page 119). Among poor, minority, inner-city communities, fewer than half get all their vaccinations by age 2, and many of those who are up to date do not receive them at recommended intervals.

Immunization at school entry is inadequate and often too late to prevent certain diseases. Practically every state requires that new entrants have completed a required series of immunizations (see Table 3.2.2, page 120).

Prevalence of all preventable diseases declined significantly during the period 1979 and 1986, following the initiation of a federal childhood immunization drive. Subsequent data, however, reveals alarming increases in all preventable diseases. Most of the increase is due to inadequate immunization.

Table 3.2.3 provides information on measles outbreaks in the United States for 1991 (see page 121). New York, Pennsylvania, California, New Jersey, Idaho, Arizona, Florida, and Utah accounted for the vast majority of all measles cases in 1991. Outbreaks occurred primarily among unvaccinated preschool-age children living in low socioeconomic areas of metropolitan areas.

Survey data suggest that nonwhite children and children whose families are of low socioeconomic status are at increased risk of being unimmunized. Beyond this, low immunization rates result from a number of factors—expense / cost of vaccines, overburdened or nonexistent public health clinics, and client factors such as physical and/or cultural isolation from the health care system.

Most children in America with private insurance do not have coverage for immunizations. In 1983, the total wholesale cost for all the recommended vaccines was $9.12 in government run programs and $27.70 in private practices. By 1993, the cost had risen to $119.02 and $247.43. Administrative costs can make the retail price $10 to $15 more per dose. When confronted with the option of paying directly for immunizations or going to a public health clinic, economics usually forces parents to choose the latter, which in turn overburdens the public health sector.

Public health clinics are often overburdened, have long lines, and require appointments and/or comprehensive physical examinations before a child can be immunized. Sometimes, doctors will immunize children only at *Well Baby* appointments and thus require parents to make additional visits to the clinic. For lower-income, working parents in particular, this missed opportunity may become a missed vaccination.

Even when vaccines are available,

Table 3.2.1. Recommended child vaccination schedule of the Public Health Service's Immunization Practices Advisory Committee.

	DTP	POLIO	MMR	HIB Option 1	HIB Option 2	HBV Option 1	HBV Option 2
Birth						■	
1-2 months						■	
2 months	■	■		■	■		■
4 months	■	■		■	■		■
6 months	■			■			
6-18 months		■					■
12 months					■		
15 months	■		■	■	■		
4-6 years	■	■	■				

Notes: HIB = Haemophilus b conjugate vaccine. HIB vaccine is given in either a 4-dose schedule (Option 1) or a 3-dose schedule (Option 2), depending on the type of vaccine used. HBV = hepatitus B vaccine. HBV can be given simultaneously with DTP, POLIO, MMR, and Haemophilus b conjugate vaccine at the same visit. DTP = diphtheria, tetanus, and pertussis vaccine, combined. Poliomyelitis vaccine may be live oral polio vaccine in drops (OPV) or killed (inactivated) polio vaccine by injection (IPV). MMR = measles, mumps, and rubella vaccine combined. Many experts recommend that DTP and polio vaccines be given at 18 months of age. MMR vaccine may be given at 12 months.

affordable, and offered, they may be refused because of cultural or religious beliefs or because of side effects—real or perceived—and the failure to understand that the benefits of immunization exceed the risks. Most states allow for exemptions from immunization requirements based on philosophical, religious, and medical reasons (see Figure 3.2.2, page 120).

Early vaccines were extremely "heat sensitive" and had to be kept under constant refrigeration from the point of manufacture to the point of administration. Improper handling could lead to ineffectiveness. Vaccines also have a finite shelf life and become impotent after a certain date. The current generation of vaccines is much more stable than previous ones, and this improvement in biochemistry as well improved data management, storage technology, and personnel training has played a large part in resolving this problem.

3.3
RUNAWAYS AND HOMELESS YOUTH

Runaways are children who leave home without securing permission or informing anyone of their whereabouts. It is very difficult to get a count of how many runaways there are among America's children. The most recent estimates (1990) from the Office of Juvenile Justice and Delinquency Prevention (OJJDP) suggest that there are approximately half a million runaways in the United States. There do not appear to be more runaways today than at the time of the last national survey in 1975. But while runaways in the past were "in search of adventure" or were acting out of youthful rebellion, runaways today are running away from problem families and situations of physical and sexual abuse and emotional neglect (Figure 3.3.1).

Not all runaway situations are of the same severity. The OJJDP presents incidence estimates according to at least two definitions—a policy focal definition and a broad scope definition. The broad scope definition

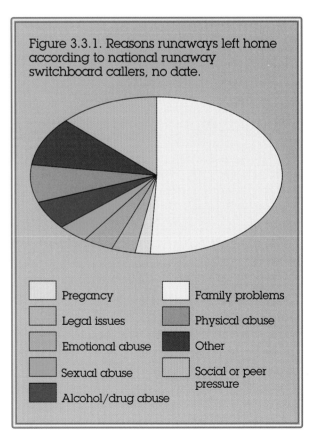

Figure 3.3.1. Reasons runaways left home according to national runaway switchboard callers, no date.

Pregancy

Legal issues

Emotional abuse

Sexual abuse

Alcohol/drug abuse

Family problems

Physical abuse

Other

Social or peer pressure

views the problem the way the affected families might define it. It includes both serious and also more minor episodes that may nonetheless be alarming to the participants. The policy focal definition defines the problem from the perspective of policy makers or social service delivery agencies. It is restricted to more serious incidences where children are at risk and protective intervention is necessary. The policy focus represents a subset of the broad scope definition. See Figures 3.3.2 and 3.3.3 for definitions and estimates of incidence for each of the two foci.

Almost all runaways are teenagers. In a comprehensive review of the literature undertaken by Posner (1991), it was noted that the median age of the runaway population in shelters was 14-16. Among "street youth," those children who avoid shelters, the median age is much higher.

Female runaways make up a slightly higher proportion of all runaways. Explanations for this finding differ. Some argue that it is an artifact of the data—the "shelter" phenomenon; others maintain that girls are more likely to be abused in the home and thus more likely to run away, still others suggest that female adolescents run away when they become pregnant. Males are, however, overrepresented among "street youth."

The racial/ethnic makeup of American runaways reflects the ethnic and racial composition of the general population of the United States. Data from federally funded runaway centers revealed 65.0 percent of that youth seeking services were white, 19.0 percent were African American, and 9.0 percent were Latino. Some locations like Hollywood, California

attract runaways from all over the country. They are drawn the by warm weather and the perception of glamour or reputation promoted by the national media. The typical center's population usually reflects the population of the surrounding area.

Youth from single-parent homes and homes in which one parent is not the biological parent are overrepresented among runaways. A large number of runaways identify at least one of their parents as having some sort of psychological or social problem, including alcoholism, drug abuse, depression, attempted suicide, a history of violence, or a criminal record. Findings regarding the socioeconomic status of runaways are mixed.

Policy efforts to intervene in the lives of runaways have been only marginally successful. Again, unlike the youth who ran away from home during the 19th and early 20th centuries, who had a relatively easy time integrating into the community and securing work roles, today's youth face greater difficulties finding a place for themselves in the economic structure.

Modern child labor laws, increased legal and illegal immigration, as well as the now common practice of a prolonged period of adolescence and the moratorium from adult responsibilities, such as work, have eliminated many of the legitimate economic roles into which young people could once fit. In order to survive, increasing

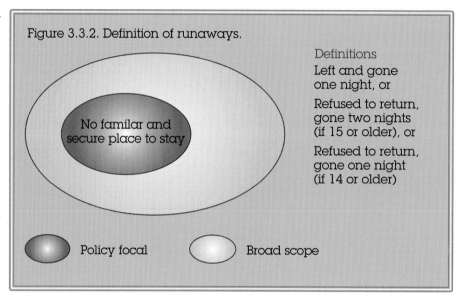

Figure 3.3.2. Definition of runaways.

No familar and secure place to stay

Definitions

Left and gone one night, or

Refused to return, gone two nights (if 15 or older), or

Refused to return, gone one night (if 14 or older)

Policy focal   Broad scope

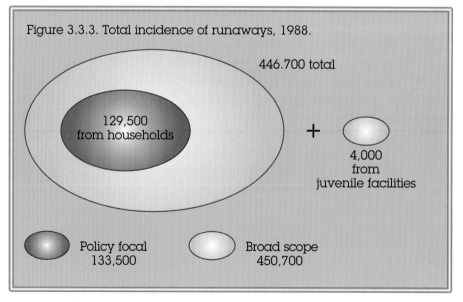

Figure 3.3.3. Total incidence of runaways, 1988.

446.700 total

129,500 from households

+   4,000 from juvenile facilities

Policy focal
133,500

Broad scope
450,700

numbers of street youth see no alternative but illegitimate economic activities, for example, prostitution, robbery, the drug trade. This increases the need for comprehensive and specialized services. Programs now recognize that the runaway incident is part of a pattern of victimization and the focus should be on families rather than on just the individual in trouble. Family reunification is a goal only after family counseling programs. Even when good programs exist, runaways may not make use of services. Often this is because they do not believe that they need help or that social service agencies will do them any good.

Health problems among runaways include inadequate nutrition, substance abuse, and inadequate medical care. In a survey of the health status of runaways in shelters, Hey (1988) found that 80.0 percent suffered from general illness (chills, fever, vomiting, diarrhea, sore throat); trauma, sensory problems, headache, nausea, stomach, gynecological afflictions, and dental problems. A disturbingly large proportion of runaways fall into one or more groups at high risk for HIV / AIDS, including gay or bisexual males, persons with multiple sexual partners, persons who abuse drugs and / or alcohol, and female partners of high-risk males (especially IV drug users). Robertson (1989) found that 20.0 percent of the sexually active runaways had a sexually transmitted disease. Most runaways (ranging from 33.0 percent to 86 percent) abuse alcohol and drugs and report getting drunk at least once a week. Because of these high-risk behaviors and the violence associated with life on the streets, the incidence of all diseases is higher than among the nonrunaway population.

It has been estimated that 20.0 to 25.0 percent of homeless teenagers are mentally ill. Almost all suffer from low self-esteem and depression. Conduct disorders and post-traumatic stress syndrome is 3 times higher among runaways than among youth who have not run away. A significant proportion of runaway youth engage in some form of self destructive behavior. Most have attempted suicide. Runaways who were abused in the family are at even greater risk of serious psychological disturbances—substance abuse, sleeping disorders, developmental delays, as well as distrust of adults and other adolescents. Given the lack of familial and institutional support systems available to youth contemplating running away, these conditions are not surprising.

A number of complicated issues surround the "rights of runaways." These issues have led to dramatic rethinking of policy at the federal and state levels.

During the 1960s, runaways were treated as lawbreakers, "mini-criminals." They were often incarcerated, put in detention homes, or adult jails. Professional child advocates viewed this as a counterproductive practice and argued that the authority of law enforcement agencies should be curtailed. Children had a right to freedom from custody. Voluntary shelters and non-secured group homes replaced jails. Children were free to come and go as they pleased. By the early 1980s, however, it was clear that the risks and dangers on the street far surpassed the rights of the child to leave a home that provided care, support, discipline, and love in search of an individual identity. Congress, which had been adamant about giving children freedom and the same rights as adults, became justifiably concerned. Though the legislation has not been altered, runaways are now seen in a new perspective—one that touches the pulse of the family.

In addition to runaways, other categories of missing and exploited children include throwaways, stranger abductees, and family abductees.

3.4

SUDDEN INFANT DEATH SYNDROME

According to the National SIDS Resource Center (NSRC), sudden infant death syndrome (SIDS) is an unpreventable and unpredictable death of an infant or young child under 1 in which a thorough postmortem examination (including a full autopsy), examination of the death scene, and review of clinical history fails to demonstrate an adequate cause of death. Currently, no international definition of SIDS exists.

In 1987, SIDS ranked third among the five leading causes of death in infants. For infants between 28 days and 1 year, SIDS is the leading cause of death. By 1990, SIDS had become the second leading cause of death (see Table 3.4.1, page 110).

While the causes of SIDS are still unknown, it is generally believed that babies who die of SIDS are born with one or more risk factors. In and of themselves, these risk factors are not "causes" but

Table 3.4.1. Infant deaths and infant mortality rates (IMR) per 1,000 live births, by cause of death.

Cause of death	Number	Percent	IMR
All causes	38,351	100.0	9.2
Birth defects	8,239	21.0	2.0
Sudden infant death syndrome	5,417	14.0	1.3
Disorders relating to short gestation and unspecified low birth weight	4,013	10.0	1.0
Respiratory distress syndrome	2,850	7.0	0.7
Newborn affected by maternal complications of pregnancy	1,655	4.0	0.4
Newborn affected by complications of placenta, cord, and membranes	975	3.0	0.2
Accidents and adverse effects	930	2.0	0.2
Infections specific to the perinatal period	875	2.0	0.2
Intrauterine hypoxia and birth asphyxia	762	2.0	0.2
Pneumonia and influenza	634	2.0	0.2
All other causes	12,001	31.0	2.9

rather are environmental and behavioral influences that are associated with the onset of ill health. In the case of SIDS, the mother's health and behavior during pregnancy and the baby's health before birth seem to influence the occurrence of SIDS. Specific maternal risk factors include cigarette smoking during pregnancy, maternal age less than 20 years, poor prenatal care, low weight gain, anemia, use of illegal drugs, and history of sexually transmitted disease or urinary tract infection. A greater number of babies who die of SIDS suffer from cyanosis (inadequate oxygenation of the blood), tachycardia (accelerated heartbeat), respiratory distress, irritability, hypothermia, poor feeding, and tachypnea (accelerated breathing). Finally, in as much as 80.0 percent of SIDS deaths occur by the age of 6 months, infants in this age group are considered to be at increased risk (see Figure 3.4.1, page 122). SIDS is a diagnosis of exclusion; it can occur only after all other alternatives have been eliminated.

Over time, the number of deaths from SIDS has remained remarkably constant. Between 1983 and 1991, though fluctuation occurred, deaths increased by only 75 (see Figure 3.4.2, page 122). The National Center for Health Statistics (NCHS) reported in 1988 that the number of SIDS deaths was 14.0 percent of all deaths among infants less than 1 year of age. Recent data from NCHS supports this estimate. Data also suggest that more deaths occur in the fall and winter (in both the Northern and Southern Hemispheres) and there is a 60 / 40 percent ratio of males to females.

For all races in the United States, the death rate attributed to SIDS between 1983 to 1994 has dropped. Among whites, the rate has followed the total trend with slightly lower numbers. The rate of SIDS among African Americans has exhibited a more dramatic decrease, dropping from 275 to 190 deaths per one-hundred thousand (see Figure 3.4.3, page 122). The death rate is consistently twice as high as that of whites (see also Figure 3.4.4).

Across the states, rates of death from SIDS range from a low of 0.64 in Connecticut to 3.18 in Montana. With the exception of Alaska, states with the highest rates are Colorado, Idaho, Montana, Nevada, Oregon, South Dakota, and Utah—primarily concentrated in the Mountain region. The last year for which SIDS data were collected by race and state is 1987.

Federal agencies and private organizations have directed their energies toward a wide array of policies and projects concerning SIDS. These include identifying those most at risk, developing approaches to prevention, collecting data on the epidemiology of SIDS, understanding various professional and community roles and levels of expertise, speeding the process by which new knowledge is transferred and incorporated into health care, development of a Medical Examiner/Coroner Information Sharing Program (MECISP), and implementing standard protocols for death investigations. The hope is that the number of deaths from SIDS will be reduced.

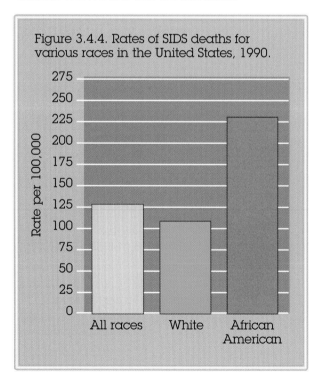

Figure 3.4.4. Rates of SIDS deaths for various races in the United States, 1990.

3.5
CHILDREN WITH HIV/AIDS

Acquired Immune Deficiency Syndrome (AIDS) poses a serious and steadily increasing public health threat to America's children. Acquired immune deficiency syndrome is transmitted to children in several ways: from infected mothers to their infants; through exposure to infected body fluids, primarily blood transfusions among adolescent hemophiliacs. The number of pediatric AIDS cases resulting from blood transfusion is expected to decrease due to increased safety of the blood supply. For those in the higher age groups, the disease is transmitted through sexual contact with a Human Immunodefiency Virus (HIV) infected partner or through intravenous drug use.

Through December 1993, 401,749 cases of AIDS were reported to the Centers for Disease Control. Of these, 5,734 were infants and children below age 13. Total deaths for this group number 3,100. Deaths from AIDS tend to be higher among minorities than whites (see Figure 3.5.1, page 123).

Figure 3.5.2 provides details of pediatric AIDS by exposure category for each of the major racial/ethnic groups. For all groups, the vast majority of pediatric AIDS cases resulted from mothers transmitting the disease to children, ranging from 94.0 percent of all cases among black (not Hispanic) to 60.0 percent among Asians/Pacific Islanders. Rates of exposure by means of hemophilia/coagulation disorder and blood transfusion are highest among whites and

Asian/Pacific Islanders.

Because adolescents engage in high-risk behaviors such as drug abuse and sexual experimentation, they are especially, vulnerable. As can be seen in Table 3.5.1, on page 123, among 13 to 19 year-olds, the highest risk of exposure for males is from "hemophilia/coagulation disorder" (47.2 percent), followed by "men who have sex with men" (35.7 percent). While not shown, females in the same age category are exposed most frequently through

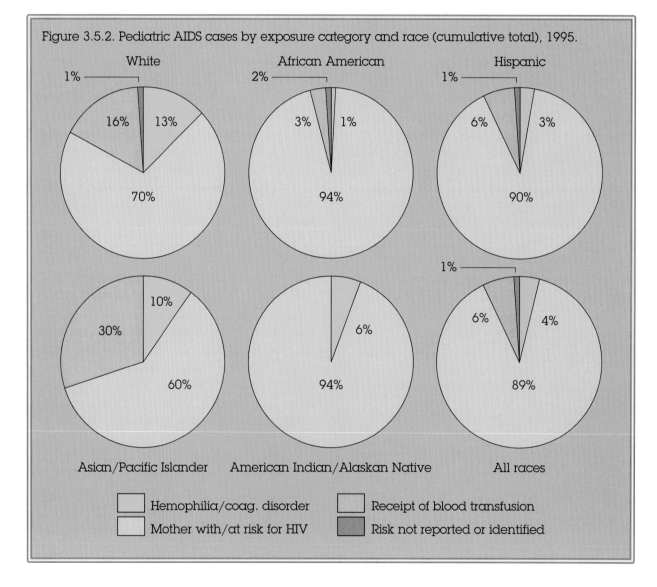

Figure 3.5.2. Pediatric AIDS cases by exposure category and race (cumulative total), 1995.

White — 1%, 16%, 13%, 70%
African American — 2%, 3%, 1%, 94%
Hispanic — 1%, 6%, 3%, 90%
Asian/Pacific Islander — 10%, 30%, 60%
American Indian/Alaskan Native — 6%, 94%
All races — 1%, 6%, 4%, 89%

Hemophilia/coag. disorder
Mother with/at risk for HIV
Receipt of blood transfusion
Risk not reported or identified

heterosexual contact. This includes sex with an injecting drug user, a bisexual male, a person with hemophilia, a transfusion recipient with HIV infection, and a HIV infected person. The next highest category identified for females in this age group is injecting drug use.

Pediatric AIDS is occurs in every state in the United States. Connecticut has the highest rates nationally, followed by New Jersey, Florida, Iowa, and Nebraska (see Figure 3.5.3, page 124). The percentage of pediatric AIDS cases ranges from 0.1 to 4.5 percent of total AIDS cases. However, for certain metropolitan areas, this percentage may be much higher. Figure 3.5.4 lists the top 10 metropolitan areas for AIDS cases in children under age 13 (see page 123).

The incidence of AIDS is highest among minority children, particularly those who face urban poverty, poor health, lack of access to health care, and general deprivation. Minority children are 7.4 percent of the total United States population under age 14, and they are 7.5 percent of the total AIDS cases. Hispanic children are 3.1 percent of the total child population, yet they account for 27.0 percent of total pediatric AIDS cases.

3.6

LEAD POISONING

Lead poisoning is one of the most common and most preventable forms of environmental hazards faced by children. Lead is ubiquitous throughout the environment. Although the toxic effects of lead have been acknowledged for generations and the production of lead dates back to antiquity, only recently has it been observed that even low levels of lead exposure may have serious effects on children's development. Generally, the ratio of children screened to the number confirmed is highest in the more industrialized, northeastern areas of the United States (see Figure 3.6.1, page 125). Most childhood lead poisoning in the United States is due to exposure to household lead-based paint or dust from leaded paint. Other sources of lead include drinking water, soil, ceramics, traditional or folk medicines, fishing sinkers, and glazed pottery. Some of the more common exposure categories—gasoline, water distribution systems, and food cans—have been eliminated or reduced. Most children who have elevated lead levels are asymptomatic. Laboratory tests are required to make an accurate diagnosis.

Low levels of lead exposure have been associated with a broad array of childhood problems ranging from diminished intellectual functioning, cognitive disarray, behavioral disorders, and deficits in motor skills (fine and gross). Presently, it appears that there may be no safe level of exposure to lead and that some effects may be irreversible.

In 1990, it was estimated that 3 million children had elevated blood lead levels in the United States. Health effects from lead vary with the blood lead level (BLL). Children with elevated blood lead levels have been associated with decreased intelligence and impaired neurobehavioral development. At higher levels, renal damage, decreased hematopoiesis, coma, seizures, and death may occur. In 1991, the Centers for Disease Control and Prevention (CDC) lowered the blood lead level of concern from 25 to 10 ug/dL (microns per deciliter) and recommended a phase-in of "virtually universal" screening of all young children. The Council of State and Territorial Epidemiologists (CSTE) approved a position statement recommending that states make elevated blood lead levels reportable to state health departments and establish surveillance for elevated blood lead levels in all age groups. Of the 29 states with multiple protocols, the vast majority are east of the Mississippi (see Figure 3.6.2, page 125). This is to be expected, as elevated lead levels are more prevalent at higher levels of industrialization and in areas with aging housing stock. Only 8 states have multiple protocols, greater than 10 ug/dL. The majority of jurisdictions required reporting values at 15 or 20 ug/dL.

Figure 3.6.3, on page 125, provides data on the mean BLL for the United States population during 1988-91 and 1976-80. A number of things are noteworthy. The first is the decline in mean BLLs over the period for all age groups. The Morbidity and Mortality Report (MMWR) reports that the mean BLL declined by 78.0 percent. In 1976-80, 53.0 percent of children aged 1-5 years had BLLs >15 ug/dL and 9.3 percent had BLLs >25 ug/dL. In the National Health and Examination Survey III (NHANES), the prevalence of children exceeding these same levels decreased to 2.7 percent and 0.5 percent respectively. Second, though lead poisoning affects all age groups, elevated BLLs are highest among infants 1-2 years and lowest among youth 12-19. Very young children and those living in deteriorated housing in inner cities are at highest risk of lead poisoning. Studies have pointed out that the effects of lead exposure are greatest among those of low socioeconomic status whose diets are high in fat. Foods high in fat are problematic because they tend to increase lead absorption in humans, whereas foods high in calcium and iron help the body absorb less lead.

The top five metropolitan areas with the highest percentage of cases with elevated BLLs are listed in Table 3.6.1 (see page 125).

Figure 3.6.4 provides information on the prevalence of elevated BLLs by race/ethnicity, income, and residence. BLLs were high among all children in low-income households in central cities. Poor, non-Hispanic black children, who reside disproportionately in center cities, are at increased risk for harmful BLLs.

The Department of Health and Human Services has defined the year 2000 objective for lead poisoning as "reducing the prevalence of blood lead levels exceeding 15 ug/dL and 25 ug/dL among children aged 6 months through 5 years to no more than 500,000 and zero respectively." For inner-city black children, special targets have been set at 75,000 children with levels between 15 and 25 ug/dL and no children with levels above 25 ug/dL. The year 2010

objective is to eliminate all elevated PbB levels among children in the United States.

3.7
THE LEGACY OF TEEN SUICIDE

It is estimated that between 100 and 200 young people per 100,000 (age 15-24) attempt suicide each year. Of these, one succeeds. Suicide is the third-ranking cause of death in the United States for youth, behind unintentional injuries and homicides (see Figure 3.7.1, page 126). In 1991, persons between the ages of 15 and 25 made up 14.4 percent of the population, but committed approximately 15 percent of the suicides. Figure 3.7.2 provides U. S. suicide

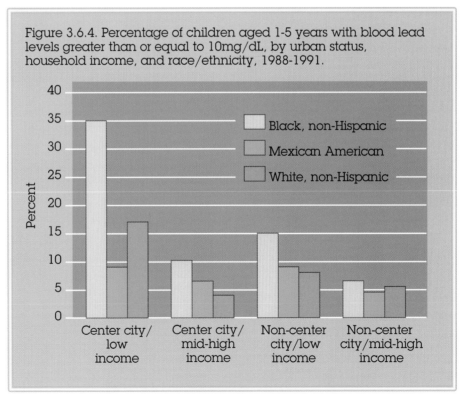

Figure 3.6.4. Percentage of children aged 1-5 years with blood lead levels greater than or equal to 10mg/dL, by urban status, household income, and race/ethnicity, 1988-1991.

rates by age per 100,000 population for the year 1994 (see page 126).

Figure 3.7.3 supports the fact that suicides increased for young people. The suicide rate rose steadily from 1980 to 1993 for both young adolescents and young adults (page 126). However, 1993 shows some sign of hope as deaths from suicides have started to decline for young adults between the ages 15 to 19.

Though there is relatively little variation in the numbers of deaths from suicides among males / females and blacks / whites in the United States, suicide death rates among Indians and Alaska Natives are significantly higher than other groups. Among Native American youths, suicide rates are particularly dramatic (see Table 3.7.1, page 114). A number of general characteristics are associated with the high incidence of suicides among American Indians:

(1) Native American males succeed at suicide most often, though most attempts are by females.

(2) Native Americans more commonly use highly lethal or violent methods (guns and hanging) to commit suicide than do other ethnic

groups in the United States. Nationally, the method most commonly used is an overdose of medication, but only about 2.0 percent of successful Indian suicides can be attributed to this means.

(3) Indian suicide, like most behaviors among other groups, can vary from one location to the next and also over time. Generally, groups with loose social integration emphasizing a high degree of individuality have higher suicide rates than those with tight integration, as do groups undergoing rapid change in social and economic conditions. Aboriginal groups, like Native Americans, are especially vulnerable to what is known to anthropologists as *acculturation stress*. This occurs when an existing cultural system is assimilated by another, and their traditional way of looking at the world is pushed to extinction.

(4) Native American families, staggered by the acculturation stress caused by the settlement of North America by Europeans since the late 16th century have been racked by problems such as high rates of divorce, desertion, arrest, and abuse of alcohol and other substances. All these symptoms of family dysfunction are also associated with increased rates of suicide.

Figure 3.7.4 compares the age-specific

suicide death rate (1989-1991) for Indian males and females (see page 126). Suicide rates for Indian males were higher for all age groups than for Indian females. The Indian male rate was at its highest (over 60 per 100,000) for males between 15 and 24. Table 3.7.1 gives suicide mortality rates by age and sex for Indian and Alaskan natives and U.S. all races.

If the changes in U.S. society since the 1960s have produced increases in suicide rates in mainstream society, it is no surprise that rates among American Indians have increased. Aside from the typical challenges of adolescence, Indian youth face additional challenges produced by their minority status, fewer economic and educational advantages, and cultural differences. According to the 1990 census, the median household income for Indian families was $19,886—much lower than the national average of $30,056. Twice as many Indians were living below the poverty level. The unemployment rate for Indians is higher than national averages, and on some reservations it is over 16.0 percent. The median age of Indians is 24.2 years, much younger than the median age of the general U.S. population. Finally, educational attainment of Indians is below national averages.

Table 3.7.1. Suicide mortality rates for Native Americans and Alaskan Natives and all races within the U.S., by age and sex, 1990 (rate per 100,000 population).

Indian and Alaskan Native

	Both sexes	Male	Female
Under 5	N/A	N/A	N/A
5 to 14	1.3	2.3	0.3
15 to 24	37.5	63.3	10.8
25 to 34	28.9	52.8	6.1
35 to 44	18.5	32.9	5.1
45 to 54	8.4	13.2	4.0
55 to 64	9.1	16.3	2.8
65 to 74	7.0	12.3	2.8
75 to 84	8.0	16.0	2.7
85 Years +	11.5	31.3	N/A

All races in the United States

	Both sexes	Male	Female
Under 5	N/A	N/A	N/A
5 to 14	0.8	1.0	0.4
15 to 24	13.2	22.0	3.9
25 to 34	15.2	24.8	5.6
35 to 44	15.3	23.9	6.8
45 to 54	14.8	23.2	6.9
55 to 64	16.0	25.7	7.4
65 to 74	17.9	32.2	6.7
75 to 84	24.9	56.1	6.3
85 Years +	22.2	65.9	5.4

3.8

CHILD AND ADOLESCENT MENTAL HEALTH

It is not known how many of America's children suffer from mental disorders. Estimates range from 12.0 percent to 22.0 percent. Even the conservative estimate of 12.0 percent translates into 9.84 million children affected by emotional maladjustment. The percentage of resident patients under the age of 18 in state and county mental hospitals is the topic of Figure 3.8.1 (see page 127).

It was not until Knitzner's 1982 landmark investigation, *Unclaimed Children,* that emotionally disturbed children became the focus of national attention. She found that the needs of approximately two-thirds of the children with serious emotional disturbances were unmet. Since then, the progress made in child mental health policy can be illustrated by the following:

(1) Only 13 states still place children on adult wards in state-run facilities (see Figure 3.8.2, page 127).

(2) Most states now have separate budgets for children's mental health.

(3) Among mental health professionals in state government there presently exists near-total agreement on the overall problems of the system (including service delivery) and a consensus on what an ideal system of care should look like.

(4) As of 1992, every state had received at least one Child and Adolescent Services System Program (CASSP) grant to stimulate child and adolescent mental health planning and enhance their capacity to deliver an appropriate range of services to seriously emotionally disturbed children and adolescents.

(5) No state is without a designated mental health representative for children and youth as well as a parent/family advocacy organization

that focuses primarily on children's mental health issues.

(6) Every state has at least one full time person dedicated exclusively to child and adolescent mental health.

Even with the remarkable progress made since 1980, a number of problems still remain. First, many children in need of help are never treated by the mental health system because of parental ignorance or embarrassment. The shortage of specialists who work in child and mental health ultimately limits the number of young people who can be treated. Fiscal restraints due to government budget cutting have forced an increase in the use of institutional rather than the less restrictive but more costly "mainstream" settings in residential neighborhoods. And finally, services to minority youth often have lacked the cultural sensitivity necessary to be effective.

3.9

TEENAGE SEXUALITY

The percentage of teenage women who are sexually active has increased. In 1982, the percentage of teenage girls between 15 and 19 who had ever had intercourse was approximately 47.0 percent. By 1990, this number had increased to 55.0 percent (see Figure 3.9.1, page 116).

In 1990, roughly one-third of all pregnancies to teens under age 15 ended in abortion. For older age groups, this num-

ber declines to about 25.0 percent. Each year, 1 in every 10 American females aged 15 to 19 has a birth or an abortion. The abortion and pregnancy rates in the United States are among the highest in the developed world, although it is likely that rates in certain Eastern European countries are comparable or higher.

In recent years, newspaper stories, magazine and journal articles, books, and TV and radio programs have made public what they describe as an "epidemic" of teenage pregnancy. The United States has the highest rates of adolescent pregnancy and childbirth among Western industrialized nations. Teenage pregnancy is without a doubt a serious problem for teenagers and families. It is also a problem for society as a whole. First, fewer teenage mothers are making the decision to get married and thus, rates of single parenting are increasing. Second, more teenage mothers are opting to keep their babies, and this has been linked to increases in the cost to public budgets in welfare and medical costs. Third, teenage pregnancy gets to the core of legal, constitutional, and human rights issues relating to access to effective fertility control. It is ironic that in the United States today, few teens have access to sex education programs that focus on prevention. Much existing instruction focuses only on the biology of reproduction and fails to address decision making under pressure. Birth control information and assistance are least accessible to the groups that need them most. Efforts to develop comprehensive programs have foundered because of restrictive school board policies and inadequate government support.

There is, however, general agreement

on the goals of public policy toward teenage pregnancy:

(1) To prevent long-term public dependency;

(2) To lower present rates of teenage pregnancy and births, especially for school age adolescents;

(3) To ensure that pregnant adolescents receive health care and that adolescent parents receive the kinds of resources and support necessary to become good parents.

Beyond this, there is little agreement on anything else. Recent legislation points to the fact that we are in an era when economic resources are limited and the sentiment has turned against social welfare nets. Although there is a consensus regarding the goals of public policy, we cannot expect the consensus to translate into new funding for social programs.

Teenage pregnancy is not new to the litany of issues confronting American policy makers. Although American teenage fertility began to increase in the late 1980's, it is still much lower than that of previous decades. Aside from the higher rates of sexual activity and more pregnancies, one of the things that contributes to the sense of "crisis" is the socioeconomic context in which births occur and the cultural ideology they challenge or the association between adolescent pregnancy and specific racial, ethnic, and income groups. Rates of adolescent premarital sexual activity are substantially higher among African Americans than among Hispanics and whites. African Americans and Hispanic teens are also less likely either to use contraception consistently or to have abortions. As a result, the rate of adolescent childbearing among African Americans is nearly 2 1/2 times higher than among whites; among Hispanic teens, it is twice as high as among whites.

Although minority groups are overrepresented in the population at greatest risk, trends are converging. More whites are following the pattern of early nonmarital childbirth that in the past was limited largely to minority communities. In 1955, only 6.0 percent of white teenage childbearing occurred outside marriage compared with 41.0 percent among African Americans. By 1990 that figure was 42.0 percent for whites and 90.0 percent for blacks. Racial and ethnic patterns also vary over time, socioeconomic class, and locale.

Until recently, fathers rarely figured in research or public policy on adolescent pregnancy. This pattern is symptomatic of deeper societal norms. The absence of men in the "problem" of adolescent pregnancy reflected the absence of men in the lives of their young families. Although males bear half of the biological responsibility for pregnancy, they do not share half of the social responsibility for child rearing. Most teenage fathers do not live with their children, and a large number are unaware of or unwilling to admit paternity. According to some, about 60.0 percent of teen fathers provide some financial assistance in the first year after birth. Similarly, about half of all children born to a single adolescent mother have contact with their biological father a year after birth. Later this involvement is sporadic and intermittent. By a child's mid-adolescence, only about 10.0 percent of never married fathers and 33.0 percent of the divorced fathers were providing any support. Overall, only 13.0 percent of teen mothers had any significant attachment with a nonresident biological father, and 69.0 percent had no such attachment.

Many young fathers attempt to provide support even as socioeconomic forces and larger structural factors such as education, employment opportunities, and incarceration make it difficult. Few public policy initiatives focus on the difficulties men face.

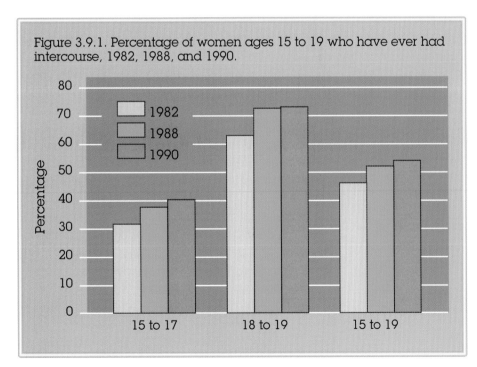

Figure 3.9.1. Percentage of women ages 15 to 19 who have ever had intercourse, 1982, 1988, and 1990.

3.10

SUBSTANCE ABUSE

Since 1990, the United States has made significant progress against overall drug use and related crime. Cocaine use has been reduced by 30.0 percent since 1992. Drug purchases have declined 23.0 percent from an estimated $64 billion in 1991 to about $49 billion in 1993.

While population-wide drug use is declining, adolescent and teen use is increasing as drugs and drug cultures become more attractive. "Today's teens are less likely to consider drug use harmful and risky, more likely to believe that drug use is widespread and tolerated, and feel more pressure to try illegal drugs than teens did just two years ago" (Partnership for a Drug-Free America, 1996). The survey attributed this reversal in attitudes to a glamorization of drugs in movies, music, and on television. It also pointed to an absence of civic leadership, at all levels, in discouraging experimentation with drugs.

In 1995, 1,106,261 Americans were arrested for drug-abuse violations. Of this number 142,475 were below the age of 18 (12.9 percent). Between 1994 and 1995, drug-abuse arrests for teens rose 17.8 percent from 120,912.

Starting in 1991, after encouraging years of decline, the number of people trying marijuana showed a marked increase for the first time since 1979. The majority of these "initiates" were young people. Other surveys confirm climbing drug use rates among youth and that first-time use is occurring at younger ages. Past-month use of alcohol, marijuana, and cocaine increased by the rate of 50.0 percent between 1992 and 1994 among youth aged 12 to 17 (see Figure 3.10.1, page 127).

By the age of 13, 24.9 percent of students had smoked a whole cigarette, 32.4 percent drank more than a few sips of alcohol, 7.6 percent had tried marijuana, and 1.2 percent had tried cocaine. With all illegal substances, males were much more likely to experiment or use at early ages.

Hispanic and white students were significantly more likely to smoke than black students; 71.3 percent of all high school students reported experimentation with cigarettes. Hispanic and black students were significantly more likely to try marijuana. Twenty-five percent of all students reported current marijuana use within the past thirty days, according to a 1995 National Risk Behavior Survey.

The level of awareness and communications surrounding adolescent use is troubling. When interviewed, only 14.0 percent of American parents suspected that their children had experimented with marijuana. This figure is in stark contrast to the 38.0 percent reported by children. Also, 34.0 percent of parents thought that their children had been offered drugs, compared to 52.0 percent confirmed by teenagers.

Many agree that communication is the key to managing and reducing the number of drug-related problems. Involvement of adults in the education of their children has a direct and positive effect in drug control. The Partnership for a Drug-Free America demonstrated that greater parental involvement discourages drug use among teenagers, particularly with regard to marijuana.

3.11

DENTAL CARE AND DENTAL CARE UTILIZATION

As fluoride toothpastes have become commonplace and communities routinely add fluoride to their water supplies, tooth decay has declined dramatically in the United States.

Despite this general improvement, minority children and children in rural areas experience slightly more dental decay and lose more teeth to decay than children in urban areas. Native American children average significantly more tooth decay than all groups combined.

Data pertaining to dental service utiliza-

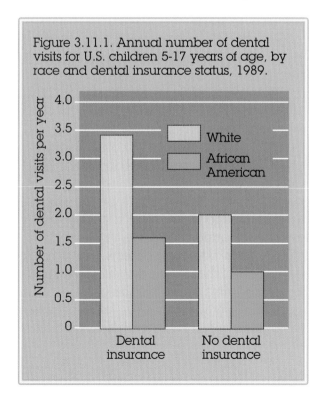

Figure 3.11.1. Annual number of dental visits for U.S. children 5-17 years of age, by race and dental insurance status, 1989.

tion are not available. What is known is that, like many other dimensions of children's lives, dental service utilization varies by race and the ability to pay (see Figure 3.11.1, page 117). In a study conducted in 1989, African American children visited the dentist fewer times than did whites. The study also showed that dental care is directly related to economic circumstances. Children supported by insurance were much more likely to seek dental care than those who had no insurance coverage. This finding was true for white and black children.

3.12

BIRTH DEFECTS

A birth defect is defined as an abnormality of structure, function or body metabolism present at birth that often results in physical or mental handicap, or is fatal. About 150,000 babies are officially reported born with birth defects in the United States each year. According to the March of Dimes, this figure underestimates the true extent since (1) birth defects cases identified after the newborn period are not accurately reported and (2) states are not required to undertake surveillance of infants born with birth defects. Though 25 states report that they have passive surveillance programs or are planning or implementing programs, only 10 states actually have active surveillance programs (see Figure 3.12.1, page 128).

There are three major categories of birth defects—structural/metabolic, congenital

infections, and a third classification that includes Rh disease and fetal alcohol syndrome. Table 3.12.1 provides estimates of the ratio of babies born with the leading types of birth defects and preventive measures. Improper development of the heart and circulatory system is the most common birth defect, afflicting 1 of every 115 babies born. Among defects for which there are no known prevention measures, PKU is the most rare with an estimated incidence of 1 in 8,000 births.

Children born with birth defects are more likely to die as infants. Birth defects are the single leading cause of infant death (see Figure 3.12.2, page 128). The largest proportion of birth defects related to infant deaths were due to heart defects, which accounted for 31.6 percent of all deaths from birth defects. This was followed by

malfunctions of the respiratory system, nervous system abnormalities, and chromosomal defects. Examples of the more common defects in each of these categories are listed in Figure 3.12.3 (see page 128).

While there is considerable variation in infant mortality rates by race, infant mortality rates due to birth defects were not significantly different for infants born to African American mothers and infants born to white mothers. In 1990, the rate of death from birth defects for infants born to white mothers was 195 per 100,000; for African Americans, it was 223 per 100,000.

Overall, deaths from birth defects decreased from 9,220 cases in 1980 to 8,239 in 1990. Virtually all categories of disorders experienced a decline with the exception of chromosomal defects, which increased from 654 in 1980 to 996 in 1990. A clearer understanding of the relationship among premature births, low birthweight babies, and birth defects is much needed.

Table 3.12.1. Leading categories of birth defects.

Birth defect	Estimated incidence	Prevention measure
Structural/metabolic		
Heart and circulation	1 in 115	
Muscles and skeleton	1 in 130	
Club foot	1 in 735	
Genital and urinary tract	1 in 135	
Nervous system and eye	1 in 235	
Neural tube defects	1 in 1,600	Folic acid
Chromosomal syndromes	1 in 635	
Down syndrome (Trisomy 21)	1 in 900	
Respiratory tract	1 in 900	
Metabolic disorders	1 in 3,500	
PKU	1 in 8,000	
Congenital infections		
Congenital syphilis	1 in 1,000	Safe sex/treatment
Congenital HIV infection	1 in 2,000	Safe sex/treatment
Congenital rubella syndrome	1 in 100,000	Immunization
Other		
Rh disease	1 in 685	Immunoglobulin
Fetal alcohol syndrome	1 in 1,000	Avoid alcohol

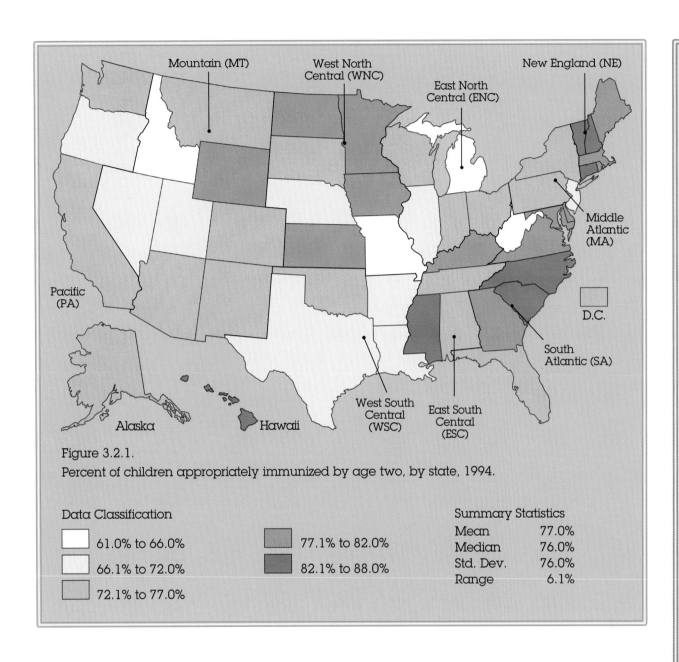

Figure 3.2.1.

Percent of children appropriately immunized by age two, by state, 1994.

Data Classification

☐	61.0% to 66.0%
☐	66.1% to 72.0%
▨	72.1% to 77.0%
▨	77.1% to 82.0%
▨	82.1% to 88.0%

Summary Statistics

Mean	77.0%
Median	76.0%
Std. Dev.	76.0%
Range	6.1%

Immunization inventory: percent of population 2 years old fully immunized against disease, 1994.

	Population 2 and under	Percent immunized
Alabama	168,195	75.0
Alaska	32,934	73.0
Arizona	175,101	77.0
Arkansas	97,770	71.0
California	1,452,250	74.0
Colorado	148,916	75.0
Connecticut	138,129	86.0
Delaware	29,271	81.0
District of Columbia	23,039	73.0
Florida	509,129	76.0
Georgia	298,321	79.0
Hawaii	50,255	86.0
Idaho	47,074	64.0
Illinois	510,109	68.0
Indiana	237,700	74.0
Iowa	114,059	81.0
Kansas	111,245	82.0
Kentucky	148,737	80.0
Louisiana	196,587	71.0
Maine	50,341	82.0
Maryland	216,136	79.0
Massachusetts	249,566	82.0
Michigan	421,559	61.0
Minnesota	199,349	81.0
Mississippi	115,656	83.0
Missouri	218,606	64.0
Montana	34,442	75.0
Nebraska	70,620	72.0
Nevada	55,666	69.0
New Hampshire	50,595	83.0
New Jersey	323,192	71.0
New Mexico	73,768	73.0
New York	757,554	77.0
North Carolina	277,079	84.0
North Dakota	28,111	81.0
Ohio	467,519	73.0
Oklahoma	133,252	76.0
Oregon	119,314	71.0
Pennsylvania	474,392	77.0
Rhode Island	40,326	82.0
South Carolina	153,847	84.0
South Dakota	32,121	74.0
Tennessee	199,290	74.0
Texas	825,524	81.0
Utah	101,444	70.0
Vermont	24,443	88.0
Virginia	267,259	81.0
Washington	217,865	74.0
West Virginia	62,153	66.0
Wisconsin	211,661	76.0
Wyoming	19,988	78.0

Table 3.2.2. Summary of state immunization requirements applicable to any or all grades K to 12, school year 1993-94.

	Diphtheria	Tetanus	Pertussis	Measles	Mumps	Rubella	Polio
Alabama					NR		
Alaska							
Arizona							
Arkansas							
California							
Colorado							
Connecticut							
Delaware							
District of Columbia							
Florida							
Georgia							
Hawaii							
Idaho	K-5	K-5	NR				
Illinois							
Indiana							
Iowa					NR		
Kansas							
Kentucky					NR		
Louisiana	NE	NE	NE	NE	NE	NE	NE
Maine			NR				
Maryland					K-1,6, & 7		
Massachusetts							
Michigan	NE	NE	NE				
Minnesota							
Mississippi							
Missouri		NR	NR				
Montana							
Nebraska							
Nevada							
New Hampshire							
New Jersey							
New Mexico					NR		
New York		NR	NR				
North Carolina					NE		
North Dakota							
Ohio							
Oklahoma					K-5		
Oregon			NR				
Pennsylvania			NR				
Rhode Island							
South Carolina					NR		
South Dakota							
Tennessee							
Texas			NR				
Utah							
Vermont					NR		
Virginia							
Washington			NR				
West Virginia	NE	NE	NE		NR		
Wisconsin							
Wyoming							

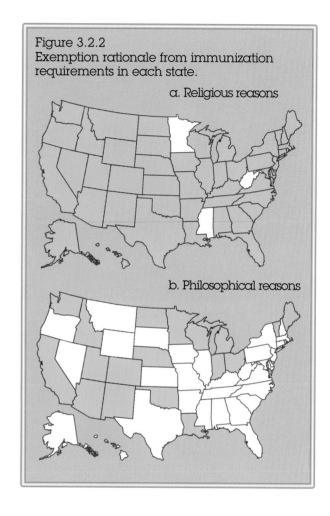

Figure 3.2.2
Exemption rationale from immunization requirements in each state.

a. Religious reasons

b. Philosophical reasons

Note: NE = immunization required of all new entrants. NR = states in yellow do not require immunization. Blank areas on this table represent the national standards whereby immunizations are required of all children in grades K-12. Pertussis vaccine is only required through age 6 years.

Table 3.2.3. Measles outbreaks with greater than 100 reported cases, 1991.

State	Counties	Date of first case	Date of last case	1991 cases	Predominant group affected	Number less than 5 years old	Percent less than 5 years old	Number unvaccinated	Percent unvaccinated
New York	Bronx King's Manhattan Queens Richmond	12/88	N/A	1,909	Preschool	1,192	62.4	1,676	87.8
Pennsylvania	Philadelphia Montgomery Bucks Chester Delaware	10/90	6/91	1,338	Preschool	632	47.2	1,079	80.6
California	Los Angeles Orange Riverside San Bernardino	8/87	5/92	1,166	Preschool	547	46.9	946	81.1
New Jersey	Essex Hudson Union Passaic Middlesex Bergen	12/90	9/91	824	Preschool	533	64.7	649	78.8
Idaho	Fremont Madison Ada Canyon Bannock Latah	2/91	9/91	465	School	91	19.6	361	77.6
Arizona	Navajo Coconino Mohave Apache Yavapai	12/90	8/91	383	Preschool	220	57.4	325	84.9
Florida	Duval Nassau St. John's Clay	4/91	1/92	176	Preschool	127	72.2	143	81.3
Utah	Davis Rich Iron Weber	3/91	8/91	149	School	45	30.2	79	53.0
New Jersey	Camden	11/90	7/91	138	Preschool	98	71.0	112	81.2
New York	Suffolk	12/90	7/91	137	Postschool	47	34.3	116	84.7
Maryland	Anne Arundel Calvert Cecil Baltimore Howard	2/91	5/91	108	School	18	16.7	85	79.0

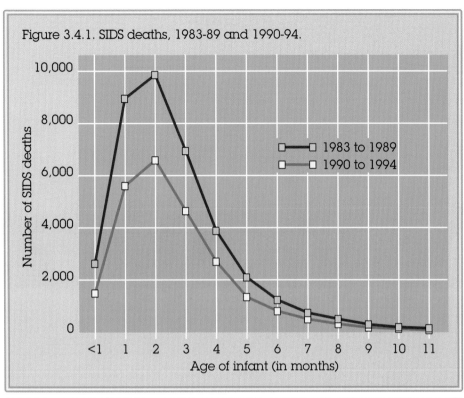

Figure 3.4.1. SIDS deaths, 1983-89 and 1990-94.

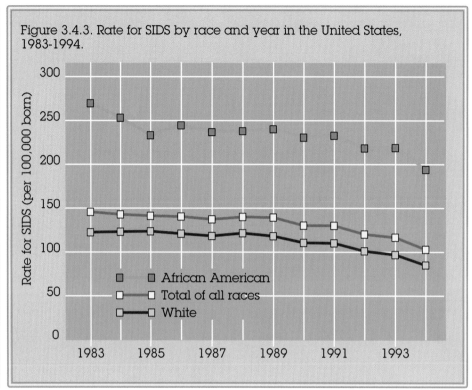

Figure 3.4.3. Rate for SIDS by race and year in the United States, 1983-1994.

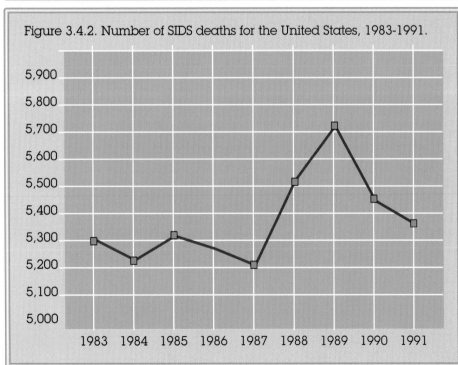

Figure 3.4.2. Number of SIDS deaths for the United States, 1983-1991.

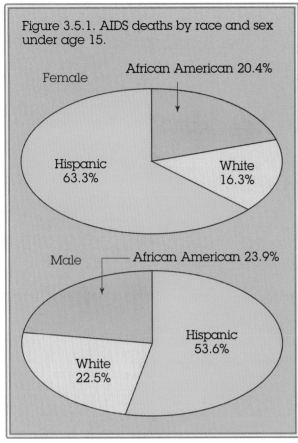

Figure 3.5.1. AIDS deaths by race and sex under age 15.

Female

African American 20.4%

Hispanic 63.3%

White 16.3%

Male

African American 23.9%

Hispanic 53.6%

White 22.5%

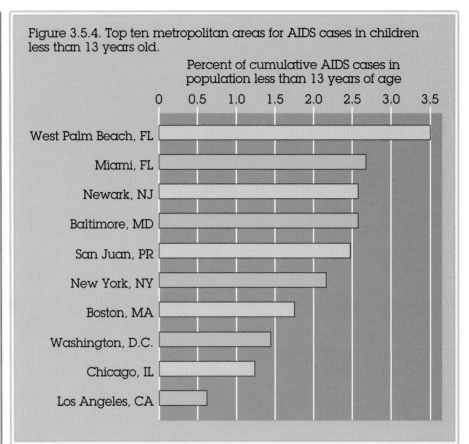

Figure 3.5.4. Top ten metropolitan areas for AIDS cases in children less than 13 years old.

Percent of cumulative AIDS cases in population less than 13 years of age

West Palm Beach, FL
Miami, FL
Newark, NJ
Baltimore, MD
San Juan, PR
New York, NY
Boston, MA
Washington, D.C.
Chicago, IL
Los Angeles, CA

Table 3.5.1. AIDS cases by age at diagnosis and exposure category, through December 1993.

Age	Men who have sex with men		Injecting drug use		Hemophilia/coagulation disorder		Heterosexual contact		Mother with/at risk for HIV infection	
	Number	Percent	Number	Percent	Number	Percent	Number	Percent	Number	Percent
Under 5	—	—	—	—	11	0.0	—	—	4,027	87
5 to 12	—	—	—	—	198	6.0	—	—	610	13
13 to 19	358	35.7	171	17.1	473	47.2	276	27.5	—	—
20 to 24	7,015	71.1	2,425	24.6	422	4.3	1,745	17.7	—	—
25 to 29	31,195	74.0	10,472	24.8	484	1.1	4,418	10.5	—	—
30 to 34	46,384	68.0	21,325	31.3	463	0.7	5,148	7.6	—	—
35 to 39	41,654	62.8	24,294	36.6	391	0.6	4,048	6.1	—	—
40 to 44	29,530	64.1	16,221	35.2	289	0.6	2,665	5.8	—	—
45 to 49	17,841	71.2	6,989	27.9	222	0.9	1,705	6.8	—	—
50 to 54	9,725	75.4	3,051	23.7	117	0.9	1,182	9.2	—	—
55 to 59	5,472	78.4	1,424	20.4	83	1.2	813	11.6	—	—
60 to 64	2,850	81.2	573	16.3	85	2.4	558	15.9	—	—
65 or older	1,628	79.6	312	15.3	104	5.1	608	29.7	—	—

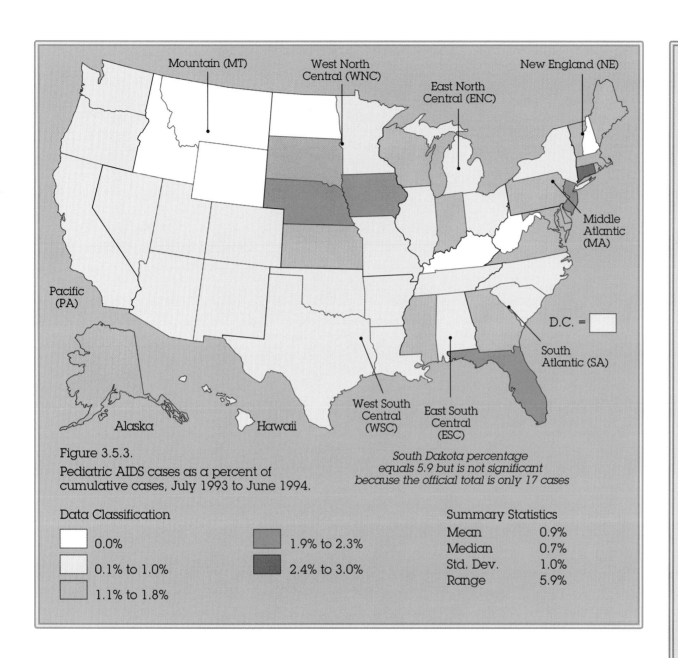

Figure 3.5.3.

Pediatric AIDS cases as a percent of cumulative cases, July 1993 to June 1994.

South Dakota percentage equals 5.9 but is not significant because the official total is only 17 cases

Data Classification

- 0.0%
- 0.1% to 1.0%
- 1.1% to 1.8%
- 1.9% to 2.3%
- 2.4% to 3.0%

D.C. =

Summary Statistics

Mean	0.9%
Median	0.7%
Std. Dev.	1.0%
Range	5.9%

Number of pediatric AIDS cases and percent of cumulative cases from July 1993 to June 1994.

	Total pediatric AIDS cases	% of total AIDS cases
Alabama	2	0.4
Alaska	1	1.4
Arizona	2	0.3
Arkansas	1	0.3
California	54	0.4
Colorado	3	0.3
Connecticut	37	2.8
Delaware	3	1.1
District of Columbia	13	0.8
Florida	157	2.0
Georgia	28	1.3
Hawaii	2	0.6
Idaho	0	0.0
Illinois	19	0.7
Indiana	9	1.2
Iowa	2	2.0
Kansas	3	1.1
Kentucky	0	0.0
Louisiana	12	1.0
Maine	2	1.5
Maryland	38	1.7
Massachusetts	22	1.1
Michigan	8	0.7
Minnesota	3	0.8
Mississippi	7	1.7
Missouri	5	0.6
Montana	0	0.0
Nebraska	2	1.9
Nevada	2	0.4
New Hampshire	0	0.0
New Jersey	103	1.9
New Mexico	1	0.6
New York	30	0.2
North Carolina	3	0.2
North Dakota	0	0.0
Ohio	7	0.5
Oklahoma	1	0.3
Oregon	2	0.3
Pennsylvania	30	1.1
Rhode Island	4	1.4
South Carolina	11	0.9
South Dakota	1	5.9
Tennessee	7	0.8
Texas	28	0.5
Utah	1	0.7
Vermont	1	1.2
Virginia	22	1.6
Washington	3	0.3
West Virginia	0	0.0
Wisconsin	6	1.5
Wyoming	0	0.0

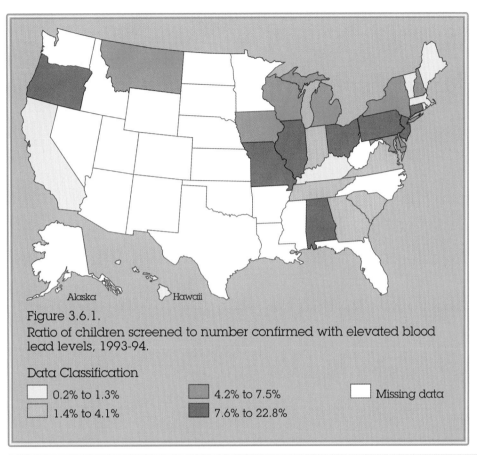

Figure 3.6.1.
Ratio of children screened to number confirmed with elevated blood lead levels, 1993-94.

Data Classification

☐ 0.2% to 1.3%		☐ 4.2% to 7.5%		☐ Missing data
☐ 1.4% to 4.1%		☐ 7.6% to 22.8%		

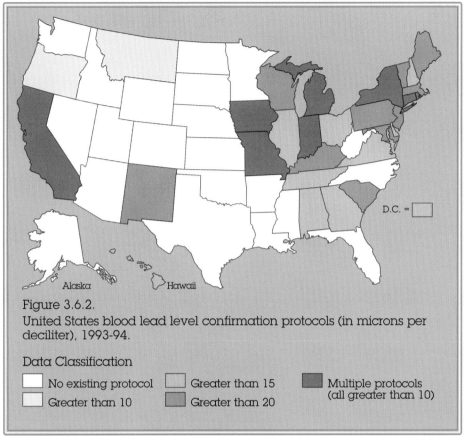

Figure 3.6.2.
United States blood lead level confirmation protocols (in microns per deciliter), 1993-94.

Data Classification

☐ No existing protocol		☐ Greater than 15		☐ Multiple protocols (all greater than 10)
☐ Greater than 10		☐ Greater than 20		

D.C. = ☐

Figure 3.6.3. Geometric mean blood lead levels (BLLs) for persons aged less than 75 years, by age group, 1976-1980 and 1988-1991.

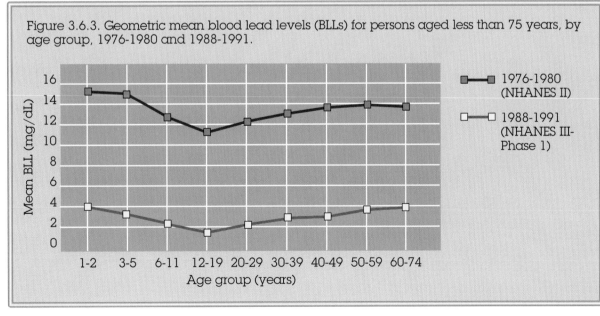

Table 3.6.1. Top 5 cities confirmed lead poisoning with levels greater than 10 microns per deciliter in children.

	Children screened	Cases confirmed	Percent confirmed
Charleston, SC	2,271	115	5.1
New York City, NY	59,106	1,754	3.0
Houston, TX	3,950	110	2.8
Detroit, MI	8,193	345	4.2
Dist. of Columbia	16,743	345	2.1

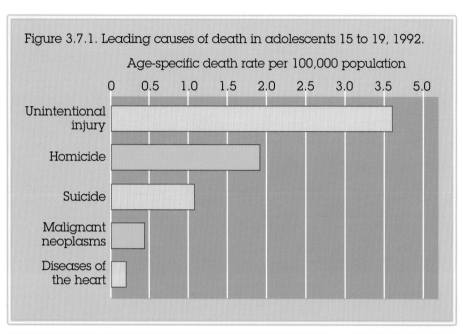

Figure 3.7.1. Leading causes of death in adolescents 15 to 19, 1992.

Age-specific death rate per 100,000 population

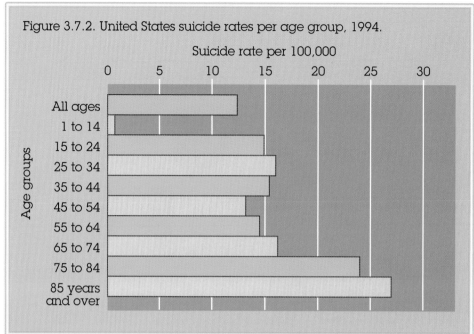

Figure 3.7.2. United States suicide rates per age group, 1994.

Suicide rate per 100,000

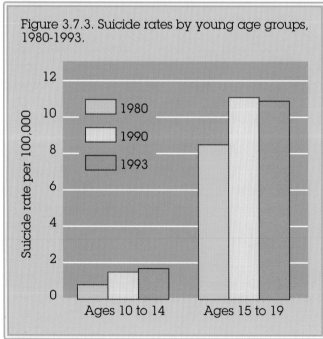

Figure 3.7.3. Suicide rates by young age groups, 1980-1993.

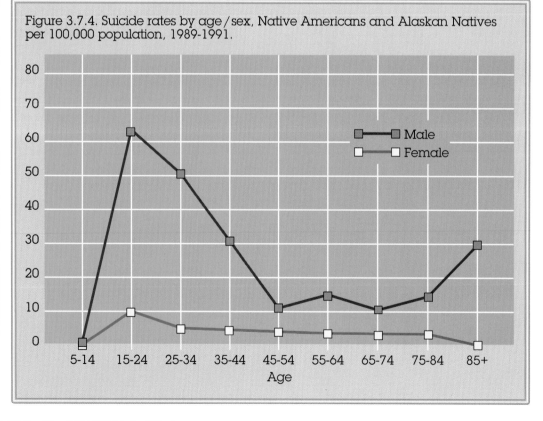

Figure 3.7.4. Suicide rates by age/sex, Native Americans and Alaskan Natives per 100,000 population, 1989-1991.

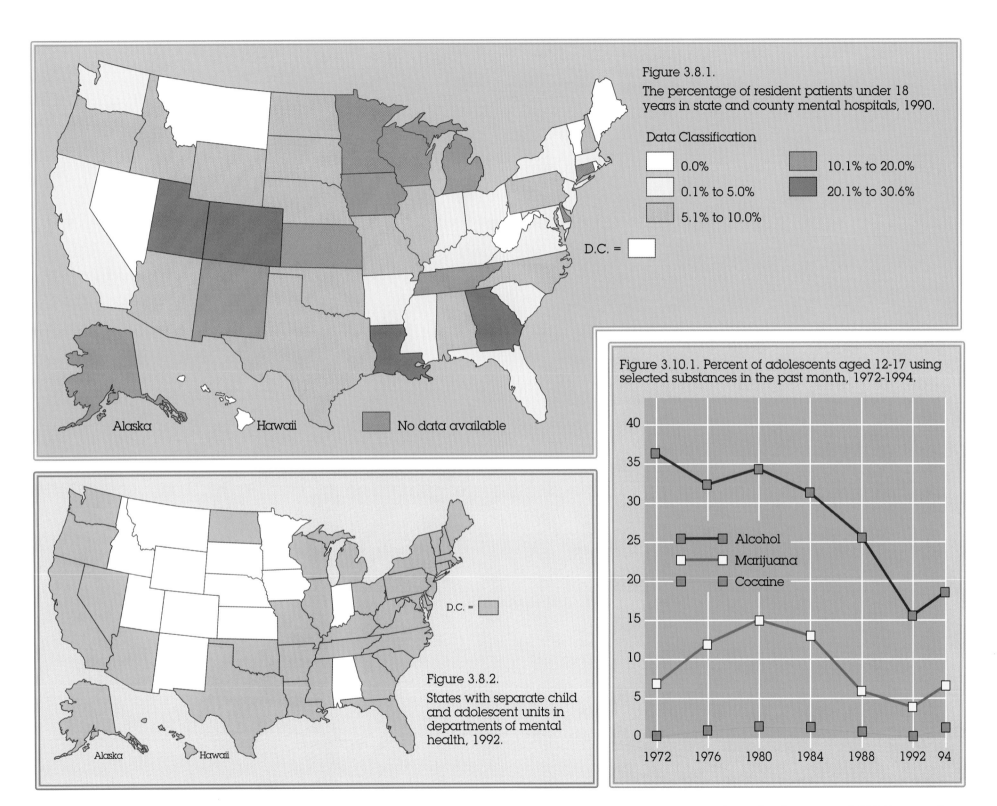

Figure 3.8.1.
The percentage of resident patients under 18 years in state and county mental hospitals, 1990.

Data Classification

0.0%

0.1% to 5.0%

5.1% to 10.0%

10.1% to 20.0%

20.1% to 30.6%

D.C. =

Alaska   Hawaii   No data available

Figure 3.10.1. Percent of adolescents aged 12-17 using selected substances in the past month, 1972-1994.

Alcohol

Marijuana

Cocaine

1972 1976 1980 1984 1988 1992 94

D.C. =

Figure 3.8.2.
States with separate child and adolescent units in departments of mental health, 1992.

Alaska   Hawaii

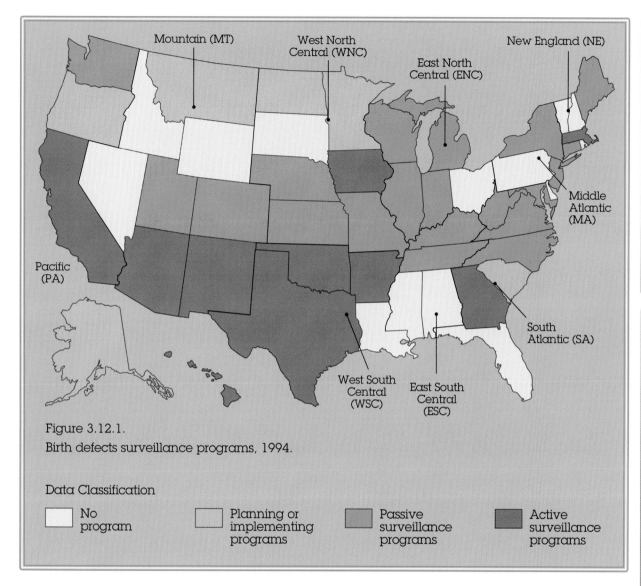

Figure 3.12.1.
Birth defects surveillance programs, 1994.

Data Classification

☐ No program

☐ Planning or implementing programs

☐ Passive surveillance programs

☐ Active surveillance programs

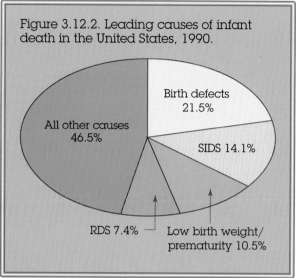

Figure 3.12.2. Leading causes of infant death in the United States, 1990.

Birth defects 21.5%

SIDS 14.1%

Low birth weight/ prematurity 10.5%

RDS 7.4%

All other causes 46.5%

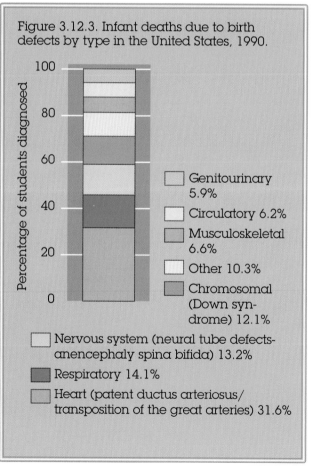

Figure 3.12.3. Infant deaths due to birth defects by type in the United States, 1990.

Percentage of students diagnosed

☐ Genitourinary 5.9%

☐ Circulatory 6.2%

☐ Musculoskeletal 6.6%

☐ Other 10.3%

☐ Chromosomal (Down syndrome) 12.1%

☐ Nervous system (neural tube defects-anencephaly spina bifida) 13.2%

☐ Respiratory 14.1%

☐ Heart (patent ductus arteriosus/ transposition of the great arteries) 31.6%

Chapter 4

Children and the Criminal Justice System

4.1

INTRODUCTION

"A child is a person who is going to carry out what you have started. He is going to sit were you are sitting and when you are gone, attend to those things you think are important. He will assume control of your cities, states and nations.... All your books are going to be judged, praised or condemned by him. The fate of humanity is in his hands."

—Abraham Lincoln

As our society changes, many things affect "business as usual." The baby boom generation (the largest proportion of our population) will soon be approaching retirement age. The young adult population will increase as the children of the baby boomers move through their adolescent years. The United States is already grappling with managing racial, ethnic, and economic diversity, and effort will only increase in the future. As well, the U. S. economy is undergoing enormous domestic and global transformations.

Communications technology is changing as well as the roles of women. As a result, the traditional socializing institutions of the community—the family, the schools, the churches—have been weakened. The rise in youth violence is intimately linked to these forces.

Adding to this is the influence of television, movies, music, newspapers and the easy availability of drugs and guns. All of these things will challenge America's ability to manage its youth.

With these changes in mind, this chapter examines children and the juvenile justice system—the goals of the system, historical approaches to dealing with juveniles, court procedures, trends in delinquency—and considers children both as victims and as victimizers. In discussing juvenile justice, we give particular attention to the philosophical debates regarding the future of the juvenile court; whether or not it can or should survive in the years ahead. Before proceeding, some background is needed on the function of the juvenile justice system and jurisdiction of the court.

4.2

THE JUVENILE COURT SYSTEM

The most important function of the juvenile codes is to specify conditions under which the state may exercise authority in a child's life—the juvenile court acts *in loco parentis*. The court has authority to: (1) supervise activities or environment within the home; (2) place children in foster care; and (3) institutionalize the child.

Juvenile court hearings have always been very different from adult court hearings—they are typically designed to be nonadversarial, informal, and confidential. The main concern has always been guided by what is in the best interests of the child—not the protection of society.

Juvenile courts may intervene in three instances. The first of these instances is one in which a youth has been accused of committing an act that would be defined as criminal for an adult—referred to as a

delinquent offense. Second, the court may also intervene in status offenses in which an act is committed that would not be defined as criminal if committed by an adult (truancy, curfew violations, and running away). Juveniles committing such acts are described as incorrigible, in need of supervision, wayward, beyond parental control, or unruly. The third instance in which the court may intervene involves instances of dependency and neglect. Here, the child is viewed by the court as being deprived and in need of support. Parental figures and the family of origin are judged incapable of resolving the problems. In this case, children are often removed from their homes for their own protection and well-being. The 1991 *Children in Custody Census* found that over 95 percent of children in custody had committed delinquent offenses. Only 5 percent were in custody because of status offenses. The United States had an overall custody rate of 221 per 100,000.

Unfortunately, there is considerable discretionary power on the part of police and court personnel in juvenile matters. Juvenile justice personnel, like the population in general, often make decisions based on social values, and those values may reflect considerable bias.

Age is probably the most important variable in determining a person's criminal intent. Our laws are based on English common law, which stated:

(1) Children under the age of 7 were deemed incapable of having criminal intent;

(2) Children who were between the ages of 7 and 14 were presumed

incapable of forming criminal intent, but the state could overcome this presumption by establishing that the child did indeed know the difference between right and wrong and that the child was aware of the consequences of his/her actions; and

(3) Children over the age of 14 were presumed capable of forming criminal intent.

Despite these seemingly precise guidelines, state legal codes exhibit fairly wide variation in the maximum age limit for childhood or the age when a person is defined as an adult (Figure 4.2.1). Codes may even differ within a state depending on the allegations made in the petition. Colorado, Delaware, North Carolina, and Vermont have the lowest maximum limit (age 16) while Wyoming has the highest (age 19). Well over half of the states designate age 18 as the age at which children lose their juvenile status.

ISSUES IN THE JUVENILE JUSTICE SYSTEM

Historically, the orientation of juvenile courts has been guided by the desire to treat and rehabilitate rather than to punish. This philosophy dates back to a time when reformers felt the need to extricate children from the harshness of the punishment meted out to older offenders. In dealing with children, the question of what is in the best interests of the child would dominate. Reformers soon agreed that if the goals of the system were to be realized without the legal and social stigmas that could emerge as a result of the child's juvenile court involvement, a cloak of confidentiality surrounding the proceedings was

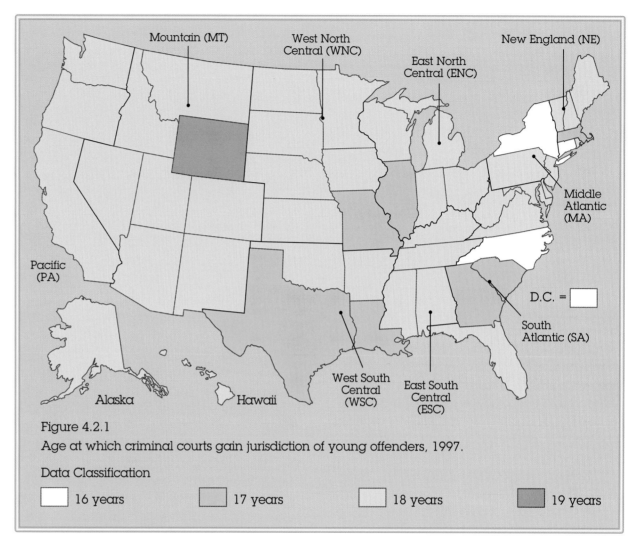

Figure 4.2.1
Age at which criminal courts gain jurisdiction of young offenders, 1997.

Data Classification

| 16 years | 17 years | 18 years | 19 years |

required. A child's unfortunate circumstances were private—to be handled only by the family and the court—oftentimes not even with an attorney present.

One of the most consistently controversial aspects of the existing juvenile justice system is the issue of confidentiality of records and record keeping. Sealing and expungement of juvenile records is the most effective way of ensuring confidentiality. Sealing, which is the act of removing a file and placing it in a central repository

that has highly restricted access, is most often the result of a court order and occurs when:

(1) a juvenile reaches the age of majority or some other age as specified in the order;

(2) a specified period of time has elapsed; or

(3) a clean record period has expired. Expungement, on the other

hand, destroys all evidence of the record. It is as though the act never occurred.

Both procedures affect the ability to construct complete juvenile criminal history records. At the same time, "open records" may not be in the best interest of the child as they color society's perceptions and deprive juveniles of equal opportunities later in life. Figure 4.2.2, on page 154, shows states which contain statutes requiring that juvenile records be either destroyed, expunged or sealed.

In roughly half of the states, both court and police records are sealed, while in only 6 are court records sealed. Once records are sealed, access or inspection is closely regulated. In 21 jurisdictions, no access is permitted without consent of the court. Included in the statutes of the states of Alabama, New Jersey, and Washington are provisions for nullifying the sealing order of the court if, subsequent to the sealing, the record subject is convicted of a crime.

Twenty-one states authorize the expungement of both law enforcement and court records. Expungement of only court records is mandated in 6 states. Because expungement is an irreversible act, however, usually a court order is required before it can occur. Only in Connecticut is there a provision for expungement of all police and court records without a formal petition of the court.

A patrol officer has considerable flexibility as to whether or not to "write up" a juvenile and thus begin a juvenile history. Discretion may often be exercised in favor of the juvenile, especially for the first contact or even the first few contacts. The result is that a juvenile may have had much more involvement with the criminal justice system than any written record or search of a juvenile history will reveal. Accordingly, whether open, sealed, or expunged, a file may not reflect a complete and accurate history of contact with the juvenile system.

Only California, Pennsylvania, and Arizona require that juvenile records contain the disposition of an arrest. Two other states—Indiana and Washington—have statutory procedures that allow individuals to audit personal records when they contain errors.

Because of the far-reaching implications that fingerprinting has for children who have had contacts with the law enforcement system, the disposition of a juvenile's fingerprints is highly contested as a confidentiality issue. Fingerprinting of juvenile offenders has traditionally been viewed as the most intrusive act of the juvenile justice system. All states, with the exception of Arizona, Massachusetts, Michigan, New Hampshire, North Carolina, Rhode Island, and Wisconsin have statutes that authorize fingerprinting of juveniles. (In Rhode Island, fingerprinting is statutorily authorized only for voluntary plans or programs and all records are given immediately to the child's parent or guardian.) The circumstances under which juveniles may be fingerprinted include:

(1) offenses that would be felonies if committed by an adult;

(2) cases when comparisons of latent fingerprints are in order;

(3) cases which require further investigation which is facilitated by fingerprinting; and/or

(4) circumstances in which consent is obtained from juveniles and parent(s).

Beyond this, what states are required to do with juvenile fingerprint records is strictly defined in state statute, administrative agency standard, court rule, or city or county ordinance. Most states have statutory provisions calling for the destruction of fingerprint records. A number, however, require that fingerprints be maintained in a central repository, particularly when the offense is a felony offense.

In recent years a number of developments have led to an erosion of support for confidentiality protections for juveniles. The first is the reemergence of a retributive penal philosophy known as "just deserts." This ideology has been prompted largely by the belief that the punishment should fit the crime. It focuses on the *criminal act* rather than the offender. Proponents argue that the age at which juveniles may be tried as adults should be lowered and that the types of crimes for which transfer to adult court is permitted should be increased. According to some, confidentiality of juvenile records and of juvenile proceedings generated inequities in treatment. The manner in which juvenile records are treated means in effect that juvenile offenders are able to enter the adult criminal justice system as first offenders. Only four states—Washington, Indiana, Michigan, and New Jersey—contain statutory provisions that allow for juvenile law enforcement records to be used in adult courts, and then the records can only be used after guilt has been established.

A second development that has shifted attitudes away from an emphasis on confidentiality is research indicating that a history of involvement in the juvenile justice system may be predictive of future involvement in crime. The best predictor of future behavior is past behavior. This research has spawned proposals for new prediction-based approaches to sentencing. Unlike "just deserts," which focuses on the criminal act, selective incapacitation seeks to predict the occurrence of criminal acts and to prevent them by imposing punishment on those deemed highly likely to commit crimes. Research suggests that there exists a small core of recalcitrant and very active offenders who are responsible for the bulk of crimes committed. Moreover, these offenders typically have histories of early and frequent encounters with juvenile authorities.

Both developments have made records, recordkeeping, and fingerprinting critical issues in the administration of juvenile justice. Figure 4.2.3, on pages 134 and 135, identifies varying state statutory provisions for dissemination and access to juvenile law enforcement records.

The waiver or transfer of juveniles to adult court is hotly debated. The juvenile justice system allows for juveniles to be tried in adult court. Roughly 5.0 percent of juvenile offenders taken into custody are referred to criminal or adult court (see Table 4.2.1, page 147). Decisions that make it possible to try a child as an adult should not be taken lightly. A transfer denies certain guarantees of the juvenile court system and allows the court to back away from the principle that children deserve care, treatment, and protection. It also allows for a child to be subjected to the death penalty, and in most states conviction in an adult court means confinement in an adult institution. Between 1985 and 1990, the number of juveniles in jails has increased (see Figure 4.2.4, page 136).

Transfers are typically granted when a juvenile court is unable to properly handle a juvenile. The chief concern is public safety. A transfer may be recommended when:

(1) A juvenile is charged with a delinquent act;

(2) The juvenile was 16 years or older at the time of the commission of the delinquent act;

(3) The alleged delinquent act is aggravated or heinous in nature;

(4) The alleged act is part of a pattern of repeated delinquent acts;

(5) There is probable cause to believe the juvenile committed acts that are to be the subject of the adult criminal proceedings if waiver and transfer are approved;

(6) The juvenile is not amenable to services provided by the family court; and/or

(7) The juvenile has been given a waiver and transfer hearing that is consistent with due process.

In addition, judges may also consider any of the following when considering a waiver or transfer:

(1) The seriousness of the alleged offense to the community and whether the protection of the community requires waiver;

(2) Whether the alleged offense was committed in an aggressive, violent or premeditated manner;

(3) Whether the alleged offense was against persons or against property (greater weight being given to offenses against persons);

(4) Whether there is evidence upon which a grand jury may be expected to return an indictment;

(5) The sophistication and maturity of the juvenile by consideration of his home, environmental situation, emotional attitude, and pattern of living; and/or

(6) The record and previous history of the juvenile including previous contacts with law enforcement, juvenile courts.

Also hotly debated is the increased use of private custody and treatment facilities for juveniles. Efforts to encourage states to institutionalize status offenders, the need to deliver specialized services such as health care, vocational training, education, and staff training has led to a "second system" of private correctional placements.

Precise information regarding the exact nature and extent of private correctional institutions is scanty, although efforts are underway to address this shortcoming. There are several concerns. First, will privately managed facilities assume the government's current liability which includes

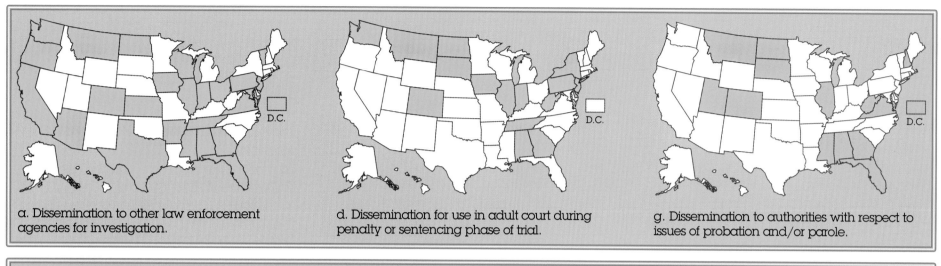

a. Dissemination to other law enforcement agencies for investigation.

d. Dissemination for use in adult court during penalty or sentencing phase of trial.

g. Dissemination to authorities with respect to issues of probation and/or parole.

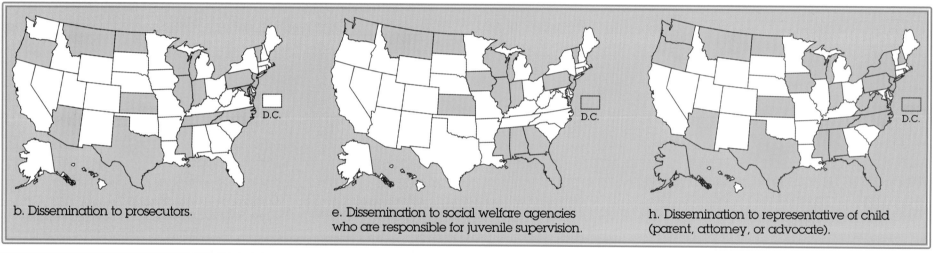

b. Dissemination to prosecutors.

e. Dissemination to social welfare agencies who are responsible for juvenile supervision.

h. Dissemination to representative of child (parent, attorney, or advocate).

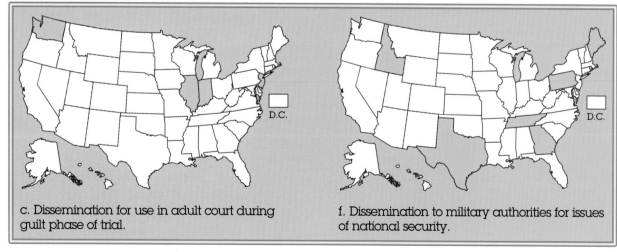

c. Dissemination for use in adult court during guilt phase of trial.

f. Dissemination to military authorities for issues of national security.

Figure 4.2.3.

Statutory provisions for dissemination and access to juvenile law enforcement records.

Yes   No

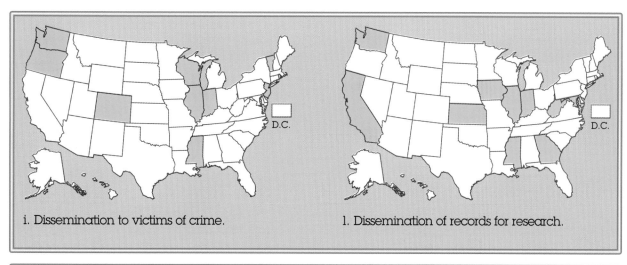

i. Dissemination to victims of crime.

l. Dissemination of records for research.

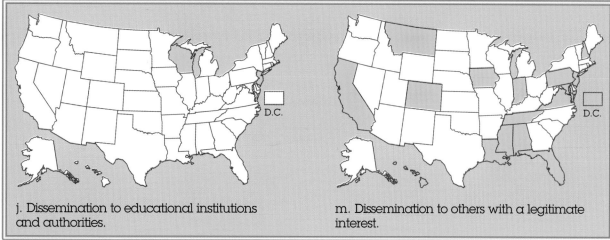

j. Dissemination to educational institutions and authorities.

m. Dissemination to others with a legitimate interest.

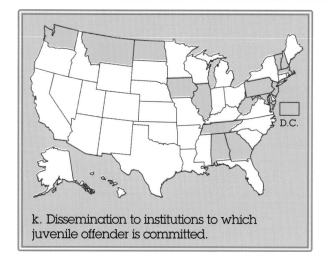

k. Dissemination to institutions to which juvenile offender is committed.

Figure 4.2.3 (cont.).

Statutory provisions for dissemination and access to juvenile law enforcement records.

☐ (shaded) Yes   ☐ No

potential for operating losses and financial shortfalls? Second, do privately run facilities offer better treatment and custody? And third, are private organizations committed to the task of rehabilitation?

Supporters of private correctional facilities maintain that nongovernmental organizations can run cost effective, safe, and clean environments for incarceration. Opponents, on the other hand, argue that fewer juveniles will be processed by professional legal administrators and that protections and judicial remedies will disappear together with "individualized attention" necessary for offender rehabilitation.

CHARACTERISTICS OF JUVENILES IN PUBLIC AND PRIVATE FACILITIES

The characteristics of juveniles confined to public facilities changed has changed dramatically in recent years. According to a report issued by the U.S. Department of Justice, Office of Juvenile Justice and Delinquency Prevention; from 1987 to 1989 the proportion of minorities has increased 13.0 percent. The biggest increases were found among African Americans (14.0 percent) and Hispanics (10.0 percent). From 1987 to 1989, the number of females held in public facilities decreased by 8.0 percent.

Approximately 10.0 percent of all juveniles were held for drug related offenses. Of these, half were held for distribution. The number of juveniles held for violent personal offenses increased over the period.

Among youth in public facilities, 95.0 percent were held for delinquent offenses, acts that would be considered criminal if committed by an adult. Of those committing delinquent acts, 41.0 percent committed crimes against property (burglary, arson, larceny theft, motor vehicle theft, vandalism, forgery, fraud, stolen property and unauthorized vehicle use). Violent and personal offenses were the next most frequent offense. Violent offenses include murder, nonnegligent manslaughter, forcible rape, robbery and aggravated assault. Personal offenses include negligent manslaughter, assault and sexual assault. Drug offenses made up only 11.0 percent of the total. Only 5.0 percent of juveniles were in custody because of status offenses (offenses that would not be considered illegal if committed by an adult) or admitted themselves voluntarily.

For youth detained in privately run facilities, 36.0 percent are being confined for delinquent offenses and 18.0 percent for status offenses. Forty seven percent are nonoffenders and voluntary commitments.

The juvenile custody rate for public facilities was 221 per 100,000 in 1989. States in the west, led by California, had higher rates for public facilities than other regions. Alaska, California, Nevada stand out as having custody rates of 300 and above (see Figure 4.2.5, page 146). For the country as a whole, Washington, D.C. stands out markedly with a custody rate of 826. Juvenile custody rates apply only to juveniles aged 10 to the upper limit of juvenile court jurisdiction.

Comparing public and private facilities in terms of their demographic composition reveals stark contrasts. The ratio of males to females is approximately 4 times higher in public facilities than in private facilities. Also, whites outnumber African Americans by 2 to 1 in private facilities. In public facilities, the numbers are roughly equal. Private

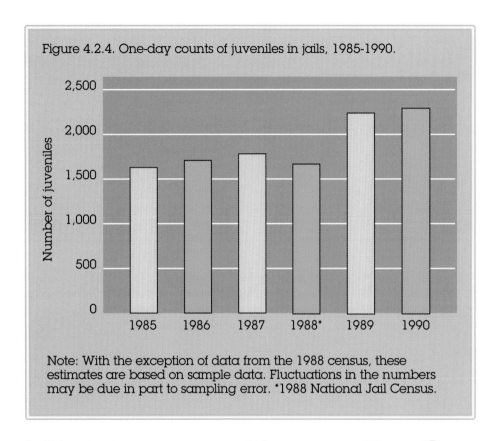

Figure 4.2.4. One-day counts of juveniles in jails, 1985-1990.

Note: With the exception of data from the 1988 census, these estimates are based on sample data. Fluctuations in the numbers may be due in part to sampling error. *1988 National Jail Census.

facilities also have a younger population; 18.0 percent of the population in private facilities is below the age of 13. For public facilities this number is 6.0 percent.

Overall, juvenile admissions to most facilities decreased or increased only slightly between 1978 and 1984 and then began to climb in the mid-1980s, resulting in an overall growth of 20.0 percent over the entire 12 years (see Figure 4.3.2, page 137). Detention centers received the vast majority of the increase. As noted, juvenile admissions to jails have also increased. One-day counts of juveniles in jails during the period 1985-1990 reveal a 50.0 percent increase in the number of juveniles admitted. This results in part from the increased popularity of the "just deserts" ideology.

4.3
CONDITIONS OF CONFINEMENT/FACILITIES FOR JUVENILE OFFENDERS

In 1988, when Congress mandated that the Office of Juvenile Justice and Delinquency Prevention (OJJDP) assess conditions of confinement for children in America's prisons, it was clear that there was a need. In 1991, the total number of juvenile facilities, both public and private, numbered 3,108, caring for 93,732 juveniles. Public facilities numbered 1,076, holding 57,542 individuals in custody while 2,032 private facilities held 36,190 juveniles according to information released by OJJDP.

Approximately 50.0 percent of publicly run facilities were administered to by state governments in 1991. The remaining half fall under local jurisdiction (see Table 4.3.1, page 147). In 1991, California had the largest number of facilities at 106 followed by New York with 78. Maine and Vermont only had one facility each.

Half of all juveniles were held in detention centers in 1991 (see Figure 4.3.1, below). They are becoming an increasingly popular destination for juvenile offenders (Figure 4.3.2). In 1979, detention centers accounted for only 43.3 percent of all juvenile placements. In 1991, that figure was 49.6 percent (see Table 4.3.2, page 139). As detention centers, reception centers, and training schools increase in number and proportion,ranches decrease significantly. In 1979, 27.3 percent of all

facilities were ranches compared to 16.5 percent in 1991.

The median facility size ranged from 22 to 86 residents. Training schools are the largest facilities, sometimes housing as many as 868 residents.

Public facilities for juvenile offenders average $1.67 billion a year for operating costs such as salaries, food, utilities, etc. In 1988, average costs per resident for one year ranged from lows of approximately $17,000 in Mississippi, Alabama, and South Dakota to highs of approximately $57,000 in the Midwest, the Northeast, and the District of Columbia. The highest costs ($78,800) occurred in Rhode Island (see Figure 4.3.3, page 148). California

stands out as having the greatest number of facilities, while the New England states have the fewest (see Figures 4.3.4, page 149. Custody rates for juveniles are highest in California and Nevada (see Figure 4.3.5, page 150).

CONDITIONS OF CONFINEMENT

Although standards for adult facilities have long been in place, standards for juvenile facilities have only recently been legislated. In the early 1990s, overcrowding became an issue for those concerned with juvenile justice. It had already been identified as an important issue in adult facilities; being linked to increases in negative behaviors and higher levels of stress

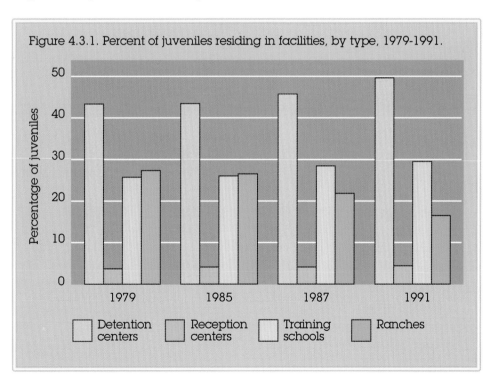

Figure 4.3.1. Percent of juveniles residing in facilities, by type, 1979-1991.

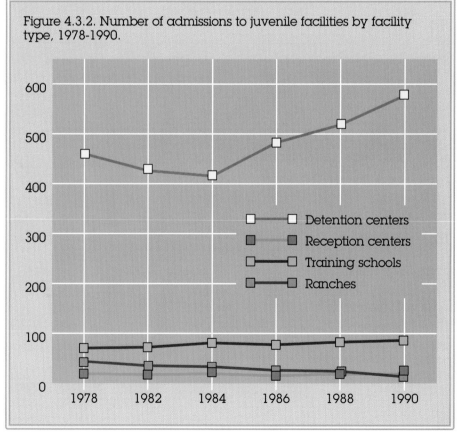

Figure 4.3.2. Number of admissions to juvenile facilities by facility type, 1978-1990.

among residents. Figure 4.3.6 provides data on the extent to which juvenile facilities conform to federal standards pertaining to adequate living space, education, security, and health/medical services (see page 151).

In 1987, only 36.0 percent of the juveniles confined were housed in facilities whose average daily population exceeded reported design capacity (Figure 4.3.7). By 1991, this number had increased to 47.0 percent. Officials began to worry that with larger numbers of juveniles entering the criminal justice system, overcrowding would increase, leading to heightened anxiety and hostility among residents. More important, it was possible that residents would resort to spending more time in their cells and have less access to rehabilitative programs.

Education is the foundation for programming in most juvenile institutions. State laws that require youngsters to attend school until a specified age apply to youth in confinement as well. Instruction may be tutoring, academic classes, individual study, or vocational classes.

Four assessment criteria are used to evaluate the quality of education in juvenile facilities: (1) provision of education; (2) qualifications of educational staff; (3) minimum class size/student teacher ratio of 15 to 1; and (4) educational assessments. The majority of all juveniles are held in facilities that conform to all applicable criteria (see Table 4.3.3, page 139). They are more likely than not to be in programs where all teachers are certified and assessments are undertaken.

Figure 4.3.8 shows the percent of confined juveniles in facilities that conform to minimum supervision (staffing) ratios over time. The NAC standard staffing ratio of 1:12 applies to all facilities except training schools. For training schools staff size standard ratio is 1:10 during waking hours and 1:20 during normal sleeping hours. Supervision standards are designed to limit escapes and walkaways, protect juveniles from harming each other, and provide a

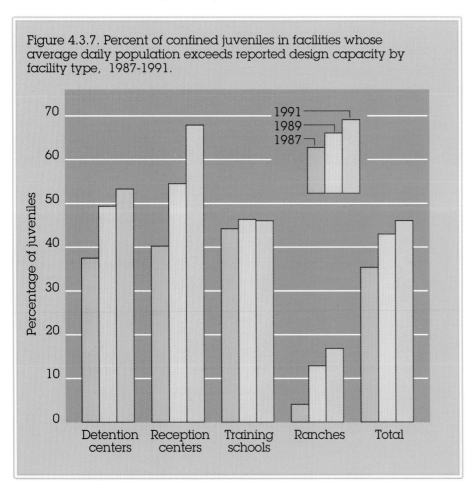

Figure 4.3.7. Percent of confined juveniles in facilities whose average daily population exceeds reported design capacity by facility type, 1987-1991.

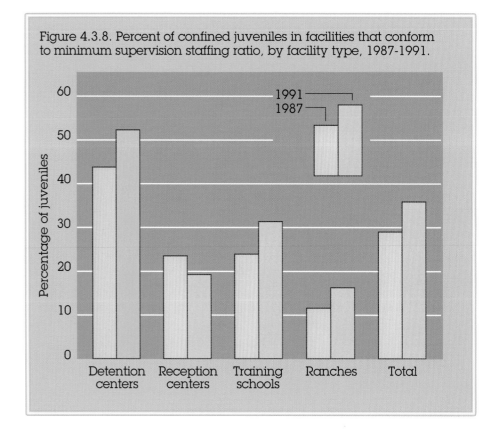

Figure 4.3.8. Percent of confined juveniles in facilities that conform to minimum supervision staffing ratio, by facility type, 1987-1991.

stable environment for training and other services. National standards express a preference for relying on staff rather than on hardware to provide security and in general require facilities to adopt the least restrictive security alternative consistent with

safety and restriction of escapes.

Conformance to staffing ratios improved for all facilities between 1987 and 1991, the one exception being reception centers (see Figure 4.3.8, page 138). In 1987, only 29.0 percent of juvenile offenders were in facilities that conformed to staffing ratios. By 1991, this number had increased to 36.0 percent. For reception centers the number of juveniles in facilities that conformed declined from 23.0 percent to 19.0 percent.

The juvenile justice system places more emphasis on rehabilitation of residents than does the adult justice system. Juveniles with severe psychological problems are an increasing source of concern in correctional institutions. Rehabilitation is thought to be more effective if residents' psychological problems can be addressed effectively. State and federal courts have ruled that children should receive psychological services, counseling,

and other mental health services from trained staff. Eighty seven percent of juveniles are in facilities that have mental health professionals available. Only 68.0 percent however are in facilities that have a counselor to resident ratio of 1:25, the designated minimum criteria.

DEATHS IN JUVENILE DETENTION AND ADULT CORRECTIONAL FACILITIES

Below are data on deaths in juvenile detention and correctional facilities by region. With the exception of death from "illness," deaths are higher in public facilities than private facilities. In both types of facilities, deaths from suicide are most common. Regionally, the west and the south stand out with the greatest percentage of juvenile deaths in the category "suicide." In neither category are the number of deaths greater than .01 percent of the total population in custody (see Table 4.3.4, page 140).

According to the U.S. Department of Justice, one-half million children are held in adult lock-ups. Ten percent of these children are under the age of 14 and many are abused and/or neglected and have committed no crime. The vast majority of children (28.0 percent of those held) are detained for status offenses such as underage drinking, disobeying parents, and/or running away.

Looking at Table 4.3.4 tells only half the story of the dangers of children in incarceration. Children are eight times more likely to commit suicide when they are in adult centers than when they are appropriately housed in juvenile detention facilities. They are also more likely to be raped, beaten, or killed by other inmates.

Table 4.3.2. Total number of juvenile facilities, 1979-1991.

Year	Detention centers	Reception centers	Facility type training schools	Ranches	Totals
1979	405.0	35.0	240.0	255.0	935.0
1983	410.0	32.5	265.0	265.0	972.5
1985	425.0	40.0	255.0	260.0	980.0
1987	450.0	40.0	280.0	215.0	985.0
1989	460.0	45.0	290.0	195.0	990.0
1991	480.0	42.5	285.0	160.0	967.5

Table 4.3.3. Percent of juveniles in facilities that conform to assessment criteria on providing basic education, by facility type, 1991.

Assessment criteria	Detention centers	Reception centers	Training schools	Ranches	Total
Provision of education	95.0	92.0	97.0	96.0	96.0
All teachers are certified	92.0	97.0	77.0	89.0	84.0
Minimum teacher to student ratio	76.0	88.0	94.0	58.0	85.0
Educational assessments	N/A	80.0	78.0	55.0	74.0
Percent of juveniles in facilities that:					
Conform to all applicable criteria	61.0	69.0	55.0	29.0	55.0
Conform to three criteria	36.0	29.0	34.0	32.0	34.0
Conform to two criteria	3.0	2.0	9.0	34.0	9.0
Conform to fewer than two criteria	0.0	0.0	2.0	5.0	2.0

Table 4.3.4. Deaths in juvenile detention and correctional facilities by region, 1988.

	Total		Illness		Suicide		Homicide		Other	
	Number	Percent	Number	Percent	Number	Percent	Number	Percent	Number	Percent
Public facilities										
Total	33	100.0	2	6.0	17	52.0	6	18.0	8	24.0
Northeast	3	100.0	0	0.0	1	33.0	1	33.0	1	33.0
Midwest	4	100.0	1	25.0	2	50.0	0	0.0	1	25.0
South	13	100.0	0	0.0	7	54.0	3	23.0	3	23.0
West	13	100.0	1	8.0	7	54.0	2	15.0	3	23.0
Private facilities										
Total	23	100.0	2	9.0	7	30.0	2	9.0	12	52.0
Northeast	4	100.0	1	25.0	1	25.0	0	0.0	2	50.0
Midwest	7	100.0	0	0.0	2	29.0	1	14.0	4	57.0
South	4	100.0	0	0.0	2	50.0	0	0.0	2	50.0
West	8	100.0	1	13.0	2	25.0	1	13.0	4	50.0

4.4

YOUTH AS AGENTS OF CRIME AND AS VICTIMS
CHILDREN AS AGENTS OF CRIME

In 1995, juveniles were responsible for 19.1 percent of all arrests. This figure is up from 16.0 percent in 1992. Table 4.4.1 lists arrests of juveniles by state (see page 156). Leading the nation in total arrests of juveniles are California, Texas, New York, Florida, and Wisconsin. Utah, North Dakota, Wisconsin, Idaho, and South Dakota lead the nation in terms of the proportion of juvenile arrests (see Figure 4.4.1, page 152). Not evident in this information, yet very disturbing, is the increase in the use of firearms in juvenile crime. Juveniles' use of guns in homicides increased from 64.0 percent to 78.0 percent between 1987 and 1991. Firearms accounted for 77.0 percent of all homicides during that period.

Juvenile involvement in violent crimes (murder, forcible rape, robbery, and aggravated assault) has also increased over time. Between 1983 and 1992, the total number of juveniles arrested for all violent crimes increased by 17.0 percent. The number of juveniles arrested for murder increased by 128.0 percent (see Table 4.4.2, page 156). In 1992, juveniles were involved in 15.0 percent of all murder arrests; 16.0 percent of all forcible rapes; 26 percent of all arrests for robbery; and 15.0 percent of all arrests for aggravated assaults.

Because the size of the juvenile population fluctuates over time, an arrest rate is preferred over number or percent of arrests. Looking at the arrest rate presents a slightly different picture. As Figure 4.4.2 shows, the juvenile violent crime arrest rate reached its highest point in 1992 (see page 141). The FBI estimates that there were 198 violent crime arrests of juveniles for every 100,000 juveniles in the U.S. population. Figures 4.4.3 through 4.4.6 on page 153 show the arrest rates for robbery as well as for each

of the three components of the Violent Crime Index (murder, forcible rape, and aggravated assault).

CHILDREN AS VICTIMS OF CRIME

While public concern continues over the epidemic of crimes committed by juveniles, national statistics indicate that young people are much more likely to be victims of violent crimes than adults (see Figure 4.4.7, page 154). Teenagers account for 14.0 percent of the population age 12 and over, yet they experienced 30.0 percent of all violent crimes. In 1992, 1.55 million violent crimes were committed against people ages 12-17. This is a 23.0 percent increase over the past five years. In 1991, one of every 10 19-year-olds had been a victim of a violent crime (see Figure 4.4.8, page 154).

There are important demographic differences among teenage victims of crime. Those who live in central cities are at higher risk of violent crime than those in suburban and nonmetropolitan areas. However, incidents involving younger crime victims

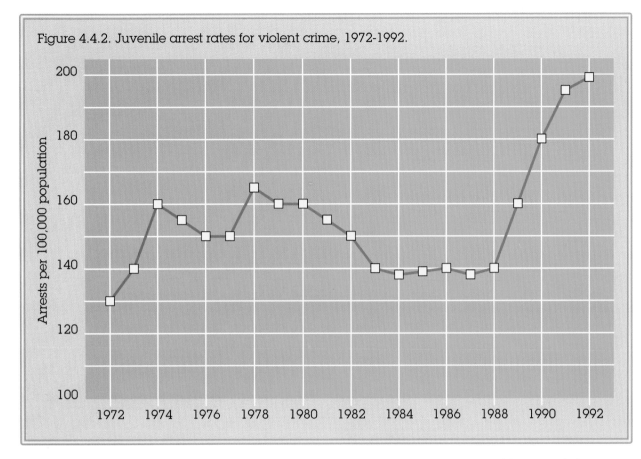

Figure 4.4.2. Juvenile arrest rates for violent crime, 1972-1992.

are increasing in more affluent suburban and rural areas. Among younger teens, the rate is 50.0 percent higher. For homicides in particular, the victimization rate is higher among males and African Americans (see Figures 4.4.9 and 4.4.10, page 142). Homicide is the leading cause of death for young African American men and women.

Young people in America face a significant risk of harm in streets, schools, work places, and at home. Violent crimes with juvenile victims were nearly as likely to occur at home (25.0 percent) as in or around school (23.0 percent). One of every 3 violent crimes committed against juveniles occurred on the street. Poor youth in

distressed inner-city neighborhoods have the highest chance of being crime victims.

According to child advocates, it is not surprising that children and youth are susceptible to having their wallets, sneakers, jackets, bikes, and countless other possessions stolen—they are the easiest of prey. They have the least money, power, and resources to protect themselves. Moreover, they are often too afraid (or don't know how) to report their attacker.

Though the figures are appalling in and of themselves, the statistical picture only addresses numbers. A more important issue is why? Why does a 15-year-old decide to kill a classmate rather than walk

away? Why is a drive-by shooting a rite of passage for youth in gangs? Why is it no longer acceptable to merely apologize or accept an apology?

YOUTH VIOLENCE AS A PUBLIC HEALTH ISSUE

Violence among children is a complex issue. The Center for Disease Control and the National Center for Injury Prevention and Control view violence as a public health problem because of its impact on the health and well-being of American youth. The public health approach identifies patterns and risk factors, implements interventions, and evaluates effectiveness on the structural or societal scale. Weakened community structures/institutions, weak parental control, absence of role models and recognition, disconnection, sustained poverty, discrimination, and lack of opportunities for education and employment are important risk factors for violence. These are discussed below.

COMMUNITY STRUCTURES AND INSTITUTIONS

Many studies reveal that increases in crime and violence are signals that the frontline institutions and the formal social controls they are charged with inculcating have failed to hold. They assert that deviance or criminality results both from the failure of formal and informal social controls. Community structures can fall short in a number of ways. They can fail to induce conformity to law-abiding norms or they can generate controls that inhibit conformity.

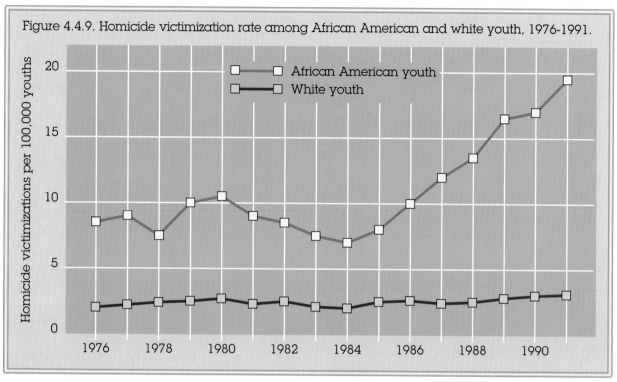

Figure 4.4.9. Homicide victimization rate among African American and white youth, 1976-1991.

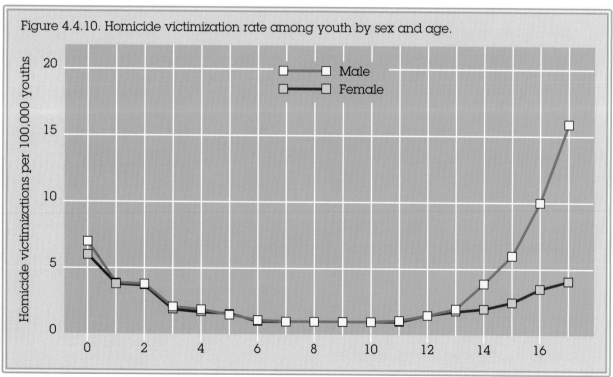

Figure 4.4.10. Homicide victimization rate among youth by sex and age.

PARENTAL CONTROL

Garbarino and Gilliam (1980), noted advocates for children, maintain that overall quality of life for families is a factor in youth violence. Families are vulnerable to stresses and frustrations imposed by the demands of everyday life. These stresses, combined with weakened community control, give rise to a peer control system. Often this peer control system supports co-offending and presents challenge to parental authority. Advocates argue that what is needed is for the nuclear family to overcome its social isolation and privacy.

ABSENCE OF ROLE AND RECOGNITION

Numerous researchers claim that many deeds of violence in U.S. society are performed by those trying to establish their self-esteem, to defend their self-image, and to demonstrate that they too are significant. Teens with little education and low self-esteem resort to *macho* displays of violence to preserve a "twisted sense of dignity." Lacking role models who exhibit other behaviors, violence becomes an acceptable mode as teens kill merely to save face.

DISCONNECTION

Teens need to interact with adults in the community to gain a sense of place and a stake in the community, as well as a useful and responsible role in it. If these are lacking, many youths may disconnect from the anchors of family, school, work, community, and the future. If teens do not view themselves as being subscribers to the social contract to which the rest of us subscribe, they will see no sense in following it.

POVERTY

There is general agreement that poverty contributes to child violence. Poverty leads to frustration and anxiety, which trigger aggression. In contemporary U.S. society, where material success is highly valued and a symbol of "worth," having too little or too few resources inevitably results in feelings of low self-esteem and self-worth. These feelings are compensated for by behaviors that display visible signs of power that are often violent.

DISCRIMINATION IN EMPLOYMENT AND EDUCATION

Society in the United States often submits its youth to confusing, conflicted, and impossible demands. When it stresses the importance of achieving certain goals but denies legitimate ways (such as job programs) to achieve those goals, discontent is to be expected. When people feel that existing norms are unjust, they withdraw support for them and seek other avenues. The result for juveniles is a conflicted culture characterized by malicious and violent activities that symbolize protest against the meaninglessness of the social experience.

At the same time that children are so engulfed in violence, they also exhibit a freshness, a vigor, and an undaunted spirit. If given an opportunity, they are eager to explore their community and test their abilities and skills.

CHILDREN AS VICTIMS OF ABUSE AND NEGLECT

The term "child abuse" for many brings to mind images of a tiny baby born to chronically poor, uneducated, often drug/alcohol addicted parents and covered with bruises, swollen welts, dirt, and filth. Not always so. The term covers a wide range of actions and failures of parents differing greatly in severity. Consider the following scenarios:

"(1) A three-year-old in Tennessee was forced by her stepfather to walk for three days and three nights until she died of exhaustion.

(2) Three children aged two to ten were found by police at 9:30 p.m. in an apartment to which police had been summoned by neighbors' complaints that the children had been left alone. The children who were barefoot and in their underwear said they had not been fed since morning, when their mother left them locked in the apartment. The mother arrived at 10:30 p.m. from her job as a cocktail waitress. She angrily protested that she had done nothing wrong.

(3) A seven-year-old in California was locked in a room and tied to a chair by her parents for her whole life; when found she weighed only 35 lbs and was only 33 inches tall and unable to talk.

(4) A judge returned a seven-year-old to her deaf parents, admonishing the protective agency that had removed her and placed her in a foster home in the belief that the parents, because of their deafness, could not give the child emotional support and the intellectual stimulation needed for development.

(5) An infant sustained permanent damage from maggots in her ears, maggots that swarmed over the feces-laden rags on which she lay."

Nowhere is there a clear-cut definition of what constitutes child abuse. When it comes to defining parental actions as abusive or neglectful, there are serious difficulties. One difficulty is philosophical. In America, there is a strong presumption for parental autonomy in child-rearing. Parents have the right to rear their children in ways they think are best. These rights are not absolute, however, and in spite of the importance of family integrity there are instances where a child's rights to basic needs—food, clothing, shelter, education, and a safe environment—outweigh the parents' rights to autonomy. Laws against child abuse and neglect are designed to regulate parental behavior. They are an implicit recognition that parents rights are limited. Still, the basic assumption in the culture is, absent evidence to the contrary, that children are best served by protecting the integrity of the family. Thus, in seeking to protect helpless children, only suspicions are reported. The parents' innocence is presumed, unless evidence substantiating the allegation is found. The consequences of "making a mistake" are irreparable for the parents, the child, and society as a whole.

Another difficulty is cultural. Child rearing practices help develop character and behaviors in children that are valued by a particular culture. These practices are a basic building block of society. Ahn (1994), in her work on cross-cultural parenting practices and ideas found widely differing views on what was considered normal and abusive behavior and methods of discipline. In the United States in particular, with its high degree of cultural diversity, the problem is heightened. Almost a third of all child protective cases in the U.S. involve minority families. This has given rise to calls for "cultural sensitivity" in dealing with issues of abuse and neglect.

The only accepted statements on the subject of cultural sensitivity are that cultural issues must be considered in examining child abuse and neglect; child abuse investigators must take culture into account in performing their role, and policies should not be made strictly from the perspective of dominant cultural values and practices.

A third difficulty is created by difficulty in detection or clinical diagnosis. Consider the following:

"(1) Parents bring their child into a hospital emergency room with a complaint of fever. During the medical examination the doctors notice round red sores on the youngster's legs which they diagnose as possible cigarette burns. They later discover that the family has recently returned from a summer retreat and that the burns are actually infected mosquito bites.

(2) A mother brings her daughter to the hospital with small black and blue marks on various parts of the child's body. Doctors perform multiple tests and can find no organic basis for the bruising. Social workers who meet the mother find her appropriately concerned and do not think her capable of abuse.

(3) A four-year-old has a second-degree burn on his hand. The mother explains that her son had been tossing his plastic car into the air and that it fell into a sink of boiling water which she had prepared for the family wash. A plastic surgeon believes that the youngster would not have been

able to hold his hand under the water long enough to receive such a burn. A psychological evaluation of the child shows that he is persistent and strong willed when pursuing activities in which he is emotionally involved." [from Bourne and Newberger (1978)].

Being able to define child abuse is an important first step in detection and prevention. Until the problem of where to draw the line is solved and all ethnic groups are fully represented in the process of definition, definitions will remain unjust and inadequate.

The nation as a whole has experienced an increase in the number of reports of child abuse/neglect (Figure 4.4.11). According to the National Center on Child Abuse and Neglect (NCCAN), in 1992 child protective service agencies received and referred for investigation nearly 1.9 million

reports of alleged child abuse and neglect involving nearly 3 million children. Approximately one-third of the children were substantiated victims of maltreatment. The rate of substantiation has increased in recent years. Among victims of child abuse, roughly 50.0 percent suffered neglect, 23.0 percent physical abuse, 14.0 percent sexual abuse, 5.0 percent emotional maltreatment, 3.0 percent medical neglect and 9.0 percent other forms of maltreatment (see Figure 4.4.12, page 155).

It is unclear whether the large increase reflects increased public awareness more so than an actual increase in child maltreatment. Substantiated cases account for less than 50.0 percent of all cases reported. Nevertheless, there were approximately 1 million substantiated cases of child maltreatment. Studies have shown that most occur in the Midwest and the Southeast. Fifteen out of every 1,000 U.S. children

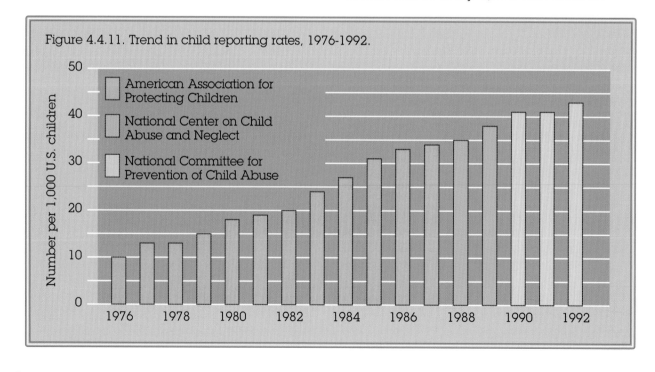

Figure 4.4.11. Trend in child reporting rates, 1976-1992.

were victims of maltreatment during 1993. Overwhelmingly, these abuses were committed by parents. Less than 2.0 percent were committed by day care/foster parents. (see Figure 4.4.13, page 155).

CHILD ABUSE FATALITIES

Every state in the United States currently has a mandatory reporting law. Despite this and the vigilance of professionals, there are still major gaps in efforts to protect children. Some children, despite injuries that are visible, are never brought to the attention of a child protective service agency. Others, though their plight is known, still suffer serious injuries in their homes.

In 1992, 133,523 abused children were removed from homes in 37 reporting states. Despite this number, courts are reluctant to terminate parental rights and remove children without exact and definitive proof of serious parental neglect or harm. Sadly, children die from neglect and abuse. The total number of fatalities nationwide for 1993 was estimated to be approximately 1,300. Since 1985, the rate of fatalities increased in most states (see Table 4.4.3, page 156). Almost half (42.0 percent) of these children were already known to the child protective services system.

Fifty-five percent of all child abuse fatalities result from physical abuse. Physical abuse includes striking, spanking, or shaking a child. Fatalities from physical abuse are followed by deaths caused by physical neglect (40.0 percent) and a combination of both activities (5.0 percent).

PRECURSORS OF CHILD MALTREATMENT

Little is known about why certain parents and caregivers abuse and/or neglect their children. However, individuals reported for child maltreatment often display a number of personality or psychodynamic problems which might be linked to abusive behavior. Often, abusive and negligent individuals have been abused themselves. Many have drug and/or alcohol problems. Others lack support from family, community, and other sources. Most are poor. Andrea Sedlak of Westat Corporation has reported that children in families with annual income of less than $15,000 are at greater risk of abuse (Sedlak 1992). Additional risk factors include family structure, family size, and metropolitan status of residential area. Poor families have insufficient resources to care for their children.

Placing blame exclusively on individuals, however, fails to consider the structural or institutional context in which abuse arises. It fails to recognize the importance of inequality and the sense of frustration, repression, and aggression that results. By concentrating on dangerous people, it denies dangerous situations (Parton 1992). It also blinds us to abusive practices of industrial, corporate, and government agencies

DEMOGRAPHICS OF CHILD VICTIMS

The National Child Abuse and Neglect Data System project (NCANDS), funded by the National Center on Child Abuse and Neglect (NCCAN) reports that the median age of child victims was 6 years; roughly 27.0 percent were ages 3 and under, and 52.0 percent were below age 7 (see Figure 4.4.14, page 155). Fifty-three percent were female and 46.0 percent were male. The racial/ethnic breakdown of child victims is disproportionately high among blacks (see Figure 4.4.15, page 155).

FAMILY PRESERVATION

Removing children who have been victims or who are alleged to be victims of abuse and neglect and placing them in foster care has long been supported by federal policy. New thinking on this issue, however, has prompted a shift in such policy, and federal funds are now being spent toward preventive and family reunification services. Both the Adoption Assistance and Child Welfare Act and the more recent Family Preservation and Support Services legislation back such reform efforts.

Definitions of Child Maltreatment

It is generally agreed that definitions of child abuse and neglect should reflect the following considerations:

(1) Physical abuse. Physical acts (such as striking, punching, kicking, biting, throwing, burning, or violent shaking) that caused or could have caused physical injury to the child. Reasonable corporal punishment, as long as it is reasonable and not excessive, is not child abuse and it is therefore not reportable;

(2) Sexual abuse. Vaginal, anal or oral intercourse; vaginal or anal penetrations; or other forms of contacts for sexual purposes;

(3) Sexual exploitation. Using a child in prostitution, pornography, or other sexually exploitative activities;

(continued on next page)

Definitions of Child Maltreatment (con't)

(4) Physical neglect. Failing to provide needed care (such as food, clothing, shelter, protection from hazardous environments, care or supervision appropriate to the child's age or development, hygiene and medical care) that caused, or over time would cause, serious harm;

(5) Abandonment. Leaving a child alone or in the care of another under circumstances that demonstrate an intentional abdication of parental responsibility; and/or

(6) Psychological maltreatment. Acts or omissions that caused or could cause serious conduct, cognitive affective or other mental disorders. (This category is often labeled emotional maltreatment.) Child Protective Services agencies generally adopt a two tiered approach to the definition of psychological maltreatment. For extreme acts such as torture and close confinement, no demonstrable harm to the child is required. For less severe acts, such as habitual scapegoating, belittling and rejecting behavior, demonstrable harm is required. Emotionally abusive behaviors can include constant rejection, terrorizing, refusal to provide basic nutriance, refusal to get help for child's psychological problems, exposing a child to corruption including drug abuse, criminal behavior, etc.; and the failure to provide physical and mental stimulation needed to grow.

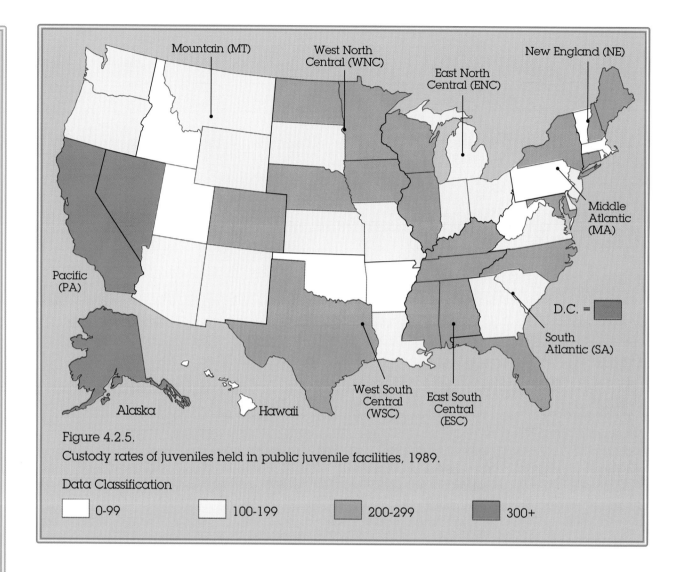

Figure 4.2.5.
Custody rates of juveniles held in public juvenile facilities, 1989.

Data Classification

| 0-99 | 100-199 | 200-299 | 300+ |

Table 4.2.1. Police disposition of juvenile offenders taken into custody, 1993 (1993 estimated population).

Population group	Total	Handled within department and released	Referred to juvenile court jurisdiction	Referred to welfare agency	Referred to other police agency	Referred to adult court
All agencies						
Number	1,286,903	329,166	865,630	19,307	11,149	61,651
Percent	100.0	25.6	67.3	1.5	0.9	4.8
All cities						
Number	1,091,890	285,795	729,947	15,659	9,121	51,368
Percent	100.0	26.2	66.9	1.4	0.8	4.7
Cities 250,000 and over						
Number	278,301	74,268	197,560	2,387	1,670	2,416
Percent	100.0	26.7	71.0	0.9	0.6	0.9
Cities 100,000 to 249,999						
Number	142,679	32,584	99,886	2,943	1,077	6,189
Percent	100.0	22.8	70.0	2.1	0.8	4.3
Cities 50,000 to 99,999						
Number	178,468	52,753	110,818	3,220	1,832	9,845
Percent	100.0	29.6	62.1	1.8	1.0	5.5
Cities 25,000 to 49,999						
Number	154,944	40,793	103,512	1,952	1,993	6,694
Percent	100.0	26.3	66.8	1.3	1.3	4.3
Cities 10,000 to 24,999						
Number	179,196	46,064	117,110	2,384	1,304	12,334
Percent	100.0	25.7	65.4	1.3	0.7	6.9
Cities under 10,000						
Number	158,302	39,333	101,061	2,773	1,245	13,890
Percent	100.0	34.8	63.8	1.8	0.8	8.8
Suburban counties						
Number	140,672	32,877	97,858	2,153	1,452	6,332
Percent	100.0	23.4	69.6	1.5	1.0	4.5
Rural counties						
Number	54,341	10,494	37,825	1,495	576	3,951
Percent	100.0	19.3	69.6	2.8	1.1	7.3
Suburban area						
Number	577,143	160,331	369,033	6,966	6,450	34,363
Percent	100.0	27.8	63.9	1.2	1.1	6.0

Table 4.3.1 Agencies administering juvenile facilities run by state authorities, 1991.

	Total facilities	State-run facilities
United States	1077	571
Alabama	22	12
Alaska	5	0
Arizona	16	11
Arkansas	10	5
California	106	95
Colorado	9	0
Connecticut	4	0
Delaware	3	0
District of Columbia	4	4
Florida	51	2
Georgia	28	1
Hawaii	2	0
Idaho	3	1
Illinois	20	13
Indiana	33	28
Iowa	12	12
Kansas	12	8
Kentucky	34	10
Louisiana	15	12
Maine	1	0
Maryland	15	1
Massachusetts	9	0
Michigan	46	27
Minnesota	19	13
Mississippi	8	6
Missouri	42	24
Montana	5	0
Nebraska	4	2
Nevada	9	7
New Hampshire	2	0
New Jersey	53	28
New Mexico	14	4
New York	78	8
North Carolina	24	15
North Dakota	3	1
Ohio	64	56
Oklahoma	16	5
Oregon	15	6
Pennsylvania	35	25
Rhode Island	2	0
South Carolina	11	1
South Dakota	6	2
Tennessee	22	5
Texas	56	40
Utah	17	1
Vermont	1	0
Virginia	61	53
Washington	30	18
West Virginia	7	2
Wisconsin	11	7
Wyoming	2	0

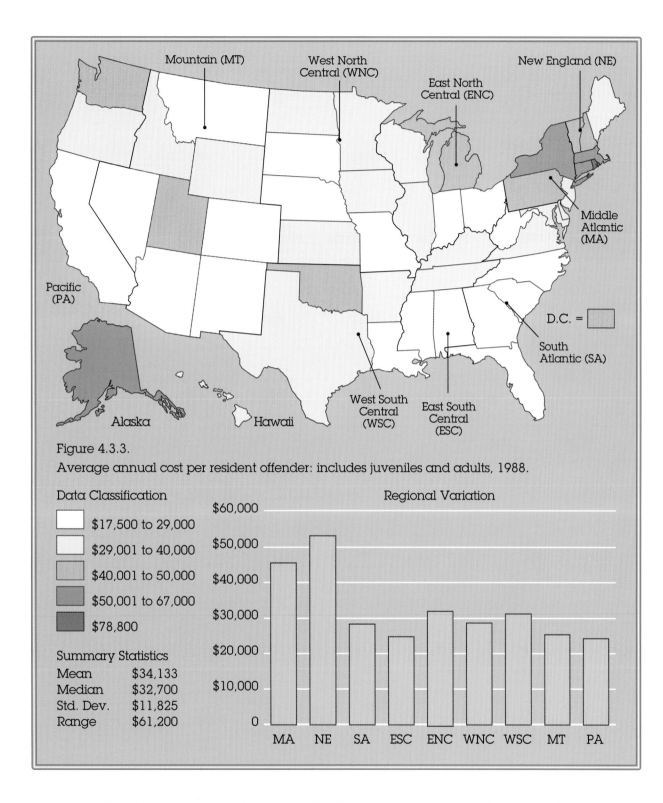

Figure 4.3.3.
Average annual cost per resident offender: includes juveniles and adults, 1988.

Data Classification

☐	$17,500 to 29,000
☐	$29,001 to 40,000
☐	$40,001 to 50,000
☐	$50,001 to 67,000
☐	$78,800

Summary Statistics

Mean	$34,133
Median	$32,700
Std. Dev.	$11,825
Range	$61,200

Regional Variation

Total and per-resident annual operating costs for adult and juvenile criminals in public facilities, 1988.

	Total annual cost (in thousands)	Cost per resident
Alabama	$16,252	$19,400
Alaska	9,925	54,500
Arizona	21,574	20,700
Arkansas	8,756	34,100
California	415,329	23,300
Colorado	14,017	26,500
Connecticut	15,812	57,500
Delaware	4,231	33,300
District of Columbia	18,051	42,600
Florida	53,385	22,900
Georgia	36,508	25,800
Hawaii	4,237	34,400
Idaho	4,938	39,500
Illinois	57,784	33,400
Indiana	31,356	21,500
Iowa	13,686	29,300
Kansas	21,778	33,100
Kentucky	18,856	32,100
Louisiana	26,269	24,600
Maine	7,733	31,400
Maryland	29,715	33,200
Massachusetts	12,592	55,500
Michigan	79,745	42,900
Minnesota	25,730	37,100
Mississippi	7,664	18,500
Missouri	23,341	26,200
Montana	5,263	27,700
Nebraska	6,421	22,000
Nevada	15,315	28,800
New Hampshire	6,063	45,900
New Jersey	65,854	35,700
New Mexico	13,051	24,600
New York	126,971	55,300
North Carolina	25,385	29,000
North Dakota	2,846	30,300
Ohio	81,363	25,300
Oklahoma	13,431	40,800
Oregon	20,529	34,300
Pennsylvania	50,489	45,700
Rhode Island	10,162	78,800
South Carolina	14,316	23,600
South Dakota	3,845	17,600
Tennessee	26,287	29,400
Texas	67,997	31,400
Utah	8,521	40,400
Vermont	1,150	50,000
Virginia	49,661	32,700
Washington	46,839	41,100
West Virginia	3,771	25,700
Wisconsin	23,401	34,800
Wyoming	5,816	36,600

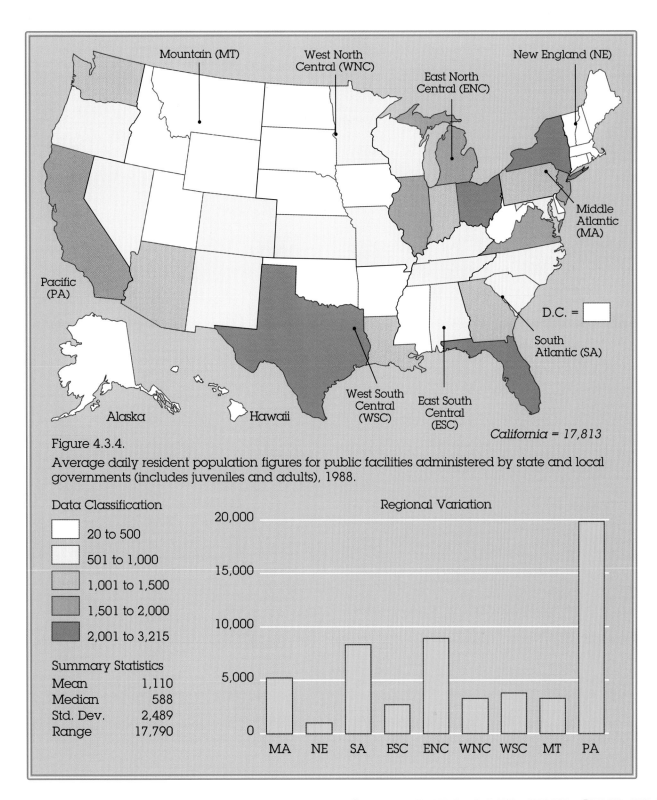

Mountain (MT)
West North Central (WNC)
East North Central (ENC)
New England (NE)
Middle Atlantic (MA)
Pacific (PA)
South Atlantic (SA)
West South Central (WSC)
East South Central (ESC)
Alaska
Hawaii
D.C. =
California = 17,813

Figure 4.3.4.

Average daily resident population figures for public facilities administered by state and local governments (includes juveniles and adults), 1988.

Data Classification

	20 to 500
	501 to 1,000
	1,001 to 1,500
	1,501 to 2,000
	2,001 to 3,215

Summary Statistics

Mean	1,110
Median	588
Std. Dev.	2,489
Range	17,790

Regional Variation

(bar chart with categories: MA, NE, SA, ESC, ENC, WNC, WSC, MT, PA; y-axis 0 to 20,000)

Number of facilities and average daily resident population (includes juveniles and adults), 1988.

	Number of facilities	Resident population
Alabama	23	837
Alaska	4	182
Arizona	17	1,041
Arkansas	7	257
California	113	17,813
Colorado	9	528
Connecticut	4	275
Delaware	3	127
District of Columbia	4	424
Florida	55	2,334
Georgia	28	1,415
Hawaii	2	123
Idaho	3	125
Illinois	20	1,730
Indiana	33	1,458
Iowa	14	467
Kansas	13	658
Kentucky	31	588
Louisiana	17	1,066
Maine	1	246
Maryland	17	895
Massachusetts	10	227
Michigan	44	1,861
Minnesota	16	694
Mississippi	8	414
Missouri	44	891
Montana	3	190
Nebraska	4	292
Nevada	9	532
New Hampshire	3	132
New Jersey	58	1,846
New Mexico	13	530
New York	92	2,297
North Carolina	24	874
North Dakota	2	94
Ohio	65	3,215
Oklahoma	16	329
Oregon	13	598
Pennsylvania	34	1,104
Rhode Island	2	129
South Carolina	11	606
South Dakota	5	219
Tennessee	21	895
Texas	56	2,166
Utah	16	211
Vermont	1	23
Virginia	64	1,520
Washington	30	1,139
West Virginia	7	147
Wisconsin	9	672
Wyoming	2	159

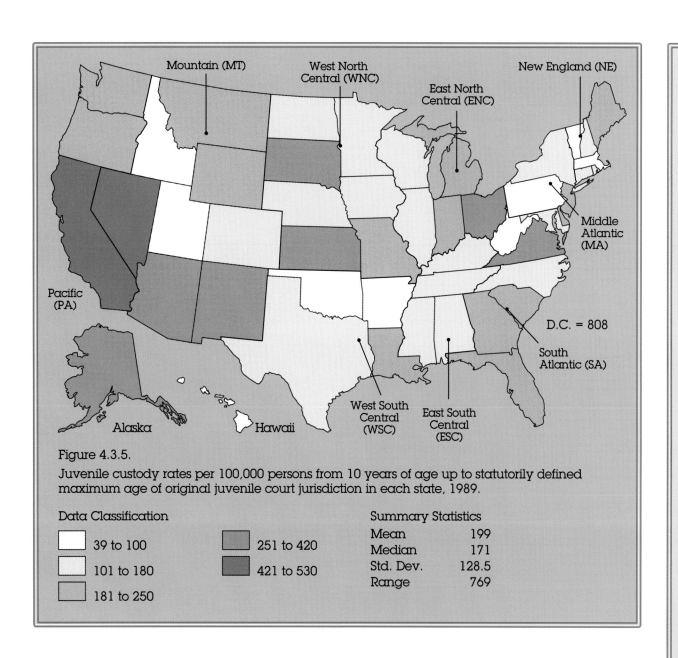

Figure 4.3.5.

Juvenile custody rates per 100,000 persons from 10 years of age up to statutorily defined maximum age of original juvenile court jurisdiction in each state, 1989.

Data Classification

☐	39 to 100	▨	251 to 420
☐	101 to 180	▨	421 to 530
☐	181 to 250		

Summary Statistics

Mean	199
Median	171
Std. Dev.	128.5
Range	769

Juvenile resident population count and custody rate, 1989.

	Number of juveniles	Custody rate (per 100,000)
Alabama	895	178
Alaska	191	324
Arizona	1,089	279
Arkansas	266	91
California	15,869	529
Colorado	566	164
Connecticut	297	124
Delaware	146	206
District of Columbia	396	808
Florida	2,284	193
Georgia	1,595	233
Hawaii	89	79
Idaho	115	85
Illinois	1,803	165
Indiana	1,340	203
Iowa	447	143
Kansas	720	264
Kentucky	614	138
Louisiana	1,074	231
Maine	262	194
Maryland	792	166
Massachusetts	227	48
Michigan	1,957	208
Minnesota	641	136
Mississippi	453	132
Missouri	1,008	207
Montana	207	223
Nebraska	299	166
Nevada	566	510
New Hampshire	136	114
New Jersey	1,957	247
New Mexico	524	283
New York	2,348	171
North Carolina	886	164
North Dakota	93	124
Ohio	3,387	273
Oklahoma	322	89
Oregon	628	208
Pennsylvania	1,125	90
Rhode Island	128	131
South Carolina	767	209
South Dakota	218	269
Tennessee	972	171
Texas	2,350	133
Utah	224	85
Vermont	24	39
Virginia	1,619	258
Washington	1,198	236
West Virginia	171	76
Wisconsin	701	130
Wyoming	137	217

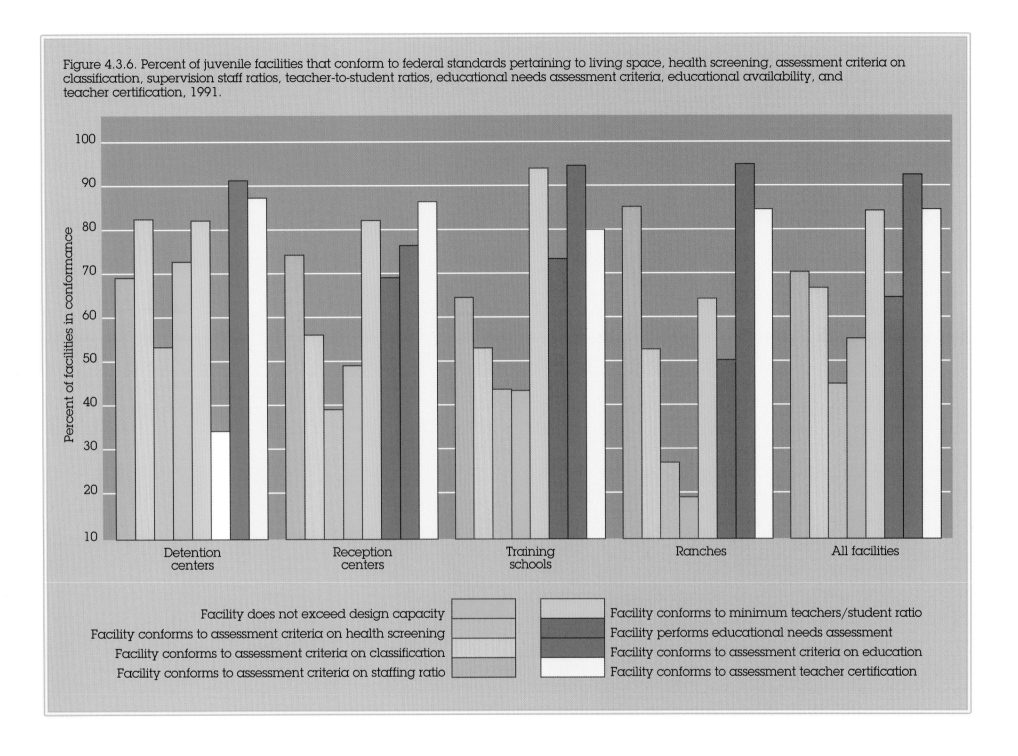

Figure 4.3.6. Percent of juvenile facilities that conform to federal standards pertaining to living space, health screening, assessment criteria on classification, supervision staff ratios, teacher-to-student ratios, educational needs assessment criteria, educational availability, and teacher certification, 1991.

Percent of facilities in conformance

100
90
80
70
60
50
40
30
20
10

Detention centers   Reception centers   Training schools   Ranches   All facilities

Facility does not exceed design capacity
Facility conforms to assessment criteria on health screening
Facility conforms to assessment criteria on classification
Facility conforms to assessment criteria on staffing ratio

Facility conforms to minimum teachers/student ratio
Facility performs educational needs assessment
Facility conforms to assessment criteria on education
Facility conforms to assessment teacher certification

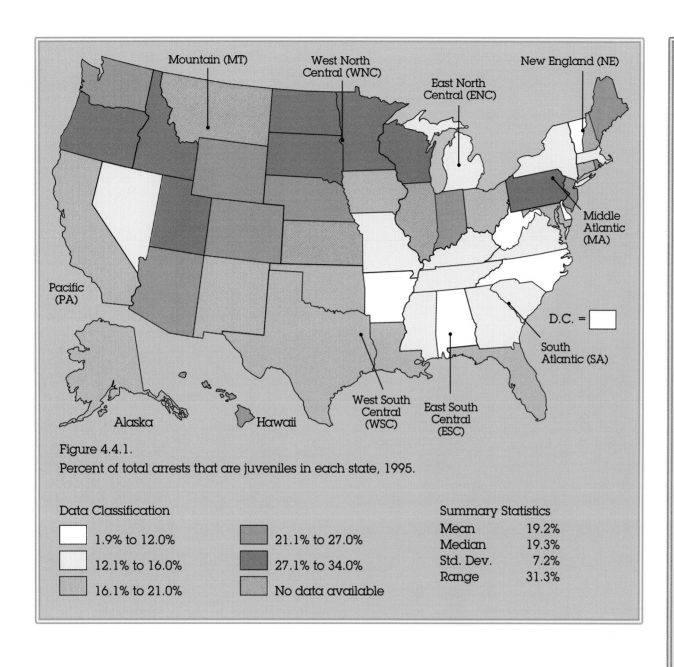

Figure 4.4.1.
Percent of total arrests that are juveniles in each state, 1995.

Data Classification

- 1.9% to 12.0%
- 12.1% to 16.0%
- 16.1% to 21.0%
- 21.1% to 27.0%
- 27.1% to 34.0%
- No data available

Summary Statistics

Mean	19.2%
Median	19.3%
Std. Dev.	7.2%
Range	31.3%

Number of juvenile arrests and the percent of total arrests that are juveniles, 1995.

	Juvenile arrests	% Juvenile arrests
Alabama	16,051	7.9
Alaska	5,647	17.0
Arizona	66,578	22.7
Arkansas	19,829	10.2
California	254,143	16.1
Colorado	41,053	24.5
Connecticut	33,259	17.8
Delaware	510	1.9
District of Columbia	3,916	9.1
Florida	147,531	19.3
Georgia	34,418	12.2
Hawaii	18,662	26.7
Idaho	23,716	30.5
Illinois	N/A	N/A
Indiana	38,434	24.0
Iowa	18,275	19.2
Kansas	n/a	N/A
Kentucky	13,585	13.6
Louisiana	37,788	19.4
Maine	7,477	22.4
Maryland	49,183	17.5
Massachusetts	22,973	14.5
Michigan	55,758	14.5
Minnesota	67,413	29.5
Mississippi	7,518	14.1
Missouri	36,309	13.8
Montana	N/A	N/A
Nebraska	17,202	21.2
Nevada	18,660	15.9
New Hampshire	N/A	N/A
New Jersey	88,724	22.2
New Mexico	9,262	21.0
New York	150,774	13.8
North Carolina	53,240	11.0
North Dakota	7,836	32.9
Ohio	63,407	20.6
Oklahoma	29,535	19.3
Oregon	34,532	29.3
Pennsylvania	19,464	27.7
Rhode Island	9,745	23.3
South Carolina	26,174	12.9
South Dakota	10,013	30.1
Tennessee	19,500	15.9
Texas	220,652	20.6
Utah	36,754	33.2
Vermont	402	10.1
Virginia	54,462	14.1
Washington	42,233	22.2
West Virginia	7,653	11.8
Wisconsin	138,396	32.1
Wyoming	6,919	23.0

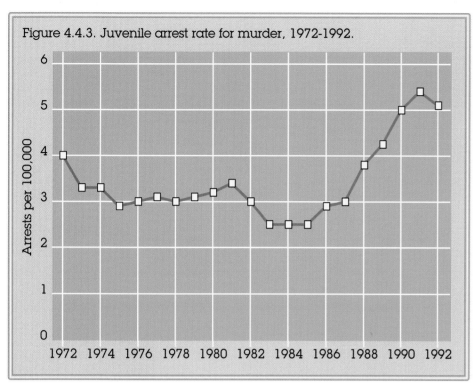

Figure 4.4.3. Juvenile arrest rate for murder, 1972-1992.

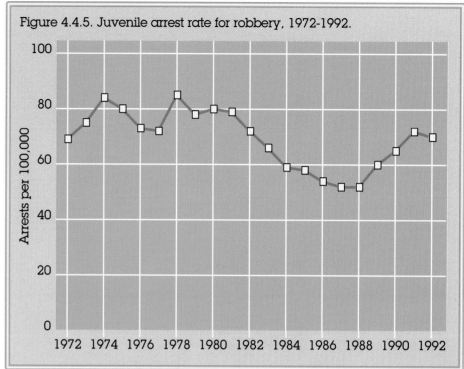

Figure 4.4.5. Juvenile arrest rate for robbery, 1972-1992.

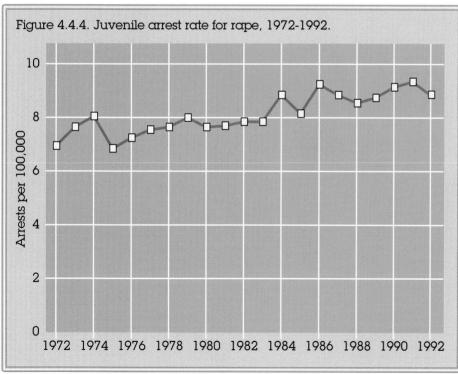

Figure 4.4.4. Juvenile arrest rate for rape, 1972-1992.

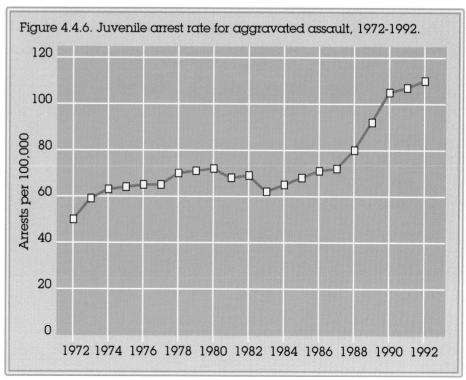

Figure 4.4.6. Juvenile arrest rate for aggravated assault, 1972-1992.

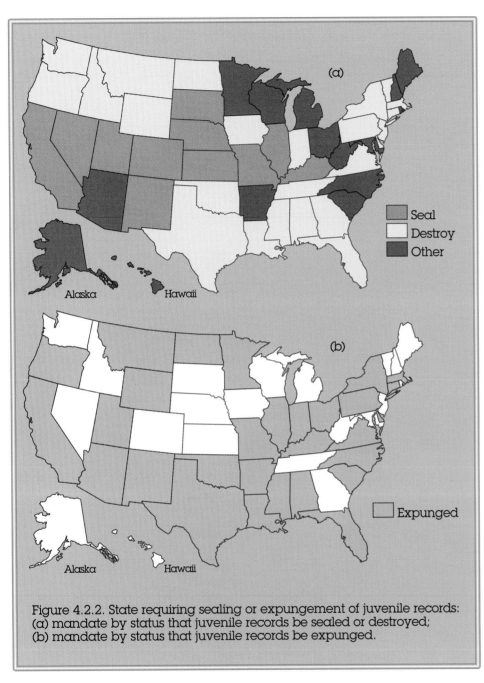

Figure 4.2.2. State requiring sealing or expungement of juvenile records:
(a) mandate by status that juvenile records be sealed or destroyed;
(b) mandate by status that juvenile records be expunged.

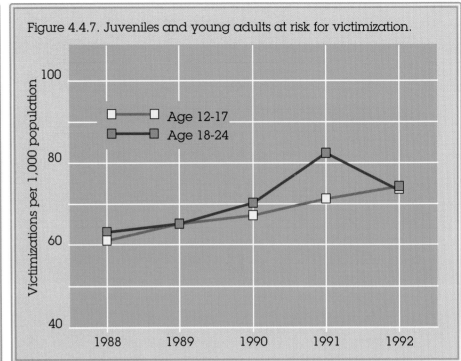

Figure 4.4.7. Juveniles and young adults at risk for victimization.

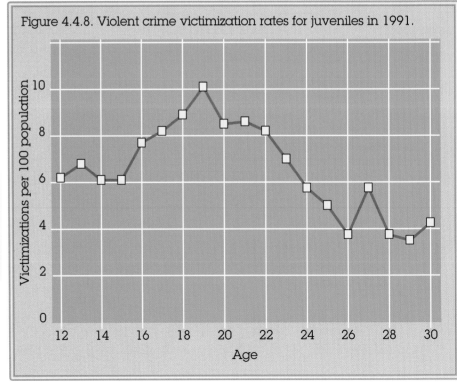

Figure 4.4.8. Violent crime victimization rates for juveniles in 1991.

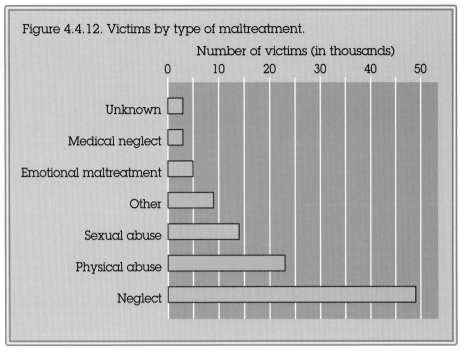

Figure 4.4.12. Victims by type of maltreatment.

Number of victims (in thousands)

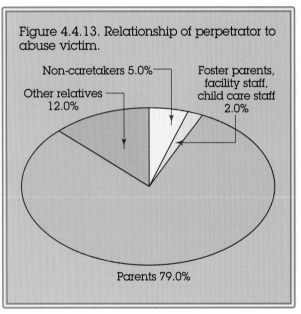

Figure 4.4.13. Relationship of perpetrator to abuse victim.

Non-caretakers 5.0%

Foster parents, facility staff, child care staff 2.0%

Other relatives 12.0%

Parents 79.0%

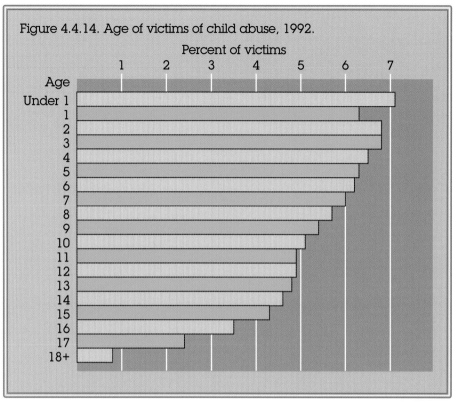

Figure 4.4.14. Age of victims of child abuse, 1992.

Percent of victims

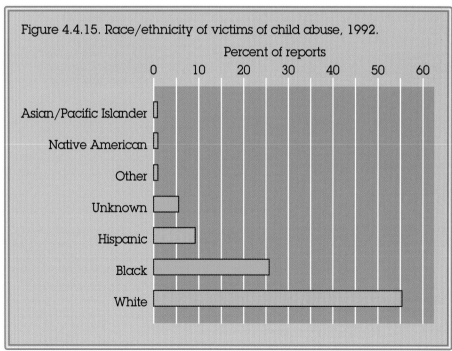

Figure 4.4.15. Race/ethnicity of victims of child abuse, 1992.

Percent of reports

Table 4.4.1. Total arrests by state and proportion of arrests that are juvenile, 1995.		
	Total	% under 18
Alabama	202,946	7.9
Alaska	33,220	17.0
Arizona	292,752	22.7
Arkansas	195,353	10.2
California	1,578,277	16.1
Colorado	167,842	24.5
Connecticut	186,902	17.8
Delaware	27,030	1.9
District of Columbia	43,239	9.1
Florida	766,240	19.3
Georgia	281,428	12.2
Hawaii	69,959	26.7
Idaho	77,839	30.5
Illinois	n/a	
Indiana	159,954	24.0
Iowa	95,070	19.2
Kansas	n/a	
Kentucky	99,981	13.6
Louisiana	194,629	19.4
Maine	33,356	22.4
Maryland	281,807	17.5
Massachusetts	158,142	14.5
Michigan	384,263	14.5
Minnesota	228,556	29.5
Mississippi	53,172	14.1
Missouri	263,054	13.8
Montana	n/a	
Nebraska	81,118	21.2
Nevada	117,434	15.9
New Hampshire	n/a	
New Jersey	400,392	22.2
New Mexico	44,049	21.0
New York	1,091,274	13.8
North Carolina	482,641	11.0
North Dakota	23,841	32.9
Ohio	307,506	20.6
Oklahoma	153,252	19.3
Oregon	117,987	29.3
Pennsylvania	70,336	27.7
Rhode Island	41,753	23.3
South Carolina	202,475	12.9
South Dakota	33,285	30.1
Tennessee	122,929	15.9
Texas	1,071,300	20.6
Utah	110,736	33.2
Vermont	3,990	10.1
Virginia	385,760	14.1
Washington	189,965	22.2
West Virginia	64,744	11.8
Wisconsin	431,689	32.1
Wyoming	30,108	23.0

Table 4.4.2. Changes in arrests of persons under age 18, 1983-1992.	
Offense	Percent change
Total	17.0
Crime index total (1)	16.0
Violent crime index (2)	57.0
Property crime index (3)	11.0
Murder	128.0
Forcible rape	25.0
Robbery	22.0
Aggravated assault	95.0
Burglary	-20.0
Larceny/theft	13.0
Motor vehicle theft	120.0
Arson	26.0
Other assaults	106.0
Forgery & counterfeiting	9.0
Fraud	-41.0
Embezzlement	35.0
Stolen property	39.0
Vandalism	34.0
Weapons	117.0
Prostitution	-54.0
Other sex offenses	41.0
Drug abuse violations	7.0
Gambling	25.0
Offenses against family/children	212.0
Driving under the influence	-52.0
Liquor laws	-12.0
Drunkenness	-47.0
Disorderly conduct	35.0
Vagrancy	36.0
All other offenses (except traffic)	3.0
Curfew & loitering	9.0
Runaways	31.0

Notes:
(1) Crime index is the combination of the violent crime index and the property crime index.

(2) Violent crime index is a combination of the offenses of murder, forcible rape, and aggravated assault.

(3) Property crime index is a combination of the offenses of burglary, larceny/theft, motor vehicle theft and arson.

Table 4.4.3. Child abuse and neglect-related fatalities, 1985 and 1993.		
	1985	1993
Alabama	n/a	25
Alaska	n/a	n/a
Arizona	n/a	24
Arkansas	9	9
California	18	n/a
Colorado	12	28
Connecticut	6	16
Delaware	2	n/a
District of Columbia	n/a	13
Florida	n/a	63
Georgia	n/a	12
Hawaii	1	0
Idaho	5	6
Illinois	53	76
Indiana	29	38
Iowa	9	6
Kansas	16	6
Kentucky	10	20
Louisiana	50	25
Maine	0	7
Maryland	8	29
Massachusetts	13	n/a
Michigan	11	n/a
Minnesota	6	n/a
Mississippi	n/a	15
Missouri	25	43
Montana	2	0
Nebraska	2	4
Nevada	6	8
New Hampshire	n/a	n/a
New Jersey	21	29
New Mexico	10	6
New York	63	n/a
North Carolina	4	n/a
North Dakota	0	2
Ohio	n/a	46
Oklahoma	16	23
Oregon	8	11
Pennsylvania	34	n/a
Rhode Island	5	7
South Carolina	21	n/a
South Dakota	4	5
Tennessee	n/a	15
Texas	113	114
Utah	8	n/a
Vermont	1	n/a
Virginia	14	43
Washington	27	9
West Virginia	n/a	5
Wisconsin	10	n/a
Wyoming	3	1

Chapter 5

Children in the Educational System

"We made a deal in this country: we're going to educate everybody's children, no matter what. And we're not holding up our end of the bargain."
—Tracy Kidder

5.1

INTRODUCTION

Recently, the United States became increasingly aware of critical issues surrounding the education of its children. The issues include changing demographics of the school-aged population, low academic performance, teacher qualifications, overall school quality, behavior in and around school facilities, and the overhaul of traditional school curriculum.

The success of individual industries, U.S. competitiveness in the global economy, and ultimately the structure and cohesiveness of American society hang in the balance of successful educational strategies. This chapter reviews the issues that are predominant in American education. A spatial description of these issues is offered in five sections—basic demographics of school-aged population, the American school system, school quality, student performance, and issues in contemporary education.

5.2

SCHOOL-AGE POPULATION
BASIC DEMOGRAPHICS

In 1960, the resident school-age popu-

lation of the United States, that is the population of children between 5 and 17 years of age, was 44,176,000. In 1997, the figure was 50,669,000—an increase of 14.7 percent. The resident school-age population, which is not to be confused with school enrollment, has slightly fewer females than males (48.8 percent versus 51.2 percent in 1997). It also has many more white youngsters (79.5 percent) than youngsters of other races (21.5 percent).

The nation's population is getting older. Median age in 1970 was 28.0 compared with 34.3 in 1995. As the U.S. ages, children make up a smaller part of the resident population. In 1970, 25.8 percent of the U.S. population was school-aged as opposed to 18.7 percent in 1995. During the same time period, children between 5 and 17 years of age dropped from 52,526,000 to 49,149,000 (6.4 percent) while younger children—those under 5 years of age—increased in numbers (17,163,000 to 19,591,000 or 14.1 percent), but decreased from 8.4 to 7.5 percent of the population.

The population of school-age children is expected to grow 5.8 percent from 50,669,000 in 1997 to 53,601,000 by 2010. By 2050, Americans of school age will account for 16.9 percent of the U.S. population having grown 31.0 percent in number from 1997.

With an estimated population of 267,645,000 people in 1997, 18.9 percent of the nation's citizens are between the ages of 5 and 17. Not surprisingly, some states are literally younger than others, with larger potential elementary and secondary enrollments (see Figure 1.1.2, page 24). The Middle Atlantic and South Atlantic regions

have fewer children, as proportions of their state populations, while Alaska, Montana, and Utah have populations of children that were proportionately larger.

Educational institutions are currently adjusting to growing enrollments and increasing ethnic diversity. Beyond the general increase in the existing minority population of the United States, eight million immigrants arrived in the United States during the last decade, bringing two million foreign students into the nation's school system. This growing number of students with unique languages and cultures is joined by a resident student population that already exhibits special characteristics associated with drug use, homelessness, and alternative life style choices. Individual groups, in turn, demand special attention that results in the formation of new policy, the need for supplemental funding, and in some cases, the enactment of federal and state legislation.

The nation's white enrollment is decreasing as a percentage of total enrollment. In 1960, 86.8 percent of America's school-age population was white as compared to 70.4 percent in 1986 and 66.1 percent in 1994. Minority enrollments, on the other hand, are increasing. Between 1986 and 1993, African American enrollment rose from 16.1 percent to 16.6 percent; Hispanic enrollment increased from 9.9 percent to 12.7 percent; Asian or Pacific Islanders went from 2.8 percent to 3.6 percent; and Native American enrollments increased to 1.1 percent from 0.9 percent of the nation's student population (see Figure 5.2.1, page 159).

America's ethnic population is not

spread evenly across the United States. Neither are its students. States of the antebellum south, for example, are disproportionately African American, with school memberships that approach and/or exceed 50 percent black (see Figure 5.2.2, page 189). Migration from these historically

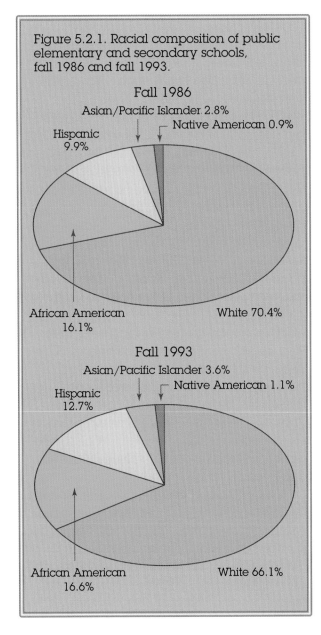

Figure 5.2.1. Racial composition of public elementary and secondary schools, fall 1986 and fall 1993.

Fall 1986

Asian/Pacific Islander 2.8%

Native American 0.9%

Hispanic 9.9%

African American 16.1%

White 70.4%

Fall 1993

Asian/Pacific Islander 3.6%

Native American 1.1%

Hispanic 12.7%

African American 16.6%

White 66.1%

black rural areas in the South has brought African American children to cities in states like Illinois, Ohio, Pennsylvania, Michigan, and New York. The overall result is a geographic distribution that sweeps south through the Mid Atlantic region and industrialized states of the East North Central along the Gulf of Mexico into Texas. California is the only other state with a noteworthy concentration of African American students. Figure 5.2.3 shows states with school memberships that are disproportionately comprised of members of America's four largest ethnic groups (see page 188).

Hispanic populations predominate in two regions of the country (see Figure 5.2.4, page 190). American citizens and illegal immigrants of Mexican origin migrate to states directly north of Mexico. In California and Texas, as a result, over one-third of all students in elementary and secondary programs are Hispanic. In New Mexico the figure is closer to 45.0 percent.

In 1993, Hispanic children ranged from 5.0 percent of children in public schools in nonmetropolitan areas to 22.0 percent of children in public schools in the central cities. Large cities, particularly in Southern California, have even larger Hispanic memberships which approach 45.0 percent in Los Angeles and 50.0 percent in San Diego. Black children ranged from 11.0 percent of students in public schools in nonmetropolitan areas to 33.0 percent of children in public schools in the central cities.

On the east coast, schools in the Middle Atlantic serve students whose families originate in and around Puerto Rico. Like their counterparts in Southern

California, urban school districts are attended by Hispanic students in large numbers. The New York City Public School District in 1996-97, for example, was 37.3 percent Hispanic.

Students with family ties to Asia and the Pacific Islands are scattered throughout the contiguous states with notable concentrations in California, Texas, Illinois, New York, and Washington (see Figure 5.2.5, page 191). The state with the largest proportion of students with ancestors originating in Asia or the Pacific Islands was Hawaii with 68.8 percent in 1996.

Native Americans are concentrated in rural areas throughout the Plains states of the lower and upper Midwest. States with large concentrations of Native American students are those which have been traditional homes for Native American populations—Montana, New Mexico, Oklahoma, and Alaska (see Figure 5.2.6, page 192). Like Hawaii, with its disproportionate student population of Asian or Pacific descent, Alaska distances itself from the contiguous states with student populations of Native Americans at 23.8 percent in 1994. American Indian, Eskimo and Aleut populations comprised 15.5 percent of Alaska's total state population during the same year.

NEW FACES THROUGH IMMIGRATION

The United States is currently receiving more immigrants per decade than at any other period in its history (see Table 5.2.1, page 195). With the arrival of new faces, 80.0 percent of whom are from countries in Latin America, Asia, and the Pacific Islands, black and white Americans represent a smaller share of the nation's population (Ascher and Burnett, 1993). In 1980, blacks and whites accounted for nearly 97.7 percent of America's population. In 1995, the figure decreased to 95.6 percent and by 2010 the figure is expected to be 93.4 percent.

Immigrant students are primarily concentrated in urban areas and enrolled in urban school districts. Table 5.2.2 is a list of the 50 largest metropolitan school districts in the United States and their corresponding enrollments (page 195). Many of these institutions have large ethnic populations and are subsequently challenged by a set of urban education issues that are unparalleled in nonmetropolitan areas.

In 1993, according to the National Center for Education Statistics (NCES), 14.5 million U.S. citizens spoke Spanish as a primary language, 5.2 million spoke a language from a European country other than Spain, 3.4 million spoke languages of Asia or the Pacific Islands, and 1.8 million Americans spoke other languages. Furthermore, between 1979 and 1989, the number of children 5 years of age and older in the United States increased 40.0 percent. The number of youngsters speaking Spanish and languages of Asia or the Pacific Islands increased more dramatically during the same period, rising to 65.0 and 98.0 percent, respectively.

America's newest citizens have large families that are highly concentrated geographically. While whites average 1.7 children per family, Mexican American families average 2.9 children; Cambodian families average 7.4; and Hmong families average 11.7 (Kellogg, 1988). Furthermore, 75.0 percent of all immigrant students live in only 5 states: Florida, Texas, California, New York, and Illinois.

CHILDREN WITH DISABILITIES

Added to increasing enrollments of minority students and immigrants are disabled children who have been included in the educational system through antidiscrimination laws. For two decades, the nation's education system has welcomed disabled children through the implementation of programs that create academic and social environments which promote achievement at, or close to, a level enjoyed by nondisabled students.

The term disabled has been used to refer to those children who have persistent and substantial differences and educational needs. Federal regulations define 13 disabilities that are eligible to be covered in federally funded special education programs, including deafness, blindness, mental retardation, serious emotional disturbance and learning disability, among others. In 1975, 8.0 percent of the primary and secondary student population received special education. Twenty years later that figure approached 12.0 percent.

In 1973, the U.S. Supreme Court ruled in *Mills v. Board of Education* that schools could not discriminate against students on the basis of disability. The ruling strengthened the position of states that had passed legislation in the 1960s and early 1970s establishing and funding special education programs. It also spurred Congress to pass, in 1975, the Education for All Handicapped Children Act (now known as IDEA or, more precisely, the Individuals with Disabilities Education Act). IDEA specified procedures regarding: (a) eligibility for special education services; (b) parental rights, individualized education programs; (c) a requirement that children be served in the least restric-

tive environment; and (d) the need for related services.

When IDEA was passed, an estimated one million children were kept out of schools because of their disabilities, while another 3.5 million were not receiving an adequate education according to Congressional hearings held that same year. It is generally acknowledged that the process of evaluating and identifying children with disabilities has been largely successful, although many with mild disabilities remain undiagnosed.

The number of students 0 to 21 years old served in federally supported programs for the disabled has increased 44.0 percent between 1976-77 and 1993-94. In 1993-94, 5,318,021 children were served nationally, an increase of 11.7 percent since 1990-91. Changes in the numbers of students served under IDEA are provided in Table 5.2.3, page 196 and Figure 5.2.7, page 193. The types of disabilities identified in students has also changed over the past 20 years.

The most common disability in 1977 was Speech/Language Impairment, with over 3.0 percent of U.S. students so labeled. In 1993, Specific Learning Disabilities replaced Speech/Language Impairment as the most common diagnosis, accounting for 45.9 percent of the students covered under IDEA (see Figure 5.2.8, page 161).

There is much debate over the legitimacy of Learning Disabilities as a diagnostic category. Some feel that the growth in the number of learning-disabled children (which actually covers several distinct conditions involving difficulties with reading, language, and mathematics) reflects an

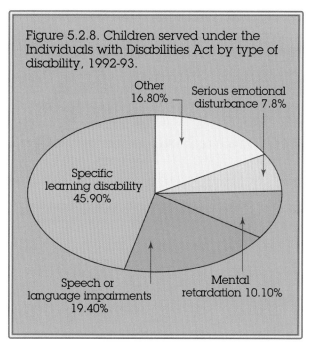

Figure 5.2.8. Children served under the Individuals with Disabilities Act by type of disability, 1992-93.

Other 16.80%

Serious emotional disturbance 7.8%

Specific learning disability 45.90%

Speech or language impairments 19.40%

Mental retardation 10.10%

The effectiveness of special education varies according to type of disability, the particular school involved and other factors. Special education classes are smaller than general education classes (15 students per teacher as opposed to 24), which facilitates more individual attention and small-group instruction. In addition, 55.0 percent of special education teachers have master's degrees (compared to 40.0 percent of general education teachers). Research has shown that the most effective strategies for students with disabilities utilizes intensive and reasonably individualized instruction with persistent monitoring of the student's progress.

The inconclusiveness of many studies has led to a movement towards "inclusion," which would abolish most special placements in favor of general education classroom interventions. Such "interventions" include peripheral interventions, designed to make individual accommodations in the general classroom; teacher consultation, in which special educators provide expertise to the general educator; modified instructional methods such as cooperative learning, peer tutoring, and cognitive strategy instruction; and whole school models which enhances the capacity of the school to integrate disabled students into the general classroom, using many of the strategies mentioned above. These interventions would require a considerable investment in resources, including teacher retraining, and supplementary curricular materials.

increased awareness of the existence and effect of these disabilities and the ineffectiveness of the educational system in providing an appropriate learning environment for affected students. Others attribute the increase to overly broad definitions of the Learning Disabled category, poorly trained teachers unable to deal with students with special needs, and the desire of states to attract government funding (see Figure 5.2.9, page 194).

African American children are found to have disabilities in greater proportion than the general population, although the majority of this disproportionate representation is found in the category of mild mental retardation (Figure 5.2.10). Poverty has also been linked with a greater incidence of a disability diagnosis. One study, conducted in 1986, found 68.0 percent of high school students with disabilities were from households with incomes of less than $25,000.

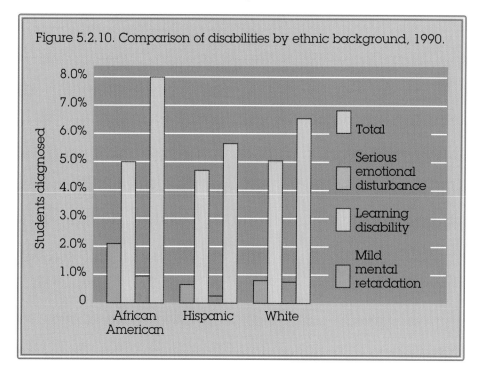

Figure 5.2.10. Comparison of disabilities by ethnic background, 1990.

Students diagnosed

Total

Serious emotional disturbance

Learning disability

Mild mental retardation

African American   Hispanic   White

5.3

THE AMERICAN SCHOOL SYSTEM
HOW SCHOOLS OPERATE

American schools are operated by different agencies—state, local, regional, state, and / or federal. Throughout the United States, regular school districts, those administered by local agencies, account for 91.0 percent of all operating agencies. This overwhelming majority is followed by regional education service agencies (7.1 percent), state operated agencies (1.2 percent), and federally operated agencies (0.7 percent).

Individual states have unique mixtures of operating agencies. New Hampshire and Kansas, for example, demonstrate contrasting school management structures. In New Hampshire, 72.4 percent of all school districts are operated by local agencies while 27.6 are operated by regional education service agencies. In Kansas, every school district is operated at the local level with no regional, state, or federal control.

At every level of control, the trend to consolidate small schools has brought about a steady and dramatic decrease in the number of schools in the United States. In 1930, there were 247,000 private and public schools as compared to 86,221 in 1994-95. The number of school districts has also decreased substantially, falling from 119,001 to 14,772 for the same time period. Table 5.3.1 on page 215 shows district sizes and the number / percent of districts within a certain size category. The table shows how smaller districts have been consolidated into larger dis-

tricts. Between 1988-89 and 1994-95, large districts grew from 177 to 207 in number while small districts decreased from 3,984 to 3,173. Supplementary information demonstrates that more students are attending larger schools. During the 1994-95 school year, 29.9 percent of all U.S. students attended schools in districts with enrollments of 25,000 or more; these super districts only comprised 1.4 percent of all districts in the United States.

Figure 5.3.1 shows the structure of the educational system in the United States. Within the structure, junior high schools are disappearing, being replaced by middle schools. Between 1983-84 and 1993-94, the number of junior high schools decreased 33.0 percent while the number of middle schools increased 39.0 percent.

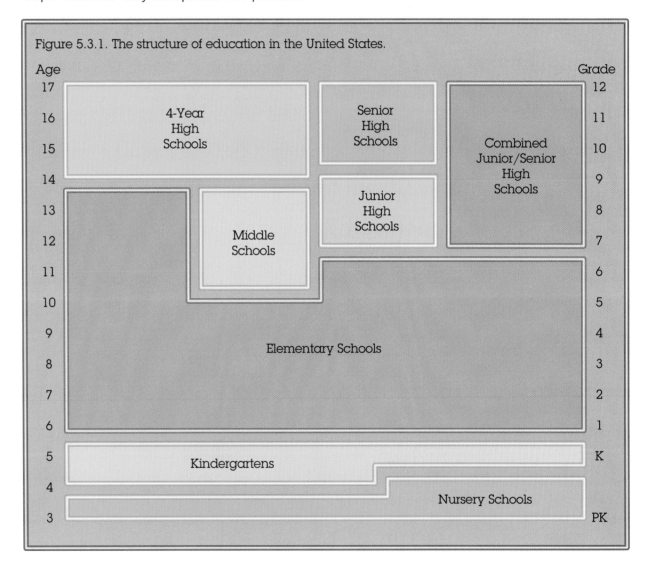

Figure 5.3.1. The structure of education in the United States.

ENROLLMENT IN THE EDUCATIONAL SYSTEM

After World War II, the number of births per year reached a peak of 4.3 million in 1957. The baby boom period between 1946 and 1964 preceded a period of declining births which reached a low of 3.1 million in 1973. Since then the number of births has gradually risen, reaching a projected 3.9 million in 1997. These trends are reflected, with lags, in the growth and decline of enrollments. Between 1970 and 1984 total public school enrollment fell about 15.0 percent; from 1984 to 1994, it rose about 13.0 percent.

In 1997, an estimated 67.0 million Americans, one in four, were enrolled in elementary and secondary schools, colleges, and universities. This figure included 37.7 million students in elementary school, 14.6 million in secondary school, and 14.6 million in colleges and universities (see Table 5.3.2, page 215).

Most students are enrolled in public educational institutions. Only 13.5 percent (5.9 million) of America's students attend private schools. Private school enrollments are higher for preprimary children (62.0 percent), than for older children and young adults. Only 13.2 percent of the nation's elementary students are enrolled in private schools, 7.3 percent are enrolled in private secondary schools, and 21.8 percent are enrolled in private institutions of higher learning.

In 1955, 22.9 percent of the nation's population was in school—a figure similar to 1995's figure of 24.9 percent.

Enrollments at all levels of instruction will increase 10.3 percent between 1995 and 2005 when the nation's K-12 school system will host 55.9 million students in both public and private schools. At elementary and secondary levels in public schools, enrollments will rise 7.6 percent from 45.1 to 48.5 million (see Table 5.3.3, page 216). Private school enrollments will show a similar rate of increases, moving from 5.7 to 6.2 million students (8.2 percent).

While enrollments increase for students of all ages, secondary level classrooms will fill at a much more rapid rate than those at the elementary level. Between 1995 and 2005, public school enrollments in grades K-8 will increase 6.5 percent. During the same period, K-8 private school enrollments will increase 6.8 percent. Public school enrollments in grades 9 through 12 will balloon 16.3 percent from 16.0 to 18.6 million as compared to private school enrollments at the same level of education, which will increase 15.4 percent from 1.3 to 1.5 million. Figure 5.3.2 traces enrollments for public elementary and secondary schools starting in 1949 with projections to year 2005.

The nation's preprimary system of education expanded significantly between 1966 and 1993 due to trends in the U.S. economy (see Figure 5.3.2a, page 164). With increases in two-earner families and families headed by working mothers, preprimary schools became full-time day care providers for many youngsters. In 1960, for example, only 5 percent of 3- to 5-year-olds attended preschool full time compared with more than 20.0 percent in 1993. As a point of reference, female participation in the workforce increased from 31.5 to 58.4 percent between 1970 and 1993 and is expected to rise to 71.8 percent by the year 2005. Simple arithmetic suggests that demand for preschool services, given increased female participation in the workforce, a younger student population, and an increasing overall school population, will at least double between now and the early part of the

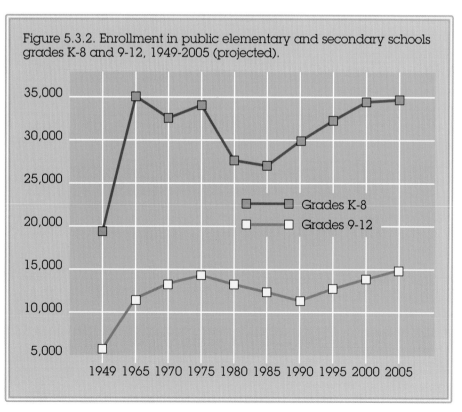

Figure 5.3.2. Enrollment in public elementary and secondary schools grades K-8 and 9-12, 1949-2005 (projected).

next century.

Enrollments do not grow or shrink uniformly from place to place. Enrollments for secondary public schools in the Pacific Northwest, California, Texas, significant portions of the South Atlantic, and the Middle Atlantic will increase most dramatically between 1993 and 2005 (see Figure 5.3.3, page 197). Much less significant enrollment changes will occur in elementary schools. In general, changes at this level of instruction will take place in the same areas of the country as those associated with grades 9 through 12 (see Figure 5.3.4, page 198).

NATIONAL COMMITMENT TO EDUCATION

The gross domestic product (GDP) of the United States has grown steadily throughout the twentieth century. The current GDP per capita is three times what is was in 1930 (1987 constant dollars). Much of the increase is relatively new. A gross domestic product per capita of $12,512 in 1960 exploded to $25,615 in 1995—an increase of 205.0 percent in chained 1992 dollars.

The proportion of the nation's gross domestic product allotted for schools at all levels of instruction has remained fairly constant at 7.3 percent since 1991-92. By comparison, this figure was 4.7 percent in 1959-1960 (see Table 5.3.4, page 216).

INTERNATIONAL COMPARISONS OF EDUCATIONAL INVESTMENT

Over time, Americans are making more of an effort to finance public education at the elementary and secondary level. An increase in the national effort index (per student revenues for elementary and secondary education from public sources as a percentage of personal income per capita)

over the last 4 decades shows 14.1 percent of the nation's personal income per capita devoted to per student revenues in 1950 compared with 26.0 percent in 1992. The United States is also among world leaders in terms of its commitment to education. Only Canada sets aside a larger portion of its GDP for education than does the United States (see Figure 5.3.5, page 199).

STATE COMMITMENT TO EDUCATION

State wealth, called gross state product (GSP), is a measure of the total output of goods and services valued at market prices.

Like GDPs of nations, state GSPs are partly comprised of "educational service expenditures," which can be calculated by dividing total state educational expenditures by overall state GSPs. Most states match U.S. commitments of GNP with comparable commitments of GSPs (see Figure 5.3.6, page 199). States with exceedingly high commitments to education are South Dakota, Wisconsin, West Virginia, Hawaii, Louisiana, Vermont, and Massachusetts. States with low commitments are Washington, Texas, Kansas, Minnesota, Illinois, Virginia, and North Carolina.

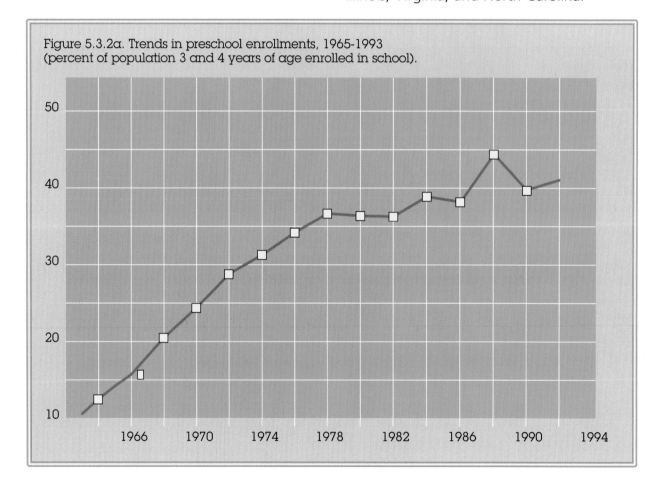

Figure 5.3.2a. Trends in preschool enrollments, 1965-1993 (percent of population 3 and 4 years of age enrolled in school).

FINANCING EDUCATION
INVESTMENT OVER TIME

Since World War II, revenues from public sources for students in elementary and secondary schools have increased substantially every decade. Total revenues increased over 4,500 percent between 1950 and 1993, rising from $5,437,044 to $248,496,276 (see Table 5.3.5, page 217). When adjusted for inflation, public revenues per student increased almost fivefold between 1950 and 1993, from $1,200 to $5,716 per student. In general, revenue increases are largely a byproduct of an educational system that has undergone a redefinition of responsibilities. Schools are now compensating for shorts falls in other institutions. For example, public policy has increased spending for disabled children and for children from poor and minority families who have failed to receive education of a quality comparable to the majority. Furthermore, women are participating in traditionally male occupations, driving up the cost of education by forcing teacher salaries to be more competitive with professions outside education.

Over the past four decades, taxpayer's ability to finance increasing education costs increased but not at the same rate as public revenue per student. In the years between 1950 and 1993, Americans watched their personal income per capita rise only 250.0 percent as compared to increases of almost 500.0 percent in public revenues per student.

SCHOOL REVENUES

America's elementary and secondary public schools receive money from federal, state, and local sources. The federal gov-ernment contributed 6.6 percent of all funds for elementary and secondary public schools in 1995. Another 46.4 percent originated from state governments and 44.3 percent were generated through local prop-erty taxes. Private sources such as gifts and fees accounted for the remaining 2.7 percent of total receipts (Figure 5.3.7).

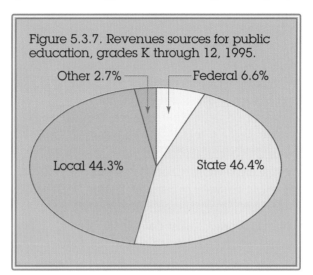

Figure 5.3.7. Revenues sources for public education, grades K through 12, 1995.

Other 2.7% — Federal 6.6%

Local 44.3% State 46.4%

In 1993, Texas, New York, and California led the nation in educational revenues (see Table 5.3.6, page 217). When combined with Illinois, Michigan, Ohio, New Jersey, Florida, Pennsylvania—similarly large urbanized states—54.2 percent of the nation's educational revenues came from Texas, New York, and California.

States meet educational needs through unique combinations of federal, state, and local funds. For most states, private and federal funds are relatively small compared with revenue streams from local and state authorities.

EDUCATIONAL EXPENDITURES

The educational dollar is divided into

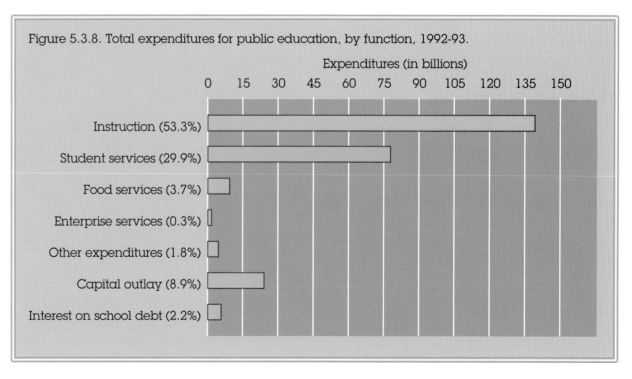

Figure 5.3.8. Total expenditures for public education, by function, 1992-93.

Expenditures (in billions)

| | 0 | 15 | 30 | 45 | 60 | 75 | 90 | 105 | 120 | 135 | 150 |

Instruction (53.3%)
Student services (29.9%)
Food services (3.7%)
Enterprise services (0.3%)
Other expenditures (1.8%)
Capital outlay (8.9%)
Interest on school debt (2.2%)

numerous cost centers (Figure 5.3.8). The largest cost center is instruction which accounts for 53.3 percent of the education dollar. Student services, which are defined as salaries, benefits, supplies, and contractual fees for staff providing social work guidance, health, psychological services, speech pathology, audiology, and other support to students, are second in terms of costs (29.9 percent).

The educational dollar is always increasing in size, much more so than enrollments. Increases in education expenditures have amounted to 416.0 percent from $118 billion in 1959-60 to $494 billion in 1995-96 when measured in 1993-94 constant dollars. In current dollars, $23.8 billion were spent in 1959-60 compared to $529.6 billion in 1995-96 (see Table 5.3.7, page 218). Referring to an earlier section of this chapter, school enrollments have also increased over the past 30 years but not nearly as quickly as figures for educational expenditures. Enrollments at all levels of education for 1997 were 66,700,000 students—an increase of only 24.4 percent over the figure of 54,394,000 in 1965.

Current outlays for elementary and secondary schools comprise 60.1 percent of all educational expenditures. This is a figure which has dropped considerably from 70.2 percent in 1959-60. As expenditures for grades K-12 have dropped, expenditures for higher education have increased in relative proportion. In 1959-60, 29.8 percent of the education dollar went to colleges and universities. In 1995-96, that figure is 39.9 percent. Of the $318.4 billion spent on elementary and secondary schools, $293.7 billion were incurred to support the operations of public schools while $24.8 billion were incurred to support private schools.

As with total expenditures on education, there is some spatial variation in terms of what is spent on instruction (see Figure 5.3.9, page 200). Once again, the Atlantic Region leads the nation in expenditures on instruction. These expenditures, plus high average teacher salaries, explain why the northeast leads the nation in expenditures per student (see Figure 5.3.10, page 201 and Figure 5.3.11, page 202).

Teacher salaries, however, cannot completely explain instructional expenditures. Decreasing class sizes and increasing enrollments drive instruction costs ever skyward for most of the country. Between 1979 and 1995, only 4 states and the District of Columbia saw statistically insignificant decreases in teacher salaries (see Figure 5.3.12, page 203). Most states increased salaries for teachers, with the largest increases occurring in the East North Central, Middle Atlantic, and New England regions.

SCHOOL EXPENDITURES COMPARED TO REVENUES

On the whole, the education system spends less than it receives. At a national level, Americans spent $274.6 billion for public elementary and secondary education during the 1993 school year. The system received $286.0 billion in the same year. Figure 5.3.13 is a map that shows ratios between expenditures and receipts for states (see page 204). Only one state, Tennessee, spends more than it receives for education. Many states break even with respect to educational financing. Others, particularly in the south and west, succeed in collecting more than they spend.

EXPENDITURES PER STUDENT

In 1994-1995, current expenditures per student in average daily attendance was $6,084 (constant 1994-95 dollars). For the 1992-1993 school year the figure was $5,904. Figure 5.3.14 shows current expenditures per pupil for 1993-94 (page 205).

MEASURING EDUCATIONAL INVESTMENT

To draw meaningful comparisons across states, educational investment is measured in two ways: (1) *public revenues per student*—revenues from public sources for a level of education, divided by the number of students enrolled at that level ; and (2) *effort*—the ratio of per student expenditure to income per capita.

Public Revenues Per Student

In 1993, revenues from public sources to support elementary and secondary education were $5,716 per student (see Table 5.3.8, page 218). This measure of resources per student varied widely across states from lows of about $3,506 in Mississippi and $3,516 in Utah to highs of about $8,952 in the District of Columbia, $9,389 in Alaska, and over $9,550 in New Jersey (see Figure 5.3.15, page 206). Excluding Alaska, industrialized states of the East North Central and the Mid-Atlantic regions spend significantly more per student than other parts of the country (see Figure 5.3.16, page 207). These areas also have inordinately high teacher salaries when those salaries are compared to personal incomes of corresponding state residents (see Figure 5.3.17, page 204).

Educational Effort

An alternative measure of public investment in education expresses the previous measure, public revenues per student, as a percentage of personal income per capita. This measure, called "educational effort," accounts for statewide variations in public support for education due to differences in the cost of living and salaries (see Table 5.3.8, page 218).

Differences between state educational effort and public revenues per student are seen when one views Figures 5.3.14 and 5.3.15 simultaneously (pages 205 and 206). In Figure 5.3.14, New Jersey and Alaska spent more than two and one half times that of Mississippi and Utah when educational commitment is measured as public revenues per student. In Figure 5.3.15, when investment is adjusted for state per capita wealth and measured as educational effort, the highest ranking states New Jersey and Alaska only outspend the lowest ranking states Mississippi and Utah by approximately 1.75.

EXPENDITURES FOR SPECIAL EDUCATION

Between 1976 and 1994, the number of students served by special education increased from 3.7 million to 5.3 million. Current estimates of total national expenditures for special education exceed $30 billion, though the last year that states were required to report these amounts was 1988, when expenditures totaled $19.2 billion. The federal government's contribution amounted to 8.0 percent of this total, far short of the projected 40.0 percent initially authorized by IDEA in 1975. The federal government bases its grant-in-aid program on each state's count of children receiving special education.

The continued funding of special education faces many challenges, primarily an increasing proportion of the student population diagnosed with disabilities. The increased need for resources at a time when funding from the federal government is being cut back has led the states to revamp their approaches to special education funding, such as census-based funding rather than special education child counts. The ostensible advantages include increased local flexibility and saving on the high cost of identification. This approach complements the "inclusion" philosophy of meeting special education needs in the context of the general education classroom. However, many feel this approach puts the needs of the special education students at risk until better accountability methods can be devised to measure the educational progress of these students.

SCHOOL QUALITY
NATIONAL EDUCATION GOALS

Good schools have good teachers, but teachers are only one component in a critical list that differentiates schools in terms of overall quality. Readiness to learn, school attainment and completion, competency, teacher preparedness, and parental participation are components that are inexorably linked to student progress. Added to this list is school safety, a topic discussed later in this chapter.

Having identified a list of critical factors affecting the quality of education in the United States, the 1995 National Educational Goals Panel announced eight goals to reform and renew American education. The panel acknowledged that education begins at birth and is a process that takes place beyond the classroom. The following is a partial list of goals and objectives to be reached by the year 2000.

l) All children in America will start school ready to learn.

2) The high school graduation rate will increase to at least 90.0 percent.

3) All students will leave grades 4, 8, and 12 having demonstrated competency over challenging subject matter including English, mathematics, science, foreign languages, civics and government, economics, arts, history, and geography, and every school in America will ensure that all students learn to use their minds well, so they may be prepared for responsible citizenship, further learning, and productive employment in our nation's modern economy.

4) The nation's teaching force will have access to programs for the continued improvement of their professional skills and the opportunity to acquire the knowledge and skills needed to instruct and prepare all American students for the next century.

5) United States students will be first in the world in mathematics and science achievement.

6) Every school in the United States will be free of drugs, violence, and the unauthorized presence of firearms and alcohol and will offer a disciplined environment conducive to learning.

7) Every school will promote partnerships that will increase parental involvement and participation in promoting the social, emotional, and academic growth of children.

We now discuss readiness to learn;

school attainment and completion; competency, teacher preparedness, and parental involvement. Issues of student performance together with issues of school safety are treated separately and more thoroughly in later sections of this chapter.

READINESS TO LEARN

A child who is in good health is *ready to learn*. The percentage of infants born in the United States with one or more health risks decreased from 37.0 to 35.0 percent between 1990 and 1992. This reduction represents a difference of at least 64,200 children who started life unchallenged by conditions associated with poor prenatal care, low maternal weight gain, and maternal smoking, alcohol, and drug use. In addition to reducing overall number, the United States was also successful in reducing the disparity between the numbers of white and African American infants born with such health risks. The disparity between white babies and Hispanic and Native American infants remained unchanged.

Immunization against preventable diseases is another factor that affects a child's ability to learn. In 1994, a baseline of 75.0 percent of all 2-year-olds were fully immunized in the United States. Full immunization consisted of four doses of diphtheria-tetanus-pertussis vaccine, three doses of polio vaccine, and one dose of measles or measles/mumps/rubella vaccine. Like the number of children born with one or more health risks, these data will be monitored until the year 2000. A state by state inventory of immunization is included as Figure 5.3.18 (page 208).

Beyond issues of health, the panel emphasized the importance of preschool education. Early education consisted of family-child reading and storytelling, and enrollment in preschool programs. The panel observed that only two-thirds of American families read or told stories to their preschoolers in 1993. That proportion increased substantially to 72 .0 percent by 1995.

The panel also noted a large and undiminishing gap between preschool participation rates for low and high income families. In 1991, less than half of 3- to 5-year-olds from families with incomes of $10,000 or less attended preschool. This was compared with 73.0 percent for families with incomes of $50,000 or more. The observed disparity of 28.0 percent remained virtually unchanged in 1995 at 27.0 percent.

SCHOOL ATTAINMENT AND COMPLETION

According to the National Educational Goals Panel, the nation must increase its school completion rate to a point where 75.0 percent of the students that do drop out will successfully complete a high school diploma or its equivalent by year 2000. The panel also concluded that the gap in high school completion rates between minority students and their nonminority counterparts must also be eliminated.

In 1994, the percent of high school dropouts among persons ages 14 to 34 was 11.2 percent see (Figure 5.3.19, page 169). Calculating the proportion of individuals who are not currently enrolled in school and have not completed high school results in the aforementioned *status dropout rate*. Status rates for African Americans and Hispanics are higher than those for whites.

Status rates, together with event dropout rates that measure the share of students who leave school without completing high school during a single year, have declined across the nation for whites and African Americans. Similar observations for Hispanics have shown no trend toward decline and have remained exceedingly high by all measures.

According to findings presented by the National Educational Goals Panel, 86.0 percent of 18- to 24-year-olds completed high school in 1990. By 1994, the completion rate had not increased but remained the same. The disparity between 18- to 24-year-olds of various backgrounds also remained the same.

COMPETENCY

Successful schools develop students who use their minds well, so they may be prepared for responsible citizenship, further learning, and productive employment in America's modern economy. The competent student regardless of race/ethnicity has a great advantage over his or her poorly prepared counterpart because educational attainment is positively associated with higher earnings and lower unemployment rates (see Figure 5.3.20, page 169). Furthermore, literacy level is positively associated with higher wages and a reduced likelihood of being unemployed. The statistics are quite clear in this matter. In 1993, the median annual earnings of males between the ages of 25 and 34 were 67.0 percent higher for those with high school diplomas than those without. For women, the observed disparity in income was 59.0 percent. Similar results have been noted with respect to higher levels of proficiency in reading.

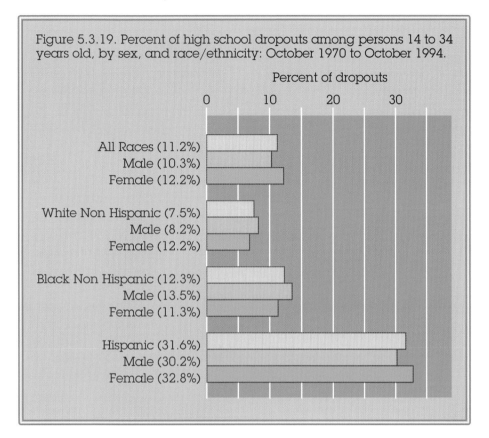

Figure 5.3.19. Percent of high school dropouts among persons 14 to 34 years old, by sex, and race/ethnicity: October 1970 to October 1994.

Percent of dropouts

All Races (11.2%)
Male (10.3%)
Female (12.2%)

White Non Hispanic (7.5%)
Male (8.2%)
Female (12.2%)

Black Non Hispanic (12.3%)
Male (13.5%)
Female (11.3%)

Hispanic (31.6%)
Male (30.2%)
Female (32.8%)

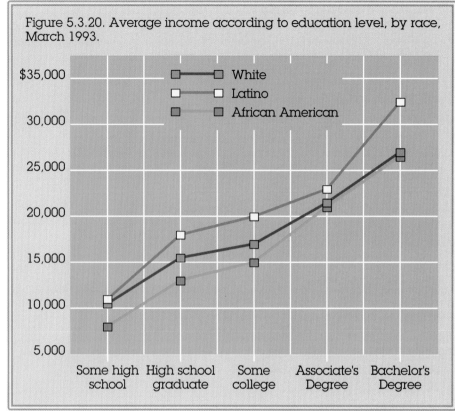

Figure 5.3.20. Average income according to education level, by race, March 1993.

White
Latino
African American

Some high school | High school graduate | Some college | Associate's Degree | Bachelor's Degree

But what are the chances of becoming competent? Unfortunately, they are often poor for economically challenged children. Poor and minority students lack proper teaching materials and "…are taught throughout their entire school careers by a steady stream of the least qualified and experienced teachers" (Darling-Hammond 1996). Furthermore, many inner city school districts have perpetually unfilled vacancies that they are unable to fill with qualified teachers. "In response, principals use substitutes, hire less qualified teachers, or cancel courses. Consequently, inner-city high school students have only about a 50.0 percent chance of having a qualified math or science teacher" (The Education Trust

1996). The Education Trust goes on to say that even qualified teachers in low-income areas suffer from a lack of basic teaching utensils such as textbooks, calculators, computers, laboratory equipment, and other supplies. In schools where student poverty is greater than 30.0 percent, 59.0 percent of teachers complain about a lack of books and other materials. Only 19.0 percent of teachers complain in more affluent schools.

TEACHER PREPAREDNESS

Obviously, good schools need good teachers. The questions surrounding teacher qualifications are twofold. First, are teachers ready to teach and, in particular,

are they ready to teach in the subject areas to which they are assigned? Second, are teachers encouraged to participate in various in-service and professional development programs?

Certification is the process by which states evaluate the credentials of teachers to ensure that they meet minimum professional standards as defined by an approved educational authority. Certification ratifies the quality of teachers' competence in subject area, educational methodology, teaching skills, and potential classroom management ability.

Currently, the vast majority of states require testing for certification of teachers. While some states develop their own standards, most follow testing guidelines developed by the National Association of State Directors of Teacher Education and Certification (NASDTEC). States assess competence in 1 to as many as 3 areas: (a) basic and professional skills; (b) content knowledge; and (c) performance based on in-class observation (see Figure 5.3.21, page 209).

The National Teachers Examination (NTE) is the most commonly used standardized test for teachers. In 1996, 21 states used the National Teachers Examination. Fourteen more administer tests specifically designed by state legislatures or boards of education (see Table 5.3.9, page 219). All states require the teacher applicant to have completed a bachelor's degree and a state-approved teacher education program. Most count credits specifying that a minimum number of credit hours be earned in certain academic subjects.

PARENTAL INVOLVEMENT

The effectiveness of the classroom is largely dependent on the preparedness of the students in the class. As students come to class prepared, teachers spend more time on instruction and less time on discipline and administrative affairs.

Parents help prepare children for school by becoming involved in school-related issues and by regulating children's out-of-school activities. Most eighth grade students—as many as 90.0 percent—report conversations with their parents about school-related issues. A similar number say that their parents check their homework and limit or regulate their social activities. Smaller numbers report parent/teacher or parent/counselor meetings (60.0 percent)

or visits to their classrooms (29.0 percent).

Becoming involved means movement in two directions. In one direction, parents move toward schools questioning administrators and teachers. They also volunteer for school committees or help in the formulation of school policy. In the opposite direction, schools contact parents about student performance, career guidance, attendance, behavior, and volunteerism.

A close examination of the types of contact between public school parents and school personnel shows that for 12th

graders, parents are much more likely to be contacted about their children's academic performance than about their behavior (Figure 5.3.22). Only 20.1 percent of all contacts between parents and schools are about concerns with behavior while 52.7 percent are concerned with academic performance (see Table 5.3.10, page 220).

OUT-OF-FIELD TEACHING ASSIGNMENT

A statistic often used to summarize poor educational quality is the number of teachers who are assigned to teach subjects for which they have no formal training. Under such circumstances, students are deprived of the most basic resource of learning (see Figure 5.3.23, page 210). This condition arises most often in poorer school districts with endemic staffing problems that require emergency "out of field" teaching assignments (see Table 5.3.11, page 221).

In 1991, only 66.0 percent of secondary school teachers held degrees in the field in which they taught (see Figure 5.3.24, page 211). That figure decreased to 63.0 percent in 1994.

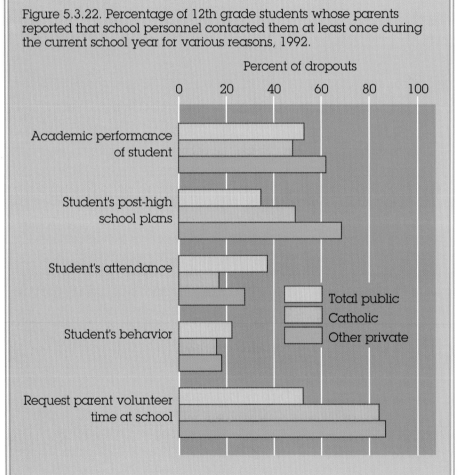

Figure 5.3.22. Percentage of 12th grade students whose parents reported that school personnel contacted them at least once during the current school year for various reasons, 1992.

More encouraging, however, are attempts to close the preparedness gap. Surveys of teachers who reported participation in various in-service or professional development programs revealed that 85.0 percent of all teachers attended development sessions on one or more topics such as uses of educational technology, methods of teaching subject field, in-depth study of teaching field, or student assessment (see Figure 5.3.25, page 212).

STUDENT/TEACHER RATIO

The number of students to the number of instructors is the pupil/teacher ratio. Pupil to teacher ratios are computed on elementary and secondary enrollment by organizational level and the number of classroom teachers by organizational level.

Since World War II, individual teachers have taught fewer and fewer students (Figure 5.3.26). The general belief is that smaller classes lead to increased attention and, thus, better education. Computed estimates for 1997 showed that teachers in both public and private elementary and secondary schools taught 17.1 students on average (see Table 5.3.12, page 220). In public schools, student/teacher ratios were 17.4 for grades K-12, 19.1 for elementary grades, and 14.9 for grade 9-12. Figures for private schools were lower respectively, with reported ratios in 1997 of 15.1, 16.7, and 11.4 students per teacher.

Student/teacher ratios depend on educational investment. They range from lows of 11:1 in New Jersey to highs of 24:1 in California (see Table 5.3.13, page 221. In general, students benefit when more teachers are employed and class sizes are small (see Figure 5.3.27, page 213).

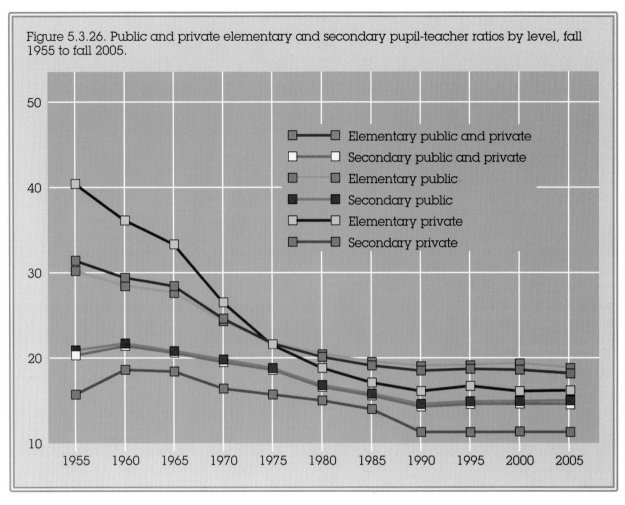

Figure 5.3.26. Public and private elementary and secondary pupil-teacher ratios by level, fall 1955 to fall 2005.

Legend:
- Elementary public and private
- Secondary public and private
- Elementary public
- Secondary public
- Elementary private
- Secondary private

INVESTMENT IN HUMAN RESOURCES
STAFF

The most important resource used in education is people. It is also the most costly. During the school year ending in 1993, public elementary and secondary schools spent approximately $254 billion. Of this amount, 83.2 percent went to pay teachers and school staff.

Elementary and secondary public schools employed 4,698,799 full-time-equivalent (FTE) school staff or 10.8 staff per 100 students in 1993. Of these, 5.7 were classroom teachers and 2.6 were support staff, such as secretaries and bus drivers. The remaining 2.5 were principals, assistant principals, school district administrators, librarians, guidance counselors, and teacher aids. In 1993, the national pupil to staff ratio was 9.1 in public elementary and secondary schools. Maine led the nation at 7.5 students per FTE staff member. Utah was at the opposite extreme with 13.4 students. In private elementary and secondary schools, each FTE staff member served 9.3 students in 1993. Catholic schools recorded a student/FTE staff member ratio of 12.2, whereas the ratio for private nonsectarian schools was only 5.3.

TEACHERS

In the United States, current (1997) middle alternative projection estimates identify 3,084,000 teachers assigned to grades K-12 in private and public schools. The vast majority of these individuals—87.4 percent or 2,694,000 teachers—work in public schools. Only 390,000 teachers are employed in the nation's private schools. In 1997, elementary schools employed more teachers than secondary schools. This statement holds trues regardless of institutional control. In public schools, 58.5 percent of all teachers instruct elementary students. In private schools, the figure is 70.0 percent.

School districts in California, Texas, Illinois, New York, and Florida engage more teachers than other states (see Figure 5.3.28, page 214). Generally, the number of teachers and a state's school-age population is directly related with variations caused by unique state student/teacher ratios.

5.4

STUDENT PERFORMANCE FACTORS AFFECTING EDUCATIONAL ACHIEVEMENT LEVELS

Low levels of achievement and attainment are rooted in social problems such as poverty, level of parental education and involvement, and the fiscal and environmental conditions in the schools. The number of years spent in poverty and the concentration of poverty in neighborhoods are associated with the likelihood of falling below expected grade level (Orland 1990). Likewise, a confluence of poverty and race constrain academic achievement.

Traditionally, children with limited English skills have performed poorly in school. In the late seventies and early eighties, 53.0 percent of children who were reported to have difficulty speaking English were enrolled below modal grade (that is, the grade in which most children of an age are enrolled at the beginning of a school year). This figure was compared to 24.0 percent of English-speaking children.

Hispanic children—those most likely to possess poor English language skills—are at an educational disadvantage for reasons that include lower parental education and a greater likelihood of living in poverty. Also, a larger percentage of Hispanic students attend disadvantaged schools with overall academic and supporting environments that are less conducive to learning (Peng 1995).

Fortunately, policy initiatives have been drafted to increase achievement levels for Hispanic students. The language perfor-

mance gap, that is, the disparity between non English speaking students and English speaking students in terms of educational attainment, has narrowed considerably in recent years with the reauthorization of the Bilingual Education Act. The Bilingual Education Act provides for competitive, voluntary, and discretionary grants to school districts to implement special education services for students whose English ability is limited. Unchanged, however, is the enduring effect of poor English skills on educational outcome. Not only do Spanish-speaking persons have higher dropout rates (31.0 percent) than English-speaking individuals or speakers of Asian or Pacific Island languages (9.0 and 11.0 percent), they are also twice as likely not to be enrolled in high school.

LEVELS OF PROFICIENCY

Indicators of what students have learned in school are perhaps the most important measures of the outcomes of education. Since its beginnings in 1969, the National Assessment of Educational Progress (NAEP) has been assessing students' rates of achievement in core curricula throughout public and private schools. Testing results compiled since 1969 provide an overview of how education has evolved while establishing a direction for policy. The NAEP also surveys the school population to establish background variables affecting the progress of students' education. The methodology used by the NAEP tests 9-, 13-, and 17-year-olds (or 4th, 8th, and 12th graders) annually in reading, writing, mathematics, and science to measure changes occurring in education.

Two emerging patterns depict decreasing proficiency scores between the early 1970s and the mid-1980s, followed by gains in achievement levels in the late 1980s and early 1990s. NAEP surveys also demonstrate a steady reduction in the achievement gap between whites and minorities.

LEVELS OF PROFICIENCY IN READING

Between 1971 and 1992, average reading scores rose for most students (see Table 5.4.1, page 222 and Table 5.4.1a, page 225). With few exceptions, girls were better readers than boys in all age groups and in all years. The same can be said for whites compared to African Americans and Hispanics. Reading proficiency scores for whites averaged higher than those for minorities for all ages groups and years.

Reading proficiency scores for minorities increased between 1971 and 1992. Gaps in scores between whites and minorities also closed. Average reading proficiency scores for 17-year-old African Americans were 52 points below whites in 1971 but only 36 points below in 1992. For Hispanic students, average reading proficiency scores for 17-year-olds were 41 points below whites in 1975 and only 26 points below in 1992.

Average 4th grade reading proficiency scores and the percent of all 4th grade students at or above proficiency are the topics of Figure 5.4.1 on page 174. State-by-state comparisons demonstrate that few states have large proportions of competent readers. White students were far more proficient than African Americans or Hispanics and Hispanics were better readers than blacks. In no state did more than 12.0 percent of African American students qualify as being proficient or above proficient. In 35 states, more than 30.0 percent of white students were proficient.

LEVELS OF PROFICIENCY IN WRITING

Between 1984 and 1992, average writing proficiency scores rose insignificantly for 4th graders and 8th graders. Scores dropped for students in 11th grade (see Table 5.4.2, page 225). Without exception, girls wrote better than boys in all age groups and in all years. Writing proficiency scores for whites averaged higher than those for African Americans and Hispanic Americans for all ages groups and years.

Between 1984 and 1992, writing proficiency scores for minorities both increased and decreased depending on age and ethnicity. Scores for African Americans dropped for 4th and 11th graders. Scores for Hispanics rose for all age groups. Gaps in scores between 17-year-old whites and African Americans widened, being 27 points in 1984 and 31 points in 1992. The opposite can be said for the relationship between Hispanic students and white students. The gap in average writing proficiency scores decreased dramatically, from 38 points in 1984 to 20 points in 1992.

LEVELS OF PROFICIENCY IN MATHEMATICS

Between 1986 and 1992, average mathematics proficiency scores rose slightly for students in all grades, with 9-year-olds showing the greatest improvement (see Table 5.4.3, page 223).

White, African American, and Hispanic students showed large improvements at all ages during the years studied. While scores for whites increased steadily between 1973 and 1992, they did so at slower rates than scores for African Americans and Hispanics. As a result, gaps in average mathematics proficiency scores between whites and ethnic groups decreased over the last 20 years.

Average 8th grade proficiency scores in mathematics and the percent of all 8th grade students at or above proficiency are the topics of Figure 5.4.2 (see page 175). State-by-state comparisons demonstrate that students enrolled in states of the upper Midwest are the nation's most proficient mathematicians. White students in this region are particularly strong.

White students were far more proficient in mathematics than African Americans or Hispanics and Hispanics outscored blacks. In no state did more than 9.0 percent of African American students qualify as being proficient or above proficient. In 15 states, more than 30.0 percent of white students were highly ranked.

LEVELS OF PROFICIENCY IN SCIENCE

Between 1970 and 1992, average science achievement scores rose significantly for all age levels (see Table 5.4.4, page 224). Boys scored higher in all years and at every age group. Science achievement scores for African Americans and Hispanics remained well below those for whites. However, gaps between 17-year-old whites and African Americans decreased from 58 points in 1977 to 48 points in 1992. Gaps between whites and Hispanics were 36 points and 34 points for the years, respectively.

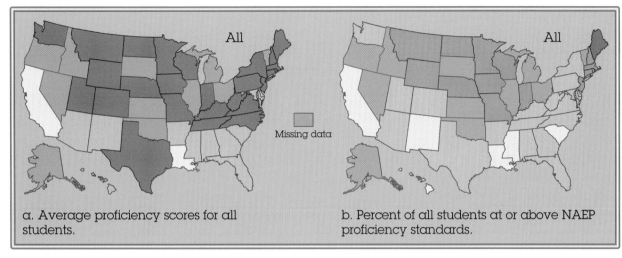

a. Average proficiency scores for all students.

b. Percent of all students at or above NAEP proficiency standards.

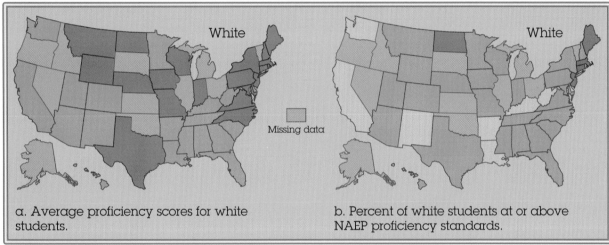

a. Average proficiency scores for white students.

b. Percent of white students at or above NAEP proficiency standards.

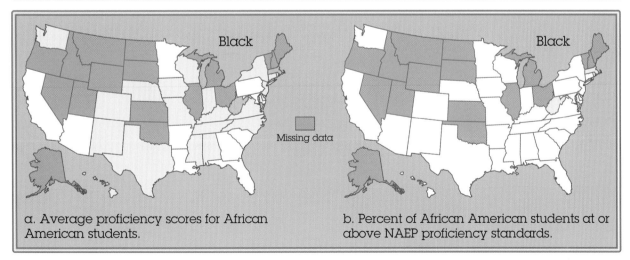

a. Average proficiency scores for African American students.

b. Percent of African American students at or above NAEP proficiency standards.

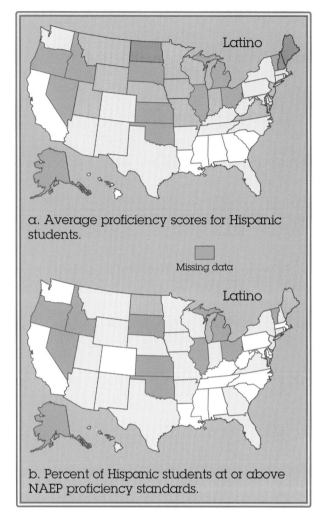

a. Average proficiency scores for Hispanic students.

b. Percent of Hispanic students at or above NAEP proficiency standards.

Figure 5.4.1.

Fourth grade reading proficiency scores, 1994.

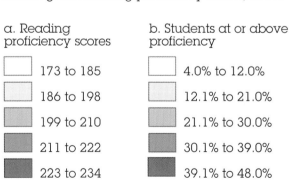

a. Reading proficiency scores	b. Students at or above proficiency
173 to 185	4.0% to 12.0%
186 to 198	12.1% to 21.0%
199 to 210	21.1% to 30.0%
211 to 222	30.1% to 39.0%
223 to 234	39.1% to 48.0%

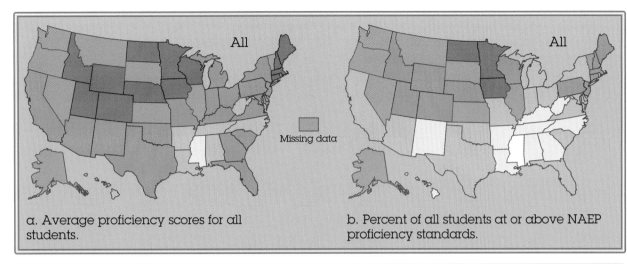

a. Average proficiency scores for all students.

b. Percent of all students at or above NAEP proficiency standards.

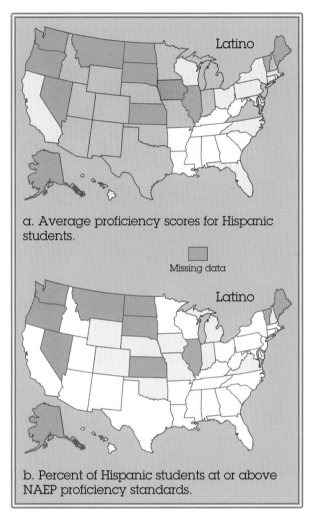

a. Average proficiency scores for Hispanic students.

b. Percent of Hispanic students at or above NAEP proficiency standards.

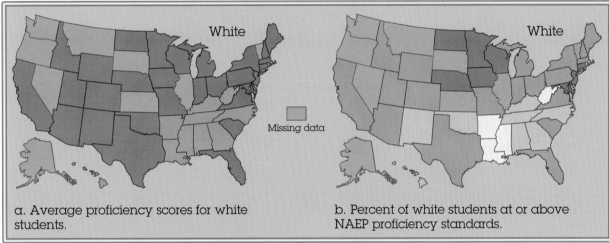

a. Average proficiency scores for white students.

b. Percent of white students at or above NAEP proficiency standards.

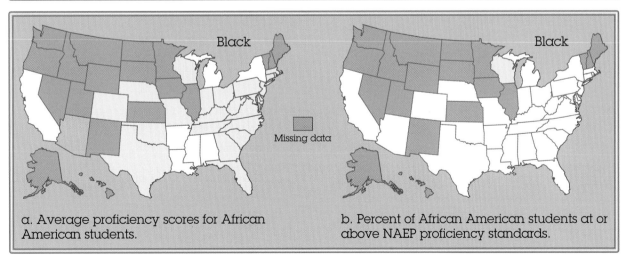

a. Average proficiency scores for African American students.

b. Percent of African American students at or above NAEP proficiency standards.

Figure 5.4.2.
Eighth grade math proficiency scores, 1992.

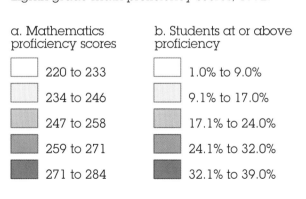

a. Mathematics proficiency scores

☐	220 to 233
☐	234 to 246
☐	247 to 258
☐	259 to 271
☐	271 to 284

b. Students at or above proficiency

☐	1.0% to 9.0%
☐	9.1% to 17.0%
☐	17.1% to 24.0%
☐	24.1% to 32.0%
☐	32.1% to 39.0%

PROFICIENCY OF U.S. STUDENTS COMPARED TO STUDENTS OF OTHER COUNTRIES

The second International Assessment of Educational Progress (IAEP) showed that U.S students compared favorably to international students in reading but unfavorably in mathematics and science. When assessing basic reading skill, 9-year-old students from the United States performed better on average on narrative domain than children from other countries (see Figure 5.4.3, page 222). Fourteen-year-old students from the United States also scored higher on expository domain than students from all countries surveyed.

Interestingly, there is far greater variation in basic literacy within countries than there is between countries. For instance, in tests evaluating narrative abilities, the difference between low proficiency students and their high proficiency counterparts was 235 points within the United States and only 62 points between the United States and West Germany. In Europe, this is explained by language and cultural differences within countries. In the United States, however, which is more homogeneous than most countries in these respects, variations are likely to be caused by gaps in investment funding.

The U.S. lags behind other nations in mathematics and science test scores (see Figure 5.4.4, page 223 and Figure 5.4.5, page 224). At age 9, U.S. students scored ahead of only Canada in mathematics and third in science. Thirteen-year-old students from the United States fared worse, ranking last in both areas. As with scores recorded for reading, in-country variations in proficiency appear to be more significant than those among countries.

As one considers international test scores, a statement published by the National Center for Education Statistics gives cause for concern. In its 1996 publication of The Condition of Education, NCES states, *"The technical skills of a nation's workers are a crucial component of its economic competitiveness. The youth of today will be tomorrow's workers and will be competing in the global marketplace. They will depend on the mathematics [and science] learned in this decade to succeed in the complex business and technological environments of the future."*

EDUCATIONAL ATTAINMENT

High school completion rates are an indicator of educational attainment. They are also a barometer of educational well-being. Since 1971, the proportion of Americans who have received high school diplomas or GEDs has increased considerably, from 77.7 percent to 86.9 percent of the total population. Females led males, with increases of 14.2 percent compared to 9.1 percent. The largest increases were those achieved by African Americans—47.6 percent. The percentage of Latinos with diplomas also increased by 18.3 percent.

In 1995, 86.9 percent of the nation's population between 25 and 29 years of age held a high school diploma or high school equivalency. Hispanics held proportionately fewer diplomas (57.2 percent) than did African Americans (86.8 percent) or whites (92.0 percent). Whites and blacks showed an increase between the years of 1992 and 1995, while the Hispanic population suffered a decrease since 1992, down to 57.2 percent from 60.9 (see Table 5.4.5, page 226).

DROPPING OUT OF SCHOOL

Examining education attainment levels is an indirect measure of the ways in which students acquire civic responsibilities, social skills, work ethics, and life skills. Included in the valuation of attainment levels are statistics portraying educational dropouts.

Students drop out of school for various reasons—the most common is a simple dislike of school. The second most common reason is that students cannot keep up with academic demands (see Table 5.4.6, page 225). For black students, the second most common reason was "could not get along with teachers."

Dropout rates are calculated in numerous ways. Calculations known as *event drop out rates* are used here to describe events for various ethnic groups. Recent drop out rates, although generally lower than those recorded in 1972, have started to increase since 1992 for all ethnic groups and groups at various levels of income.

Among ethnic groups, Hispanic students drop out most frequently (see Figure 5.4.6, page 177). Students from low-income families, particularly those from inner cities, are also at greater risk of dropping out with dropout rates for individuals with low incomes are six and one-half times greater than those for individuals with high incomes (see Figure 5.4.7, page 177).

Students from families originating in Asia or the Pacific Islands drop out infrequently with only 4.0 percent of that student population quitting school in 1992. Finally, there appears to be a significant relationship between dropping out and family status. Students from intact families drop out less frequently than do students from fractured families.

5.5

ISSUES IN CONTEMPORARY EDUCATION
THE ECONOMICALLY
CHALLENGED STUDENT

By the late 1980s, the gap between the wealthiest and poorest Americans widened to its largest extent since 1947 (Reed and Sautter 1990). Currently, the American lower class includes more than 40.0 percent of the nation's population. The places the United States ahead of all industrialized nations in terms of those who are perpetually poor.

Children are the poorest of all Americans. One out of five children lives in a family with an income below the poverty line. Forty-six percent of black children live in poverty, as do 39.0 percent of all Hispanic children. In urban neighborhoods, 30.0 percent of all children fall below the poverty line compared to only 13.0 percent of children in suburban communities and 22.0 percent of children in rural areas.

With this uneven distribution of the nation's poor, children affected by poverty are likely to be spatially concentrated in some schools and largely absent from others (see Figure 5.5.1, 178). Urban students are more likely to be attending schools with high concentrations of low income students (see Figure 5.5.2, page 178). One-third of the nation's poor students, 40.0 percent of the nation's African American students, and 30.0 percent of the nation's Hispanic students are enrolled in under-resourced urban school districts.

The effects of poverty on education outcomes are well documented. A high concentration of low income students in an urban school is related to less desirable student performance as poor students are exposed to a variety of risks. Among risks associated with poverty are inadequate medical care, increased exposure to personal injury due to school and neighborhood

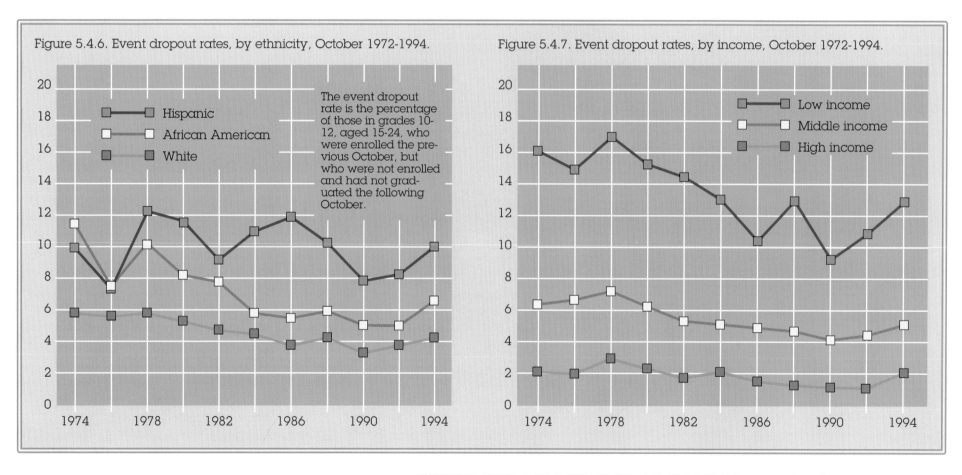

Figure 5.4.6. Event dropout rates, by ethnicity, October 1972-1994.

Hispanic
African American
White

The event dropout rate is the percentage of those in grades 10-12, aged 15-24, who were enrolled the previous October, but who were not enrolled and had not graduated the following October.

Figure 5.4.7. Event dropout rates, by income, October 1972-1994.

Low income
Middle income
High income

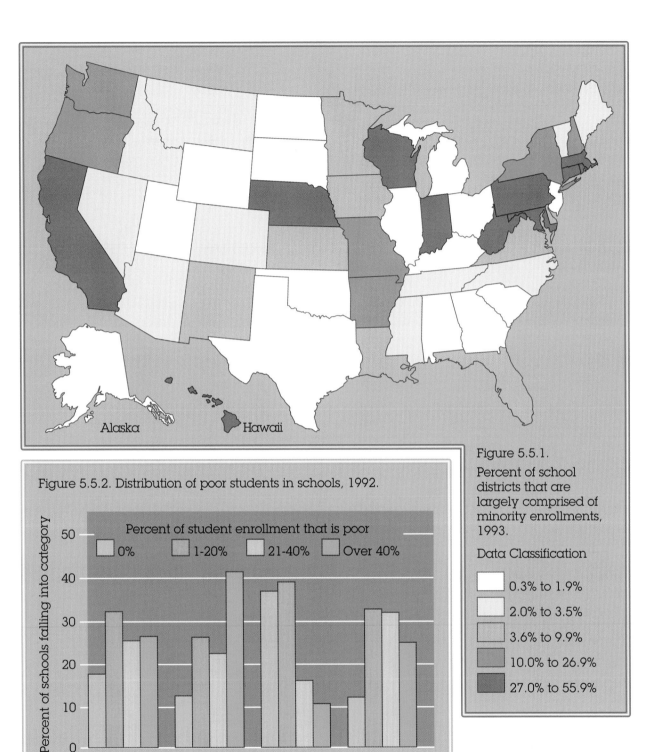

Figure 5.5.1.
Percent of school districts that are largely comprised of minority enrollments, 1993.

Data Classification

☐ 0.3% to 1.9%
☐ 2.0% to 3.5%
☐ 3.6% to 9.9%
☐ 10.0% to 26.9%
☐ 27.0% to 55.9%

Figure 5.5.2. Distribution of poor students in schools, 1992.

Percent of student enrollment that is poor
☐ 0% ☐ 1-20% ☐ 21-40% ☐ Over 40%

violence, and risk-taking behavior such as premarital relations and drug use.

EDUCATIONAL INVESTMENT GAPS

Historically, state funding for K-12 education has increased and local funding has decreased (see Figure 5.5.3, page 227). Since potential school district revenues are based on the relative tax wealth of a given district, less wealthy districts are forced to tax themselves at higher rates to generate revenues equivalent to those in more affluent districts. When increased taxation cannot happen due to real financial constraints in poorer communities, gaps in educational investment occur. Concerning these gaps The Education Trust writes, "resources such as well-educated teachers, up-to-date textbooks, challenging curricula, ongoing professional development of teachers, computers and laboratory equipment are not distributed equitably" (1996).

Poorer districts contribute less to schools and, therefore, individual students. On a national level, schools with less than 5.0 percent of their children in poverty spent $6,565 per student as compared to $5,173 per student in schools with more than 25.0 percent of their children in poverty. Even with adjustments for local costs and needs, an investment gap of $5,209 in low poverty schools and $4,044 in schools with high poverty rates exists (National Center for Education Statistics, 1995).

Similar investment gaps are found in schools based on their minority enrollments. With local adjustments for costs and needs, schools with low minority enrollments spent $4,389 per student in 1995 while schools with high minority enrollments spent less—$4,103.

Measuring Educational Investment Gaps

Disparity of funding is the district-to-district variation in per-pupil spending. It is calculated by dividing the standard deviation within a state by the average spending in that state. Among states, spatial patterns of disparity are minimal, and disparities are generally low with the exceptions of Alaska, Missouri, and Ohio (see Figure 5.5.4, page 228).

Safe, Disciplined, and Substance-Free Schools
Violence in Schools

Numerous studies produced in the 1990s, supported by anecdotal evidence obtained in educator/student interviews, document a dramatic increase in school violence across the United States. More than 3 million crimes are now committed annually on or near school property, according to the National Crime Survey (Whitaker and Bastian 1991). In another survey, Lou Harris and Associates (1994) found that one 1 of every 4 students and 1 in 10 teachers had been victims of violence in the nation's schools. In addition to the escalation in the number of violent incidents, crimes themselves are more violent. A 1993 University of Michigan study found that 9.0 percent of eighth graders carried a weapon of some sort (gun, knife, or club) during the previous month, and that an estimated 270,000 guns are in American schools on any given day. The effect of such weaponry can be seen in the results of numerous studies. More than 400,000 students between the ages of 12 and 19 claimed to have been victims of violent crime (U. S. Bureau of Justice Statistics, 1991). The National School Safety Center, which monitors violence in the nation's schools, reported 46 violent deaths in schools nationwide in the 1993-94 school year. These statistics reflect a climate of fear that seems to be common in schools (see Table 5.5.1, page 227). The Lou Harris survey found that, in addition to the almost 40.0 percent of students who carried a weapon for self-protection in high-crime neighborhoods, more than 10.0 percent had cut classes or stayed away from school because of fear of crime.

Spatial Distribution of School Violence

School violence is not confined to large urban schools in troubled neighborhoods (Table 5.5.2). In 1994, 82.0 percent of all school districts reported significant increases in violence, with 39.0 percent reporting a shooting or knifing incident (National Association of School Boards, 1992). A survey of over 1,200 school principals in 1992 found that while 64.0 percent of urban principals reported an increase in crime in the previous 5 years, 54.0 percent of suburban principals, 43.0 percent of small town principals, and 34.0 percent of rural principals also reported increases in school violence (Garibaldi, et al 1996.).

Causes of the Violence

Although several explanations have been offered for what the 1992 National Association of School Boards (NASB) study labeled an epidemic of violence in the schools, many experts agree that the *culture of violence* that seemed to explode in the 1980s, especially in the inner city, is the primary culprit. Violence in schools is essentially a mirror for violence in society at large. Between 1970 and 1990, the number of youth killed in the United States with firearms more than doubled, from 1,059 in 1970 to 2,162 in 1990. The greater willingness to use force, often deadly force, is attributed to several factors.

Table 5.5.2. Percent of students responding to questions about crime on or near school campuses, 1993.

	Type of school district		
	Urban	Suburban	Rural
Students who said they were victims at school			
Violent crimes	8.0	7.0	7.0
Property crimes	2.0	2.0	1.0
Students who said they were afraid of attacks			
At school	24.0	20.0	22.0
To & from school	19.0	13.0	13.0
Students who said they avoided certain places at school out of fear			
	8.0	6.0	6.0
Students who had taken a weapon or other object to school for protection			
	8.0	6.0	6.0

In the NASB study, changing family circumstances, particularly single-parent households, were cited by 77.0 percent of the respondents as the main cause of school violence. One-third of all American infants are born to unwed mothers, a figure that reaches 68.0 percent for African American babies. These children of single-parent households account for 70.0 percent of the caseloads in juvenile courts. According to the National Crime Prevention Council in Washington, "kids are terribly disconnected and isolated from the fundamental building blocks of family, community, school, and church." Marian Wright Edelman of the Children's Defense Fund observes that "never has America permitted children to rely on guns and gangs rather than parents and neighbors for protection and love."

The number of gangs in Los Angeles County alone doubled to around 800 in just 6 years between 1985 and 1991, according to the *Los Angeles Times*. In one analysis, gangs offer "identity, friendship, protection, and excitement—not to mention money and sex" (Harper 1989). An integral component of the gang culture is the drug trade, which offers fast money but involves a deep immersion in violent turf wars with rival gangs. This street violence is ubiquitous. At the Boston City Hospital pediatric clinic in 1992, 10.0 percent of the children treated had witnessed a shooting or stabbing before age 6. A survey by the University of Alabama conducted in 1991 found that 43.0 percent of inner city children surveyed had witnessed a homicide. A sociologist who conducted the UAB study noted that this environment "has significant developmental implications for these children," that they have become desensitized to violence and grief.

The ability to easily obtain guns allows this culture of violence to thrive. Tulane University researchers conducted surveys which found that 35.0 percent of inner-city youths carried guns at least occasionally and 70.0 percent indicated that there was a gun in the family (Sheley 1995). These researchers argue that today's gun culture grew out of the drug culture of the 1980s, that many became armed as they entered into the drug distribution network, and that other teens armed themselves out of fear of those in the drug trade.

The NASB report also found that violence in the media was to blame "as a way that young people come to accept violence as a natural part of life." The American Psychological Association estimates that the average child watches 8,000 murders and 100,000 other violent acts on television by the time he or she finishes elementary school. The glamour of violence depicted on many TV shows, and especially Hollywood movies, has contributed to an ethos of violence that one Ball State University researcher found reflected in the 74.0 percent of students who approved of hitting a sibling after being hit first. Students at an antiviolence forum held in North Carolina in 1993 complained to the governor that violent TV shows, movies and music lyrics often promote violence.

The Threat to Education

Violence defeats education through physical and psychological intimidation. Not only are children being hurt, but experts fear that this increasingly hostile climate is robbing every child of the social and intellectual atmosphere needed to become successful students as well as productive members of society. With widespread violence in so many schools comes not only concern for the physical and psychological safety of students and teachers but a fear that the classroom in this environment is not conducive to learning. In a University of Michigan study, 17.0 percent of 10th grade students reported that during an average week, misbehavior by other students often interferes with their own learning (1992). In another study conducted the same year, 46.0 percent of secondary school teachers reported that disruptive student behavior interferes with their teaching (National Center for Education Statistics, 1992). The fear engendered by the threat of violence is reflected in the fact that 45.0 percent of public school students avoid school grounds, 43.0 percent avoid rest rooms, and 20.0 percent avoid hallways when possible.

Answering Violence

The violence that is so pervasive in the nation's schools has precipitated numerous responses, from disciplinary measures and tighter security measures in schools to Acts of Congress. Metal detectors, surveillance cameras, and other methods designed to keep school property free of weapons are being used widely (see Table 5.5.3, page 227).

By 1994, some 50 urban school systems employed metal detectors to screen their students for weapons. However, many lament their use, feeling they lead to a fortress mentality. Also, some theorize that if students know they must pass through a detector they will get a weapon into school by some other means, for instance passing it through an open window. Chicago's school system instituted a roving schedule of metal detector placement to deter students by keeping them off guard. This measure, and close cooperation with city police, was a key component of a program started in 1990 called Schools are for Education (SAFE). Two years after its inception, there had not been a single shooting in the city's schools.

Some school districts opt to excise the worst of the disruptive students, with some placing them in special schools in an attempt at rehabilitation. Schools in Boston, Miami, Houston, and other areas have such programs which counsel students in violence prevention and attempt to involve the parents in the treatment. The Dallas school system combined this method with conflict resolution training and high tech security systems in its schools. One particular building was designed and built as a state-of-the-art example of a security conscious school, with wide, bright hallways and straight lines to prevent dark hiding places. Crimes decreased in the school district from 1,730 in the 1991-92 school year to 1,085 in 1993-94.

Others believe that the long-term solution to violence in the schools is in deploying methods such as teaching conflict resolution to students and teachers, including peer mediation to resolve conflicts nonviolently. In touting the Safe Schools Act of 1993, introduced by President Clinton, U.S. Secretary of Education Richard Riley emphasized that, although a good portion of the $175 million would go toward the purchase of metal detectors and other safety measures, violence prevention, peer mediation, and summer and after-school programs would be an integral part of the effort. He called for the involvement of parents, grandparents, neighbors, and businesses as well as educators and politicians to help reclaim the schools and their communities.

Other national efforts have also called attention to the problem of school violence. The National Education Association, in 1993, called for a $500 million national program to combat the problem, including security and prevention methods just discussed, as well as special educational programs for disruptive students and smaller classroom student-teacher ratios. In the same year, philanthropist Walter Annenberg pledged $500 million to restructure the nation's public schools. The bulk of the money was to go to educational organizations involved in the reform of school bureaucracies and the improvement of curriculums and student achievement.

Organizations such as the Coalition of Essential Schools and Educators for Social Responsibility have emerged to take a leading role in revamping the way the classroom is run. A program called "Resolving Conflict Creatively," developed by Educators for Social Responsibility, has been deployed in over 200 schools nationwide. The curriculum incorporates instruction on listening attentively, dealing with anger, and overcoming racial stereotypes, while submitting to peer mediation to resolve conflicts. The Coalition for Essential Schools, founded in 1984, has over 500 participating schools involved in its programs. The Coalition shifts the emphasis from traditional rote memorization drills, to a system where teachers "coach" students to think creatively in order to increase their achievement. The reduction of bureaucratic impediments to learning and the restructured and more personalized approach to teaching create a more challenging atmosphere for the student that many feel is the ultimate solution to combating violence in the nation's schools.

SCHOOL DISCIPLINE

Education experts and the American public agree that schools that lack discipline are neither safe nor conducive to learning. In an educational issues poll, Americans chose "fighting, violence, and gangs" and "lack of discipline" as equal problems at the top of a list of educational concerns (Rose, *et al.* 1996). Teachers and school administrators warn that unless problems of discipline are addressed, educational reform is impossible.

In 1993, the U.S. Department of Education surveyed parents and students about their perceptions of school safety and discipline (National Household Education Survey, 1993). The survey measured academic challenge, enjoyment of school, respect between teachers and students, discipline maintained by teachers and administrators, and norms of achievement among peers. The results showed that perceptions vary with the characteristics of the school, the students grade, and the racial composition of the school (see Table 5.5.4, page 232). Students who attend private school, and their parents, report a more positive learning environment than those attending public schools. They also see schools as being more disciplined.

Positive responses with respect to classroom discipline decreased with age and school size. Older students—those in high school—thought that discipline was worse than did students in elementary school. Also, students in large schools were less pleased than those in schools with less than 300 students.

A longitudinal study followed 8th graders on issues such as disruptions in class interfering with learning, discipline, and the quality of teaching. Students who felt that class disruptions interfered with their ability to learn decreased over time. When asked if the school they attended was unsafe, only 10.4 percent of 12th graders said they strongly agreed or agreed with this statement. This figure fluctuated over the time of the study, starting at 11.8 percent and falling to 8.0 percent in 1990. When asked if discipline was fair in their school 69.1 percent of students agreed or strongly agreed, rising to 70.2 percent in 1990 before dropping to 68.0 percent by the time they were in 12th grade. Students agreed or strongly agreed that the teaching was good, this figure rising from 80.2 percent in 1988 to 85.4 percent in 1992.

Teachers were also surveyed about their perceptions of problems in school. Once again, public school teachers and private school teachers saw similar problems in different ways. The contrast between teachers was significant in the areas of student challenge and apathy, vandalism, drugs and drinking, tardiness and absenteeism, and social problems such as poverty and family conflicts. Public school teachers saw poverty as a major problem (19.5 percent) compared with only 2.7 percent of private school teachers (see Table 5.5.5, page 232). Public school teachers also complained about students being unprepared

for class by a margin of 28.8 percent to 4.1 percent of private school teachers.

Substance Abuse in the Classroom

Over ninety percent of all Americans regard drugs as a more serious problem than welfare, health care, or the Federal budget deficit. In partial response to this concern, Congress enacted legislation called "Improving America's Schools" which includes "Goals 2000," an ambitious agenda that seeks to make schools conducive to learning through the eradication of drugs.

After a decade of declining drug use, the use of illegal drugs by adolescents increased significantly between 1992 and 1994 (see Figure 5.5.5, page 229). These increases are driven primarily by the use of marijuana, which rose steadily for students between 12 and 17 years of age (see Figure 5.5.6, page 229).

Use of hallucinogenic substances follows patterns established for marijuana (see Figure 5.5.7, page 229). After initial declines between 1979 and 1992, yearly and monthly use increased between between 1992 and 1994. Monthly use of cocaine increased between 1992 and 1994 after declining years (see Figure 5.5.8, page 229). Heroin use, on the other hand, increased dramatically among students between 1993 and 1994. The percentage of students using heroin nearly tripled in this one year (see Figure 5.5.9, page 230).

Alcohol and cigarette use has also jumped in recent years. In the case of alcohol, which has always been the most abused substance among students, use increased in 1992 and has continued to rise (see Figure 5.5.10, page 230). In 1995,

80.7 percent of high school students acknowledged lifetime use of alcohol, 73.7 percent claimed use within the last 12 months, and 51.3 percent acknowledged use during the previous 30 days (see Table 5.5.6, page 233).The increasing use of cigarettes has been far more dramatic, reaching all-time highs in 1994 (see Figure 5.5.11, page 230).

Children at Risk of School Failure

According to the National Household Education Survey, a child is at risk of school failure when he or she is African American or Hispanic, comes from poverty, speaks a language other than English at home, has only one parent, belongs to a large family (6 or more members), and/or is born to a parent under the age of 18 (Hofferth et al., 1994). Other factors that place children at risk are divorce, being born to an unwed mother, and/or having a mother with less than a high school education (Zill, 1992, Hofferth et al., 1994).

While every child with risk factors does not do poorly in school, risk factors predispose children to poor academic performance. At-risk children repeat grades, require special education services, are suspended frequently, and/or drop out of school more often than children who are not at risk (Zill, 1992). Furthermore, at-risk children have difficulty making the transition to adulthood and the workplace (Pallas et al., 1989).

Since the 1970s, the number of at-risk children has increased due to changes in work and family life. Of the 4 million babies born each year, nearly 1 in 8 is born to a teenage mother, 1 in 4 is born to a mother without a high school diploma, 1 in

4 is born into poverty, 1 in 4 is born to an unwed mother, and 1 in 14 is born with low birth weight (Zill, 1992).

Given the above statistics, between 10.0 and 25.0 percent of the U.S. population exhibits at least one at-risk indicator (Pallas et al., 1989). Children with more than one risk factor are considered to be educationally disadvantaged or at risk of school failure.

EDUCATING CHILDREN AT RISK

The National Education Goals Report (NEGR) states "all children in America will start school ready to learn [by the year 2000]." The objective associated with this goal is that all disadvantaged and disabled children will have the same access to high quality preschool programs as do children who are not at risk. A second objective is that every parent will become a child's first teacher and devote time each day to helping preschoolers learn, and parents will have access to the training and support that they need to accomplish this objective. Objective three states that all children will receive the nutrition, physical activity, and health care needed to arrive at school with healthy minds and bodies in order to maintain the mental alertness necessary to be prepared to learn, and that the number of low-birth weight babies will be significantly reduced through enhanced prenatal health systems.

According to the report, 35.0 percent of all U.S. children in 1992 were born with one or more health risks, 75.0 percent of 2-year-olds were fully immunized against preventable childhood diseases, and 66.0 percent of America's parents read or told stories to their 3- to 5-year-olds.

Issues of immunization in education are discussed in an earlier section of this chapter, and exact figures for parental participation in preschool education and intellectual stimulation through family reading and storytelling are not complete at a state level. What is available are data showing the proportion of children in each state that were born with one or more health risks (see Figure 5.5.12, page 231).

STUDENTS ATTRACTED TO PARTNERS OF THE SAME SEX

Children attracted to partners of the same sex are one of America's most isolated groups. According to the U.S. Bureau of the Census, 7.2 million Americans under the age of 20 are gay or lesbian. Many of this number are in their early teens, with first-time same sex experiences at an average age of 15.2 for males and 13.1 for females (Herdt and Boxer 1993).

The process of "coming out," albeit courageous, is often painful. Half of all lesbian and gay youth, who come out at an average age of 16, reported that their parents rejected them because of their sexual preferences. One in four was forced to leave their home, contributing to a street population of youth that is 25.0 percent gay or lesbian. Those who stay at home and in school often experience emotional trauma. Eight percent of gay and lesbian children reported severe emotional isolation. Every day, 13 Americans between the ages of 15 and 24 commit suicide, and gay and lesbian youths account for 30.0 percent of that figure.

School districts have failed to react successfully to a growing gay and lesbian population. Nearly half of all gay males have been harassed in school as have 28.0 percent of lesbian students (Hetrick-Martin Institute, 1993). Twenty-eight percent of high school students have been forced to drop out of school due to what they describe as relentless harassment based on sexual preference. A 1987 study conducted by the South Carolina Guidance Counselor's Association noted that 8 out of every 10 prospective teachers and two-thirds of all existing guidance counselors expressed negative feelings about homosexuality. Furthermore, 1,600 school districts have adopted sex education programs that present sexual abstinence and monogamy within heterosexual marriage as the only sexual choices available to teenagers.

In 1997, only the state of Massachusetts outlawed discrimination against gay and lesbian students. One hundred gay and lesbian support groups have formed in the nation's high schools. Fifteen U.S. colleges and universities have gay and lesbian task forces, and 248 have nondiscrimination policies that include sexual orientation.

LATCHKEY CHILDREN

The labor force participation of women and mothers has been rising since 1950. Between 1970 and 1993, the rate of participation of married mothers with children under 6 years old increased from 30.3 to 59.9 percent (Figure 5.5.13). Married mothers with children older than 6 years of age also entered the workforce in record numbers with participation rates of 49.2 percent and 74.9 percent for the same years (see Figure 5.5.14, 185). Collectively, 75.0 percent of married women with children between 6 and 17 were either employed or looking for work in 1993. Divorced mothers are being employed in larger proportions than married mothers. While 59.9 percent of married mothers with children under 6 and 74.9 percent with children between 6 and 17 years of age worked, divorced mothers participated in the work force in numbers that were recorded at 68.1 percent and 83.6 percent respectively.

As mothers, single, separated, divorced, or married, enter the workplace in record numbers, parents are confronted with the difficult task of providing child care after school hours. The term "latchkey children" is used to describe children of working parents for whom accommodations are not found and, therefore, care for themselves before or after school or during school vacations.

Estimated to be 2 to 5 million strong in 1997, this miniature society of self-caring

individuals is creating growing demands for high-quality child care, before- and after-school programs, and sick-child services that have not been met with increased resources. The National Committee for the Prevention of Child Abuse notes that only 900,000 of the 7.5 million children under the age of 6 whose mothers are working are enrolled in day care centers. The remaining 6.6 million children either care for themselves or are cared for by relatives or nonfamily members in a variety of *ad hoc* arrangements.

As the likelihood of being in self care varies, so do issues of child welfare for various age groups. Self-care issues for younger children revolve mainly around safety and emotional security. Sadly, many young children in self care feel emotionally isolated, rejected, alienated, or afraid. They also run greater risks of being hurt or abused in the absence of adult supervision.

For older children—those 11 to 15 years old—developmental opportunities are lost, being replaced by questionable activities such as hanging out, watching television, and visiting shopping malls.

HOME SCHOOLING

In addition to the 52 million American children who attend public and private schools, a small but growing number are educated at home. According to the National Center for Education Statistics, the number of children in home instruction seems to have grown from about 15,000 in the early seventies to well over 245,000 today. Current figures constitute about 0.5 percent of the total number of students in school.

The reasons for home schooling vary. Some parents object to the political or cultural values they perceive to exist in public and private schools. The largest and fastest growing group—devout Christians—feel that public education does not adequately address matters of religious nature. Other home schooling advocates are committed to "alternative" lifestyles—those characterized by natural childbirth at home, natural foods, natural fibers, etc. Other reasons include parents' recognizing that special needs of children not being fulfilled in schools or children not reaching full potential in structured classroom instruction. Regardless of specific rationale, a common thread among all home school advocates is the firm belief that parents should be deeply involved in the education and development of their own children.

LAWS APPLYING TO HOME SCHOOLS
Until the mid 1980s, compulsory edu-

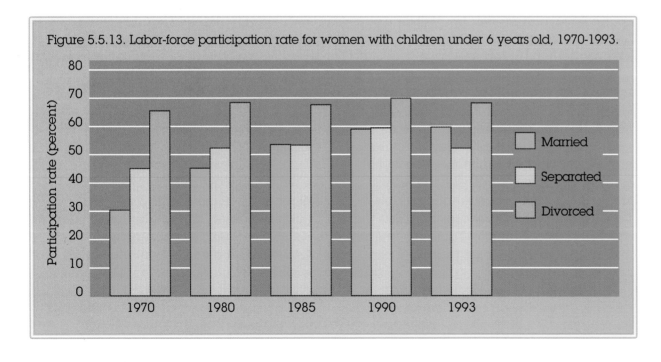

Figure 5.5.13. Labor-force participation rate for women with children under 6 years old, 1970-1993.

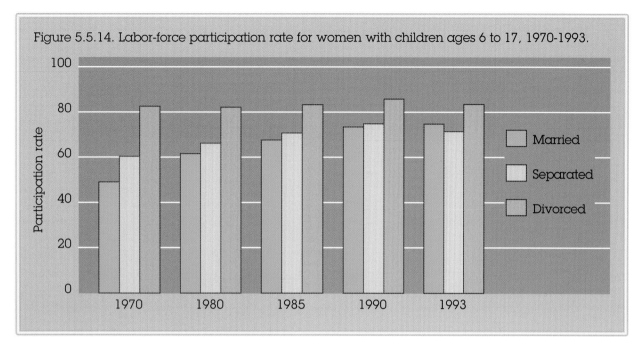

Figure 5.5.14. Labor-force participation rate for women with children ages 6 to 17, 1970-1993.

Participation rate

Married
Separated
Divorced

1970   1980   1985   1990   1993

cation laws, crafted over a century ago to combat truancy, did not recognize home schooling as a viable alternative to established education programs. Since, every state has adopted some form of legislation to legitimize home schooling. In 1991, 22 states required certification of the home-teacher. Another 23 states required pupil testing. In general, laws regulating home instruction are found in states' compulsory education requirements and are administered by branches of state government or local education agencies (see Table 5.5.7, page 233). Twenty-two of the fifty states require teacher certification and twenty-three require mandatory pupil testing. In many cases, state regulations are passed along to localities for implementation.

State legislatures, court systems, the ACLU, and the NEA are generally supportive of home schooling. The ACLU protects the constitutional right to home school while

the NEA supports rigorous regulation. In separate instances, some states have attempted to move home school policy in a liberally interpreted direction, but court responses have varied considerably, often seeking greater regulatory power and more stringent requirements. A source of variation resides in the interpretation of what defines "school" or "equivalent instruction." Some courts have decided that home schooling does not conform to compulsory attendance requirements within education laws while other courts have declared that education laws have been too vague or too broad in their definitions of "school" and "requirements of attendance."

Gifted and Talented Children

In a study addressing educational stagnation, the U.S. Department of Education concluded that there is a "quiet crisis" threatening American students who have

been encouraged to bring home good grades but have not been challenged to master higher level course work or skills. Both international testing and testing by the National Assessment of Educational Progress (NAEP) support this conclusion by demonstrating that, when compared to students of other nations, American students achieve below average test scores, participate in less rigorous curriculum, read fewer demanding books, do less homework, and enter the work force or higher education with less preparation.

Affected disproportionately by this trend to mediocrity are gifted or talented children who are defined by the Office of Educational Research and Improvement (OERI) of the U.S. Department of Education as "children and youth who give evidence of high performance capability in areas such as intellectual, creative, artistic, or leadership capacity, or in specific academic fields, and who require services or activities not ordinarily provided by the school in order to fully develop such capabilities." Gifted students are found to be working well below their capabilities and are not being provided an experience that allows them to reach their full potential.

The Department of Education outlines a series of steps to reverse the "quiet crisis" within American schools. Recommendations include: (1) setting curriculum standards that provide challenging opportunities to learn; (2) increasing access to early childhood education and increasing opportunities for disadvantaged and minority children; (3) broadening the definition of "gifted;" (4) emphasizing teacher development; and (5) matching international performances. The Office of Educational

Research and Improvement also calls for increased funding, noting that only 2 cents of every 100 dollars allocated for K-12 education was spent on special opportunities for talented students.

INITIATIVES TO DEVELOP PROGRAMS FOR THE GIFTED AND TALENTED STUDENTS

By 1994, 37 states mandated legislation to define and address the needs of gifted and talented students (Table 5.5.8). Only 7 states required special programs 20 years ago. Most states identify exceptional students using eligibility criteria sanctioned by the U.S. Department of Education. These eligibility processes employ broad guidelines that look at a variety of qualities beyond intellectual ability. They are based on the prevailing theory that intelligence is complex, takes many forms, and therefore is not measurable by single criterion alone.

While a multicriteria approach to identifying gifted children is the theoretical choice of educators, it is rarely implemented at the state or local level. In practice, State Education Agencies (SEAs) require only student IQ scores—sometimes supported by teacher recommendations—to justify funding. This flawed evaluation process predominates despite research that demonstrates disparities in IQ scores between ethnic groups and students from poor families compared with affluent nonminority students. In effect, current screening practices tend to eliminate minority and economically disadvantaged children, females, students with disabilities, underachievers, and those displaying artistic potential, from programs for which they are otherwise qualified.

Table 5.5.8. Gifted and talented students and programs, 1994.

	State programs Mandated	State programs Discretionary	Gifted and talented students receiving services	Gifted and talented students as a percent of enrollment
Alabama			16,522	2.4
Alaska	X		4,696	4.0
Arizona	X		39,200	—
Arkansas	X		34,710	8.0
California		X	290,000	5.0
Colorado	X		—	—
Connecticut	X		16,871	3.5
Delaware	X		—	5.0
Dist. of Columbia		X	—	9.0
Florida	X		74,572	3.5
Georgia	X		—	5.0
Hawaii	X		18,000	11.0
Idaho	X		—	1.3
Illinois	X		166,234	5.0
Indiana		X	85,192	8.9
Iowa	X		—	4.0
Kansas	X		—	3.1
Kentucky	X		52,600	5.0
Louisiana	X		24,000	3.2
Maine	X		10,100	5.0
Maryland		X	90,222	12.0
Massachusetts		X	—	—
Michigan		X	225,154	14.0
Minnesota		X	55,467	7.2
Mississippi	X		21,678	4.3
Missouri	X		24,877	5.0
Montana	X		—	—
Nebraska		X	18,600	10.0
Nevada	X	X	8,343	2.0
New Hampshire	X		—	—
New Jersey	X		—	—
New Mexico	X		—	—
New York	X		135,000	6.0
North Carolina	X		88,450	8.0
North Dakota		X	1,107	1.0
Ohio	X		244,670	13.0
Oklahoma	X		61,082	10.0
Oregon	X		—	8.5
Pennsylvania	X		79,756	4.6
Rhode Island		X	—	3.5-5.0
South Carolina	X		52,000	10.0
South Dakota	X		6,515	4.4
Tennessee	X		18,626	2.0
Texas	X		248,769	7.0
Utah	X		—	—
Vermont		X	—	—
Virginia	X		121,598	9.2
Washington		X	38,781	1.5
West Virginia	X		—	3.5
Wisconsin	X		—	15.0
Wyoming		X	—	3.0

FUNDING PROGRAMS FOR GIFTED AND TALENTED STUDENTS

Each state policy regarding funding for gifted and talented students is different in terms of how financial support is provided. Some states mandate programs but do not provide financial support, while others identify local education agencies (LEAs) and grant organizations as funding sources. Gifted and talented programs are also partly supported through federal grants from the Office of Educational Research and Improvement (OERI). These grants are administered through the Jacob H. Javits Gifted and Talented Students Education Program which was mandated in 1988 by an amendment to the Education Act of 1965. The purpose of the Javits Program is to support research, demonstration projects, and personnel training to identify and meet the special educational needs of gifted and talented students. The Javits Program is currently funded with an annual budget of just under $10 million, which is available to SEAs and local programs through a grant application process.

ETHNIC DISTRIBUTION OF GIFTED AND TALENTED STUDENTS

Concluding this section are an interesting series of tables (see Tables 5.5.9 to 5.5.13, pages 234 to 236). They show special placements for students of various ethnic backgrounds. Each table represents a particular ethnic group. Table 5.5.9 on page 234, for example, represents white students, with 5 columns of data. Column 1 is the proportion of each state's enrollment that is white. Columns 2, 3, and 4 are the percentages of white students in special placements. Column 5 is the per-cent of white children who are suspended from school.

Worth noting are the relationships between the placements and enrollments and placements and suspensions. They speak highly to the issue of equal opportunity for students of all backgrounds. In Alabama, for example, 62.0 percent of the state's enrollment is white, yet 89.0 percent of the state's "gifted and talented" are white. Shifting to Table 5.5.10 on page 234, which represents African American placements, another relationship is evident. Using Delaware as an example, 29.0 percent of all students are African American, while only 8.0 percent are placed in programs for the "gifted and talented." Furthermore, 44.0 percent of the state's special placements are black, as are 48.0 percent of those suspended.

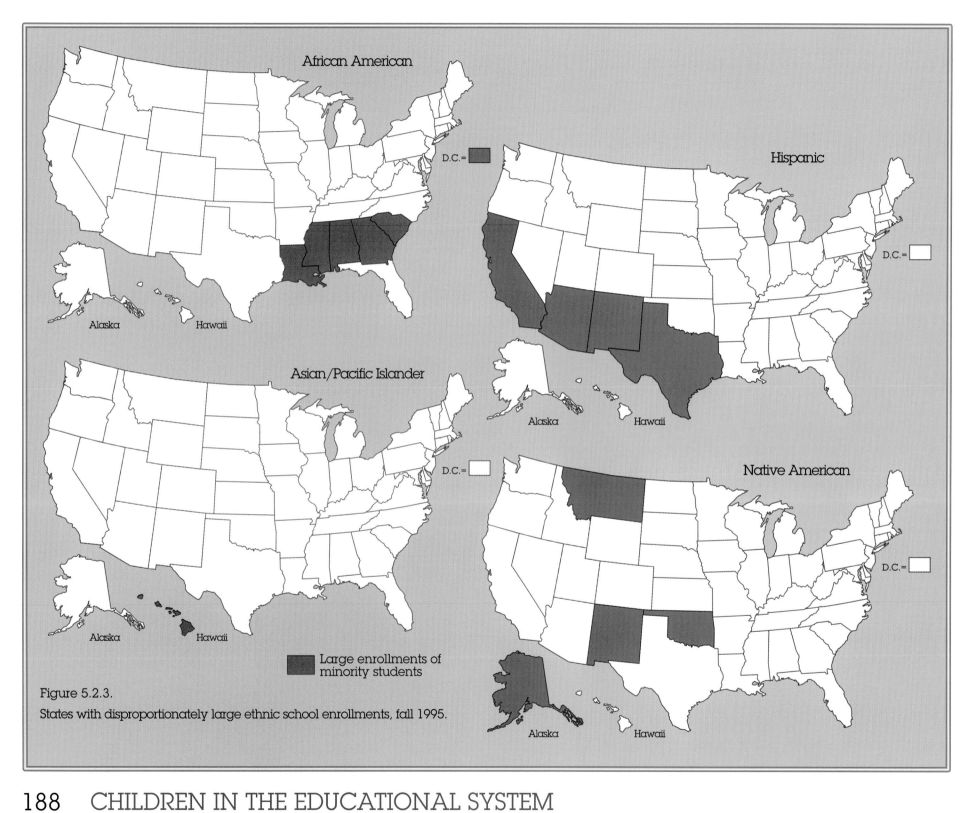

African American

Hispanic

D.C.=

D.C.=

Asian/Pacific Islander

Alaska   Hawaii

Native American

D.C.=

D.C.=

Alaska   Hawaii

Alaska   Hawaii

Alaska   Hawaii

Large enrollments of
minority students

Figure 5.2.3.
States with disproportionately large ethnic school enrollments, fall 1995.

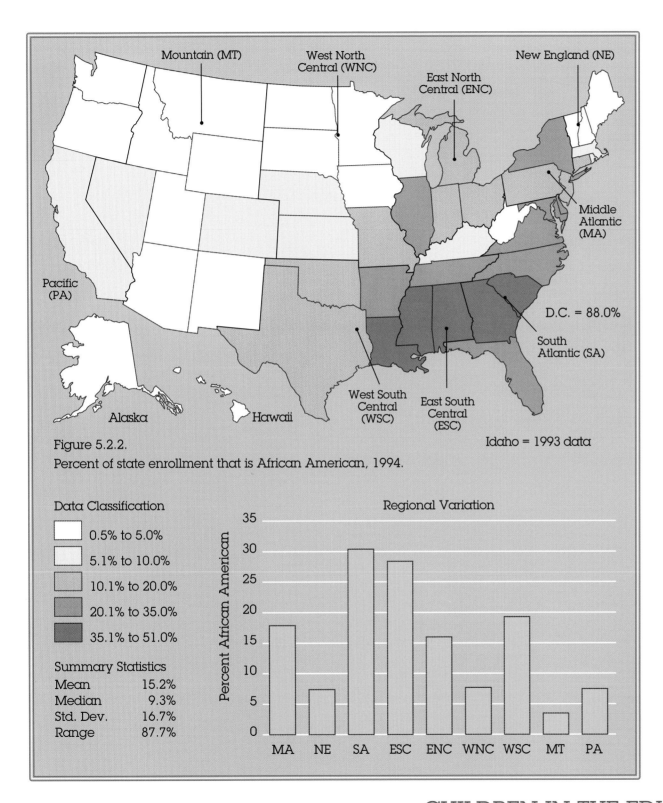

Figure 5.2.2.
Percent of state enrollment that is African American, 1994.

Percent of state enrollment that is African American, 1994.

	Total enrollment	% African American
Alabama	734,288	35.8
Alaska	125,948	4.8
Arizona	709,453	4.3
Arkansas	444,271	23.9
California	5,327,231	8.7
Colorado	625,062	5.4
Connecticut	496,298	13.3
Delaware	105,547	29.1
District of Columbia	80,678	88.0
Florida	2,040,763	25.0
Georgia	1,235,304	37.5
Hawaii	180,410	2.7
Idaho	236,774	0.3
Illinois	1,893,078	21.0
Indiana	965,633	11.2
Iowa	498,519	3.2
Kansas	457,614	8.4
Kentucky	655,265	9.7
Louisiana	800,560	45.7
Maine	216,995	0.7
Maryland	772,638	34.7
Massachusetts	877,726	8.0
Michigan	1,599,377	17.5
Minnesota	810,233	4.5
Mississippi	505,907	50.9
Missouri	866,378	15.8
Montana	163,009	0.5
Nebraska	285,097	5.8
Nevada	235,800	9.3
New Hampshire	185,360	0.8
New Jersey	1,151,307	18.6
New Mexico	322,292	2.4
New York	2,733,813	20.2
North Carolina	1,133,231	30.5
North Dakota	119,127	0.8
Ohio	1,807,319	15.1
Oklahoma	604,076	10.4
Oregon	516,611	2.5
Pennsylvania	1,744,082	13.9
Rhode Island	145,676	7.0
South Carolina	643,696	41.7
South Dakota	142,825	0.8
Tennessee	866,557	23.0
Texas	3,608,262	14.3
Utah	471,365	0.7
Vermont	102,755	0.7
Virginia	1,045,471	26.2
Washington	915,952	4.6
West Virginia	314,383	3.9
Wisconsin	844,001	9.3
Wyoming	100,899	1.0

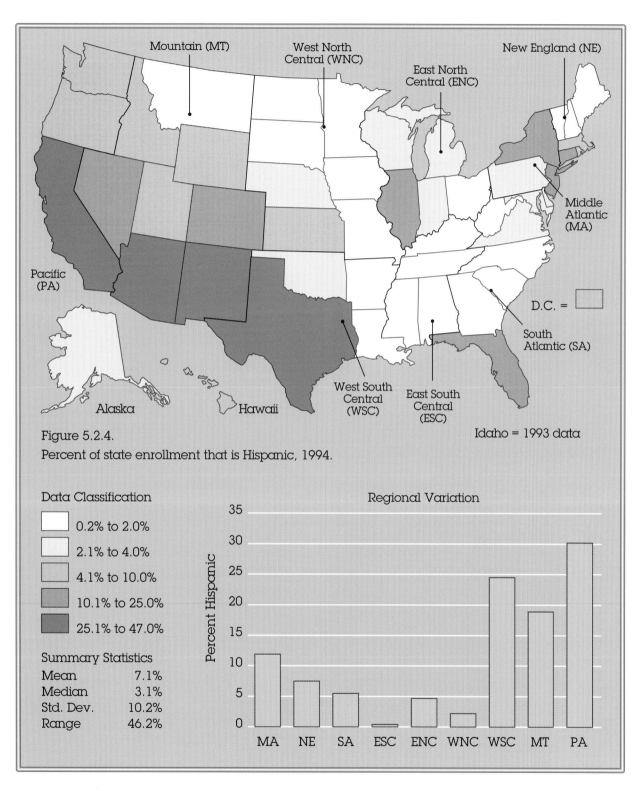

Figure 5.2.4.

Percent of state enrollment that is Hispanic, 1994.

Data Classification

☐	0.2% to 2.0%
☐	2.1% to 4.0%
☐	4.1% to 10.0%
☐	10.1% to 25.0%
☐	25.1% to 47.0%

Summary Statistics

Mean	7.1%
Median	3.1%
Std. Dev.	10.2%
Range	46.2%

Percent of state enrollment that is Hispanic, 1994.

	Total enrollment	Percent Hispanic
Alabama	734,288	0.4
Alaska	125,948	2.6
Arizona	709,453	28.7
Arkansas	444,271	1.1
California	5,327,231	37.9
Colorado	625,062	17.6
Connecticut	496,298	11.4
Delaware	105,547	3.6
District of Columbia	80,678	6.6
Florida	2,040,763	14.4
Georgia	1,235,304	1.8
Hawaii	180,410	4.9
Idaho	236,774	4.9
Illinois	1,893,078	11.6
Indiana	965,633	2.2
Iowa	498,519	1.8
Kansas	457,614	5.7
Kentucky	655,265	0.3
Louisiana	800,560	1.1
Maine	216,995	0.4
Maryland	772,638	3.1
Massachusetts	877,726	9.0
Michigan	1,599,377	2.6
Minnesota	810,233	1.8
Mississippi	505,907	0.3
Missouri	866,378	0.9
Montana	163,009	1.4
Nebraska	285,097	3.8
Nevada	235,800	15.5
New Hampshire	185,360	1.1
New Jersey	1,151,307	13.1
New Mexico	322,292	46.4
New York	2,733,813	16.9
North Carolina	1,133,231	1.5
North Dakota	119,127	0.8
Ohio	1,807,319	1.4
Oklahoma	604,076	3.7
Oregon	516,611	6.3
Pennsylvania	1,744,082	3.4
Rhode Island	145,676	9.5
South Carolina	643,696	0.6
South Dakota	142,825	0.7
Tennessee	866,557	0.6
Texas	3,608,262	36.1
Utah	471,365	4.8
Vermont	102,755	0.3
Virginia	1,045,471	3.0
Washington	915,952	7.4
West Virginia	314,383	0.2
Wisconsin	844,001	3.1
Wyoming	100,899	6.1

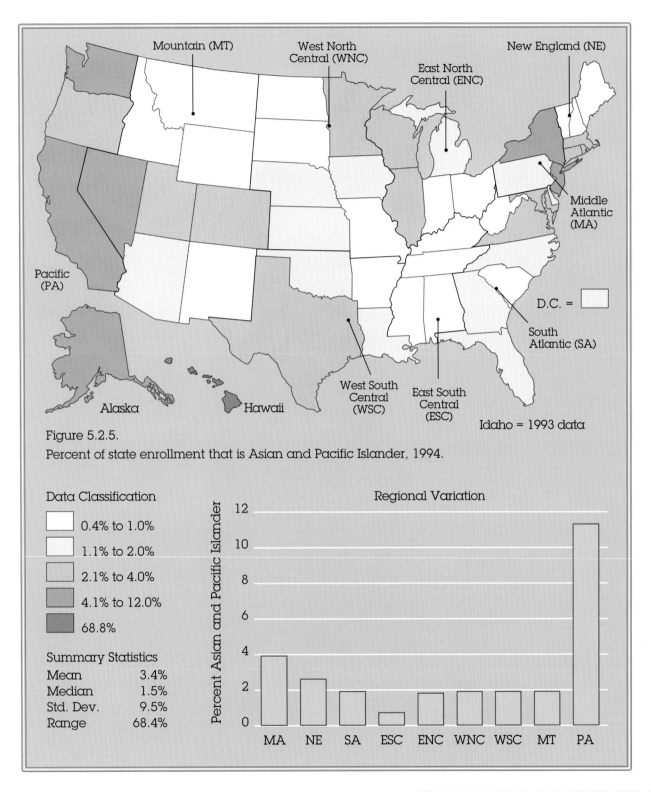

Figure 5.2.5.
Percent of state enrollment that is Asian and Pacific Islander, 1994.

Data Classification

- 0.4% to 1.0%
- 1.1% to 2.0%
- 2.1% to 4.0%
- 4.1% to 12.0%
- 68.8%

Summary Statistics

Mean	3.4%
Median	1.5%
Std. Dev.	9.5%
Range	68.4%

Regional Variation

Percent of state enrollment that is Asian/Pacific Islander, 1994.

	Total enrollment	Percent Asian
Alabama	734,288	0.6
Alaska	125,948	4.1
Arizona	709,453	1.7
Arkansas	444,271	0.7
California	5,327,231	11.2
Colorado	625,062	2.5
Connecticut	496,298	2.4
Delaware	105,547	1.7
District of Columbia	80,678	1.3
Florida	2,040,763	1.7
Georgia	1,235,304	1.5
Hawaii	180,410	68.8
Idaho	236,774	0.8
Illinois	1,893,078	3.0
Indiana	965,633	0.8
Iowa	498,519	1.5
Kansas	457,614	1.9
Kentucky	655,265	0.6
Louisiana	800,560	1.3
Maine	216,995	0.8
Maryland	772,638	3.8
Massachusetts	877,726	3.7
Michigan	1,599,377	1.5
Minnesota	810,233	3.7
Mississippi	505,907	0.5
Missouri	866,378	1.0
Montana	163,009	0.8
Nebraska	285,097	1.2
Nevada	235,800	4.2
New Hampshire	185,360	1.0
New Jersey	1,151,307	5.2
New Mexico	322,292	1.0
New York	2,733,813	4.8
North Carolina	1,133,231	1.2
North Dakota	119,127	0.7
Ohio	1,807,319	1.0
Oklahoma	604,076	1.2
Oregon	516,611	3.2
Pennsylvania	1,744,082	1.7
Rhode Island	145,676	3.2
South Carolina	643,696	0.7
South Dakota	142,825	0.8
Tennessee	866,557	0.9
Texas	3,608,262	2.3
Utah	471,365	2.1
Vermont	102,755	0.9
Virginia	1,045,471	3.4
Washington	915,952	6.3
West Virginia	314,383	0.4
Wisconsin	844,001	2.6
Wyoming	100,899	0.8

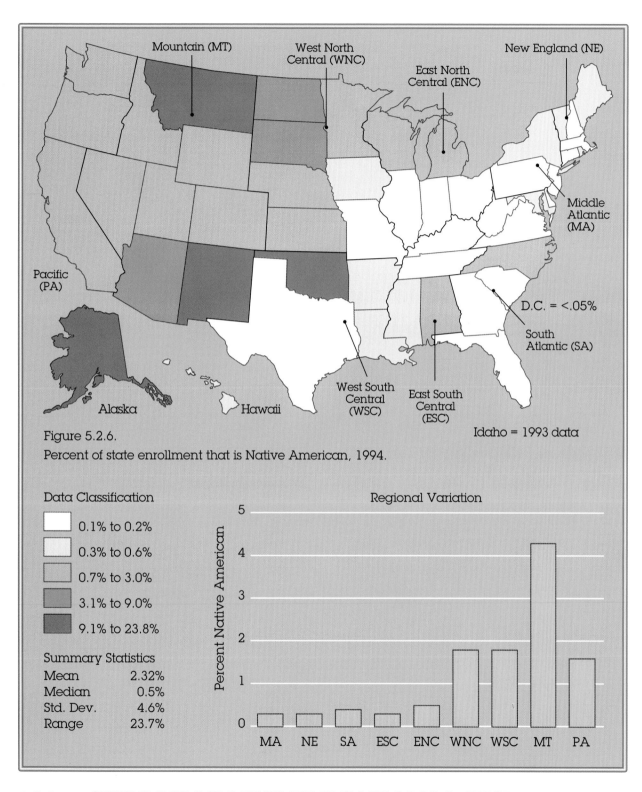

Figure 5.2.6.
Percent of state enrollment that is Native American, 1994.

Data Classification

- ☐ 0.1% to 0.2%
- ☐ 0.3% to 0.6%
- ☐ 0.7% to 3.0%
- ☐ 3.1% to 9.0%
- ☐ 9.1% to 23.8%

Summary Statistics

Mean	2.32%
Median	0.5%
Std. Dev.	4.6%
Range	23.7%

Regional Variation (Percent Native American by region: MA, NE, SA, ESC, ENC, WNC, WSC, MT, PA)

Idaho = 1993 data

Percent of state enrollment that is Native American, 1994.

	Total enrollment	% Native American
Alabama	734,288	0.8
Alaska	125,948	23.8
Arizona	709,453	7.0
Arkansas	444,271	0.3
California	5,327,231	0.9
Colorado	625,062	1.0
Connecticut	496,298	0.2
Delaware	105,547	0.2
District of Columbia	80,678	<0.1
Florida	2,040,763	0.2
Georgia	1,235,304	0.1
Hawaii	180,410	0.4
Idaho	236,774	1.3
Illinois	1,893,078	0.1
Indiana	965,633	0.2
Iowa	498,519	0.4
Kansas	457,614	1.0
Kentucky	655,265	0.1
Louisiana	800,560	0.5
Maine	216,995	0.5
Maryland	772,638	0.3
Massachusetts	877,726	0.2
Michigan	1,599,377	1.1
Minnesota	810,233	1.9
Mississippi	505,907	0.4
Missouri	866,378	0.2
Montana	163,009	9.6
Nebraska	285,097	1.3
Nevada	235,800	2.0
New Hampshire	185,360	0.2
New Jersey	1,151,307	0.2
New Mexico	322,292	10.4
New York	2,733,813	0.4
North Carolina	1,133,231	1.5
North Dakota	119,127	7.6
Ohio	1,807,319	0.1
Oklahoma	604,076	14.3
Oregon	516,611	1.9
Pennsylvania	1,744,082	0.1
Rhode Island	145,676	0.5
South Carolina	643,696	0.2
South Dakota	142,825	13.6
Tennessee	866,557	0.1
Texas	3,608,262	0.2
Utah	471,365	1.4
Vermont	102,755	0.5
Virginia	1,045,471	0.2
Washington	915,952	2.6
West Virginia	314,383	0.1
Wisconsin	844,001	1.3
Wyoming	100,899	2.8

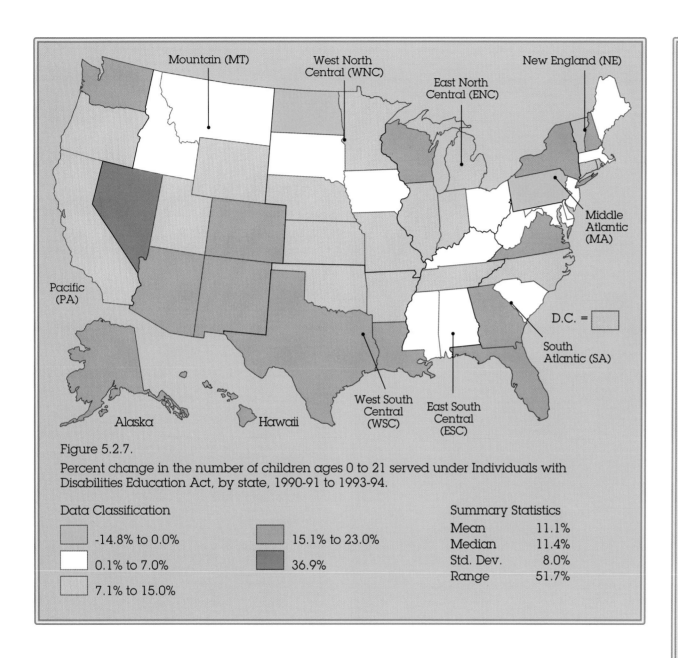

Figure 5.2.7.

Percent change in the number of children ages 0 to 21 served under Individuals with Disabilities Education Act, by state, 1990-91 to 1993-94.

Data Classification

	-14.8% to 0.0%
	0.1% to 7.0%
	7.1% to 15.0%

	15.1% to 23.0%
	36.9%

Summary Statistics

Mean	11.1%
Median	11.4%
Std. Dev.	8.0%
Range	51.7%

Percent change in the number of children (0-21 years of age) served under the IDEA, by state, 1990-91 to 1993-94.

	Total children 1993-94	Percent change
Alabama	99,760	5.1
Alaska	18,006	22.1
Arizona	69,530	21.5
Arkansas	53,187	11.2
California	533,807	13.7
Colorado	66,595	16.6
Connecticut	71,863	11.3
Delaware	15,196	6.3
District of Columbia	6,994	11.2
Florida	289,539	22.7
Georgia	123,143	20.7
Hawaii	15,248	15.8
Idaho	23,536	6.9
Illinois	257,986	7.9
Indiana	127,961	11.6
Iowa	63,373	4.4
Kansas	50,438	11.6
Kentucky	80,539	1.4
Louisiana	86,931	18
Maine	29,350	4.9
Maryland	97,998	6.6
Massachusetts	160,275	3.7
Michigan	181,251	8.6
Minnesota	90,918	12.4
Mississippi	64,153	5.3
Missouri	114,008	11.8
Montana	18,401	7
Nebraska	37,112	13.3
Nevada	25,242	36.9
New Hampshire	23,354	18.8
New Jersey	190,003	4.8
New Mexico	43,474	20.6
New York	365,697	18.9
North Carolina	136,513	10.9
North Dakota	12,440	-0.5
Ohio	219,875	7
Oklahoma	73,130	11.4
Oregon	63,212	14.6
Pennsylvania	210,826	-3.9
Rhode Island	23,582	11.9
South Carolina	81,930	5.4
South Dakota	15,907	6.1
Tennessee	119,146	13.6
Texas	411,917	17.5
Utah	51,950	8.8
Vermont	10,452	-14.8
Virginia	131,599	15.5
Washington	101,254	18.6
West Virginia	44,528	3.2
Wisconsin	102,412	17.8
Wyoming	12,480	11.4

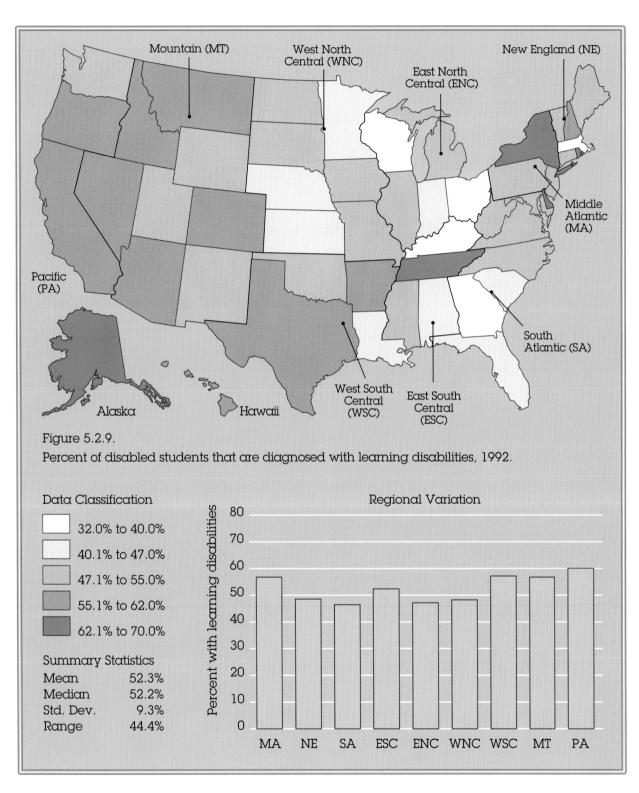

Figure 5.2.9.
Percent of disabled students that are diagnosed with learning disabilities, 1992.

Data Classification

	32.0% to 40.0%
	40.1% to 47.0%
	47.1% to 55.0%
	55.1% to 62.0%
	62.1% to 70.0%

Summary Statistics

Mean	52.3%
Median	52.2%
Std. Dev.	9.3%
Range	44.4%

Percent of disabled students that are diagnosed with learning disabilities, 1992.

	Total students diagnosed	Percent with learning disabilities
Alabama	36,020	41.1
Alaska	7,202	63.9
Arizona	32,725	60.2
Arkansas	24,563	59.4
California	273,840	61.3
Colorado	29,039	56.2
Connecticut	30,577	54.3
Delaware	6,921	69.7
Dist. of Columbia	1,936	76.9
Florida	103,016	45.0
Georgia	31,594	32.5
Hawaii	7,240	58.8
Idaho	11,730	60.9
Illinois	97,673	54.6
Indiana	45,075	43.6
Iowa	25,889	47.4
Kansas	18,313	45.6
Kentucky	23,417	35.1
Louisiana	30,404	45.0
Maine	11,728	47.9
Maryland	42,259	52.6
Massachusetts	46,433	36.7
Michigan	74,144	52.0
Minnesota	31,797	44.5
Mississippi	29,247	52.4
Missouri	50,613	52.1
Montana	9,201	58.3
Nebraska	14,900	46.0
Nevada	11,045	60.9
New Hampshire	11,171	62.0
New Jersey	88,061	53.8
New Mexico	17,516	49.6
New York	174,590	62.9
North Carolina	54,629	47.8
North Dakota	5,683	52.2
Ohio	76,010	39.8
Oklahoma	31,910	51.5
Oregon	28,078	61.2
Pennsylvania	83,918	47.4
Rhode Island	12,345	65.5
South Carolina	30,189	43.1
South Dakota	6,130	49.4
Tennessee	64,455	64.9
Texas	196,501	59.8
Utah	23,722	54.0
Vermont	4,704	54.4
Virginia	53,263	49.3
Washington	38,598	50.3
West Virginia	18,598	47.1
Wisconsin	25,912	33.7
Wyoming	5,555	54.9

Table 5.2.1. Ten-year flows of immigration to the United States and their impact on the total United States population, 1830-1990.

Census decade	Total population (in millions)	Immigrants (in millions)	Percent of U.S. population
		Immigration during prior decade	
1830 through 1840	12,900,000	100,000	0.8
1840 through 1850	17,100,000	600,000	3.5
1850 through 1860	23,200,000	1,700,000	7.3
1860 through 1870	31,400,000	2,600,000	8.3
1870 through 1880	38,600,000	2,300,000	6.0
1880 through 1890	50,200,000	2,800,000	5.6
1890 through 1900	63,000,000	5,200,000	8.3
1900 through 1910	76,200,000	3,700,000	4.9
1910 through 1920	92,200,000	8,900,000	9.7
1920 through 1930	106,000,000	5,800,000	5.5
1930 through 1940	123,200,000	4,100,000	3.3
1940 through 1950	132,200,000	500,000	0.4
1950 through 1960	151,300,000	1,000,000	0.7
1960 through 1970	179,300,000	2,500,000	1.4
1970 through 1980	203,300,000	3,800,000	1.9
1980 through 1990	226,500,000	7,000,000	3.1
1990 through 1994	248,700,000	9,000,000	3.6

NOTE: Included in estimates of immigration are illegal aliens, agricultural workers, and persons seeking asylum in the United States.

Table 5.2.2. Enrollment of fifty largest school districts, fall 1993.

Name of district	State	Enrollment	Minority pupils
New York City	New York	1,005,521	82.5%
Los Angeles Unified	California	639,129	87.9%
City of Chicago	Illinois	409,499	88.6%
Dade County	Florida	308,465	83.9%
Philadelphia	Pennsylvania	207,667	78.3%
Houston ISD	Texas	200,445	87.6%
Broward County	Florida	189,862	47.5%
Hawaii Public Schools	Hawaii	180,529	76.3%
Detroit Public Schools	Michigan	173,295	93.4%
Clark County	Nevada	145,327	34.9%
Dallas ISD	Texas	142,652	86.3%
Fairfax County	Virginia	135,413	32.1%
Hillsborough County	Florida	135,104	40.0%
San Diego City Unified	California	127,258	67.8%
Palm Beach County	Florida	122,145	42.6%
Duval County	Florida	119,785	42.9%
Prince George's County	Maryland	115,918	78.2%
Orange County	Florida	113,638	44.4%
Montgomery County	Maryland	113,429	42.0%
Baltimore City	Maryland	113,354	84.2%
Memphis City	Tennessee	105,978	82.4%
Pinellas County	Florida	100,135	22.9%
Baltimore County	Maryland	96,402	26.1%
Milwaukee City	Wisconsin	95,259	73.0%
Jefferson County	Kentucky	93,529	32.3%
Albuquerque	New Mexico	92,697	52.8%
Orleans Parish	Louisiana	85,983	93.7%
Charlotte-Mecklenburg	North Carolina	82,842	45.0%
Jefferson County	Colorado	82,760	12.3%
DeKalb County	Georgia	81,468	77.2%
DC Public Schools	District of Columbia	80,678	96.0%
Granite	Utah	79,746	10.7%
Cobb County	Georgia	77,563	19.0%
Long Beach Unified	California	76,783	77.5%
Gwinnett County	Georgia	76,482	15.7%
Fresno Unified	California	76,349	73.0%
Virginia Beach City	Virginia	74,880	28.8%
Cleveland City	Ohio	73,633	77.6%
Wake County	North Carolina	73,263	31.0%
Nashville-Davidson County	Tennessee	72,483	44.0%
Fort Worth ISD	Texas	72,114	69.6%
Austin ISD	Texas	71,664	59.0%
Jordan	Utah	70,256	5.4%
Polk County	Florida	69,718	29.9%
Anne Arundel County	Maryland	69,020	20.1%
Mesa Unified	Arizona	67,639	20.5%
Mobile County	Alabama	66,580	49.5%
El Paso ISD	Texas	64,141	80.2%
Columbus City	Ohio	63,877	53.9%
Boston City	Maryland	63,738	80.7%

Table 5.2.3. Number of children served under Individuals with Disabilities Education Act and Chapter 1 of the Education Consolidation and Improvement Act, State Operated Programs, by age group and state, 1990-91, 1991-92 and 1993-94.

	Age 0 to 21			Age 0 to 5			Percent change 1990-91 to 1993-94
	1990-91	1991-92	1992-93	1990-91	1991-92	1992-93	age 0 to 21
Alabama	94,945	96,975	99,760	7,498	8,344	9,161	5.1
Alaska	14,745	16,106	18,006	1,813	2,089	2,633	22.1
Arizona	57,235	61,076	69,530	4,936	5,784	7,685	21.5
Arkansas	47,835	49,018	53,187	5,274	5,648	6,972	11.2
California	469,282	494,058	533,807	40,489	44,351	52,061	13.7
Colorado	57,102	60,357	66,595	4,894	5,444	7,011	16.6
Connecticut	64,562	66,192	71,863	6,142	6,471	7,875	11.3
Delaware	14,294	14,435	15,196	1,579	1,677	1,953	6.3
Dist. of Columbia	6,290	7,104	6,994	411	588	600	11.2
Florida	236,013	253,606	289,539	16,387	18,289	31,017	22.7
Georgia	101,997	107,660	123,143	7,333	8,378	11,869	20.7
Hawaii	13,169	14,163	15,248	1,273	1,577	1,890	15.8
Idaho	22,017	22,755	23,536	3,129	3,209	3,654	6.9
Illinois	239,185	245,931	257,986	26,122	27,353	30,346	7.9
Indiana	114,643	118,924	127,961	8,937	9,874	12,874	11.6
Iowa	60,695	61,510	63,373	6,329	6,391	6,633	4.4
Kansas	45,212	47,063	50,438	4,308	4,952	6,421	11.6
Kentucky	79,421	81,681	80,539	11,008	12,989	13,668	1.4
Louisiana	73,663	78,760	86,931	7,541	8,600	11,083	18
Maine	27,987	27,891	29,350	2,895	2,497	2,873	4.9
Maryland	91,940	92,520	97,998	10,409	10,615	12,018	6.6
Massachusetts	154,616	156,633	160,275	17,014	18,293	21,163	3.7
Michigan	166,927	172,238	181,251	14,963	18,370	19,748	8.6
Minnesota	80,896	83,028	90,918	10,529	11,205	12,725	12.4
Mississippi	60,934	61,197	64,153	5,704	4,731	5,896	5.3
Missouri	101,955	105,521	114,008	4,889	6,491	9,108	11.8
Montana	17,204	18,038	18,401	1,934	2,071	2,131	7
Nebraska	32,761	35,975	37,112	2,961	3,356	3,728	13.3
Nevada	18,440	20,530	25,242	1,742	2,364	3,215	36.9
New Hampshire	19,658	21,047	23,354	2,077	2,153	2,561	18.8
New Jersey	181,319	184,621	190,003	17,190	17,445	18,025	4.8
New Mexico	36,037	38,207	43,474	2,247	2,652	3,631	20.6
New York	307,458	324,677	365,697	26,353	31,511	46,243	18.9
North Carolina	123,126	127,867	136,513	10,700	11,984	15,042	10.9
North Dakota	12,504	12,679	12,440	1,374	1,377	1,336	-0.5
Ohio	205,440	210,268	219,875	12,487	13,629	16,347	7
Oklahoma	65,653	68,576	73,130	5,359	5,983	6,627	11.4
Oregon	55,149	56,702	63,212	3,581	3,943	5,859	14.6
Pennsylvania	219,428	214,035	210,826	23,156	22,236	24,248	-3.9
Rhode Island	21,076	21,588	23,582	2,112	2,263	2,798	11.9
South Carolina	77,765	79,872	81,930	8,346	9,199	10,571	5.4
South Dakota	14,987	15,284	15,907	2,366	2,463	2,518	6.1
Tennessee	104,898	111,315	119,146	7,536	10,926	11,799	13.6
Texas	350,636	367,860	411,917	30,955	33,082	38,059	17.5
Utah	47,747	50,009	51,950	4,565	5,043	5,256	8.8
Vermont	12,263	11,101	10,452	1,200	1,130	1,232	-14.8
Virginia	113,971	122,647	131,599	11,791	13,359	14,271	15.5
Washington	85,395	91,286	101,254	11,409	12,462	14,392	18.6
West Virginia	43,135	44,338	44,528	3,630	4,372	5,298	3.2
Wisconsin	86,930	91,742	102,412	12,213	12,885	15,648	17.8
Wyoming	11,202	11,935	12,480	1,571	1,726	1,911	11.4

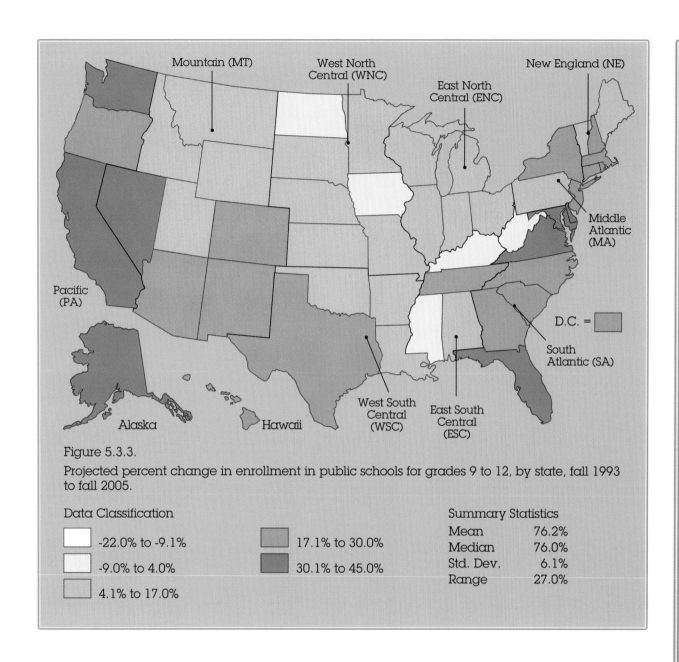

Figure 5.3.3.

Projected percent change in enrollment in public schools for grades 9 to 12, by state, fall 1993 to fall 2005.

Data Classification

- -22.0% to -9.1%
- -9.0% to 4.0%
- 4.1% to 17.0%
- 17.1% to 30.0%
- 30.1% to 45.0%

Summary Statistics

Mean	76.2%
Median	76.0%
Std. Dev.	6.1%
Range	27.0%

Projected percent change in enrollment in public schools for grades 9-12, by state, fall 1993 to fall 2005.

	1993 enrollment grades 9-12	Projected change
Alabama	198,651	15.3
Alaska	32,347	34.2
Arizona	183,041	29.3
Arkansas	126,558	10.3
California	1,424,094	44.1
Colorado	165,132	29.9
Connecticut	127,666	21.0
Delaware	28,930	31.2
District of Columbia	19,244	22.9
Florida	525,569	30.8
Georgia	324,879	24.6
Hawaii	48,772	19.9
Idaho	69,775	15.3
Illinois	536,749	15.4
Indiana	286,567	11.7
Iowa	150,513	3.1
Kansas	127,906	11.4
Kentucky	187,950	3.4
Louisiana	213,070	5.7
Maine	60,467	8.2
Maryland	203,141	33.7
Massachusetts	232,208	26.9
Michigan	439,409	13.8
Minnesota	233,253	12.2
Mississippi	137,219	3.5
Missouri	244,207	10.7
Montana	46,341	7.5
Nebraska	81,671	9.7
Nevada	60,746	41.0
New Hampshire	49,149	24.8
New Jersey	307,781	29.7
New Mexico	96,005	18.7
New York	813,204	17.4
North Carolina	305,060	29.7
North Dakota	35,000	2.5
Ohio	517,122	9.7
Oklahoma	162,982	12.2
Oregon	148,470	26.5
Pennsylvania	510,969	13.9
Rhode Island	38,629	23.0
South Carolina	176,745	18.9
South Dakota	40,544	4.9
Tennessee	236,542	19.0
Texas	927,209	20.9
Utah	141,439	10.7
Vermont	27,927	8.6
Virginia	278,124	32.0
Washington	255,528	35.0
West Virginia	98,599	-5.8
Wisconsin	248,284	9.2
Wyoming	29,497	9.1

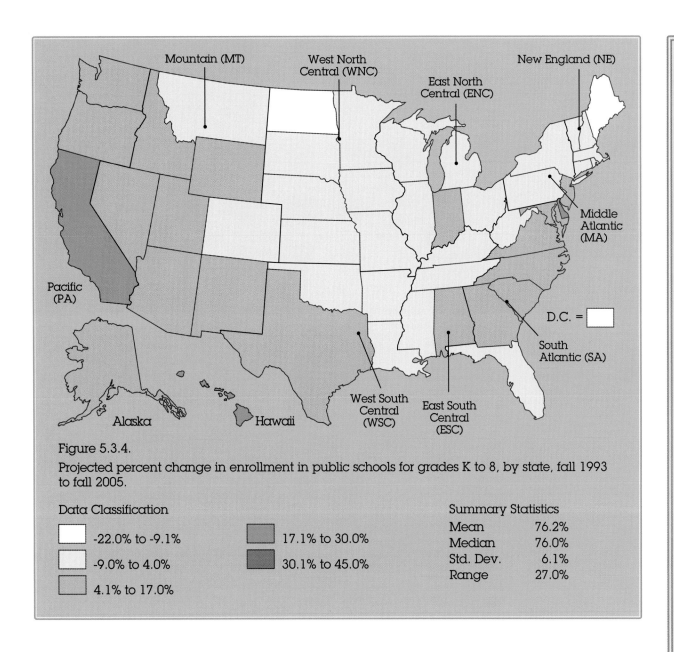

Figure 5.3.4.

Projected percent change in enrollment in public schools for grades K to 8, by state, fall 1993 to fall 2005.

Data Classification

☐	-22.0% to -9.1%
☐	-9.0% to 4.0%
☐	4.1% to 17.0%
☐	17.1% to 30.0%
☐	30.1% to 45.0%

Summary Statistics

Mean	76.2%
Median	76.0%
Std. Dev.	6.1%
Range	27.0%

D.C. = ☐

Projected percent change in enrollment in public schools for grades K-8, by state, fall 1993 to fall 2005.

	1993 Enrollment grades K-8	Projected change
Alabama	535,637	15.0
Alaska	93,601	13.4
Arizona	526,412	7.6
Arkansas	317,713	1.6
California	3,903,137	19.9
Colorado	459,930	3.7
Connecticut	368,632	-1.2
Delaware	76,617	28.2
District of Columbia	61,434	-22.0
Florida	1,515,194	3.6
Georgia	910,425	9.3
Hawaii	131,638	18.2
Idaho	166,999	7.1
Illinois	1,356,329	3.7
Indiana	679,066	4.8
Iowa	348,006	-5.9
Kansas	329,708	-0.3
Kentucky	467,315	1.5
Louisiana	587,490	-0.2
Maine	156,528	-11.9
Maryland	569,497	11.6
Massachusetts	645,518	-7.9
Michigan	1,159,968	2.3
Minnesota	576,980	-7.0
Mississippi	368,688	-1.0
Missouri	622,171	-4.3
Montana	116,668	-1.3
Nebraska	203,426	-3.5
Nevada	175,054	9.6
New Hampshire	136,211	-8.7
New Jersey	843,526	8.3
New Mexico	226,287	11.9
New York	1,920,609	-0.8
North Carolina	828,171	7.6
North Dakota	84,127	-12.6
Ohio	1,290,197	-2.7
Oklahoma	441,094	-3.6
Oregon	368,141	11.8
Pennsylvania	1,233,113	-5.1
Rhode Island	107,047	-7.4
South Carolina	466,951	7.4
South Dakota	102,281	-4.0
Tennessee	630,015	2.9
Texas	2,681,053	8.4
Utah	329,926	12.8
Vermont	74,828	-6.1
Virginia	767,347	8.8
Washington	660,424	14.1
West Virginia	215,784	-1.8
Wisconsin	595,717	-6.0
Wyoming	71,402	6.0

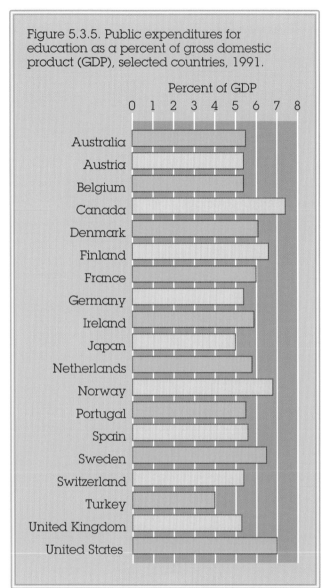

Figure 5.3.5. Public expenditures for education as a percent of gross domestic product (GDP), selected countries, 1991.

Percent of GDP

	0	1	2	3	4	5	6	7	8
Australia									
Austria									
Belgium									
Canada									
Denmark									
Finland									
France									
Germany									
Ireland									
Japan									
Netherlands									
Norway									
Portugal									
Spain									
Sweden									
Switzerland									
Turkey									
United Kingdom									
United States									

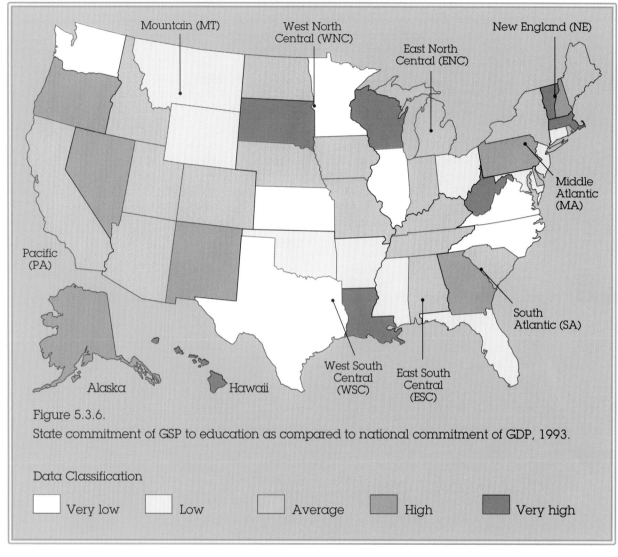

Figure 5.3.6.
State commitment of GSP to education as compared to national commitment of GDP, 1993.

Data Classification

Very low   Low   Average   High   Very high

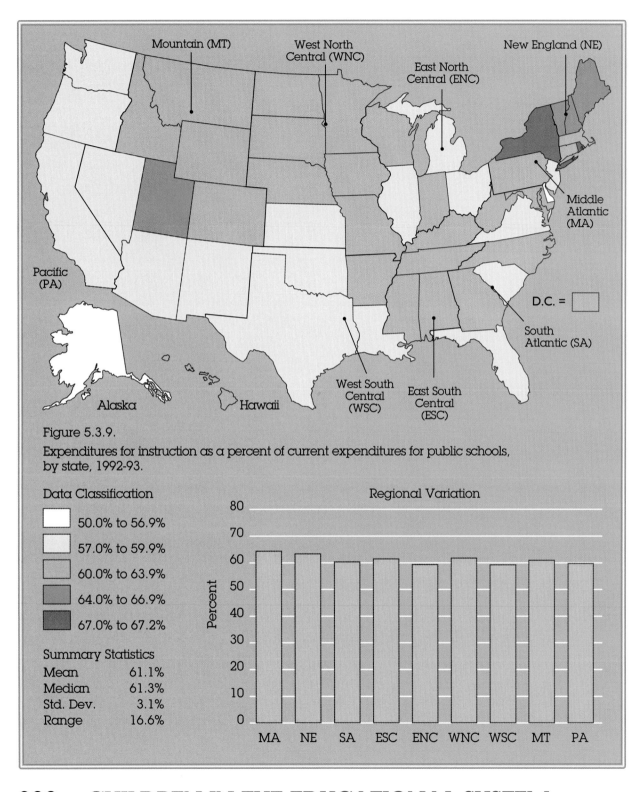

Figure 5.3.9.

Expenditures for instruction as a percent of current expenditures for public schools, by state, 1992-93.

Data Classification

☐	50.0% to 56.9%
☐	57.0% to 59.9%
☐	60.0% to 63.9%
☐	64.0% to 66.9%
☐	67.0% to 67.2%

Summary Statistics

Mean	61.1%
Median	61.3%
Std. Dev.	3.1%
Range	16.6%

Regional Variation

Expenditures for instruction as a percent of current expenditures for public schools, by state, 1992-1993.

	Current expenditures (in millions)	Percent instruction
Alabama	2,610	62.2
Alaska	967	51.2
Arizona	2,753	58.4
Arkansas	1,703	62.8
California	24,219	59.9
Colorado	2,919	61.4
Connecticut	3,737	63.4
District of Columbia	599	62.6
Delaware	670	50.6
Florida	9,661	58.1
Georgia	5,273	63.0
Hawaii	946	61.3
Idaho	804	62.7
Illinois	9,942	59.2
Indiana	4,797	62.2
Iowa	2,459	62.2
Kansas	2,224	58.6
Kentucky	2,823	60.7
Louisiana	3,199	59.6
Maine	1,217	66.2
Maryland	4,556	61.9
Massachusetts	5,281	61.3
Michigan	9,532	58.1
Minnesota	4,135	64.0
Mississippi	1,600	62.3
Missouri	3,710	60.7
Montana	785	62.0
Nebraska	1,430	61.9
Nevada	1,035	59.1
New Hampshire	972	65.2
New Jersey	9,915	59.0
New Mexico	1,240	58.6
New York	20,898	67.2
North Carolina	4,930	61.6
North Dakota	508	61.4
Ohio	9,572	57.2
Oklahoma	2,442	59.0
Oregon	2,849	59.7
Pennsylvania	10,944	63.6
Rhode Island	934	67.0
South Carolina	2,690	59.3
South Dakota	553	61.3
Tennessee	3,139	60.8
Texas	15,121	58.8
Utah	1,376	66.1
Vermont	625	65.0
Virginia	5,228	59.7
Washington	4,679	59.8
West Virginia	1,626	61.9
Wisconsin	4,954	63.4
Wyoming	547	61.1

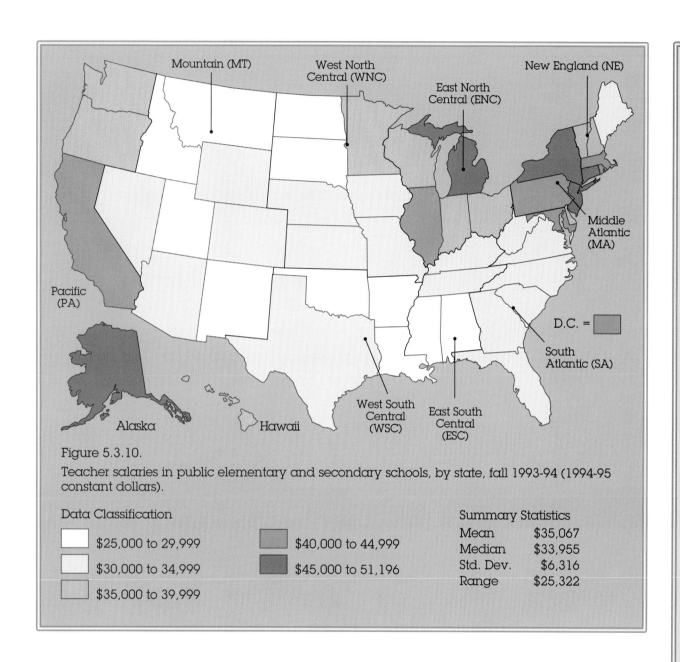

Figure 5.3.10.

Teacher salaries in public elementary and secondary schools, by state, fall 1993-94 (1994-95 constant dollars).

Data Classification

☐	$25,000 to 29,999	◼	$40,000 to 44,999
☐	$30,000 to 34,999	◼	$45,000 to 51,196
☐	$35,000 to 39,999		

Summary Statistics

Mean	$35,067
Median	$33,955
Std. Dev.	$6,316
Range	$25,322

Teacher salaries in public elementary and secondary schools, by state (1994-1995 constant dollars).

	Average teacher salaries	
	1990-91	1993-94
Alabama	26,846	30,545
Alaska	43,406	47,864
Arizona	30,773	32,223
Arkansas	23,735	28,950
California	39,118	40,667
Colorado	31,819	34,571
Connecticut	43,398	50,598
Delaware	35,246	39,076
District of Columbia	39,362	43,142
Florida	30,555	32,590
Georgia	28,950	32,198
Hawaii	33,548	37,443
Idaho	25,510	29,784
Illinois	34,642	39,445
Indiana	32,931	36,799
Iowa	27,949	31,511
Kansas	28,188	32,085
Kentucky	29,115	32,272
Louisiana	26,170	26,811
Maine	28,531	31,972
Maryland	38,312	40,661
Massachusetts	36,090	40,976
Michigan	37,800	46,575
Minnesota	33,128	35,948
Mississippi	24,609	26,818
Missouri	27,636	31,209
Montana	26,696	28,785
Nebraska	26,592	30,922
Nevada	35,269	38,010
New Hampshire	31,273	34,721
New Jersey	38,411	47,038
New Mexico	25,800	28,394
New York	42,080	47,612
North Carolina	29,165	30,793
North Dakota	23,574	26,317
Ohio	31,964	36,971
Oklahoma	24,378	28,745
Oregon	32,295	38,871
Pennsylvania	36,057	44,510
Rhode Island	38,220	40,729
South Carolina	28,174	30,366
South Dakota	22,363	26,037
Tennessee	28,248	31,270
Texas	28,100	31,223
Utah	25,415	28,919
Vermont	29,714	35,207
Virginia	32,692	33,907
Washington	32,975	36,160
West Virginia	25,966	31,944
Wisconsin	33,077	37,617
Wyoming	28,996	31,285

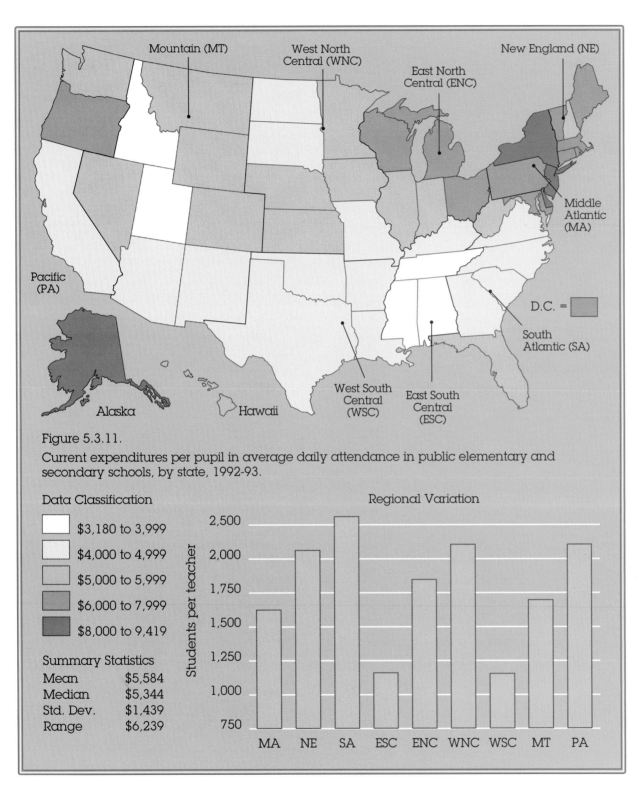

Figure 5.3.11.

Current expenditures per pupil in average daily attendance in public elementary and secondary schools, by state, 1992-93.

Data Classification

- $3,180 to 3,999
- $4,000 to 4,999
- $5,000 to 5,999
- $6,000 to 7,999
- $8,000 to 9,419

Summary Statistics

Mean	$5,584
Median	$5,344
Std. Dev.	$1,439
Range	$6,239

Regional Variation

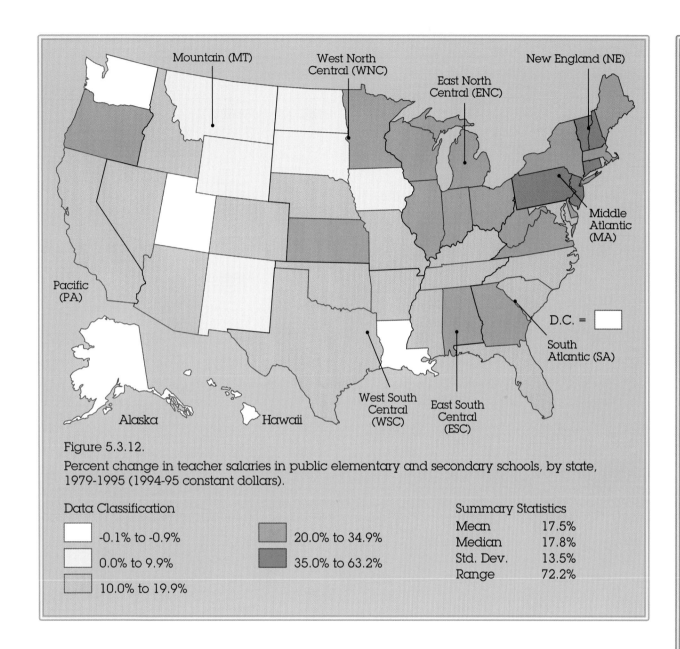

Mountain (MT)
West North Central (WNC)
New England (NE)
East North Central (ENC)
Middle Atlantic (MA)
Pacific (PA)
South Atlantic (SA)
Alaska
Hawaii
West South Central (WSC)
East South Central (ESC)
D.C. =

Figure 5.3.12.

Percent change in teacher salaries in public elementary and secondary schools, by state, 1979-1995 (1994-95 constant dollars).

Data Classification

-0.1% to -0.9%

0.0% to 9.9%

10.0% to 19.9%

20.0% to 34.9%

35.0% to 63.2%

Summary Statistics

Mean	17.5%
Median	17.8%
Std. Dev.	13.5%
Range	72.2%

Percent change in teacher salaries in public elementary and secondary schools, by state.

	Percent change	
	1979-1995	1991-1995
Alabama	23.1	1.3
Alaska	-9.0	1.8
Arizona	10	6.8
Arkansas	19.2	8.6
California	16.5	7.4
Colorado	10.1	3.3
Connecticut	63.2	3.8
Delaware	24.9	1.3
District of Columbia	-0.1	2.4
Florida	18.9	5.0
Georgia	22.3	1.0
Hawaii	-0.2	0.6
Idaho	12.9	4.0
Illinois	20.4	1.4
Indiana	20.8	0.5
Iowa	7.0	0.4
Kansas	31.7	1.3
Kentucky	14.7	1.3
Louisiana	-0.3	8.8
Maine	25.8	0.2
Maryland	19.5	5.5
Massachusetts	25.9	1.1
Michigan	24.5	9.7
Minnesota	21.4	3.4
Mississippi	17.2	3.0
Missouri	17.8	0.5
Montana	2.2	4.0
Nebraska	17.7	3.5
Nevada	10.3	4
New Hampshire	38.7	1.1
New Jersey	40.8	9.0
New Mexico	0.1	2.0
New York	23.1	0.7
North Carolina	13.6	6.0
North Dakota	2.5	0.6
Ohio	24.0	3.0
Oklahoma	10.1	5.0
Oregon	22.8	7.2
Pennsylvania	39.0	9.9
Rhode Island	16.8	5.1
South Carolina	19.9	4.0
South Dakota	8.8	3.7
Tennessee	15.5	1.4
Texas	14.4	1.1
Utah	-0.7	1.3
Vermont	50.1	5.5
Virginia	23.9	7.7
Washington	-0.9	2.4
West Virginia	20.2	9.5
Wisconsin	20.4	1.3
Wyoming	0.9	3.9

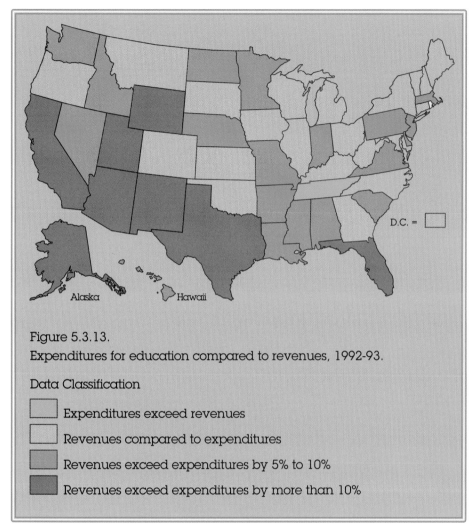

Figure 5.3.13.
Expenditures for education compared to revenues, 1992-93.

Data Classification

Expenditures exceed revenues

Revenues compared to expenditures

Revenues exceed expenditures by 5% to 10%

Revenues exceed expenditures by more than 10%

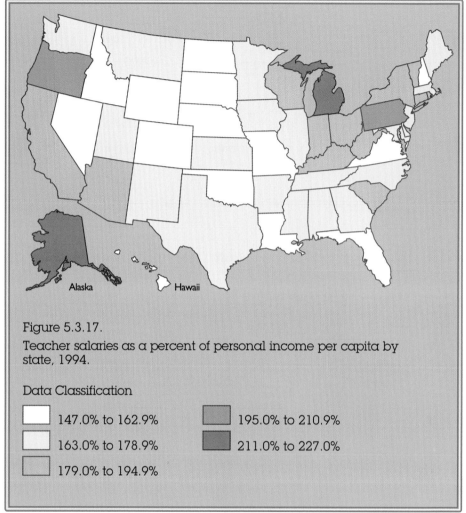

Figure 5.3.17.
Teacher salaries as a percent of personal income per capita by state, 1994.

Data Classification

147.0% to 162.9%   195.0% to 210.9%

163.0% to 178.9%   211.0% to 227.0%

179.0% to 194.9%

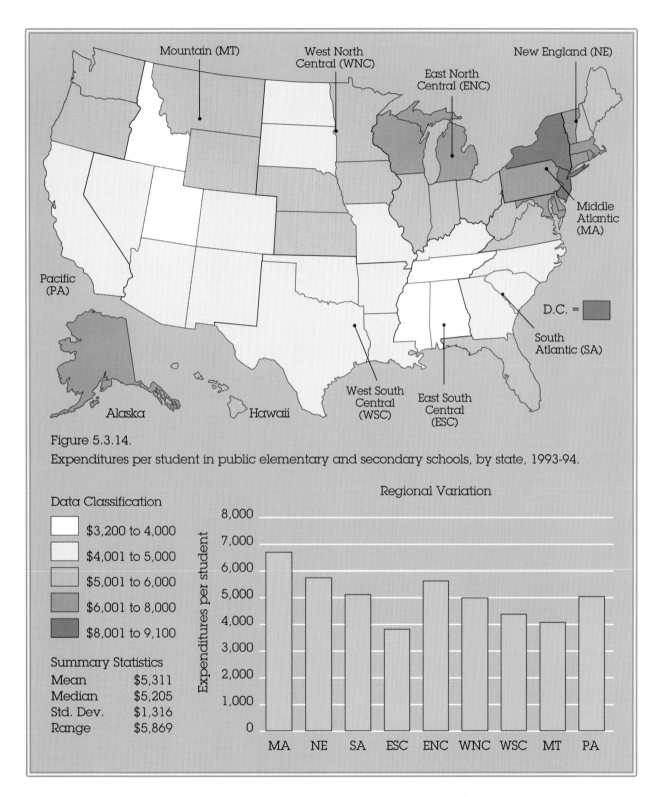

Figure 5.3.14.

Expenditures per student in public elementary and secondary schools, by state, 1993-94.

Data Classification

- $3,200 to 4,000
- $4,001 to 5,000
- $5,001 to 6,000
- $6,001 to 8,000
- $8,001 to 9,100

Summary Statistics

Mean	$5,311
Median	$5,205
Std. Dev.	$1,316
Range	$5,869

Regional Variation

D.C. =

Mountain (MT)	
West North Central (WNC)	
East North Central (ENC)	
New England (NE)	
Middle Atlantic (MA)	
Pacific (PA)	
South Atlantic (SA)	
West South Central (WSC)	
East South Central (ESC)	

Expenditures per student in public elementary and secondary schools, by state, 1993-1994.

	Current expenditures (in thousands)	Amount per student
Alabama	1,002,515	3,826
Alaska	2,809,713	7,960
Arizona	1,782,645	4,104
Arkansas	2,911,304	4,013
California	25,140,639	4,719
Colorado	2,954,793	4,727
Connecticut	3,943,894	7,947
Delaware	713,427	6,101
District of Columbia	643,915	8,843
Florida	10,331,896	5,063
Georgia	5,643,843	4,569
Hawaii	998,143	5,533
Idaho	10,076,889	3,628
Illinois	5,064,685	5,323
Indiana	2,527,434	5,245
Iowa	859,088	5,070
Kansas	2,325,247	5,081
Kentucky	2,952,119	4,505
Louisiana	3,309,020	4,133
Maine	5,637,337	5,569
Maryland	4,783,023	6,191
Massachusetts	1,208,411	6,423
Michigan	9,816,830	6,138
Minnesota	4,328,093	5,342
Mississippi	3,981,614	3,410
Missouri	1,725,386	4,596
Montana	822,015	5,043
Nebraska	1,007,129	5,310
Nevada	5,145,420	4,661
New Hampshire	10,448,096	5,433
New Jersey	1,323,459	9,075
New Mexico	22,059,949	4,106
New York	522,377	8,069
North Carolina	1,513,971	4,540
North Dakota	1,099,058	4,385
Ohio	9,612,678	5,319
Oklahoma	2,659,460	4,403
Oregon	2,852,723	5,522
Pennsylvania	11,236,417	6,443
Rhode Island	990,094	6,797
South Carolina	2,790,878	4,336
South Dakota	584,894	4,095
Tennessee	3,305,579	3,815
Texas	16,193,722	4,488
Utah	1,511,205	3,206
Vermont	5,441,388	6,266
Virginia	643,828	5,205
Washington	4,892,690	5,342
West Virginia	5,170,343	5,292
Wisconsin	1,663,868	6,126
Wyoming	558,353	5,534

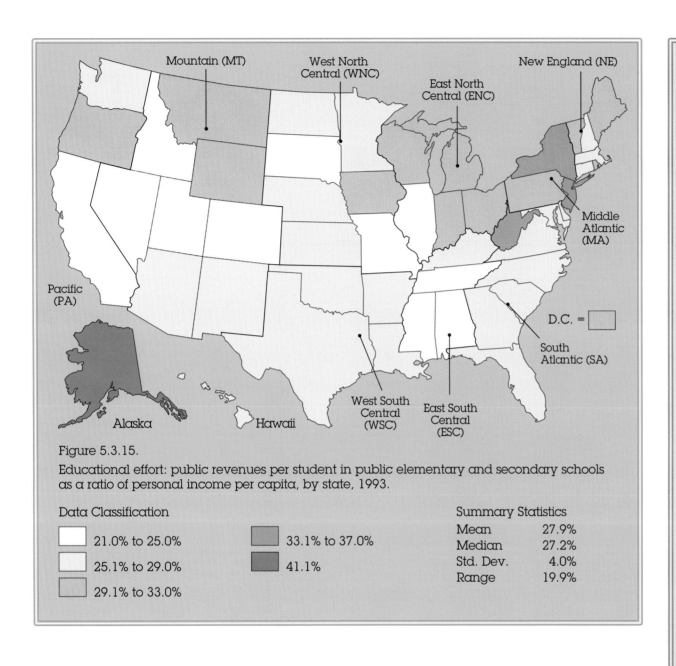

Mountain (MT)   West North Central (WNC)   East North Central (ENC)   New England (NE)

Middle Atlantic (MA)

Pacific (PA)

D.C. =

South Atlantic (SA)

Alaska   Hawaii   West South Central (WSC)   East South Central (ESC)

Figure 5.3.15.

Educational effort: public revenues per student in public elementary and secondary schools as a ratio of personal income per capita, by state, 1993.

Data Classification

21.0% to 25.0%

25.1% to 29.0%

29.1% to 33.0%

33.1% to 37.0%

41.1%

Summary Statistics

Mean	27.9%
Median	27.2%
Std. Dev.	4.0%
Range	19.9%

Educational effort: public revenues per student in public schools as a ratio of personal income per capita, 1993.

	Personal income per capita	Educational effort
Alabama	17,234	23.6
Alaska	22,846	41.1
Arizona	18,121	26.5
Arkansas	16,143	27.0
California	21,821	24.1
Colorado	21,564	24.8
Connecticut	28,110	28.5
Delaware	21,481	27.9
District of Columbia	29,438	30.4
Florida	20,857	26.7
Georgia	19,278	25.2
Hawaii	23,354	25.3
Idaho	17,646	21.5
Illinois	22,582	24.7
Indiana	19,203	30.3
Iowa	18,315	29.5
Kansas	20,139	25.8
Kentucky	17,173	27.3
Louisiana	16,667	26.2
Maine	18,895	32.6
Maryland	24,044	26.5
Massachusetts	24,563	27.3
Michigan	20,453	32.9
Minnesota	21,063	27.5
Mississippi	14,894	23.5
Missouri	19,463	25.0
Montana	17,322	29.9
Nebraska	19,726	28.4
Nevada	22,729	21.9
New Hampshire	22,659	25.3
New Jersey	26,967	35.4
New Mexico	16,297	27.2
New York	24,623	33.5
North Carolina	18,702	25.3
North Dakota	17,488	26.5
Ohio	19,688	30.9
Oklahoma	17,020	27.0
Oregon	19,443	31.2
Pennsylvania	21,351	32.4
Rhode Island	21,096	31.5
South Carolina	16,923	28.1
South Dakota	17,666	23.9
Tennessee	18,434	21.2
Texas	19,189	25.2
Utah	16,180	21.7
Vermont	19,467	31.9
Virginia	21,634	25.9
Washington	21,887	27.4
West Virginia	16,209	36.1
Wisconsin	19,811	32.0
Wyoming	19,539	31.1

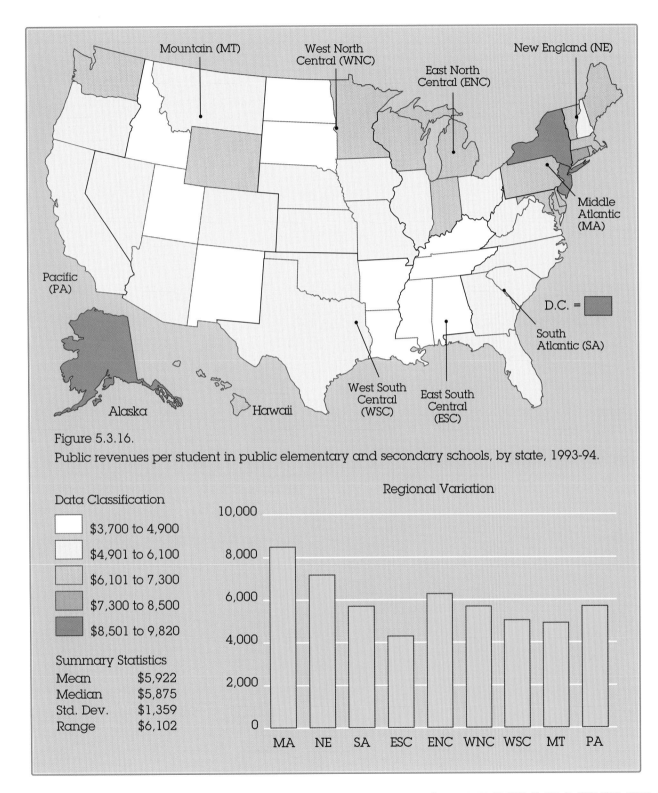

Figure 5.3.16.

Public revenues per student in public elementary and secondary schools, by state, 1993-94.

Data Classification

- $3,700 to 4,900
- $4,901 to 6,100
- $6,101 to 7,300
- $7,300 to 8,500
- $8,501 to 9,820

Summary Statistics

Mean	$5,922
Median	$5,875
Std. Dev.	$1,359
Range	$6,102

Regional Variation

Revenues per student in public elementary and secondary schools, 1993-94.

	Revenues (in thousands)	Amount per student
Alabama	3,121,320	4,251
Alaska	1,159,259	9,204
Arizona	3,550,177	5,004
Arkansas	2,014,900	4,535
California	29,050,409	5,453
Colorado	3,368,596	5,389
Connecticut	4,103,218	8,268
Delaware	684,411	6,484
District of Columbia	735,722	9,119
Florida	11,927,112	5,844
Georgia	6,630,693	5,368
Hawaii	1,128,456	6,255
Idaho	955,081	4,034
Illinois	11,322,719	5,981
Indiana	5,918,601	6,129
Iowa	2,782,621	5,582
Kansas	2,695,033	5,889
Kentucky	3,194,404	4,875
Louisiana	3,608,436	4,507
Maine	1,327,946	6,120
Maryland	5,145,236	6,659
Massachusetts	6,227,191	7,095
Michigan	11,134,083	6,962
Minnesota	5,160,259	6,369
Mississippi	1,879,377	3,715
Missouri	4,526,828	5,225
Montana	877,807	5,385
Nebraska	1,674,836	5,875
Nevada	1,268,826	5,381
New Hampshire	1,097,159	5,919
New Jersey	11,301,907	9,817
New Mexico	1,562,447	4,848
New York	23,775,186	8,697
North Carolina	5,560,314	4,907
North Dakota	563,352	4,729
Ohio	10,499,236	5,809
Oklahoma	3,077,911	5,095
Oregon	3,074,679	5,952
Pennsylvania	12,601,361	7,225
Rhode Island	1,022,861	7,021
South Carolina	3,200,412	4,972
South Dakota	647,026	4,530
Tennessee	3,649,630	4,212
Texas	18,744,302	5,195
Utah	1,785,758	3,788
Vermont	703,939	6,851
Virginia	6,162,835	5,895
Washington	5,723,616	6,249
West Virginia	1,879,452	5,978
Wisconsin	5,661,241	6,708
Wyoming	673,906	6,679

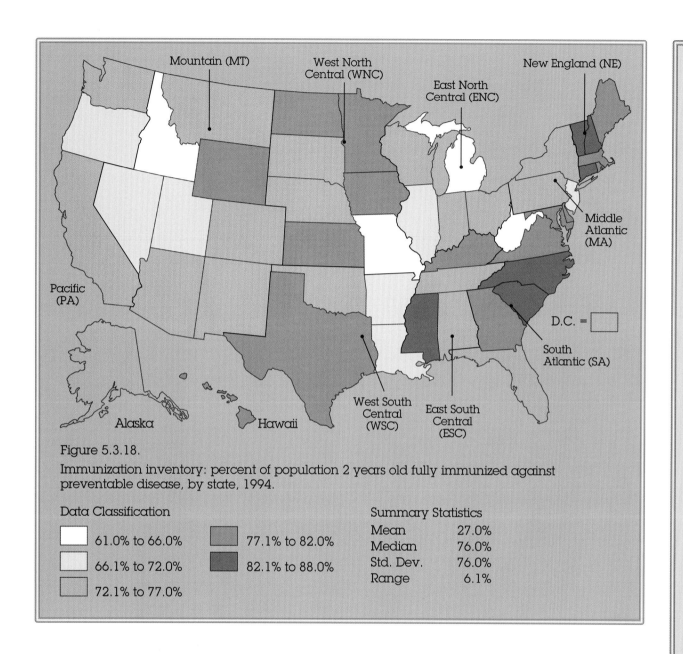

Figure 5.3.18.

Immunization inventory: percent of population 2 years old fully immunized against preventable disease, by state, 1994.

Data Classification

☐ 61.0% to 66.0%	☐ 77.1% to 82.0%
☐ 66.1% to 72.0%	■ 82.1% to 88.0%
☐ 72.1% to 77.0%	

Summary Statistics

Mean	27.0%
Median	76.0%
Std. Dev.	76.0%
Range	6.1%

Immunization inventory: percent of population 2 years old fully immunized against disease, 1994.

	Population 2 and under	% 2-year olds immunized
Alabama	168,195	75
Alaska	32,934	73
Arizona	175,101	77
Arkansas	97,770	71
California	1,452,250	74
Colorado	148,916	75
Connecticut	138,129	86
Delaware	29,271	81
District of Columbia	23,039	73
Florida	509,129	76
Georgia	298,321	79
Hawaii	50,255	86
Idaho	47,074	64
Illinois	510,109	68
Indiana	237,700	74
Iowa	114,059	81
Kansas	111,245	82
Kentucky	148,737	80
Louisiana	196,587	71
Maine	50,341	82
Maryland	216,136	79
Massachusetts	249,566	82
Michigan	421,559	61
Minnesota	199,349	81
Mississippi	115,656	83
Missouri	218,606	64
Montana	34,442	75
Nebraska	70,620	72
Nevada	55,666	69
New Hampshire	50,595	83
New Jersey	323,192	71
New Mexico	73,768	73
New York	757,554	77
North Carolina	277,079	84
North Dakota	28,111	81
Ohio	467,519	73
Oklahoma	133,252	76
Oregon	119,314	71
Pennsylvania	474,392	77
Rhode Island	40,326	82
South Carolina	153,847	84
South Dakota	32,121	74
Tennessee	199,290	74
Texas	825,524	81
Utah	101,444	70
Vermont	24,443	88
Virginia	267,259	81
Washington	217,865	74
West Virginia	62,153	66
Wisconsin	211,661	76
Wyoming	19,988	78

a.

b.

c.

Participating state

Figure 5.3.21.
States requiring testing for certification of
teachers: a) basic skills tests; b) content
knowledge; and c) in-class observations,
1996.

Alaska   Hawaii

Alaska   Hawaii

Alaska   Hawaii

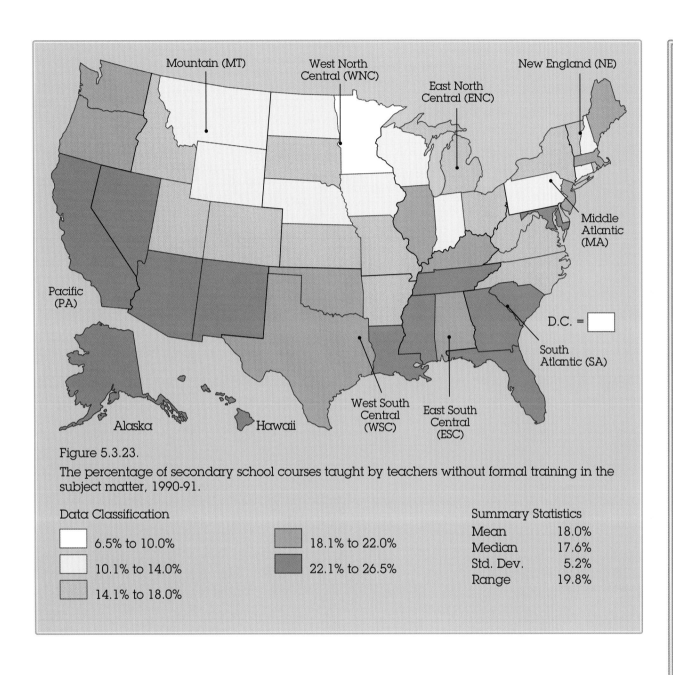

Figure 5.3.23.

The percentage of secondary school courses taught by teachers without formal training in the subject matter, 1990-91.

Data Classification

☐	6.5% to 10.0%
☐	10.1% to 14.0%
☐	14.1% to 18.0%
☐	18.1% to 22.0%
☐	22.1% to 26.5%

Summary Statistics

Mean	18.0%
Median	17.6%
Std. Dev.	5.2%
Range	19.8%

Percent of secondary school courses taught by teachers without formal training in the subject matter, 1990-91.

	Secondary teachers, fall 1990	Percent of courses
Alabama	14,820	18.9
Alaska	2,038	25.0
Arizona	8,517	24.5
Arkansas	12,446	14.1
California	56,801	25.5
Colorado	15,839	15.8
Connecticut	13,312	12.2
Delaware	2,941	16.0
District of Columbia	2,532	6.8
Florida	41,279	26.4
Georgia	20,106	23.1
Hawaii	3,228	23.8
Idaho	5,092	17.6
Illinois	28,934	19.0
Indiana	23,201	12.7
Iowa	12,589	13.0
Kansas	11,530	16.9
Kentucky	11,367	21.7
Louisiana	N/A	26.2
Maine	5,122	21.5
Maryland	19,944	25.6
Massachusetts	28,077	19.2
Michigan	38,395	17.4
Minnesota	20,099	6.7
Mississippi	10,803	25.4
Missouri	24,751	15.3
Montana	2,830	13.4
Nebraska	8,135	10.1
Nevada	3,639	22.4
New Hampshire	3,573	10.8
New Jersey	26,737	19.8
New Mexico	4,291	23.9
New York	65,135	17.5
North Carolina	21,058	17.4
North Dakota	2,550	10.1
Ohio	45,649	17.6
Oklahoma	15,716	18.9
Oregon	9,867	20.9
Pennsylvania	45,556	11.4
Rhode Island	3,979	15.7
South Carolina	12,125	23.1
South Dakota	3,023	17.9
Tennessee	12,576	26.5
Texas	102,669	18.2
Utah	6,446	16.4
Vermont	3,119	15.1
Virginia	25,826	18.0
Washington	16,168	21.9
West Virginia	7,760	15.3
Wisconsin	17,890	11.5
Wyoming	3,460	13.5

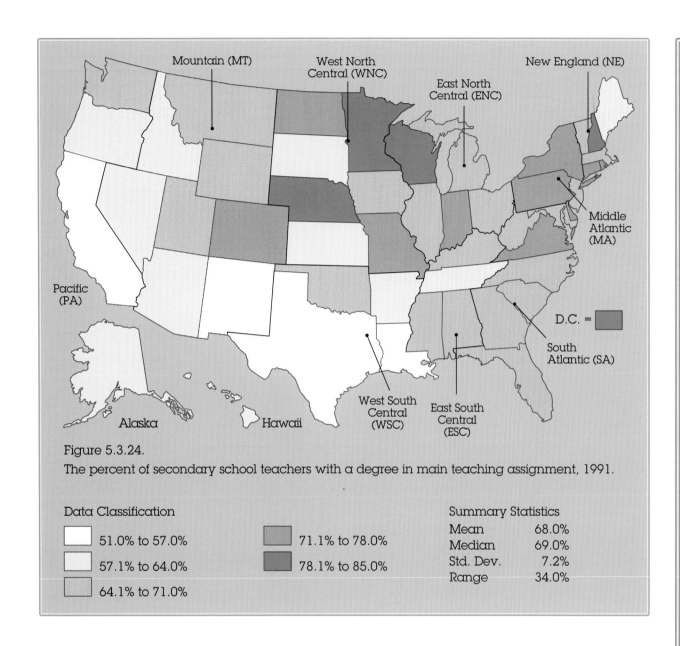

Figure 5.3.24.

The percent of secondary school teachers with a degree in main teaching assignment, 1991.

Data Classification

☐ 51.0% to 57.0%	☐ 71.1% to 78.0%
☐ 57.1% to 64.0%	☐ 78.1% to 85.0%
☐ 64.1% to 71.0%	

Summary Statistics

Mean	68.0%
Median	69.0%
Std. Dev.	7.2%
Range	34.0%

Percent of secondary school teachers with a degree in main teaching assignment, 1991.

	Secondary teachers, year 1990-91	Percent with degree
Alabama	14,820	70
Alaska	2,038	60
Arizona	8,517	63
Arkansas	12,446	62
California	56,801	56
Colorado	15,839	74
Connecticut	13,312	76
Delaware	2,941	73
District of Columbia	2,532	85
Florida	41,279	66
Georgia	20,106	67
Hawaii	3,228	62
Idaho	5,092	62
Illinois	28,934	69
Indiana	23,201	73
Iowa	12,589	71
Kansas	11,530	62
Kentucky	11,367	65
Louisiana	N/A	51
Maine	5,122	64
Maryland	19,944	70
Massachusetts	28,077	69
Michigan	38,395	70
Minnesota	20,099	80
Mississippi	10,803	67
Missouri	24,751	72
Montana	2,830	69
Nebraska	8,135	82
Nevada	3,639	62
New Hampshire	3,573	80
New Jersey	26,737	69
New Mexico	4,291	53
New York	65,135	74
North Carolina	21,058	68
North Dakota	2,550	73
Ohio	45,649	68
Oklahoma	15,716	65
Oregon	9,867	64
Pennsylvania	45,556	78
Rhode Island	3,979	72
South Carolina	12,125	69
South Dakota	3,023	62
Tennessee	12,576	59
Texas	102,669	54
Utah	6,446	68
Vermont	3,119	71
Virginia	25,826	72
Washington	16,168	65
West Virginia	7,760	66
Wisconsin	17,890	79
Wyoming	3,460	69

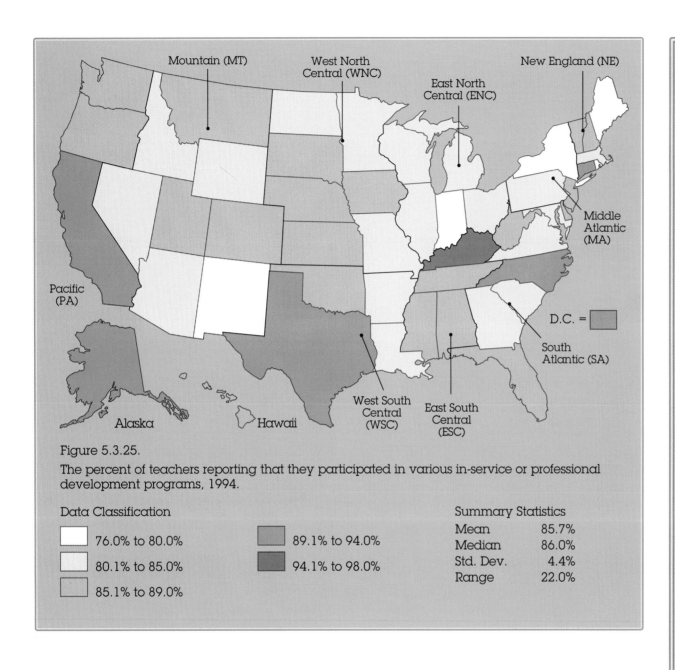

Figure 5.3.25.

The percent of teachers reporting that they participated in various in-service or professional development programs, 1994.

Data Classification

- 76.0% to 80.0%
- 80.1% to 85.0%
- 85.1% to 89.0%
- 89.1% to 94.0%
- 94.1% to 98.0%

Summary Statistics

Mean	85.7%
Median	86.0%
Std. Dev.	4.4%
Range	22.0%

Percent of public school teachers reporting that they participated in various programs, 1994.

	Public school teachers, 1994	Percent that participated
Alabama	42,789	86
Alaska	7,205	90
Arizona	38,132	85
Arkansas	26,181	84
California	225,001	94
Colorado	34,894	88
Connecticut	35,316	92
Delaware	6,416	86
District of Columbia	6,110	92
Florida	110,674	88
Georgia	77,914	82
Hawaii	10,240	88
Idaho	12,582	84
Illinois	110,830	81
Indiana	55,496	80
Iowa	31,775	89
Kansas	30,579	89
Kentucky	38,784	98
Louisiana	47,599	83
Maine	15,404	80
Maryland	46,565	84
Massachusetts	60,489	82
Michigan	80,522	82
Minnesota	46,958	85
Mississippi	28,866	88
Missouri	56,606	81
Montana	10,079	86
Nebraska	19,774	87
Nevada	13,414	81
New Hampshire	12,109	89
New Jersey	85,258	87
New Mexico	19,025	79
New York	182,273	76
North Carolina	71,592	93
North Dakota	7,796	84
Ohio	109,085	83
Oklahoma	39,406	88
Oregon	26,208	86
Pennsylvania	102,988	82
Rhode Island	10,066	77
South Carolina	39,437	81
South Dakota	9,985	86
Tennessee	47,406	87
Texas	234,213	93
Utah	19,524	87
Vermont	7,566	89
Virginia	72,853	85
Washington	46,439	89
West Virginia	21,024	88
Wisconsin	54,054	84
Wyoming	6,698	85

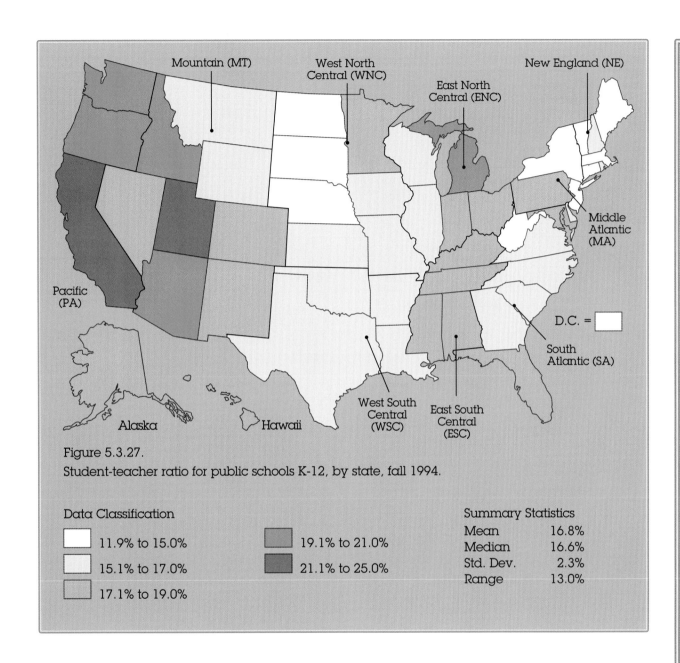

Figure 5.3.27.
Student-teacher ratio for public schools K-12, by state, fall 1994.

Data Classification

☐	11.9% to 15.0%
☐	15.1% to 17.0%
☐	17.1% to 19.0%
☐	19.1% to 21.0%
☐	21.1% to 25.0%

Summary Statistics

Mean	16.8%
Median	16.6%
Std. Dev.	2.3%
Range	13.0%

Student-teacher ratio for public schools K-12, by state, fall 1994.

	Total enrollment (in thousands)	Student/ teacher ratio
Alabama	734,288	17.4
Alaska	125,948	17.8
Arizona	709,453	19.1
Arkansas	444,271	15.5
California	5,327,231	24.9
Colorado	625,062	18.6
Connecticut	496,298	14.8
Delaware	105,547	17.0
District of Columbia	80,678	12.9
Florida	2,040,763	18.1
Georgia	1,235,304	16.3
Hawaii	180,410	17.9
Idaho	236,774	19.4
Illinois	1,893,078	16.9
Indiana	965,633	17.5
Iowa	498,519	15.8
Kansas	457,614	15.3
Kentucky	655,265	17.5
Louisiana	800,560	16.6
Maine	216,995	14.4
Maryland	772,638	17.6
Massachusetts	877,726	14.2
Michigan	1,599,377	20.4
Minnesota	810,233	17.5
Mississippi	505,907	17.7
Missouri	866,378	15.5
Montana	163,009	16.4
Nebraska	285,097	14.6
Nevada	235,800	18.7
New Hampshire	185,360	16.3
New Jersey	1,151,307	13.6
New Mexico	322,292	17.9
New York	2,733,813	15.0
North Carolina	1,133,231	16.4
North Dakota	119,127	14.8
Ohio	1,807,319	17.5
Oklahoma	604,076	15.4
Oregon	516,611	20.4
Pennsylvania	1,744,082	17.5
Rhode Island	145,676	16.2
South Carolina	643,696	16.6
South Dakota	142,825	14.6
Tennessee	866,557	17.7
Texas	3,608,262	15.9
Utah	471,365	21.8
Vermont	102,755	11.9
Virginia	1,045,471	15.1
Washington	915,952	20.6
West Virginia	314,383	14.9
Wisconsin	844,001	15.5
Wyoming	100,899	15.3

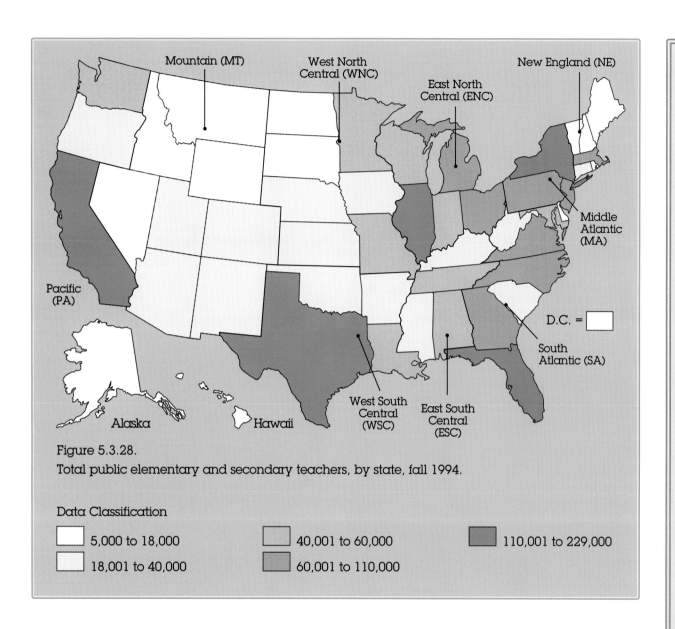

Mountain (MT)

West North Central (WNC)

East North Central (ENC)

New England (NE)

Middle Atlantic (MA)

Pacific (PA)

D.C. =

South Atlantic (SA)

Alaska

Hawaii

West South Central (WSC)

East South Central (ESC)

Figure 5.3.28.
Total public elementary and secondary teachers, by state, fall 1994.

Data Classification

5,000 to 18,000

18,001 to 40,000

40,001 to 60,000

60,001 to 110,000

110,001 to 229,000

Public elementary and secondary school teachers, 1994.

	Elementary teachers	Secondary teachers
Alabama	24,168	18,423
Alaska	4,666	2,539
Arizona	27,595	10,537
Arkansas	13,884	12,160
California	142,795	58,586
Colorado	18,008	16,886
Connecticut	20,745	9,340
Delaware	3,215	3,201
District of Columbia	3,497	2,173
Florida	48,150	40,893
Georgia	56,211	21,703
Hawaii	5,770	4,425
Idaho	6,388	6,018
Illinois	66,462	28,619
Indiana	27,527	25,251
Iowa	18,663	12,021
Kansas	14,823	12,763
Kentucky	27,054	11,730
Louisiana	26,916	12,176
Maine	10,524	4,880
Maryland	25,792	20,773
Massachusetts	22,342	29,922
Michigan	34,846	36,701
Minnesota	23,980	22,948
Mississippi	15,071	8,864
Missouri	29,054	26,782
Montana	7,009	3,070
Nebraska	11,368	8,406
Nevada	6,784	5,058
New Hampshire	8,158	3,951
New Jersey	47,280	26,439
New Mexico	11,265	4,342
New York	91,408	63,928
North Carolina	42,480	24,700
North Dakota	5,223	2,573
Ohio	72,005	36,912
Oklahoma	18,735	16,517
Oregon	14,128	8,484
Pennsylvania	46,919	43,798
Rhode Island	4,597	4,090
South Carolina	26,820	12,617
South Dakota	6,098	2,738
Tennessee	33,039	12,795
Texas	116,999	85,987
Utah	9,041	8,056
Vermont	3,131	2,952
Virginia	43,905	28,948
Washington	24,077	18,247
West Virginia	10,212	7,244
Wisconsin	37,235	16,819
Wyoming	3,289	3,401

Table 5.3.1. Public school districts and enrollment, by size of district, 1988-89 to 1994-95.

	Districts in 1988-89		Districts in 1992-93		Districts in 1993-94		Districts in 1994-95	
	Number	Percent	Number	Percent	Number	Percent	Number	Percent
Total	15,376	100	15,025	100	14,881	100	14,772	100
25,000 or more	177	1.2	202	1.3	206	1.4	207	1.4
10,000 to 24,999	473	3.1	510	3.4	525	3.5	542	3.7
5,000 to 9,999	924	6.0	955	6.4	973	6.5	996	6.7
2,500 to 4,999	1,907	12.4	2,002	13.3	2,008	13.5	2,013	13.6
1,000 to 2,499	3,529	23.0	3,530	23.5	3,570	24.0	3,579	24.2
600 to 999	1,813	11.8	1,798	12.0	1,785	12.0	1,777	12.0
300 to 599	2,266	14.7	2,200	14.6	2,162	14.5	2,113	14.3
1 to 299	3,984	25.9	3,465	23.1	3,294	22.1	3,173	21.5
Size not reported	303	2.0	363	2.4	358	2.4	372	2.5

Table 5.3.2. Enrollment in educational institutions, by level and control of institution, fall 1980 to fall 2000.

Level of instruction and type of control	Fall				Projected Fall				
	1980	1985	1990	1995	1996	1997	1998	1999	2000
All levels	58,305	57,226	60,267	64,572	66,081	66,996	67,807	68,570	69,165
Public	50,335	48,901	52,061	55,770	57,139	57,929	58,615	59,251	59,747
Private	7,971	8,325	8,206	8,801	8,943	9,067	9,192	9,319	9,418
Elementary and secondary	46,208	44,979	46,448	50,362	51,683	52,400	52,921	53,342	53,668
Public	40,877	39,422	41,217	44,662	45,885	46,524	46,988	47,365	47,656
Private	5,331	5,557	5,232	5,700	5,798	5,876	5,933	5,977	6,012
Grades K-8	31,639	31,229	33,973	36,516	37,330	37,772	38,109	38,303	38,484
Public	27,647	27,034	29,878	32,085	32,837	33,226	33,522	33,692	33,852
Private	3,992	4,195	4,095	4,431	4,493	4,547	4,587	4,610	4,632
Grades 9-12	14,570	13,750	12,475	13,845	14,353	14,628	14,811	15,039	15,184
Public	13,231	12,388	11,338	12,576	13,049	13,299	13,466	13,673	13,804
Private	1,339	1,362	1,137	1,269	1,304	1,329	1,346	1,367	1,380
Higher education	12,097	12,247	13,819	14,210	14,398	14,596	14,886	15,228	15,497
Public	9,457	9,479	10,845	11,108	11,254	11,405	11,627	11,886	12,091
Private	2,640	2,768	2,974	3,101	3,145	3,191	3,259	3,342	3,406

Note: 1995 data is based on "Early Estimates" surveys for public elementary and secondary schools. Elementary and secondary enrollment includes enrollments in local public school systems and in most private schools (religiously affiliated and nonsectarian); excludes subcollegiate departments of institutions of higher education, residential schools for exceptional children, and federal schools. Excludes preprimary pupils in schools that do not offer first grade or above. Enrollments for grades K-8 include kindergarten and some nursery school pupils. Enrollments for higher education include full-time and part-time students enrolled in degree-credit and nondegree-credit programs in universities and 2-year and 4-year colleges, unclassified students below the baccalaureate level, and unclassified postbaccalaureate students.

Table 5.3.3. Enrollment in grades K-12 in public elementary and secondary schools, by region and state, fall 1995 to fall 2005.

	1995	1997	1999	2001	2003	2005	% change 1995 to 2005
Alabama	743	762	785	809	830	841	13.2
Alaska	133	140	145	149	151	153	15
Arizona	765	808	828	835	831	838	9.5
Arkansas	451	456	459	462	465	466	3.3
California	5,626	5,976	6,234	6,447	6,642	6,808	21
Colorado	655	683	699	707	711	711	8.5
Connecticut	519	532	539	541	539	537	3.5
Delaware	112	121	127	133	138	139	24.1
District of Columbia	79	76	73	71	72	72	-8.9
Florida	2,173	2,279	2,328	2,341	2,332	2,336	7.5
Georgia	1,296	1,346	1,379	1,404	1,422	1,434	10.6
Hawaii	200	209	215	218	219	226	13
Idaho	243	248	252	255	258	262	7.8
Illinois	1,937	1,989	2,014	2,032	2,038	2,044	5.5
Indiana	980	999	1,012	1,025	1,037	1,038	5.9
Iowa	505	508	503	497	492	487	-3.6
Kansas	477	484	486	485	483	484	1.5
Kentucky	660	664	668	670	672	672	1.8
Louisiana	794	794	793	793	798	801	0.9
Maine	219	218	215	211	208	206	-5.9
Maryland	816	857	888	908	921	929	13.8
Massachusetts	915	943	949	945	935	921	0.7
Michigan	1,657	1,686	1,709	1,720	1,724	1,725	4.1
Minnesota	841	854	853	843	829	821	-2.4
Mississippi	505	507	504	503	505	506	0.2
Missouri	891	902	901	895	888	884	-0.8
Montana	167	168	168	168	167	168	0.6
Nebraska	291	295	294	293	291	290	-0.3
Nevada	260	279	290	294	292	294	13.1
New Hampshire	194	198	198	195	193	192	-1
New Jersey	1,199	1,255	1,291	1,317	1,332	1,339	11.7
New Mexico	341	355	361	366	370	376	10.3
New York	2,817	2,895	2,928	2,936	2,925	2,914	3.4
North Carolina	1,181	1,229	1,267	1,296	1,315	1,320	11.8
North Dakota	118	117	114	112	111	110	-6.8
Ohio	1,832	1,857	1,861	1,861	1,857	1,844	0.7
Oklahoma	615	622	619	614	612	614	-0.2
Oregon	538	558	574	586	597	606	12.6
Pennsylvania	1,809	1,848	1,857	1,846	1,824	1,805	-0.2
Rhode Island	152	156	156	155	154	152	0
South Carolina	658	676	688	700	712	716	8.8
South Dakota	148	151	150	147	144	144	-2.7
Tennessee	892	916	931	941	948	948	6.3
Texas	3,725	3,839	3,915	3,971	4,022	4,070	9.3
Utah	480	487	493	502	514	527	9.8
Vermont	105	106	106	105	103	103	-1.9
Virginia	1,097	1,146	1,181	1,208	1,226	1,233	12.4
Washington	969	1,020	1,056	1,085	1,108	1,123	15.9
West Virginia	310	308	305	304	304	303	-2.3
Wisconsin	884	901	899	888	870	861	-2.6
Wyoming	102	102	102	102	104	107	4.9
United States	45076	46525	47362	47891	48235	48500	7.6

Table 5.3.4. Total expenditures of educational institutions related to the gross domestic product (GDP), by level of institution, 1959-1960 to 1995-96.

School year	GDP (in billions)	School expenditures as a percent of GDP
1959-60	507.2	4.7
1961-62	544.8	5.2
1963-64	617.4	5.6
1965-66	719.1	6.1
1967-68	833.6	6.7
1969-70	951.4	6.9
1970-71	1,035.6	7.3
1971-72	1,125.4	7.2
1972-73	1,237.3	7.0
1973-74	1,382.6	6.9
1974-75	1,496.9	7.3
1975-76	1,630.6	7.3
1976-77	1,819.0	6.9
1977-78	2,026.9	6.8
1978-79	2,291.4	6.5
1979-80	2,557.5	6.5
1980-81	2,784.2	6.6
1981-82	3,115.9	6.3
1982-83	3,242.1	6.5
1983-84	3,514.5	6.5
1984-85	3,902.4	6.3
1985-86	4,180.7	6.4
1986-87	4,422.2	6.6
1987-88	4,692.3	6.7
1988-89	5,049.6	6.9
1989-90	5,438.7	7.0
1990-91	5,743.8	7.2
1991-92	5,916.7	7.3
1992-93	6,244.4	7.3
1993-94	6,550.2	7.3
1994-95	6,931.4	7.3
1995-96	7,245.8	7.3

Note: 1994 data are preliminary. 1995 data are estimated.

Table 5.3.5. Revenues for public elementary and secondary schools, by source of funds, 1919-1920 to 1992-93.

	Total revenues (000s)	Percent from federal	Percent from state	Percent from local
1919-20	970,121	0.3	16.5	83.2
1929-30	2,088,557	0.4	16.9	82.7
1939-40	2,260,527	1.8	30.3	68.0
1941-42	2,416,580	1.4	31.4	67.1
1943-44	2,604,322	1.4	33.0	65.6
1945-46	3,059,845	1.4	34.7	63.9
1947-48	4,311,534	2.8	38.9	58.3
1949-50	5,437,044	2.9	39.8	57.3
1951-52	6,423,816	3.5	38.6	57.9
1953-54	7,866,852	4.5	37.4	58.1
1955-56	9,686,677	4.6	39.5	55.9
1957-58	12,181,513	4.0	39.4	56.6
1959-60	14,746,618	4.4	39.1	56.5
1961-62	17,527,707	4.3	38.7	56.9
1963-64	20,544,182	4.4	39.3	56.3
1965-66	25,356,858	7.9	39.1	53.0
1967-68	31,903,064	8.8	38.5	52.7
1969-70	40,266,923	8.0	39.9	52.1
1970-71	44,511,292	8.4	39.1	52.5
1971-72	50,003,645	8.9	38.3	52.8
1972-73	52,117,930	8.7	40.0	51.3
1973-74	58,230,892	8.5	41.4	50.1
1974-75	64,445,239	9.0	42.2	48.8
1975-76	71,206,073	8.9	44.6	46.5
1976-77	75,322,532	8.8	43.4	47.8
1978-79	87,994,143	9.8	45.6	44.6
1979-80	96,881,165	9.8	46.8	43.4
1980-81	105,949,087	9.2	47.4	43.4
1981-82	110,191,257	7.4	47.6	45.0
1982-83	117,497,502	7.1	47.9	45.0
1983-84	126,055,419	6.8	47.8	45.4
1984-85	137,294,678	6.6	48.9	44.4
1985-86	149,127,779	6.7	49.4	43.9
1986-87	158,523,693	6.4	49.7	43.9
1987-88	169,561,974	6.3	49.5	44.1
1988-89	192,016,374	6.2	47.8	46.0
1989-90	208,547,573	6.1	47.1	46.8
1990-91	223,340,537	6.2	47.2	46.7
1991-92	234,588,732	6.6	46.4	47.0
1992-93	248,496,276	6.9	45.6	47.4

Note: Local sources include a relatively small amount from nongovernmental sources (gifts and tuition and transportation fees from patrons). These sources accounted for 2.7 percent of total revenues in 1992-93.

Table 5.3.6. Source of revenues for public elementary and secondary schools, by state, 1992-93.

	Total revenues (000s)	% from federal	% from state	% from local	% from private
Total	$248,496,276	6.9	45.6	44.7	2.7
Alabama	2,982,753	11.6	58.1	22.2	8.1
Alaska	1,182,527	14.6	64.9	18.3	2.2
Arizona	3,402,888	8.8	41.5	47.4	2.3
Arkansas	1,933,846	9.6	57.1	28.6	4.7
California	28,039,018	0.8	62.2	28.6	1.2
Colorado	3,337,266	4.9	4.2	49.7	3.4
Connecticut	3,971,766	3.5	38.9	54.9	2.8
Delaware	631,885	6.9	66.1	25.3	1.6
Dist. of Columbia	722,230	10.4	0.0	89.1	0.5
Florida	11,369,988	8.3	48.5	39.1	4.1
Georgia	5,997,559	7.7	50.4	39.9	0.2
Hawaii	1,067,810	7.6	90.1	0.6	1.6
Idaho	896,846	8.4	61.1	28.5	0.2
Illinois	10,575,035	7.1	28.5	6.2	2.4
Indiana	5,625,542	5.2	52.1	39.5	3.1
Iowa	2,694,532	5.4	48.2	40.5	5.9
Kansas	2,373,507	5.5	49.7	4.2	2.8
Kentucky	3,071,172	10.1	6.7	22.1	0.8
Louisiana	3,490,001	11.7	53.8	31.9	2.6
Maine	1,337,730	6.2	50.7	4.2	1.1
Maryland	4,923,313	5.4	39.4	52.1	3.1
Massachusetts	5,881,335	5.6	32.7	59.6	0.2
Michigan	10,766,136	6.2	30.6	61.4	1.9
Minnesota	4,698,237	4.8	48.1	43.2	3.8
Mississippi	1,773,823	17.1	53.7	25.4	3.8
Missouri	4,260,954	6.4	38.3	51.1	4.1
Montana	845,249	9.2	53.8	3.3	0.4
Nebraska	1,597,612	6.3	33.2	54.4	6.2
Nevada	1,176,376	4.7	34.2	57.5	3.6
New Hampshire	1,062,532	3.1	7.9	86.6	2.3
New Jersey	10,994,535	4.2	41.4	52.1	2.3
New Mexico	1,429,383	12.6	73.7	11.3	2.5
New York	22,574,304	0.6	39.2	53.3	1.5
North Carolina	5,356,917	8.1	63.3	24.7	0.4
North Dakota	551,527	11.9	43.1	39.6	5.3
Ohio	10,993,728	5.8	3.8	52.3	3.9
Oklahoma	2,770,975	7.1	6.0	28.3	4.6
Oregon	3,135,734	6.3	37.8	53.1	2.9
Pennsylvania	12,060,334	6.1	4.0	51.8	0.2
Rhode Island	968,667	0.6	40.6	52.7	0.7
South Carolina	3,061,004	9.3	4.7	39.2	4.4
South Dakota	603,085	11.6	27.2	58.1	3.1
Tennessee	3,394,425	10.3	45.6	3.7	7.1
Texas	17,446,887	7.5	4.0	49.6	2.9
Utah	1,657,433	7.1	5.8	31.4	3.5
Vermont	637,740	5.5	31.1	61.6	1.9
Virginia	5,867,838	6.2	32.1	58.8	2.8
Washington	5,499,862	5.6	71.3	20.1	0.3
West Virginia	1,841,575	7.7	6.7	23.8	1.5
Wisconsin	5,346,988	4.4	38.3	55.3	1.9
Wyoming	613,864	5.8	50.3	42.3	1.7

Table 5.3.7. Estimated total expenditures of educational institutions, by level, control of institution, and source of funds, 1959-1960 to 1995-96 (in billions of current dollars).

Level and control of institution	1959-60 Amount	1959-60 Percent	1980-81 Amount	1980-81 Percent	1995-96 Amount	1995-96 Percent
All levels of instruction						
Public and private	23.8	100.0	182.9	100.0	529.6	100.0
Public	19.5	81.9	150.7	82.4	426.4	80.5
Private	4.3	18.1	32.2	17.6	103.2	19.5
Elementary and secondary schools						
Public and private	16.7	100.0	112.3	100.0	318.5	100.0
Public	15.6	93.4	104.1	92.7	293.7	92.2
Private	1.1	6.6	8.2	7.3	24.8	7.8
Institutions of higher education						
Public and private	7.1	100.0	70.6	100.0	211.1	100.0
Public	3.9	54.9	46.6	66.0	132.7	62.9
Private	3.2	45.1	24.0	34.0	78.4	37.1

Table 5.3.8. Personal income per capita (PIC), revenues per students, and educational effort by state, 1993 (1993 current dollars).

	Personal income per capita	State rank PIC	Revenues per student	Educational effort
Total	$20,817	—	$5,716	27.5
Alabama	17,234	41	4,061	23.6
Alaska	22,846	7	9,389	41.1
Arizona	18,121	36	4,796	26.5
Arkansas	16,143	49	4,353	27.0
California	21,821	12	5,262	24.1
Colorado	21,564	14	5,339	24.8
Connecticut	28,110	1	8,003	28.5
Delaware	21,481	15	5,987	27.9
Dist. of Columbia	29,438	—	8,952	30.4
Florida	20,857	19	5,571	26.7
Georgia	19,278	29	4,855	25.2
Hawaii	23,354	6	5,918	25.3
Idaho	17,646	38	3,788	21.5
Illinois	22,582	10	5,586	24.7
Indiana	19,203	30	5,826	30.3
Iowa	18,315	35	5,405	29.5
Kansas	20,139	21	5,187	25.8
Kentucky	17,173	42	4,687	27.3
Louisiana	16,667	45	4,359	26.2
Maine	18,895	32	6,165	32.6
Maryland	24,044	5	6,372	26.5
Massachusetts	24,563	4	6,701	27.3
Michigan	20,453	20	6,731	32.9
Minnesota	21,063	18	5,799	27.5
Mississippi	14,894	50	3,506	23.5
Missouri	19,463	27	4,866	25.0
Montana	17,322	40	5,185	29.9
Nebraska	19,726	23	5,604	28.4
Nevada	22,729	8	4,989	21.9
New Hampshire	22,659	9	5,732	25.3
New Jersey	26,967	2	9,550	35.4
New Mexico	16,297	46	4,435	27.2
New York	24,623	3	8,257	33.5
North Carolina	18,702	33	4,727	25.3
North Dakota	17,488	39	4,630	26.5
Ohio	19,688	24	6,083	30.9
Oklahoma	17,020	43	4,587	27.0
Oregon	19,443	28	6,070	31.2
Pennsylvania	21,351	16	6,915	32.4
Rhode Island	21,096	17	6,649	31.5
South Carolina	16,923	44	4,754	28.1
South Dakota	17,666	37	4,223	23.9
Tennessee	18,434	34	3,915	21.2
Texas	19,189	31	4,835	25.2
Utah	16,180	48	3,516	21.7
Vermont	19,467	26	6,206	31.9
Virginia	21,634	13	5,613	25.9
Washington	21,887	11	6,005	27.4
West Virginia	16,209	47	5,858	36.1
Wisconsin	19,811	22	6,335	32.0
Wyoming	19,539	25	6,084	31.1

Table 5.3.9. States requiring testing for initial certification of teachers, by authorization and test used, 1996.

	Authority	Test used	Assessment for certification		
			Basic skills	Content knowledge	In-class observation
Alabama	State Board	State	■	■	■
Alaska	—	—			
Arizona	Legislature	State	■		
Arkansas	Legislature	NTE	■	■	■
California	Legislature	State	■	■	■
Colorado	Legislature	California Achievement	■	■	■
Connecticut	State Board	State	■		■
Delaware	State Board	P.-P.S.T.	■		■
District of Columbia	—	—	■	■	■
Florida	Legislature	State	■	■	■
Georgia	State Board	State		■	■
Hawaii	State Board	NTE	■	■	■
Idaho	Legislature	NTE		■	■
Illinois	Legislature	State	■	■	■
Indiana	Legislature	NTE	■	■	
Iowa	—	—			
Kansas	Legislature	To be determined	■		■
Kentucky	Legislature	NTE	■	■	■
Louisiana	Legislature	NTE	■	■	■
Maine	Legislature	NTE		■	■
Maryland	State Board	NTE		■	
Massachusetts	Legislature	To be determined	■	■	
Michigan	Legislature	To be determined	■		■
Minnesota	—	—	■		
Mississippi	Legislature	NTE	■	■	■
Missouri	Legislature	To be determined	■	■	■
Montana	Board of Education	NTE	■	■	
Nebraska	Legislature	To be determined	■		■
Nevada	State Board	To be determined	■		■
New Hampshire	State Board	NTE	■		
New Jersey	State Board	NTE		■	■
New Mexico	State Board	NTE	■	■	■
New York	State Board	NTE		■	■
North Carolina	State Board	NTE	■	■	■
North Dakota	—	—	■		■
Ohio	State Board	NTE	■	■	■
Oklahoma	Legislature	State	■	■	■
Oregon	O.T.S.P.C.	C.B.E.S.T.	■	■	■
Pennsylvania	State Board	State	■	■	
Rhode Island	State Board	NTE	■		■
South Carolina	Legislature	NTE and State	■	■	■
South Dakota	State Board	NTE			■
Tennessee	State Board	NTE	■	■	■
Texas	Legislature	State	■	■	■
Utah	—	—			■
Vermont	—	—			■
Virginia	Legislature	NTE	■	■	■
Washington	State Board	To be determined	■		■
West Virginia	State Board	State	■	■	■
Wisconsin	S.P.I.	To be determined	■		■
Wyoming	—	—			■

Note:
O.T.S.P.C.= Oregon Teacher Standards and Practice Commission

S.P.I.= Superintendent of Public Instruction

NTE = National Teacher Examination

State = State developed test

C.B.E.S.T.= California Basic Education Skills Test

P.-P.S.T.= Pre-professional Skills Test (Praxis).

Table 5.3.10. Percentage of 12th grade students whose parents reported that school personnel contacted them at least once during the current school year for various reasons, by race/ethnicity, 1992.

Reason school contacted parents	Percent of parents contacted by school personnel					
	Total	White	African American	Hispanic	Asian	Native American
Student's academic performance	52.7	52.9	49.0	55.8	47.5	61.6
Student's academic program	43.8	44.0	44.6	41.7	38.5	54.7
Student's post-high school plans	37.1	37.2	38.2	35.8	33.2	44.5
Student's attendance	37.0	36.7	34.3	39.7	42.0	40.2
Student's behavior	20.1	18.7	29.2	19.4	17.4	28.1
Request parents volunteer time at school	55.0	58.5	52.0	38.6	47.0	42.4
Inform parents how to help student with school work	22.3	21.3	29.7	20.4	21.4	29.8

Table 5.3.12. Public and private elementary and secondary teachers and pupil-teacher ratios, by level, fall 1955 to fall 2005 (projected).

Teachers (000s)	Public and private schools			Public and private schools			Public and private schools		
	K to 12	Elementary	Secondary	K to 12	Elementary	Secondary	K to 12	Elementary	Secondary
1955-56	1,286	827	459	1,141	733	408	145	94	51
1960-61	1,600	991	609	1,408	858	550	192	133	59
1970-71	2,292	1,283	1,009	2,059	1,130	929	233	153	80
1980-81	2,485	1,401	1,084	2,184	1,189	995	301	212	89
1985-86	2,549	1,483	1,066	2,206	1,237	969	343	246	97
1990-91	2,753	1,680	1,073	2,398	1,426	972	356	254	101
1995-96	2,971	1,784	1,187	2,595	1,520	1,075	375	264	112
1997-98	3,084	1,850	1,234	2,694	1,576	1,118	390	273	117
2000-01	3,228	1,936	1,292	2,820	1,650	1,170	408	286	122
2005-06	3,371	1,984	1,387	2,947	1,691	1,255	424	293	131
Pupil-teacher ratios									
1955-56	27.4	31.4	20.3	26.9	30.2	20.9	31.7	40.4	15.7
1960-61	26.4	29.4	21.4	25.8	28.4	21.7	30.7	36.1	18.6
1970-71	22.4	24.6	19.5	22.3	24.3	19.8	23.0	26.5	16.4
1980-81	18.6	20.1	16.6	18.7	20.4	16.8	17.7	18.8	15.0
1985-86	17.6	19.1	15.6	17.9	19.5	15.8	16.2	17.1	14.0
1990-91	16.9	18.5	14.3	17.2	19.0	14.6	14.7	16.1	11.3
1995-96	17.1	18.7	14.6	17.4	19.1	14.9	15.1	16.7	11.3
1997-98	17.1	18.7	14.6	17.4	19.1	14.9	15.1	16.7	11.4
2000-01	16.9	18.5	14.4	17.1	18.8	14.7	14.9	16.4	11.3
2005-06	16.6	18.0	14.5	16.8	18.3	14.9	14.7	16.2	11.3

Note: Data for teachers are expressed in full-time equivalents. Distribution of unclassified teachers by level is estimated. Distribution of elementary and secondary school teachers by level is determined by reporting units. Kindergarten includes a relatively small number of nursery school teachers and students. Some data have been revised from previously published figures. Because of rounding, details may not add to totals.

Table 5.3.11. Teachers teaching "out of field," by state, 1995.			
	Overall percent of teachers out of field	Disparity in percent of out-of-field teachers	
		Between affluent and poor schools	Between schools with large and small minority enrollments
Alabama	18.9	15.5	13.4
Alaska	25.0	26.9	24.5
Arizona	24.5	17.2	3.2
Arkansas	14.1	-0.1	4.4
California	25.5	0.8	0.6
Colorado	15.8	-10.5	-3.3
Connecticut	12.2	23.8	12.9
Delaware	16.0	52.6	n/a
Dist. of Columbia	6.8	n/a	n/a
Florida	26.4	21.6	5.5
Georgia	23.1	11.0	-1.3
Hawaii	23.8	-0.5	n/a
Idaho	17.6	0.8	n/a
Illinois	19.0	22.4	9.9
Indiana	12.7	3.8	12.4
Iowa	13.0	8.0	n/a
Kansas	16.9	10.9	n/a
Kentucky	21.7	23.9	-22.9
Louisiana	26.2	18.8	-6.7
Maine	21.5	14.2	n/a
Maryland	25.6	14.4	7.5
Massachusetts	19.2	14.3	4.3
Michigan	17.4	20.7	6.0
Minnesota	6.7	-3.1	6.2
Mississippi	25.4	16.7	4.1
Missouri	15.3	-3.5	4.7
Montana	13.4	-6.3	-10.2
Nebraska	10.1	-4.2	-5.7
Nevada	22.4	-2.0	-9.0
New Hampshire	10.8	n/a	n/a
New Jersey	19.8	3.7	4.3
New Mexico	23.9	5.4	n/a
New York	17.5	19.7	11.9
North Carolina	17.4	7.7	-2.7
North Dakota	10.1	4.7	25.4
Ohio	17.6	16.3	6.9
Oklahoma	18.9	1.0	1.5
Oregon	20.9	23.2	n/a
Pennsylvania	11.4	-4.7	-4.9
Rhode Island	15.7	10.1	n/a
South Carolina	23.1	12.9	2.7
South Dakota	17.9	10.0	12.4
Tennessee	26.5	23.9	-5.0
Texas	18.2	12.3	-2.9
Utah	16.4	-5.1	0.6
Vermont	15.1	n/a	n/a
Virginia	18.0	10.9	-13.5
Washington	21.9	5.7	7.0
West Virginia	15.3	-15.8	n/a
Wisconsin	11.5	-5.0	6.5
Wyoming	13.5	15.7	n/a

Table 5.3.13. Student/teacher ratio, public elementary and secondary schools, by state, fall 1994.

	Student/teacher ratio
Alabama	17.4
Alaska	17.8
Arizona	19.1
Arkansas	15.5
California	24.9
Colorado	18.6
Connecticut	14.8
Delaware	17.0
District of Columbia	12.9
Florida	18.1
Georgia	16.3
Hawaii	17.9
Idaho	19.4
Illinois	16.9
Indiana	17.5
Iowa	15.8
Kansas	15.3
Kentucky	17.5
Louisiana	16.6
Maine	14.4
Maryland	17.6
Massachusetts	14.2
Michigan	20.4
Minnesota	17.5
Mississippi	17.7
Missouri	15.5
Montana	16.4
Nebraska	14.6
Nevada	18.7
New Hampshire	16.3
New Jersey	13.6
New Mexico	17.9
New York	15.0
North Carolina	16.4
North Dakota	14.8
Ohio	17.5
Oklahoma	15.4
Oregon	20.4
Pennsylvania	17.5
Rhode Island	16.2
South Carolina	16.6
South Dakota	14.6
Tennessee	17.7
Texas	15.9
Utah	21.8
Vermont	11.9
Virginia	15.1
Washington	20.6
West Virginia	14.9
Wisconsin	15.5
Wyoming	15.3

Figure 5.4.3. Distribution of scale scores on reading literacy assessment, by age and country, school year, 1991-92.

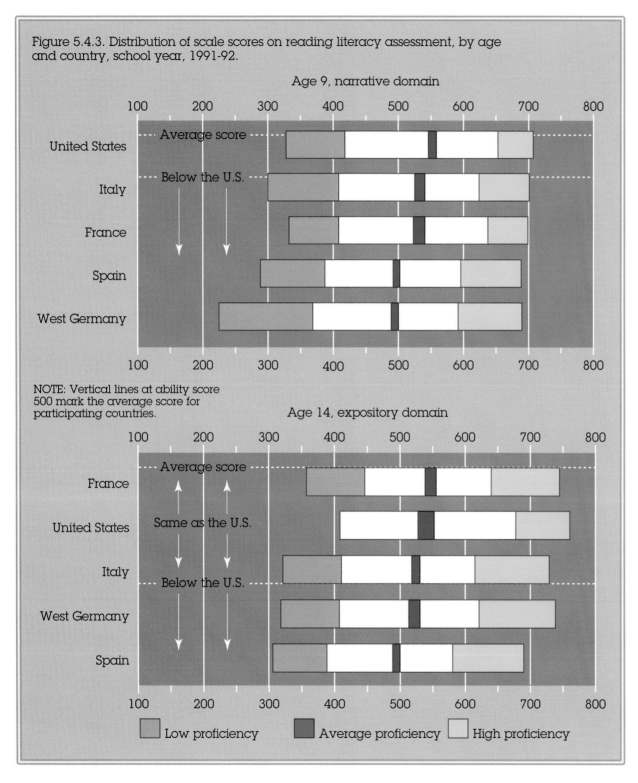

Age 9, narrative domain

NOTE: Vertical lines at ability score 500 mark the average score for participating countries.

Age 14, expository domain

Low proficiency   Average proficiency   High proficiency

Table 5.4.1. Average reading proficiency (scale score), by age, ethnicity, and sex, selected years, 1975-1992.

	Age 9	Age 13	Age 17
Total			
1975	210	256	286
1980	215	258	286
1984	211	257	289
1988	212	258	290
1990	209	257	290
1992	210	260	290
Male			
1975	204	250	280
1980	210	254	282
1984	208	253	284
1988	208	252	286
1990	204	250	284
1992	206	254	284
Female			
1975	216	262	291
1980	220	263	289
1984	214	262	294
1988	216	263	294
1990	214	263	296
1992	215	265	296
White			
1975	217	262	293
1980	221	264	293
1984	218	263	295
1988	218	261	295
1990	217	262	297
1992	218	266	297
Black			
1975	181	226	241
1980	188	233	243
1984	186	236	264
1988	189	243	274
1990	182	242	267
1992	184	238	261
Hispanic			
1975	183	232	252
1980	190	237	261
1984	187	240	268
1988	194	240	271
1990	189	238	275
1992	192	239	271

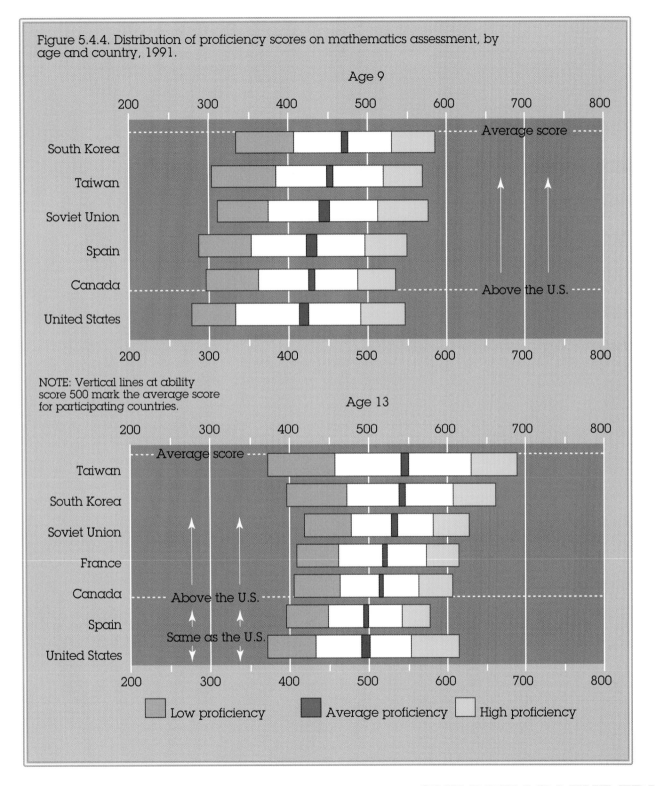

Figure 5.4.4. Distribution of proficiency scores on mathematics assessment, by age and country, 1991.

Age 9

South Korea
Taiwan
Soviet Union
Spain
Canada
United States

Average score
Above the U.S.

NOTE: Vertical lines at ability score 500 mark the average score for participating countries.

Age 13

Taiwan
South Korea
Soviet Union
France
Canada
Spain
United States

Average score
Above the U.S.
Same as the U.S.

☐ Low proficiency   ■ Average proficiency   ☐ High proficiency

Table 5.4.3. Average mathematics proficiency (scale score), by age, ethnicity, and sex, selected years, 1973-1992.

	Age 9	Age 13	Age 17
Total			
1973	219	266	304
1978	219	264	300
1982	219	269	298
1986	222	269	302
1990	230	270	305
1992	230	273	307
Male			
1973	210	265	309
1978	217	264	304
1982	217	269	302
1986	222	270	305
1990	229	271	306
1992	231	274	309
Female			
1973	220	267	301
1978	221	265	297
1982	222	268	296
1986	222	268	299
1990	230	270	303
1992	228	272	304
White			
1973	225	274	310
1978	224	272	306
1982	224	274	304
1986	227	274	308
1990	235	276	310
1992	235	279	312
Black			
1973	190	228	270
1978	192	230	268
1982	185	240	272
1986	202	249	279
1990	208	249	288
1992	208	250	286
Hispanic			
1973	202	239	277
1978	203	238	276
1982	204	252	277
1986	205	254	283
1990	214	255	284
1992	212	259	292

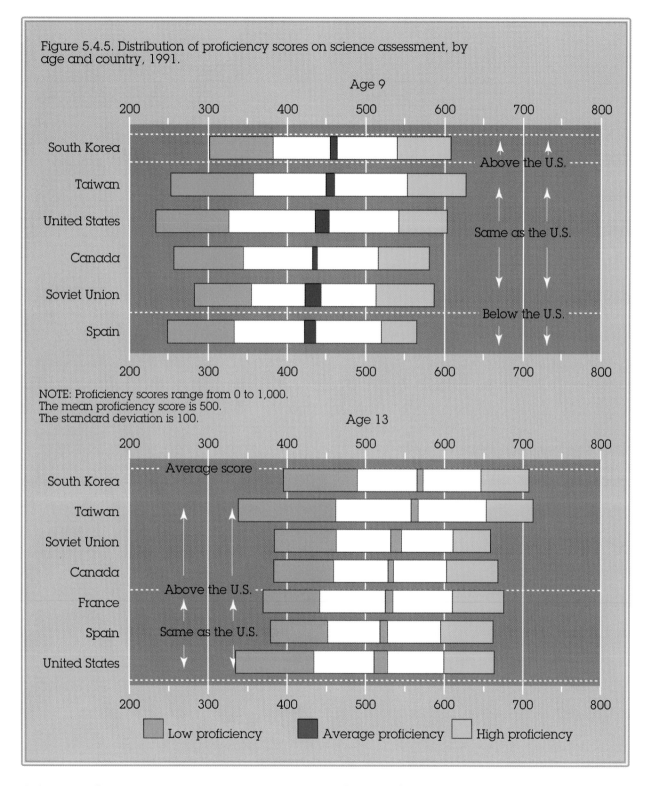

Figure 5.4.5. Distribution of proficiency scores on science assessment, by age and country, 1991.

Age 9

Above the U.S.

Same as the U.S.

Below the U.S.

NOTE: Proficiency scores range from 0 to 1,000.
The mean proficiency score is 500.
The standard deviation is 100.

Age 13

Average score

Above the U.S.

Same as the U.S.

Low proficiency   Average proficiency   High proficiency

Table 5.4.4. Average science proficiency (scale score), by age, ethnicity, and sex, selected years, 1973-1992.

	Age 9	Age 13	Age 17
Total			
1973	220	250	296
1977	220	247	290
1982	221	250	283
1986	224	251	288
1990	229	255	290
1992	231	258	294
Male			
1973	223	252	304
1977	222	251	297
1982	221	256	292
1986	227	256	295
1990	230	258	296
1992	235	260	299
Female			
1973	218	247	288
1977	218	244	282
1982	221	245	275
1986	221	247	282
1990	227	252	285
1992	227	256	289
White			
1973	231	259	304
1977	230	256	298
1982	229	257	293
1986	232	259	298
1990	238	264	301
1992	239	267	304
Black			
1973	177	205	250
1977	175	208	240
1982	187	217	235
1986	196	222	253
1990	196	226	253
1992	200	224	256
Hispanic			
1973	N/A	N/A	N/A
1977	192	213	262
1982	189	226	249
1986	199	226	259
1990	206	232	262
1992	205	238	270

Table 5.4.1a. Average reading proficiency (scale score), selected years, 1971-1992.

	All students			Male			Female		
	Age 9	Age 13	Age 17	Age 9	Age 13	Age 17	Age 9	Age 13	Age 17
1971	208	255	285	201	250	279	214	261	291
1975	210	256	286	204	250	280	216	262	291
1980	215	258	286	210	254	282	220	263	289
1984	211	257	289	208	253	284	214	262	294
1988	212	258	290	208	252	286	216	263	294
1990	209	257	290	204	250	284	214	263	296
1992	210	260	290	206	254	284	215	265	296

	White			African American			Hispanic		
	Age 9	Age 13	Age 17	Age 9	Age 13	Age 17	Age 9	Age 13	Age 17
1971	214	261	291	170	222	239	—	—	—
1975	217	262	293	181	226	241	183	232	252
1980	221	264	293	188	233	243	190	237	261
1984	218	263	295	186	236	264	187	240	268
1988	218	261	295	189	243	274	194	240	271
1990	217	262	297	182	242	267	189	238	275
1992	218	266	297	184	238	261	192	239	271

Table 5.4.2. Average writing proficiency (scale score), by grade, ethnicity, and sex, selected years, 1984-1992.

Total	Grade 4	Grade 8	Grade 11
1984	204	267	290
1988	206	264	291
1990	202	257	287
1992	207	274	287
Male			
1984	200	258	281
1988	199	254	282
1990	195	246	276
1992	198	264	279
Female			
1984	208	276	299
1988	213	274	299
1990	209	268	298
1992	216	285	296
White			
1984	211	272	297
1988	215	269	296
1990	211	262	293
1992	217	279	294
African American			
1984	182	247	270
1988	173	246	275
1990	171	239	268
1992	175	258	263
Hispanic			
1984	188	247	259
1988	190	250	274
1990	184	246	277
1992	189	265	274

Table 5.4.6. Percentage of 10th to 12th grade dropouts who reported various reasons for dropping out of school, by sex and race/ethnicity, 1992.

Reason for dropping out	Total	Male	Female	Hispanic	Black	White
Did not like school	42.9	43.6	42.2	48.0	28.8	45.5
Could not get along with teachers	22.8	24.6	21.1	24.6	27.8	21.5
Could not get along with students	14.5	17.7	11.6	15.6	18.4	13.6
Did not feel safe in school	6.0	7.0	5.1	8.3	8.5	4.8
Felt like I didn't belong	24.2	25.8	22.7	16.0	25.9	26.6
Could not keep up with schoolwork	31.3	32.7	29.9	35.0	25.6	30.3
Was failing school	38.7	43.4	34.5	40.6	39.5	36.6
Did not like new school	10.6	10.8	10.7	12.3	9.1	10.2
Was suspended/expelled	15.5	21.6	10.0	10.1	24.4	15.4
Could not work and go to school	22.8	26.9	19.1	20.4	15.4	24.6
Found a job	28.5	35.9	21.8	34.1	19.1	27.5
Had to support family	11.2	10.4	11.9	15.8	11.8	9.9
Wanted to have a family	7.5	6.4	8.4	9.1	4.6	8.2
Was pregnant	26.8	—	26.8	30.6	34.5	25.6
Become parent(s)	14.7	7.7	21.0	19.6	21.0	12.4
Got married	12.1	3.7	19.7	13.4	2.0	15.1
Had to care for family member	11.9	9.5	14.0	8.5	14.7	10.7
Wanted to travel	8.1	8.2	8.0	6.6	7.3	7.1
Friends dropped out	8.0	8.5	7.5	7.6	6.7	8.6
Had a drug and/or alcohol problem	4.4	6.1	2.8	1.8	2.1	5.9

Table 5.4.5. Percent of population with high school diploma or equivalency, by race and gender, 1971-1995.

Year	Total Population			White			African American			Hispanic		
	Total	Male	Female	Total	Male	Female	Total	Male	Female	Total	Male	Female
1971	77.7	79.1	76.5	81.7	83.0	80.5	58.8	56.7	60.5	48.3	51.3	45.7
1972	79.8	80.5	79.2	83.4	84.1	82.7	64.1	61.7	66.0	47.6	47.1	47.9
1973	80.2	80.6	79.8	84.0	84.2	83.9	64.1	63.2	64.9	52.3	54.2	50.6
1974	81.9	83.1	80.8	85.5	86.0	85.0	68.4	71.5	65.8	54.1	55.9	52.5
1975	83.1	84.5	81.7	86.6	88.0	85.2	71.1	72.3	70.1	53.1	52.2	53.9
1976	84.7	86.0	83.5	87.7	89.0	86.4	74.0	72.8	74.9	58.1	57.6	58.4
1977	85.4	86.6	84.2	88.6	89.2	88.0	74.5	77.5	72.0	58.0	61.9	54.6
1978	85.3	86.0	84.6	88.5	88.8	88.2	77.4	78.7	76.3	56.5	58.5	54.6
1979	85.6	86.3	84.9	89.2	89.8	88.5	74.7	74.0	75.3	57.1	55.5	58.6
1980	85.4	85.4	85.5	89.2	89.1	89.2	76.7	74.8	78.3	57.9	57.0	58.8
1981	86.3	86.5	86.1	89.8	89.7	89.9	77.6	78.8	76.6	59.8	59.1	60.4
1982	86.2	86.3	86.1	89.1	89.1	89.1	81.0	80.4	81.5	61.0	60.6	61.2
1983	86.0	86.0	86.0	89.3	89.3	89.3	79.5	79.0	79.9	58.4	57.8	58.9
1984	85.9	85.6	86.3	89.4	89.4	89.4	79.1	75.9	81.7	58.6	56.7	60.1
1985	86.2	85.9	86.4	89.5	89.2	89.9	80.5	80.6	80.5	61.0	58.6	63.1
1986	86.1	85.9	86.4	89.6	88.7	90.4	83.5	86.4	81.0	59.1	58.2	60.0
1987	86.0	85.5	86.4	89.4	88.9	90.0	83.5	84.5	82.6	59.8	58.6	61.0
1988	85.9	84.7	87.1	89.7	88.4	90.9	80.9	80.9	80.9	62.3	59.9	64.8
1989	85.5	84.4	86.5	89.3	88.2	90.4	82.3	80.5	83.8	61.0	61.0	61.1
1990	85.7	84.4	87.0	90.1	88.6	91.6	81.8	81.4	82.0	58.2	56.6	59.9
1991	85.4	84.9	85.8	89.8	89.2	90.5	81.8	83.6	80.1	56.7	56.4	57.2
High school diploma or equivalency certificate												
1992	86.3	86.1	86.5	90.6	90.3	91.1	80.9	82.7	79.3	60.9	61.1	60.6
1993	86.7	86.0	87.4	91.2	90.7	91.8	82.7	84.8	80.8	60.9	58.2	63.9
1994	86.1	84.5	87.6	91.1	90.0	92.3	84.1	82.8	85.3	60.3	58.0	63.0
1995	86.9	86.3	87.4	92.5	92.0	93.0	86.8	88.4	85.3	57.2	55.7	58.7

Note: 12 years of schooling completed for 1971-91 and high school diploma or equivalency certificate for 1992-95.
Beginning in 1992, the Current Population Survey changed the questions it used to obtain the
educational attainment of respondents. See the supplemental note to this indicator for further discussion.

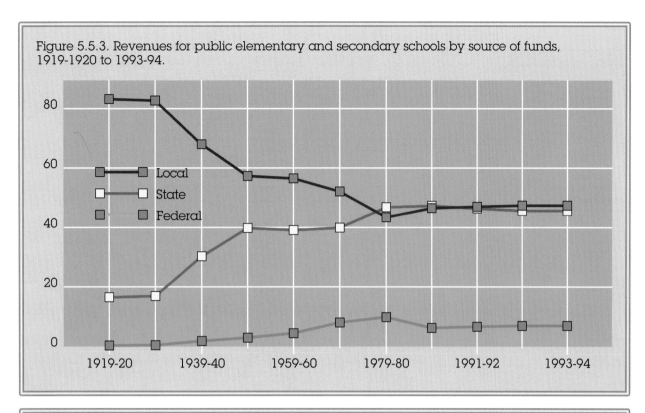

Figure 5.5.3. Revenues for public elementary and secondary schools by source of funds, 1919-1920 to 1993-94.

Table 5.5.1. Percent of high school students who reported experience with violence on school property, 1993.

	Race/ethnicity			Grade			
	White	Black	Hispanic	Nine	Ten	Eleven	Twelve
Feel too unsafe to go to school	3.0	7.1	10.1	6.1	5.2	3.3	3.0
Carried a weapon on school property	10.9	15.0	13.3	12.6	11.5	11.9	10.8
Threatened or injured with a weapon on school property	6.3	11.2	8.6	9.4	7.3	7.3	5.5
In a physical fight on school property	15.0	22.0	17.9	23.1	17.2	13.8	11.4
Property stolen or deliberately damaged on school property	32.0	35.5	32.2	37.2	32.8	32.3	28.9

Table 5.5.3. Steps school principals have taken to prevent violence in the classroom.

	Urban	Suburban	Rural
Instituted strict enforcement of discipline policies	60.0	50.0	42.0
Closed the campus	20.0	20.0	19.0
Banned gang clothing and insignias	38.0	24.0	9.0
Restricted use of school facilities after school hours	21.0	12.0	12.0
Issued ID cards to students	17.0	14.0	6.0
Instituted mandatory multicultural education	24.0	15.0	4.0
Banned racial/ethnic insignias	18.0	12.0	5.0
Instituted use of metal detectors	10.0	1.0	1.0
Installed surveillance cameras	5.0	4.0	1.0
Formed volunteer parent patrol groups	8.0	2.0	1.0
Instituted use of school uniforms	6.0	1.0	0.0

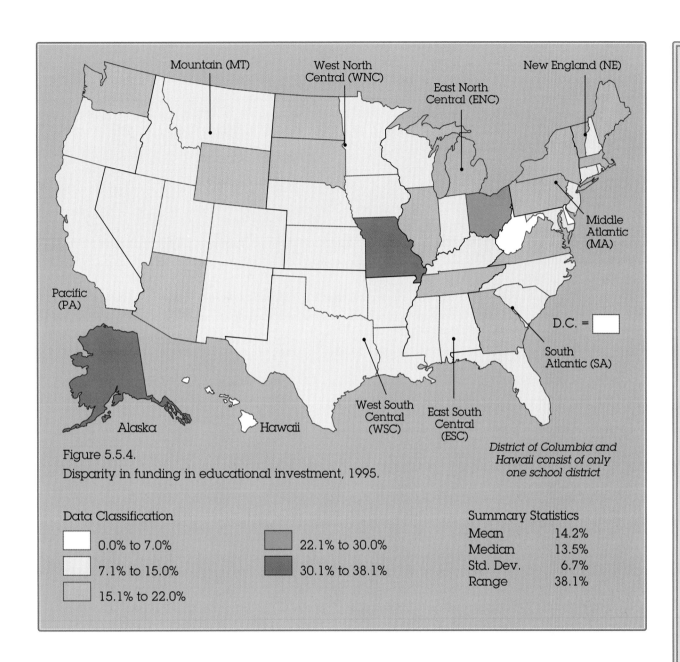

Figure 5.5.4.
Disparity in funding in educational investment, 1995.

Data Classification

☐	0.0% to 7.0%
☐	7.1% to 15.0%
☐	15.1% to 22.0%
☐	22.1% to 30.0%
☐	30.1% to 38.1%

Summary Statistics

Mean	14.2%
Median	13.5%
Std. Dev.	6.7%
Range	38.1%

Disparity in funding and difference between high-spending and low-spending districts, 1995.

	Spending gap between districts	Disparity in funding
Alabama	1,255	11.8
Alaska	7,657	38.1
Arizona	2,078	15.5
Arkansas	2,078	13.7
California	1,392	12.0
Colorado	1,788	12.0
Connecticut	3,239	12.9
Delaware	994	6.0
District of Columbia	0	0.0
Florida	1,186	8.4
Georgia	2,845	17.3
Hawaii	0	0.0
Idaho	1,499	13.8
Illinois	1,776	15.9
Indiana	1,808	14.6
Iowa	1,176	8.3
Kansas	2,107	13.7
Kentucky	1,293	11.6
Louisiana	1,499	12.1
Maine	2,333	21.9
Maryland	2,472	13.0
Massachusetts	3,545	21.9
Michigan	3,368	20.7
Minnesota	2,738	15.0
Mississippi	1,058	11.4
Missouri	4,876	34.0
Montana	963	11.4
Nebraska	1,981	14.3
Nevada	583	9.0
New Hampshire	2,326	14.9
New Jersey	3,556	13.5
New Mexico	1,808	14.9
New York	5,122	21.6
North Carolina	1,204	8.9
North Dakota	1,545	15.2
Ohio	2,878	27.4
Oklahoma	1,265	12.6
Oregon	2,217	13.4
Pennsylvania	3,933	18.8
Rhode Island	1,755	8.0
South Carolina	1,294	10.7
South Dakota	1,830	15.2
Tennessee	1,491	16.2
Texas	1,500	12.5
Utah	1,142	12.5
Vermont	3,812	16.7
Virginia	2,534	20.3
Washington	1,523	8.9
West Virginia	781	5.3
Wisconsin	1,901	12.5
Wyoming	2,572	15.8

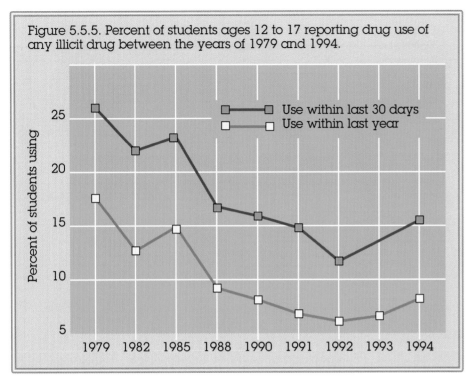

Figure 5.5.5. Percent of students ages 12 to 17 reporting drug use of any illicit drug between the years of 1979 and 1994.

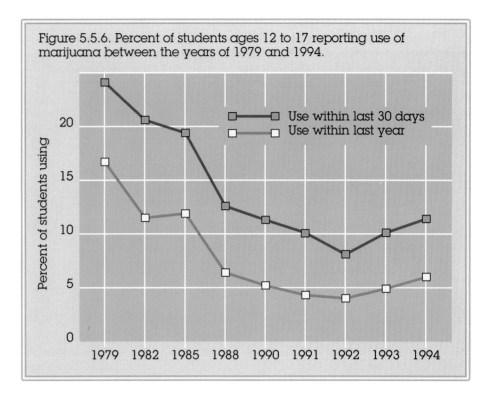

Figure 5.5.6. Percent of students ages 12 to 17 reporting use of marijuana between the years of 1979 and 1994.

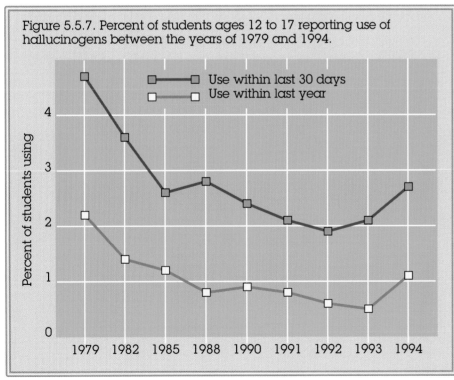

Figure 5.5.7. Percent of students ages 12 to 17 reporting use of hallucinogens between the years of 1979 and 1994.

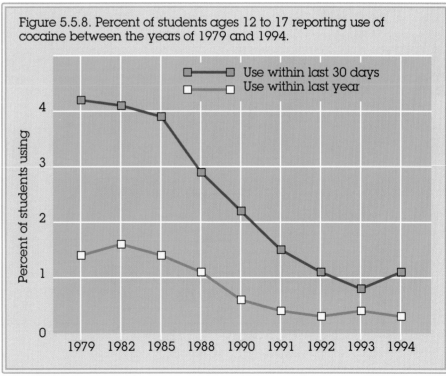

Figure 5.5.8. Percent of students ages 12 to 17 reporting use of cocaine between the years of 1979 and 1994.

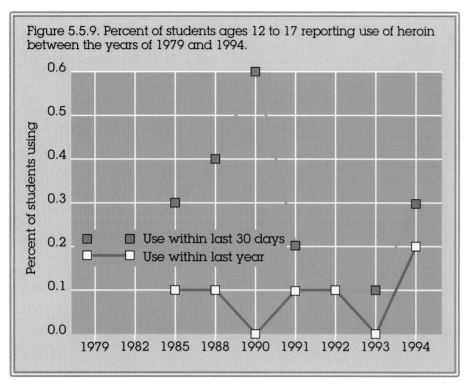

Figure 5.5.9. Percent of students ages 12 to 17 reporting use of heroin between the years of 1979 and 1994.

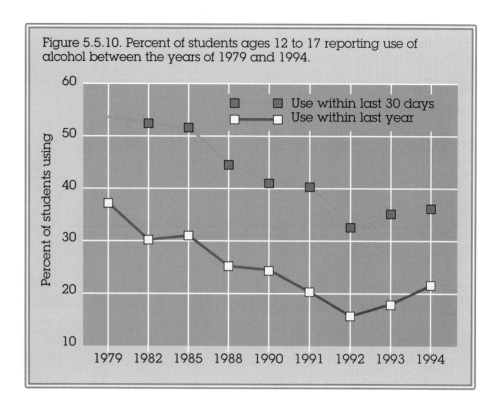

Figure 5.5.10. Percent of students ages 12 to 17 reporting use of alcohol between the years of 1979 and 1994.

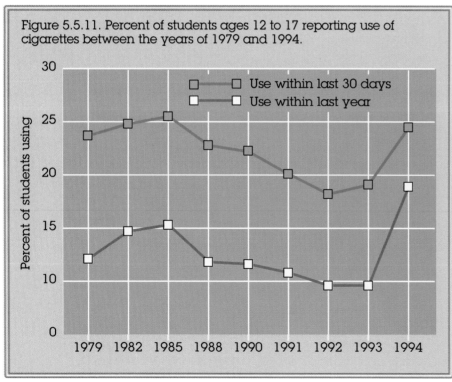

Figure 5.5.11. Percent of students ages 12 to 17 reporting use of cigarettes between the years of 1979 and 1994.

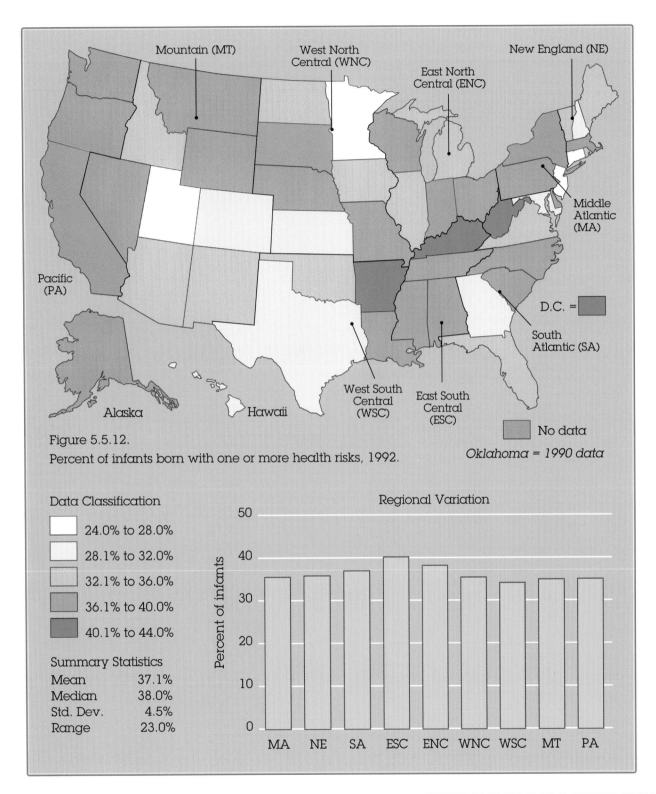

Figure 5.5.12.
Percent of infants born with one or more health risks, 1992.

Oklahoma = 1990 data

Data Classification

	24.0% to 28.0%
	28.1% to 32.0%
	32.1% to 36.0%
	36.1% to 40.0%
	40.1% to 44.0%

Summary Statistics

Mean	37.1%
Median	38.0%
Std. Dev.	4.5%
Range	23.0%

D.C. =

No data

Children born and percent of infants born with one or more health risks, 1992.

	Live births	Percent born with risks
Alabama	62,260	39
Alaska	11,726	37
Arizona	68,829	37
Arkansas	34,820	42
California	601,730	N/A
Colorado	54,535	33
Connecticut	47,573	25
Delaware	10,656	40
District of Columbia	10,960	48
Florida	191,713	37
Georgia	111,116	35
Hawaii	19,864	30
Idaho	17,362	35
Illinois	191,396	35
Indiana	84,140	N/A
Iowa	38,469	39
Kansas	38,027	32
Kentucky	53,840	45
Louisiana	70,707	39
Maine	16,057	35
Maryland	77,815	31
Massachusetts	87,231	42
Michigan	144,089	38
Minnesota	65,607	28
Mississippi	42,681	40
Missouri	76,301	41
Montana	11,472	38
Nebraska	23,397	38
Nevada	22,374	38
New Hampshire	15,990	35
New Jersey	119,909	31
New Mexico	27,922	37
New York	287,887	N/A
North Carolina	103,967	40
North Dakota	8,811	36
Ohio	162,247	41
Oklahoma	47,557	36
Oregon	42,035	39
Pennsylvania	164,625	39
Rhode Island	14,500	36
South Carolina	56,192	43
South Dakota	11,018	N/A
Tennessee	73,614	38
Texas	320,845	32
Utah	37,200	29
Vermont	7,737	38
Virginia	97,198	35
Washington	79,450	34
West Virginia	22,170	43
Wisconsin	70,670	42
Wyoming	6,723	41

Table 5.5.4. Percentage of students in grades 6-12 who report agreement or strong agreement with statements about the school discipline, by school and by family characteristics.

Characteristics	Good classroom discipline is maintained by	
	teacher	principal
Total	81.0	89.0
Educational level		
Elementary school	89.0	94.0
Middle or junior h.s.	85.0	91.0
Senior high school	77.0	87.0
Combined	84.0	88.0
School type		
Public—assigned	81.0	88.0
Public—chosen	80.0	89.0
Private	89.0	96.0
School size		
Under 300	87.0	92.0
300–599	83.0	90.0
600–999	79.0	88.0
1,000 or more	79.0	88.0
Race and school racial composition		
White in mostly white	84.0	91.0
White in racially mixed	82.0	90.0
White in mostly nonwhite	73.0	88.0
Black in mostly black	70.0	83.0
Black in racially mixed	74.0	85.0
Black in mostly nonblack	80.0	87.0
Other race/ethnicity	82.0	88.0
Student's race/ethnicity		
White, non-Hispanic	83.0	90.0
Black, non-Hispanic	74.0	85.0
Hispanic	82.0	88.0
Other races	83.0	88.0
Parent's highest education		
Less than h.s.	82.0	87.0
H.S. diploma or equivalent	80.0	88.0
Voc./Tech. some college	81.0	88.0
College graduate	84.0	92.0
College+ or professional	82.0	93.0
Household urbanicity		
Urban-inside	80.0	89.0
Urban-outside	81.0	88.0
Rural	83.0	89.0

Table 5.5.5. Percent of teachers indicating item is a serious problem in their school, by type and control of school, 1993-94.

Problem area	Public school teachers		Private school teachers	
	Elementary	Secondary	Elementary	Secondary
Student tardiness	6.3	18.3	1.8	4.3
Student absenteeism	7.2	27.1	0.8	5.2
Teacher absenteeism	1.3	1.9	0.7	1.2
Students cutting class	1.3	11.9	0.2	2.4
Physical conflicts among students	7.8	8.6	0.9	2.1
Robbery or theft	3.0	5.8	0.4	1.4
Vandalism of school property	5.2	9.0	0.9	2.0
Student pregnancy	1.1	18.4	0.2	1.1
Student use of alcohol	1.6	23.1	0.3	11.0
Student drug abuse	1.0	14.2	0.2	4.0
Student possession of weapons	1.2	5.6	0.2	0.6
Verbal abuse of teachers	8.6	14.8	0.7	2.8
Student disrespect for teachers	15.3	23.6	2.2	4.2
Students dropping out	1.2	14.1	0.3	1.3
Student apathy	15.6	38.0	2.2	9.7
Lack of academic challenge	4.2	10.4	1.0	2.5
Lack of parental involvement	23.0	34.5	2.8	7.1
Parental alcoholism/drug abuse	12.9	12.3	1.6	4.2
Poverty	20.8	15.9	2.2	3.2
Racial tension	4.0	6.7	0.6	1.7
Students come unprepared to learn	24.3	36.0	2.6	7.6

Table 5.5.6. Percent of high school seniors reporting drug use, by type of drug and frequency of use, 1980-1995.

	Year graduated			
	1980	1985	1990	1995
Percent reporting having ever used drugs				
Alcohol	93.2	92.2	89.5	80.7
Any illicit drug abuse	65.4	60.6	47.9	48.4
Marijuana only	26.7	20.9	18.5	20.3
Any illicit drug other than marijuana	38.7	39.7	29.4	28.1
Cocaine	15.7	17.3	9.4	6.0
Heroin	1.1	1.2	1.3	1.6
LSD	9.3	7.5	8.7	11.7
Marijuana/hashish	60.3	54.2	40.7	41.7
PCP	9.6	4.9	2.8	2.7
Percent reporting use of drugs in the past 12 months				
Alcohol	87.9	85.6	80.6	73.7
Any illicit drug abuse	53.1	46.3	32.5	39.0
Marijuana only	22.7	18.9	14.6	19.6
Any illicit drug other than marijuana	30.4	27.4	17.9	19.4
Cocaine	12.3	13.1	5.3	4.0
Heroin	0.5	0.6	0.5	1.1
LSD	6.5	4.4	5.4	8.4
Marijuana/hashish	48.8	40.6	27.0	34.7
PCP	4.4	2.9	1.2	1.8
Percent reporting use of drugs in the past 30 days				
Alcohol	72.0	65.9	57.1	51.3
Any illicit drug abuse	37.2	29.7	17.2	23.8
Marijuana only	18.8	14.8	9.2	13.8
Any illicit drug other than marijuana	18.4	14.9	8.0	10.0
Cocaine	5.2	6.7	1.9	1.8
Heroin	0.2	0.3	0.2	0.6
LSD	2.3	1.6	1.9	4.0
Marijuana/hashish	33.7	25.7	14.0	21.2
PCP	1.4	1.6	0.4	0.6

Table 5.5.7. Home-schooled children and requirements in the U.S., 1991.

	Home-schooled children	Statutory language	Certification of teacher	Mandatory pupil testing
Alabama	N/A	yes	yes	no
Alaska	1,000	yes	yes	yes
Arizona	N/A	yes	yes	yes
Arkansas	2,500	yes	no	yes
California	6,000	yes	yes	no
Colorado	N/A	yes	yes	no
Connecticut	289	yes	no	yes
Delaware	367	yes	no	no
District of Columbia	10	—	—	—
Florida	7,555	yes	no	no
Georgia	5,024	yes	yes	no
Hawaii	272	yes	yes	yes
Idaho	N/A	yes	no	no
Illinois	529	yes	no	no
Indiana	882	yes	no	no
Iowa	N/A	yes	yes	no
Kansas	2,700	yes	no	no
Kentucky	N/A	yes	no	no
Louisiana	2,121	yes	no	no
Maine	1,300	yes	no	yes
Maryland	1,500	yes	no	no
Massachusetts	N/A	yes	no	yes
Michigan	675	yes	yes	no
Minnesota	3,538	yes	yes	no
Mississippi	600	yes	no	no
Missouri	N/A	yes	no	no
Montana	906	yes	no	no
Nebraska	3,509	yes	yes	no
Nevada	682	yes	yes	yes
New Hampshire	711	yes	no	yes
New Jersey	1,000	yes	no	no
New Mexico	N/A	yes	no	yes
New York	4,975	yes	yes	yes
North Carolina	4,145	yes	yes	yes
North Dakota	483	yes	yes	yes
Ohio	2,729	yes	yes	yes
Oklahoma	N/A	yes	no	no
Oregon	4,578	yes	no	no
Pennsylvania	2,552	yes	yes	yes
Rhode Island	N/A	yes	no	yes
South Carolina	743	yes	yes	yes
South Dakota	1,176	yes	no	yes
Tennessee	1,248	yes	yes	no
Texas	N/A	yes	no	no
Utah	N/A	yes	no	yes
Vermont	680	yes	no	yes
Virginia	2,934	yes	yes	yes
Washington	4,696	yes	yes	yes
West Virginia	684	yes	yes	no
Wisconsin	6,298	yes	no	no
Wyoming	470	yes	no	yes

Table 5.5.9. Special placements of white students, 1992.

	Percent				
	K to 12 enrollment	AP math & science	Gifted & talented	Special education	Suspensions
Alabama	62.0	72.0	89.0	60.0	38.0
Alaska	65.0	82.0	84.0	60.0	67.0
Arizona	60.0	70.0	81.0	60.0	53.0
Arkansas	74.0	78.0	81.0	67.0	53.0
California	42.0	50.0	58.0	50.0	36.0
Colorado	74.0	77.0	80.0	71.0	56.0
Connecticut	73.0	84.0	81.0	69.0	51.0
Delaware	66.0	83.0	85.0	52.0	48.0
Dist. of Columbia	4.0	3.0	3.0	2.0	2.0
Florida	60.0	71.0	86.0	58.0	49.0
Georgia	60.0	73.0	87.0	45.0	36.0
Hawaii	24.0	25.0	27.0	24.0	13.0
Idaho	—	97.0	95.0	83.0	83.0
Illinois	65.0	79.0	74.0	67.0	58.0
Indiana	86.0	85.0	93.0	85.0	73.0
Iowa	93.0	93.0	95.0	93.0	81.0
Kansas	83.0	84.0	93.0	83.0	62.0
Kentucky	89.0	91.0	93.0	88.0	82.0
Louisiana	52.0	59.0	80.0	45.0	38.0
Maine	98.0	98.0	98.0	98.0	95.0
Maryland	59.0	66.0	72.0	59.0	53.0
Massachusetts	79.0	87.0	82.0	88.0	68.0
Michigan	78.0	91.0	90.0	80.0	71.0
Minnesota	89.0	92.0	88.0	86.0	76.0
Mississippi	48.0	77.0	90.0	42.0	33.0
Missouri	82.0	87.0	90.0	79.0	61.0
Montana	88.0	94.0	93.0	86.0	83.0
Nebraska	88.0	94.0	87.0	86.0	71.0
Nevada	71.0	80.0	86.0	71.0	74.0
New Hampshire	97.0	94.0	98.0	97.0	96.0
New Jersey	63.0	70.0	74.0	64.0	49.0
New Mexico	41.0	69.0	73.0	40.0	31.0
New York	58.0	74.0	56.0	54.0	47.0
North Carolina	66.0	83.0	91.0	61.0	50.0
North Dakota	90.0	94.0	83.0	86.0	65.0
Ohio	83.0	80.0	75.0	82.0	60.0
Oklahoma	72.0	73.0	82.0	68.0	58.0
Oregon	87.0	89.0	92.0	89.0	85.0
Pennsylvania	82.0	86.0	92.0	76.0	52.0
Rhode Island	81.0	88.0	93.0	94.0	94.0
South Carolina	57.0	78.0	84.0	46.0	38.0
South Dakota	85.0	95.0	96.0	87.0	82.0
Tennessee	76.0	72.0	87.0	73.0	60.0
Texas	48.0	49.0	70.0	53.0	33.0
Utah	92.0	92.0	94.0	87.0	77.0
Vermont	98.0	95.0	98.0	99.0	98.0
Virginia	68.0	76.0	85.0	70.0	54.0
Washington	80.0	78.0	86.0	81.0	74.0
West Virginia	95.0	96.0	97.0	95.0	90.0
Wisconsin	84.0	95.0	92.0	83.0	66.0
Wyoming	89.0	95.0	96.0	83.0	80.0

Table 5.5.10. Special placements of African American students, 1992.

	Percent				
	K to 12 enrollment	AP math & science	Gifted & talented	Special education	Suspensions
Alabama	36.0	22.0	9.0	40.0	61.0
Alaska	5.0	2.0	1.0	6.0	11.0
Arizona	4.0	4.0	2.0	6.0	7.0
Arkansas	24.0	20.0	18.0	32.0	46.0
California	9.0	4.0	5.0	13.0	20.0
Colorado	5.0	4.0	4.0	8.0	16.0
Connecticut	13.0	5.0	11.0	18.0	32.0
Delaware	29.0	4.0	8.0	44.0	48.0
Dist. of Columbia	89.0	95.0	94.0	95.0	95.0
Florida	25.0	9.0	6.0	29.0	40.0
Georgia	37.0	18.0	10.0	45.0	63.0
Hawaii	3.0	1.0	1.0	3.0	2.0
Idaho	—	0.0	0.0	1.0	1.0
Illinois	21.0	4.0	13.0	24.0	32.0
Indiana	11.0	11.0	5.0	14.0	24.0
Iowa	3.0	1.0	2.0	5.0	15.0
Kansas	8.0	7.0	3.0	11.0	27.0
Kentucky	10.0	6.0	5.0	12.0	18.0
Louisiana	45.0	29.0	15.0	53.0	60.0
Maine	1.0	0.0	0.0	1.0	2.0
Maryland	34.0	13.0	15.0	38.0	44.0
Massachusetts	8.0	1.0	8.0	7.0	17.0
Michigan	17.0	2.0	6.0	16.0	25.0
Minnesota	4.0	1.0	4.0	7.0	16.0
Mississippi	51.0	20.0	7.0	58.0	66.0
Missouri	16.0	7.0	7.0	20.0	37.0
Montana	1.0	0.0	0.0	1.0	1.0
Nebraska	6.0	2.0	9.0	7.0	18.0
Nevada	9.0	5.0	4.0	14.0	7.0
New Hampshire	1.0	1.0	1.0	2.0	2.0
New Jersey	19.0	4.0	12.0	23.0	37.0
New Mexico	2.0	1.0	1.0	3.0	4.0
New York	20.0	5.0	20.0	27.0	36.0
North Carolina	30.0	11.0	7.0	37.0	48.0
North Dakota	1.0	2.0	1.0	1.0	
Ohio	15.0	13.0	22.0	16.0	38.0
Oklahoma	10.0	13.0	6.0	18.0	27.0
Oregon	2.0	1.0	1.0	3.0	4.0
Pennsylvania	14.0	8.0	5.0	19.0	41.0
Rhode Island	7.0	4.0	3.0	4.0	3.0
South Carolina	41.0	16.0	15.0	54.0	61.0
South Dakota	1.0	0.0	0.0	1.0	1.0
Tennessee	23.0	24.0	11.0	27.0	39.0
Texas	14.0	19.0	9.0	19.0	63.0
Utah	1.0	0.0	0.0	1.0	3.0
Vermont	1.0	1.0	0.0	1.0	
Virginia	26.0	7.0	10.0	26.0	42.0
Washington	4.0	3.0	2.0	6.0	8.0
West Virginia	4.0	1.0	1.0	5.0	10.0
Wisconsin	9.0	1.0	4.0	12.0	26.0
Wyoming	1.0	1.0	1.0	2.0	5.0

Table 5.5.11. Special placements of Hispanic students, 1992.

	Percent				
	K to 12 enrollment	AP math & science	Gifted & talented	Special education	Suspensions
Alabama	0.0	0.0	0.0	0.0	0.0
Alaska	2.0	2.0	1.0	2.0	4.0
Arizona	28.0	17.0	10.0	24.0	30.0
Arkansas	1.0	1.0	0.0	0.0	0.0
California	37.0	11.0	17.0	32.0	38.0
Colorado	17.0	13.0	12.0	19.0	26.0
Connecticut	11.0	2.0	4.0	13.0	16.0
Delaware	3.0	2.0	2.0	4.0	4.0
Dist. of Columbia	6.0	1.0	2.0	3.0	3.0
Florida	14.0	10.0	5.0	12.0	10.0
Georgia	2.0	1.0	0.0	1.0	1.0
Hawaii	5.0	3.0	2.0	4.0	3.0
Idaho	—	1.0	2.0	9.0	14.0
Illinois	11.0	3.0	6.0	8.0	9.0
Indiana	2.0	1.0	1.0	1.0	2.0
Iowa	2.0	1.0	1.0	1.0	2.0
Kansas	5.0	3.0	2.0	5.0	7.0
Kentucky	0.0	1.0	0.0	0.0	0.0
Louisiana	1.0	1.0	1.0	1.0	1.0
Maine	0.0	0.0	0.0	0.0	0.0
Maryland	32.0	2.0	3.0	2.0	2.0
Massachusetts	9.0	1.0	3.0	4.0	14.0
Michigan	2.0	1.0	1.0	2.0	3.0
Minnesota	2.0	1.0	1.0	2.0	2.0
Mississippi	0.0	0.0	1.0	0.0	0.0
Missouri	1.0	1.0	1.0	1.0	1.0
Montana	1.0	0.0	1.0	2.0	2.0
Nebraska	4.0	1.0	2.0	3.0	4.0
Nevada	14.0	5.0	4.0	11.0	12.0
New Hampshire	1.0	1.0	0.0	1.0	2.0
New Jersey	13.0	3.0	5.0	12.0	13.0
New Mexico	46.0	23.0	21.0	43.0	50.0
New York	17.0	3.0	15.0	18.0	16.0
North Carolina	1.0	1.0	0.0	1.0	1.0
North Dakota	1.0	1.0	1.0	1.0	0.0
Ohio	1.0	1.0	1.0	1.0	1.0
Oklahoma	3.0	3.0	2.0	3.0	3.0
Oregon	6.0	3.0	2.0	5.0	7.0
Pennsylvania	3.0	1.0	1.0	5.0	7.0
Rhode Island	9.0	3.0	2.0	2.0	3.0
South Carolina	1.0	1.0	0.0	0.0	0.0
South Dakota	1.0	1.0	0.0	0.0	1.0
Tennessee	1.0	1.0	0.0	0.0	0.0
Texas	36.0	24.0	16.0	28.0	34.0
Utah	5.0	2.0	3.0	7.0	14.0
Vermont	0.0	0.0	0.0	0.0	0.0
Virginia	3.0	2.0	1.0	2.0	2.0
Washington	7.0	4.0	3.0	8.0	10.0
West Virginia	0.0	0.0	0.0	0.0	0.0
Wisconsin	3.0	1.0	1.0	3.0	6.0
Wyoming	6.0	3.0	3.0	8.0	14.0

Table 5.5.12. Special placements of Asian American students, 1992.

	Percent				
	K to 12 enrollment	AP math & science	Gifted & talented	Special education	Suspensions
Alabama	1.0	5.0	2.0	0.0	0.0
Alaska	4.0	12.0	4.0	2.0	4.0
Arizona	2.0	6.0	4.0	1.0	1.0
Arkansas	1.0	2.0	1.0	0.0	0.0
California	11.0	35.0	20.0	4.0	5.0
Colorado	2.0	6.0	3.0	1.0	1.0
Connecticut	2.0	9.0	4.0	1.0	1.0
Delaware	2.0	12.0	5.0	1.0	0.0
District of Columbia	1.0	2.0	1.0	0.0	0.0
Florida	2.0	9.0	3.0	1.0	1.0
Georgia	1.0	8.0	3.0	0.0	0.0
Hawaii	68.0	70.0	70.0	69.0	81.0
Idaho	—	2.0	2.0	5.0	1.0
Illinois	3.0	14.0	7.0	1.0	1.0
Indiana	1.0	4.0	2.0	0.0	0.0
Iowa	2.0	5.0	2.0	1.0	1.0
Kansas	2.0	6.0	2.0	0.0	1.0
Kentucky	1.0	3.0	1.0	0.0	0.0
Louisiana	1.0	11.0	4.0	0.0	1.0
Maine	1.0	2.0	1.0	0.0	0.0
Maryland	4.0	19.0	10.0	1.0	1.0
Massachusetts	4.0	12.0	7.0	1.0	1.0
Michigan	1.0	6.0	3.0	1.0	0.0
Minnesota	4.0	6.0	6.0	1.0	2.0
Mississippi	1.0	2.0	2.0	0.0	0.0
Missouri	1.0	5.0	2.0	0.0	0.0
Montana	1.0	1.0	1.0	0.0	0.0
Nebraska	1.0	2.0	2.0	0.0	1.0
Nevada	4.0	10.0	6.0	1.0	3.0
New Hampshire	1.0	4.0	1.0	0.0	0.0
New Jersey	5.0	23.0	9.0	1.0	1.0
New Mexico	1.0	5.0	2.0	1.0	0.0
New York	5.0	18.0	8.0	1.0	1.0
North Carolina	1.0	5.0	2.0	0.0	0.0
North Dakota	1.0	2.0	1.0	0.0	1.0
Ohio	1.0	6.0	2.0	0.0	0.0
Oklahoma	1.0	5.0	2.0	0.0	1.0
Oregon	3.0	7.0	4.0	1.0	1.0
Pennsylvania	2.0	6.0	3.0	0.0	1.0
Rhode Island	3.0	5.0	1.0	0.0	0.0
South Carolina	1.0	5.0	1.0	0.0	0.0
South Dakota	1.0	2.0	1.0	0.0	2.0
Tennessee	1.0	3.0	2.0	0.0	0.0
Texas	2.0	9.0	4.0	1.0	1.0
Utah	2.0	5.0	3.0	1.0	4.0
Vermont	1.0	3.0	1.0	0.0	0.0
Virginia	3.0	15.0	4.0	1.0	1.0
Washington	6.0	13.0	8.0	2.0	4.0
West Virginia	0.0	2.0	1.0	0.0	0.0
Wisconsin	2.0	2.0	2.0	1.0	1.0
Wyoming	1.0	1.0	1.0	0.0	0.0

Table 5.5.13. Special placements of Native American students, 1992.

	K to 12 enrollment	AP math & science	Gifted & talented	Special education	Suspensions
			Percent		
Alabama	1.0	0.0	0.0	0.0	0.0
Alaska	27.0	3.0	10.0	29.0	15.0
Arizona	7.0	2.0	3.0	11.0	9.0
Arkansas	0.0	0.0	0.0	0.0	1.0
California	1.0	1.0	1.0	1.0	1.0
Colorado	1.0	1.0	1.0	1.0	1.0
Connecticut	0.0	0.0	0.0	0.0	0.0
Delaware	0.0	0.0	0.0	0.0	0.0
District of Columbia	0.0	0.0	0.0	0.0	0.0
Florida	0.0	0.0	0.0	0.0	0.0
Georgia	0.0	0.0	0.0	0.0	0.0
Hawaii	0.0	0.0	0.0	0.0	0.0
Idaho	—	0.0	1.0	3.0	3.0
Illinois	0.0	0.0	0.0	0.0	0.0
Indiana	0.0	0.0	0.0	0.0	0.0
Iowa	0.0	0.0	0.0	1.0	1.0
Kansas	1.0	0.0	0.0	1.0	3.0
Kentucky	0.0	0.0	0.0	0.0	0.0
Louisiana	1.0	0.0	0.0	1.0	1.0
Maine	1.0	0.0	0.0	1.0	2.0
Maryland	0.0	0.0	0.0	0.0	0.0
Massachusetts	0.0	0.0	0.0	0.0	0.0
Michigan	1.0	0.0	1.0	1.0	1.0
Minnesota	2.0	0.0	1.0	4.0	4.0
Mississippi	0.0	0.0	0.0	0.0	1.0
Missouri	0.0	0.0	0.0	0.0	0.0
Montana	10.0	4.0	6.0	11.0	14.0
Nebraska	1.0	0.0	1.0	3.0	6.0
Nevada	2.0	0.0	0.0	3.0	5.0
New Hampshire	0.0	0.0	0.0	0.0	0.0
New Jersey	0.0	0.0	0.0	0.0	0.0
New Mexico	10.0	3.0	3.0	14.0	16.0
New York	0.0	0.0	0.0	0.0	0.0
North Carolina	2.0	0.0	0.0	1.0	1.0
North Dakota	8.0	1.0	14.0	13.0	32.0
Ohio	0.0	0.0	0.0	0.0	0.0
Oklahoma	14.0	6.0	9.0	11.0	11.0
Oregon	2.0	1.0	1.0	2.0	3.0
Pennsylvania	0.0	0.0	0.0	0.0	0.0
Rhode Island	0.0	0.0	0.0	0.0	0.0
South Carolina	0.0	0.0	0.0	0.0	0.0
South Dakota	13.0	2.0	3.0	11.0	15.0
Tennessee	0.0	0.0	0.0	0.0	0.0
Texas	0.0	0.0	0.0	0.0	0.0
Utah	1.0	0.0	0.0	4.0	2.0
Vermont	1.0	1.0	0.0	1.0	1.0
Virginia	0.0	0.0	0.0	0.0	0.0
Washington	3.0	2.0	1.0	4.0	3.0
West Virginia	0.0	0.0	0.0	0.0	0.0
Wisconsin	1.0	1.0	1.0	2.0	2.0
Wyoming	3.0	0.0	0.0	2.0	2.0

Conclusions

Children: Our Future

REVISITING THE ISSUES

In the recent past there has been an increasing number of papers, monographs, and books on America's children. As recently as 1994, a major conference was held devoted exclusively to the issue of developing indicators of Children's Well Being (*e.g.* GNP, GDP). These indicators were to be similar to the commonly used indicators of national economic well being. The conference was sponsored by the Institute for Research on Poverty; Child Trends, Inc.; the Office of the Assistant Secretary for Planning and Evaluation in Department of Health and Human Services; the National Institute of Child Health and Human Development; and the Annie E. Casey Foundation. In attendance were policy makers, academicians, and researchers from a wide range of organizations and institutions from around the country. Their work resulted in a publication, *America's Children: Key National Indicators of Well Being*. Additionally, the Annie E. Casey Foundation publishes each year its *Kidscount* reference. Numerous other organizations have held national conferences focusing on issues of children. Given the commitment of the persons involved in the discussion, the excellent work being done, and the volume of literature produced, we are privileged to be able to contribute to the important work being undertaken.

The chapters in *GROWING UP IN AMERICA* graphically display data at the state level. We present a spatial examination of several dimensions of children's lifes in America. For America's children, we sought to paint a portrait of who they are, how they live, their health, education and involvement in crime. In some instances we succeeded; in other instances, diversity was so great that the concept of "America's children" proved ill-conceived for the task. In examining the diversity of children's experiences and the ways in which their lives and futures are differentially shaped within varied spatial, political and economic structures; we conclude that one of the biggest obstacles to understanding the condition of America's children is the tendency to think that the American child exists. Differences in life quality for children in America are profound. Powerful structures such as residential location, race/ethnicity, class, gender, nationality, and "ableism" exert themselves in ways that have far reaching implications. There is a large discontinuity between the lives of poor children and the lives of "well off" children; the lives of able children and their disabled counterparts, and the lives of children of color and their white peers. Moreover, for certain subgroups of children (the rural poor, the "at risk" child, the children of migrant workers), life cannot be captured by traditional statistics.

Similarly, our work has shown that just as there are many faces to America's children, there are many visions of what childhood in America should be like. We agree on very little. In seeking to insure a common vision of childhood, U.S. laws guarantee certain rights—equal education, adequate standard of living, accessible health care, equal representation—but only to varying degrees and never completely. The U.N. Convention on the Rights of the Child (which offers a comprehensive statement of international norms to guide the efforts of those who work with children was unanimously adopted by the General Assembly of the United Nations and over 100 countries). It has not been signed by the U.S. Exactly what the U.S. objects to is unclear.

Some of what we found points to very disturbing trends. Other findings are more encouraging.

Recent congressional legislation has given states important roles to play in shaping the future of children in America. This is a highly significant development and while it is obviously impossible to do full justice in the space available here to the complexity of this shift in responsibility, it is nonetheless important to note that the resurgence of states' rights also brings with it considerable responsibility. Moreover, the enormous variation we discovered in the performance of states in caring for their children points to considerable inequalities in children's lives. It is an over simplification to point out that states are not starting from the same "place." Arriving at the point where there is a consensus vision of what childhood in America should be like and we can speak of "the American child," requires considerable thought. The challenge is how to best inform our vision of what we want to accomplish. Nonetheless, this new political reality will certainly have an energizing effect for subsequent debate.

While much has been said, much has yet to be done.

Appendix

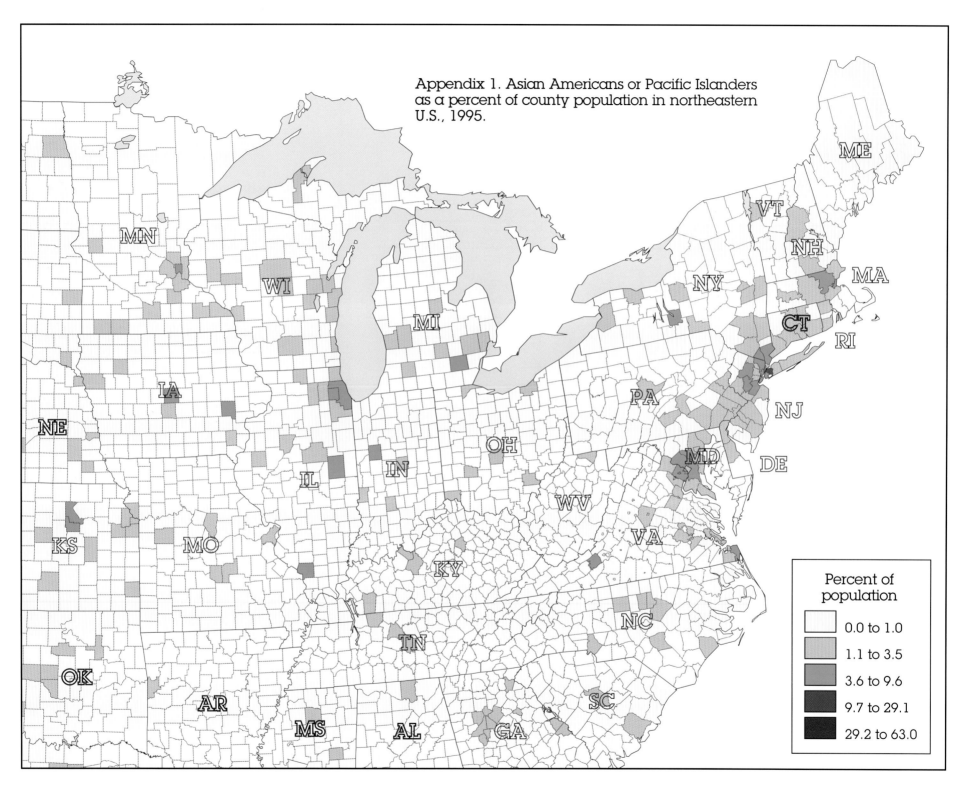

Appendix 1. Asian Americans or Pacific Islanders as a percent of county population in northeastern U.S., 1995.

Percent of population

0.0 to 1.0
1.1 to 3.5
3.6 to 9.6
9.7 to 29.1
29.2 to 63.0

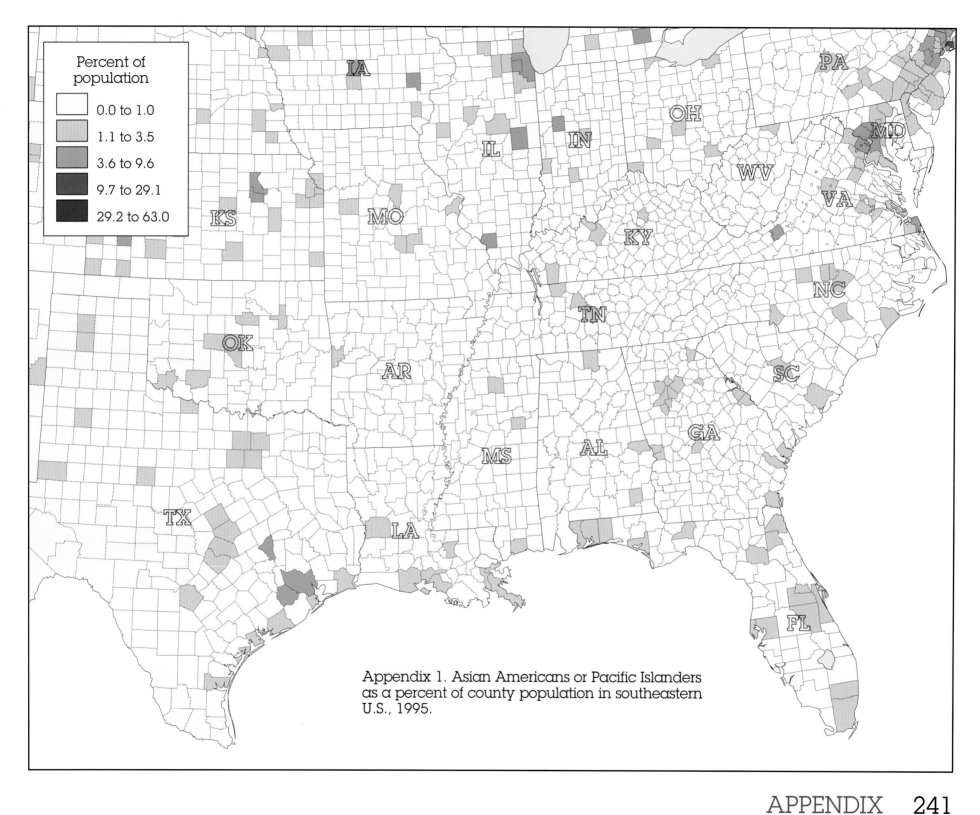

Percent of population

0.0 to 1.0
1.1 to 3.5
3.6 to 9.6
9.7 to 29.1
29.2 to 63.0

Appendix 1. Asian Americans or Pacific Islanders as a percent of county population in southeastern U.S., 1995.

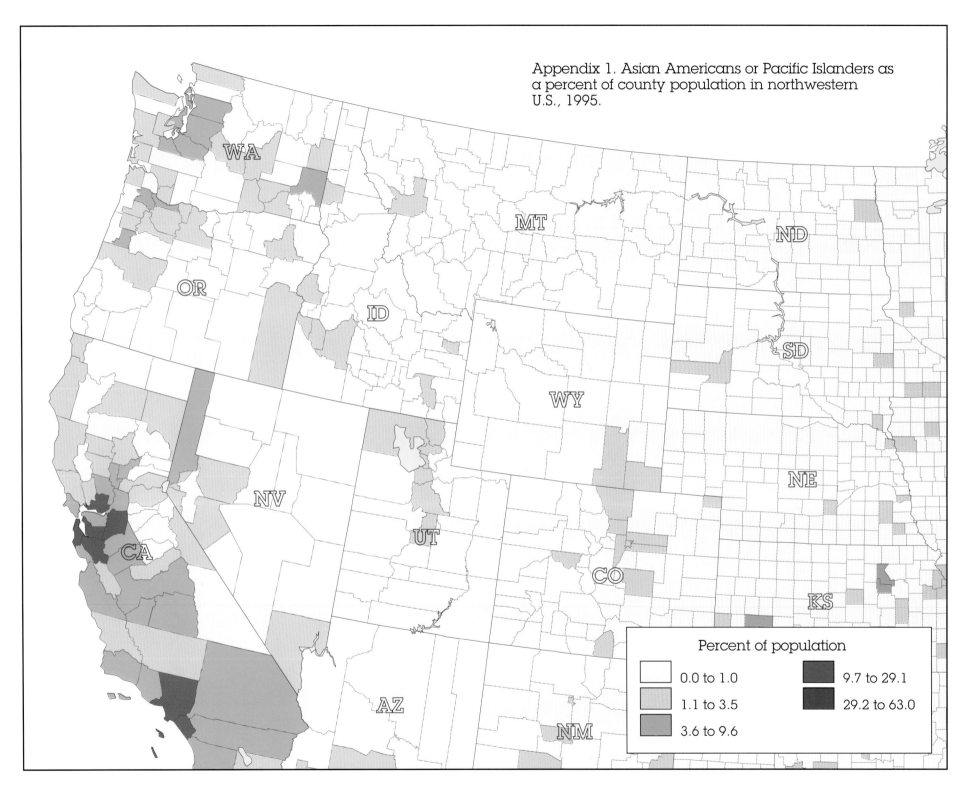

Appendix 1. Asian Americans or Pacific Islanders as a percent of county population in northwestern U.S., 1995.

Percent of population

0.0 to 1.0	9.7 to 29.1
1.1 to 3.5	29.2 to 63.0
3.6 to 9.6	

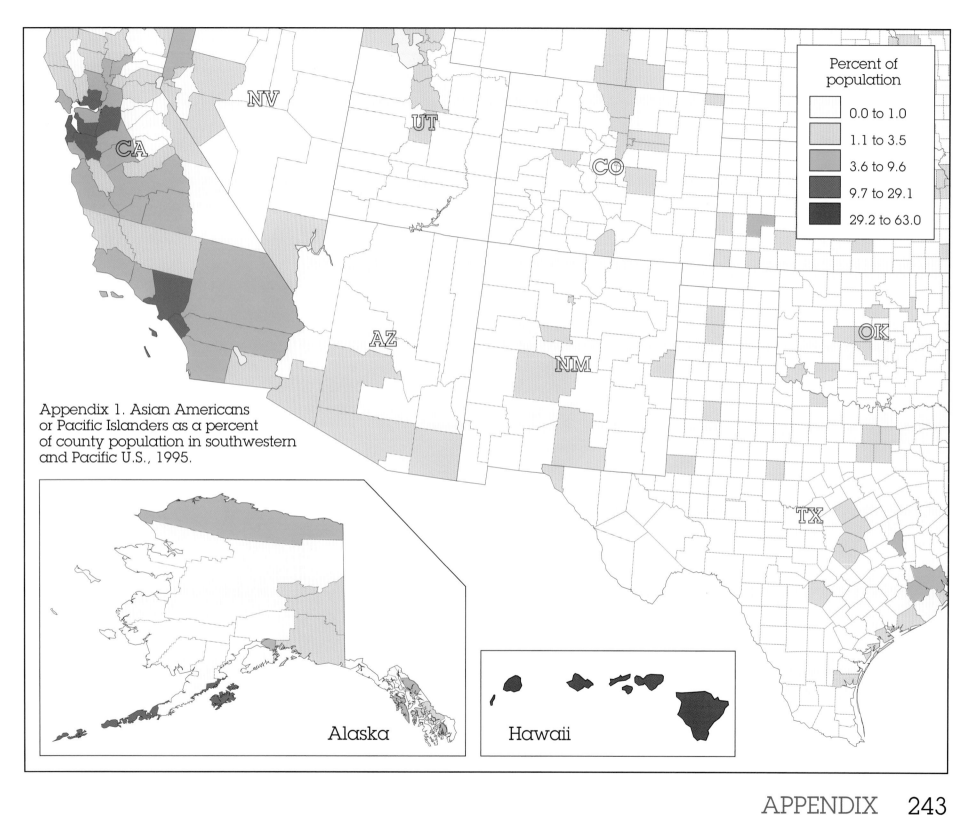

Percent of population

- 0.0 to 1.0
- 1.1 to 3.5
- 3.6 to 9.6
- 9.7 to 29.1
- 29.2 to 63.0

NV

UT

CO

CA

AZ

NM

OK

TX

Appendix 1. Asian Americans or Pacific Islanders as a percent of county population in southwestern and Pacific U.S., 1995.

Alaska

Hawaii

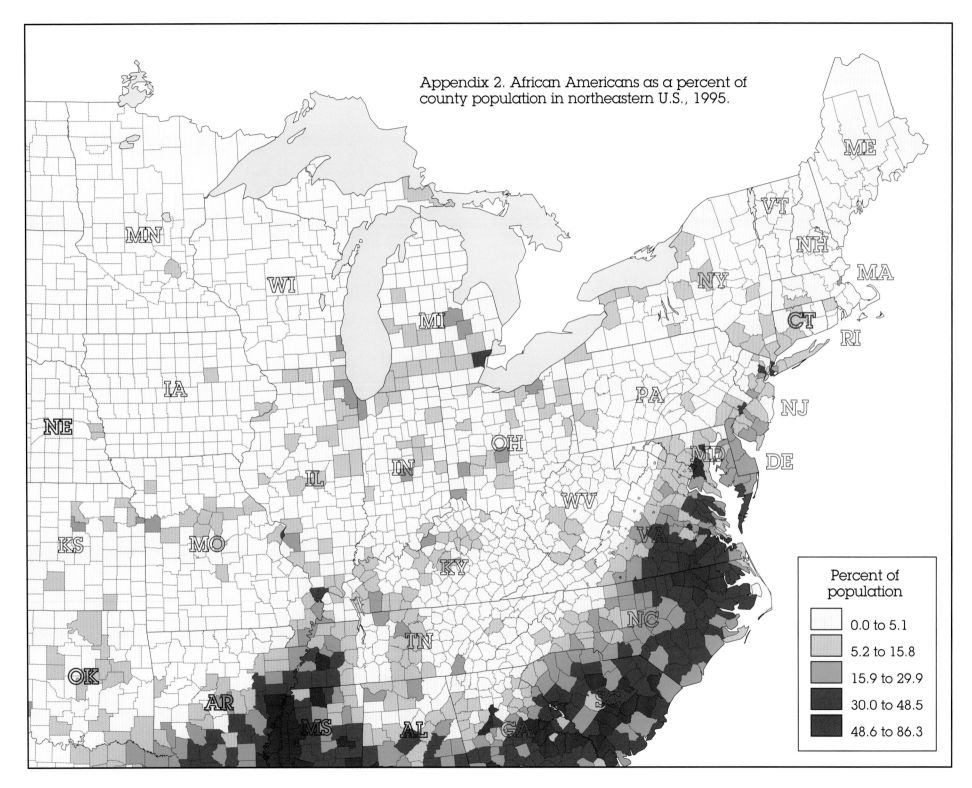

Appendix 2. African Americans as a percent of
county population in northeastern U.S., 1995.

Percent of
population

0.0 to 5.1

5.2 to 15.8

15.9 to 29.9

30.0 to 48.5

48.6 to 86.3

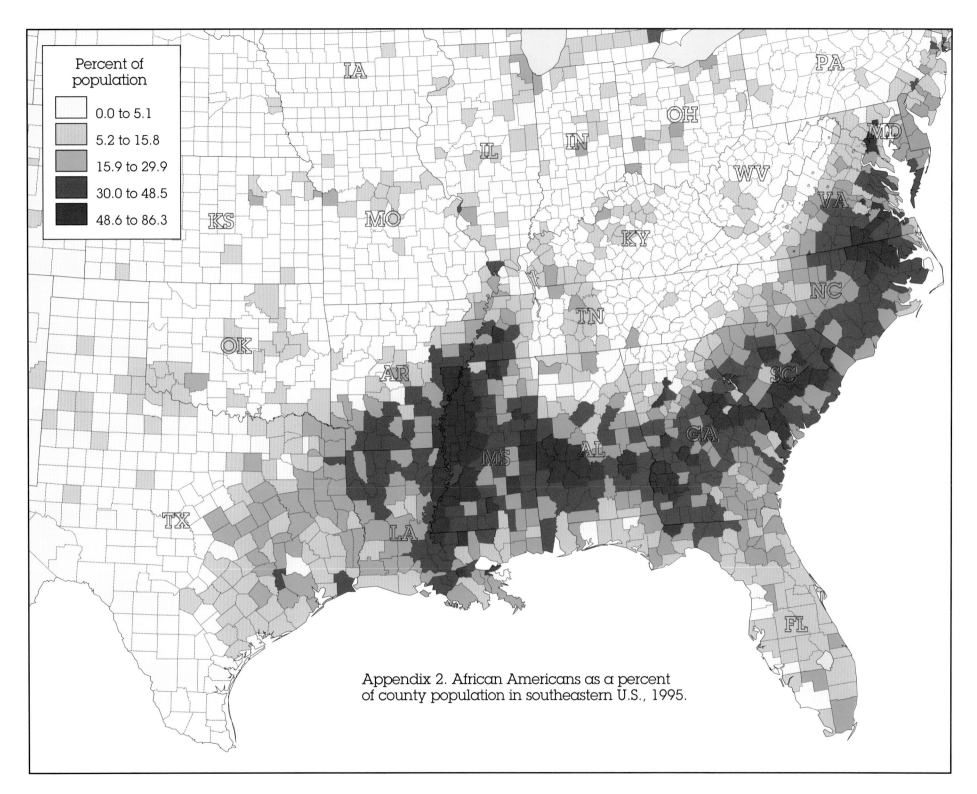

Percent of population

0.0 to 5.1
5.2 to 15.8
15.9 to 29.9
30.0 to 48.5
48.6 to 86.3

Appendix 2. African Americans as a percent of county population in southeastern U.S., 1995.

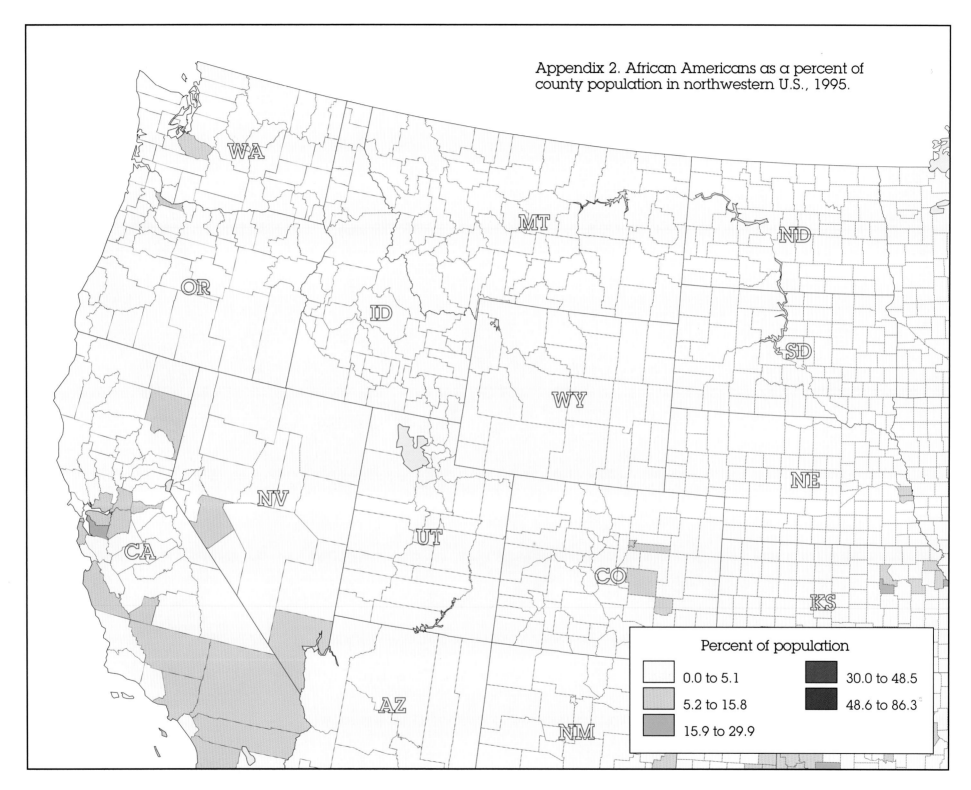

Appendix 2. African Americans as a percent of county population in northwestern U.S., 1995.

Percent of population

0.0 to 5.1	30.0 to 48.5
5.2 to 15.8	48.6 to 86.3
15.9 to 29.9	

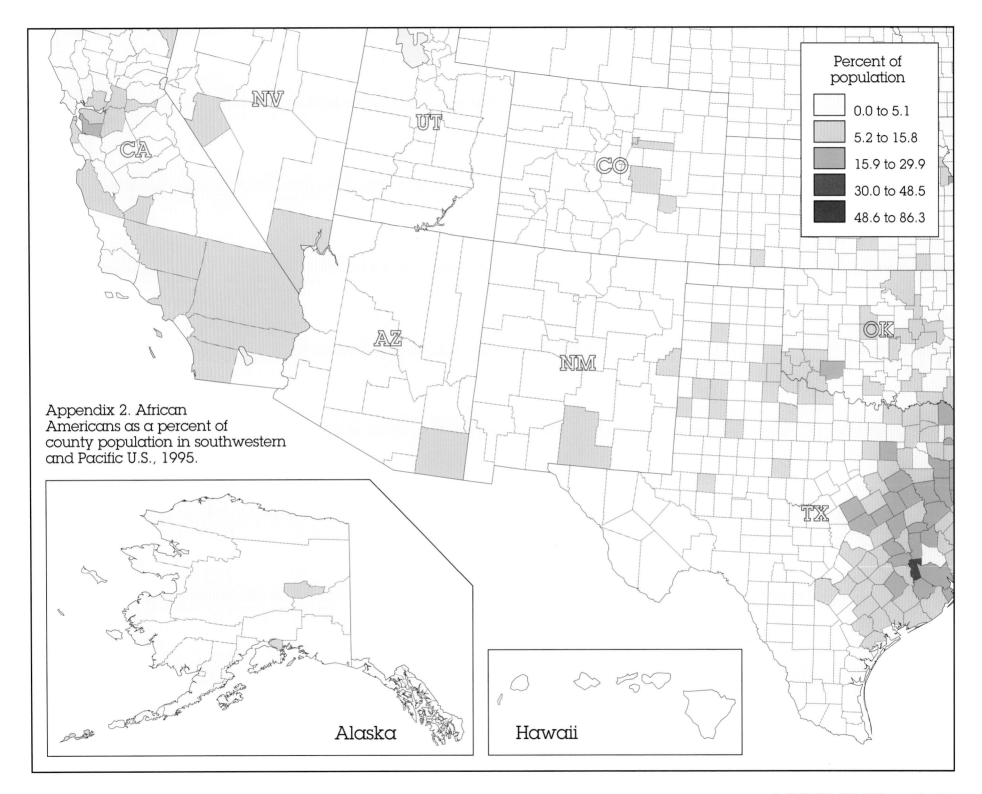

Appendix 2. African
Americans as a percent of
county population in southwestern
and Pacific U.S., 1995.

Percent of
population

0.0 to 5.1
5.2 to 15.8
15.9 to 29.9
30.0 to 48.5
48.6 to 86.3

NV
UT
CA
CO
AZ
NM
OK
TX

Alaska

Hawaii

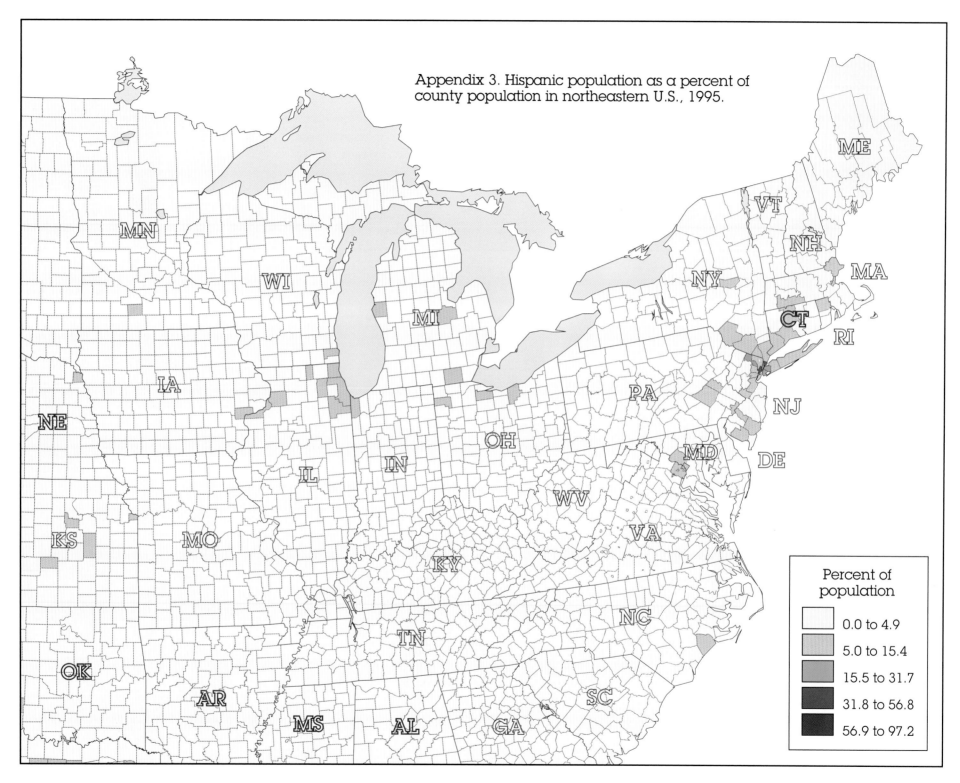

Appendix 3. Hispanic population as a percent of county population in northeastern U.S., 1995.

Percent of population

- 0.0 to 4.9
- 5.0 to 15.4
- 15.5 to 31.7
- 31.8 to 56.8
- 56.9 to 97.2

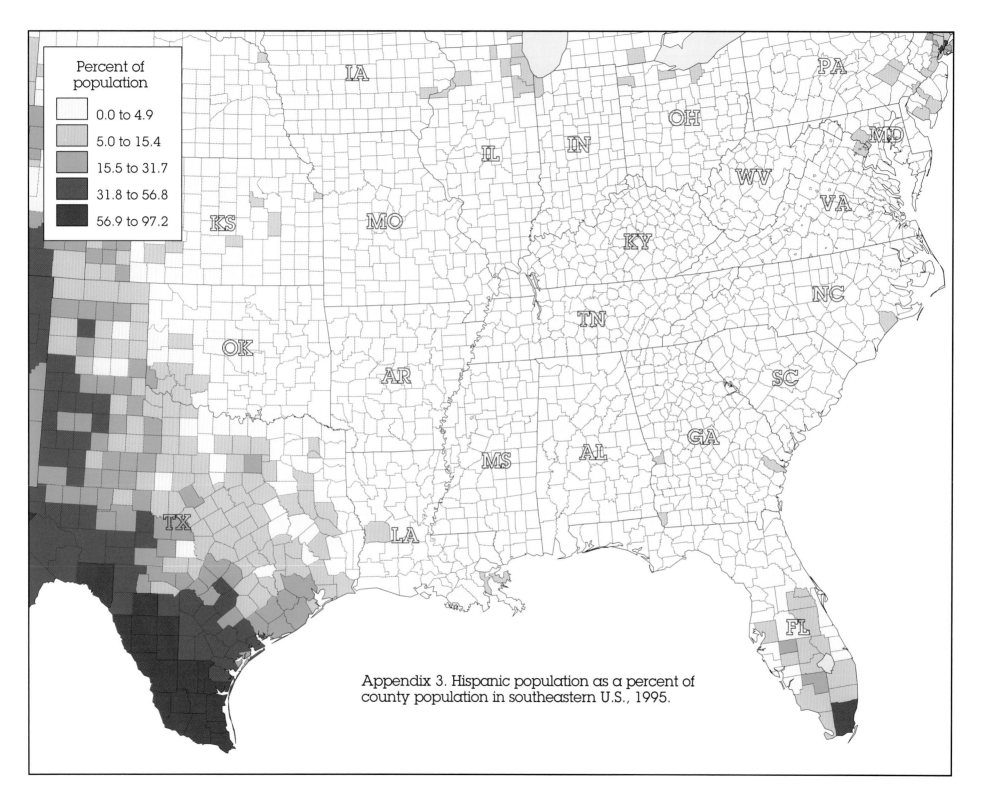

Appendix 3. Hispanic population as a percent of county population in southeastern U.S., 1995.

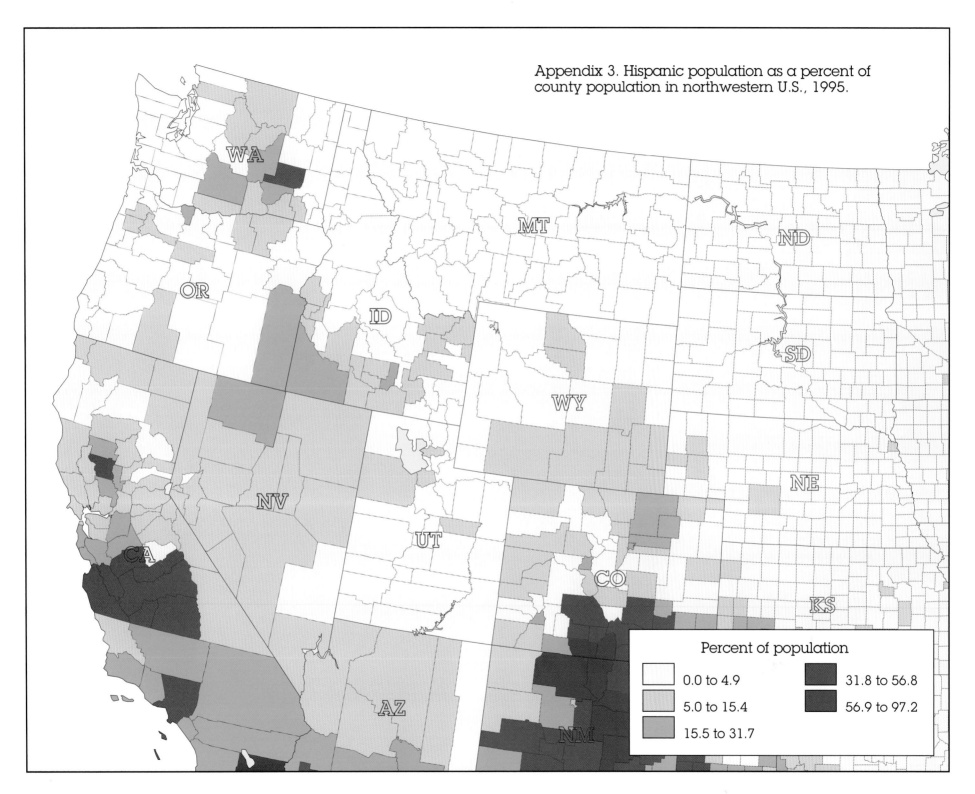

Appendix 3. Hispanic population as a percent of county population in northwestern U.S., 1995.

Percent of population

0.0 to 4.9	31.8 to 56.8
5.0 to 15.4	56.9 to 97.2
15.5 to 31.7	

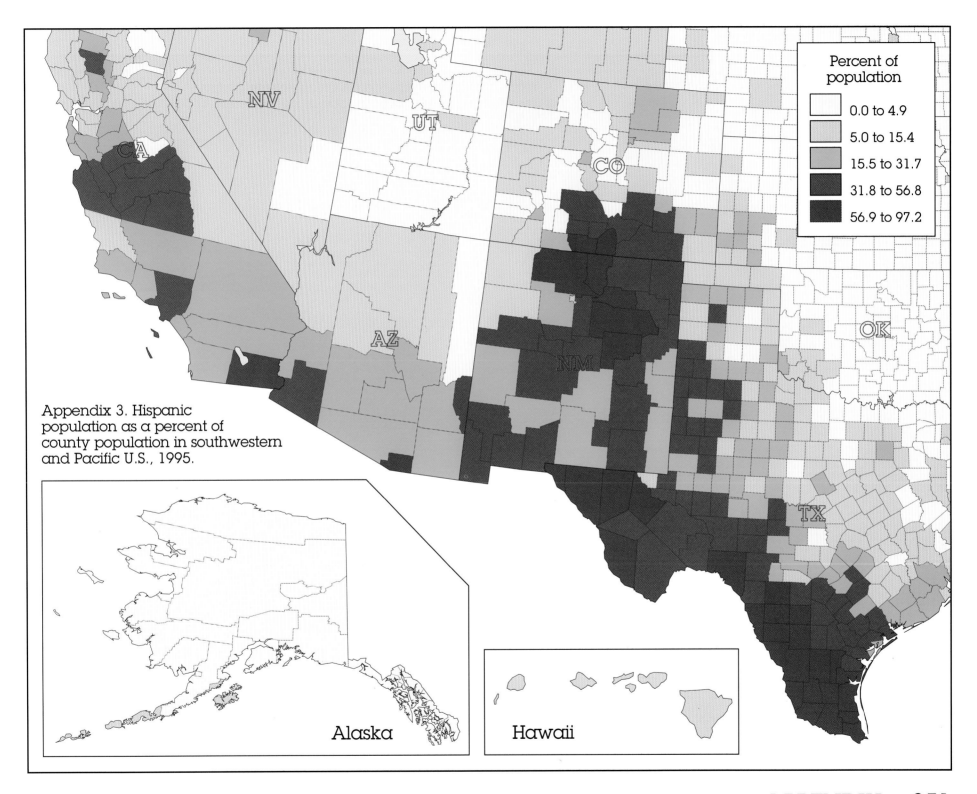

Appendix 3. Hispanic population as a percent of county population in southwestern and Pacific U.S., 1995.

Percent of population

0.0 to 4.9
5.0 to 15.4
15.5 to 31.7
31.8 to 56.8
56.9 to 97.2

NV
UT
CO
CA
AZ
NM
OK
TX

Alaska

Hawaii

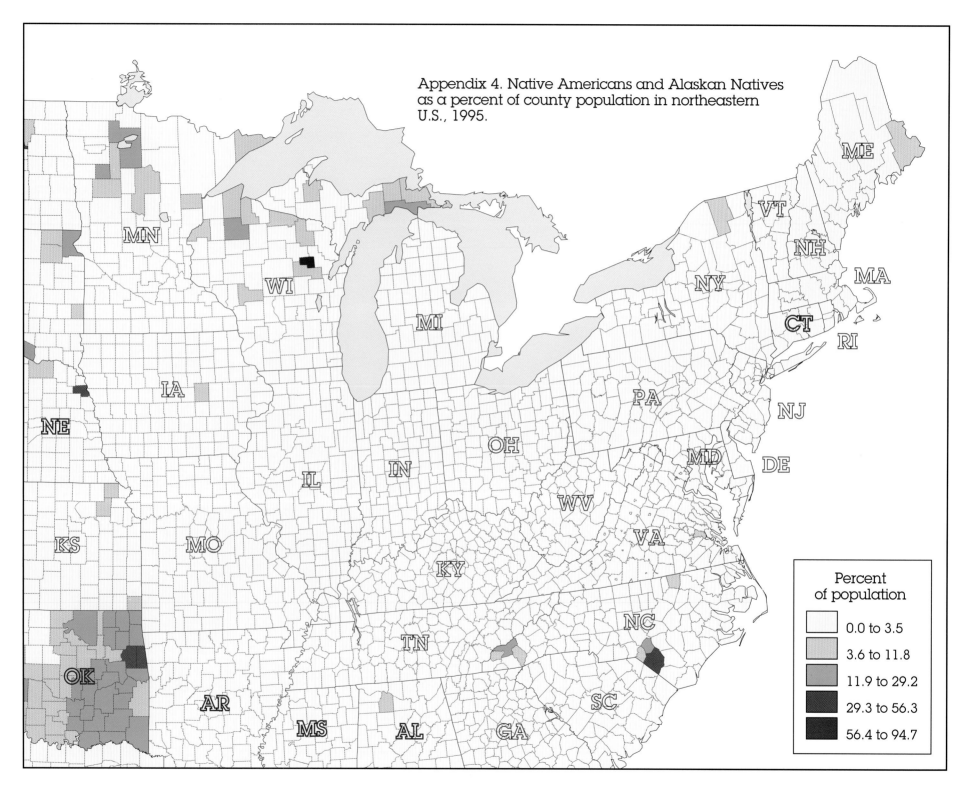

Appendix 4. Native Americans and Alaskan Natives as a percent of county population in northeastern U.S., 1995.

Percent of population

0.0 to 3.5
3.6 to 11.8
11.9 to 29.2
29.3 to 56.3
56.4 to 94.7

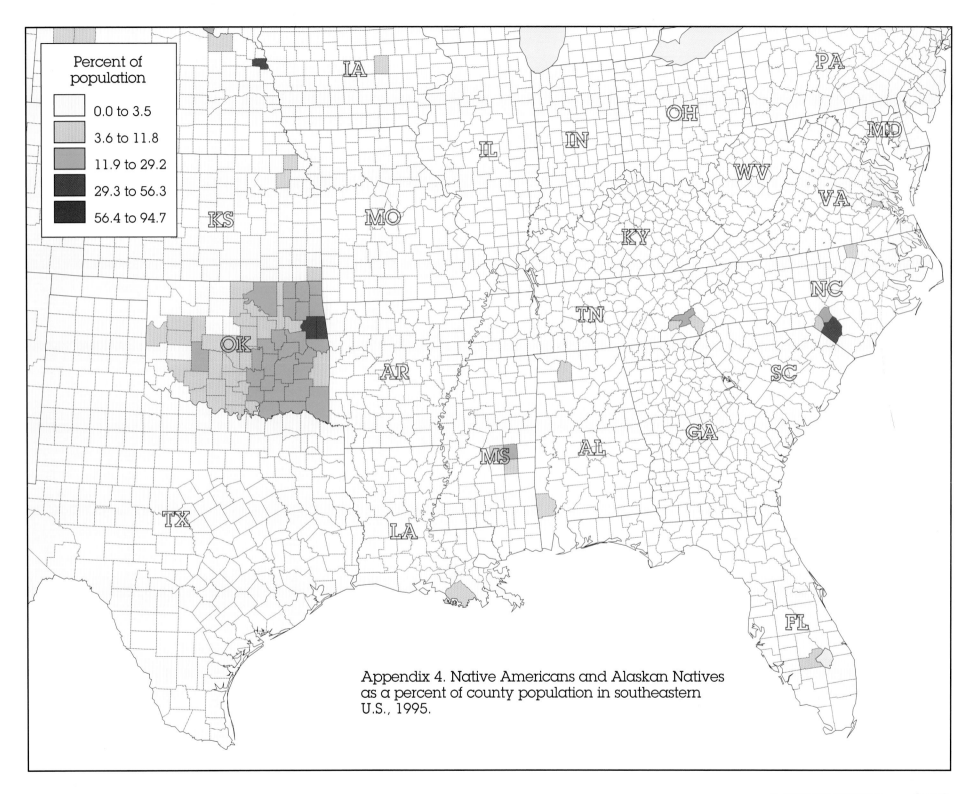

Appendix 4. Native Americans and Alaskan Natives as a percent of county population in southeastern U.S., 1995.

Percent of population

0.0 to 3.5
3.6 to 11.8
11.9 to 29.2
29.3 to 56.3
56.4 to 94.7

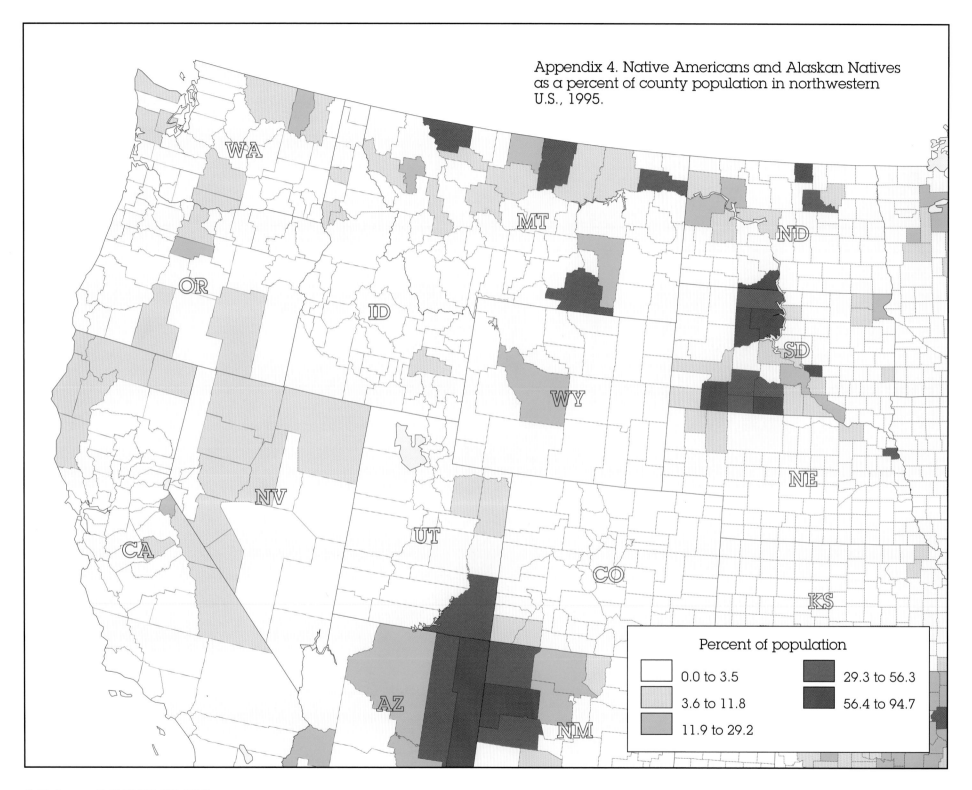

Appendix 4. Native Americans and Alaskan Natives as a percent of county population in northwestern U.S., 1995.

Percent of population

0.0 to 3.5	29.3 to 56.3
3.6 to 11.8	56.4 to 94.7
11.9 to 29.2	

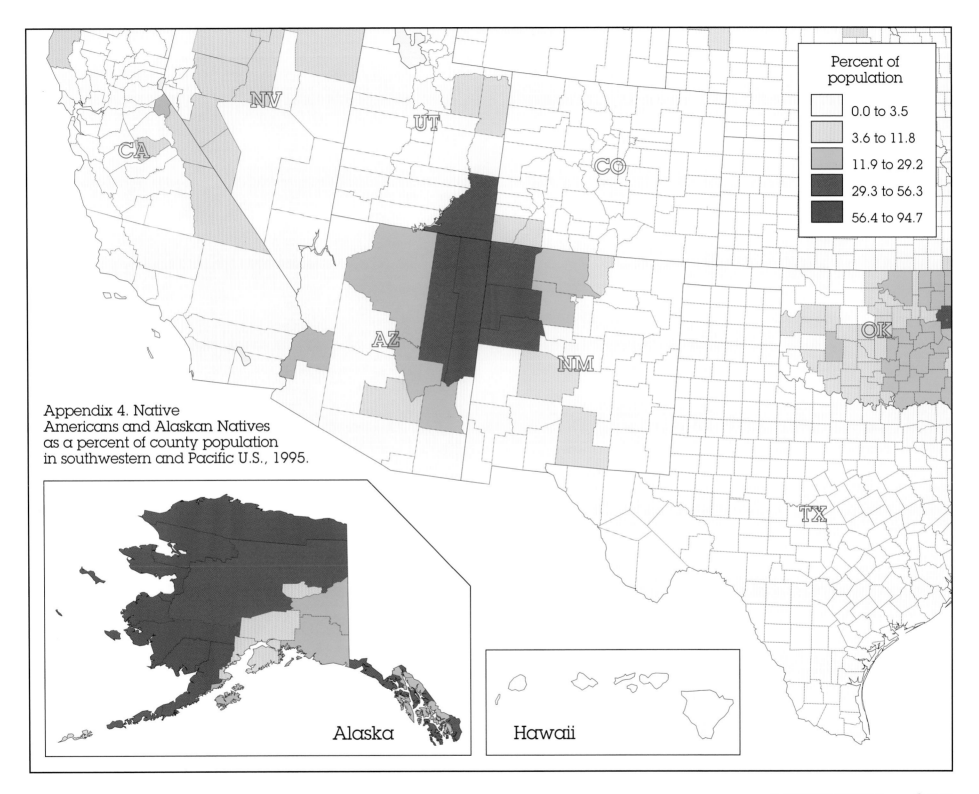

Appendix 4. Native
Americans and Alaskan Natives
as a percent of county population
in southwestern and Pacific U.S., 1995.

Percent of
population

0.0 to 3.5
3.6 to 11.8
11.9 to 29.2
29.3 to 56.3
56.4 to 94.7

NV
CA
UT
CO
AZ
NM
OK
TX

Alaska

Hawaii

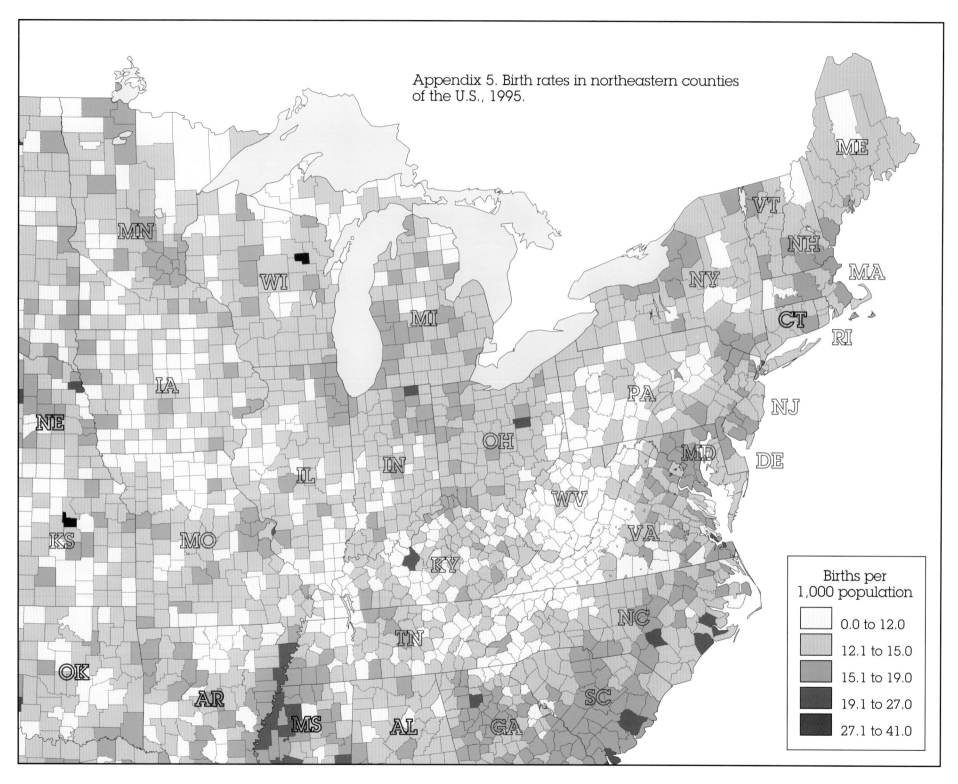

Appendix 5. Birth rates in northeastern counties of the U.S., 1995.

Births per
1,000 population

0.0 to 12.0

12.1 to 15.0

15.1 to 19.0

19.1 to 27.0

27.1 to 41.0

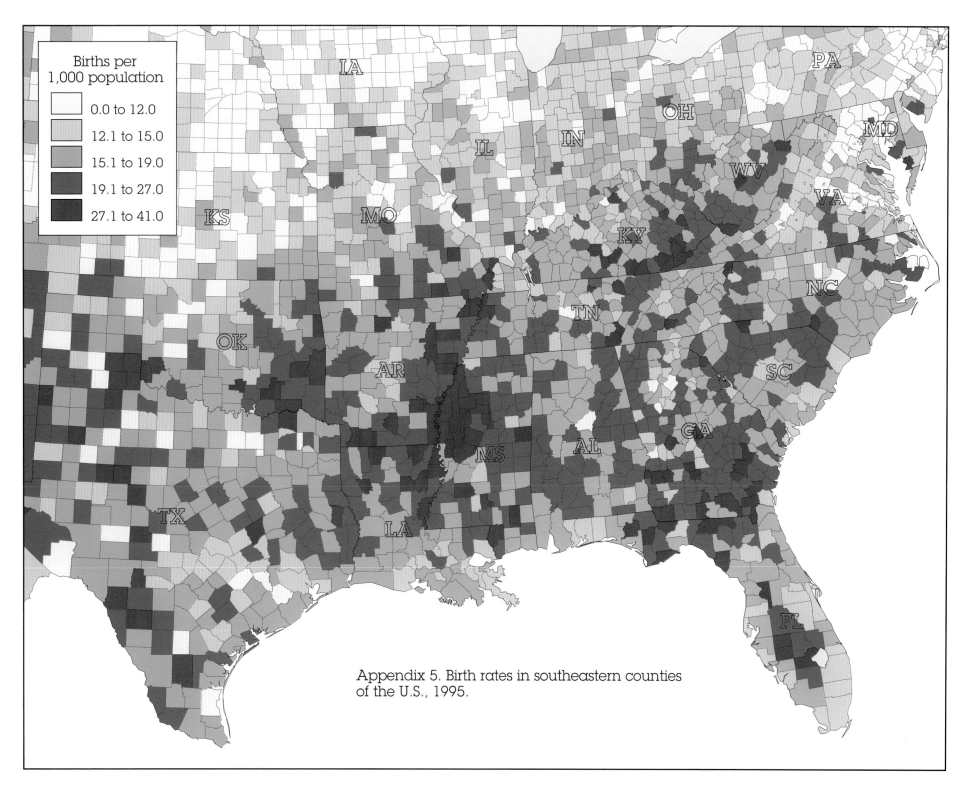

Appendix 5. Birth rates in southeastern counties of the U.S., 1995.

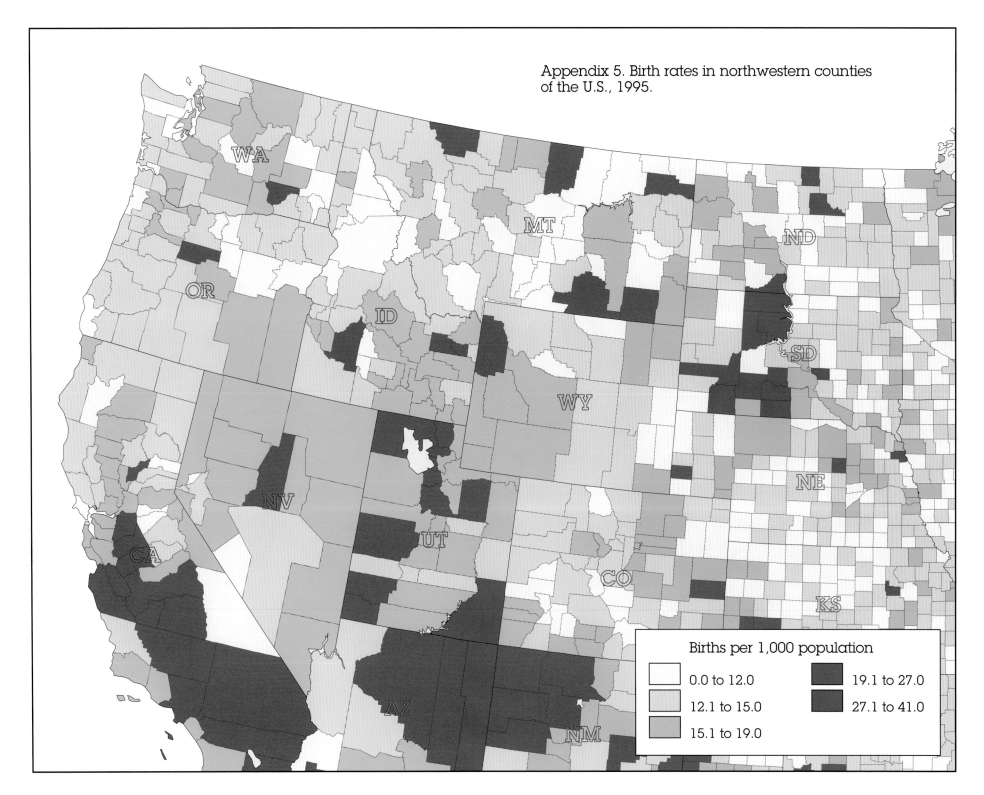

Appendix 5. Birth rates in northwestern counties of the U.S., 1995.

Births per 1,000 population

- 0.0 to 12.0
- 12.1 to 15.0
- 15.1 to 19.0
- 19.1 to 27.0
- 27.1 to 41.0

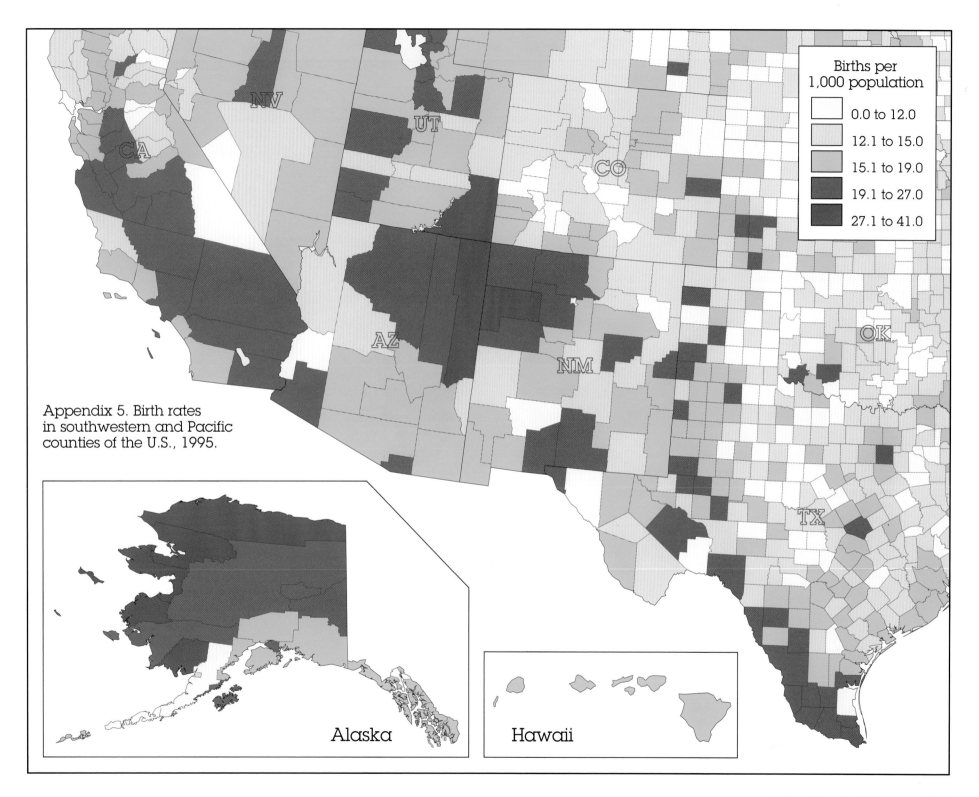

Appendix 5. Birth rates
in southwestern and Pacific
counties of the U.S., 1995.

Births per
1,000 population

0.0 to 12.0
12.1 to 15.0
15.1 to 19.0
19.1 to 27.0
27.1 to 41.0

Alaska

Hawaii

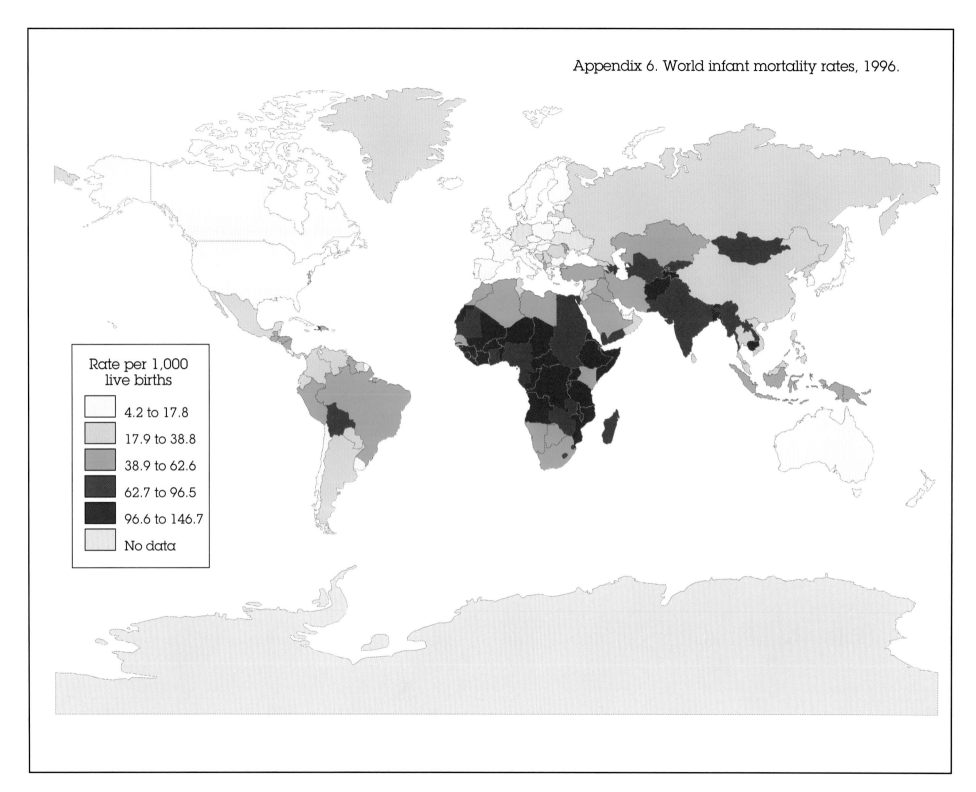

Appendix 6. World infant mortality rates, 1996.

Rate per 1,000
live births

- 4.2 to 17.8
- 17.9 to 38.8
- 38.9 to 62.6
- 62.7 to 96.5
- 96.6 to 146.7
- No data

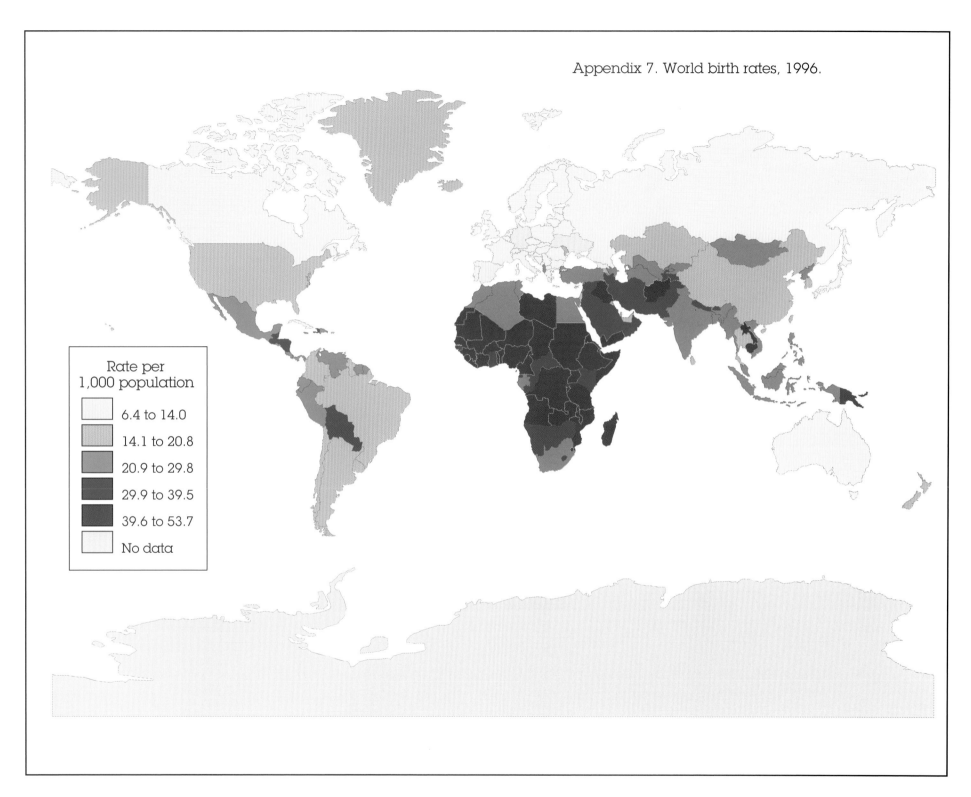

Appendix 7. World birth rates, 1996.

Rate per
1,000 population

6.4 to 14.0
14.1 to 20.8
20.9 to 29.8
29.9 to 39.5
39.6 to 53.7
No data

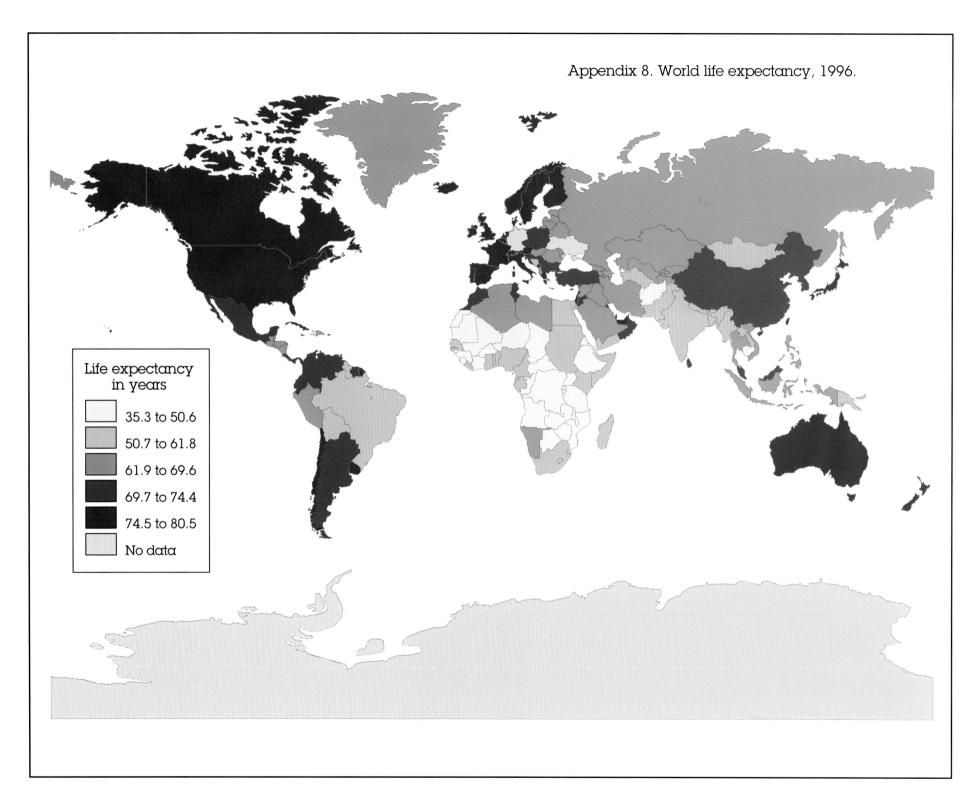

Appendix 8. World life expectancy, 1996.

Life expectancy
in years

35.3 to 50.6

50.7 to 61.8

61.9 to 69.6

69.7 to 74.4

74.5 to 80.5

No data

Sources & References

Sources

Introduction

Figure 1
U.S. Bureau of the Census. *Statistical Abstract of the United States, 1996*. U.S. Department of Commerce, 1996; U.S. Bureau of the Census. "Population Paper Listing 41, Resident Population, by Age and Race: 1960 to 1995." *Current Population Reports, P25-1095*. U.S. Department of Commerce, 1996.

Figure 2
U.S. Bureau of the Census. *Historical Poverty Tables— Persons* HTTP://WWW. CENSUS.GOV/HHES/POVER-TY/HISTPOV/HSTPOV3.HTML 30 July 1997.

Table 1
U.S. Bureau of the Census. *Statistical Abstract of the United States, 1996*. U.S. Department of Commerce, 1996; U.S. Bureau of the Census. "Marital Status and Living Arrangements: March 1994." *Current Population Reports, Series P20-484*. U.S. Department of Commerce, 1994.

Chapter 1

Figure 1.1.1
U.S. Bureau of the Census. *Current Population Reports Series P25-1111*. U.S. Department of Commerce, 1995.

Figure 1.1.2
U.S. Bureau of the Census. *Current Population Reports Series P25-1111*. U.S. Department of Commerce, 1995.

Figure 1.1.3
U.S. Bureau of the Census. *County and City Data Book, 1994*. U.S. Department of Commerce, 1994.

Figure 1.1.3a
U.S. Bureau of the Census. *County and City Data Book, 1994*. U.S. Department of Commerce, 1994.

Figure 1.1.4
U.S. Bureau of the Census. *Current Population Reports Series P25-1111*. U.S. Department of Commerce, 1995.

Figure 1.2.1
Duncan, Cynthia, M., ed.

(1992). *Rural Poverty in America*. New York: Auburn House.

Figure 1.2.2
Duncan, Cynthia, M., ed. (1992). *Rural Poverty in America*. New York: Auburn House.

Figure 1.2.3
Duncan, Cynthia, M., ed. (1992). *Rural Poverty in America*. New York: Auburn House.

Figure 1.2.4
Duncan, Cynthia, M., ed. (1992). *Rural Poverty in America*. New York: Auburn House.

Figure 1.2.5
Office of Elementary and Secondary Education, Office of Migrant Education. *Migrant Education Program Allocations (5 year period)*. U.S. Department of Education. HTTP://WWW.ED.GOV/OFFICE S/OESE/MEP/STATEINFO.HTML August 8, 1997.

Figure 1.2.6
U.S. Department of Education. Office of Elementary and Secondary Education, Office of Migrant Education. *Migrant Education Program Allocations (5 year period)*. HTTP://WWW.ED.GOV/OFFICE S/OESE/MEP/STATEINFO 8 September 1997.

Figure 1.3.1
U.S. Bureau of the Census. *Statistical Abstract of the United States, 1996*. U.S. Department of Commerce, 1996.

Figure 1.3.2
U.S. Bureau of the Census. *Statistical Abstract of the United States, 1994*. U.S. Department of Commerce, 1994.

Figure 1.3.3
U.S. Bureau of the Census. *Statistical Abstract of the United States, 1994*. U.S. Department of Commerce, 1994.

Figure 1.3.4
U.S. Bureau of the Census. *Statistical Abstract of the United States, 1996*. U.S. Department of Commerce, 1996.

Figure 1.3.5
U.S. Bureau of the Census. *Statistical Abstract of the United States, 1996*. U.S. Department of Commerce, 1996.

Figure 1.3.6
U.S. Bureau of the Census. *Statistical Abstract of the United States, 1996*. U.S. Department of Commerce, 1996.

Figure 1.3.7
U.S. Bureau of the Census. *Statistical Abstract of the United States, 1996*. U.S. Department of Commerce, 1996.

Figure 1.4.1
National Center for Health Statistics. *Vital Statistics of the United States*, annual; U.S. Department of Health and Human Services, 1993.

Figure 1.4.2
National Center for Health Statistics. *Vital Statistics of the United States*, annual; U.S. Department of Health and Human Services, 1993.

Figure 1.5.1
U.S. Bureau of the Census. *Statistical Abstract of the United States, 1996*. U.S. Department of Commerce, 1996.

Figure 1.5.2
U.S. Bureau of the Census. *Statistical Abstract of the United States, 1996*. U.S. Department of Commerce, 1996.

Figure 1.5.3
U.S. Bureau of the Census. *Statistical Abstract of the United States, 1996*. U.S. Department of Commerce, 1996.

Figure 1.5.4
U.S. Bureau of the Census. *Statistical Abstract of the United States, 1996*. U.S. Department of Commerce, 1996.

Figure 1.5.5
U.S. Bureau of the Census. *Statistical Abstract of the United States, 1996*. U.S. Department of Commerce, 1996.

Figure 1.5.6
U.S. Bureau of the Census. *Statistical Abstract of the United States, 1996*. U.S. Department of Commerce, 1996.

Figure 1.5.7
U.S. Bureau of the Census. *Statistical Abstract of the United States, 1996*. U.S. Department of Commerce, 1996.

Figure 1.5.8
U.S. Bureau of the Census.

Statistical Abstract of the United States, 1996. U.S. Department of Commerce, 1996.

Figure 1.6.1
Flango, Victor E. , and Carol Flango. "Adoption Statistics by State." *Childwelfare 72, 3 May/June 1993*. Child Welfare League of America, 1993.

Figure 1.6.2
Committee on Ways and Means. *1993 Green Book, 14th edition*. U.S. House of Representatives, 1993.

Figure 1.6.3
Committee on Ways and Means. *1993 Green Book, 14th edition*. U.S. House of Representatives, 1993.

Figure 1.6.4
Hollinger, Joan Heifetz. "Adoption Law." *The Future of Children*. 3 (1). Los Altos: Center for the Future of Children, 1993.

Figure 1.6.5
Committee on Ways and Means. *1993 Green Book, 14th edition*. U.S. House of Representatives, 1993.

Table 1.1.1
U.S. Bureau of the Census. *Current Population Reports Series P25-1111*. U.S. Department of Commerce, 1995.

Table 1.1.2
U.S. Bureau of the Census. *Current Population Reports Series P25-1092*. U.S. Department of Commerce, 1992.

Table 1.1.3
U.S. Bureau of the Census. *Current Population Reports Series P25-1092*. U.S. Department of Commerce, 1992.

Table 1.1.4
U.S. Bureau of the Census. *Current Population Reports Series P25-1092*. U.S. Department of Commerce, 1992.

Table 1.2.1
Duncan, Cynthia, M., ed. (1992). *Rural Poverty in America*. New York: Auburn House.

Table 1.2.2
U.S. Bureau of the Census. *Statistical Abstract of the United States, 1996*. U.S. Department of Commerce, 1996.

Table 1.2.3
U.S. Bureau of the Census. *Current Population Reports and Invisible Children: A Portrait of Migrant Education in the United States, A Final Report of the National Commission on Migrant Education*. U.S. Department of Commerce, 1992.

Table 1.2.4
U.S. Bureau of the Census. *Current Population Reports and Invisible Children: A Portrait of Migrant Education in the United States, A Final Report of the National Commission on Migrant Education*. U.S. Department of Commerce, 1992.

Table 1.3.1
U.S. Bureau of the Census. *Statistical Abstract of the United States, 1996*. U.S. Department of Commerce, 1996.

Table 1.4.1
The State of the World's Children 1990. New York: UNICEF, 1993.

Table 1.4.2
National Center for Health Statistics. *Vital Statistics of the United States*, annual; U.S. Department of Health and Human Services, 1993.

Table 1.4.3
Centers for Disease Control and Prevention. *Morbidity and Mortality Weekly Report*, 42 (9). U.S. Department of Health and Human Services, 1994.

Table 1.4.4
National Center for Health Statistics. *Advance report of final mortality statistics, 1990. Monthly Vital Statistics Report*, 41 (9). Supplement. U.S. Department of Health and Human Services, 1993.

Table 1.4.5
National Center for Health Statistics. *Vital Statistics of the United States*, annual; U.S. Department of Health and Human Services, 1993.

Table 1.4.6
National Center for Health Statistics. *Vital Statistics of the United States*, annual; U.S. Department of Health and Human Services, 1993.

Table 1.5.1
U.S. Bureau of the Census, *Statistical Abstract of the United States, 1996*. U.S. Department of Commerce, 1996.

Table 1.2.3
U.S. Bureau of the Census. *Current Population Reports and Invisible Children: A Portrait of Migrant Education in the United States, A Final Report of the National Commission on Migrant Education*. U.S. Department of Commerce, 1992.

Table 1.6.1
Committee on Ways and Means. *1993 Green Book, 14th edition*. U.S. House of Representatives, 1993.

Table 1.6.2
"State Child Welfare Abstracts 1980-1985," Maximus Inc. prepared for Office of Social Services Policy. Assistant Secretary for Planning and Evaluation, HHS, December 1987; VCIS data.

Table 1.6.3
Committee on Ways and Means. *1993 Green Book, 14th edition*. U.S. House of Representatives, 1993.

Table 1.6.4
Committee on Ways and Means. *1993 Green Book, 14th edition*. U.S. House of Representatives, 1993.

Table 1.6.5
Committee on Ways and Means. *1993 Green Book, 14th edition*. U.S. House of Representatives, 1993.

Table 1.6.6
Committee on Ways and Means. *1993 Green Book, 14th edition*. U.S. House of Representatives, 1993.

Table 1.6.7
Committee on Ways and Means. *1993 Green Book, 14th edition*. U.S. House of Representatives, 1993.

Table 1.6.8
Committee on Ways and Means. *1993 Green Book, 14th edition*. U.S. House of Representatives, 1993.

Table 1.6.9
Committee on Ways and Means. *1993 Green Book, 14th edition*. U.S. House of Representatives, 1993.

Chapter 2

Figure 2.1.1
Hernandez, Donald J. *America's Children Resources From Family, Government and the Economy*. New York: Russell Sage Foundation, 1993.

Figure 2.1.2
U.S. Bureau of the Census. *Historical Poverty Tables— Persons* HTTP://WWW. CENSUS.GOV/HHES/POVER-TY/HISTPOV/HSTPOV3.HTML 30 July 1997.

Figure 2.1.3
National Center for Children in Poverty. *Long Term Young Child Poverty Trends: Alarming Growth, Changing Demographics, Working Families in Poverty*. Columbia School of Public Health. HTTP://CPMCNET. COLUMBIA.EDU/DEPT/NCEP/R EPORTS/LONGTERM.HTML 30 June 1997.

Figure 2.1.4
National Center for Children in Poverty. *Long Term Young Child Poverty Trends: Alarming Growth, Changing Demographics, Working Families in Poverty*. New York: Columbia School of Public Health. HTTP://CPMCNET. COLUMBIA.EDU/DEPT/NCEP/R EPORTS/LONGTERM.HTML 30 June 1997.

Figure 2.3.1
National Center for Children in Poverty. *Child Poverty News & Issues*, 5 (3). Columbia School of Public Health, 1995.

Figure 2.3.2
Eller, T. J. "Dynamics of Economic Well-Being: Poverty, 1992-1993 Who Stays Poor? Who Doesn't?" *Current Population Reports, P70-55*, 1996.

Figure 2.3.3
Eller, T. J. "Dynamics of Economic Well-Being: Poverty, 1992-1993. Who Stays Poor? Who Doesn't?" *Current Population Reports, P70-55*, 1996.

Figure 2.3.4
U.S. Bureau of the Census. *U.S.1990 Census of Population and Housing*. U.S. Department of Commerce, 1993.

Figure 2.3.5
U.S. Bureau of the Census. *U.S.1990 Census of Population and Housing*. U.S. Department of Commerce, 1993.

Figure 2.3.6
U.S. Bureau of the Census. *U.S.1990 Census of Population and Housing*. U.S. Department of Commerce, 1993.

Figure 2.3.7
U.S. Bureau of the Census. *U.S.1990 Census of Population and Housing*. U.S. Department of Commerce, 1993.

Figure 2.3.8
U.S. Bureau of the Census.

U.S.1990 Census of Population and Housing. U.S. Department of Commerce, 1993.

Figure 2.3.9
Eller, T. J. "Dynamics of Economic Well-Being: Poverty, 1992-1993. Who Stays Poor? Who Doesn't?" *Current Population Reports*. P70-55, 1996.

Figure 2.4.1
National Center for Children in Poverty. *Long Term Young Child Poverty Trends: Alarming Growth, Changing Demographics, Working Families in Poverty*. Columbia School of Public Health. HTTP://CPMCNET. COLUMBIA.EDU/DEPT/NCEP/R EPORTS/LONGTERM.HTML 30 June 1997.

Figure 2.4.2
National Center for Children in Poverty. "Number of Poor Children Under Six Increased From 5 to 6 Million 1987-1992." *Child Poverty News & Issues*, 5 (1), 1995.

Figure 2.4.3
National Center for Children in Poverty. "Number of Poor Children Under Six Increased From 5 to 6 Million 1987-1992." *Child Poverty News & Issues*, 5 (1), 1995.

Figure 2.4.4
National Center for Children in Poverty. *Long Term Young Child Poverty Trends: Alarming Growth, Changing Demographics, Working Families in Poverty*. Columbia School of Public Health. HTTP://CPMCNET. COLUMBIA.EDU/DEPT/NCEP/R EPORTS/LONGTERM.HTML 30 June 1997.

Figure 2.4.5
Committee on Ways and Means. *1993 Green Book, 14th edition*. U.S. House of Representatives, 1993.

Figure 2.5.1
A Tale of Two Nations: The Creation of American "Poverty Nomads." New York: Homes for the Homeless, 1996.

Figure 2.5.2
A Tale of Two Nations: The Creation of American "Poverty Nomads." New York: Homes for the Homeless, 1996.

Figure 2.5.3
A Tale of Two Nations: The Creation of American "Poverty Nomads." New York: Homes for the Homeless, 1996.

Figure 2.6.1
U.S. Bureau of the Census. "Trends in Child Care Arrangements of Working Mothers." *Current Population Reports, P-23, No. 117*, various years.

Figure 2.6.2
U.S. Bureau of the Census. *Current Population Reports, P-23, No. 117*, various years.

Figure 2.6.3
U.S. Bureau of the Census. "Trends in Child Care Arrangements of Working Mothers." *Current Population Reports, P-23, No. 117*, various years.

Figure 2.6.4
U.S. Bureau of the Census. "Trends in Child Care Arrangements of Working Mothers." *Current Population Reports, P-23, No. 117*, various years.

Figure 2.6.5
Casper, L. M. (1996). "Who's Minding Our Preschoolers?" *Current Population Reports, P-70-53*. U.S. Bureau of the Census.

Figure 2.6.6
Holcomb, Betty, Catherine Cartwright, Shaun Dreisbach, and Anne L. Fritz (1997). "Child Care: How Does Your State Rate?" *Working Mother*, July/August.

Figure 2.6.7
Holcomb, Betty, Catherine Cartwright, Shaun Dreisbach, and Anne L. Fritz (1997). "Child Care: How Does Your State Rate?" *Working Mother*, July/August.

Figure 2.6.8
Holcomb, Betty, Catherine Cartwright, Shaun Dreisbach, and Anne L. Fritz (1997). "Child Care: How Does Your State Rate?" *Working Mother*, July/August.

Figure 2.6.9
Holcomb, Betty, Catherine Cartwright, Shaun Dreisbach, and Anne L. Fritz (1997). "Child Care: How Does Your State Rate." *Working Mother*, July/August.

Figure 2.6.10
Holcomb, Betty, Catherine Cartwright, Shaun Dreisbach, and Anne L. Fritz (1997). "Child Care: How Does Your State Rate?" *Working Mother*, July/August.

Figure 2.6.11
Holcomb, Betty, Catherine Cartwright, Shaun Dreisbach, and Anne L. Fritz (1997). "Child Care: How Does Your State Rate?" *Working Mother*, July/August.

Figure 2.6.12
Holcomb, Betty, Catherine Cartwright, Shaun Dreisbach, and Anne L. Fritz (1997). "Child Care: How Does Your State Rate?" *Working Mother*, July/August.

Figure 2.7.1
Committee on Ways and Means. *1996 Green Book, 17th edition*. U.S. House of Representatives, 1996.

Figure 2.7.2
Committee on Ways and Means. *1996 Green Book, 17th edition*. U.S. House of Representatives, 1996.

Figure 2.7.3
Committee on Ways and Means. *1996 Green Book, 17th edition*. U.S. House of Representatives, 1996.

Figure 2.7.4
Committee on Ways and Means. *1996 Green Book, 17th edition*. U.S. House of Representatives, 1996.

Figure 2.7.5
Committee on Ways and Means. *1996 Green Book, 17th edition*. U.S. House of Representatives, 1996.

Figure 2.7.6
Committee on Ways and Means. *1996 Green Book, 17th edition*. U.S. House of Representatives, 1996.

Figure 2.7.7
National Center for Children in Poverty. "Study Maps State Strategies to Spur Responsible Fatherhood." *News and Issues, Summer 1997*, 7 (1). Columbia School of Public Health, 1997.

Table 2.2.1
U.S. Bureau of the Census. *Current Population Survey March 1996*. U.S. Department of Commerce, 1996.

Table 2.2.2
U.S. Bureau of the Census. *Current Population Survey March 1996*. U.S. Department of Commerce, 1996.

Table 2.3.1
Duncan, G., and W. Rogers. *Demographic Analysis of Childhood Poverty*. Committee on Ways and

Table 2.3.2
Duncan, G., and W. Rogers. *Demographic Analysis of Childhood Poverty*. Committee on Ways and Means. *1993 Green Book, 14th edition*. U.S. House of Representatives, 1993.

Table 2.4.1
Brandon, Peter (1993). "The Connection Between Family Structure and Entitlements Affecting Poor Young Children." *Focus*, 15 (3), Winter 1993-94.

Table 2.4.2
Brandon, Peter (1993). "The Connection Between Family Structure and Entitlements Affecting Poor Young Children." *Focus*, 15 (3), Winter 1993-94.

Table 2.4.3
Brandon, Peter (1993). "The Connection Between Family Structure and Entitlements Affecting Poor Young Children." *Focus*, 15 (3), Winter 1993-94.

Table 2.5.1
The U.S. Conference of Mayors. *A Status Report on Hunger and Homelessness in American Cities: 1996*, 1996.

Table 2.5.2
The U.S. Conference of Mayors. *A Status Report on Hunger and Homelessness in American Cities: 1996*, 1996.

Table 2.5.3
The U.S. Conference of Mayors. *A Status Report on Hunger and Homelessness in American Cities: 1996*, 1996.

Table 2.5.4
The U.S. Conference of Mayors. *A Status Report on Hunger and Homelessness in American Cities: 1996*, 1996.

Table 2.6.1
Committee on Ways and Means. *1996 Green Book, 17th edition*. U.S. House of Representatives, 1996.

Table 2.6.2
Committee on Ways and Means. *1996 Green Book, 17th edition*. U.S. House of Representatives, 1996.

Table 2.6.3
Committee on Ways and Means. *1996 Green Book, 17th edition*. U.S. House of Representatives, 1996.

Table 2.6.4
Bureau of Labor Statistics. *Employee Benefits Survey*. U.S. Department of Labor. HTTP://STATS.BLS.GOV/NEWS. RELEASE/EBS3.TO3.HTML 25 August 1997.

Table 2.6.5
Holcomb, Betty, Catherine Cartwright, Shaun Dreisbach, and Anne L. Fritz (1997). "Child Care: How Does Your State Rate?" *Working Mother*, July/August.

Table 2.7.1
Committee on Ways and Means. *1996 Green Book, 17th edition*. U.S. House of Representatives, 1996.

Table 2.7.2
Committee on Ways and Means. *1996 Green Book, 17th edition*. U.S. House of Representatives, 1996.

Table 2.7.3
Committee on Ways and Means. *1996 Green Book, 17th edition*. U.S. House of Representatives, 1996.

Table 2.7.4
Committee on Ways and Means. *1996 Green Book, 17th edition*. U.S. House of Representatives, 1996.

Table 2.7.5
Committee on Ways and Means. *1996 Green Book, 17th edition*. U.S. House of Representatives, 1996.

Table 2.7.6
Committee on Ways and Means. *1996 Green Book, 17th edition*. U.S. House of Representatives, 1996.

Table 2.7.7
Committee on Ways and Means. *1996 Green Book, 17th edition*. U.S. House of Representatives, 1996.

Chapter 3

Figure 3.1.1
U.S. Bureau of the Census. *Current Population Survey*. U.S. Department of Commerce, Three-year merged 1989, 1990, and 1991.

Figure 3.1.2
Health Care Financing Administration: *Statistical Report on Medical Care: Eligibles, Recipients, Payments and Services, HCFA form 2082*. U.S. Department of Health and Human Services, 1994.

Figure 3.1.3
Health Care Financing
Administration. *Statistical
Report on Medical Care:
Eligibles, Recipients, Payments
and Services, HCFA form
2082*. U.S. Department of
Health and Human Services,
1994.

Figure 3.1.4
Health Care Financing
Administration. *Statistical
Report on Medical Care:
Eligibles, Recipients, Payments
and Services, HCFA form
2082*. U.S. Department of
Health and Human Services,
1994.

Figure 3.1.5
U.S. Bureau of the Census.
*Statistical Abstract of the
United States, 1996*. U.S.
Department of Commerce,
1996.

Figure 3.2.1
National Education Goals
Panel. "National Education
Goals Report." *Building a
Nation of Learners 1995*,
1995. ; U.S. Bureau of the
Census. *Current Population
Survey*. U.S. Department of
Commerce, 1994.

Figure 3.2.2
Centers for Disease Control
and Prevention. "Summary of
State Immunization
Requirements Applicable to
Any or All Grades K-12. 1993-
94 School Year." *State
Immunization Requirements
1993-94*. U.S. Department of
Health and Human Services,
1995.

Figure 3.3.1
National Runaway
Switchboard. Chicago, 1994.

Figure 3.3.2
Finkelhor, David, et al.
*Missing, Abducted, Runaway,
and Thrownaway Children in
America*. Office of Juvenile
Justice and Delinquency
Prevention, U.S. Department
of Justice, 1990.

Figure 3.3.3
Finkelhor, David, et al.
*Missing, Abducted, Runaway,
and Thrownaway Children in
America*. Office of Juvenile
Justice and Delinquency
Prevention, U.S. Department
of Justice, 1990.

Figure 3.4.1
Centers for Disease Control
and Prevention. *Morbidity and
Mortality Weekly Report*, 45,
(40). U.S. Department of
Health and Human Services,
1995.

Figure 3.4.2
National Sudden Infant Death
Syndrome Resource Center.
What Is SIDS?. National
Center for Education in
Maternal and Child Health,
1993.

Figure 3.4.3
U.S. National Center for
Health Statistics. *Vital
Statistics of the United States,
Annual; and Monthly Vital
Statistics Report*. U.S.
Department of Health and
Human Services, 1994.

Figure 3.4.4
U.S. National Center for
Health Statistics. *Vital
Statistics of the United States,
Annual; and Monthly Vital
Statistics Report*. U.S.
Department of Health and
Human Services, 1994.

Figure 3.5.1
Centers for Disease Control
and Prevention. *HIV / AIDS
Surveillance Report, U.S. HIV
and AIDS cases reported
through June 1994*. U.S.
Department of Health and
Human Services, 1994.

Figure 3.5.2
Centers for Disease Control
and Prevention. *HIV / AIDS
Surveillance Report, U.S. HIV
and AIDS cases reported
through June 1994*. U.S.
Department of Health and
Human Services, 1994.

Figure 3.5.3
Centers for Disease Control
and Prevention. *HIV / AIDS
Surveillance Report, U.S. HIV
and AIDS cases reported
through December 1993*. U.S.
Department of Health and
Human Services, 1994.

Figure 3.5.4
Centers for Disease Control
and Prevention. *HIV / AIDS
Surveillance Report, U.S. HIV
and AIDS cases reported
through June 1994*. U.S.
Department of Health and
Human Services, 1994.

Figure 3.6.1
Tibbs, Nancy (1995). *Ratio of
Children Screened to Number
Confirmed with Elevated
Blood Lead Levels, 1993-
1994*. Unpublished data sup-
plied upon request. Lead

Poisoning Prevention Branch,
Division of Environmental
Hazards and Health Effects,
National Center for
Environmental Health, Centers
for Disease Control and
Prevention.

Figure 3.6.2
Tibbs, Nancy (1995). *United
States Blood Lead Level
Confirmation Protocols (in
microns per deciliter) 1993-
1994*. Unpublished data sup-
plied upon request. Lead
Poisoning Prevention Branch,
Division of Environmental
Hazards and Health Effects,
National Center for
Environmental Health, Centers
for Disease Control and
Prevention.

Figure 3.6.3
Centers for Disease Control
and Prevention. "National
Health and Nutrition
Examination Survey (NHANES)
II and III—Phase 1, United
States, 1976-1980 and 1988-
1991." *Morbidity and
Mortality Report, 43*. U.S.
Department of Health and
Human Services, 1994.

Figure 3.6.4
Centers for Disease Control
and Prevention. "National
Health and Nutrition
Examination Survey (NHANES)
II and III-Phase 1, United
States, 1976-1980 and 1988-
1991." *Morbidity and
Mortality Report, 43*. U.S.
Department of Health and
Human Services, 1994.

Figure 3.7.1
Maternal and Child Health
Bureau. *Child Health USA '94*.
Health Resources & Services
Administration, U.S.
Department of Health and
Human Services, 1995.

Figure 3.7.2
Singh, G. K., et al. "Annual
Summary of Births, Marriages,
Divorces, and Deaths: United
States, 1994." *Monthly Vital
Statistics Report, 43* (13).
National Center for Health
Statistics, 1995.

Figure 3.7.3
U.S. National Center for
Health Statistics. *Vital
Statistics of the United States,
Annual; and Monthly Vital
Statistics Report*. U.S.
Department of Health and
Human Services, 1994.

Figure 3.7.4
Indian Health Service. *Trends
in Indian Health–1994*. U.S.
Department of Health and
Human Services, 1995.

Figure 3.8.1
Center for Mental Health
Services. *Additions and
Resident Patients at End of
Year, State and County Mental
Hospitals, by Age and
Diagnosis, by State, United
States, 1992*. U.S. Department
of Health and Human
Services, 1994.

Figure 3.8.2
Knitzer, Jane. *Unclaimed
Children: The Failure of Public
Responsibility to Children and
Adolescents in Need of
Mental Health Services*.
Children's Defense Fund,
Publications Department,
1992.

Figure 3.9.1
U.S. National Center for
Health Statistics. *Vital
Statistics of the United States,
Annual; and Monthly Vital
Statistics Report*. U.S.
Department of Health and
Human Services, 1994.

Figure 3.10.1
National Center for Education
Statistics. *The Digest of
Education Statistics, 1996*.
Office of Educational Research
and Improvement, U.S.
Department of Education,
1996.

Figure 3.11.1
National Center for Health
Statistics. *Health United States
1994*. U.S. Department of
Health and Human Services,
1995.

Figure 3.12.1
Division of Birth Defects and
Developmental Disabilities.
*State and Local Programs in
Birth Defect Surveillance
Program Contacts*.
Department of Health and
Human Services, 1994.

Figure 3.12.2
U.S. National Center for
Health Statistics. *Vital
Statistics of the United States,
Annual; and Monthly Vital
Statistics Report*. U.S.
Department of Health and
Human Services, 1994.

Figure 3.12.3
U.S. National Center for
Health Statistics. *Vital
Statistics of the United States,
Annual; and Monthly Vital
Statistics Report*. U.S.
Department of Health and
Human Services, 1994.

Table 3.2.1
Maternal and Child Health
Bureau. *Child Health USA '93*.
U.S. Public Health Service,
Department of Health and
Human Services, 1994.

Table 3.2.2
Franklin, P., et al. *Building a
National Immunization
System: A Guide to
Immunization Services and
Resources*. Children's Defense
Fund. Washington, D.C.,
1994.

Table 3.2.3
Atkinson, William L., et al.
(1992). "Measles
Surveillance–United States,
1991." U.S. Department of
Health and Human Services,
Reprinted from *CDC
Surveillance Summaries, 41*,
No. SS-6.

Table 3.4.1
U.S. National Center for
Health Statistics. *Vital
Statistics of the United States,
Annual; and Monthly Vital
Statistics Report*. U.S.
Department of Health and
Human Services, 1994.

Table 3.5.1
Centers for Disease Control
and Prevention. *HIV / AIDS
Surveillance Report, U.S. HIV
and AIDS cases reported
through December1993*. U.S.
Department of Health and
Human Services, 1994.

Table 3.6.1
Tibbs, Nancy (1995). *Top
Cities Confirmed Lead
Poisoning Levels Greater Than
10 Microns Per Deciliter In
Children*. Unpublished data
supplied upon request. Lead
Poisoning Prevention Branch,
Division of Environmental
Hazards and Health Effects,
National Center for
Environmental Health, Centers
for Disease Control and
Prevention.

Table 3.7.1
Indian Health Service. *Trends
in Indian Health–1994*. U.S.
Department of Health and
Human Services, 1995.

Table 3.12.1
Division of Birth Defects and
Developmental Disabilities.
*State and Local Programs in
Birth Defect Surveillance
Program Contacts*.
Department of Health and
Human Services, 1994.

Chapter 4

Figure 4.2.1
Szymanski, Linda A. *Upper Age
of Juvenile Court Jurisdiction
Statutes Analysis*. National
Center for Juvenile Justice,
1987.

Figure 4.2.2
Bureau of Justice Statistics.
*Juvenile Records and
Recordkeeping Systems,
Appendix K*. U.S. Department
of Justice, 1992.

Figure 4.2.3
Bureau of Justice Statistics.
*Juvenile Records and
Recordkeeping Systems,
Appendix K*. U.S. Department
of Justice, 1992.

Figure 4.2.4
Office of Juvenile Justice and
Delinquency Prevention. *1-Day
Counts of Juveniles in Jails,
1985-1990, Annual Survey of
Jails*. U.S. Department of
Justice, 1993; Bureau of
Justice Statistics, *Fact Sheet
#2*. U.S. Department of
Justice, 1993.

Figure 4.2.5
Office of Juvenile Justice and
Delinquency Prevention.
*Annual Survey of Jails. Bureau
of Justice Statistics, 1985-90*.
U.S. Department of Justice,
1991.

Figure 4.3.1
Office of Juvenile Justice and
Delinquency Prevention, U.S.
Department of Justice.
*Conditions of Confinement:
Juvenile Detention and
Corrections Facilities*. Abt
Associates, 1994.

Figure 4.3.2
Office of Juvenile Justice and
Delinquency Prevention, U.S.
Department of Justice.
*Conditions of Confinement:
Juvenile Detention and
Corrections Facilities*. Abt
Associates, 1994.

Figure 4.3.3
Allen-Hagen, Barbara. "Public
Juvenile Facilities: Children in
Custody 1989." *Juvenile
Justice Bulletin*. OJJDP *Update
on Statistics*. U.S. Department
of Justice, 1991.

Figure 4.3.4
Allen-Hagen, Barbara. "Public
Juvenile Facilities: Children in
Custody 1989." *Juvenile
Justice Bulletin*. OJJDP *Update
on Statistics*. U.S. Department
of Justice, 1991.

Figure 4.3.5
Allen-Hagen, Barbara. "Public Juvenile Facilities: Children in Custody 1989." *Juvenile Justice Bulletin. OJJDP Update on Statistics.* U.S. Department of Justice, 1991.

Figure 4.3.6
Office of Juvenile Justice and Delinquency Prevention, U.S. Department of Justice. *Conditions of Confinement: Juvenile Detention and Corrections Facilities.* Abt Associates, 1994.

Figure 4.3.7
Office of Juvenile Justice and Delinquency Prevention, U.S. Department of Justice. *Conditions of Confinement: Juvenile Detention and Corrections Facilities."* Abt Associates, 1994.

Figure 4.3.8
Office of Juvenile Justice and Delinquency Prevention, U.S. Department of Justice. *Conditions of Confinement: Juvenile Detention and Corrections Facilities.* Abt Associates, 1994.

Figure 4.4.1
Federal Bureau of Investigation. *1995 Crime in the United States.* Criminal Justice Information Services Division, 1996.

Figure 4.4.2
Snyder, Howard N., *Juvenile Violent Crime Arrest Rates 1972-1992. Fact Sheet #14,* U.S. Office of Juvenile Justice and Delinquency Prevention, U.S Department of Justice, 1994.

Figure 4.4.3
Snyder, Howard N., *Juvenile Violent Crime Arrest Rates 1972-1992. Fact Sheet #14,* U.S. Office of Juvenile Justice and Delinquency Prevention, U.S Department of Justice, 1994.

Figure 4.4.4
Snyder, Howard N., *Juvenile Violent Crime Arrest Rates 1972-1992. Fact Sheet #14,* U.S. Office of Juvenile Justice and Delinquency Prevention, U.S Department of Justice, 1994.

Figure 4.4.5
Snyder, Howard N., *Juvenile Violent Crime Arrest Rates 1972-1992. Fact Sheet #14,* U.S. Office of Juvenile Justice and Delinquency Prevention, U.S Department of Justice, 1994.

Figure 4.4.6
Snyder, Howard N., *Juvenile Violent Crime Arrest Rates 1972-1992. Fact Sheet #14,* U.S. Office of Juvenile Justice and Delinquency Prevention, U.S Department of Justice, 1994.

Figure 4.4.7
Moone, Joseph. *Juvenile Victimization: 1987-1992, Fact Sheet #17.* U.S. Office of Juvenile Justice and Delinquency Prevention, U.S. Department of Justice, 1994.

Figure 4.4.8
Moone, Joseph. "Juvenile Victimization: 1987-1992." *Fact Sheet #17.* U.S. Office of Juvenile Justice and Delinquency Prevention, U.S. Department of Justice, 1994.

Figure 4.4.9
Allen-Hagen, Barbara, Melissa Sickmund, and Howard N. Snyder, "Juveniles and Violence: Juvenile Offending and Victimization." *Fact Sheet #19.* U.S. Office of Juvenile Justice and Delinquency Prevention, U.S. Department of Justice, 1994.

Figure 4.4.10
Allen-Hagen, Barbara, Melissa Sickmund, and Howard N. Snyder. "Juveniles and Violence: Juvenile Offending and Victimization." *Fact Sheet #19.* U.S. Office of Juvenile Justice and Delinquency Prevention, U.S. Department of Justice, 1994.

Figure 4.4.11
Allen-Hagen, Barbara, Melissa Sickmund, and Howard N. Snyder. "Juveniles and Violence: Juvenile Offending and Victimization." *Fact Sheet #19.* U.S. Office of Juvenile Justice and Delinquency Prevention, U.S. Department of Justice, 1994.

Figure 4.4.12
National Center on Child Abuse and Neglect. *Child Maltreatment 1992: Reports From the States to the National Center on Child Abuse and Neglect.* U.S. Department of Health and Human Services, 1994.

Figure 4.4.13
National Center on Child Abuse and Neglect. *Child Maltreatment 1992: Reports From the States to the National Center on Child Abuse and Neglect.* U.S. Department of Health and

Human Services, 1994.

Figure 4.4.14
National Center on Child Abuse and Neglect. *Child Maltreatment 1992: Reports From the States to the National Center on Child Abuse and Neglect.* U.S. Department of Health and Human Services, 1994.

Figure 4.4.15
National Center on Child Abuse and Neglect. *Child Maltreatment 1992: Reports From the States to the National Center on Child Abuse and Neglect.* U.S. Department of Health and Human Services, 1994.

Table 4.2.1
Federal Bureau of Investigation. "Crime in the United States 1995." *Uniform Crime Reports.* U.S. Department of Justice, 1996.

Table 4.3.1
Office of Juvenile Justice and Delinquency Prevention. "Public Juvenile Facilities: Children in Custody 1989." *Juvenile Justice Bulletin. OJJDP Update on Statistics.* U.S. Department of Justice, 1991.

Table 4.3.2
Office of Juvenile Justice and Delinquency Prevention. "Public Juvenile Facilities: Children in Custody 1989." *Juvenile Justice Bulletin. OJJDP Update on Statistics.* U.S. Department of Justice, 1991.

Table 4.3.3
Office of Juvenile Justice and Delinquency Prevention, U.S. Department of Justice. *Conditions of Confinement: Juvenile Detention and Corrections Facilities.* Abt Associates, 1994.

Table 4.3.4
Krisberg, Barry, and R. Decomo (1993). *Juveniles Taken Into Custody: Fiscal Year 1991 Report.* Office of Juvenile Justice and Delinquency Prevention, Office of Justice Programs, U.S Department of Justice.

Table 4.4.1
Federal Bureau of Investigation. *1995 Crime in the United States.* Criminal Justice Information Services Division, 1996.

Table 4.4.2
Snyder, Howard N. (1994). *1992 Juvenile Arrests. Fact Sheet #13.* U.S. Office of Juvenile Justice and

Delinquency Prevention, U.S Department of Justice.

Table 4.4.3
National Center on Child Abuse Prevention Research. *Current Trends in Child Abuse Reporting and Fatalities: The Results of the 1993 Annual Fifty State Survey.* National Committee to Prevent Child Abuse. Chicago, 1994.

Chapter 5

Figure 5.2.1
National Center for Education Statistics. *The Digest of Education Statistics, 1996.* Office of Educational Research and Improvement, U.S. Department of Education, 1996.

Figure 5.2.2
National Center for Education Statistics. *The Digest of Education Statistics, 1996.* Office of Educational Research and Improvement, U.S. Department of Education, 1996.

Figure 5.2.3
National Center for Education Statistics. *The Digest of Education Statistics, 1996.* Office of Educational Research and Improvement, U.S. Department of Education, 1996.

Figure 5.2.4
National Center for Education Statistics. *The Digest of Education Statistics, 1996.* Office of Educational Research and Improvement, U.S. Department of Education, 1996.

Figure 5.2.5
National Center for Education Statistics. *The Digest of Education Statistics, 1996.* Office of Educational Research and Improvement, U.S. Department of Education, 1996.

Figure 5.2.6
National Center for Education Statistics. *The Digest of Education Statistics, 1996.* Office of Educational Research and Improvement, U.S. Department of Education, 1996.

Figure 5.2.7
National Center for Education Statistics. *The Digest of Education Statistics, 1996.* Office of Educational Research and Improvement, U.S.

Delinquency Prevention, U.S Department of Justice.

Department of Education, 1996.

Figure 5.2.8
National Center for Education Statistics. *The Digest of Education Statistics, 1996.* Office of Educational Research and Improvement, U.S. Department of Education, 1996.

Figure 5.2.9
National Center for Education Statistics. *The Digest of Education Statistics, 1996.* Office of Educational Research and Improvement, U.S. Department of Education, 1996.

Figure 5.2.10
Office of Special Education and Rehabilitative Services. *Annual Report to Congress on the Implementation of the Individuals with Disabilities Act.* U.S. Department of Education, 1995.

Figure 5.3.1
National Center for Education Statistics. *The Digest of Education Statistics, 1996.* Office of Educational Research and Improvement, U.S. Department of Education, 1996.

Figure 5.3.2
National Center for Education Statistics. *The Digest of Education Statistics, 1996.* Office of Educational Research and Improvement, U.S. Department of Education, 1996.

Figure 5.3.2a
National Center for Education Statistics, *Common Core of Data Surveys.* U.S. Department of Education, 1994.

Figure 5.3.3
National Center for Education Statistics, *Common Core of Data Surveys.* U.S. Department of Education, 1994.

Figure 5.3.4
National Center for Education Statistics, *Common Core of Data Surveys.* U.S. Department of Education, 1994.

Figure 5.3.5
National Center for Education Statistics. *The Digest of Education Statistics, 1992.* Office of Educational Research and Improvement, U.S. Department of Education, 1992.

Figure 5.3.6
National Center for Education Statistics. *The Digest of Education Statistics, 1996.* Office of Educational Research and Improvement, U.S. Department of Education, 1996.

Figure 5.3.7
National Center for Education Statistics. *The Digest of Education Statistics, 1996.* Office of Educational Research and Improvement, U.S. Department of Education, 1996.

Figure 5.3.8
National Center for Education Statistics, *The Digest of Education Statistics, 1995.* Office of Educational Research and Improvement, U.S. Department of Education, 1995.

Figure 5.3.9
National Center for Education Statistics, *Common Core of Data Surveys.* U.S. Department of Education, 1994.

Figure 5.3.10
National Center for Education Statistics, *The Digest of Education Statistics, 1996.* Office of Educational Research and Improvement, U.S. Department of Education, 1996.

Figure 5.3.11
National Center for Education Statistics. *The Digest of Education Statistics, 1996.* Office of Educational Research and Improvement, U.S. Department of Education, 1996; U.S. Bureau of the Census. *Statistical Abstract of the United States.* U.S. Department of Commerce, 1995.

Figure 5.3.12
National Center for Education Statistics. *The Digest of Education Statistics, 1996.* Office of Educational Research and Improvement, U.S. Department of Education, 1996.

Figure 5.3.13
National Center for Education Statistics. *The Digest of Education Statistics, 1994.* Office of Educational Research and Improvement, U.S. Department of Education, 1994.

Figure 5.3.14
National Center for Education Statistics. *The Digest of*

Education Statistics, 1996. Office of Educational Research and Improvement, U.S. Department of Education, 1996.

Figure 5.3.15
National Center for Education Statistics. *The Digest of Education Statistics, 1996*. Office of Educational Research and Improvement, U.S. Department of Education, 1996.

Figure 5.3.16
National Center for Education Statistics. *The Digest of Education Statistics, 1996*. Office of Educational Research and Improvement, U.S. Department of Education, 1996.

Figure 5.3.17
National Center for Education Statistics. *The Digest of Education Statistics, 1996*. Office of Educational Research and Improvement, U.S. Department of Education, 1996.

Figure 5.3.18
National Center for Education Statistics. *The Digest of Education Statistics, 1996*. Office of Educational Research and Improvement, U.S. Department of Education, 1996.

Figure 5.3.19
National Center for Education Statistics. *Statistics of State School Systems, and Core Data Surveys*. U.S. Department of Education, 1995.

Figure 5.3.20
National Center for Education Statistics. *The Digest of Education Statistics, 1996*. Office of Educational Research and Improvement, U.S. Department of Education, 1996.

Figure 5.3.21
National Center for Education Statistics. *The Digest of Education Statistics, 1996*. Office of Educational Research and Improvement, U.S. Department of Education, 1996.

Figure 5.3.22
National Center for Education Statistics. *The Digest of Education Statistics, 1996*. Office of Educational Research and Improvement, U.S. Department of Education, 1996.

Figure 5.3.23
National Center for Education Statistics. *The Digest of Education Statistics, 1996*. Office of Educational Research and Improvement, U.S. Department of Education, 1996; U.S. Bureau of the Census. *Statistical Abstract of the United States, 1996*. U.S. Department of Commerce, 1996.

Figure 5.3.24
Centers for Disease Control and Prevention. "1994 National Immunization Survey." *Morbidity and Mortality Weekly Report, August, 1995*. U.S. Department of Health and Human Services. 1995.

Figure 5.3.25
National Center for Education Statistics. *The Digest of Education Statistics, 1996*. Office of Educational Research and Improvement, U.S. Department of Education, 1996.

Figure 5.3.26
National Center for Education Statistics. *The Digest of Education Statistics, 1995*. Office of Educational Research and Improvement, U.S. Department of Education, 1995; National Center for Education Statistics. *Projections of Education Statistics to 2005*. Office of Educational Research and Improvement, U.S. Department of Education, 1995.

Figure 5.3.27
National Center for Education Statistics. *The Digest of Education Statistics, 1996*. Office of Educational Research and Improvement, U.S. Department of Education, 1996.

Figure 5.3.28
National Center for Education Statistics. *The Digest of Education Statistics, 1996*. Office of Educational Research and Improvement, U.S. Department of Education, 1996.

Figure 5.4.1
National Center for Education Statistics. *A First Look: NAEP Reading*, revised edition. U.S. Department of Education, 1995.

Figure 5.4.2
National Center for Education Statistics. *NAEP, Trends in Academic Progress*. U.S. Department of Education, 1994.

Figure 5.4.3
National Center for Education Statistics. *NAEP, Trends in Academic Progress*. U.S. Department of Education, 1994.

Figure 5.4.4
National Center for Education Statistics. *NAEP, Trends in Academic Progress*. U.S. Department of Education, 1994.

Figure 5.4.5
National Center for Education Statistics. *NAEP, Trends in Academic Progress*. U.S. Department of Education, 1994.

Figure 5.4.6
National Center for Education Statistics. *The Condition of Education 1996*. U.S. Department of Education, 1996.

Figure 5.4.7
National Center for Education Statistics. *The Condition of Education 1996*. U.S. Department of Education, 1996.

Figure 5.5.1
National Center for Education Statistics. *The Condition of Education 1996*. U.S. Department of Education, 1996.

Figure 5.5.2
National Center for Education Statistics. *The Condition of Education 1996*. U.S. Department of Education, 1996.

Figure 5.5.3
National Center for Education Statistics. *Digest of Education Statistics 1995*. U.S. Department of Education, 1995.

Figure 5.5.4
The Education Trust. *Education Watch: The 1996 Education Trust State and National Data Book*. Washington, D.C., 1996.

Figure 5.5.5
National Center for Education Statistics. *The Digest of Education Statistics 1996*. U.S. Department of Education, 1996.

Figure 5.5.6
National Center for Education Statistics. *The Digest of Education Statistics 1996*. U.S. Department of Education, 1996.

Figure 5.5.7
National Center for Education Statistics. *The Digest of Education Statistics 1996*. U.S. Department of Education, 1996.

Figure 5.5.8
National Center for Education Statistics. *The Digest of Education Statistics 1996*. U.S. Department of Education, 1996.

Figure 5.5.9
National Center for Education Statistics. *The Digest of Education Statistics 1996*. U.S. Department of Education, 1996.

Figure 5.5.10
National Center for Education Statistics. *The Digest of Education Statistics 1996*. U.S. Department of Education, 1996.

Figure 5.5.11
National Center for Education Statistics. *The Digest of Education Statistics 1996*. U.S. Department of Education, 1996.

Figure 5.5.12
National Center for Education Statistics. *The Digest of Education Statistics 1996*. U.S. Department of Education, 1996.

Figure 5.5.13
U.S. Bureau of the Census. *Statistical Abstract of the United States*. U.S. Department of Commerce, various years; U.S. Department of Labor Statistics. *Special Labor Force Reports*, and unpublished data. U.S. Department of Commerce, various years.

Figure 5.5.14
U.S. Bureau of the Census. *Statistical Abstract of the United States*. U.S. Department of Commerce, various years; U.S. Department of Labor Statistics. *Special Labor Force Reports*, and unpublished data. U.S. Department of Commerce, various years.

Table 5.2.1
U.S. Bureau of the Census. *Statistical Abstract of the United States, 1994*, CD ROM. 1995.

Table 5.2.2
National Center for Education Statistics. *The Digest of Education Statistics 1995*. U.S. Department of Education, 1995.

Table 5.2.3
National Center for Education Statistics. *The Digest of Education Statistics 1995*. U.S. Department of Education, 1995.

Table 5.3.1
National Center for Education Statistics. *The Digest of Education Statistics, 1996*. Office of Educational Research and Improvement, U.S. Department of Education, 1996.

Table 5.3.2
National Center for Education Statistics. "Fall Enrollment in Institutions of Higher Education." *Common Core of Data and Surveys; Integrated Postsecondary Education Data System (IPEDS), Fall Enrollment Surveys, and Projections of Education Statistics to 2006*. U.S. Department of Education, 1996.

Table 5.3.3
National Center for Education Statistics. *Projections of Education Statistics to 2005*. U.S. Department of Education, 1995.

Table 5.3.4
National Center for Education Statistics. *The Digest of Education Statistics, 1996*. U.S. Department of Education, 1996.

Table 5.3.5
National Center for Education Statistics. *The Digest of Education Statistics, 1995*. U.S. Department of Education, 1995.

Table 5.3.6
National Center for Education Statistics. *The Digest of Education Statistics, 1995*. U.S. Department of Education, 1995.

Table 5.3.7
National Center for Education Statistics. *The Digest of Education Statistics, 1995*. U.S. Department of Education, 1995.

Table 5.3.8
U.S. Bureau of Economic Analysis. *Survey of Current Business*, August issues; and unpublished data.

Table 5.3.9
National Center for Education Statistics. *The Digest of Education Statistics, 1995*. U.S. Department of Education, 1995.

Table 5.3.10
National Center for Education Statistics. *The Digest of Education Statistics, 1995*. U.S. Department of Education, 1995.

Table 5.3.11
National Center for Education Statistics. *Projections of Education Statistics to 2005*. U.S. Department of Education, 1995.

Table 5.3.12
National Center for Education Statistics. *Projections of Education Statistics to 2005*. U.S. Department of Education, 1995.

Table 5.3.13
National Center for Education Statistics. *The Digest of Education Statistics, 1996*. U.S. Department of Education, 1996.

Table 5.4.1
National Center for Education Statistics. *The Condition of Education 1996*. U.S. Department of Education, 1996.

Table 5.4.1a
National Center for Education Statistics. *The Condition of Education 1996*. U.S. Department of Education, 1996.

Table 5.4.2
National Center for Education Statistics. *The Condition of Education 1996*. U.S. Department of Education, 1996.

Table 5.4.3
National Center for Education Statistics. *The Condition of Education 1996*. U.S. Department of Education, 1996.

Table 5.4.4
National Center for Education Statistics. *The Condition of Education 1996*. U.S. Department of Education, 1996.

Table 5.4.5
National Center for Education Statistics. *The Condition of Education 1996*. U.S. Department of Education, 1996.

Table 5.4.6
National Center for Education Statistics. *The Condition of Education 1996*. U.S. Department of Education, 1996.

Table 5.5.1
Centers for Disease Control and Prevention. "The Youth Risk Behavior Surveillance System, 1993." National Center for Chronic Disease, Prevention and Health Promotion, Division of Adolescent and School Health, U.S. Department of Health and Human Services, 1995.

Table 5.5.2
Centers for Disease Control and Prevention. "The Youth Risk Behavior Surveillance System, 1993." National Center for Chronic Disease, Prevention and Health Promotion, Division of Adolescent and School Health, U.S. Department of Health and Human Services, 1995.

Table 5.5.3
National Center for Education Statistics. *The Digest of Education Statistics 1996*. U.S. Department of Education, 1996.

Table 5.5.4
National Center for Education Statistics. *National Household Education Survey*. U.S. Department of Education, 1993.

Table 5.5.5
National Center for Education Statistics. *The Digest of Education Statistics 1996*. U.S. Department of Education, 1996.

Table 5.5.6
National Center for Education Statistics. *The Digest of Education Statistics 1996*. U.S. Department of Education, 1996; University of Michigan, "Monitoring the Future." Institute for Social Research, unpublished data.

Table 5.5.7
Lines, Patricia M. *Estimating the Home Schooled Population*. U.S. Department of Education. Office of Research, 1991.

Table 5.5.8
Council of State Directors of Programs for the Gifted. "The 1994 State of the States Gifted and Talented Education Report." Helena, MT. 1996.

Table 5.5.9
National Center for Education Statistics. *The Digest of Education Statistics 1996*. U.S. Department of Education, 1996.

Table 5.5.10
National Center for Education Statistics. *The Digest of Education Statistics 1996*. U.S. Department of Education, 1996.

Table 5.5.11
National Center for Education Statistics. *The Digest of Education Statistics 1996*. U.S. Department of Education, 1996.

Table 5.5.12
National Center for Education Statistics. *The Digest of Education Statistics 1996*. U.S. Department of Education, 1996.

Table 5.5.13
National Center for Education Statistics. *The Digest of Education Statistics 1996*. U.S. Department of Education, 1996.

References

Introduction

Children's Defense Fund. *America's Children Falling Behind: The U.S. and the Convention on the Rights of the Child.*, 1992

Cohen, Cynthia, and Howard Davidson, eds. (1990). *Children's Rights in America: UN Convention on the Rights of the Child Compared with U.S. Law.* American Bar Association, Center on Children and the Law. Defense for Children International—USA. American Bar Association.

Hermann, Kenneth, Jr. (1991). *Social Workers and the United Nations Convention on the Rights of the Child.* National Association of Social Workers, Inc. CCC Code: 0037-8046/91.

National Commission on Children. *Speaking of Kids.* Report of the National Opinion Research Project, 1991.

Presidential Working Group on the Unmet Legal Needs of Children and Their Families. *America's Children at Risk: A National Agenda for Legal Action*, 1993.

U.S. Department of Health and Human Services of the Assistant Secretary for Planning and Evaluation. *Trends in the Well Being of*

America's Children and Youth: 1996. Washington, D.C., 1996.

Chapter 1

Bianchi, Suzanne (1990). "America's Children: Mixed Prospects." *Population Bulletin,* 45 (1).

Bureau of the Census. *We the American... Asians.* U.S. Department of Commerce, Economics and Statistics Administration. WE-3., 1993.

Bureau of the Census. *We the American... Blacks.* U.S. Department of Commerce, Economics and Statistics Administration. WE-1., 1993.

Bureau of the Census. *We the American... Children.* U.S. Department of Commerce, Economics and Statistics Administration. WE-10., 1993.

Bureau of the Census. *We the American... Hispanics.* U.S. Department of Commerce, Economics and Statistics Administration. WE-2., 1993.

Bureau of the Census. *We the American... Pacific Islanders.* U.S. Department of Commerce, Economics and Statistics Administration. WE-4., 1993.

Bureau of the Census. *We the... First Americans.* U.S. Department of Commerce, Economics and Statistics Administration. WE-5., 1993.

Child Welfare League of America. *The Child Welfare Stat Book.* Washington, D.C., 1993.

Festinger, Trudy (1986). *Necessary Risk: A Study of Adoptions and disrupted Adoptive Placements.* Washington, D.C.: Child Welfare League of America, Inc.

Gardner, Robert (1985). "Asian Americans: Growth, Change, and Diversity." *Population Bulletin,* 40 (4).

Hernandez, Donald J. (1993). *America's Children Resources from Family, Government and the Economy.* New York: Russell Sage Foundation.

Hernandez, Donald J. "Changing Demographics: Past and Future Demands for Early Childhood Programs." *The Future of Children,* 5 (3), Winter 1995. HTTP://WWW.FUTURE-OFCHILDREN.ORG/LTO/06_LTO.HTML

McHale, Magda, et al. (1979). "World of Children." *Population Bulletin.* Washington, D.C.

Nelson, Katherine (1985). *On the Frontier of Adoption: A Study of Special Needs Adoptive Families.* Washington, D.C.: Child Welfare League of America, Inc.

O'Hare, William (1992). "America's Minorities—The Demographics of Diversity." *Population Bulletin,* 46 (4).

O'Hare, William, et al. (1991). "African Americans in the 1990s." *Population Bulletin,* 46 (1).

UNICEF. United Nations Children's Fund. *The State of the World's Children: 1995.* Oxford University Press. Began publication in 1980.

Chapter 2

Bane, Mary Jo, and David T. Ellwood (1989). "One Fifth of the Nation's Children: Why Are They Poor?" *Science,* September 8.

Baugher, Eleanor, and Leatha Lamison-White (1995). *Poverty in the United States: 1995.* U.S. Department of Commerce. *Current Population Reports,* P60-194.

Bianchi, Suzanne, and Daphne Spain (1996). "Women Work, and Family in America." *Population Bulletin,* 51 (3). Washington, D.C.

Boocook, Sarane. "Early Childhood Programs in Other Nations: Goals and Outcomes." *Future of Children,* 5 (3). Winter 1995.

Carnegie Corporation of New York. Task Force on Meeting the Needs of Young Children. *Starting Points: Meeting the Needs of our Youngest Children: The Report of the Carnegie Task Force,* 1994.

Casper, Lynne M (1996). "Who's Minding Our Preschoolers?" U.S. Department of Commerce. *Current Population Reports,* P70-53, 1996.

Casper, Lynne M (1997). "What Does it Cost to Mind Our Preschoolers?" *U.S. Census Bureau,* P70-52, 1997.

Center For the Future of Children, the David and Lucile Packard Foundation. *The Future of Children: Adoption,* 3 (1), Spring 1993.

Center For the Future of Children, the David and Lucile Packard Foundation. *The Future of Children: Welfare to Work,* 7 (1), Spring 1997.

Children's Defense Fund. *Welfare Reform Briefing Book.* January, 1995.

Collins, Ann, and J. Lawrence Aber (1996). "State Welfare Waiver Evaluations: Will They Increase Our Understanding of the Impact of Welfare Reform on Children?" National Center for Children in Poverty. *Child Poverty News & Issues,* 6 (1), Summer.

Duncan, Greg J., and Willard Rodgers (1987). "Single-parent Families: Are Their Economic Problems Transitory or Persistent?" *Family Planning Perspectives,* 19 (4), July/August.

Duncan, Greg J., and Willard Rodgers (1988). "Longi-tudinal Aspects of Childhood Poverty." *Journal of Marriage and the Family,* 50.

Duncan, Greg J., and Willard Rodgers (1991). "Has Children's Poverty Become more Persistent?" *American Sociological Review,* 1991, 56, August.

Federal Interagency Forum on Child and Family Statistics. *America's Children: Key National Indicators of Well-Being,* 1997.

Fuchs, Victor, and Diane Reklis (1992). "America's Children: Economic Perspectives and Policy Options." *Science,* 255, 1992.

Garbarino, James (1995). "The Meaning of Poverty in the World of Children." *American Behavioral Scientist,* 35 (3).

Ginzberg, Eli, with James K. Anderson, and John L. Herma (1962). *The Optimistic Tradition and American Youth.* New York & London: Columbia University Press, 1962.

Goodman, William (1995). "Boom in Day Care Industry." *Monthly Labor Review,* 118 (8).

Goodwillie, Susan (1993). *Voices from the Future.* New York: Crown Publishers Inc.

Gustafsson, Siv S., and Frank P. Stafford (1995). "Links Between Early Childhood Programs and Maternal Employment in Three Countries." *The Future of Children,* 5 (3). HTTP://WWW.FUTUREOF CHILDREN.ORG/LTO/09_LTO.HTML

Hamm, S. Randall, et al. (1994). *Child, Parent, and State: Law and Policy Reader.* Under the sponsorship of the University of Pennsylvania Law Review. Philadelphia: Temple University Press.

Havemann, Judith (1996). "Some States are Hobbled in Race to Welfare Reform." *Washington Post,* 22 October 1996.

Holcomb, Betty, et al. (1997). "Childcare, How Does Your State Rate?" *Working Mother,* July/Aug, pp. 22-46.

Kimmich, Madeleine (1985). *America's Children, Who Cares? Growing Needs and Declining Assistance in the Reagan Era.* Washington, D.C.: The Urban Institute Press.

Knitzer, Jane (1995). "Unclaimed Children: The Future of Public Policies for Children and Adolescents in Need of Mental Health Services." National Center for Children in Poverty. *Child Poverty News & Issues,* 5 (1), Winter.

Lichter. Daniel T., and Erica L.Gardner (1996). "Welfare Reform and the Poor Children of Working Parents." *Focus,* Fall / Winter 65-70.

National Center for Education Statistics. *Child Care and Early Education Program Participation of Infants, Toddlers, and Preschoolers.* National Data Resource Center. HTTP://WWW.ED.GOV/NCES/PUBS/95213.HTML#FOOTNOTE2

National Commission on Children. *Next Steps for Children and Families. Protecting Vulnerable Children and their Families.* Washington, D.C., 1993a.

Nelson, Katherine A. (1985). *On the Frontier of Adoption: A Study of Special-Needs Adoptive Families.* Child Welfare League of America, Inc.

Norton, Arthur (1987) "Families and Children in the Year 2000." *Children Today,* July/August, 6-9.

Orshansky, Mollie (1963). "Children of the Poor" *Social Security Bulletin,* 26, July.

Rogers, Joseph, and G. Larry Mays (1987). *Juvenile Delinquency and Juvenile Justice.* New York: John Wiley and Sons.

Seltzer, Judith A., and Daniel R. Meyer (1996). "Child Support and Children's Well-being." *Focus,* Spring 31-36.

Snyder, Thomas, and Carol Fromboluti (1993). *Youth Indicators, 1993. Trends in the Well Being of American Youth.* National Center for Education Statistics. U.S. Department of Education. Office of Educational Research and Improvement. NCES 93-242.

St. Pierre, Robert, et al. (1993). *National Evaluation of the Even Start Program, Report on Effectiveness.* U.S. Department of Education, Office of Policy and Planning.

U.S. Bureau of the Census. *Child Care Arrangements.* Statistical Brief. HTTP://WWW.CENSUS.GOV/POPULATION/WWW/POP-PROFILE/CHILDCARE.HTML 7 July 1997

U.S. Bureau of the Census. *Definitions of Income and Poverty Terms. Poverty Definitions.* HTTP://WWW.CENSUS.GOV/INCOME/DEFS/POVERTY.HTML

U.S. Bureau of the Census. *Overview of the SIPP Program. Household Economic Statistics.* HTTP://WWW.CENSUS.GOV.HHES/SIPPDESC.HTML 22 August 1997

U.S. Bureau of the Census. *Who Receives Child Support? Statistical Brief.* HTTP://WWW.CENSUS.GOV/SOCDEMO/WWW/CHILDSUPP.HTML

U.S. Bureau of the Census. *Work Related Expenditures in a New Measure of Poverty.* Poverty Measurement Working Papers. HTTP://WWW.CENSUS.GOV/HHES/POVERTY/POVMEAS/WRKEXPEN.HTML 7 July 1997

U.S. Department of Health and Human Services. *Characteristics and Financial Circumstances of AFDC Recipients, FY 1992.* Administration for Children and Families, Office of Family Assistance. 1992.

U.S. Department of Health and Human Services. *Head Start Information Kit.* Administration On Children, Youth and Families Head Start Bureau.

Weinberg, David H (1996). *Poverty Measurement: Changing the Way the United States Measures Income and Poverty.* U.S. Census Bureau.

Chapter 3

Adams, William, et al. (1993). "Decline of Childhood Haemophilus Influenzae Type b (Hib) Disease in the Hib Vaccine Era." *JAMA,* 269 (2), pp. 221-226.

Alliance to End Childhood Lead Poisoning and Conservation Law Foundation. Model State Law. Lead Poisoning Prevention Act, 1993.

American Academy of Pediatrics. *An Action Blueprint for Business: Forging New Partnerships to Make a Difference in Maternal and Child Health.*

National Commission to Prevent Infant Mortality. Washington Business Group on Health, 1993.

Bennefield, Robert (1996). *Who Loses Coverage and for How Long? Current Population Reports. P70-54.* Household Economic Studies. U.S. Department of Commerce, Economics and Statistics Administration, Washington, D.C.

Center For the Future of Children, the David and Lucile Packard Foundation. *The Future of Children: Special Education for Students with Disabilities,* 6 (1), Spring 1996.

Centers for Disease Control (1992). *Guidelines for Assessing Vaccination Levels of the 2-year-old Population in a Clinic Setting.* U.S. Department of Health and Human Services. Public Health Service.

Centers for Disease Control. *Preventing Lead Poisoning in Young Children: A Statement by the CDC, October, 1991.* U.S. Department of Health and Human Services, 1991.

Centers for Disease Control and Prevention. *HIV/AIDS Surveillance Report. U.S. AIDS Cases Reported through March 1993.* Issued May 1993, 5 (1). U.S. Department of Health and Human Services. Public Health Service. Centers for Disease Control and Prevention. National Center for Infectious Diseases, Division of HIV/AIDS, 1993.

CIGNA Corp. No date. *Infant Health in America: Everybody's Business. A Report.* Conducted by the Center for Risk Management and Insurance Research—Georgia State University and the Center for Health Policy Studies, Columbia, MD.

Cochi, Stephen (1994). "Overview of Policies Affecting Vaccine Use in Child Day Care." Supplement to *Pediatrics,* 94 (6) (part 2 of 2), pp. 994-996.

Cutts, Felicity, et al. (1992). "Monitoring Progress toward U.S. Preschool Immunization Goals." *JAMA,* 267 (14), pp. 1952-1955.

Davis, Maryann, Susan Yelton, and Judith Katz Leavy (1995). *State Child and Adolescent Mental Health: Administration, Policies and Laws.* The Research and Training Center for Children's Mental Health.

Dietz, Vance, et al. (1994). "Potential Impact on Vaccination Coverage Levels by Administering Vaccines Simultaneously and Reducing Dropout Rates." *Archives of Pediatrics and Adolescent Medicine,* 148, pp. 943-948.

Farizo, Karen, et al. (1990). "Poliomyelitis in the United States: A Historical Perspective and Current Vaccination Policy." *Journal of American College Health,* 39 (3), pp. 137-143.

Henshaw, Stanley (1993). "Teenage Abortion, Birth and Pregnancy Statistics by State, 1988. A Research Note." *Family Planning Perspectives,* 25 (3).

Henshaw, Stanley (1996). *U.S. Teenage Pregnancy Statistics.* Unpublished paper.

Hersh, Bradley, et al. (1992). "The Geographic Distribution of Measles in the United States, 1980 Through 1989." *JAMA,* 267 (14), pp. 1936-1941.

Hinman, Alan, et al. (1992). "When, Where, and How Do Immunizations Fail?" *Annals of Epidemiology,* 2 (6), pp. 805-812.

Hughes, Dana, et al. (1988). "The Health of America's Children." *Maternal and Child Health Data Book.* Adolescent Pregnancy Prevention: Prenatal Care Campaign. Children's Defense Fund.

Hutchings, John (1988). "Pediatric Aids: An Overview." *Children Today,* May/June, 1988.

Indian Health Service. *Regional Differences in Indian Health, 1994.* U.S. Department of Health and Human Services. Public Health Service Indian Health Service. Office of

Planning, Evaluation, and Legislation, 1994.

Jones, Elise, et al. (1985). "Teenage Pregnancy in Developed Countries: Determinants and Policy Implications." *Family Planning Perspectives,* 17 (2).

Lee, Philip R., and Bruce Vladeck (1994) "From the Health Care Financing Administration and the U.S. Public Health Service." *JAMA,* 271 (16), p. 1230.

Liu, Joseph (1992). "The Health of America's Children: 1992." *Maternal and Child Health Data Book.* Children's Defense Fund. Washington, D.C.

Manderscheid, Ronald, and Mary Sonnenschein (1994). *Mental Health, United States, 1994.* U.S. Department of Health and Human Services. Substance Abuse and Mental Health Services Administration. Center for Mental Health Services.

March of Dimes Birth Defects Foundation. *March of Dimes StatBook—Statistics for Healthier Mothers and Babies,* 1993.

May, Philip (1987). "Suicide Among American Indian Youth: A Look at the Issues." *Children Today.*

Miller, C. Arden, Amy Fine, and Sharon Adams-Taylor (1989). *Monitoring Children's Health.* American Public Health Association.

Mott, Frank, et al. (1996). "The Determinants of First Sex by Age 14 in a High Risk Adolescent Population." *Family Planning Perspectives,* 28 (1).

National Center for Environmental Health: Division of Birth Defects and Developmental Disabilities. *State and Local Programs in Birth Defect Surveillance Program Contacts.* Prepared by Larry Edmonds. Washington, D.C., 1994.

National Center for Health Statistics. "Number, Percentage, and Rate of Infant Deaths for the Ten Leading Causes of Infant Death by Race, 1990." *March of Dimes Statbook.* 1993.CIGNA Corp. No date. *Infant Health in America:*

Everybody's Business. A Report. Conducted by the Center for Risk Management and Insurance Research—Georgia State University and the Center for Health Policy Studies, Columbia, MD.

National Network of Runaway and Youth Services. *Runaway and Homeless Youth Fact Sheet.* The National Network of Runaway and Youth Services, Washington, D.C., 1994.

O'Hare, William (1992). "America's Minorities—The Demographics of Diversity." *Population Bulletin,* 47 (4).

Posner, Marc (1991). *Runaway Youth and Interagency Collaboration: A Review of the Literature.* Unpublished paper submitted to Family and Youth Services bureau, Administration for Children, Youth and Families. The Office of Human Development Services, United States Department of Health and Human Services, Washington, D.C., 1991.

Presidential Working Group on the Unmet Legal Needs of Children and Their Families. *America's Children at Risk: A National Agenda for Legal Action, 1993.*

Robinson, Bryan (1988). *Teenage Fathers.* Lexington Books.

Sutter, Roland, et al. (1992). "Pertussis Hospitalizations and Mortality in the United States, 1985-1988." *JAMA,* 267 (3), pp. 386-391.

Tesman, Johanna, and Amanda Hills (1994). "Developmental Effects of Lead Exposure in Children." *Social Policy Report, Society for Research in Child Development,* 8 (3).

The Alan Guttmacher Institute. *Facts in Brief: Teenage Reproductive Health in the U.S.* New York and Washington, D.C., 1994.

U.S. Department of Health and Human Services. *The National Adolescent Student Health Survey: A Report on the Health of America's Youth.* American School Health Association, Association for the Advancement of Health Education, Society for Public Health Education, Inc., 1989.U.S. Department of

Health and Human Services: National Center for Health Statistics. "Adolescent Mortality." *Child Health USA,* 1994.

U.S. Department of Health and Human Services. *National Plan for Research on Child and Adolescent Mental Disorders. A Report Requested by the U.S. Congress.* Submitted by the National Advisory Mental Health Council, 1990.

U.S. Department of Health and Human Services. *Sudden Infant Death Syndrome: Trying to Understand the Mystery.* National Sudden Infant Death Syndrome Resource Center, 1994.

U.S. Department of Health and Human Services / Public Health Service. "Behaviors Related to Unintentional and Intentional Injuries Among High School Students—United States, 1991." *Morbidity and Mortality Weekly Report, Centers for Disease Control,* 41 (41), 1992.

U.S. Department of Health and Human Services / Public Health Service. "Blood Lead Levels in the U.S., 1988-1991." *Morbidity and Mortality Weekly Report, Centers for Disease Control,* 43 (30), 1994.

U.S. Department of Health and Human Services / Public Health Service. "Health Risk Behaviors Among Persons Aged 12-21 Years in the U.S. 1992." *Morbidity and Mortality Weekly Report, Centers for Disease Control,* 43 (13), 1994.

U.S. Department of Health and Human Services / Public Health Service. "HIV Instruction and Selected HIV risk Behaviors Among High School Students—United States." *Morbidity and Mortality Weekly Report, Centers for Disease Control,* 41 (46), 1992.

U.S. Department of Health and Human Services / Public Health Service. "Influenza—United States." *Morbidity and Mortality Weekly Report, Centers for Disease Control,* 41 (SS-1), 1993.

U.S. Department of Health and Human Services / Public Health Service. "Measles—

United States." *Morbidity and Mortality Weekly Report, Centers for Disease Control,* 42 (19), 1992.

U.S. Department of Health and Human Services / Public Health Service. "Sexual Behavior Among High School Students in the United States, 1990." *Morbidity and Mortality Weekly Report, Centers for Disease Control,* 40 (51- 52), 1992.

U.S. Department of Health and Human Services / Public Health Service. "Summary of Notifiable Diseases, United States, 1992." *Morbidity and Mortality Weekly Report, Centers for Disease Control,* 41 (55), 1993.

U.S. Department of Health and Human Services / Public Health Service. "Surveillance of Children's Blood Lead Levels—United States, 1991." *Morbidity and Mortality Weekly Report, Centers for Disease Control,* 41 (34), 1992.

U.S. Department of Health and Human Services / Public Health Service. "Tetanus Surveillance—United States, 1989-1990." *Morbidity and Mortality Weekly Report, Centers for Disease Control,* 41 (SS-8), 1992.

U.S. Department of Health and Human Services / Public Health Service. "Tobacco, Alcohol, and Other Drug Use Among High School Students—United States, 1991." *Morbidity and Mortality Weekly Report, Centers for Disease Control,* 41 (37), 1992.

U.S. Department of Justice. *Missing, Abducted, Runaway, and Thrownaway Children in America.* First Report: Numbers and Characteristics National Incidence Studies. Office of Justice Programs. Office of Juvenile Justice and Delinquency Prevention, 1990.

Wyszewainski, Leon, and Stephen Mick. eds. (1984). *Medical Care Chartbook, 9th edition.* Health Administration Press, A division of the Foundation of the American College of Healthcare Executives.

Zell, Elizabeth, et al. (1994). "Low Vaccination Levels of U.S. Preschool and School-age Children: Retrospective Assessments of Vaccination Coverage, 1991-1992." *JAMA,* 271 (11), pp. 833-839.

Chapter 4

Ahn, Helen Noh (1994). *Cultural Diversity and the Definition of Child Abuse in Child Welfare, Research Review 1.* (Richard Barth, Jill Berrick, and Neil Gilbert, eds.). New York: Columbia University Press.

American Humane Association/ Children's Division. *Child Abuse and Neglect Data.* AHA Fact Sheet #1, 1994.

Berger, Ronald J (1996). *The Sociology of Juvenile Delinquency.* Chicago: Nelson-Hall.

Besharov, Douglas (1987). "Policy Guidelines for Decision Making in Child Abuse and Neglect." *Children Today,* Nov.-Dec.

Bourne, Richard (1978). *Child Abuse and Neglect: An Overview in Critical Perspectives on Child Abuse.* (Bourne, Richard, and Eli Newberger, eds.). Lexington Books.

Butts, Jeffrey (1994). *Delinquency Cases in Juvenile Court, 1992.* Office of Juvenile Justice and Delinquency Prevention, Fact Sheet #18.

Center For the Future of Children, the David and Lucile Packard Foundation. *The Future of Children: The Juvenile Court,* 6 (3), Winter 1996.

Davis, Liane (1991). *Violence and Families.* National Association of Social Workers, Inc. CCC Code: 0037-8046/91.

Empey, LaMar (1978). *American Delinquency: Its Meaning and Construction.* The Dorsey Press.

Garbarino, James, and G. Gilliam (1980). *Understanding Abusive Families.* Lexington: D.C. Health and Co.

Giovannoni, Jeanne, and Rosina Becerra (1979). *Defining Child Abuse.* New York: The Free Press.

Hotaling, Gerald, and David Finkelhor (1988). *The Sexual Exploitation of Missing Children: A Research Review.* U.S. Department of Justice. Office of Juvenile Justice and Delinquency Prevention. Washington, D.C.

Krisberg, Barry, and James Austin (1993). *Reinventing Juvenile Justice.* Russell Sage Publications.

McCurdy, Karen, and Deborah Daro (1994). *Current Trends in Child Abuse Reporting and Fatalities: The Results of the 1993 Annual Fifty State Survey.* Prepared by the National Center on Child Abuse Prevention Research, a Program of the National Committee to Prevent Child Abuse. Working Paper #808.

National School Safety Center News Service. "Annual Study Shows 3 Million Crimes on School Campuses." *School Safety,* October 1991.

Office of Juvenile Justice and Delinquency Prevention. "Conditions of Confinement: Juvenile Detention and Corrections Facilities." *Research Report,* 1994.

Office of Juvenile Justice and Delinquency Prevention. "Conditions of Confinement: Juvenile Detention and Corrections Facilities." *Research Summary, 1994.*

Office of Juvenile Justice and Delinquency Prevention. "Juvenile and Adult Records: One System, One Record?" *Juvenile Justice Bulletin OJJPD Update on Statistics.* U.S. Department of Justice, 1990.

Office of Juvenile Justice and Delinquency Prevention. *Juvenile Court Statistics 1991.* Prepared by National Center for Juvenile Justice, May 1994.

Office of Juvenile Justice and Delinquency Prevention. "Juveniles Taken Into Custody: Fiscal Year 1991 Report." *Juvenile Justice Bulletin OJJPD Update on Statistics.* U.S. Department of Justice, 1991.

Office of Juvenile Justice and Delinquency Prevention. "Juvenile Violent Crime Arrest Rates 1972-1992." *Juvenile Justice Bulletin OJJPD Update on Statistics.* U.S. Department of Justice, 1994.

Office of Juvenile Justice and Delinquency Prevention. "Offenders in Juvenile Court, 1990." *Juvenile Justice Bulletin. OJJDP Update on Statistics.* U.S. Department of Justice 1993.

Office of Juvenile Justice and Delinquency Prevention. "Public Juvenile Facilities Children in Custody 1989." *Juvenile Justice Bulletin OJJPD Update on Statistics.* U. S. Department of Justice, 1991.

Parton, Nancy (1992) "The Contemporary Politics of Child Protection." *Journal of Social Welfare and Family Law,* 2.

Rogers, Joseph W. and G. Larry Mays (1987) *Juvenile Delinquency and Juvenile Justice.* New York: John Wiley & Sons.

Schmittroth, Linda, ed. (1994). *Statistical Record of Children.* Detroit: Gale Research Inc.

Sedlak, Andrea (1992). *Demographic Research and Child Abuse.* Paper presented at the Centennial Convention of the American Psychological Association, Washington, D.C.

Sullivan, John J., and Joseph L. Victor, eds. (1989). *Criminal Justice 1989/1990.* Connecticut: The Dushkin Publishing Group.

Thornberry, Terence (1994). *Violent Families and Youth Violence.* Office of Juvenile Justice and Delinquency Prevention. Fact Sheet #21.

U.S. Department of Health and Human Services. *Child Maltreatment 1992: Reports from the States to the National Center on Child Abuse and Neglect.* Administration for Children and Families. Washington, D.C., 1992.

U.S. Department of Justice. *America's Missing and Exploited Children: Their Safety and their Future.* Office of Juvenile Justice and

Delinquency Prevention; Report and Recommendations of the U.S. Attorney General's Advisory Board on Missing Children. National Institute for Juvenile Justice and Delinquency Prevention, Washington, D.C., 1986.

U.S. Department of Justice. *Criminal Justice Information Policy Juvenile Records and Recordkeeping Systems.* Bureau of Justice Statistics, 1988.

U.S. Department of Justice. *Teenage Victims: A National Crime Survey Report.* Office of Justice Programs, May, 1991.

U.S. Department of Justice: Office of Justice Programs. *School Crime: A National Crime Victimization Survey Report.* Bureau of Justice Statistics, September 1991.

Whitaker, Catherine J., and Lisa D. Bastian (1991). *Teenage Victims, A National Crime Survey Report.* Office of Justice Programs, U.S. Department of Justice.

Wong, Debra (1987). "Preventing Child Sexual Assault." *Children Today,* November/December.

Chapter 5

"A Bullet for Teacher." *The Economist,* 24 July 1993.

"Schools are Relatively Safe, U.S. Study Says." *The New York Times,* 19 November 1995, A40.

"More Students, In a Study, See Unsafe Schools." *The New York Times,* 15 July 1995.

Acsher, Carol, and Gary Burnett (1993). *Current Trends and Issues in Urban Education, 1993.* ERIC Clearinghouse on Urban Education, Institute for Urban and Minority Education. Trends and Issues (19).

Associated Press. "Survey Finds School Violence Hits 1 in 4 Students." *The New York Times,* 17 December 1993, A37.

Bureau of Justice Statistics. *School Crime.* U.S. Department of Justice. http://www.ojp.us.doj.gov/pub/bjs/ascii/sc.txt 12 June 1997.

Cantrell, Robert P., and Mary Lynn Cantrell (1993). "Countering Gang Violence in American Schools." *Principal, 14,* November.

Celis, William (1993). "Suburban and Rural Schools Learning That Violence Isn't Confined to the Cities." *The New York Times,* 21 April 1993, L+ B11.

Cole, Robert M., ed. (1995). *Educating Everybody's Children.* Association for Supervision and Curriculum Development. Alexandria, VA.

Darling-Hammond, Linda (1996). "The Quiet Revolution: Rethinking Teacher Development." *Educational-Leadership,* 53 (6).

Education Watch: The 1996 Education Trust State and National Data Book. The Education Trust. Washington, D.C., 1996.

Franklin, Paula, et al. (1994). *Building a National Immunization System: A Guide to Immunization Services and Resources.* Children's Defense Fund. Washington, D.C.

Education Watch: The 1996 Education Trust State and National Data Book. The Education Trust, Washington, D.C., 1996.

Garibaldi, Antoine M., Loren Blanchard, and Gregory Osborn (1996). "Reducing Violence and Conflict in New Orleans Public Schools." *Challenge: Journal of Research on African American Men,* 7 (1).

Gerald, Debra E., and William J. Hussar (1991). *Projections of Education Statistics to 2002.* U.S. Department of Education: National Center for Education Statistics, Office of Educational Research and Improvement.

Gerald, Debra E., and William J. Hussar (1995). *Projections of Education Statistics to 2002.* U.S. Department of Education: National Center

for Education Statistics, Office of Educational Research and Improvement.

Harper, Suzanne (1989). *"LA's Gang-Busters—Lessons Learned." School Safety.*

Herdt, Gilbert, and Andrew Boxer (1993). *Children of Horizons: How Gay and Lesbian Teens Are Leading a New Way Out of the Closet.* Boston: Beacon Press.

Hernandez, Raymond (1996). "Pataki Proposes Letting Teachers Suspend Students." *The New York Times,* 5 March 1996, A1+.

Hofferth, Sandra L (1992). "Price, Quality, and Income in Child Care Choice." *Journal of Human Resources,* 27 (1).

Holmstrom, D (1994). "Violent Crime is Down–But Not in Public Schools." *The Christian Science Monitor,* 13 January 1994.

Hull, Jon D. (1993). "The Knife in the Book Bag." *Time Magazine,* 8 February 1993.

Kellogg, J. B. (1988). "Forces of Change." *Phi Delta Kappan,* 70 (3), pp. 118-128.

Mahaffey, Foyne (1994). "Eliminate Violence in the Classroom." *Utne Reader,* January/February 1994.

Mattson, Mark T. (1994). *Fact Book on Elementary, Middle and Secondary Schools, 1993.* Scholastic, Inc.

McCarthy, Colman (1993). "Epidemic of Violence." *The Washington Post,* 13 February 1993, A31.

National Center for Education Statistics. *Access to Early Childhood Programs for Children at Risk.* U.S. Department of Education, 1994.

National Center for Education Statistics. *Crime and Violence in Our Schools an Overview of Statistics.* U.S. Department of Education. http://ed.gov/UPDATES/FACT-209.HTML 18 June 1997.

National Center for Education Statistics. *Digest of Education Statistics,.* U.S. Department of Education, various years.

National Center for Education Statistics. *Dropout Rates in

the United States: 1993.* U.S. Department of Education, 1994.

National Center for Education Statistics. *Findings from The Condition of Education 1996: Teachers' Working Conditions.* U.S. Department of Education. http://ed.gov/NCES/pubs/97371.HTML 19 June 1997.

National Center for Education Statistics. *Language Characteristics and Schooling in the United States, A Changing Picture: 1979 and 1989.* U.S. Department of Education, 1993.

National Center for Education Statistics. *Making the Cut: Who Meets Highly Selective College Entrance Criteria?.* U.S. Department of Education. http://ed.gov/NCES/pubs/95732.HTML 16 June 1997.

National Center for Education Statistics. *1989, Education Indicators.* U.S. Department of Education, 1989.

National Center for Education Statistics. *Parents' Reports of School Practices to Involve Families.* U.S. Department of Education. http://ed.gov/NCES/pubs/97327.html 18 June 1997.

National Center for Education Statistics. *Research on School-Level Expenditures.* U.S. Department of Education. http://ed.gov/NCES/pubs/9619ch2.html 25 June 1997.

National Center for Education Statistics. *Urban Schools: The Challenge of Location and Poverty, Executive Summary.* U.S. Department of Education, 1996.

National Center for Education Statistics. *What Are the Most Serious Problems in Schools?.* U.S. Department of Education. http://ed.gov/NCES/pubs/93149.html 23 June 1997.

National School Safety Center. *School Safety Update.* Pepperdine University, October, 1991.

Nordland, Rod (1992). "Deadly Lessons." *Newsweek,* 9 March 1992.

Office of Educational Research and Improvement. National

Excellence: A Case for Developing America's Talent. U.S. Department of Education. http://Gopher.ed.gov:70/00/publications/full_text/931201.dos. 5 June 1997.

Office of National Drug Control Policy. *National Drug Control Strategy.* Executive Office of the President, 1991.

Orland, M. E. (1990). Demographics of disadvantage. In J. I. Goodland and P. Keating, eds., *Access to Knowledge: An Agenda for Our Nation's Schools.* New York: The College Board. (ERIC Document Reproduction Service No. ED 337 509).

Pallas, Aaron M. (1989). "The Changing Nature of the Disadvantaged Population: Current Dimensions and Future Trends." *Educational Researcher,* 18 (5), June/July.

Peng, Samuel S., Deeann Wright, and Susan T. Hill (1995). *Understanding Racial-Ethnic Differences in Secondary School Science and Mathematics Achievement.* National Center for Education Statistics, U.S. Department of Education.

Pond, Elizabeth F., and Charlotte M. Gilbert (1987). "A Support Group Offers Help for Parents of Hyperactive Children." *Children Today.*

Rose, Lowell, Alec Gallup, and Stanley Elam (1996). *The 28th Annual Phi Delta Kappa-Gallup Poll of the Public's Attitudes Toward Public Schools.*

Reed, S., and R.C. Sautter (1990). "Children of Poverty: The status of 12 million young Americans." *Phi Delta Kappan, Special Report,* 17 (10), k1-k11.

Safe and Drug-Free Schools Program. *About Safe & Drug-Free Schools Program.* U.S. Department of Education. 12 June 1997. http://www.ed.gov/offices/OESE/SDFS/aboutSDFS.html

Safe, Disciplined and Drug-Free Schools. U.S. Department of Education. 18 June 1997. http://www.ed.gov/updates/PresEDPlan/part7.html

Sheley, Joseph F., et al. (1995). *Weapon Related Victimization in Selected Inner-City high School Samples. A Final Summary Report Presented to the National Institute of Justice.* Department of Justice, Washington, D.C., International Institute of Justice.

Star Schools Program, Biennial Evaluation Report-FY 93-94. U.S. Department of Education. 10 June 1997. http://www.ed.gov/pubs/biennial/617.html

Toch, Thomas, Ted Gest, and Monika Guttman (1993). "Violence in Schools." *U.S. News and World Report,* 8 November 1993.

U.S. Bureau of the Census. "Who's Minding the Kids." U.S. Department of Commerce. *Current Population Reports.* P-70, 1987.

Zill, Nicholas (1992). *Trends in Family Life and Children's School Performance.* Child Trends, Inc. Washington D.C.

Conclusions

Federal Interagency Forum on Child and Family Statistics. *America's Children: Key National Indicators of Well Being.* Washington, D.C. 1997.

Herrmann, Kenneth Jr. (1991). Social Workers and the United Nations Convention on the Rights of the Child. National Association of Social Workers, Inc. CCC Code: 0037-8046/91.

The Annie E. Casey Foundation. *Kidscount Data Book. State Profiles of Child Well Being.* Baltimore, 1995.

INDEX

A

Aber, J. Lawrence, 65
abortion, teenage, 115-116
abuse
    alcohol
        and child abuse and neglect,
            145
        educational goals regarding,
            167
        among parents of runaways,
            108
        among runaways, 109
        among students, 182, 230, 233
    child
        abandonment, 146
        child and parent rights, 143
        cultural difficulties, 143-144
        demographics of victims, 145
        diagnosis or detection, 144
        effect of economic
            deprivation, 4
        emotional/psychological, 144,
            146, 155
        fatalities, 145, 156
        general points in defining,
            145-146
        government programs, 3
        and homelessness, 66
        and juvenile court system, 130
        medical, 144, 155
        philosophy behind, 143
        physical, 107, 144, 145-146,
            155
        precursors, 145
        race/ethnicity of victims, 155
        reporting rates, 144
        and runaways, 107
        scenarios, 143, 144
        sexual, 107, 144, 145, 155
        by type of maltreatment, 144,
            155
        victim/abuser relationship, 155
        victims by age, 155
    spouse, 66
    substance abuse
        AIDS cases due to, 123
        and child abuse and neglect,
            145
        educational goals regarding,
            167
        and HIV/AIDS, 111
        and homelessness, 66, 68

among parents of runaways,
    108
and poverty, 178
among runaways, 109
in schools, 182
among students, 182, 229-230
and suicide, 114
trends, 117, 127
acculturation stress, 114
ACLU (American Civil Liberties
    Union), 185
Acquired Immune Deficiency
    Syndrome (AIDS), 111-112,
    123, 124
    cases by age and exposure
        category, 123
    cities with high rates of
        pediatric, 123
    deaths by race and sex under
        age 15, 123
    demographics, 111-112
    pediatric
        cases by state, 124
        by exposure category and
            race, 111
        as percent of cumulative
            cases, 124
adolescence
    defining, 6
    leading causes of death, 126
    pregnancy, 115-116
    premarital sexual activity, 116,
        178
    runaways, 108
    sexuality, 115-116
    substance abuse during, 117
    suicide, 113-114, 126
    as victims of crime, 140
    violence of
        and disconnection from
            adults, 142
        as public health issue, 141-143
Adoption Information Improve-
    ment Project (AIIP), 19
adoptions
    access to confidential records,
        54
    assistance legislation, 145
    confidentiality laws, 20, 54
    demographics, 19-21
    employer assistance, 76
    and foster care, 19-23
    monthly assistance claims, 53

national level information, 23
number of children, 53
percent of finalized, 55
special needs children, 20
transracial, 20-21
Adoption Technical Assistance
    Project (ATAP), 20
adult care food program, 74-75
adult court, juveniles in, 133, 147
AFDC. See Aid to Families with
    Dependent Children (AFDC)
African American children. See also
    African Americans
    criminal justice system
        as abuse victims, 155
        homicide victimization, 141-142
        as juvenile offenders, 135
        in private juvenile facilities,
            136
    demographics
        child mortality rates, 16, 46
        foster care and adoption, 20
        infant mortality rates, 14-16,
            45, 46
        living in poverty, 4
        as percent of U.S. population,
            16-17, 18
        population by state, 49, 52
        population description, 18
    education
        births to unwed mothers, 180
        disabilities, 161
        experience with school
            violence, 227
        high school completion rates,
            176, 226
        high school dropout rates,
            168, 169, 176, 177, 225
        incidence of health risks at
            birth, 168
        mathematics proficiency by
            age, 223
        mathematics proficiency by
            state, 175
        as percent of school enroll-
            ment, 158-159
        reading proficiency by age,
            222, 225
        reading proficiency by state,
            174
        school enrollment by state,
            188
        school failure risk, 182

school/parent contact, 220
school placement of gifted,
    234
school suspensions, 234
science proficiency by age,
    224
states with large school
    enrollments, 189
writing proficiency by age,
    225
health
    adolescent childbearing, 116
    deaths due to birth defects,
        118
    dental care, 117, 118
    incidence of health risks at
        birth, 168
    lead poisoning, 113
    pediatric AIDS, 111
    as percent of runaways, 108
    rate of SIDS among, 110, 122
    and teenage sexuality, 116
living conditions
    household characteristics and
        poverty, 63-64
    Medicaid recipients, 78
    poverty of, as percent of total
        by state, 86
    and substance abuse, 117
    time spent living in poverty,
        63-64
African Americans. See also African
    American children
    births to unwed mothers, 18
    and civil rights movement, 8
    family structure, 18
    income by education level, 169
    migrant workers, 11
    percent exiting poverty, 85
    as percent of homeless
        population, 68
    as percent of Northeastern U.S.
        counties, 244
    as percent of Northwestern U.S.
        counties, 246
    as percent of Pacific U.S.
        counties, 247
    as percent of Southeastern U.S.
        counties, 245
    as percent of Southwestern U.S.
        counties, 247
age. See also elderly
    of adult versus juvenile, 131

age (continued)
  and American Indian suicide, 114
  of child abuse and neglect victims, 145
  of children in foster care, 22, 56
  and determining criminal intent, 130-131
  distribution of time spent in poverty by, 64
  and exiting poverty, 64, 85
  of homeless, 67
  of homeless children, 66, 68
  homicide victimization rate by, 142
  in juvenile facilities, 136
  mathematical proficiency by ethnicity and sex, 223
  median U.S., 158
  Medicaid recipients by, 81
  of mother
    and AFDC benefits, 102
    and child care expense, 75
  and Native Alaskan suicide, 114
  of poor versus non-poor parents, 93
  poverty rates by, 61
  reading proficiency by ethnicity and sex, 222
  reading proficiency by sex and, 225
  risk of victimization by, 154
  school violence experience by race and, 227
  science proficiency by ethnicity and sex, 224
  suicide rates by, 126
  writing proficiency by ethnicity and sex, 225
aged. See elderly
aggravated assault, juvenile arrest rate for, 153
Agriculture, U.S. Department of, 61
Ahn, Helen Noh, 143
AIDS, 111-112, 123, 124
  cases by age and exposure category, 123
  cities with high rates of pediatric, 123
  deaths by race and sex under age 15, 123
  demographics, 111-112

pediatric
  cases by state, 124
  by exposure category and race, 111
  as percent of cumulative cases, 124
Aid to Families with Dependent Children (AFDC). See also Temporary Assistance to Needy Families (TANF)
  administrative expenditures, 82
  benefits as percent of poverty guidelines, 81
  benefits by state, 100, 101
  changes due to PRWORA, 102
  child care funding, 74-75, 77
  child care support, 73
  historical enrollment trends, 80
  and in-kind welfare programs, 77, 78
  and Medicaid, 104-105
  for migrant children, 11, 13
  percent of women returning to, 81
  recipients and payments by state, 37
  recipients as a percent of U.S. population, 80
  recipients' leaving, 82
  Title IV-E, 22-23, 56, 57
  welfare funding for, 78
AIIP (Adoption Information Improvement Project), 19
Alabama
  child care welfare reform, 71
  juvenile offender housing costs, 137
  rural population, 10
  sealing of juvenile records, 132
Alabama, University of, 180
Alaska. See also Native Alaskans
  American Indian children, 18
  educational investment gaps, 179
  juvenile custody rate, 136
  migrant children, 13
  Native American students, 159
  native children, 18-19
  proportion of children in population, 158
  public revenues per student, 166
  SIDS cases, 110
Alaskan natives. See Native

Alaskans
alcohol abuse. See also substance abuse
  and child abuse and neglect, 145
  educational goals regarding, 167
  among parents of runaways, 108
  among runaways, 109
  among students, 182, 230, 233
Aleut children. See Native Alaskan children
American Academy of Pediatrics, 98
American Association for Protecting Children, 144
American Civil Liberties Union (ACLU), 185
American Indian children. See also American Indians; Native American children
  Indian Child Welfare Act of 1978, 20
  living in poverty, 4
  pediatric AIDS, 111
  as percent of school enrollments, 159
  as percent of U.S. population, 16-17, 18
American Indians. See also American Indian children; Native Americans
  age of, 114
  demographics, 114
  education, 114
  family structure, 18
  income, 114
  population description, 18-19
  poverty, 19, 114
  suicide, 113-114, 126
  unemployment, 114
American Psychological Association, 180
American Public Welfare Association (APWA), 20
America's Children: Key National Indicators of Well Being, 238
Annenberg, Walter, 181
APSA (adolescent premarital sexual activity), 116
APWA (American Public Welfare Association), 20
Arizona
  American Indian children, 18
  fingerprinting of juveniles, 132

juvenile record laws, 132
measles outbreak, 106, 121
urban population of, 11
youth versus elderly population, 13, 42
Arkansas, rural population, 10
arrests, juvenile
  number of, as percent total arrests, 152
  states with highest, 140
  total, by state, 140, 156
  for violent crimes, 141, 153
Asian American children. See also Asian Americans; Pacific Islander children
  as abuse victims, 155
  demographics
    as percent of U.S. population, 16-17, 18
    population by state, 52
    population description, 17-18
  education
    high school dropout rate, 172, 176
    as percent of school enrollment, 159
    school enrollment by state, 191
    school/parent contact, 220
    school placement of gifted, 235
    school suspensions, 235
    states with large school enrollments of, 189
  living conditions
    as percent of population by state, 48
    poverty of, as percent of total by state, 87
  pediatric AIDS cases, 111, 124
Asian Americans. See also Asian American children; Pacific Islanders
  family structure, 18
  as percent of homeless population, 68
  as percent of Northeastern U.S. counties, 240
  as percent of Northwestern U.S. counties, 242
  as percent of Pacific U.S. counties, 243
  as percent of Southeastern U.S.

Asian Americans (continued)
counties, 241
as percent of Southwestern U.S. counties, 243
assault, juvenile arrest rate for aggravated, 153
ATAP (Adoption Technical Assistance Project), 20
At-Risk Child Care, 74-75, 77
Australia
gross domestic product for education, 199
income inequality, 63
Austria
child care support in, 73
gross domestic product for education, 199
income inequality, 63

B

baby boom, 163
Ball State University, 180
Bartelt, David, *Homelessness in Pennsylvania: How Can This Be?,* 66
Belgium
gross domestic product for education, 199
income inequality, 63
young child poverty rates, 64, 91
Bilingual Education Act, 172
birth defects, 118, 128
birth rates
in Northeastern U.S. counties, 256
in Northwestern U.S. counties, 258
in Pacific U.S. counties, 259
in Southeastern U.S. counties, 257
in Southwestern U.S. counties, 259
U.S. annual, 163
worldwide, 261
births to unwed mothers
African American, 18
and children's school failure risk, 182-183
effect of increase in, 3
and expected years of child poverty, 63
and violence, 180

welfare effect on, 60
white, 19
black children. *See* African American children
blacks. *See* African Americans
Blanchard, Loren, 179
blood lead level (BLL), 112, 125. *See also* Lead poisoning
Boston City Hospital, 180
Bourne, Richard, 144
Boxer, Andrew, 183
Britain. *See* Great Britain
broad scope definition of runaways, 107-108
Bureau of the Census, 61, 62, 78
Bureau of Justice Statistics, 179
Burnett, Gary, 159

C

California
criminal justice system
juvenile arrests in, 140
juvenile custody rate, 136
juvenile record laws, 132
public juvenile facilities, 137
demographics
African American children, 18
American Indian children, 18
Asian American children, 18
Hispanic children, 17
migrant children, 13
Title IV-E money spent, 22
urban population, 11
education
African American students, 159
Asian American students, 159
educational revenues, 165
high number of teachers, 172
Hispanic students, 159
immigrant students, 160
secondary school enrollment, 164
student/teacher ratios, 171
health
measles outbreak, 106, 121
runaways, 108
Cambodian children. *See* Asian American children
Canada
gross domestic product for education, 164, 199

income inequality, 63
mathematics proficiency by age, 176, 223
science proficiency by age, 224
young child poverty rates, 64, 91
capital punishment for juveniles, 133
Casey, Annie E., Foundation, 238
Casper, Lynne, "What Does it Cost to Mind Our Preschoolers?", 75
CASSP (Child and Adolescent Services System Program), 115
CDC (Centers for Disease Control and Prevention), 111-112
Center for Budget and Policy Priorities, 79, 80
Centers for Disease Control and Prevention (CDC), 111-112
child abuse and neglect
defining
child and parents' rights in, 143
cultural difficulties in, 143-144
general points in, 145-146
diagnosis or detection of, 144
effect of economic deprivation on, 4
fatalities, 145, 156
government programs, 3
and homelessness, 66
and juvenile court system, 130
philosophy behind, 143
precursors of, 145
reporting rates, 144
and runaways, 107
scenarios, 143, 144
types of
abandonment, 146
emotional/psychological, 144, 146, 155
medical, 144, 155
physical, 107, 144, 145-146, 155
sexual, 107, 144, 145, 155
victims
by age, 155
demographics, 145
race/ethnicity of, 155
relationship to abuser, 155
by type of maltreatment, 144, 155
Child and Adolescent Services System Program (CASSP), 115
child care
accreditation standards, 72

arrangements used, 95
and changes in parents' employment, 69
and development block grants, 70-71, 77
employers subsidizing, 76
financing, 73-76
food programs, 74-75
government programs, 3
latchkey children, 183-184
major areas of concern, 74-75
primary caregiver data, 68, 69, 70, 95
PRWORA changes, 79-80
social issues, 68-69
spending for family, 75
state spending, 99
child care centers
employer subsidized, 76
inspection frequency by state, 96
limits for adult/infant ratio in, 96
limits for adult/toddler ratio, 99
NAEYC accredited, 97
percent of children served by, 69
quality, 69, 74
child care workers
child abuse and neglect by, 145, 155
high turnover of, 75
child mortality. *See also* infant mortality rates
by child abuse and neglect, 145, 156
due to birth defects, 118, 128
from HIV/AIDS, 111
in juvenile detention facilities, 139-140
leading causes of, 46, 126, 128
from lead poisoning, 112
from low birth weight, 15
rates, 4, 16, 46
from respiratory distress syndrome (RDS), 15
from sudden infant death syndrome (SIDS), 15, 109-110, 122
suicide, 16
homosexual youth, 183
in juvenile detention facilities, 140
rates by age, 126
in runaway population, 109
teenage, 113-114

child mortality (continued)
 trend in rate of, 4
children. See also adolescence;
 female children; specific
 racial/ethnic groups
 average number of, per family,
  160
 decreasing percentage of, 8-9
 defining, 6
 effect of child care on, 68
 and elderly, comparison of, 2,
  13, 38, 42
 exploited, 109
 and growth of elderly population, 2
 homeless
  number of, 94
  percent of, 68, 69
  profiles of, 94
 missing, 109
 as percent of state population,
  24, 25
 perspective of, on poverty, 62
 population by state, 39-41
 poverty rates for, 3, 61
 runaway, 107-109
 school-age population, 24, 158-160
 state-funded programs for, 65-
  66, 92
 as victims of abuse and neglect,
  143-145, 155, 156
 worsening status of, 4
Children in Custody Census, 130
Children's Bureau, 19
Children's Defense Fund, 2, 60, 180
Children's Well-Being indicators,
 238
child support, state enforcement
 of, 101
Child Trends, Inc., 238
Child Welfare Act, 145
Child Welfare League of America,
 19, 78
Child Welfare Services Program
 (Title IV-B), 22
Chinese children. See Asian American children
cigarettes, students' use of, 182, 230
city comparisons
 disposition of juvenile offenders,
  147
 homelessness, 68, 94
 lead poisoning, 125

minority students, 195
pediatric AIDS cases, 123
school district enrollments, 195
civil rights movement, 8
Clinton, Bill, 77, 181
Coalition of Essential Schools, 181
cocaine, percent of students using,
 182, 229, 233
Colorado
 age of juvenile status, 131
 SIDS cases, 110
community structure and youth
 violence, 141
confidentiality
 of adoption records, 54
 in juvenile court system, 130,
  131-133, 154
Connecticut
 expungement of juvenile
  records, 132
 minority children, 11
 pediatric AIDS cases, 112, 124
 SIDS cases, 110
Consumer Price Index, 2
Cornell University Family Life
 Development Center, 62
Council of Economic Advisors, 61
Council of State and Territorial
 Epidemiologists (CSTE), 112
counties
 low-income nonmetropolitan,
  10, 12
 rural versus urban juvenile
  offenders, 147
county populations
 African Americans as percent of,
  244-247
 Asian Americans as percent of,
  240-243
 children as percent of, 9, 25
 children as percent of U.S., 26-33
 Hispanics as percent of, 248-251
 Native Alaskans as percent of,
  252-255
 Native Americans as percent of,
  252-255
 Pacific Islanders as percent of,
  240-243
courts
 juvenile
  causes for intervention by, 130
  characteristics of juveniles in,
   135-136

confidentiality in, 130, 131-
 133, 154
fingerprinting, 132
goals, 130, 131
public versus private facilities,
 133-134, 136-137, 139-140
record keeping in, 131-133,
 134-135, 154
referral of juveniles to adult
 court, 133
juveniles in adult, 133, 147
juveniles in criminal, 133, 147
CPS (Current Population Survey), 62
crime. See also violence
 among runaways, 109
 children as victims of, 140-141,
  154-156
 committed by youth, 140, 141,
  152-153, 156
 victimization of students, 179-
  181, 227
criminal court, juveniles in, 133, 147
criminal intent, age, and determining, 130-131
criminal justice system
 conditions of confinement/
  facilities, 136-139
 juvenile court system, 130-136,
  147
 runaways and, 109
 states' costs for adults and juveniles in, 148
 youth as agents and as victims
  of crime, 140-145
criminal records among parents of
 runaways, 108
CSTE (Council of State and Territorial Epidemiologists), 112
cultural illiteracy, 4
cultural sensitivity in child abuse
 issues, 144
culture of violence, 179
Current Population Survey (CPS), 62
CWSP (Child Welfare Services
 Program), 22

D

Darling-Hammond, Linda, 169
death of children. See child mortality
death penalty for juveniles, 133

Delaware, age of juvenile status,
 131
delinquent acts, 136. See also
 juvenile entries
delinquent offenses, 130. See also
 juvenile entries
Demographic Analysis of Child
 hood Poverty (Rogers), 63
demographics of children
 changing racial/ethnic makeup,
  16-19
 dependency ratio, 13-14, 38-42
 foster care and adoptions, 19-23
 infant and child mortality, 14-16,
  43-46
 migrant farm workers, 11
 as percent of U.S. population, 8-9
 rural-urban contrasts, 10-13
 school-age population, 24, 158-
  160
 spatial distribution, 9
Denmark
 gross domestic product for
  education, 199
 income inequality, 63
 young child poverty rates, 64, 91
dental care, 117-118
dependency ratio, 13-14, 38-42
depression
 among homeless children, 68
 among parents of runaways, 108
 in runaway population, 109
detention centers
 educational standards, 138-139,
  151
 number of admissions, 137
 number of juvenile, 139
 percent conforming to federal
  standards, 151
 percent of juveniles residing in,
  137
developing countries, preschool
 programs in, 73
development block grants for child
 care, 70-71, 74-75, 77
diphtheria and tetanus toxoids and
 pertussis (DTP) vaccine, 105-107,
 168
disabilities
 children with
  classroom interventions for,
   161
  in foster care, 22, 56

disabilities (continued)
    inclusion, 161
    Medicaid expenditures, 104
    preschool for, 183
    by race, 161
    school enrollment, 160-161
    special education funding, 167
    SSI benefits, 78
    definition, 160
    in heads of household, and
        poverty, 63
    mental retardation, 161
    serious emotional disturbances,
        161
    specific learning, 160, 161, 194
    speech/language impairment,
        160, 161
discipline in schools, 181-182, 232
disconnection, youth/adult, as fac-
    tor in youth violence, 142
discrimination
    protection for disabled children,
        160
    sexual orientation, 183
    against youth in employment
        and education, 143
diseases. See also health care;
    immunizations
    HIV/AIDS, 111-112, 123, 124
    related to SIDS, 110
    in runaway population, 109
    U.S. prevention of, 106-107
District of Columbia. See Washing-
    ton, D.C.
divorce
    and children's school failure risk,
        182
    effect of high rates, 3
    and suicide, 114
    and working mothers, 184
domestic violence, 66. See also vio-
    lence
dropout rates
    event, 168, 169, 176, 177
    homosexuals', 183
    by reason, sex, and race, 225
    Spanish-speaking students, 172
drug abuse. See alcohol abuse;
    substance abuse
drug offenses by juveniles, 135-
    136, 180
DTP vaccine, 105-107, 168
Duncan, Greg J., 63

E

early childhood, defining, 6
early childhood education. See also
    education
    for disabled children, 183
    government funding, 70-71
    international, 71-73
    participation related to income,
        168
    and readiness to learn, 168
    state government programs, 65,
        92
    trends, 163-164
early school years, defining, 6
earned income tax credit (EITC)
    effect on child poverty, 60
    welfare funding for, 78
economy. See also income; poverty
    effect of global restructuring
        on child poverty, 60
    effect of inflation on children's
        programs, 2
    gross domestic product in, 4,
        164, 199, 216
    and homelessness, 66
    slave, and population of
        children, 9
education. See also early childhood
    education; Head Start; schools;
    special education; teachers
    African American children, 18
    American Indian children, 18-19
    American Indians, 114
    annual total spending, 171
    Asian American children, 18
    children at risk of failure, 182-
        183
    discrimination against youth in,
        143
    economically challenged
        students, 177-178
    enrollment, 163-164, 213
    financing of
        expenditures by function, 165-
            166
        expenditures for gifted
            students, 186, 187
        expenditures per student, 166,
            178-179, 205
        investment gaps in, 178-179,
            227, 228
        investment over time, 165, 217

by level of instruction, 218
measuring investment, 166-167
public versus private, 218
school expenditures versus
    revenues, 166, 204, 205
school revenues, 165, 207
by source of funds, 217, 218,
    227
sources by state, 217
special education, 167
gifted and talented children,
    185-187, 234-236
of head of household, and
    poverty, 63
Hispanic children, 17
and homelessness, 66, 68
home schooling, 184-185, 233
homosexual students, 183
human resources spending, 171-
    172
income by race and, 169
international comparisons, 164,
    199
investment gaps, 178-179, 227,
    228
in juvenile facilities
    assessment criteria for, 138
    staffing ratios in, 138-139, 151
    standards conformity in, 138-
        139, 151
latchkey children, 183-184
of migrant children, 11, 13
national commitment to educa-
    tion, 164
of parents
    and child care expense, 76
    and homelessness, 67
    and school discipline, 232
of poor versus non-poor parents,
    93
quality, 167-171
safety, discipline, and substance
    abuse in, 179-182
school-age population
    demographics, 158-159
    disabled children, 160-161
    immigrants, 158, 159-160
    institutional adjustments, 158
sex, 115, 183
state commitment to, 164, 199
structure, 162
student performance
    educational achievement, 172

high school completion rates,
    176, 226
levels of proficiency, 172-176,
    185
school dropouts, 168, 169, 176,
    177, 225
student/teacher ratio, 171, 220,
    221
white children, 19
Education, U.S. Department of,
    181, 185, 186
educational effort, 167, 206, 218
Education Consolidation and
    Improvement Act, 196
Education for All Handicapped
    Children Act, 160
The Education Trust, 169, 178
Educators for Social Responsibility,
    181
8th-grade proficiency testing, 172-
    176
EITC (earned income tax credit)
    effect on child poverty, 60
    welfare funding for, 78
Elam, Stanley, 181-182, 232
elderly
    and children, comparison of, 2,
        13, 38, 42
    Medicaid expenditures for, 104
    population of youth versus, 42
    poverty rates, 3, 60, 61
elementary schools, 162-164, 232.
    See also education; schools
emotional neglect of children,
    107
employee benefits, subsidized child
    care, 76
employers, subsidizing child care,
    76
employment. See also unemploy-
    ment
    changing pattern of parents', 69
    and child care, 68
    discrimination against youth in,
        143
    and homelessness, 67
    of homeless population, 68
    improvement in, and homeless-
        ness, 66
    and poverty, 65
    PRWORA requirements for, 79
entitlements, by family type, 93
Eskimo children. See Native

Alaskan children
ethnicity. *See* race/ethnicity
event drop out rates, 168, 169, 176, 177
exploited children, 109
expungement of juvenile records, 131-132, 154

F

families. *See also* family structure; single-parent families
  average number of children, 160
  child care arrangements used by, 95
  as factor in youth violence, 142
  homelessness, 66-69
  mother-only, 3
  as percent of homeless population, 68
  persistent poverty in, 63
  single parent, and expected years of child poverty, 63, 85
  size of, and children's school success, 182-183
  trend in rate of single-parent, 4
  two parent, and expected years of child poverty, 63, 85
family abductee children, 109. *See also* runaways
family child care, 97. *See also* child care centers
family preservation and support services legislation, 145
family structure. *See also* families; single-parent families; two-parent families
  of AFDC recipients, 102
  African American, 18
  American Indian, 18
  Asian American, 18
  change in percent of working mothers, 69
  and child abuse and neglect, 145
  and child care, 68
  distribution of poor by, 85
  entitlements by, 93
  and exiting poverty, 64, 85
  female heads, 93, 105
  and high school dropout rate, 176
  Hispanic, 17

and infant mortality, 15
  poor versus non-poor female family head, 93
  trends in children's, 95
  and violence, 180
  white, 19
farming and population of children, 9
fatalities. *See* child mortality; infant mortality
fathers. *See also* males; parents
  and adolescent pregnancy, 116
  and child support, 101
federal government. *See* government, federal
female children. *See also* children; females
  high school completion rates, 176, 226
  high school dropout rates, 169, 176, 177, 225
  homicide victimization rate, 142
  homosexuality in, 183
  as juvenile offenders, 135
  versus male children in juvenile facilities, 136
  mathematics proficiency by age, 223
  as percent of school-age children, 158
  reading proficiency by age, 222, 225
  runaways, 108
  science proficiency by age, 224
  SIDS cases, 110
  as victims of abuse and neglect, 145
  writing proficiency by age, 225
females. *See also* female children; mothers
  as family heads, 93, 105
  high school dropout rates, 169, 176, 177, 225
  homicide victimization rate, 142
  as juvenile offenders, 135
  versus male children in juvenile facilities, 136
  mathematics proficiency by age, 223
  as percent of school-age children, 158
  reading proficiency by age, 222, 225

runaways, 108
science proficiency by age, 224
SIDS cases, 110
as victims of abuse and neglect, 145
writing proficiency by age, 225
fertility rates for racial and ethnic groups, 9, 25
Fijian children. *See* Asian American children
Filipino children. *See* Asian American children
financing
  of child care, 73-76
  of education
    expenditures by function, 165-166
    expenditures for gifted students, 186, 187
    expenditures per student, 166, 178-179, 205
    investment gaps, 178-179, 227, 228
    investment over time, 165, 217
    by level of instruction, 218
    measuring investment, 166-167
    public versus private, 218
    school expenditures versus revenues, 166, 204, 205
    school revenues, 165, 207
    by source of funds, 218, 227
    special education, 167
    of schools
      by source of funds, 217
      sources by state, 217
fingerprinting of juveniles, 132
Finland
  gross domestic product for education, 199
  income inequality, 63
  young child poverty rates, 64, 91
firearms. *See* guns; violence
fiscal conservatism, 2-3
Florida
  African American children, 18
  educational revenues, 165
  high number of teachers, 172
  Hispanic children, 17
  immigrant students, 160
  juvenile arrests, 140
  measles outbreak, 106, 121
  migrant children, 13
  migrant workers, 11

pediatric AIDS cases, 112, 124
youth versus elderly population, 13, 42
Food Stamp Program. *See also* welfare
  effect on child poverty, 60
  entitlements for young children, 93
  for migrant children, 11
  PRWORA changes to, 80, 81, 102
  received by poor versus non-poor parents, 93
  welfare funding for, 77
foster care
  child abuse and neglect in, 145, 155
  children entering and leaving, 56
  demographics, 21
  and homelessness, 66
  monthly maintenance rates by state, 57
  population by state, 54, 55
  for special needs children, 55
  Title IV-E expenditures, 22-23, 56
France
  child care support, 73
  gross domestic product for education, 199
  income inequality, 63
  reading proficiency by age, 222
  young child poverty rates, 64, 91
The Future of Children, 74, 77, 78

G

gangs, 180
GAO (Government Accounting Office), 23
Garbarino, James, 62, 142
Garibaldi, Antoine M., 179
gay youth, 183
GDP (gross domestic product), 4, 164, 199, 216
gender. *See* fathers; females; males; mothers
General Accounting Office, 4, 66
geographic regions
  Middle Atlantic
    children in population, 158
    secondary school enrollment, 164

geographic regions *(continued)*
  Midwest
    child abuse and neglect, 144
    juvenile detention facility
      deaths, 140
    juvenile offender housing
      costs, 137
    mathematics proficiency, 173,
      224
  Northeast
    African American county
      populations, 244
    Asian American county
      populations, 240
    birth rates by county, 256
    child care expense, 76
    expenditures per student, 166
    Hispanic county populations,
      248
    juvenile detention facility
      deaths, 140
    juvenile offender housing
      costs, 137
    lead poisoning, 112
    Native Alaskan county popula-
      tions, 252
    Native American county popu-
      lations, 252
    Pacific Islander county popula-
      tions, 240
  Northwest
    African American county pop-
      ulations, 246
    Asian American county popu-
      lations, 242
    birth rates by county, 258
    Hispanic county populations,
      250
    Native Alaskan county popula-
      tions, 254
    Native American county popu-
      lations, 254
    Pacific Islander county popula-
      tions, 242
  Pacific
    African American county pop-
      ulations, 247
    Asian American county popu-
      lations, 243
    birth rates by county, 259
    Hispanic county populations,
      251
    Native Alaskan county popula-

tions, 255
    Native American county popu-
      lations, 255
    Pacific Islander county popula-
      tions, 243
  Pacific Northwest, secondary
    school enrollment, 164
  South
    child care expense, 76
    expected years of poverty, 63
    juvenile detention facility
      deaths, 140
    percent of children, 9
    rural poverty, 10
  South Atlantic
    children in population, 158
    secondary school enrollment,
      164
  Southeast
    African American county pop-
      ulation, 245
    Asian American county popu-
      lations, 241
    birth rates by county, 257
    child abuse and neglect, 144
    Hispanic county populations,
      249
    Native Alaskan county popula-
      tions, 253
    Native American county popu-
      lations, 253
    Pacific Islander county popula-
      tions, 241
  Southwest
    African American county pop-
      ulations, 247
    Asian American county popu-
      lations, 243
    birth rates by county, 259
    Hispanic county populations,
      251
    Native Alaskan county popula-
      tions, 255
    Native American county popu-
      lations, 255
    Pacific Islander county popula-
      tions, 243
  West, juvenile detention facility
    deaths, 140
  West South Central U.S., percent
    of children, 9
Georgia
  African American children, 18

infant mortality rates, 14
migrant workers, 11
rural population, 10
Germany
  child care support, 73
  gross domestic product for
    education, 199
  income inequality, 63
  young child poverty rates, 64, 91
gifted students, 185-187, 234-236
Gilliam, G., 142
global economic restructuring,
  effect on child poverty, 60
Goals 2000 legislation, 182
Goldstein, Ira, *Homelessness in
  Pennsylvania: How Can This Be?*,
  66
government. *See also* politics
  federal
    Bilingual Education Act, 172
    child care funding, 73-76
    child care payments by state, 71
    child versus adult spending by,
      38
    commitment to children, 3
    disability discrimination laws,
      160
    Goals 2000 legislation, 182
    gross domestic product for
      education, 164, 199, 216
    immunization drive, 106
    Improving America's Schools
      legislation, 182
    operation of schools, 162
    response to child welfare, 3
    revenues for schools, 217
    Safe Schools Act of 1993, 181
    school funding, 165
    school legislation, 158, 160,
      172, 182
    standards for juvenile care
      facilities, 137-139, 151
  programs
    for adoption of special needs
      children, 20
    for child abuse and neglect, 3
    child care, 3, 70-71
    and decrease in child poverty,
      60
    dependency ratio effect on,
      13-14
    early childhood, 70-71
    European, 3

health care (*See* Medicaid)
    for homelessness, 66-69
    housing, 3
    job training, 3
    nutrition, 3
    Omnibus Budget Reconcilia-
      tion Act, 3
    and poverty, 8, 20, 22
    for special education, 3
    sponsoring preschool services,
      72-73
    supporting child care, 73-76
    Title IV-B, 22
    Title IV-E, 20, 22-23, 56, 57
    welfare, 77-81
  state and local
    agencies handling juvenile
      facilities, 147
    child care spending, 99
    early childhood education, 65-
      66, 92
    funding for child care, 73-76
    gifted student programs, 187
    gross state product for educa-
      tion, 164, 199
    Head Start programs, 65, 92
    home school legislation, 185
    homosexuality discrimination
      legislation, 183
    immunization requirements,
      106, 120
    juvenile detention facilities,
      137, 147-149
    mental health facilities, 115,
      127
    operation of schools, 162
    responsibility for children, 3,
      238
    revenues for schools, 217
    school funding, 165
    school legislation, 158
    welfare management, 78-79
Government Accounting Office
  (GAO), 23
Great Britain. *See also* United
  Kingdom
  gross domestic product for
    education, 199
  income inequality, 63
  young child poverty rates, 64, 91
Great Depression, 60
gross domestic product (GDP), 4,
  164, 199, 216

gross state product (GSP), 164, 199
guns. *See also* violence
    educational goals regarding, 167
    in juvenile crimes, 140
    number of youth killed by, 180
    students/youths carrying, 180, 182
Gustafsson, Siv, 73

H

Haemophilus influenzae type b
    (Hib) vaccine, 106-107
Haitian migrant workers, 11
hallucinogens, student use of, 182,
    229, 233
handguns. *See* guns; violence
Harper, Suzanne, 180
Harris, Lou, and Associates, 179
Havemann, Judith, 70-71
Hawaii
    Asian American children, 18
    Asian American students, 159
    GSP commitment to education,
        164
    minority versus white children,
        17
Head Start. *See also* early child-
        hood education
    overview, 72, 74-75
    as safety net, 73
    state government programs for,
        65, 92
    welfare funding for, 77-78
health, public, youth violence
    as issue of, 141-143
Health and Human Services, U.S.
    Department of, 113, 238
    Migrant Education Program, 11,
        13
    Migrant School Record Transfer
        System, 11, 13
health care
    birth defects, 118, 128
    children's supplemental, 65, 92
    dental care, 117-118
    and education, 168, 183
    entitlements for young children,
        93
    in foster care, 22, 56
    government programs, 3
    and homelessness, 66
    immunizations, 105-107, 119-121

requirements for child care, 98
in juvenile detention facilities,
    139-140
leading causes of death, 46
and lead poisoning, 112-113, 125
Medicaid
    eligibility requirements, 104
    overview, 104-105
    payments by eligibility group,
        105
    PRWORA changes to, 80, 102
    reasons for increase in, 105
    recipient characteristics, 81
    recipients and payments by
        eligibility groups, 104
    users by eligibility group, 105
    welfare funding for, 78
mental, 109, 114-115, 127, 139
for migrant children, 11, 13
and poverty, 177
prenatal, and infant mortality, 15
risks at birth, 183, 231
for runaways, 109
substance abuse (*See* substance
    abuse)
sudden infant death syndrome
    (SIDS), 109-110, 122
teenage sexuality, 115-116
teen suicide, 113-114, 126
health insurance
    children lacking, 4
    children under age 19 by type of,
        104
    for dental care, 117, 118
    private versus public, 104
hemophilia, AIDS cases due to, 123
hepatitis B vaccine, 106-107
Herdt, Gilbert, 183
heroin, percent of students using,
    182, 230, 233
Hetrick-Martin Institute, 183
Hib vaccine, 106-107
high schools. *See also* education;
    schools
    completion rates, 4, 168, 176,
        226
    dropout rates, 168, 169, 176,
        177, 225
    dropout reasons, 225
    Hispanic enrollment in, 172
    structure of, 162
    student perspective on discipline,
        232

Hispanic children. *See also*
    Hispanics
    criminal justice system
        as abuse victims, 155
        as juvenile offenders, 135
    demographics
        living in poverty, 5
        migrant farm workers, 11, 13
        as percent of population by
            state, 47
        as percent of U.S. population,
            16-17, 18
        population by state, 52
        population description, 17
    education
        disabilities, 161
        educational achievement, 172
        experience with school
            violence, 227
        high school completion rates,
            176, 226
        high school dropout rates, 168,
            169, 172, 176, 177, 225
        incidence of health risks at
            birth, 168
        living in poverty, 177
        mathematics proficiency by
            age, 223
        mathematics proficiency by
            state, 175
        as percent of school enroll-
            ment, 158-159
        reading proficiency by age,
            222, 225
        reading proficiency by state,
            174
        school enrollment by state, 190
        school failure risk, 182
        school/parent contact, 220
        school placement of gifted, 235
        school suspensions, 235
        science proficiency by age, 224
        states with large school enroll-
            ments, 189
        writing proficiency by age, 225
    health
        lead poisoning, 113
        pediatric AIDS cases, 111, 112
        and substance abuse, 117
        and teenage sexuality, 116
    poverty of, as percent of total by
        state, 88
Hispanics. *See also* Hispanic

children; Latinos
    family structure, 17
    percent exiting poverty, 85
    as percent of homeless popula-
        tion, 68
    as percent of Northeastern U.S.
        counties, 248
    as percent of Northwestern U.S.
        counties, 250
    as percent of Pacific U.S. coun-
        ties, 251
    as percent of Southeastern U.S.
        counties, 249
    as percent of Southwestern U.S.
        counties, 251
HIV (Human Immunodeficiency
    Virus), 111-112, 123, 124. *See
    also* AIDS
Hmong children. *See* Asian Ameri-
    can children
Holland. *See* Netherlands
homelessness
    of children under 16, 94
    composition of population in,
        68-69
    demographics, 67
    estimation of U.S., 4
    and homosexuality, 183
    number of residences prior to, 67
    and runaways, 107
    trends, 66-69
*Homelessness in Pennsylvania:
    How Can This Be?*, 66
home schooling, 184-185, 233
Homes for the Homeless, Inc., 67
homicide. *See also* crime; violence
    African American and white
        children as victims of, 142
    children witnessing, 180
    juvenile arrest rate for, 153
    in juvenile detention facilities,
        140
    juveniles' use of guns in, 140
    trend in rate of teen, 4
    victimization rate by age, 142
homosexuality. *See also* sexuality
    AIDS cases due to, 123
    and homelessness, 183
    in-school harassment due to, 183
Hong Kong, preschool programs,
    73
housing. *See also* homelessness
    government programs, 3

housing (continued)
   for migrant children, 11, 13
   rural, 10, 34, 63, 117
   subsidized, for young children, 93
   urban, 10-11, 34, 63, 93, 106-107
   waiting period for public, 68
   welfare funding, 78
Human Immunodefiency Virus
   (HIV), 111-112, 123, 124

I

IAEP (International Assessment of
   Educational Progress), 176
Idaho
   African American children, 18
   juvenile arrests, 140
   measles outbreak, 106, 121
   SIDS cases, 110
IDEA (Individuals with Disabilities
   Education Act), 160, 167, 193, 196
Illinois
   African American children, 18
   African American students, 159
   Asian American students, 159
   educational revenues, 165
   GSP commitment to education,
     164
   high number of teachers, 172
   Hispanic children, 17
   immigrant students, 160
illiteracy, cultural, 4. See also reading proficiency testing
immigrants
   and population of children, 9
   PRWORA benefit changes for,
     80-81, 102
   and U.S. education system, 158
immigration
   by area of origin, 17
   effect on U.S. educational
     system, 158, 159-160
   high, contributing to homeless-
     ness, 66
   historical statistics by decade, 195
   as percent of U.S. population by
     decade, 195
Immigration and Naturalization
   Service, 19
immunizations. See also health care

children's lack of, 106-107
children with complete, 119, 208
diphtheria and tetanus toxoids
   and pertussis (DTP), 105-107,
   168
and education, 183
effect on ability to learn, 168
exemption rationale, 120
Haemophilus influenzae type b
   (Hib), 106-107
hepatitis B, 106-107
measles-mumps-rubella (MMR),
   106-107, 168
oral polio vaccine, 106-107, 168
recommended schedule for, 107
requirements, 98, 105-107, 120,
   168
Improving America's Schools
   legislation, 182
IMR. See infant mortality rates
inclusion, for disabled children,
   161, 167
income. See also poverty
   for American Indians, 114
   children by levels of, 60
   counties with low, 10, 12
   definitions of, for poverty
     estimates, 84
   and early childhood education
     participation, 168
   by educational level and race, 169
   event dropout rates by, 176, 177
   inequality, 62-63, 65
   international comparison of
     family, 62-63
   positive effect of education on,
     168
   versus public revenues per
     student, 165
   rural versus urban, 10, 11
income transfers, effect of, on
   estimates of poverty, 84
Indiana, juvenile records laws, 132
Indian children. See American
   Indian children; Asian American
   children; Native American
   children
Indian Child Welfare Act of 1978, 20
Individuals with Disabilities Education Act (IDEA), 160, 167, 193, 196
infant mortality rates (IMR). See
   also child mortality

African American, 18
Asian American, 46
by cause of death, 110
decrease in U.S., 4
demographics, 14-16, 43-46
due to birth defects, 118
Hispanic, 17, 46
for migrant children, 13
Native American, 46
by race and cause, 45
by state, 43, 44
worldwide, 260
inflation, effect on children's
   programs, 2
Institute for Research on Poverty,
   238
insurance. See health insurance;
   Medicaid
International Assessment of
   Educational Progress (IAEP),
   176
international comparisons. See also
     worldwide statistical informa-
     tion
   child care, 71-73
   children's quality of life, 62
   education, 185
   of educational investments, 164,
     199
   family income, 63
   infant mortality rates, 14
   mathematics proficiency by age,
     176, 223
   reading proficiency by age, 176,
     222
   science proficiency by age, 176,
     224
   of young child poverty, 91
Inuit children. See Native Alaskan
   children
Iowa
   pediatric AIDS cases, 112, 124
   youth versus elderly population,
     13, 42
Ireland
   gross domestic product for
     education, 199
   income inequality, 63
Israel, income inequality, 63
Italy
   child care support, 73
   income inequality, 63

reading proficiency by age, 222
young child poverty rates, 64, 91

J

jails, juveniles in, 133, 136
Japan
   gross domestic product for
     education, 199
   preschool programs, 73
Japanese children. See Asian American children
Javits, Jacob J., Gifted and Talented
   Students Education Program, 187
job training, government programs
   for parents, 3
junior high schools, 162, 232. See
   also education; schools
just deserts penal philosophy, 132,
   133, 136
Justice, U.S. Department of, 135
justice system. See criminal justice
   system; juvenile court system
juvenile arrests
   number of, as percent of total
     arrests, 152
   states with highest, 140
   total, by state, 140, 156
   for violent crimes, 141, 153
juvenile court system
   causes for intervention by, 130
   characteristics of juveniles in,
     135-136
   confidentiality in, 130, 131-133,
     154
   fingerprinting, 132
   goals, 130, 131
   public versus private facilities,
     133-134, 136-137, 139-140
   recordkeeping in, 131-133, 134-
     135, 154
   referral of juveniles to adult
     court, 133
juvenile custody rate, 136, 146, 150
juvenile detention facilities
   admissions by facility type, 137
   conditions of confinement, 137-
     139, 151
   deaths in, 139-140
   percent of residents by type, 137
juvenile offenders

characteristics, 135-136
cost of housing, 137
crimes committed by, 135-136
number of and custody rate per state, 150
police disposition of, 147

K

Kansas
  GSP commitment to education, 164
  school district operation, 162
Kellogg, J. B., 160
Kentucky
  child poverty rates in, 60
  rural population in, 10
Kidder, Tracy, 158
Kidscount, 238
kindergartens, 162. *See also* early childhood education
Knitzer, Jane, 65
  unclaimed Children, 115
Korea. *See* South Korea
Korean children. *See* Asian American children

L

language
  as barrier to migrant children, 11, 13
  and educational achievement, 172
  primary, of U.S. citizens, 160
  and risk of school failure, 182
Laotian children. *See* Asian American children
latchkey children, 183-184
Latino children. *See* Hispanic children
Latinos. *See also* Hispanics
  income by education level, 169
  as percent of runaways, 108
laws. *See* legislation
lead poisoning, 112-113, 125
learning disabilities, 160, 161, 194
LEAs (local education agencies), 187

legislation
  adoption assistance, 145
  adoption confidentiality, 20, 54
  family preservation and support services, 145
  Goals 2000, 182
  home school, 185
  homosexuality discrimination, 183
  school, 158, 160, 172, 182
lesbian youth, 183
life expectancies
  increase in U.S., 4
  worldwide, 262
Lincoln, Abraham, 130
Links Between Early Childhood Programs and Maternal Employment in Three Countries (Gustafsson and Stafford), 73
literacy assessment. *See* reading proficiency testing
local education agencies (LEAs), 187
local government. *See* government, state and local
Los Angeles Times, 180
Louisiana
  child care welfare reform, 71
  child poverty rates, 60, 61
  GSP commitment to education, 164
  rural population, 10
low birth weight
  infant death from, 15
  and mother's age and race, 16
  and risk of school failure, 183
LSD, student use of, 182, 229, 233
Luxembourg, income inequality, 63
Luxembourg Income Study, 62

M

Maine
  infant mortality rates, 14
  public juvenile facilities, 137
  pupil/staff ratio, 171
  white children, 19
major metropolitan statistical areas (MSAs), 9, 24
male children. *See also* children; males versus female children in

juvenile facilities, 136
  high school completion rates, 176, 226
  high school dropout rates, 169, 176, 177, 225
  homicide victimization of, 141-142
  homosexuality in, 183
  mathematics proficiency by age, 223
  as percent of school-age children, 158
  reading proficiency by age, 222, 225
  runaways, 108
  science proficiency by age, 224
  SIDS cases, 110
  as victims of abuse and neglect, 145
  writing proficiency by age, 225
males. *See also* fathers; male children
  versus female children in juvenile facilities, 136
  high school dropout rates, 169, 176, 177, 225
  homicide victimization of, 141-142, 142
  mathematics proficiency by age, 223
  as percent of school-age children, 158
  reading proficiency by age, 222, 225
  runaways, 108
  science proficiency by age, 224
  SIDS cases, 110
  as victims of abuse and neglect, 145
  writing proficiency by age, 225
March of Dimes, 118
marijuana, percent of students using, 182, 229, 233
marital status. *See also* divorce
  of parents, 95
  of poor vs. non-poor parents, 93
  and women's employment, 70
  of working women, 70
Maryland, measles outbreak, 106, 121
Massachusetts
  fingerprinting of juveniles, 132

GSP commitment to education, 164
Hispanic children, 17
homosexuality discrimination legislation, 183
mathematics proficiency testing, 173, 175, 225
measles-mumps-rubella (MMR) vaccine, 106-107, 168
measles outbreaks, 106, 121
"Measuring Poverty: Issues and Approaches" (Weinberg), 61
MECISP (Medical Examiner/Coroner Information Sharing Program), 110
Medicaid
  eligibility requirements, 104
  overview, 104-105
  payments by eligibility group, 105
  PRWORA changes to, 80, 102
  reasons for increase in, 105
  recipient characteristics, 81
  recipients and payments by eligibility groups, 104
  users by eligibility group, 105
  welfare funding for, 78
medical care. *See* health care; Medicaid
Medical Examiner/Coroner Information Sharing Program (MECISP), 110
men. *See* males
mental health, 109, 114-115, 127, 139
mental illness
  and child abuse and neglect, 145
  as educational disability, 161
  in juvenile detention facilities, 139
  in parents of runaways, 108
  as percent of homeless population, 68
  in runaways, 109
mental retardation, 161
MEP (Migrant Education Program), 11, 13, 35, 36
metal detectors, in schools, 180-181
metropolitan households. *See* urban households
Mexican migrant workers, 11
Michigan
  African American students, 159

Michigan (continued)
  American Indian children, 18
  educational revenues, 165
  fingerprinting of juveniles, 132
  juvenile records laws, 132
  migrant children, 13
Michigan, University of, 179, 180
Middle Atlantic U.S.
  proportion of children in popula-
    tion, 158
  secondary school enrollment,
    164
middle schools, 162, 232
Midwestern U.S.
  child abuse and neglect, 144
  juvenile detention facility
    deaths, 140
  juvenile offender housing costs,
    137
  mathematics proficiency, 173,
    224
Migrant Clinicians Network, 13
Migrant Education Program (MEP),
  11, 13, 35, 36
migrant farm workers
  children of, 11, 13
  streams of, 34
Migrant School Record Transfer
  System (MSRTS), 11, 13
migrant workers
  African Americans, 11
  Haitian, 11
  Mexican, 11
  Puerto Rican, 11
Mills v. Board of Education, 160
Minnesota, GSP commitment to
  education, 164
minorities. *See also* race/ethnicity
  dental care, 117
  disparity in teacher preparedness,
    221
  and expenditures per student,
    179
  fertility rates, 9, 25
  informal adoptions, 19
  as juvenile offenders, 135
  mental health services, 115
  pediatric AIDS risk, 112
  as percent of school-age popula-
    tion, 158-159
  as percent of U.S. children, 9
  school demographics, 177-178
  unimmunized children, 106-107

in urban households, 10-11
missing children, 109. *See also* run-
  aways
Mississippi
  African American children, 18
  child poverty rates, 60, 61
  juvenile offender housing costs,
    137
  public revenues per student, 166
  rural population, 10
Missouri, educational investment
  gaps, 179
Mistral, Gabriela, 2
MMR vaccine, 106-107, 168
MMWR (Morbidity and Mortality
  Report), 112
modal grade, 172
Montana
  African American children, 18
  Native American students, 159
  proportion of children in popula-
    tion, 158
  SIDS cases, 110
Morbidity and Mortality Report
  (MMWR), 112
mortality rates. *See* child mortality;
infant mortality rates
mother-only families, 3
  contributing to child poverty, 60
mother-only households, and
  poverty, 64, 85
mothers. *See also* females; parents
  age
    and AFDC benefits, 102
    and child care expense, 75
    and low birth weight, 16
  births to unwed, 3, 18, 19, 60, 63,
    180, 182-183
  childhoods of homeless, 67
  education
    and child care expense, 76
    and children's school success,
      182-183
  health
    and behavior, and SIDS, 110
    transmitting AIDS to children,
      111, 123
  infant mortality and diet of, 15
  race, and low birth weight, 16
  teenage
    and children's school success,
      183
    and expected years of child

poverty, 63
  pregnancy and abortion, 115
working
  and age of youngest child, 70
  and changes to early child-
    hood programs, 163-164
  children's status, 4
  history of, 8, 69
  and latchkey children, 183-184
  marital status of, 70
  married versus divorced, 184
  percent of, with young
    children, 76, 184
movies, promoting violence, 180
MSAs (major metropolitan statistical areas), 9, 24
MSRTS (Migrant School Record
  Transfer System), 11, 13
murder. *See* homicide
music, promoting violence, 180

N

NAEP (National Assessment of Edu-
  cational Progress), 172-173, 174,
  175, 185
NAEYC (National Association for
  the Education of Young
  Children), 97
NASB (National Association of
  School Boards), 179, 180
NASDTEC (National Association of
  State Directors of Teacher Educa-
  tion and Certification), 170
National Academy of Sciences,
  Committee on National Statistics,
  62
National Assessment of Educa-
  tional Progress (NAEP), 172-173,
  174, 175, 185
National Association of Black Social
  Workers, 20-21
National Association for the Educa-
  tion of Young Children (NAEYC),
  97
National Association for Family
  Child Care, 97
National Association of School
  Boards (NASB), 179, 180
National Association of State
  Directors of Teacher Education

and Certification (NASDTEC), 170
National Center for Children in
  Poverty (NCCP), 62, 64, 65
National Center for Education Sta-
  tistics (NCES), 160, 178, 180, 184
National Center for Health Statis-
  tics (NCHS), 110
National Center for Social Statis-
  tics, 19
National Center on Child Abuse
  and Neglect (NCCAN), 144, 145
National Child Abuse and Neglect
  Data System project (NCANDS),
  145
National Commission on Children,
  2-3
National Commission on Migrant
  Education, 11
National Committee for the
  Prevention of Child Abuse, 184
National Council for Adoption, 19
National Crime Prevention Council,
  180
National Crime Survey, 179
National Educational Goals Panel,
  167, 168
National Education Association
  (NEA), 181, 185
National Education Goals Report
  (NEGR), 182
National Health and Examination
  Survey III (NHANES), 113
National Household Education
  Survey, 181, 182
National Institute of Child Health
  and Human Development, 238
National Research Council, 61
National School Safety Center, 179
National SIDS Resource Center
  (NSRC), 109
National Teachers Examination
  (NTE), 170
Native Alaskan children. *See also*
  American Indian children;
  Native Alaskans; Native
  American children
  demographics, 18-19
  pediatric AIDS cases, 111
  as percent of school enrollments,
    159
  suicide by age and sex, 114
  suicide rate, 113, 126
Native Alaskans. *See also* American

Indians; Native Alaskan
children; Native Americans
as percent of Northeastern U.S.
counties, 252
as percent of Northwestern U.S.
counties, 254
as percent of Pacific U.S. counties, 255
as percent of Southeastern U.S.
counties, 253
as percent of southwestern U.S.
counties, 255
suicide rate, 126
Native American children. *See also*
American Indian children;
Native Alaskan children;
Native Americans
demographics
Indian Child Welfare Act of
1978, 21
as percent of population by
state, 50
population by state, 52
education
incidence of health risks at
birth, 168
as percent of school enrollment, 158-159
school enrollments by state, 192
school/parent contact, 220
school placement of gifted,
236
school suspensions, 236
states with large school enrollments of, 189
health
dental care among, 117
suicide among, 126
suicide by age and sex, 114
poverty of, as percent of total by
state, 89
Native Americans. *See also* American Indians; Native Alaskans;
Native American children
as abuse victims, 155
as percent of homeless population, 68
as percent of Northeastern U.S.
counties, 252
as percent of Northwestern U.S.
counties, 254
as percent of Pacific U.S. counties, 255

as percent of Southeastern U.S.
counties, 253
as percent of Southwestern U.S.
counties, 255
suicide rate, 126
NCANDS (National Child Abuse and
Neglect Data System project), 145
NCCAN (National Center on Child
Abuse and Neglect), 144, 145
NCCP (National Center for Children
in Poverty), 65
NCES (National Center for Education Statistics), 160
NCHS (National Center for Health
Statistics), 110
NEA (National Education Association), 181, 185
Nebraska, pediatric AIDS cases,
112, 124
neglect. *See* child abuse and
neglect
NEGR (National Education Goals
Report), 182
Netherlands
child care support, 73
gross domestic product for education, 199
income inequality, 63
Nevada
infant mortality rates, 14
juvenile custody rate, 136
SIDS cases, 110
newborns. *See also* infant
mortality rates; low birth
weight
definition of, 6
New Hampshire
fingerprinting of juveniles, 132
infant mortality rates, 14
school district operation, 162
white children, 19
New Jersey
educational revenues, 165
Hispanic children, 17
juvenile records laws, 132
measles outbreak, 106, 121
migrant workers, 11
minority children, 11
pediatric AIDS cases, 112, 124
population of, in urban areas, 11
public revenues per student, 166
sealing of juvenile records, 132
student/teacher ratios, 171

New Mexico
American Indian children, 18
child poverty rates, 60
Hispanic students, 159
Native American students, 159
New York
child poverty rates in, 60
criminal justice system
juvenile arrests in, 140
public juvenile facilities in, 137
demographics
African American children in, 18
American Indian children in, 18
Asian American children in, 18
Hispanic children in, 17
migrant workers, 11
minority children in, 11
Title IV-E money spent in, 22
education
African American students in,
159
Asian American students in,
159
educational revenues, 165
Hispanic students in, 159
immigrant students in, 160
number of teachers in, 172
measles outbreak, 106, 121
NHANES (National Health and
Examination Survey III), 113
North Carolina
age of juvenile status, 131
American Indian children, 18
fingerprinting of juveniles, 132
GSP commitment to education,
164
migrant workers, 11
rural population, 10
North Dakota
infant mortality rates, 14
juvenile arrests, 140
Northeastern U.S.
African American county populations, 244
Asian American county populations, 240
birth rates by county, 256
child care expense, 76
expenditures per student, 166
Hispanic county populations,
248
juvenile detention facility
deaths, 140

juvenile offender housing costs,
137
lead poisoning, 112
Native Alaskan county populations, 252
Native American county populations, 252
Pacific Islander county populations, 240
Northwestern U.S.
African American county populations, 246
Asian American county populations, 242
birth rates by county, 258
Hispanic county populations, 250
Native Alaskan county populations, 254
Native American county populations, 254
Pacific Islander county populations, 242
Norway
gross domestic product for education, 199
income inequality, 63
young child poverty rates, 64, 91
NSRC (National SIDS Resource
Center), 109
NTE (National Teachers Examination), 170
nursery schools. *See* early childhood education
nutrition
adult and child care food
programs, 74-75
and child care, 73
government programs, 3
link to lead poisoning, 113

O

Office of Educational Research and
Improvement (OERI), 185, 186, 187
Office of Juvenile Justice and
Delinquency Prevention (OJJDP),
107, 136, 137
Office of the Assistant Secretary
for Planning and Evaluation, 238
Ohio
African American students, 159

Ohio *(continued)*
    educational investment gaps, 179
    educational revenues, 165
OJJDP (Office of Juvenile Justice and Delinquency Prevention), 107, 136, 137
Oklahoma
    American Indian children, 18
    Native American students, 159
Omnibus Budget Reconciliation Act, 3
OPV vaccine, 106-107, 168
oral polio vaccine (OPV), 106-107, 168
Oregon
    migrant children, 13
    SIDS cases, 110
Orland, M. E., 172
Orshansky, Mollie, 61
Orshansky thresholds, 61
overcrowding, in juvenile detention facilities, 137-138, 151

P

Pacific Islander children. *See also* Asian American children; Pacific Islanders
    high school dropout rate, 172, 176
    pediatric AIDS cases, 111
Pacific Islanders. *See also* Asian Americans; Pacific Islander children
    as percent of Northeastern U.S. counties, 240
    as percent of Northwestern U.S. counties, 242
    as percent of Pacific U.S. counties, 243
    as percent of Southeastern U.S. counties, 241
    as percent of Southwestern U.S. counties, 243
    population description, 17-18
Pacific Northwestern U.S., secondary school enrollment, 164
Pacific U.S.
    African American county populations, 247

Asian American county populations, 243
birth rates by county, 259
Hispanic county populations, 251
Native Alaskan county populations, 255
Native American county populations, 255
Pacific Islander county populations, 243
Paige, Satchel, 60
Pallas, Aaron M., 183
parents. *See also* fathers; mothers
    child abuse and neglect by, 145, 155
    demographics of homeless, 67
    education of Hispanic, 172
    employment of, and child poverty, 60
    knowledge of children's drug use, 117
    marital status of, 95
    paying for child care, 73
    reading to children, 183
    of runaways, 108
    school involvement by, 170, 181, 184-185, 220
    as teachers, 183
Partnership for a Drug Free America, 117
Parton, Nancy, 145
PCP, student use by, 182, 229, 233
peer mediation, 181
Peng, Samuel S., 172
Pennsylvania
    African American students, 159
    educational revenues, 165
    juvenile record laws, 132
    measles outbreak, 106, 121
    migrant children, 13
    migrant workers, 11
    youth versus elderly population, 13, 42
personal income per capita (PIC), 218
personal offenses by juveniles, 135-136
Personal Responsibility and Work Opportunity Reconciliation Act, 77, 79-81, 102
physical abuse. *See* child abuse and neglect

PIC (personal income per capita), 218
playground surface requirements, 98
poisoning, lead, 112-113, 125
policy definition of runaways, 108
polio vaccine, 106-107, 168
politics. *See also* government
    dependency ratio effect on, 13-14
    fiscal conservatism, 2-3
population, U.S. *See also* specific groups
    dependency ratio in, 13-14, 42
    elderly versus children, comparison of, 42
    proportion of children and elderly, 2
    by region
        African American, 244-247
        Alaskan Natives, 252-255
        Asian American, 240-243
        Hispanic, 248-251
        Native Americans, 252-255
        Pacific Islander, 240-243
Portugal, gross domestic product for education, 199
Posner, Marc, 108
post-traumatic stress syndrome, in runaways, 109
    and criminal justice system
        child abuse and neglect, 145
        as factor in youth violence, 143
    definition of, 61
    demographics
        American Indian, 19, 114
        Asian families, 18
        children versus elderly living in, 14, 38
        percent of, 4
        primary residence location rates, 10
        rates for elderly living in, 3
        in rural areas, 10, 12
        rural versus urban, 34
        in urban households, 11
    and education
        children's disabilities, 161
        distribution of students living in, 178
        educational achievement, 172
        effect of poverty on education, 169, 177-178
        expenditures per student, 178

        as problem in schools, 182
        and risk of school failure, 182-183
    effect of taxes and transfers on estimates of, 84
    explanations for, 60
    government programs aiding, 8, 20, 22 (*See also* Welfare)
    and health
        lead poisoning, 113
        unimmunized children, 106-107
    and living conditions
poverty
    AFDC recipients as percent of children in, 80
    after Great Depression, 60
    age and race distribution of time spent in, 64
    characteristics of parents, 65, 93
    children versus elderly living in, 60, 61
    child's perspective on, 62
    consequences of young, 64
    current measurement method for, 61-62
    decline in elderly living in, 60, 61
    distribution of, by family type, 85
    factors influencing years of, 63
    homelessness, 66
    increase in young, 64-65, 91
    international comparison of young, 64, 91
    Medicaid recipients by level of, 81
    number and rate of children under 6 in, 82, 83
    percent of people exiting, 64, 85
    proposed changes to measurement methods, 62
    by race and state, 86-90
    rates by age, 61
    rates for U.S. young child, 91
    trends in U.S. child, 62-63
    years lived in, by race, 63-64
poverty thresholds, 61-62, 84
pregnancy
    mother's behavior during, and SIDS, 110
    teenage, 115-116

preschools. *See* early childhood education

primary residence. *See also* housing
 income by, 11
 poverty rates by location of, 10

private detention facilities
 deaths in, 139-140
 for juvenile offenders, 133, 135-136
 number of, 136-137

private health insurance, 104, 106-107

private schools. *See also* education; schools
 enrollment in, 163, 215
 financing of, 218
 number of teachers in, 172
 pupil/staff ratios, 171-172
 students' perspective on discipline, 182, 232
 student/teacher ratios, 171

proficiency testing, 172-176, 185
 8th grade, 172-176
 4th grade, 172-176
 mathematics, 173, 175, 225
 reading, 173, 174, 222, 225
 science, 173, 224
 student, 172-176, 185
 12th grade, 172-176
 writing, 173, 225

prostitution, among runaways, 109

PRWORA, 77, 79-81, 102

puberty, defining, 6

public detention facilities
 costs of running, 137
 deaths in, 139-140
 number and population of, 149
 number of, 136
 number of agencies regulating, 147
 residents in, 133, 135-136, 146
 states' annual costs for, 148

public health, youth violence as issue of, 141-143

public health clinics, 106

public health insurance, 104. *See also* Medicaid

public housing. *See* housing

public revenues per student, 165, 166, 206, 207, 218

public schools. *See* education; schools

Puerto Rican migrant workers, 11

pupil/staff ratios, 171

pupil/teacher ratios, 171, 220, 221

R

race/ethnicity. *See also* specific race or ethnicity
 of child abuse and neglect victims, 145
 demographics
  adoption across, 20-21
  child mortality rate by cause, 46
  of children in foster care, 22, 56
  composition of U.S. children, 16-17, 52
  fertility rates, 9, 25
  infant mortality rate by cause, 45
  poverty, 4-5
 education
  composition of public schools, 158
  experience with school violence, 227
  gifted student distributions, 187, 234-236
  high school completion rates, 176, 226
  high school dropout rate, 169, 176, 177, 225
  and income, 169
  mathematical proficiency by sex and age, 223
  reading proficiency by age and sex, 222
  school suspensions, 234-236
  science proficiency by age and sex, 224
  students' perspective on discipline, 232
  writing proficiency by age and sex, 225
 health
  pediatric AIDS by exposure category, 111
  rates for SIDS, 122
 living conditions
  distribution of time spent in poverty, 64
  and exiting poverty, 64, 85
  Medicaid recipients, 81

 of poor versus non-poor parents, 93
  poverty rates, 65
  years lived in poverty, 63-64

ranches for juvenile offenders
 educational standards, 138-139, 151
 federal standards conformity percent, 151
 number of, 139
 number of admissions to, 137
 percent of juveniles in, 137

rape, juvenile arrest rate for, 153

RDS (respiratory distress syndrome), 15

reading proficiency testing, 173, 174, 222, 225

reception centers
 educational standards, 138-139, 151
 number of admissions to, 137
 number of juvenile, 139
 percent conforming to federal standards, 151
 percent of juveniles residing in, 137

Reed, S., 177

regions. *See* geographic regions

rehabilitation, 139

religious beliefs
 and population of children, 9
 as reason for home schooling, 184

Resolving Conflict Creatively program, 181

respiratory distress syndrome (RDS), 15

revenues. *See* financing; public revenues per student

Rhode Island
 fingerprinting of juveniles, 132
 infant mortality rates, 14
 juvenile offender housing costs, 137
 population of, in urban areas, 11

rights
 child, 143
 parent, 143

Rights of the Child Convention, 3

Riley, Richard, 181

risk factors, for school failure, 182-183

robbery, juvenile arrest rate for, 153

Rogers, Willard, *A Demographic Analysis of Childhood Poverty*, 63

Rose, Lowell, 181-182, 232

runaways, 107-109

rural households. *See also* rural-urban contrasts
 dental care, 117
 economic status, 10
 poverty, 34, 63

rural-urban contrasts
 crime against children, 140-141
 demographics of children, 10-13
 income, 10
 juvenile offenders, 147
 poverty and education, 34, 177-178
 school violence, 179
 students' perspective on discipline, 232

Ryan, Phyllis, *Homelessness in Pennsylvania: How Can This Be?*, 66

S

Safe Schools Act of 1993, 181

SAFE (Schools Are for Education), 181

safety
 of latchkey children, 184
 in schools, 179-182

Saint-Exupéry, Antoine de, 104

Samoan children. *See* Asian American children

SAT scores, 4

Sautter, R. C., 177

school districts, 162, 169, 178, 215. *See also* schools

schools. *See also* education; teachers
 discipline, 181-182, 232
 enrollment trends, 163-164, 197, 198, 216
 expenditures of gross domestic product, 216
 expenditures per student, 202
 full-time-equivalent (FTE) staff investment, 171-172
 home schooling, 184-185, 233
 minority demographics, 177-178
 number of, in U.S., 162

schools *(continued)*
  proficiency testing, 172-176
  public versus private
    enrollment, 163, 215
    number of teachers, 172
    pupil/staff ratio, 171-172
    student/teacher ratios, 171, 220
  quality of
    affluent versus poor, 221
    competency of students, 168-169
    national educational goals, 167-168
    parental involvement, 170, 181, 220
    readiness to learn, 168
    school attainment and completion, 168
    student performance, 172-176
    student safety, 179-182
    teacher preparedness, 169-170, 170-171, 210, 212, 221
  revenues, 165, 207
  students' perspective on discipline, 232
  students' suspension rates by race and state, 234-236
  substance abuse in, 182
  violence in, 179-181
Schools Are for Education (SAFE), 181
science proficiency testing, 173, 224
sealing of juvenile records, 131-132, 154
seasonal farm workers. *See* migrant farm workers
SEAs (State Education Agencies), 186
secondary schools, 163-164, 164
Section 8 rent subsidies, 78
Sedlack, Andrea, 145
segregation, effect on children, 8
selective incapacitation penal philosophy, 133
self-esteem, as factor in youth violence, 142
sex. *See* females; males
sex education, 115, 183
sexual abuse/exploitation. *See* child abuse and neglect
sexual harassment, 183
sexuality. *See also* homosexuality
  AIDS cases due to, 123

  and poverty, 178
  of runaways, 109
  teenage, 115-116
Sheley, Joseph F., 180
shelters
  families returning to, 67
  homeless children living in, 66
  for runaways, 108
SIDS (sudden infant death syndrome), 15, 109-110, 122
SIIP, 75
Singapore, preschool programs, 73
single men, as percent of homeless population, 68
single-parent families, 3. *See also* families
  AFDC benefits, 102
  and children's school failure risk, 182-183
  contributing to child poverty, 60
  and expected years of child poverty, 63, 85
  and homelessness, 68
  percent of children in, 95
  as percent of homeless population, 68
  runaways from, 108
  with teenage mothers, 115
  trend in rate of, 4
single women as percent of homeless population, 68
SIPP (Survey of Income and Program Participation), 62, 63
slave economy, and population of children, 9
smoking by students, 182, 230
social controls and youth violence, 141
Social Security Administration, 61
Social Security Insurance, and Medicaid, 104-105
societal changes, effects of, 2-3
socioeconomic status and infant mortality, 15
South Atlantic U.S.
  percent of children, 9
  proportion of children in population, 158
  secondary school enrollment, 164
South Carolina
  migrant workers, 11
  rural population, 10
South Carolina Guidance

  Counselor's Association, 183
South Dakota
  African American children, 18
  GSP commitment to education, 164
  Hispanic children, 17
  juvenile arrests, 140
  juvenile offender housing costs, 137
  SIDS cases, 110
Southeastern U.S.
  African American county populations, 245
  Asian American county populations, 241
  birth rates by county, 257
  child abuse and neglect, 144
  Hispanic county populations, 249
  Native Alaskan county populations, 253
  Native American county populations, 253
  Pacific Islander county populations, 241
Southern U.S.
  child care expense, 76
  expected years of poverty, 63
  juvenile detention facility deaths, 140
  percent of children, 9
  rural poverty, 10
South Korea
  mathematics proficiency by age, 223
  preschool programs, 73
  science proficiency by age, 224
Southwestern U.S.
  African American county populations, 247
  Asian American county populations, 243
  birth rates by county, 259
  Hispanic county populations, 251
  Native Alaskan county populations, 255
  Native American county populations, 255
  Pacific Islander county populations, 243
Soviet Union
  mathematics proficiency by age, 223
  science proficiency by age, 224

Spain
  gross domestic product for education, 199
  mathematics proficiency by age, 223
  reading proficiency by age, 222
  science proficiency by age, 224
  young child poverty rates, 64, 91
spatial distribution of children, 9
special education. *See also* disabilities; education
  class structure, 161
  expenditures for, 167
  government programs, 3
  percent of student population receiving, 160
  teachers, 161
  for violent students, 181
special needs children, 20, 55. *See also* disabilities
Special Supplemental Food Program for Women, Infants, and Children, 77
Speech/Language Impairment, 160, 161
spouse abuse, 66
SSI (Supplemental Security Income)
  PRWORA changes to, 80, 102
  recipients and payments by state, 37
  welfare funding, 78
Stafford, Frank, 73
state and local government. *See* government, state and local
state comparisons. *See also* specific states
  criminal justice system
    age of juvenile status, 131
    costs for facilities, 148
    facility administration, 147
    facility populations, 149
    juvenile arrests, 140, 152, 156
    juvenile custody rate, 150
    juvenile resident count, 150
    number of facilities, 149
    public facility costs, 148
  demographics
    AFDC and SSI recipients and payments, 37
    African American children population, 49
    Asian American children population, 48

state comparisons (continued)
   children as percent of population, 25
   children by race, 52
   Hispanic children population, 47
   infant mortality rate, 43, 44
   Migrant Education Program, 35, 36
   Native American children population, 50
   population ages 5-17, 40
   population under age 18, 41
   white children population, 51
education
   children served under IDEA, 193, 196
   disabled children served, 196
   disabled students, 194
   educational effort, 206, 218
   expenditures for instruction, 200
   expenditures per student, 205
   gifted children placement by race, 234-236
   gifted students and programs, 186
   grades K-12 enrollment 1995-2000, 216
   home schooling requirements, 233
   investment gaps, 228
   learning disabilities, 194
   number of home schooled children, 233
   number of public school teachers, 214
   out-of-field teacher assignments, 210
   out-of-field teachers, 221
   percent change in teacher salaries, 203
   percent of enrollment by race, 188, 190-192
   percent of fully immunized children, 208
   percent of infants with health risks, 231
   personal income per capita, 206, 218
   projected change in enrollments, 197, 198

revenues per public school student, 207
revenues per student, 218
school suspensions by race, 234-236
source of school revenues, 217
student/teacher ratio, 213, 221
teacher certification testing, 219
teacher education/assignment, 211
teacher salaries, 201
teacher training, 212
health
   pediatric AIDS cases, 124
   percent of fully immunized children, 119
   percent of infants with health risks, 231
living conditions
   AFDC and poverty guidelines, 81
   child care center inspections, 96
   children in poverty by race, 86-90
   children under 6 in poverty, 83
   federal payments for child care, 71
   foster care expenditures, 56, 57
   foster care populations, 55
State Education Agencies (SEAs), 186
status dropout rates, 168, 169. See also dropout rates
status offenses by juveniles, 135-136
Status Report on Hunger and Homelessness in America's Cities, 66
stranger abductee children, 109. See also runaways
stress, acculturation, 114
students. See also education; schools
   alcohol abuse, 182, 230, 233
   drug abuse, 182, 229-230
   expenditures per, 166, 178-179, 205
   gifted and talented, 185-187, 234-236
   perspective on discipline, 232
   proficiency testing, 172-176, 185

public revenues per, 165, 166, 206, 207, 218
use of cigarettes, 182, 230
student/teacher ratios, 171, 181, 220, 221
substance abuse. See also alcohol abuse
   AIDS cases due to, 123
   among parents of runaways, 108
   among runaways, 109
   among students, 182, 229-230
   and child abuse and neglect, 145
   educational goals regarding, 167
   and HIV/AIDS, 111
   and homelessness, 66, 68
   and poverty, 178
   in schools, 182
   and suicide, 114
   trends, 117, 127
substitute care. See foster care
suburban households. See urban households
sudden infant death syndrome (SIDS), 15, 109-110, 122
suicide
   adolescence, 113-114, 126
   American Indian, 114
   child mortality due to, 16
   homosexual youth, 183
   in juvenile detention facilities, 140
   Native Alaskan, 114
   parents of runaways, 108
   rates by age, 126
   in runaway population, 109
   trend in rate of, 4
Supplemental Security Income (SSI)
   PRWORA changes to, 80, 102
   recipients and payments by state, 37
   welfare funding for, 78
surfactant medications, effect on infant mortality rates, 15
Survey of Income and Program Participation (SIPP), 62, 63
Survey Research Center (University of Michigan), 63
Sweden
   child care support, 73
   gross domestic product for education, 199
   income inequality, 63
   young child poverty rates, 64, 91

Switzerland
   gross domestic product for education, 199
   income inequality, 63

T

Tahitian children. See Asian American children
Taiwan
   mathematics proficiency by age, 223
   preschool programs, 73
   science proficiency by age, 224
TANF (Temporary Assistance to Needy Families), 77, 79-80, 81-102. See also Aid to Families with Dependent Children (AFDC)
taxes. See also earned income tax credit (EITC)
   effect of, on estimates of poverty, 84
TCC (transitional child care assistance), 74-75, 77
teachers. See also education; schools
   certification of, 169-170, 185, 209, 219
   development session participation, 171, 212
   educational requirements, 170
   expenditures for, 165-166, 200, 204
   national educational goals, 167
   number of, in U.S., 172, 214
   out-of-field assignments, 170-171, 210, 221
   parents as, 183
   perception of school problems, 182
   in poor school districts, 169
   reducing school violence, 181
   salaries
      average, by state, 201
      percent of change in, 203
      as percent of personal income per capita, 204
   special education, 161
   testing of, 169-170, 185, 209, 219
teenagers. See adolescence
teeth, care of, 117-118

television, violence on, 180
Temporary Assistance to Needy Families (TANF), 77, 79-80, 81, 102
Tennessee
  rural population, 10
  school expenditures versus revenues, 166
testing
  student proficiency, 172-176, 185
  of teachers, 169-170, 185, 209, 219
Texas
  African American children, 18
  American Indian children, 18
  Asian American children, 18
  Asian American students, 159
  child poverty rates, 60
  educational revenues, 165
  GSP commitment to education, 164
  Hispanic children, 17
  Hispanic students, 159
  immigrant students, 160
  infant mortality rates, 14
  juvenile arrests, 140
  migrant children, 13
  migrant workers, 11
  number of teachers, 172
  secondary school enrollment, 164
Thai children. See Asian American children
throwaway children, 109. See also runaways
Title IV-B, 22
Title IV-E, 20, 22-23, 56, 57
Title XX social services block grant, 74-75
tobacco, students' use of, 182, 230
Tongan children. See Asian American children
training schools
  educational standards, 138-139, 151
  number of admissions, 137
  number of juvenile, 139
  percent conforming to federal standards, 151
  percent of juveniles residing in, 137
transfer of juveniles to adult court, 133

transitional child care assistance (TCC), 74-75, 77
transracial adoption, 20-21
Tulane University, 180
Turkey, gross domestic product for education, 199
12th-grade proficiency testing, 172-176
two-parent families
  percent of children in, 95
  poverty, 3, 63, 65, 85

U

Unclaimed Children (Knitzer), 115
unemployment. See also employment
  among American Indians, 114
  as cause of poverty, 65
Uniform Adoption Act, 20
United Kingdom. See also Great Britain
  gross domestic product for education, 199
  income inequality, 63
  young child poverty rates, 64, 91
United Nations, 3
  Convention on the Rights of the Child, 238
United States
  distribution of children in, 9
  income inequality, 63
  regions (See geographic regions)
  social insurance, 4
  wealth, 4
University of Alabama, 180
University of Michigan, 179, 180
University of Wisconsin Madison Institute for Research on Poverty, 65
unwed mothers. See births to unwed mothers
urban households. See also rural-urban contrasts
  expected years of poverty, 63
  minorities in, 10-11
  poor versus non-poor parents, 93
  poverty, 10-11, 34
  versus rural, 10
  unimmunized children, 106-107
Urban Institute, The, 79

Utah
  juvenile arrests, 140
  measles outbreak, 106, 121
  population of, in urban areas, 11
  proportion of children in population, 158
  public revenues per student, 166
  pupil/staff ratio, 171
  SIDS cases, 110

V

vaccinations, 105-107, 168. See also immunizations
VCIS (Voluntary Cooperative Information System), 19, 21, 22
Vermont
  African American children, 18
  age of juvenile status, 131
  child care welfare reform, 71
  GSP commitment to education, 164
  Hispanic children, 17
  infant mortality rates, 14
  public juvenile facilities, 137
veterans as percent of homeless population, 68
victimization. See also child abuse and neglect; crime; violence
  of juveniles, 141-145, 155, 156
    by age, 140, 154
    violent crime rates, 140, 154
  of students, 179-181, 227
Vietnam conflict, effect on transracial adoptions, 21
Vietnamese children. See Asian American children
violence. See also crime; homicide
  and criminal justice system
    absence of role and recognition, 142
    community structures and institutions, 141
    disconnection of teens and adults, 142
    employment and education discrimination, 143
    forces linked to youth, 130
    juvenile detention facilities, 139
    parental control, 142
    poverty, 143

  youth as agents of and victims of, 140-141, 152-156
  domestic, 66
  and education
    causes of, 179-180
    culture of, 179
    educational goals regarding, 167
    movies promoting, 180
    music promoting, 180
    poverty, 178
    prevention of, 180-181, 227
    spatial distribution of, 179
    statistics, 179, 227
    television promoting, 180
    violence as threat to education, 180, 182
    weapons in schools, 179, 180
  and homelessness, 68
  offenses by juveniles, 135-136
  among parents of runaways, 108
Virginia, GSP commitment to education, 164
Voluntary Cooperative Information System (VCIS), 19, 21, 22

W

waiver of juveniles to adult court, 133
Washington, D.C.
  changes to teacher salaries, 166
  infant mortality rate, 14
  juvenile custody rate, 136
  juvenile offender housing costs, 137
  minority versus white children, 17
  public revenues per student, 166
Washington (state)
  American Indian children, 18
  Asian American students, 159
  GSP commitment to education, 164
  juvenile record laws, 132
  migrant children, 13
weapons in schools, 179, 180. See also guns; violence
Weinberg, Daniel, "Measuring Poverty: Issues and Approaches," 61

welfare. *See also* Aid to Families with Dependent Children (AFDC); Food Stamp program; Medicaid
  alternatives, 79
  benefits decrease, 3
  and child care, 69
  child care reform, 70-71
  direct (cash) assistance programs, 78-81
  effect on child poverty, 60
  entitlements for young children, 93
  in-kind programs, 77-78
  percent of women leaving, 81
  received by poor versus non-poor parents, 93
Welfare Reform Act of 1996, 3
Well Baby appointments, 106
Western U.S.
  dependency ratio, 13
  juvenile detention facility deaths, 140
  percent of children, 9
West Germany, reading proficiency by age in, 176, 222
West South Central U.S. percent of children, 9
West Virginia
  child poverty rates, 60, 61
  GSP commitment to education, 164
  white children, 19
  youth versus elderly population, 13, 42
"What Does it Cost to Mind Our Preschoolers?" (Casper), 75
Whitaker, Catherine J., 179

white children. *See also* whites
  criminal justice system
    as abuse victims, 155
    homicide victimization, 142
    in private juvenile facilities, 136
  demographics
    child mortality rates, 16
    foster care and adoption, 20
    infant mortality rates, 14-16, 45, 46
    as percent of population by state, 51
    as percent of U.S. population, 16-17
    population by state, 52
    population description, 19
  education
    disabilities, 161
    experience with school violence, 227
    high school completion rates, 176, 226
    high school dropout rates, 168, 169, 176, 177, 225
    incidence of health risks at birth, 168
    mathematics proficiency by age, 223
    mathematics proficiency by state, 175
    as percent of school-age population, 158
    as percent of school enrollment, 158-159
    reading proficiency by age, 222, 225
    reading proficiency by state, 174

    school/parent contact, 220
    school placement of gifted, 234
    school suspensions, 234
    science proficiency by age, 224
    writing proficiency by age, 225
  health
    adolescent childbearing, 116
    deaths due to birth defects, 118
    dental care, 117, 118
    lead poisoning, 113
    pediatric AIDS cases, 111
    as percent of runaways, 108
    rate of SIDS, 110, 122
    substance abuse, 117
  living conditions
    poverty, as percent of total by state, 90
    poverty, household characteristics, 63
    time spent in poverty, 63
whites. *See also* white children
  births to unwed mothers, 19
  family structure, 19
  income by education level, 169
  percent exiting poverty, 85
  as percent of homeless population, 68
WIC program, 77
Wisconsin
  child care welfare reform, 71
  fingerprinting of juveniles, 132
  GSP commitment to education, 164
  juvenile arrests, 140
Wisconsin, University of, at Madison Institute for Research

on Poverty, 65
women. *See* females; working women/mothers
working women/mothers
  age of youngest child, 70
  changes to early childhood programs, 163-164
  children's status, 4
  history, 8, 69
  latchkey children, 183-184
  marital status, 70
  married versus divorced, 184
  percent of, with young children, 76, 184
World War II
  annual birth rate after, 163
  effect on children, 8
  increasing education revenues after, 165
  student-teacher ratios since, 171
worldwide statistical information. *See also* international comparisons
  birth rates, 261
  infant mortality rates, 260
  life expectancy, 262
Wright Edelman, Marian, 2, 180
writing proficiency testing, 173, 225
Wyoming
  African American children, 18
  age of juvenile status, 131

Z

Zill, Nicholas, 182, 183